Atlas *of the* World

Atlas *of the* World

ATLAS OF THE WORLD

Produced by

AND Cartographic Publishers Ltd
Alberto House
Hogwood Lane
Finchampstead
Berkshire RG40 4RF
United Kingdom

www.info@andmap.co.uk

ISBN 1 84178 015 4
RRR
10 9 8 7 6 5 4 3 2 1

Senior Cartographic Editor: Craig Asquith
Cartographic Editor: Veronica Beattie
Assistant Cartographic Editors: Jenny Gill, Nikki Sargeant

Cartographic Production Manager: Caroline Beckley
Senior Cartographer: Glyn Rozier
Cartographers: Ben Brown, Ross Clode, Caleb Gould, Rachel Hopper, Adam Meara, Lee Rowe
DTP: Richard Fox

Satellite images: PP ©WorldSat International Inc, Ontario, Canada

Preliminary and front section:
Editor: Alexa Stace
Copy Editor: Robert Armstrong

Design: Michael Leaman
Illustration: Sienna Artworks

Photographic credits:
p11 NASA, p13 R Royer/Science Photo Library, p15 R Edmaier/Science Photo Library, p17 K Svenson/Science Photo Library, p18 N Komine/Science Photo Library.

Printing by Leefung-Asco. Printers Ltd. China

CONTENTS

Key map 6

An Introduction to our World 8-31
- Our star and our neighbours 10
- The Earth and the Moon 12
- A world in motion 14
- Shaping the Earth 16
- Contrasting conditions 18
- Peopling the globe 20
- The population explosion 22
- Belief and understanding 24
- The world at work 26
- On the move 28
- The legacy of industry 30

The British Isles in maps 32-39
- Key to map symbols 33
- Administrative areas of Great Britain 34
- Ireland 35
- Great Britain: North 36
- Great Britain: South 38

The World in maps 40-160
- Key to map symbols 41
- World *political* 42
- Europe *a view from space* 44
- Europe *flags and statistics* 46
- Europe *political* 48
  - Scandinavia 50
  - Central Europe 52
  - Germany 54
  - Benelux 56
  - British Isles 58
  - France 60
  - Spain and Portugal 62
  - The Alpine States 64
  - Italy 66
  - The Balkans 68
  - Greece and Western Turkey 70
  - European Russia 72
- Asia *a view from space* 74
- Western Asia *flags and statistics* 76
- Eastern Asia *flags and statistics* 78
- Asia *political* 80
  - Northwest Asia 82
  - Northeast Asia 84
  - Eastern China 86
  - Japan and Korea 88
  - Southeast Asia 90
  - Malaysia and Indonesia 92
  - Southern Asia 94
  - The Middle East 96
  - Turkey 98
  - Israel and the Gulf States 100
- Africa *a view from space* 102
- Northern Africa *flags and statistics* 104
- Central and Southern Africa *flags and statistics* 106
- Africa *political* 108
  - Northeast Africa 110
  - Northwest Africa 112
  - West Africa 114
  - Central Africa 116
  - Southern Africa 118
- Oceania *a view from space* 120
- Oceania *flags and statistics* 122
- Oceania *political* 124
  - Australia 126
  - New Zealand 128
- North America *a view from space* 130
- North America *flags and statistics* 132
- North America *political* 134
  - Canada 136
  - United States 138
  - Northwest United States 140
  - Northeast United States 142
  - Southeast United States 144
  - Southwest United States 146
  - Central America and the Caribbean 148
- South America *a view from space* 150
- South America *flags and statistics* 152
- South America *political* 154
  - Northern South America 156
  - Southern South America 158
- Polar Regions 160

Index 161–208
- How to use the index 161
- Glossary 162
- Index to names 163

KEY MAP

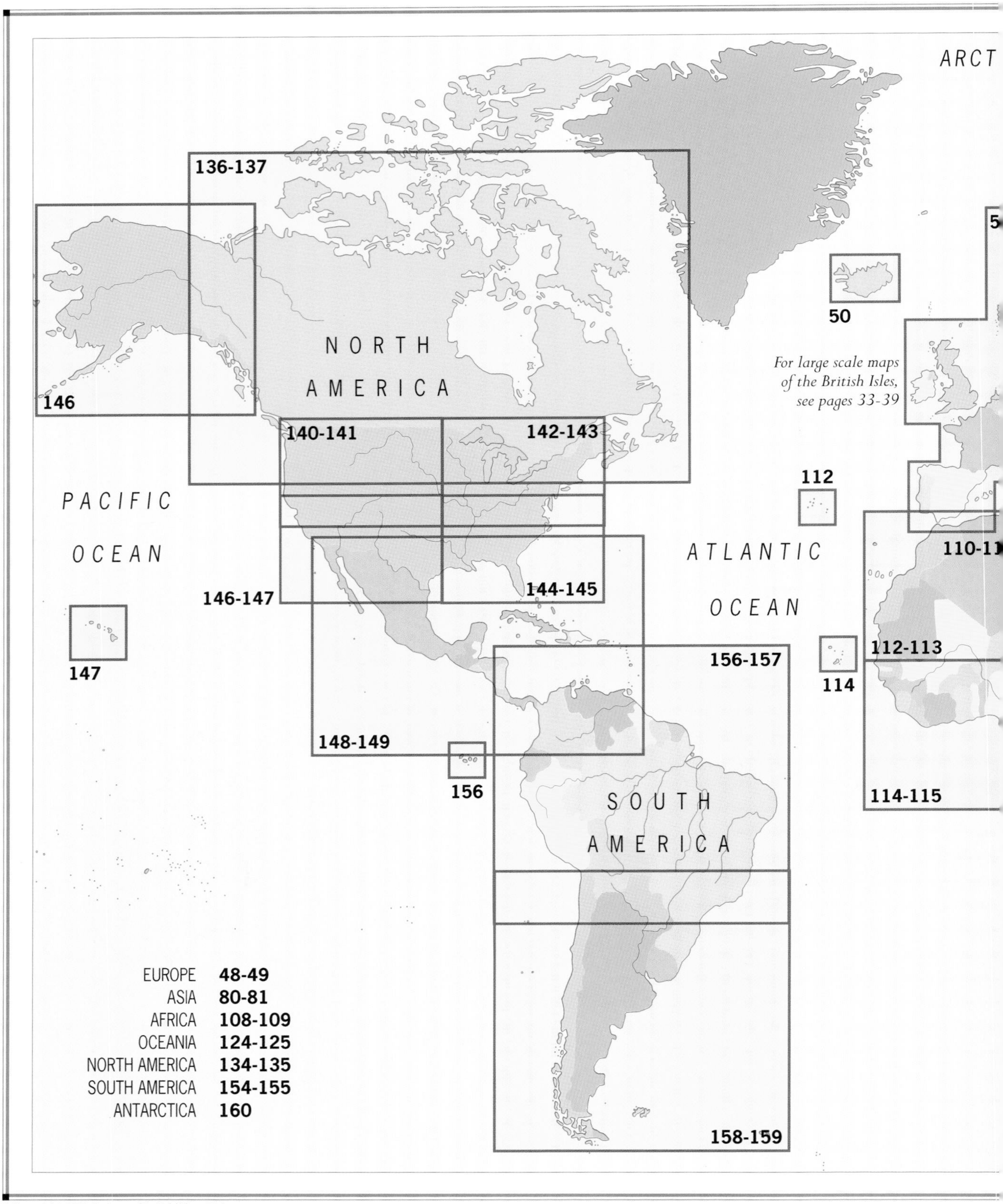

ARCT
136-137
146
NORTH AMERICA
140-141
142-143
PACIFIC OCEAN
146-147
144-145
147
148-149
156
ATLANTIC OCEAN
50
For large scale maps of the British Isles, see pages 33-39
112
110-11
112-113
114
114-115
156-157
SOUTH AMERICA
158-159
EUROPE 48-49
ASIA 80-81
AFRICA 108-109
OCEANIA 124-125
NORTH AMERICA 134-135
SOUTH AMERICA 154-155
ANTARCTICA 160

KEY TO CONTINENTAL RECORD SYMBOLS

- Highest point
- Lowest point
- Lowest average annual rainfall
- Highest average annual rainfall
- Longest river
- Largest lake

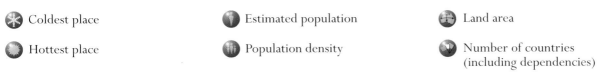

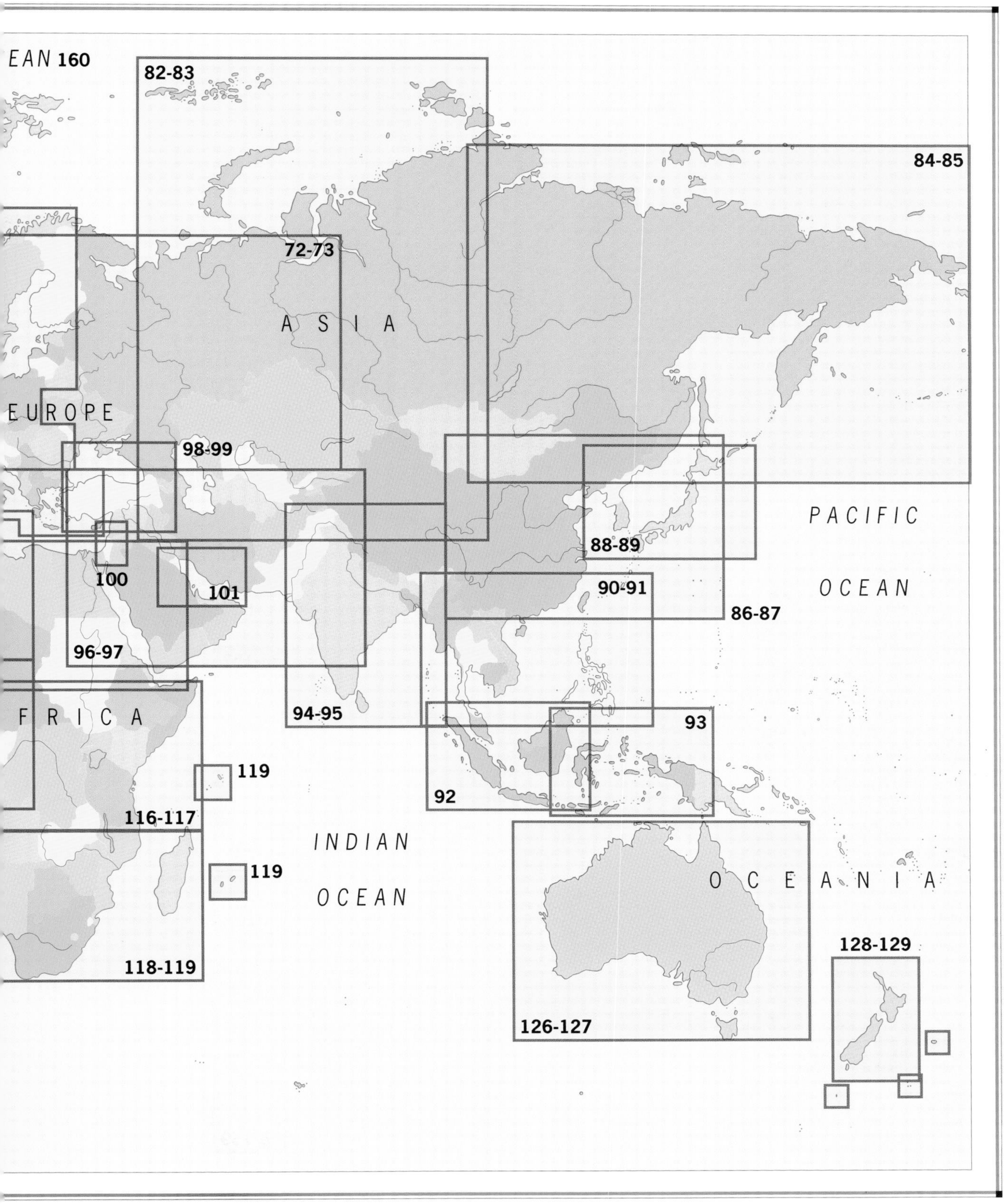
EAN 160
82-83
84-85
72-73
ASIA
EUROPE
98-99
PACIFIC
OCEAN
88-89
90-91
86-87
100
101
96-97
94-95
FRICA
93
92
119
116-117
INDIAN
OCEAN
119
OCEANIA
128-129
118-119
126-127

The first eight symbols show the most extreme value of the feature described, as well as its location. If that description is in ***bold****, it is not only the continental record, but also the World record.*

- Coldest place
- Hottest place
- Estimated population
- Population density
- Land area
- Number of countries (including dependencies)

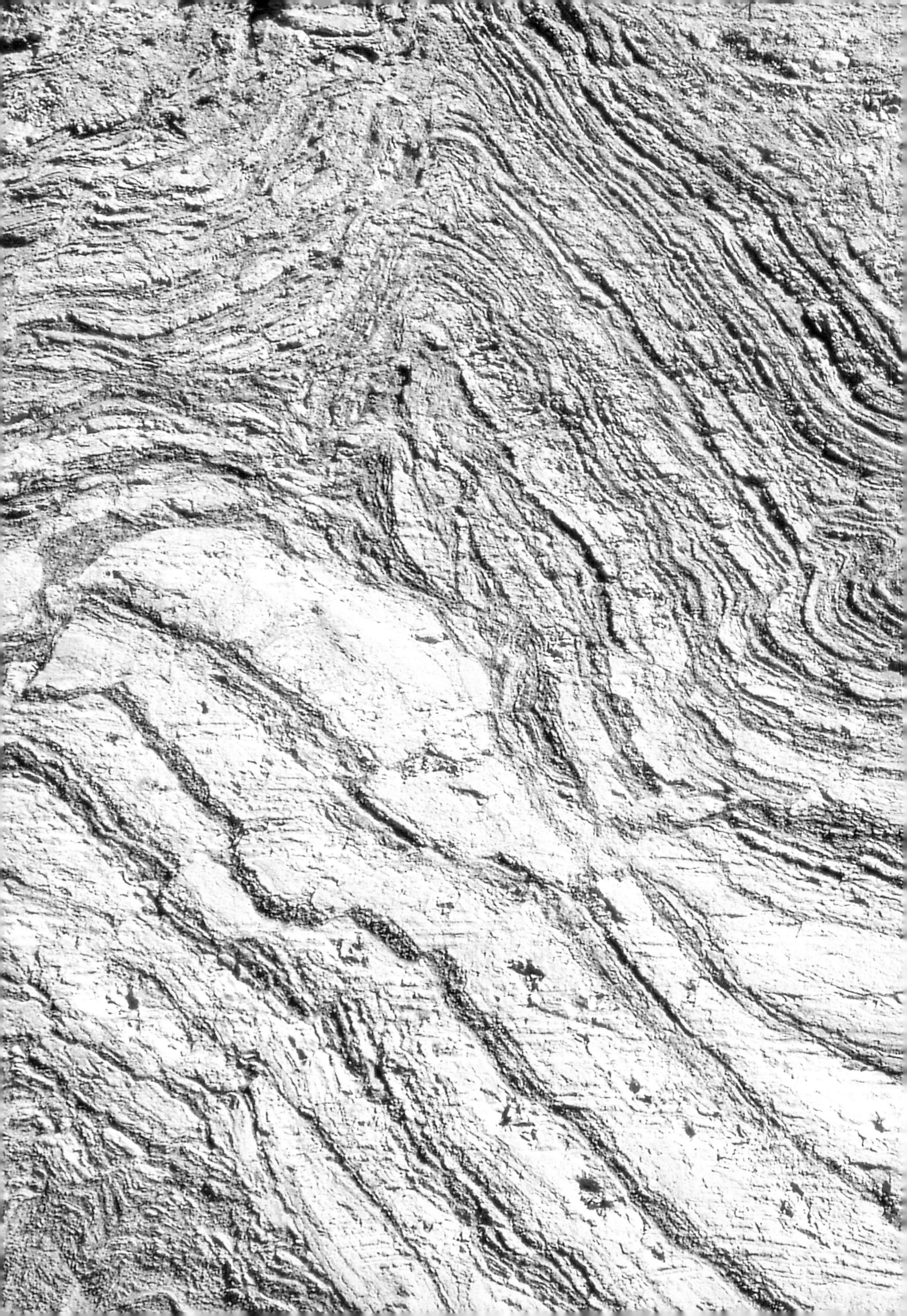

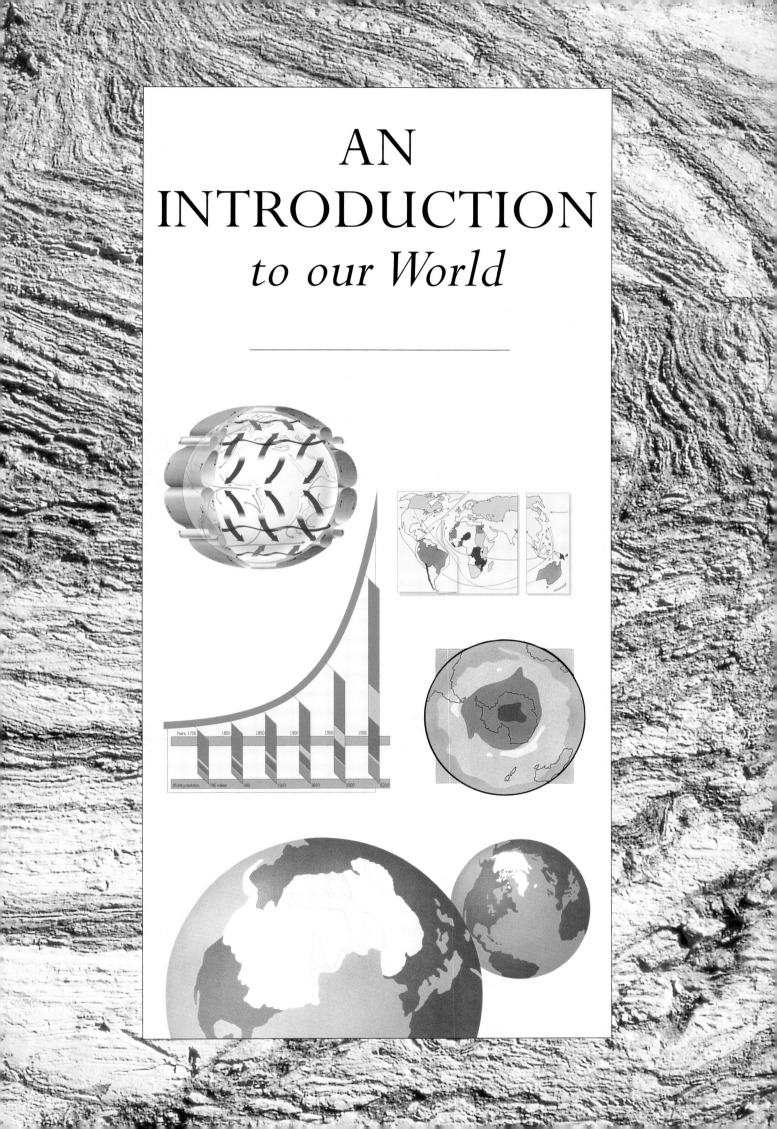

AN INTRODUCTION *to our World*

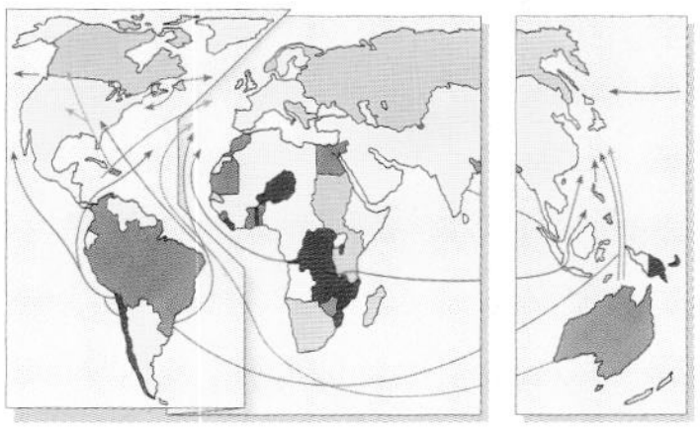

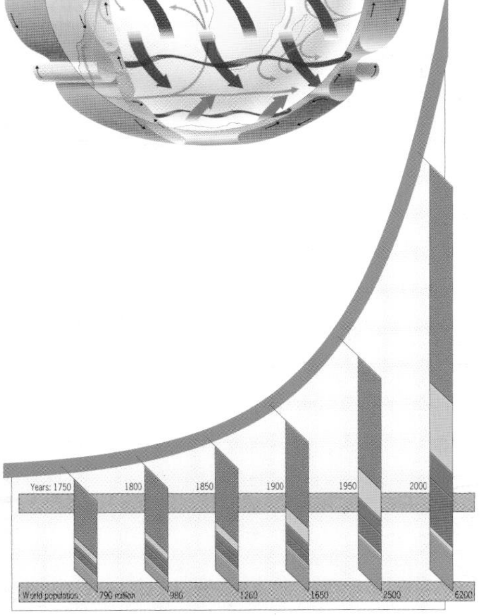

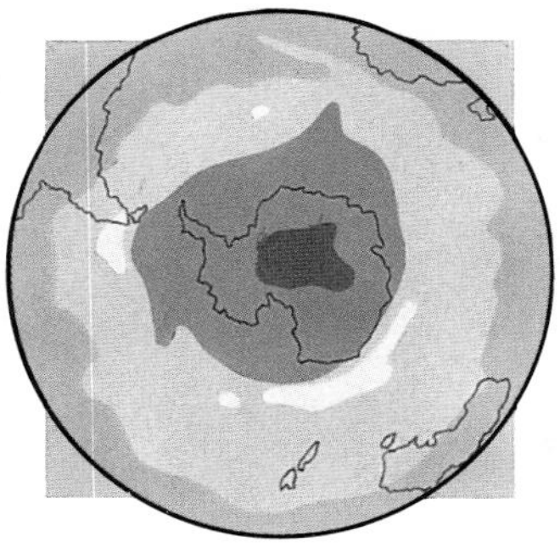

OUR STAR & OUR NEIGHBOURS

THE EARTH IS ONE MEMBER OF A SOLAR SYSTEM of nine planets orbiting our local star – the Sun. All these bodies formed from a single cloud of gas and dust around 4.5 billion years ago as it was compressed, possibly by shockwaves from a giant supernova explosion. The centre of the cloud collapsed most rapidly, becoming denser and attracting more material until eventually it reached a point so hot and dense that nuclear reactions began inside it. These reactions continue today and are the source of the sunlight that heats our planet and sustains life. The Sun is critical to the regulation of our climate and environment – fine alterations in Earth's orbit are thought to cause periodic ice ages, so we are fortunate that the Sun is not likely to change drastically for another 5 billion years.

On a shorter scale, the Sun's output does have slight fluctuations. A cycle of sunspot formation (comparatively cool regions of the Sun's surface caused by magnetic activity), reaches a maximum every 11 years. From 1645–1705 almost no sunspots were seen, a dip in solar activity which coincided with a 'mini-Ice Age' of unusually low temperatures on Earth.

Once the Sun had formed, a disk of material would have been left outside the newly-formed star, which condensed to form the planets. Particles in the gas and dust cloud collided and stuck together, becoming increasingly larger bodies. Eventually these 'proto-planets' were pulled into a spherical shape by their increasing gravity.

The Solar System we see today reflects the composition of that gas and dust cloud, and divides into two regions. The inner portion contains the four terrestrial (Earth-like) planets – from Mercury orbiting close to the Sun, through Venus and Earth, to Mars. Beyond the orbit of Mars lies the asteroid belt, a ring of rocky debris, outside which are the gas giants, enormous planets created where the cloud bulged with huge quantities of gas.

The inner rocky worlds

The terrestrial planets are all very different. Mercury is a small, baking world, quite similar to our own Moon, and covered in craters. Venus is shrouded in a thick atmosphere of carbon dioxide and toxic

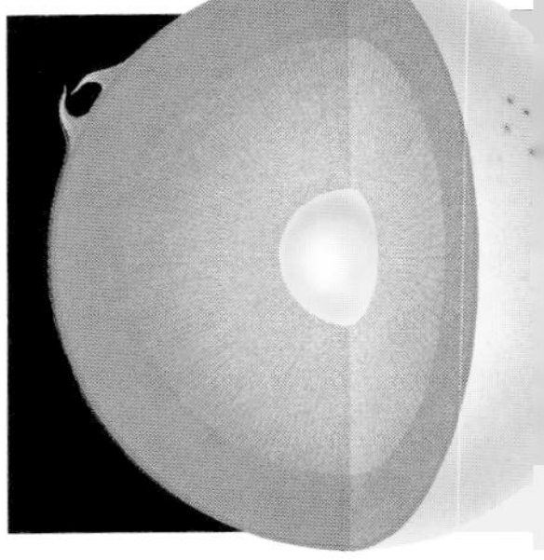

▶ THE SUN
The Sun is a massive ball of hydrogen gas **[B]**, *1.39 million km across. Energy is generated at its heart, where temperatures exceed 15 million°C, by nuclear fusion – the joining together through a chain reaction of two hydrogen atoms to form one helium. In the process, a large amount of excess energy is released, carried to the surface of the Sun in giant convection cells, and then radiated across the Solar System from the top of the 'photosphere' – the visible disk of the Sun, with a temperature of 5500°C.*

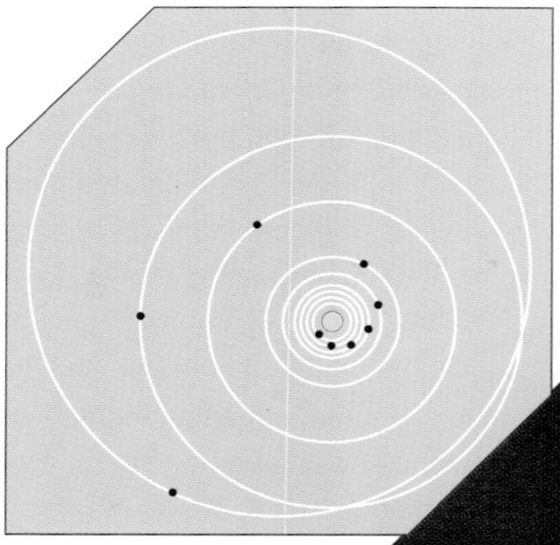

◀ THE SOLAR SYSTEM
The solar system consists of 9 planets **[A]**: *Pluto* [1], *the smallest, is the furthest away from the Sun, though once in every 248.6 years its orbit crosses inside Neptune's path. Neptune* [2], *the outermost of the gas giants, has a diameter of 49,400km, and orbits every 164.8 years.*

Uranus [3] *is similar in size to Neptune and orbits every 84 years. All the gas giants have ring systems, but Uranus's are second only to Saturn's. The planet is tilted at over 98° to the plane of the*

Solar System, so it seems to roll around its orbit. Saturn [4] is noted for its spectacular ring system – the planet has a diameter of 105,000km, while the rings stretch out to 300,000km. It orbits the Sun every 29.5 years, and has a huge family of satellites.

Jupiter [5] orbits the Sun every 11.9 years. With a diameter of 137,400km it is the largest planet in the Solar System. It has complex weather systems, including the Great Red Spot, a storm with a diameter larger than the Earth's.

Between Jupiter and Mars is the asteroid belt [6], rocky debris left over from the Solar System's formation. Inside it lie the terrestrial planets. Mars [7], the red planet, circles the Sun in 1.9 years, and has a diameter of 6790km. Its surface is scoured by massive dust storms, and it shows evidence of running water on the surface in its past. Next in towards the Sun is our own blue planet, the Earth [8], with a diameter of 12,700km. Within the orbit of the Earth lies its near twin Venus [9], circling the Sun in 225 days, and with a diameter of 12,100km. The atmosphere of Venus, however, is a poisonous mixture of carbon dioxide and other gases, with clouds of sulphuric acid. Mercury [10] is the second smallest planet with a diameter of only 4,880km, and a solar orbit that lasts 88 days. Its proximity to the Sun (58 million km) makes it a scorched world with no atmosphere, and a cratered surface similar to that of the Moon. It orbits the Sun once every 88 days.

molecules, with a surface pressure 95 times that of Earth's atmosphere, and temperatures of 470°C. Beyond the Earth's orbit, Mars is famous as the Red Planet – a colour given by rust in its surface dust. Although smaller than Earth, there is evidence that Mars once had a thick atmosphere, and that water ran on its surface – although now it is frozen into polar ice-caps.

The gas giants

The outer Solar System contains worlds quite different from those nearer the Sun – the gas giants. Largest of these is Jupiter, more massive than all the other planets in the Solar System put together, with churning weather systems that include the Great Red Spot, a storm large enough to engulf Earth. Beyond Jupiter lies Saturn, with its spectacular ring system of icy particles, and then the smaller giants Uranus and Neptune. Space probes have shown that Jupiter, Uranus and Neptune also have thin ring systems, although these are nothing to match Saturn's spectacle.

All four of these worlds have large families of moons orbiting round them. Jupiter has a vast family of moons, including Io, the most volcanic body in the Solar System, whose eruptions launch yellow plumes of sulphur into space, scarring its surface with streaks. The most interesting member of Uranus's satellite system is Miranda – a small, deeply-cratered world which displays so many variations in terrain that it must have suffered some great cataclysm in the past. Neptune's giant satellite Triton has active geysers shooting water, ammonia and methane 8km above its surface.

◀ *The Sun is just one of over 200 billion stars in the vast spiral of the Milky Way galaxy, like every other star that we see with the naked eye in the night sky. It lies roughly two-thirds of the way towards the edge of the galactic disc, orbiting the centre at a speed of 250 kilometres per second, taking 200 million years to complete each revolution. This view is what the galaxy would look like to an observer outside. But because of our position in the plane, we see the dense star clouds as a pale band across the sky.*

THE EARTH & THE MOON

THE EARTH'S SATELLITE, THE MOON, IS SO LARGE by comparison with our own world (at 3746km, it is over one-quarter the Earth's diameter) that astronomers consider the two together as a 'double planet'. This massive size and proximity means that the Moon has a great influence on the Earth itself, for example through the tides.

The origins of the Moon are open to debate – some believe that the Moon is a chunk of debris flung off when the still-molten Earth collided with another body the size of Mars, in the early days of the Solar System. Since then, the two bodies have had very different histories. The Moon's small size meant that it cooled more quickly and its low gravity made it unable to hold onto an atmosphere – the factor which has been crucial in shaping our own planet's terrain. In fact, the Moon has altered so little that it provides valuable information about the history of the early Solar System. The lack of an atmosphere also means that, unlike Earth, the Moon is not shielded from the extremes of heat from the Sun. Temperatures at noon climb to 150°C, while at night they can plummet to -200°C. These acute differences can even cause moonquakes as the surface stretches and contracts.

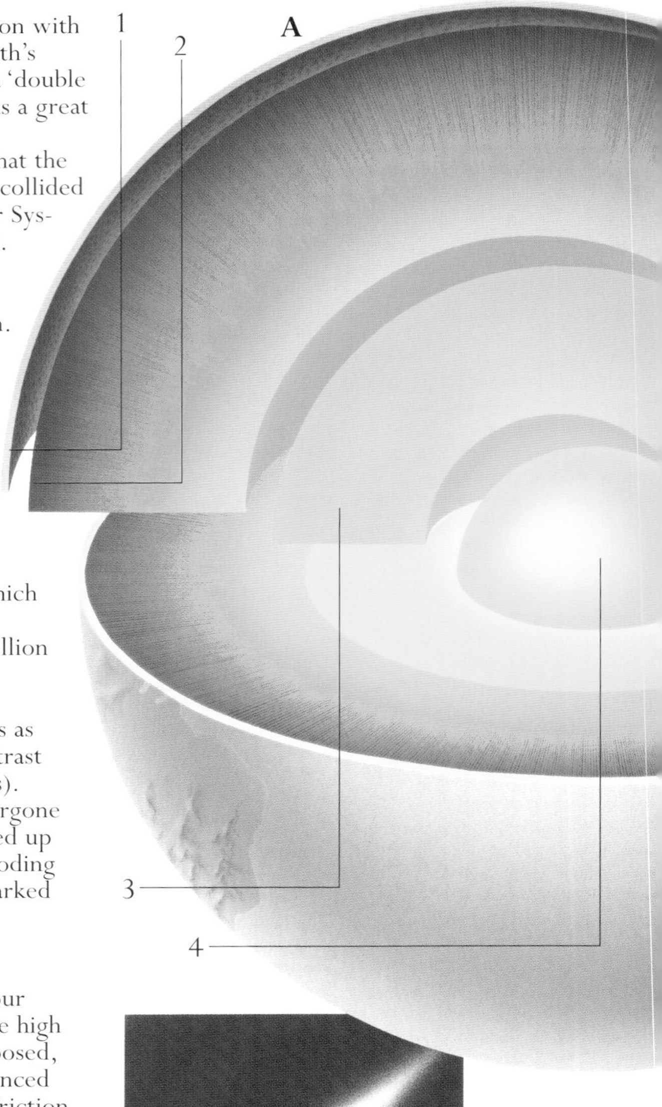

A familiar face

The Moon's surface divides into two distinct types of terrain, which can be easily distinguished with the naked eye from Earth. The bright highlands are highly cratered areas created more than 4 billion years ago during an era of bombardment by rock particles from space. The numbers of these particles dwindled until only a few massive chunks were left, which created enormous impact basins as they crashed into the Moon's surface. The gnarled highlands contrast sharply with the smoother, darker Maria (from the Latin for seas). After the cratering had died away, the Moon seems to have undergone a brief period of intense volcanic activity. Red-hot fissures opened up across its surface, out of which huge volumes of lava poured, flooding low-lying areas. These lava lakes solidified to form the Maria, marked by only a few, very small craters.

Lunar attraction

The changing direction of the Sun and Moon from Earth cause our monthly cycle of tides. Twice a month, at full and new moon, the high Spring Tides occur, with Moon and Sun lined up, or directly opposed, so the tidal effect is at its strongest. Such tidal effects have influenced the Earth-Moon system as a whole. Over millions of years, the friction of the oceans' movement has slowed the lunar 'day', so it now lasts exactly as long as the time the Moon takes to orbit Earth, with the result that it always keeps the same face turned towards us. Fossil records show that there were once 400 days in each Earth year, so the same effect must also be

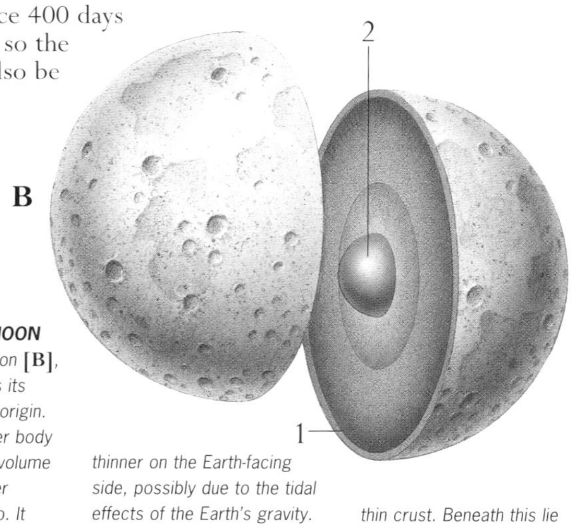

▶ ***STRUCTURE OF THE MOON***
The Earth's satellite, the Moon **[B]**, *has a structure that reflects its different size, and possibly origin. Because it is a much smaller body – around one-twentieth the volume of the Earth – it has a higher surface area to volume ratio. It cooled down more rapidly early in the history of the Solar System, and is now inactive. The lunar crust [1] is actually thicker than Earth's – an average of 70km, though it is thinner on the Earth-facing side, possibly due to the tidal effects of the Earth's gravity. This could be a possible explanation of why the smooth 'seas' are found far more on this side, formed from eruptions of lava through the thin crust. Beneath this lie layers of solidified, cold rock, which decrease in rigidity. At the centre there may be a cold core [2], although its existence is still debated.*

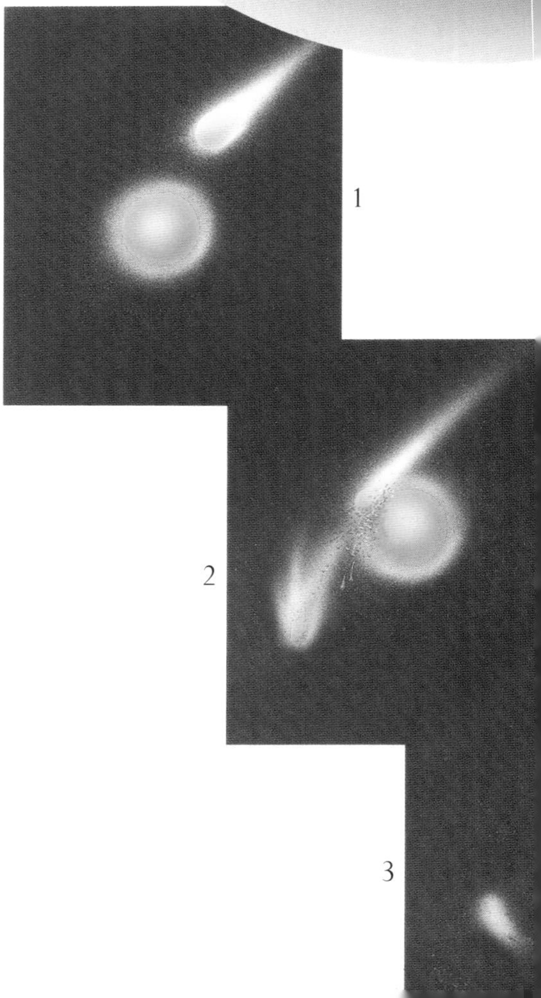

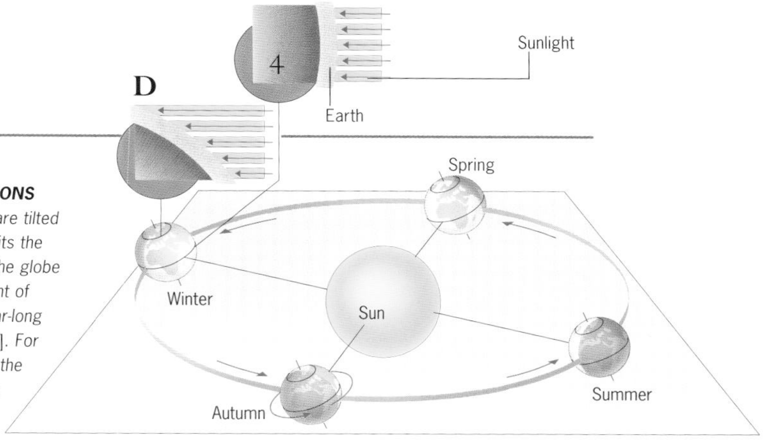

▶ THE EARTH'S SEASONS
The Poles of the Earth are tilted at 23.5° **[D]**. *As it orbits the Sun, different parts of the globe receive a varying amount of sunlight through the year-long cycle of the seasons [3]. For six months of the year, the Northern Hemisphere is tilted towards the Sun, which therefore appears higher in the sky, giving warmer temperatures and longer days [1]. Six months later, when the Northern Hemisphere is tilted in the other direction, the days are shorter and the Sun stays closer to the horizon [2]. The situation is reversed in the Southern Hemisphere. The Tropics of Cancer and Capricorn are lines around the globe at the lines of latitude +/- 23.5°. They mark the northernmost and southernmost points where the Sun appears directly overhead.*

◀ THE STRUCTURE OF THE EARTH
The Earth has the shape of a squashed ball or a spheroid **[A]**. *It has a diameter at the poles of 12,703km, but is wider at the Equator, thrown outward by the rapid daily spin which causes a 'bulge'. The crust [1], on which lie the continents and oceans, is a thin layer of rock varying in depth between 10 and 20km. Below this lies a mantle [2], divided into two regions. The upper mantle extends down to 3000km, and divides into the mainly solid lithosphere and the mostly molten aesthenosphere. Beyond this, the molten rock of the upper and lower mantle extends down towards the molten outer [3] and solid inner [4] cores of iron and nickel, around 7000km across, at the centre of the Earth. It is the rotation of this core that is believed to generate the Earth's magnetic field, in an effect similar to that of a dynamo.*

slowing its rotation as well. Hence in the distant future, the spin of the Earth could be so slow that its day and year are equal, so that one scorched side of the planet will permanently face the Sun.

Complete coverage

Very occasionally, as the Moon orbits around the Earth and it in turn moves around the Sun, all three bodies – Sun, Earth and Moon – line up exactly and an eclipse is seen. If the Earth blocks out the Sun shining onto the full Moon, a rather unspectacular lunar eclipse happens.
Far more spectacular are solar eclipses, when the new Moon passes right across the face of the Sun. By chance the Moon and Sun have discs in the sky that are almost the same size. This means that total solar eclipses can only be seen for short periods of time from tiny regions of the Earth. The effect is breathtaking as the Moon covers the bright central disk of the Sun, and reveals the wispy white corona of gas streaming out from the Sun's surface.

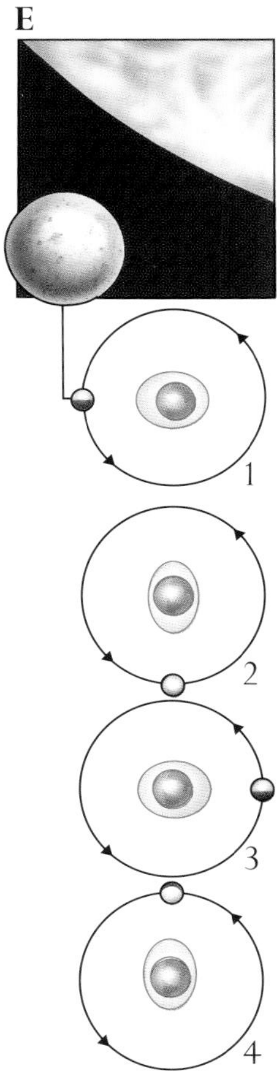

◀ HOW THE MOON BEGAN
The Moon orbits too far from the Earth to be a captured asteroid. Instead, it is thought to have been formed when a body the size of Mars collided with the still-molten Earth during the formation of the Solar System, some 5 billion years ago [1].

The collision resulted in a stream of debris being thrown off into orbit round the Earth [2], and this eventually condensed to form the Moon [3]. The iron-rich cores of the two original bodies combined and remained within the Earth, becoming its very dense central region, whilst the Moon formed from the two lighter outer sections. This may explain why the Earth is thought to have a more complicated structure than the Moon, and also the lack of iron in Moon rock.

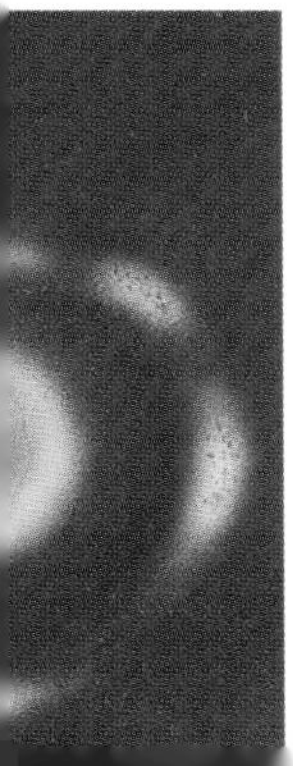

◀ HOW THE MOON AFFECTS THE EARTH'S TIDES
The proximity of the Moon to the Earth, coupled with its size, causes strong gravitational forces between the two worlds, which is shown in the tides **[E]**.

As the Moon exerts a gravitational pull on the Earth, it draws the seas towards it, and creates a bulge in the seawater on one side of the planet. At the same time, the Earth itself is attracted towards the Moon, pulling it away from the sea on the opposite side of the globe and creating a smaller tidal bulge on the opposite side. Because the Moon is relatively slow-moving, the tidal bulges in the sea remain in almost the same place, while the Earth rotates under them [1,2,3,4]. As each bulge passes a point on the Earth roughly once each day, seashores experience two high and two low tides each day (although the shape of an inlet can alter their spacing). As the Moon circles the Earth once a month, the tides occur at different times each day.

▼ During the brief minutes of the eclipse, the corona of the Sun can be seen.

Normally this is an invisible halo, made up of two distinct regions of gas which overlap, the K-corona and the F-corona. The latter reaches out many millions of kilometres from the Suns surface while the K-corona extends for a mere 75,000km.

A WORLD IN MOTION

WE THINK OF THE GROUND AS BEING STEADY AND IMMOVABLE: in fact the surface of the Earth is in a constant state of movement, propelled by the intense heat of the interior. Although our planet is 12,700km wide, the crust on which the continents and oceans lie is only a few tens of kilometres thick at its deepest. This thin crust is broken into slabs or plates, which float on top of an inner molten layer, the mantle. Where these plates collide with each other or slowly draw apart are areas of violent activity, subject to earthquakes and studded with volcanoes. This drama is not restricted to dry land: satellite photography has shown that the two-thirds of Earth's surface under the ocean is just as fascinating, with features such as chains of volcanic mountains that stretch for 60,000km around the globe.

The idea that the continents are slowly moving was first put forward to explain how the coastlines of different continents appear to fit together like pieces of a jigsaw puzzle. For example, the eastern coast of South America nestles snugly into the western coast of Africa. Such continental drifts can be traced back to a point around 250 million years ago, when all the land masses on Earth were joined into a supercontinent called Pangaea (from the Greek for all earth), surrounded by a single vast sea, the Tethys Ocean. This supercontinent slowly disintegrated into the major land masses we know today.

Geologists call their model for the movements of the Earth's crust plate tectonics. This describes the surface, both continents and ocean floor, as being split into plates whose movements are driven by the churning of the molten rock in the inner mantle. The largest plates are as wide as the Pacific Ocean, while others are much smaller. Their thickness varies from around 10km beneath the oceans, to 30km under major land masses, and up to 60km where a plate has to support the weight of a mountain range. In general, ocean floor plates are made of dense basaltic rocks, while the continents are formed from less dense granite.

Earthquakes

Most of the areas where plates are separating are hidden beneath the ocean. At the fault between the plates molten rock wells up through a fissure and solidifies, creating new ocean floor. Only in a few places can this process be seen on dry land, notably in the volcanoes of Iceland, which sits on a fault called the Mid-Atlantic Ridge.

Plates can meet in a number of ways. At earthquake zones they grind past each other in opposite directions, being compressed so that they store huge amounts of energy. This is released in calamitous movements of the ground – earthquakes. The most famous earthquake zone of all, the San Andreas Fault in California, is a region where the North American and Pacific Plates are moving past each other. Earthquake prediction hinges on the theory that major quakes are preceded by 'quiet' periods during which the plates lock together, and store up the energy. Not all the plate boundaries are earthquake or volcano zones – the Himalayas are the result of a head-on collision between the relatively fast-moving Indo-Australian Plate, and the Eurasian Plate. These two continental plates buckled upwards, forming the mountain range, and halting the Indo-Australian plate's movement.

Conversely, not all volcanoes are at plate boundaries. The volcanic Hawaiian Islands,

*▼ **PANGAEA***

The continents of the world have not always looked as they do today **[A]**. *The process of plate tectonics means that that they have migrated across the surface of the Earth. 200 million years ago, in the Jurassic era, all the land masses were joined in a single supercontinent, Pangaea [1]. Eventually, 120 million years ago, Pangaea split in two, the northern Laurasia made up of present-day North America and Eurasia, and the southern Gondwana, comprising South America, Africa, Australia and India [2].*

By 40 million years ago the world had taken on a familiar look, although India had yet to collide with Eurasia (and create the Himalayas in the process) and Australia was still located very close to Antarctica [3].

A

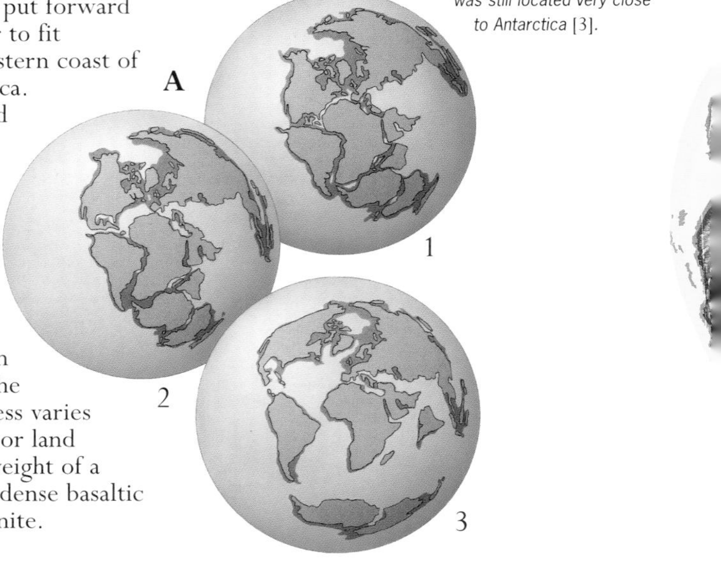

*▼ **PLATE TECTONICS***

The processes of plate tectonics can be seen most clearly on a section of ocean floor **[B]**. *At a subduction zone [1], an oceanic plate meets a much thicker continental plate and is forced down into the Earth's upper mantle. The heat in this zone melts the upper basalt layer of the oceanic plate, forming liquid magma which then rises to the surface and is vented through volcanoes.*

At a mid-oceanic ridge [2] new crust is constantly being generated where two plates are separating. Magma rises up from the Earth's mantle, forcing its way through cracks in the crust, and solidifying. As the cracks expand, a striated ocean floor is formed. When the new crust solidifies, traces of iron in it align with the Earth's magnetic field and so preserve a record of the various reversals in the field over millions of years.

A hot spot volcano [3] forms where the crust thins above a hot plume rising from the inner mantle. It is only the latest in a string of volcanoes that form as the oceanic plate moves over the stationary plume. The earlier volcanoes become extinct, subsiding to volcanic islands with coral fringes, and eventually become atolls, where only the ring of coral remains above the surface of the ocean.

B

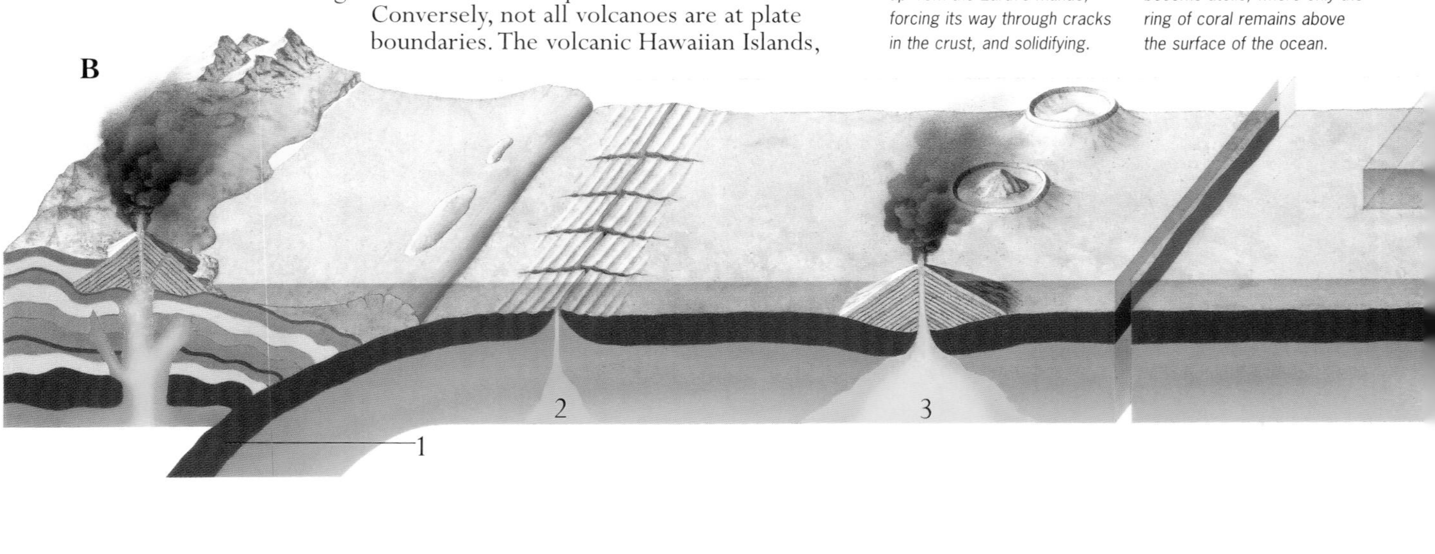

D

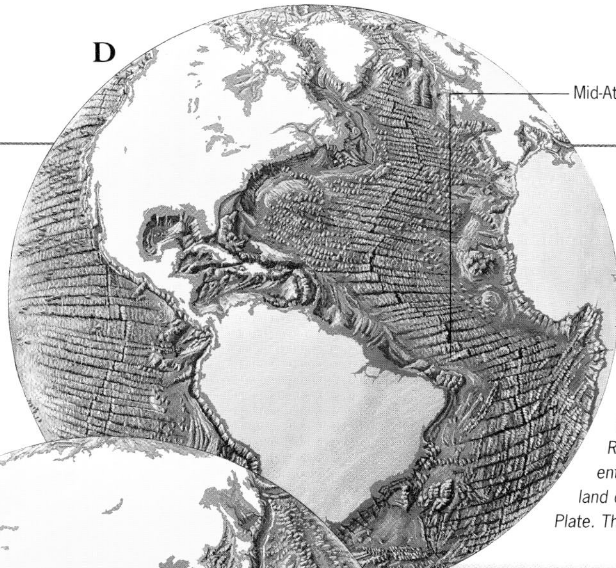
Mid-Atlantic Ridge

◀ THE ATLANTIC AND THE PACIFIC
The floors of the two largest oceans reveal important differences in their structures.

The Atlantic Ocean **[D]** *is divided by the Mid-Atlantic Ridge that runs for its entire length, from Greenland down to the Antarctic Plate. This is a region where the Earth's crust is stretching, new floor being pumped out so that the Atlantic is gradually widening. As the rock is pulled apart, large slabs sink, creating the series of rifts that run parallel to the ridge along its length. Only in a few places does the ridge emerge above the sea, most spectacularly in Iceland, the shape of which is constantly being redefined by volcanic activity.*

In contrast, the floor of the Pacific Ocean **[E]** *shows signs of many different seismic activities. It is surrounded by the so-called 'ring of fire' – volcanic zones where the oceanic plates dive below continental ones and create volcanoes. At other places, oceanic plates converge, creating trenches where one plate dives below the other, such as the Marianas Trench, the deepest place on Earth.*

E

Marianas Trench

THE SEVEN SEAS

The phrase 'the seven seas' dates back to the seas known to Muslim voyagers before the fifteenth century. Nowadays, the waters of the world are divided into seven oceans – the North Pacific, the South Pacific, the North Atlantic, the South Atlantic, the Indian, the Arctic and the Antarctic. But divisions such as these are in reality arbitrary, as all these waters can just as easily be considered as parts of one continuous global ocean.

The Pacific Ocean
Water Area:
180,000,000 square kilometres
Volume:
724,000,000 cubic kilometres
Average Depth: *3940 metres*

The Atlantic Ocean
Water Area:
106,000,000 square kilometres
Volume:
355,000,000 cubic kilometres
Average Depth: *3310 metres*

The Indian Ocean
Water Area:
75,000,000 square kilometres
Volume:
292,000,000 cubic kilometres
Average Depth: *3840 metres*

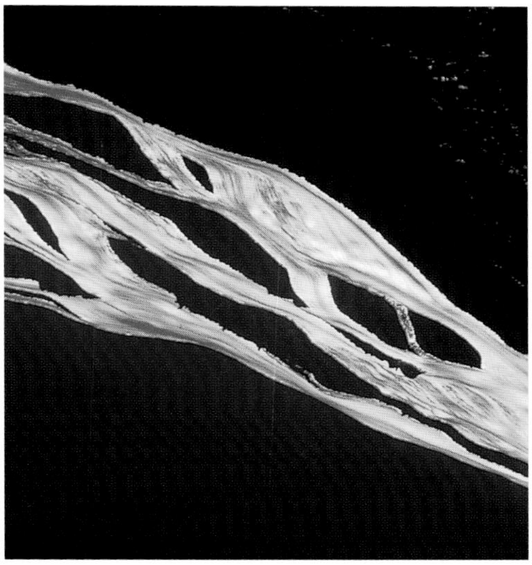

◀ Lava which erupts from the earth's surface can take on a number of forms. Aa, or block lava, is runny, and quickly forms a hard pastry-like crust when it cools. Pahoehoe lava has a sheen to it like satin and often consolidates in rope-like forms. When this kind of lava comes into contact with the sea it takes on the form of a jumbled heap of pillows, hence its name pillow lava.

▼ SEA CHANGE
A coastal region **[C]** *is shaped by the forces of longshore drift. Sand is pushed along the shore by ocean currents to build up spits [1], bars [2] and sometimes enclosing bays to form lagoons.*

A river carries vast amounts of sediment out to sea, which is deposited to form a delta [3]. Under the sea, the accumulation of sediment forms the continental shelf [4], a region that slopes gently out from the coastline for about 75km, to depths of 100-200m. In places it is cut through by submarine gorges, formed either by rivers when the sea level was lower or by the undercutting effect of river currents flowing out to sea. The shelf gives way to the steep continental slope, which dives to depths of several kilometres. From the base of the slope, the continental rise extends up to 1000km from the coast into the ocean.

C

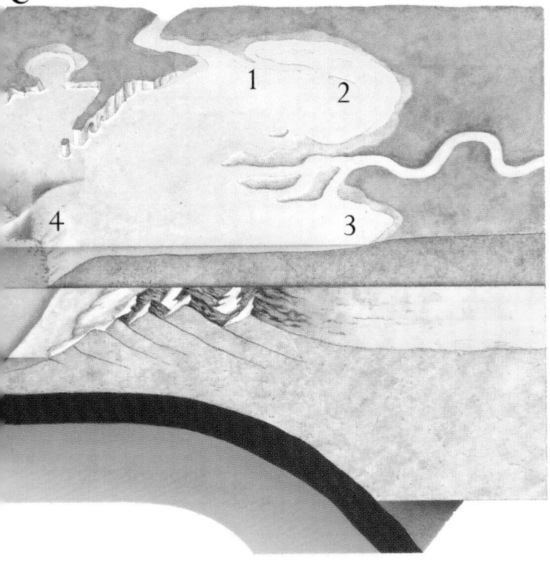

for instance, lie in the middle of the Pacific Plate. This chain of volcanic mountains is caused by a semi-permanent 'hot spot' where molten magma rises from the depths of the mantle through the crust, and spews out of a volcano. Although the hot spot in the mantle is stationary, the Pacific Plate, and with it the volcano, is continually moving. Hawaii itself is only the most recent in a chain of 107 volcanic vents formed by the plume. As the plate moves on, each volcano becomes extinct, and a new one forms further along the chain. Many thousands of these 'hot spot' volcanoes are known – mostly beneath the ocean surface – so there must be hundreds of hot plumes in the mantle to have created them all.

While plates are being destroyed in the subduction zones where they collide, new plate material is being produced all the time deep beneath the ocean surface. The sea floor is just as geologically fascinating as the continental land surface, and is still awaiting full exploration.

Occasionally, the volcanic activity of the mid-oceanic ridges reaches the surface, and forms islands. At other places, hot gases venting from the depths of the Earth create pools of warmth on the ocean floor, where life can flourish.

SHAPING THE EARTH

OVER BILLIONS OF YEARS, THE HARSH landscape created by geological activity such as plate tectonics and volcanism has been softened and sculpted by the eroding forces of ice, water and air. Glaciers have ground out valleys, and rivers have carved huge gorges, including America's Grand Canyon. At the same time the steady pounding of the seas and oceans eats away and remodels coastlines.

Studies of the changing climate in the past show that the Earth has gone through periodic 'ice ages' when the ice-caps pushed into temperate regions closer to the Equator. These periods were critical in shaping the landscape that we see today – during the last Ice Age, which ended 10,000 years ago, an ice sheet covered most of Northern Europe, Asia and North America. The ice ages can be dated by drilling out an ice core from a polar cap. Each year a layer of new ice is laid down, which in colder years – during ice ages – is thicker. These records surprisingly reveal that over the last 4 million years, successive ice ages have gripped Earth for longer than the warmer periods in between.

Variations in the Earth's climate are thought to be the result of cyclical changes in its orbit, which becomes more, then less, elongated. According to these models the Earth's average temperature should currently be on the increase – which means that the measured increases in temperature cited as evidence of global warming and the greenhouse effect may have a natural cause.

Getting in shape

During the ice ages, massive glaciers formed across the globe. As these vast, slow-moving rivers of ice rolled forward, the sheer weight of ice ground down rocks in their paths, leaving a softened, altered landscape once they had retreated. These forces are still at work today: on Greenland and in Antarctica there are many glaciers which eventually find their way to the sea, where they break up into icebergs.

Although glaciers are the most dramatic form of erosion, there are others: over longer periods, rivers and seas can cut through rock and carve out valleys. Even rain has a profound cumulative effect on rock. Raindrops dissolve gases from the atmosphere and become dilute acid, chemically attacking igneous rocks formed from volcanic lava. In time, the particles broken off build up to great depths and are converted by pressure and heat into sedimentary rocks such as limestone. When these are subjected to the intense heat of the Earth's crust they become metamorphic rocks, such as marble and slate.

▼ A WOBBLING WORLD
The climate of the Earth is not constant but gradually varies over time in cycles of thousands of years **[B]**. *The shape of the Earth's orbit around the Sun can vary between an almost perfect circle* [1] *and a pronounced ellipse* [2] *over a cycle of around 100,000 years. When the orbit is more elliptical, the climate of the Earth is more extreme. At the same time, another cycle changes the angle of tilt of the planet between a minimum 21.8° and a maximum 24.4°* **[C]**. *At the maximum inclination, every 22,000 years, the climate is most extreme, and the seasons are especially marked, with the Poles pointing further away from the Sun during winter. When the effects of these cycles are combined, they lead to ice ages of varying severity, the last of which ended around 10,000 years ago.*

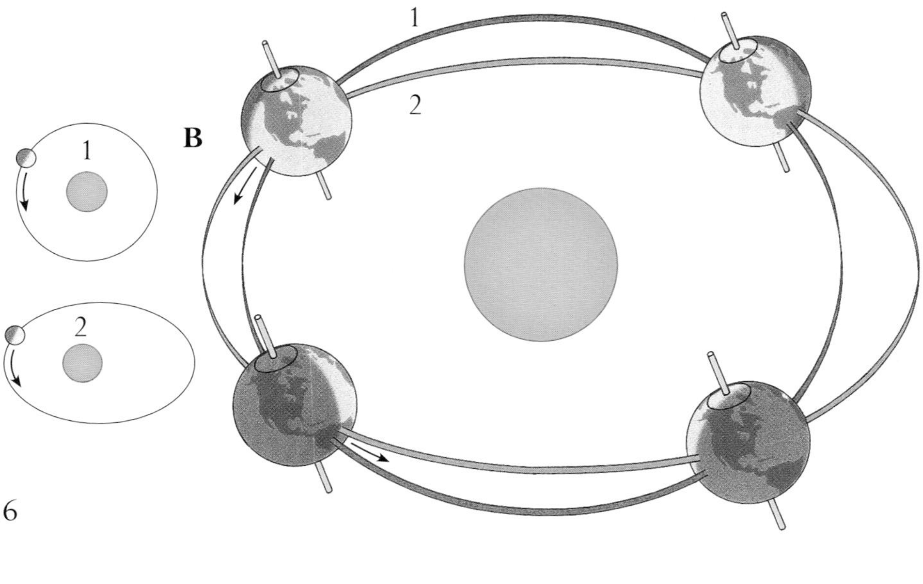

▶ EARTH SCRAPER
Glaciers **[A]** *are dramatic rivers of ice slowly creeping down valleys and carving mountain ranges into a series of sharp peaks. They usually originate where ice or hard-packed snow builds up in a cirque* [1], *a basin near a mountain top. After a sufficient mass has built up, it will start to move under its own gravity, wearing down rocks by pressure, scraping and frost action, to form glacial spoil called 'moraines'. The boulders of moraine underneath the glacier act as abrasives, scouring the landscape. Lateral moraines* [2] *are rocks cut away and pulled along at the sides of the glacier. Where two ice-rivers meet, the lateral moraines can join to form a medial moraine* [3] *– a stripe of rubble down the centre of the glacier. As the glacier grinds along over rocks and boulders, the stresses induced can open up deep and jagged splits called crevasses* [4]. *A glacier terminates at a snout* [5] *which may empty into the sea, or a great lake. On dry land the shape of the snout depends on the climatic conditions, and especially the rate at which the snout melts compared with the rate at which the glacier advances. If the the two rates are exactly balanced, the snout*

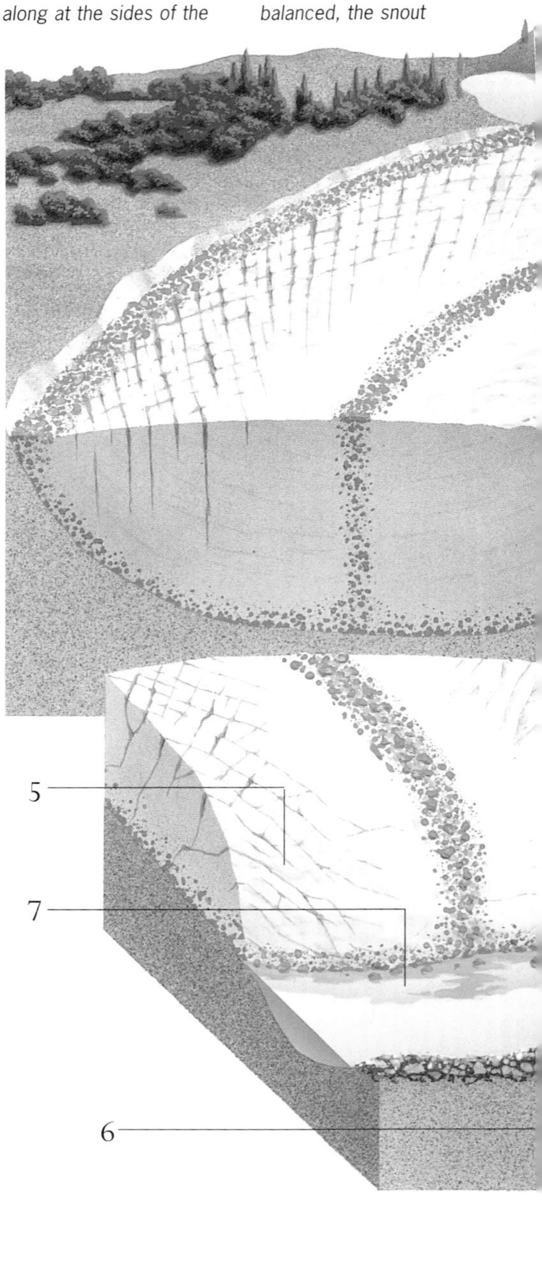

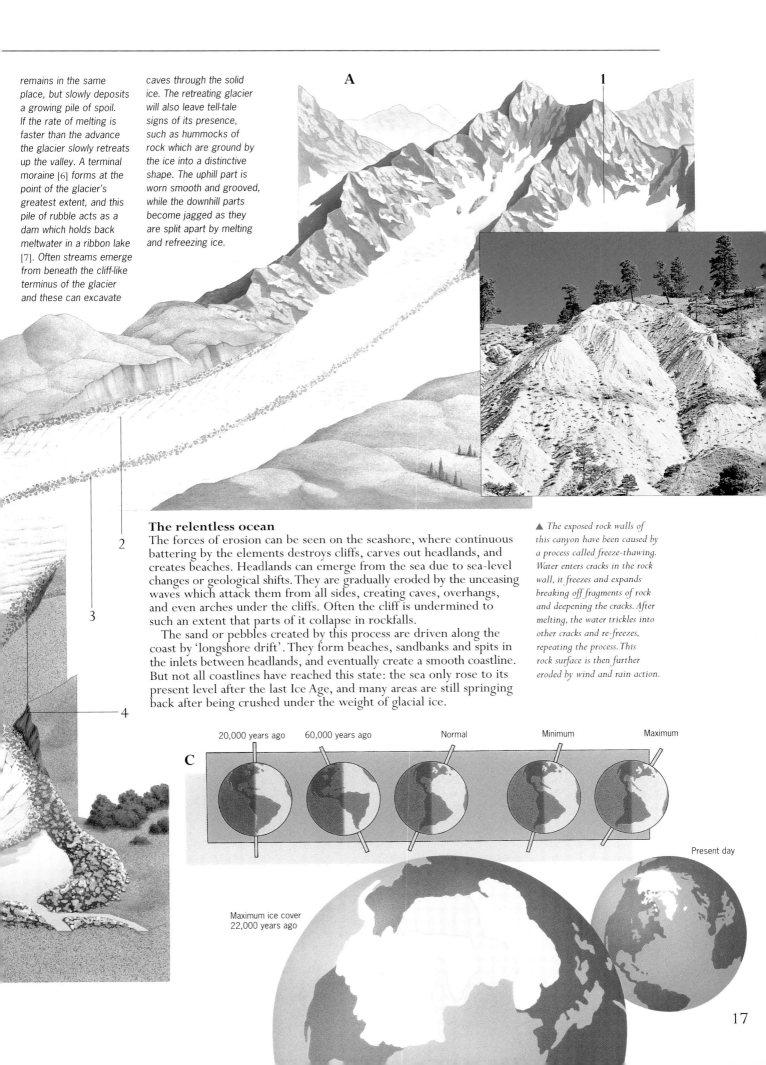

remains in the same place, but slowly deposits a growing pile of spoil. If the rate of melting is faster than the advance the glacier slowly retreats up the valley. A terminal moraine [6] forms at the point of the glacier's greatest extent, and this pile of rubble acts as a dam which holds back meltwater in a ribbon lake [7]. Often streams emerge from beneath the cliff-like terminus of the glacier and these can excavate caves through the solid ice. The retreating glacier will also leave tell-tale signs of its presence, such as hummocks of rock which are ground by the ice into a distinctive shape. The uphill part is worn smooth and grooved, while the downhill parts become jagged as they are split apart by melting and refreezing ice.

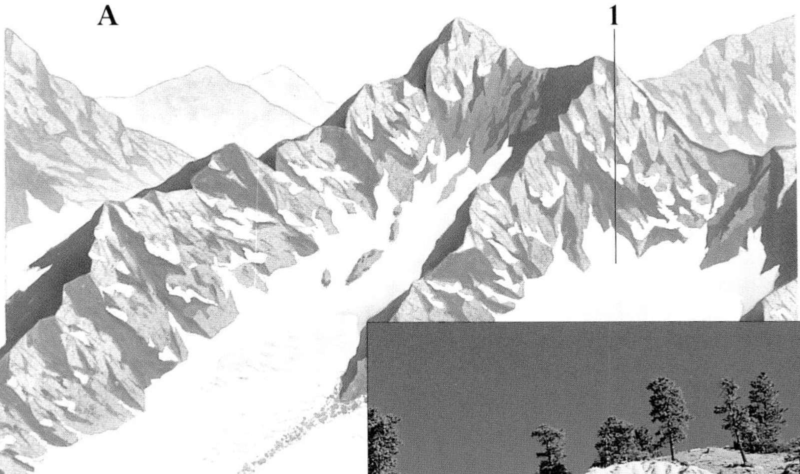

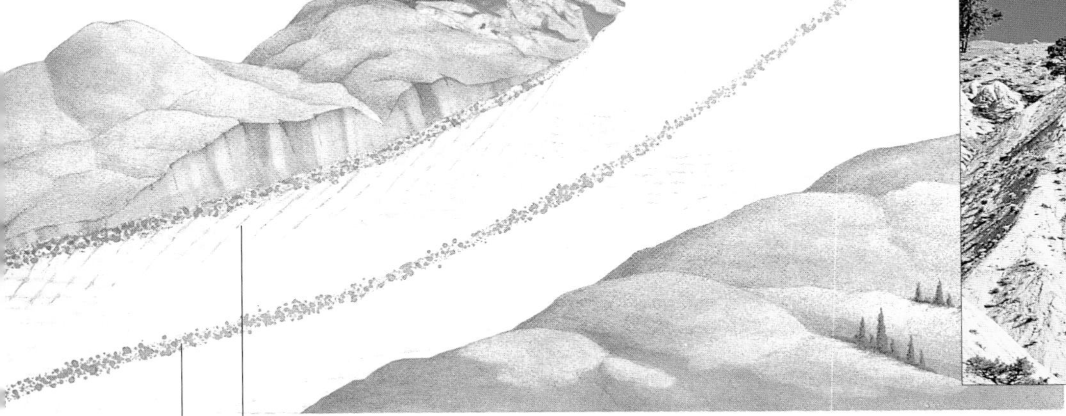

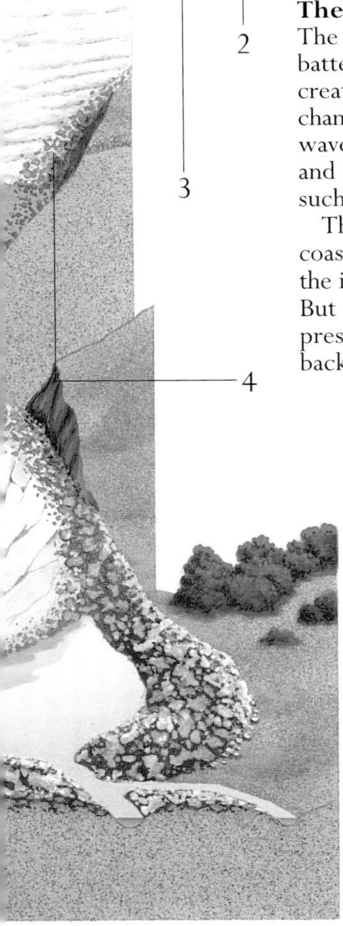

▲ *The exposed rock walls of this canyon have been caused by a process called freeze-thawing. Water enters cracks in the rock wall, it freezes and expands breaking off fragments of rock and deepening the cracks. After melting, the water trickles into other cracks and re-freezes, repeating the process. This rock surface is then further eroded by wind and rain action.*

The relentless ocean

The forces of erosion can be seen on the seashore, where continuous battering by the elements destroys cliffs, carves out headlands, and creates beaches. Headlands can emerge from the sea due to sea-level changes or geological shifts. They are gradually eroded by the unceasing waves which attack them from all sides, creating caves, overhangs, and even arches under the cliffs. Often the cliff is undermined to such an extent that parts of it collapse in rockfalls.

The sand or pebbles created by this process are driven along the coast by 'longshore drift'. They form beaches, sandbanks and spits in the inlets between headlands, and eventually create a smooth coastline. But not all coastlines have reached this state: the sea only rose to its present level after the last Ice Age, and many areas are still springing back after being crushed under the weight of glacial ice.

C
20,000 years ago
60,000 years ago
Normal
Minimum
Maximum

Present day
Maximum ice cover
22,000 years ago

CONTRASTING CONDITIONS

We talk so much about the weather because of its infinite changeability. As the Sun's radiation heats up the Equatorial zones of the planet much more than the Polar regions, it creates wide temperature contrasts. The hottest places on Earth can be a blistering 50°C in the shade, while in the depths of an Antarctic winter, levels as low as -70°C have been recorded. This variable heat produces hot air at the Equator, which rises, while cooler air further north and south sinks under it, producing wind patterns that stretch across the globe. These in turn create swirling eddies of air that can absorb water vapour over the sea, forming clouds, and deposit it as rain over land. Such air currents couple with the variable heat of the Sun to produce the wide variety of climates found on Earth, ranging from hot, rainless deserts to cool, wet, temperate coastal regions.

The atmosphere of the Earth just after it formed was an unbreatheable mixture of hydrogen and helium. In time this was replaced by an equally unbreatheable mixture belched out from volcanoes, which in turn has been modified by lifeforms to the air we breathe today. This is made up of 78 per cent nitrogen, 21 per cent oxygen, and a small proportion of carbon dioxide, which plants then recycle into oxygen. The remainder of the atmosphere is water vapour and small traces of other gases. The balance is a delicate one, perfectly suited to life as it has evolved, and the entire planet – both living things and minerals – is needed to maintain it.

The outer limits of the atmosphere stretch 2400 km above the surface, but the lower 15km, the troposphere, is the densest, holding nearly all the atmosphere's water vapour – which condenses under different conditions to create clouds. Beyond this region, up to 40 km high, lies the stratosphere, which contains a thin ozone layer that blocks out harmful ultraviolet radiation.

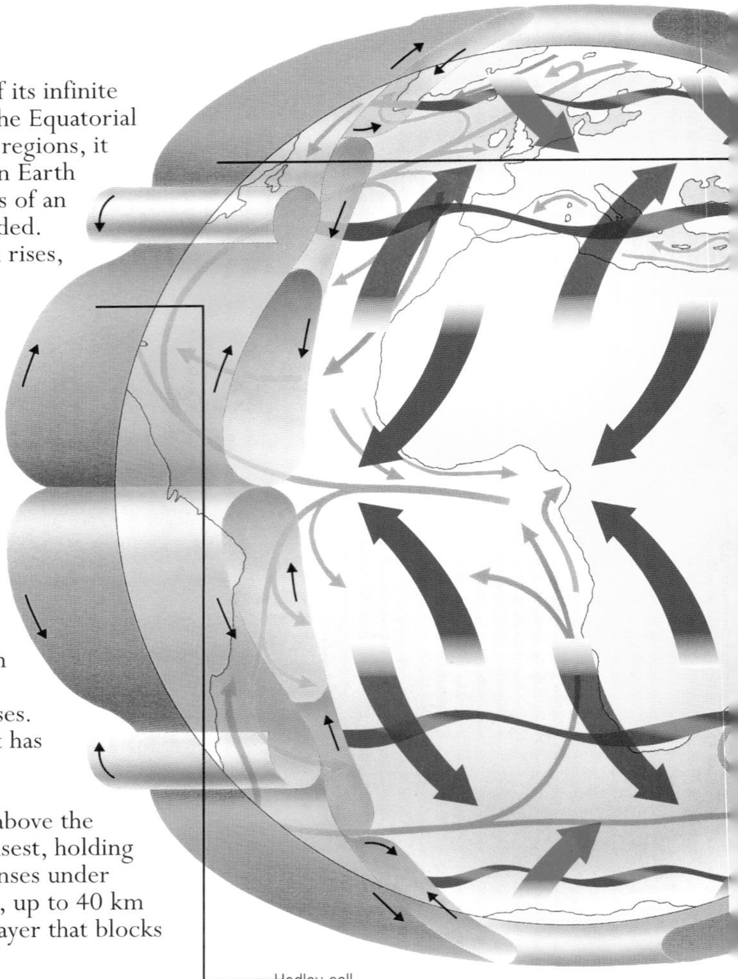

▲ CREATING WINDS
The amount of heat absorbed at the Equator is much greater than at the Poles. The temperature difference creates giant circulation cells which transfer heat from the Equator to the Poles **[A]**. *The Hadley cell is driven by hot air rising from the Equator which cools and returns to the surface at 30° latitude. Some of this returning air is drawn back towards the Equator, creating the trade winds. The Ferrel cell guides warm air towards the Poles, creating winds which the Earth's rotation skews to become the Westerlies. Where these winds meet cold air blowing directly from the Pole, frontal depressions form giving unsettled weather. At the cell boundaries jet streams form – channels of high winds which encircle the planet. This circulation from the Equator to the Poles is complicated by the Earth's rotation, creating the Coriolis force which bends winds to the right in the Northern Hemisphere, and to the left in the Southern Hemisphere.*

Climate types

Land near the Equator has weather patterns typified by those of southern Asia. For six months of the year cold dry winds blow from the land out to sea, giving arid conditions and little rain. In the summer the wind reverses direction and starts to blow warm air off the ocean. This air is heavy with water vapour and triggers torrential rainstorms over land.

Weather in the temperate latitudes of northern Europe is dominated by the jet stream, a band of high winds at altitudes of about 12km. It forms where warm air from the tropics meets cold Polar air, creating a jet of air travelling at speeds around 200kmh in summer, 400kmh in winter. The jet stream's direction develops in a similar way to a slowly flowing river, meandering and forming eddies. These are seen as high-pressure anticyclones, wind systems that create clear, dry weather, or low pressure depressions with associated clouds and weather fronts.

The circulation patterns of the oceans are just as important in regulating climate. In general, the oceans circulate in large eddies, clockwise in the Northern Hemisphere, anticlockwise in the Southern. One of the

▶ Deserts can be created in many ways, and they may be hot or cold. The Antarctic, being one of the driest places in the world, is classed as a cold desert. The Sahara and the Arabian Deserts are classic examples of hot deserts. The photograph shows a sand dune system in the Namib Desert in Southern Africa. Winds blowing over the land constantly shift dunes in ever changing patterns.

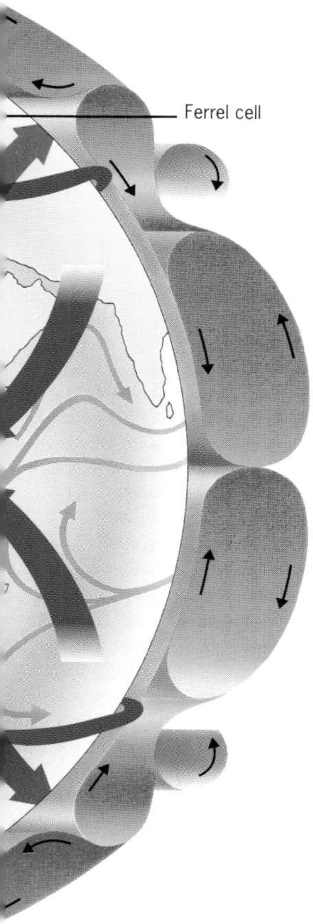
Ferrel cell

▶ *A tornado can form during a very severe thunderstorm* **[C]**. *Hot air evaporating off land or sea rises rapidly through the atmosphere, condensing to form clouds. As surface air rushes inward the low pressure at the centre of the storm, the spin of the Earth makes the whole complex spin, producing a typhoon or hurricane (right). Tornadoes occur when the fast-rising thermals, which create a storm, begin to spin even more quickly, perhaps in response to the local geography. As the thermal winds up on itself, it draws a funnel of cloud down from the bottom of the storm towards the ground, where the winds often exceed 200kmh. The extreme low pressure sucks up material from the ground, flinging it out at the top of the tornado, sometimes to land several kilometres away. Waterspouts are similar vortices that form over water.*

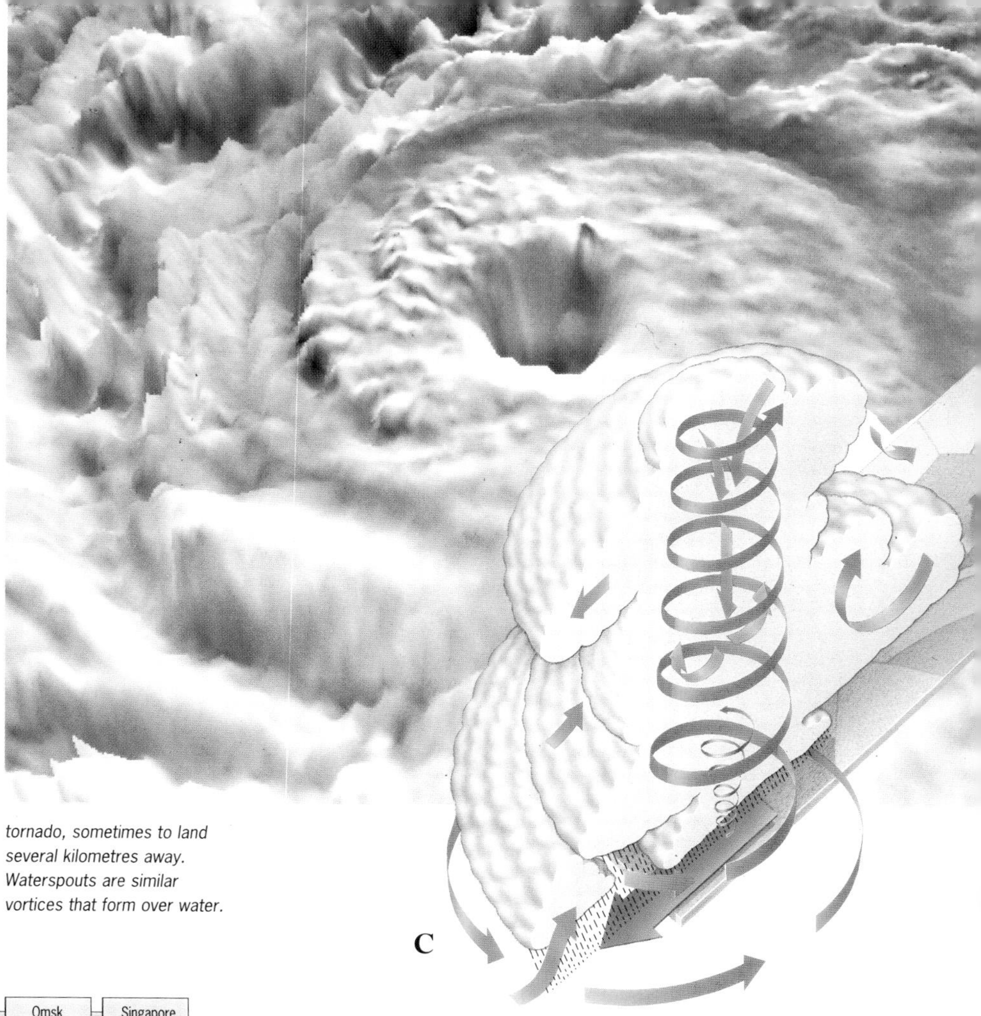

C

▶ ***VARIETY OF CLIMATE***
The patterns of rainfall and temperature around the world divide the Earth into different regions of vegetation **[B]**. *Seven cities around the world illustrate the wide variety of weather these produce.*

New York has an east coast continental climate, with cold winters, hot summers and steady rainfall all year round. London's climate is marine west coast, similarly wet to New York's but with less variation between summer and winter temperatures. Omsk has typical steppe climate, with low rainfall and very cold winters followed by hot summers. Singapore's tropical climate gives almost constant hot and very wet weather. Manaus in Brazil's region of tropical savanna has constant high temperatures, with very dry summer months. A desert climate like that of Alice Springs has very high average temperatures (with a slight dip during the southern winter months), but almost no rain throughout the year. The Nigerian capital, Lagos, has a constantly hot tropical rainforest climate, characterised by its extremely wet summer months.

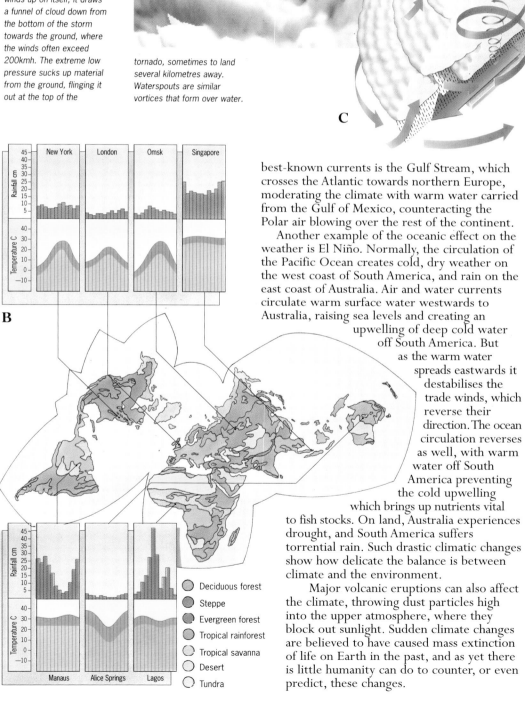

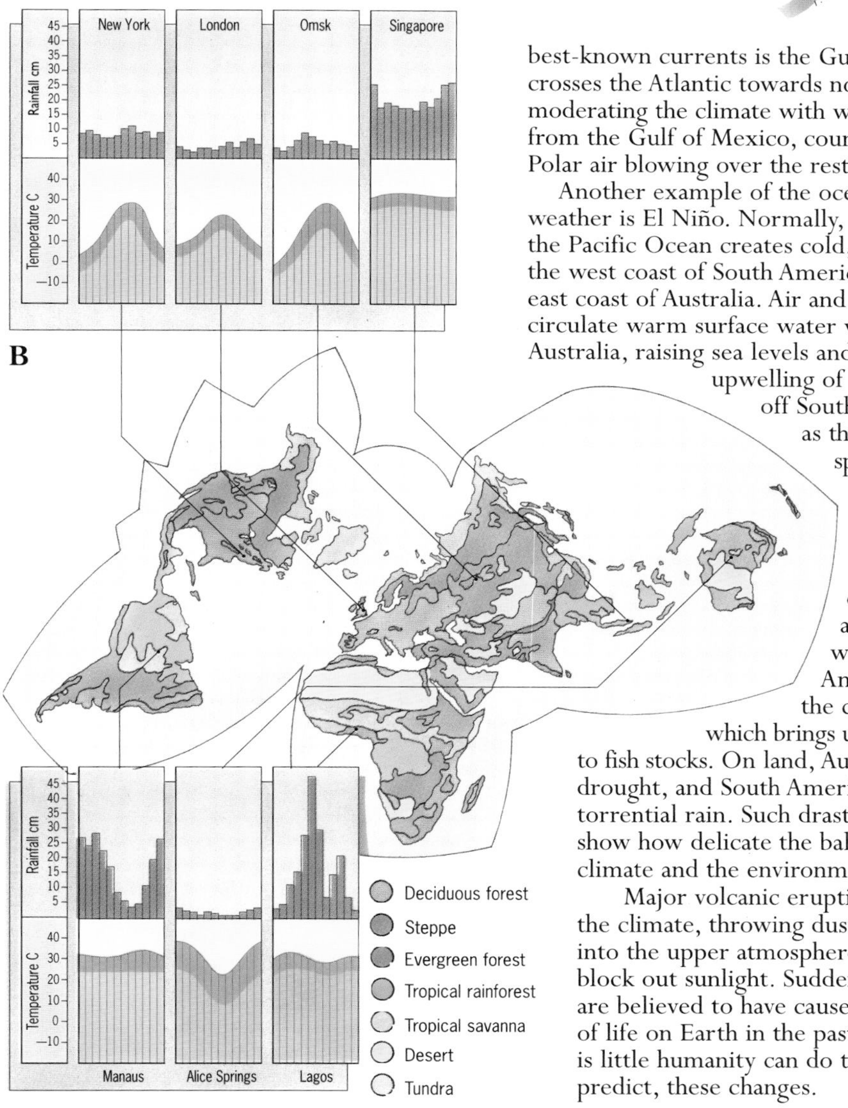
New York
London
Omsk
Singapore
Rainfall cm
45
40
35
30
25
20
15
10
5
Temperature C
40
30
20
10
0
–10
Manaus
Alice Springs
Lagos
Deciduous forest
Steppe
Evergreen forest
Tropical rainforest
Tropical savanna
Desert
Tundra

B

best-known currents is the Gulf Stream, which crosses the Atlantic towards northern Europe, moderating the climate with warm water carried from the Gulf of Mexico, counteracting the Polar air blowing over the rest of the continent.

Another example of the oceanic effect on the weather is El Niño. Normally, the circulation of the Pacific Ocean creates cold, dry weather on the west coast of South America, and rain on the east coast of Australia. Air and water currents circulate warm surface water westwards to Australia, raising sea levels and creating an upwelling of deep cold water off South America. But as the warm water spreads eastwards it destabilises the trade winds, which reverse their direction. The ocean circulation reverses as well, with warm water off South America preventing the cold upwelling which brings up nutrients vital to fish stocks. On land, Australia experiences drought, and South America suffers torrential rain. Such drastic climatic changes show how delicate the balance is between climate and the environment.

Major volcanic eruptions can also affect the climate, throwing dust particles high into the upper atmosphere, where they block out sunlight. Sudden climate changes are believed to have caused mass extinction of life on Earth in the past, and as yet there is little humanity can do to counter, or even predict, these changes.

PEOPLING THE GLOBE

THE ORIGINS OF HUMANKIND ARE VERY HARD TO DETERMINE. The fossil record of our ancestors is very patchy, and thus the story involves large amounts of guesswork. Archaeologists believe that between 7 and 10 million years ago, a human ancestor, called Ramapithecus, developed from the same stock as chimpanzees and gorillas. The route from these creatures to modern man can be traced in terms of changing skeletons. Bipedal motion required a sturdy pelvis, while the increasing intelligence of these progenitors can be followed through increasing brain capacities. Ramapithecus was succeeded by Australopithecus, whose later form is named Homo habilis, the handy man, because fossil evidence shows that it used simple tools.

Homo erectus appeared in Africa 1.7 million years ago and spread to the rest of the world roughly 1 million years ago. They were almost as tall as modern humans, with skull capacities twice as large as Homo habilis. This species lived longer in Asia than in Africa – it includes Peking Man, who lived 250,000 years ago. It was gradually succeeded by our species, Homo sapiens, which appeared in Africa more than 500,000 years ago. The expansion was a slow drift as bands of hunter-gatherers followed prey animals. There can have been no population pressure: 10,000 years ago the world population was between 5 and 10 million, about the population of New York City today. As people settled in various places, climate and food sources led them to evolve differently. For example, those in very hot Equatorial countries kept a dark skin to protect them from ultraviolet sunlight; those in colder climates developed lighter skins to maximise the effect of a weaker sun – vitamin D, essential to bone growth, is gained from sunlight.

At first only Africa, Asia and the warmer parts of Europe were colonised: America and Australia remained empty for thousands of years. Movement between continental land masses was made possible by climate changes. During the last Ice Age, much of the world's water was locked into the ice caps. Sea levels dropped dramatically, what is now the Bering Strait became a land passage, and vast stretches of ocean became navigable by small boats.

Hunters to farmers

For two million years, human ancestors lived as hunter-gatherers, following a nomadic pattern of life, with a diet of animals and seasonal fruits. This changed between 20,000 and 10,000 years ago with the development of agriculture. About 15,000 years ago, as temperatures rose, primitive

▼ THE ICE AGE

In the Ice Age, parts of Europe were covered in glacial sheets and the North Sea was a great plain **[A]**. *The climate and terrain were very like Alaska today, and herds of reindeer roamed the area. These were a main food source for groups of hunter-gatherers, traces of whom have been found in Europe, mostly in the warmer areas (southern Spain, south-west France and along main rivers). These people followed the deer herds on their grazing migrations, augmenting their diet with small game as well as vegetables, berries and grains. As the climate became warmer various groups settled near coasts to become fisher-gatherers.*

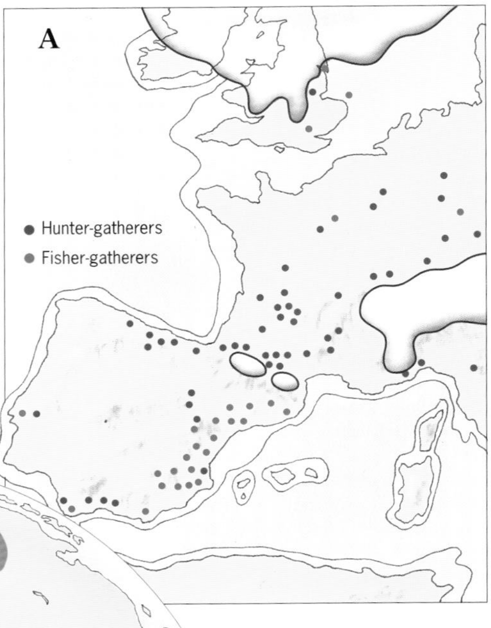

A
Hunter-gatherers
Fisher-gatherers

◀ HOMO SAPIENS

From central and southern Africa Homo sapiens spread out to populate the whole world **[B]**. *The first migration spread from Africa eastwards across to Asia. Routes branched off to northern Africa and southern Europe. A second wave occurred 15,000 years ago, when glaciation provided a land bridge across the Bering Strait, allowing movement from northern Asia to the Americas.*

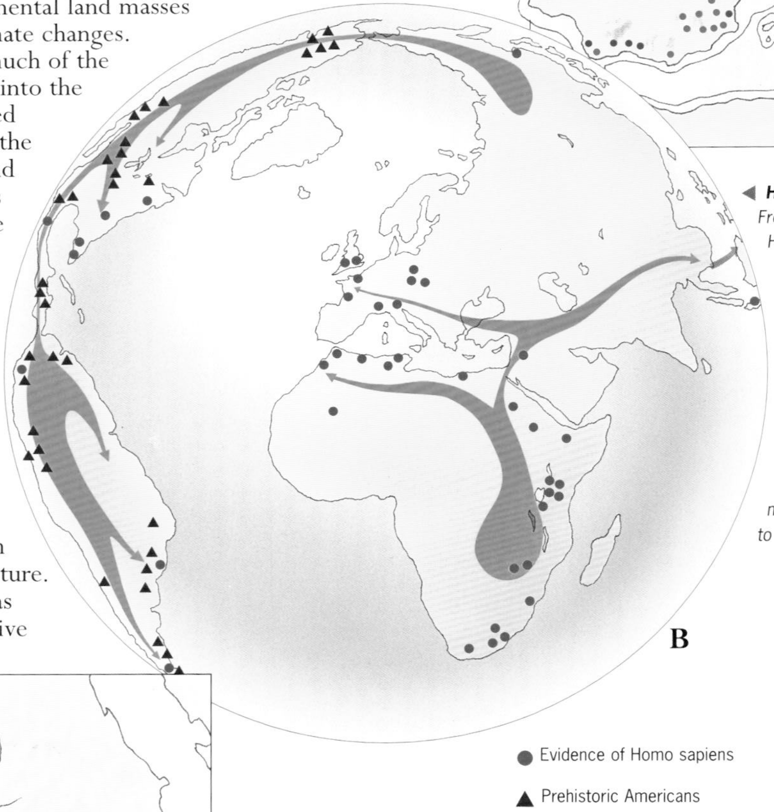

B
Evidence of Homo sapiens
Prehistoric Americans

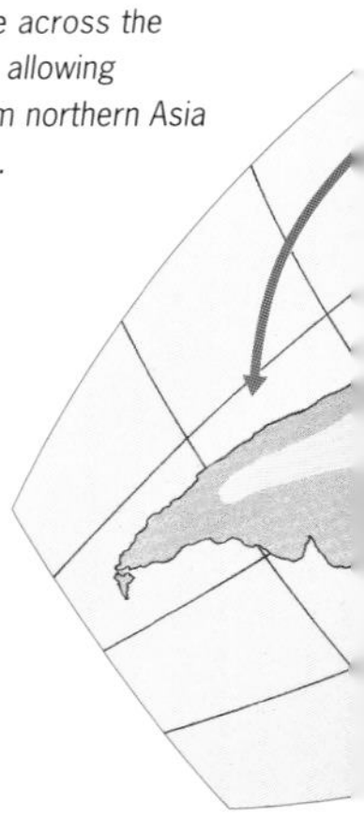

C

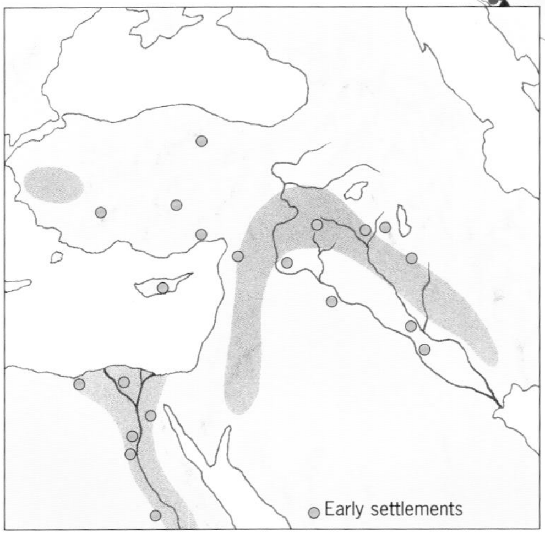

Early settlements

◀ THE FIRST FARMERS

The first farming settlements, which developed into the first cities, were probably founded around 10,000 years ago in the 'Fertile Crescent' **[C]**, *a band of land stretching from the Mediterranean to the rivers Tigris and Euphrates, in modern Jordan, Lebanon, Syria, Turkey and Iraq. Civilisation also flowered along the banks of the river Nile, similarly suited to agriculture. From simple farmsteads grew villages, towns, cities and eventually whole civilisations.*

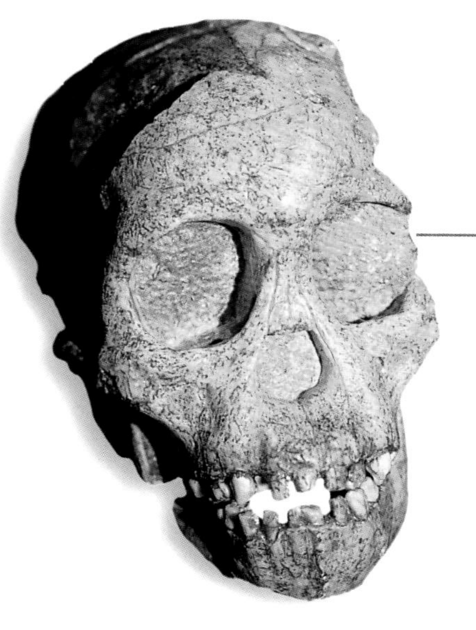

▲ *This skull of* Australopithicus africanus *is over 2 million years old.* Africanus *was the first hominid to leave the forest for the open plain.*

farming practices began to appear wherever the climate allowed it. The most important of these were Mesopotamia, the crescent between the rivers Tigris and Euphrates in modern Iraq, south-eastern Turkey and eastern Syria, the Nile valley, Central America and north-east China. Once wandering groups settled down the population soared, increasing from 5 to 300 million in 8000 years.

Small farming settlements developed into villages, then towns, then cities. Social and political organisations developed to control large groups of people. Gradually, the great civilisations grew, in the fertile fields of these first settlements. Along the Nile Valley, the Egyptians started to build a sophisticated culture around 3000BC, at the same time as the Sumerians were developing a system of city states in Mesopotamia. Similar civilisations appeared in China and Central America. Influences from these civilisations rippled outwards, laying down the pattern for the shape of the modern world.

▶ ***OUT OF AFRICA***

It is now considered that the ancestors of humankind first appeared in Africa **[D]**. *As well as indications of early Homo sapiens, the evidence for Africa's claims to be the cradle of humanity comes from fossils of Australopithecus and Homo erectus found in South Africa, Olduvai Gorge in Kenya, and Ethiopia. These are older than any others so far discovered in the world and so it seems likely that the human beings who evolved in Africa gradually spread out to other parts of the world. This is corroborated by fossils of a later date found in India, Java and China which indicate the direction of migration out of Africa. Early Homo sapiens fossils have also been found in China, southern Europe, North and South America and the Middle East. In Europe, the fossils found so far are confined to early forms of Homo sapiens and Neanderthal man, whose traces have been found in Germany, Hungary, France, Belgium, Greece, Czechoslovakia, Russia and the Middle East.*

D

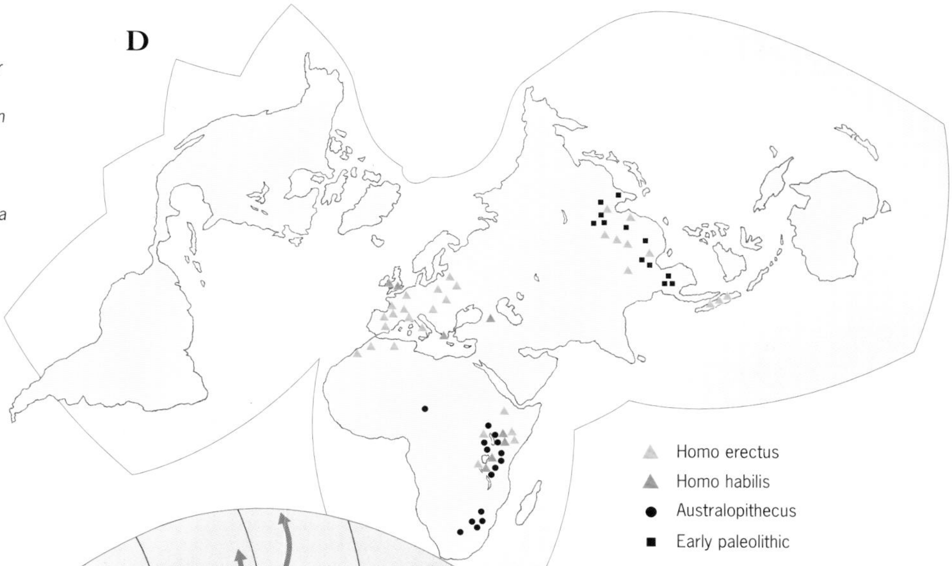
Homo erectus
Homo habilis
Australopithecus
Early paleolithic

E

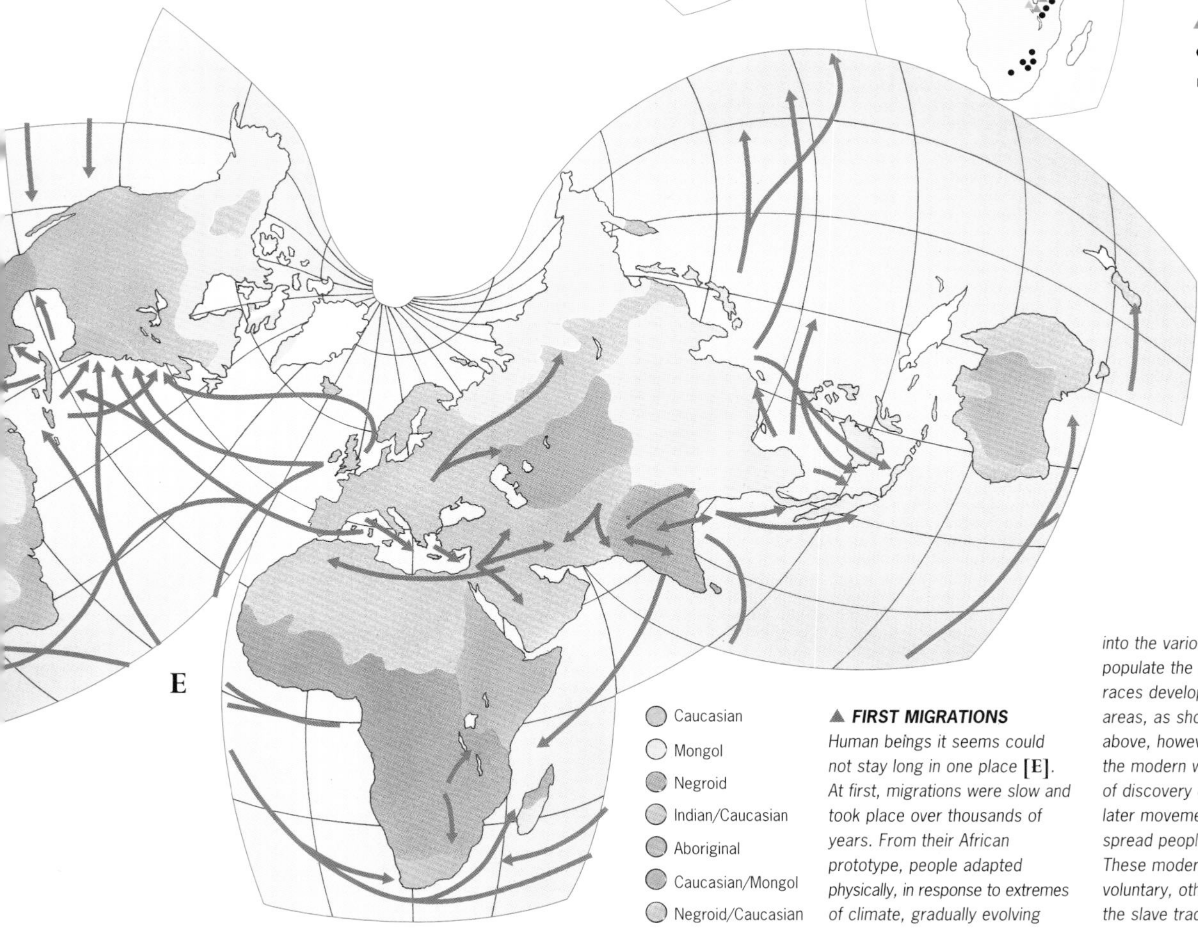
Caucasian
Mongol
Negroid
Indian/Caucasian
Aboriginal
Caucasian/Mongol
Negroid/Caucasian

▲ ***FIRST MIGRATIONS***

Human beings it seems could not stay long in one place **[E]**. *At first, migrations were slow and took place over thousands of years. From their African prototype, people adapted physically, in response to extremes of climate, gradually evolving into the various races that populate the world today. These races developed in certain areas, as shown on the map above, however, the forces of the modern world from the age of discovery onwards created later movements that have spread people around the world. These modern migrations, some voluntary, others enforced as in the slave trade, are also shown.*

THE POPULATION EXPLOSION

There are 6 billion people in the world today. This figure is rising at a rate of 140 million each year, an increase of more than the population of Japan. But until comparatively recently, the rate of increase of the world population was low. Two thousand years ago, there were an estimated 300 million people on Earth; by 1650 this had increased to a mere 500 million. Then in only 200 years this number had doubled, and in the 150 years since then it has increased five-fold. In spite of recurrent famine and war, the world population seems set on an inexorable upward curve, doubling every 39 years.

This population explosion is a result of social developments since the Industrial Revolution. Proportionally there are the same number of births each year – or perhaps fewer. But the advances of improved sanitation and nutrition made possible by the industrial and scientific advances of the 18th and 19th centuries meant that fewer babies died at birth and that people lived longer.

At first these changes were confined to the countries of the developed world, in Europe and America, but as they have spread around the world, the population has ballooned. Now in most European countries the population remains stable, mainly because of the availability of reliable contraception. Indeed, in some countries the birth rate has fallen below the number needed to maintain stability; this will result in a top-heavy 'age pyramid', with too many grandparents and not enough grandchildren to support them. Some countries, such as France and Sweden, have tried to encourage people to have more babies through maternity payments and tax discounts for large families.

In the developing world the situation is different. There are many cultural and religious objections to the use of contraception. In a traditional agricultural community, too, a large family was desirable. As well as ensuring that the parents would have surviving children to look after them, many children provided a workforce to farm the land. But fewer people now live on the land, as farming becomes mechanised; and a large family in an urban industrialised setting just creates more mouths to feed. China, the most populated country in the world, has solved the problem, rationing families to one child each.

The rush to the cities

All over the world, more people live in cities than in the country, because it is no longer possible to make a living working on the land. As a consequence cities have proliferated. The process is not a new one: after the Industrial Revolution industrial towns gradually expanded until they merged to form huge conurbations. In terms of population density, a vast swathe of northern Europe

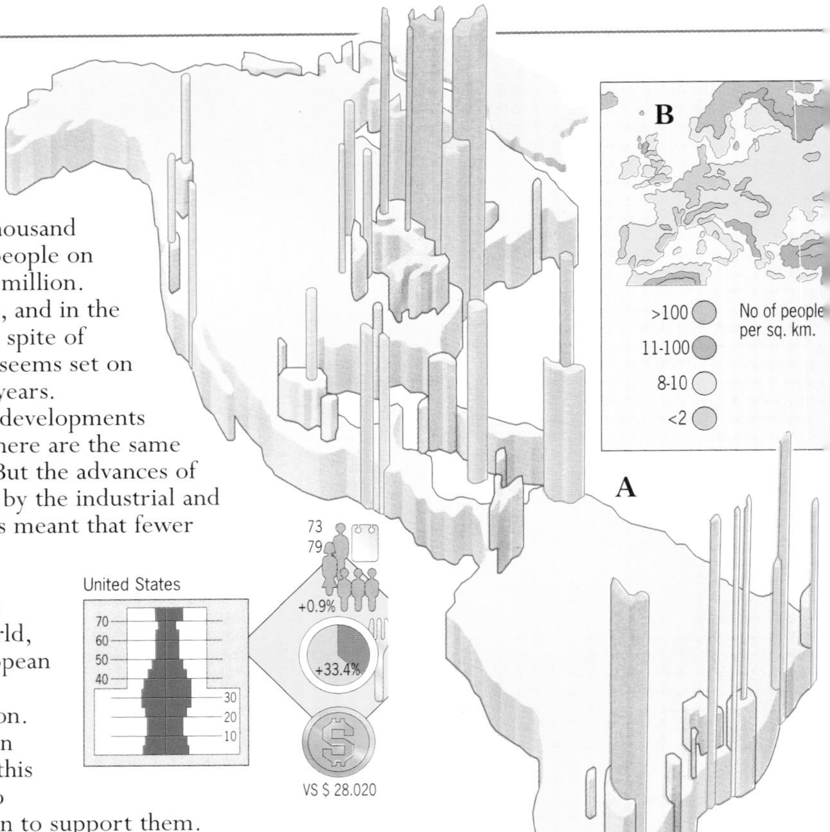

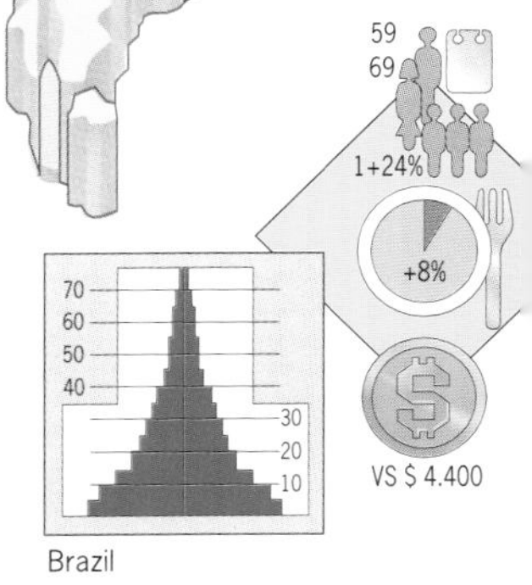

▲ GLOBAL POPULATION

The global population is distributed in clumps and clusters around the world. In hotter countries, most people live on a narrow ribbon along the coast, leaving vast arid inner tracts of land under-populated. In cooler countries, the population is able to spread itself more evenly about the landmass. The map makes clear the huge numbers of people living all across China and India, in contrast with the comparatively sparse population of much of the United States. The graphics around illustration **[A]** *show for each continent the rate of population growth, the average longevity of men and women, the gross national product per capita (a measure of wealth), and the calorific intake per head as a percentage of an adult's average daily requirement. These illustrate the gap in health and wealth between the developed world and the*

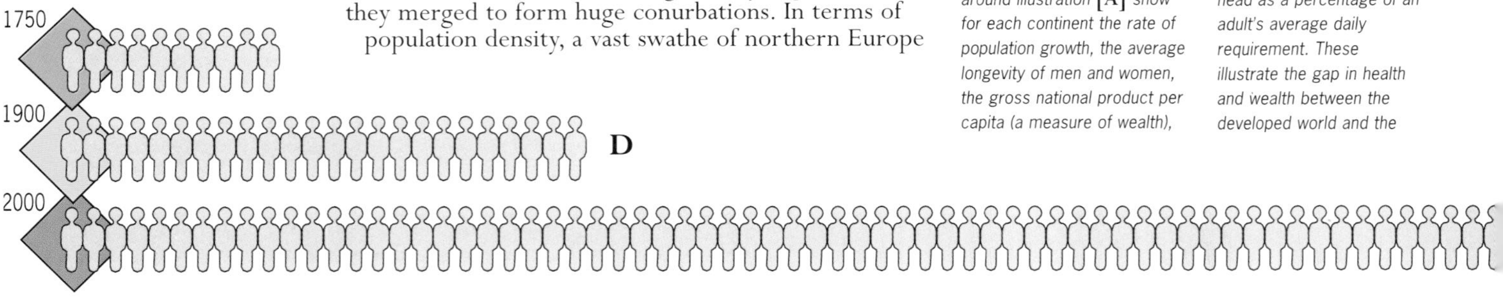

▲ GROWTH 1750–2000

The growth of the human population can be shown **[D]** *by demonstrating the number of people that would occupy each 2km² of land of the Earth's surface at various eras: 1750, 1900 and an estimation of the figure for the year 2000.*

▶ POPULATION GROWTH

The Earth's population has swollen from a mere 250 million 1000 years ago (roughly the present-day population of the United States) to 6 billion today.

For most of the intervening period growth was very slow, and there were even slight declines caused by plagues such as the Black Death. However, from about the time of the Industrial Revolution the rate of growth increased, accelerating further with each improvement in hygiene and healthcare.

A graph of world population growth over the past 300 years **[C]** *can be split to show how the relative increases in each continent have been staggered. Throughout recorded history, the population of Asia has been greater than that of all the other continents combined. However, during the 19th century the population of Europe grew at twice the rate of Asia's, thanks mainly to the improvements in living conditions brought about by scientific advances and the Industrial Revolution. This rate of growth has slowed in Europe this century, whereas that of Asia has accelerated spectacularly – its population seems likely to have tripled in the fifty years from 1950. Over the last two centuries the populations of North and South America have been*

*ʼhough there are
ɟividual areas with
ɒnser population,
ɒrope is the continent
ɫh the highest
ɒpulation density* **[B]**.
*ɪncludes Monaco,
ɫh more than
ɒ,000 people
ammed into
ch km².*

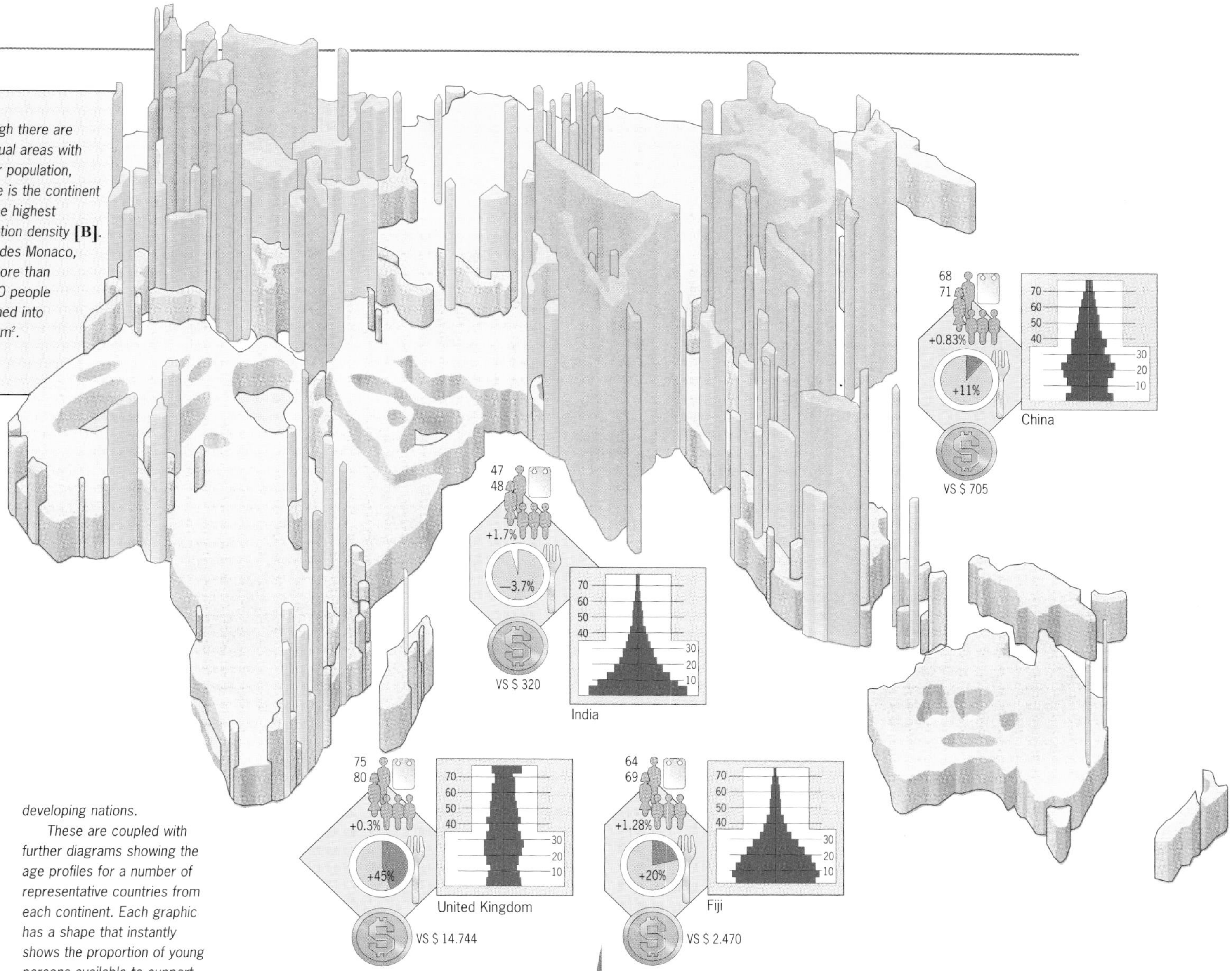

developing nations.

These are coupled with further diagrams showing the age profiles for a number of representative countries from each continent. Each graphic has a shape that instantly shows the proportion of young persons available to support aging parents and grandparents. In Brazil and Kenya, the pronounced pyramid shape indicates a high birth rate providing large numbers of young people supporting a dwindling older population. For the UK and USA, the shape is dramatically different – more a column than a pyramid, with the birth rate barely keeping up with the long-living older generation. The diagram for the USA shows a bulge of middle-aged people, the product of the 'baby boom', a period of high birth-rate after World War 2. In China, a rigorous family planning regime has resulted in a taper at the young end of its curve, beginning to have an effect on the shape of the pyramid.

increasing just as fast. In the 19th century this was due to immigration, whereas this century's gains can be attributed to better health and hygiene, improvements which have gradually spread to the developing world.

C

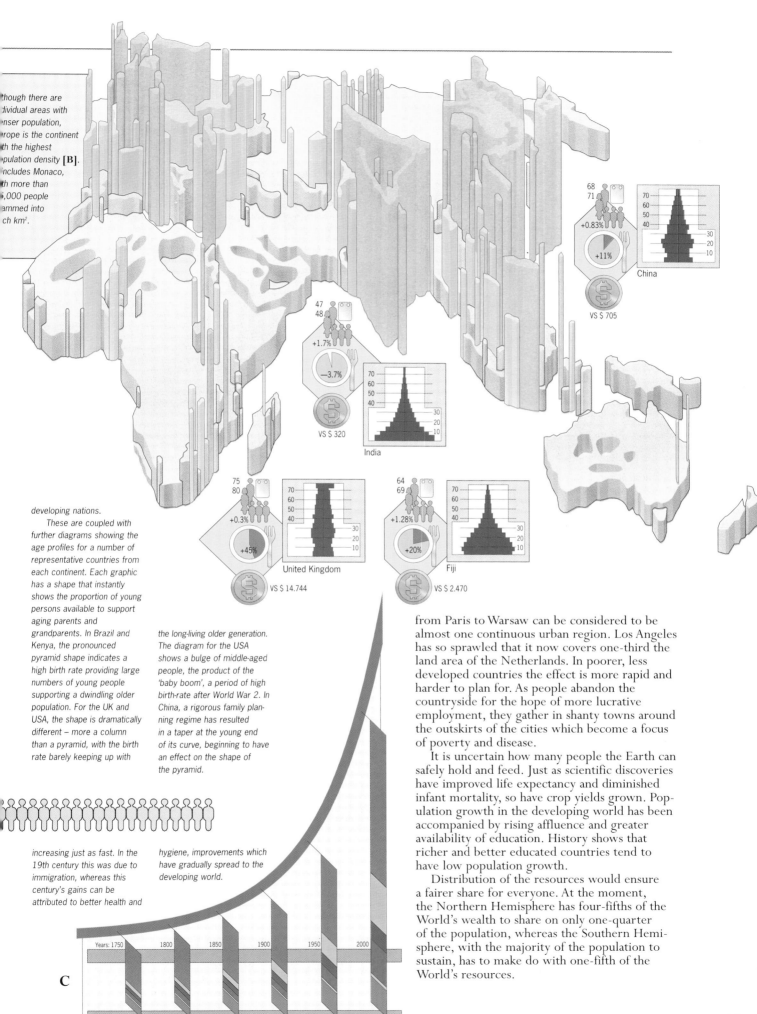

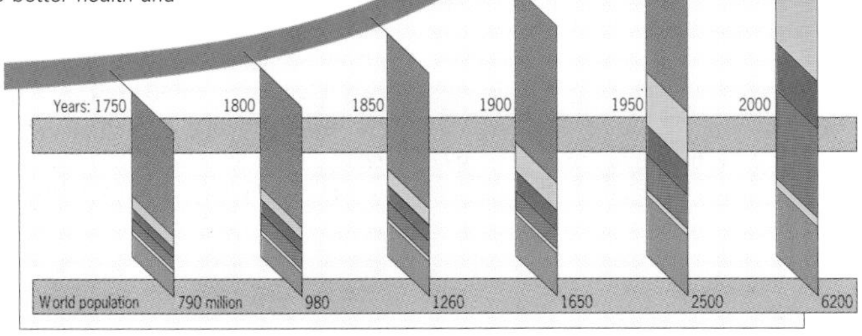

from Paris to Warsaw can be considered to be almost one continuous urban region. Los Angeles has so sprawled that it now covers one-third the land area of the Netherlands. In poorer, less developed countries the effect is more rapid and harder to plan for. As people abandon the countryside for the hope of more lucrative employment, they gather in shanty towns around the outskirts of the cities which become a focus of poverty and disease.

It is uncertain how many people the Earth can safely hold and feed. Just as scientific discoveries have improved life expectancy and diminished infant mortality, so have crop yields grown. Population growth in the developing world has been accompanied by rising affluence and greater availability of education. History shows that richer and better educated countries tend to have low population growth.

Distribution of the resources would ensure a fairer share for everyone. At the moment, the Northern Hemisphere has four-fifths of the World's wealth to share on only one-quarter of the population, whereas the Southern Hemisphere, with the majority of the population to sustain, has to make do with one-fifth of the World's resources.

BELIEF & UNDERSTANDING

MODERN COUNTRIES HAVE BEEN SHAPED POLITICALLY by many forces and movements, the most important being religion and language. Religion has been a central aspect of human society since before the earliest written records – fertility sculptures dating from the Ice Age indicate a need to recognise and pacify a spirit that brought forth the sun and rain, made crops grow and ensured a plentiful supply of food. The ancient Near-Eastern civilisations, particularly Egypt, had a multitude of different gods for each aspect of human life or death. This polytheism was continued in the Greek and Roman traditions, in contrast with monotheism, belief in a single all-powerful god, exemplified by Judaism and first recorded around 1200BC.

Today there are eleven major formal religions in the world: Christianity; Judaism; Islam; Hinduism; Buddhism and Jainism; Zoroastrianism; Confucianism; Taoism; Shinto and Sikhism. Of these Christianity is the most widespread, with over a billion followers. It has three major divisions: Roman Catholic, Protestant and Greek Orthodox, and 300 different denominations.

Christianity staked a political claim very early in the history of the developed world, being adopted as the official religion of the Roman Empire in AD324 by the emperor Constantine. The religion instantly changed from being a local Near-Eastern cult to the majority religion of Europe. It became more widespread over 1000 years later through the zeal of European colonists. The Portuguese and Spanish took Catholicism to South America, while the French, English and Dutch brought a variety of denominations to North America. The British took Anglicanism to Africa, India and China and the Dutch took Calvinism to South Africa and Malaysia.

More than words

There are over 3000 spoken languages in the world, a figure that does not include dialects. Of these, just over 100 have more than a million speakers, and only 13 have over 50 million speakers. Some of these are spoken by very large numbers of people (more than 800 million people speak Mandarin Chinese) concentrated in one country. Others – notably Portuguese, Spanish and English – are spoken in many places as a result of the colonial past. Just as explorers brought their religion with them, they also brought their language. Languages spread across the world through different mechanisms today. The growth of international trade has meant that a few languages – mostly English, and to a lesser extent French, Spanish and German – have become standard for business.
The film, television and music industries have been instrumental in making American English understood almost worldwide. American English is also the language of electronics and computing.
As electronic communication grows through the Internet and other networks, it is interesting to speculate on what will happen to language in the freedom of cyberspace; perhaps a new, worldwide lingua franca of the Internet will emerge, allowing everyone to communicate as long as they have the technology.

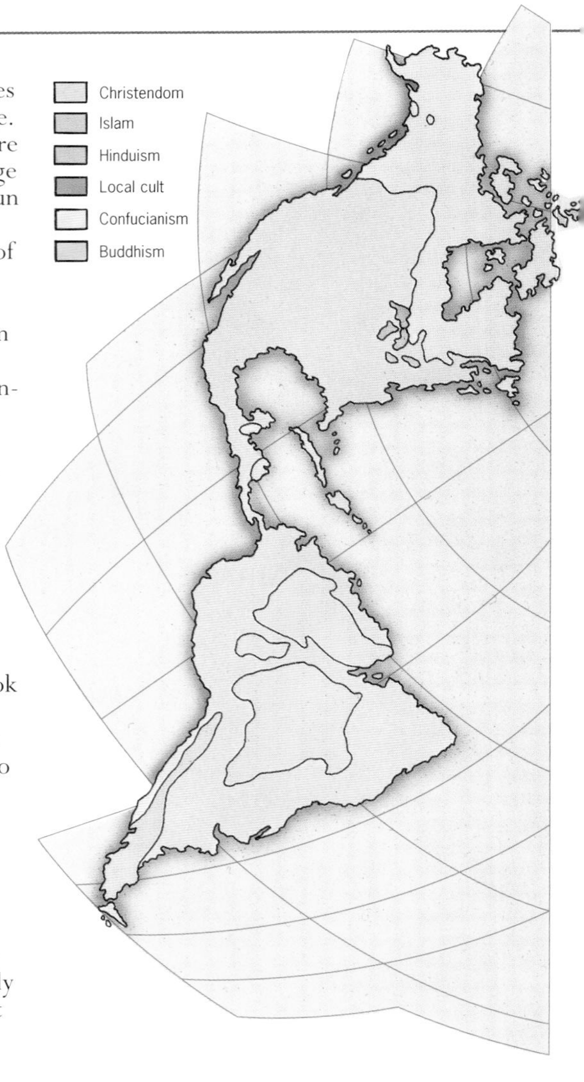

Christendom
Islam
Hinduism
Local cult
Confucianism
Buddhism

▲ ***MAIN BELIEF SYSTEMS***
The main illustration shows the distribution of the adherents to the main belief systems of the world **[A]**. *The areas that carry no shading are not dominated by any of these main systems of belief: this does not mean that they are free of religion, merely that they are dominated by local or tribal traditions.*

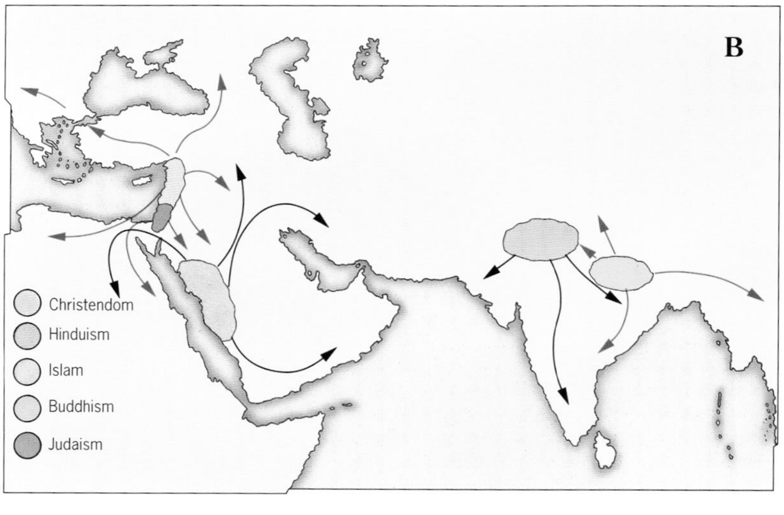

B
Christendom
Hinduism
Islam
Buddhism
Judaism

▶ ***SPREAD OF RELIGIONS***
The great religions all originated in a comparatively small area of the globe **[B]**, *but have spread in different directions to be practised by the majority of the world's population.*

Hinduism and Buddhism are the world's oldest religions. Hinduism arose in prehistoric India. Strictly speaking it is not a single religion, but a group of different bodies of belief. Today there are roughly 733 million Hindus worldwide.

Buddhism was founded in the 6th century BC, also in India, but spread eastwards and is now practised in various forms all over East Asia with large numbers of adherents in Tibet, China and Japan. The number of Buddhists in the world has been estimated at 315 million.

Judaism can be traced from before 1200BC. Jewish people have spread sorldwide from Israel, partly driven by periodic persecution. In particular, during the Nazi holocaust, 6 million Jews perished. Today Jews number 18 million worldwide.

Islam was was created in Arabia in the 7th century, and spread through migration, conversion and conquest. There are an estimated 1 billion Muslims worldwide.

Christianity, which also began in Palestine as a Jewish sect, has spread most around the world, through conquest and conversion. Today it is the most popular religion worldwide, the different denominations numbering 1.8 billion adherents.

▼ WORLD RELIGIONS

A map of the religions of the world cannot have sharp boundaries like those of a political chart **[A]**, *as many countries contain people from a multitude of different faiths. Christianity was founded 2000 years ago, based on the belief that Jesus Christ was the son of God sent to save the people on earth. Christians practise active evangelism.*

Judaism was founded about 3000 years ago. Jews consider themselves to be the Chosen People of God, and to be Jewish you have to be born of a Jewish mother.

Buddhism was founded in the 6th century BC by Gautama Buddha. The teaching is to follow an eight-fold path of behaviours to reach enlightenment. Anyone can become a Buddhist. It is gaining great popularity in the West.

Hinduism was founded in prehistoric India. It teaches that to reach perfection, people have to be born into many different lives and therefore one should respect all life forms.

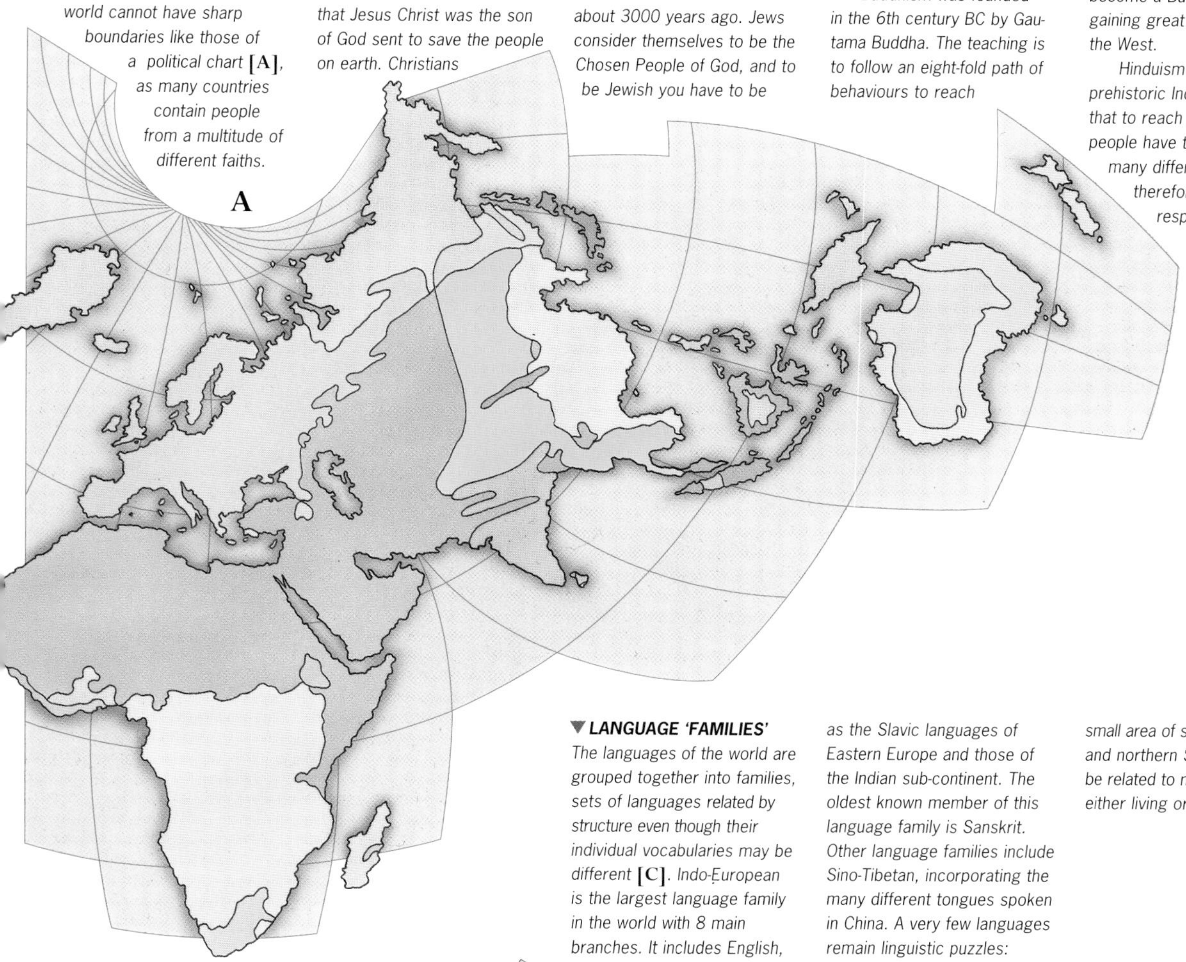

Many different kinds of worship exist among the tribal peoples of North and South America, Australia and the Pacific Islands, Asia and India. Their rituals and ceremonies are closely bound up in the fertility of the land and the spiritual life of the tribe. In contrast, many people in the developed countries are turning against the idea of monotheistic, paternal religion altogether – some through the pagan and Druid traditions of pre-Christianity.

▼ LANGUAGE 'FAMILIES'

The languages of the world are grouped together into families, sets of languages related by structure even though their individual vocabularies may be different **[C]**. *Indo-European is the largest language family in the world with 8 main branches. It includes English, French and German as well as the Slavic languages of Eastern Europe and those of the Indian sub-continent. The oldest known member of this language family is Sanskrit. Other language families include Sino-Tibetan, incorporating the many different tongues spoken in China. A very few languages remain linguistic puzzles: Basque, which is spoken in a small area of south-west France and northern Spain appears to be related to no other language either living or dead.*

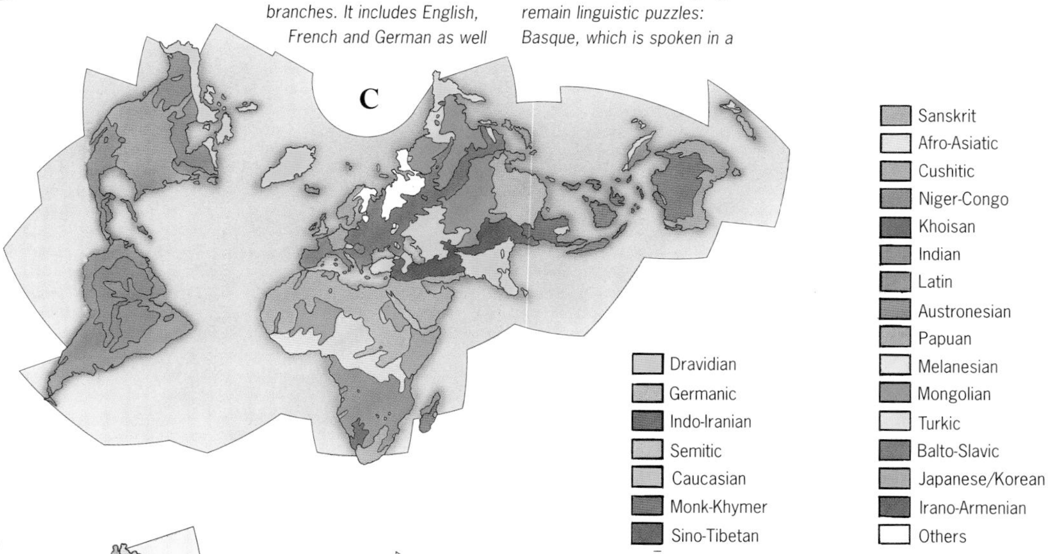

C
Sanskrit
Afro-Asiatic
Cushitic
Niger-Congo
Khoisan
Indian
Latin
Austronesian
Papuan
Melanesian
Mongolian
Turkic
Balto-Slavic
Japanese/Korean
Irano-Armenian
Others
Dravidian
Germanic
Indo-Iranian
Semitic
Caucasian
Monk-Khymer
Sino-Tibetan

◀ COLONIAL INFLUENCE

The influence of colonialism can be traced on a map showing the official languages of the countries of the world **[D]**. *Spanish and Portuguese are spoken in South and Central America; English in North America, India and parts of Africa. French is still the official language in most of its former colonies – and for historical reasons remains the language of diplomacy. More people speak Mandarin Chinese than any other language.*

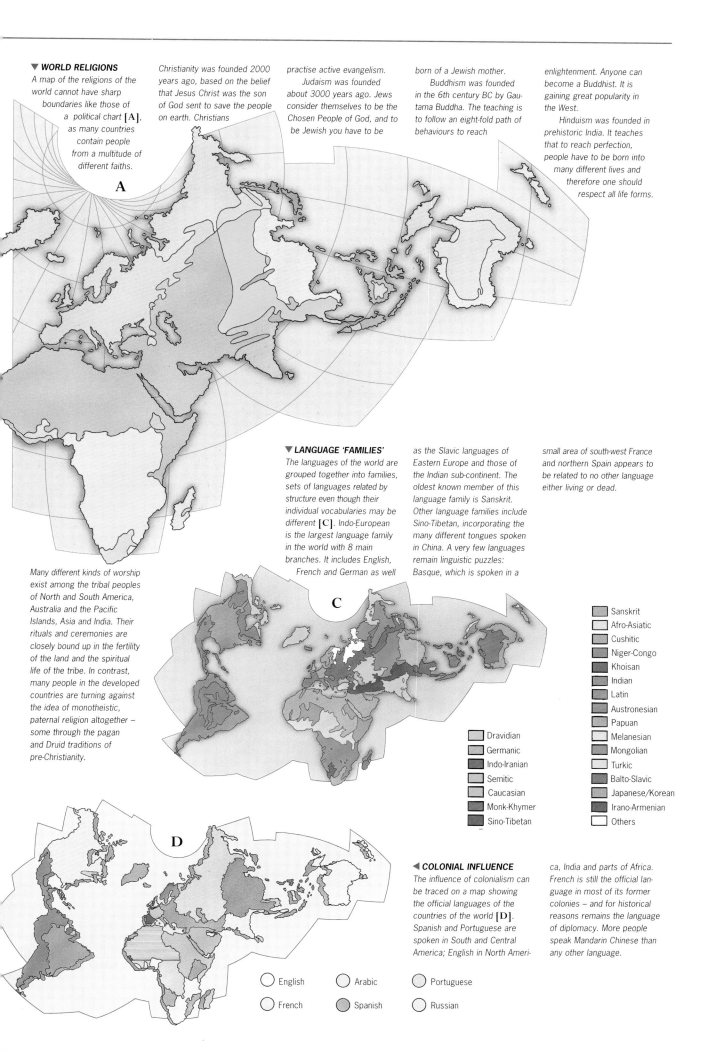

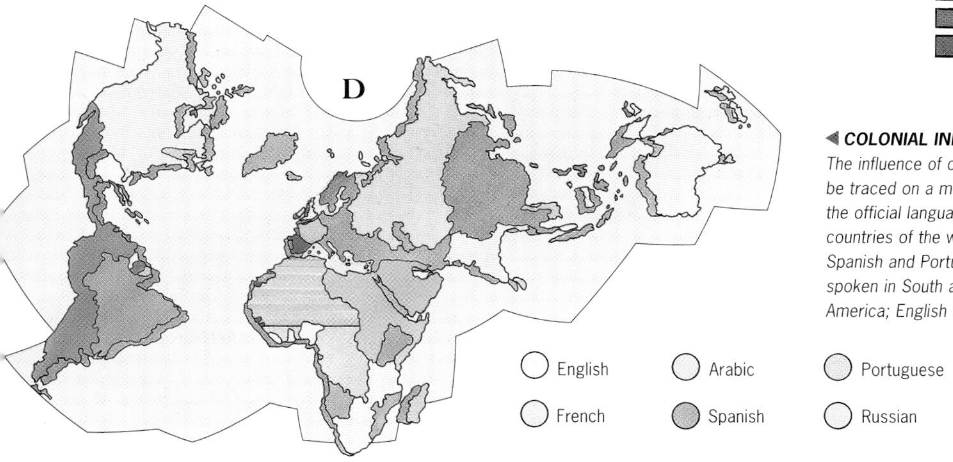

D
English
Arabic
Portuguese
French
Spanish
Russian

THE WORLD AT WORK

THE DEVELOPMENT OF SOCIETY can be looked at as a series of industrial revolutions, as man has learned to use the Earth's resources. Ancient history divides up into three such stages: the Stone Age, when humans first learned to make stone tools and began to practise agriculture; the Bronze Age, when pure metals were first refined and used; and the Iron Age, when man discovered how to extract iron from rock and cast or forge it into tools and weapons.

The greatest industrial leaps have come in the past three centuries. New scientific discoveries led to the construction of the first steam engines, which transformed industry as well as transport. Iron was then overtaken by steel, and the chemical and electrical industries developed. Plastics, electrical transistors and silicon chips became part of everyday life. Each new wave of industries has had a far-reaching effect on society: employment rises and falls, new methods of transport become available and global trade opens up. With each 'revolution' a world economy is brought closer, fuelling an ever-increasing demand for energy.

The source of power

The first Industrial Revolution depended on coal to produce the iron and fire the steam engines. Today, the vast majority of the world's energy still comes from fossil fuels such as coal, oil and natural gas which are a finite resource. Coal is still burnt to generate electricity, supplying about 28 per cent of our total energy needs. The internal combustion engine has created an insatiable demand for petroleum. Today, oil reserves supply 40 per cent of the world's energy, and natural gas 20 per cent. As well as being a finite resource, fossil fuels are a major source of pollution, contributing to the greenhouse effect and the global warming that it brings. In the long term, other sources of energy will have to be found.

Energy alternatives

Nuclear power comes from the splitting of heavy uranium atoms, accompanied by the release of energy in a process called 'fission'. In many countries this energy has been harnessed to electricity needs, but there are many problems, particularly the long-term storage of waste products. Research continues into nuclear fusion, the process which powers the Sun. Although much more difficult to achieve, this could be a cleaner way of generating cheap energy. There are pollution-free energy sources. Hydro-electric power is used in countries such as Switzerland, where water provides more than half of all energy requirements, but it can have a great impact on the environment, flooding valleys and destroying eco-systems. Tidal power exploits the energy of the sea in a similar way. Windmills were one of our earliest sources of power. Today, wind-farms are sited on exposed coasts or on offshore spits, and some countries hope to be able to generate 10–20 per cent of energy needs in this way in the next decade or so. California, for instance, has tens of thousands of wind turbines.

The demand for energy is highest in the USA and western Europe, which are heavily industrialised and also have a large consumer society. At the same time, increasing consumption of oil has led to the rise in power and wealth of Middle-Eastern countries where two-thirds of the world's reserves are located.

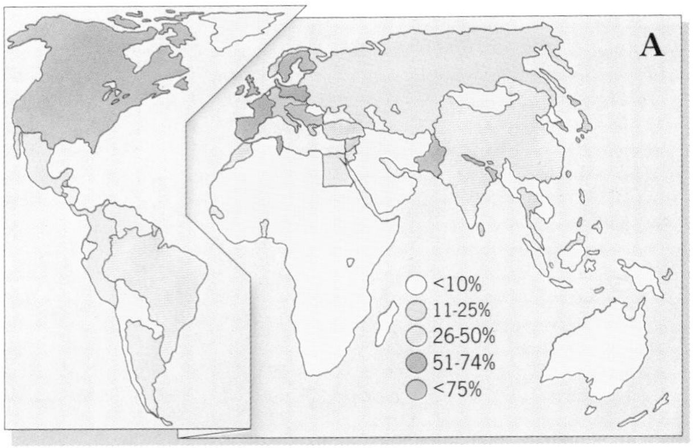
A
<10%
11-25%
26-50%
51-74%
<75%

▲ ***THE GLOBAL ECONOMY*** *The engine-houses of today's global economy are those countries that produce the most consumer goods. Map* **[A]** *is shaded according to the percentage of each country's total exports that are manufactured goods. It clearly demonstrates that the most successful manufacturing economies are concentrated in the richer northern hemisphere of the world. Almost the whole of Europe and North America have figures over 50%, but the best performers are in Central Europe and the Far East. These include traditionally industrial nations, such as Germany and Japan, as well as fast -growing economies like Korea, Taiwan and the Czech Republic.*

The world's biggest producers of food are its largest countries in terms of area and population. However, although there is an overall excess of food, some countries, particularly in Africa, are still susceptible to famine. The reasons for this are both political and environmental. Traditionally farmed areas of land are often cleared to make way for so-called 'cash crops', and instead of using the land for self-sufficiency, an export-driven economy is created, with newly-displaced farmers to support. At the other extreme, the United States farms staple crops successfully on a massive scale, producing surpluses which can then be sold on to smaller countries.

◀ ***ENERGY*** *The driving-force of an economy is energy,* **[B]** *so the balance between the energy a country produces – in the form of coal, oil and other fuels – and the amount it consumes is vital. This table shows the ratio for the main regions of the world. In many areas the balance is even, but some, such as Europe, produce 12% of world energy, but consume 17%.*

▲ *Wind turbines, pictured here in Palm Springs in California USA, are being viewed as an increasingly viable way of producing energy. Europe, especially Holland and Germany, has a number of these eco-friendly farms.*

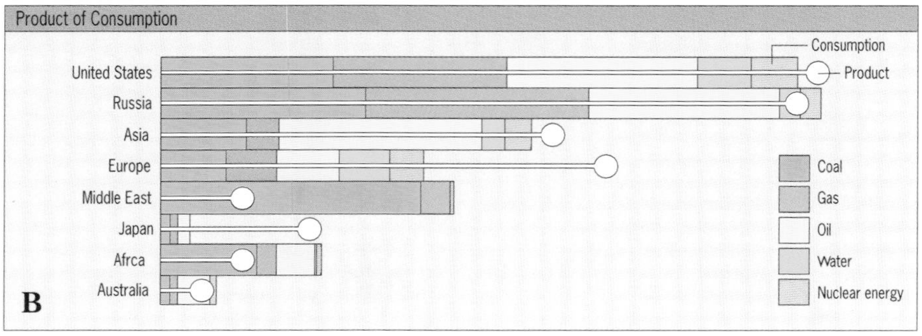
Product of Consumption
Consumption
Product
United States
Russia
Asia
Europe
Middle East
Japan
Afrca
Australia
Coal
Gas
Oil
Water
Nuclear energy
B

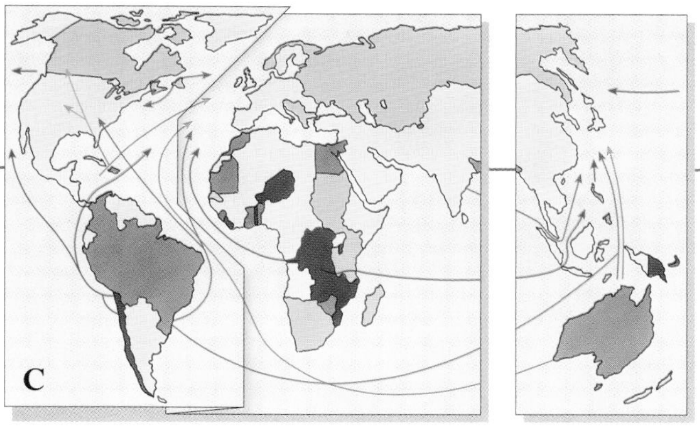

▲ MINERALS

Mineral deposits can often be the key to a nation's economy **[C]**. *Jamaica has extensive bauxite and alumina deposits – the raw material for the production of aluminium – which account for almost half the country's total exports.*

Mineral deposits are not only valued for their practical uses: gemstones can also bring in considerable income. Central and Southern Africa were the world's largest producers but are now threatened by the deposits in Australia, and those in Russia which have yet to be fully exploited, but which could flood and destabilise the market. If in the future the market is flooded with Russian diamonds, the market could collapse.

Many other minerals and metal ores are concentrated only in rocks which have undergone extensive weathering, or around mountain ranges, which have seen intense metamorphic processes in the past.

The Industrial Revolution, which began in Britain, soon spread through the rest of Europe. Apart from America, the industrialisation of the rest of the world was the result of investment by colonial European powers, taking advantage of cheap labour and raw materials, and faster, cheaper transport which turned the world into a single complex economy.

In the last fifty years the rest of the world has also developed major industries, overtaking the West. Japan became one of the world's great economic powers by heavy investment in new technology, and other nations are following its example. The pattern is now reversed as Far-Eastern companies open manufacturing plants in the West to provide goods for the lucrative consumer markets. Often, these plants assemble imported components, but they also provide access to the major economic blocs, such as the United States and the European Union, which impose quotas and tariffs on imported goods.

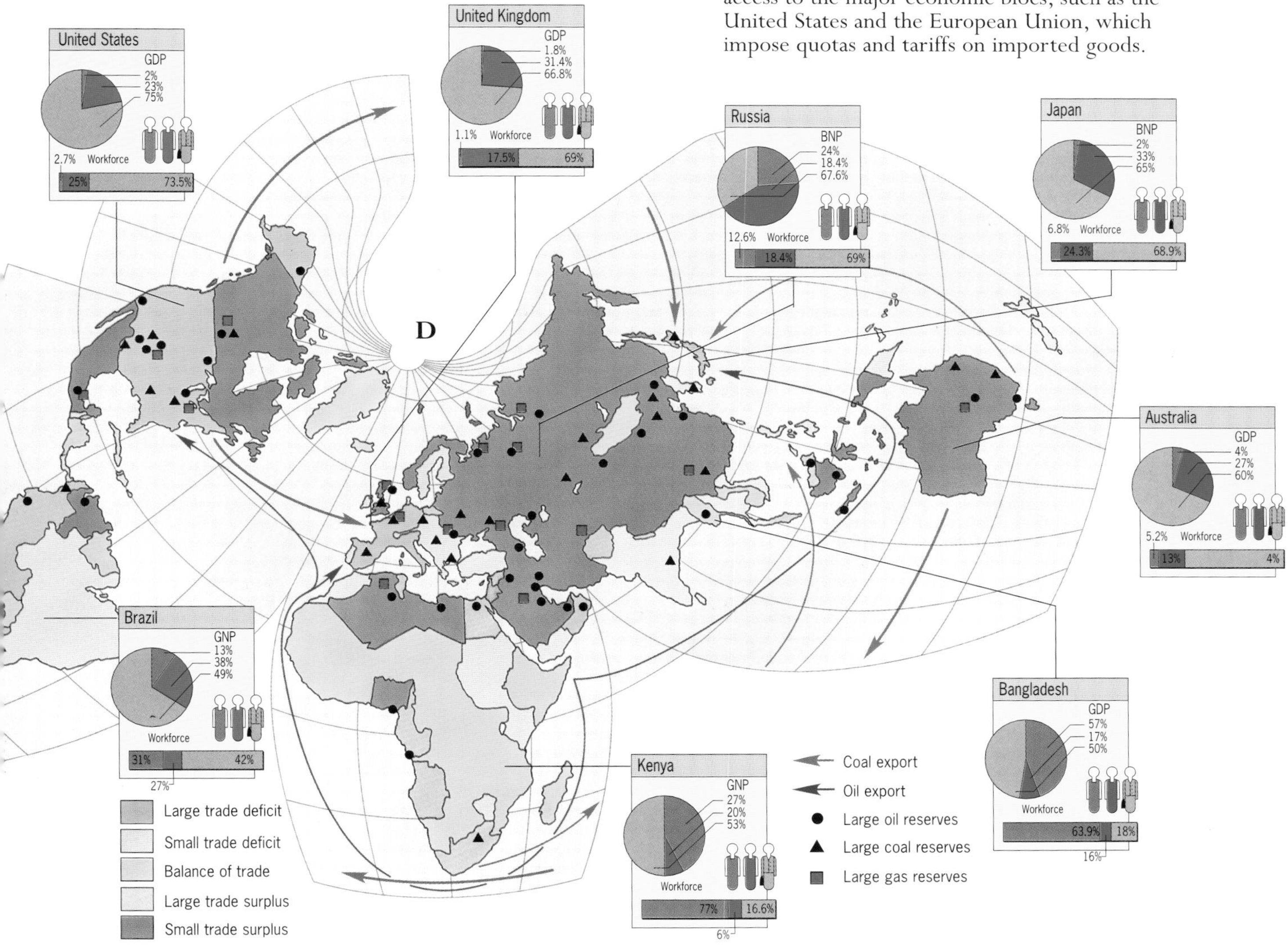

▲ THE LABOUR FORCE

The relative economic development of various countries can be seen by comparing the numbers of people employed in different types of work, and the contribution to the gross domestic product (GDP) made by each **[D]**. *Developing countries such as Bangladesh have a high proportion of labour involved in agriculture, which is responsible for a comparatively high proportion of GDP. Nigeria is similar, but its extensive oil reserves account for a higher industrial contribution to GDP.*

As countries make more use of natural resources, more of the population is employed in heavy industry, creating more wealth, while improvements in agriculture lead to increased efficiency, and a reduction in the numbers employed. The agricultural output tends to remain steady, so that its contribution as a percentage of GDP decreases. In the most developed nations the majority of the workforce is employed in the manufacture and service sectors.

The graphics in the illustration **[C]** *show the labour forces of several countries. The bar at the bottom gives the percentage involved in the agricultural (brown), industrial (blue) and service (grey) sectors, while the pie chart shows the contribution that each of these sectors makes to the GDP of that country.*

ON THE MOVE

ONCE THE MAJORITY OF HUMANITY HAD SETTLED DOWN into permanent villages, towns and cities, they began to devise ways to travel between them to trade and treaty. It was quickly realised that whoever controlled trade routes or devised the quickest means of transport would be at an advantage. Just as today, communications were all-important.

At first, people could only move as far as they could walk in a day, at most 32km. Around 8000 years ago, as farming was becoming established, some domesticated animals were employed as a means of transport. This did not make travel much faster, but enabled more goods to be carried or pulled along on sleds.

The great transportation breakthrough was of course the wheel, which was invented about 5000 years ago somewhere in the eastern Mediterranean. The earliest known example of wheeled transport is an Egyptian chariot, built about 2000BC. Horsedrawn chariots formed a rapid transport communications network in all the great empires and kingdoms, where rulers needed to know what was going on all over their territory.

Chariots could go faster if they had straight roads to run along. The first road network was established c1122BC in China under the emperor Chou, but the most famous road system, traces of which still exist today, was established in the Roman Empire. In engineering terms, probably the most impressive road system was built by the Incas of Peru. Built entirely of dry stone, the 4800km system wound over the steep slopes of the western Andes. These roads were for messengers on horse or foot: the Incas never used the wheel for transport.

Ships and the sea

The development of sea travel parallels that of roads. Empires that needed good internal communications along roads also needed to reach trading partners quickly and efficiently by sea. The oar was developed around the same time and in the same part of the world as the wheel. At once a propellant and a steering device, the oar made it possible to control speed and direction. The Phoenicians, a people from the eastern Mediterranean, combined oars with sail power in the galley, a long ship powered by a row of oars along each side. This eventually developed into the the Greek and Roman trireme, with three rows of oars on each side, which needed 200 rowers to power it.

Between the 14th and the 17th centuries ships and sea trading shaped the world. In 1300 northern European shipbuilders invented the rudder: before that, ships had been steered by a set of oars at the stern. In the mid-1400s, the Portuguese developed the three-masted ship, which at once increased sail-power, but kept the sails small enough to be easily handled. From the 15th to 17th centuries, these ships were used and developed by many nations, and oceans were criss-crossed by Portuguese, Dutch, Spanish and English ships claiming new colonies and discovering new trade routes.

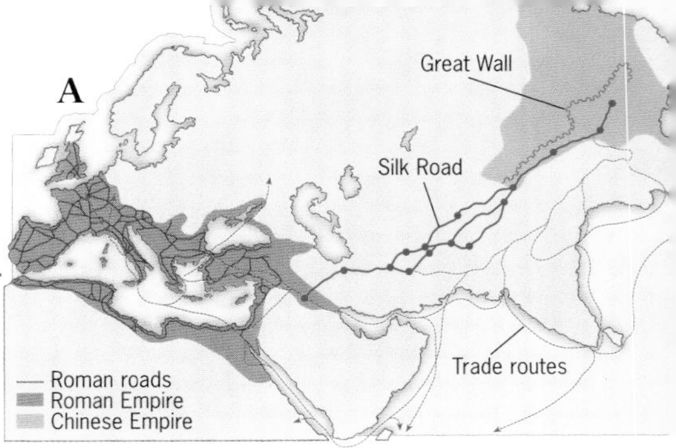

▲ ***EARLY ROAD SYSTEMS***
In the first few centuries of the Christian era, the landmass of Eurasia was dominated by empires at its east and west extremes **[A]**. *Transport was central to both these realms. In Europe, the Romans built an extensive network of roads which allowed troops, administrators, tax-collectors and traders to travel quickly from one end of the empire to the other.*

Under the Han dynasty, China began extensive trade. As well as extensive sea trading routes, there was the old Silk Road linking oases across the deserts of central Asia, along which caravans carried China's silks and spices as far as the Greek and Roman worlds.

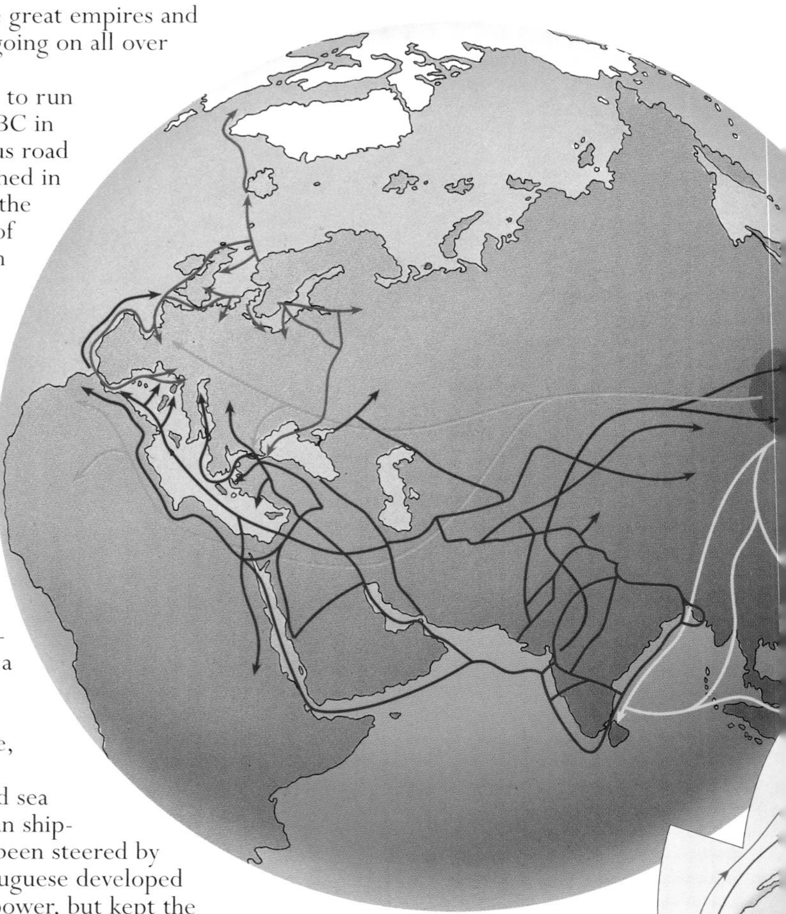

Arab trade routes
Origin of the stirrup
Spread of the stirrup
Chinese trade routes
Viking voyages

▲ ***THE DARK AGES***
The fall of the Roman Empire was a signal for mass movement across the known world. Arab traders opened trade routes that extended from Spain to China.

During the Dark Ages, both Europe and Asia were subject to raids by the Mongols, whose use of the stirrup gave them a mastery of warfare on horseback. The invention of the stirrup had spread from India to the Mongols by the 4th century, and to Europe three centuries later **[B]**. *The Mongolian war bands swept eastwards towards Europe, displacing Huns, Vandals, Goths, Ostrogoths, Visigoths and Alans who moved into the western part of Europe, in turn displacing the Franks who moved from what is now Germany into France. The native Gauls and Celts were pushed up into the corners of Brittany.*

The Vikings used their ocean-going longboats to raid many European coastal areas as well as penetrating inland along the great rivers. Some may have even reached the coast of North America.

TRANSPORT

Throughout history, certain craft have had a profound effect on transportation [D]. The SS Great Britain, built by Isambard Brunel in 1845, was the first propeller-driven ship to cross the Atlantic. Columbus had sailed across the same ocean 350 years earlier in the tiny Santa Maria, a three-masted ship typical of the sort built in the 1400s by Mediterranean shipwrights.

It was rigged to be easy to sail against the wind, making epic voyages of discovery possible.

Railway transport became a possibility with the invention in 1804 of the first steam railway engine by Richard Trevithick. A century later, the Model T Ford became the world's first production line automobile, making the car available to ordinary people.

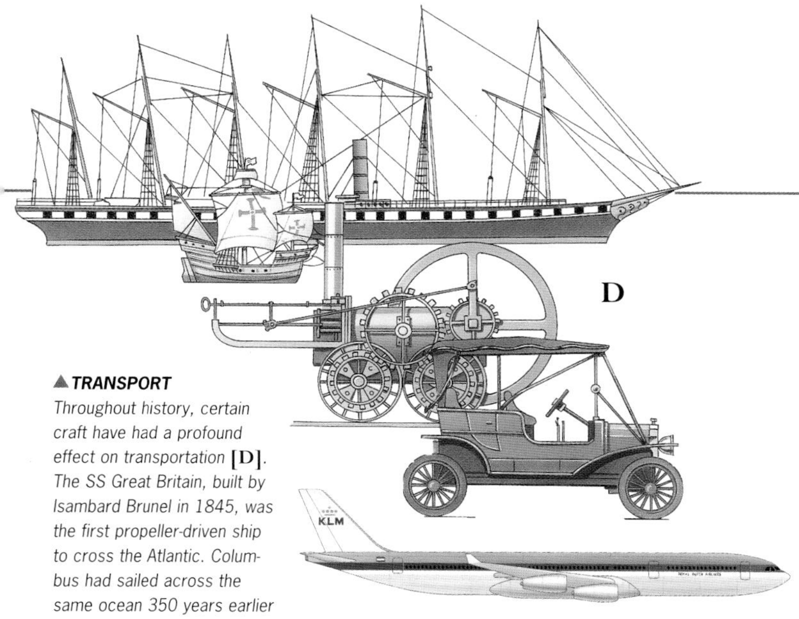

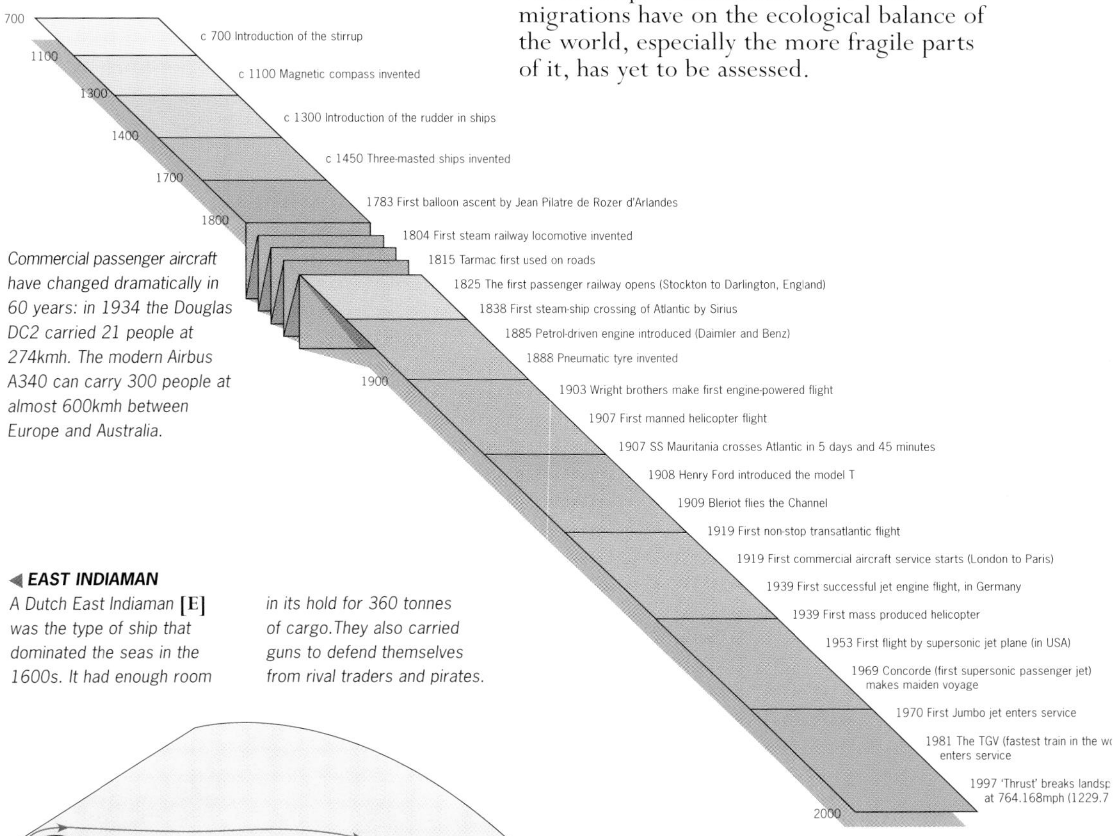

Commercial passenger aircraft have changed dramatically in 60 years: in 1934 the Douglas DC2 carried 21 people at 274kmh. The modern Airbus A340 can carry 300 people at almost 600kmh between Europe and Australia.

The modern age

For almost 3500 years, transport was based on natural power, but the invention of the steam engine revolutionised travel. Railways transformed the face of the earth and steamships plied the same routes as their sailing sisters, but did it much faster. The invention of the motor car in 1885 and manned powered flight in 1903 opened the door to universal transport.

Until the 20th century, few people travelled. Today, many people travel long distances to work; many more travel for leisure; and tourism is big business. Air travel has shrunk the world, but the impact these mass short-term migrations have on the ecological balance of the world, especially the more fragile parts of it, has yet to be assessed.

c 700 Introduction of the stirrup
c 1100 Magnetic compass invented
c 1300 Introduction of the rudder in ships
c 1450 Three-masted ships invented
1783 First balloon ascent by Jean Pilatre de Rozer d'Arlandes
1804 First steam railway locomotive invented
1815 Tarmac first used on roads
1825 The first passenger railway opens (Stockton to Darlington, England)
1838 First steam-ship crossing of Atlantic by Sirius
1885 Petrol-driven engine introduced (Daimler and Benz)
1888 Pneumatic tyre invented
1903 Wright brothers make first engine-powered flight
1907 First manned helicopter flight
1907 SS Mauritania crosses Atlantic in 5 days and 45 minutes
1908 Henry Ford introduced the model T
1909 Bleriot flies the Channel
1919 First non-stop transatlantic flight
1919 First commercial aircraft service starts (London to Paris)
1939 First successful jet engine flight, in Germany
1939 First mass produced helicopter
1953 First flight by supersonic jet plane (in USA)
1969 Concorde (first supersonic passenger jet) makes maiden voyage
1970 First Jumbo jet enters service
1981 The TGV (fastest train in the w... enters service
1997 'Thrust' breaks landsp... at 764.168mph (1229.7...

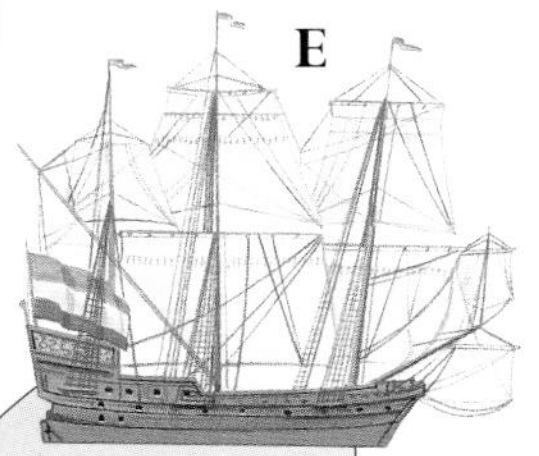

EAST INDIAMAN

A Dutch East Indiaman [E] was the type of ship that dominated the seas in the 1600s. It had enough room in its hold for 360 tonnes of cargo. They also carried guns to defend themselves from rival traders and pirates.

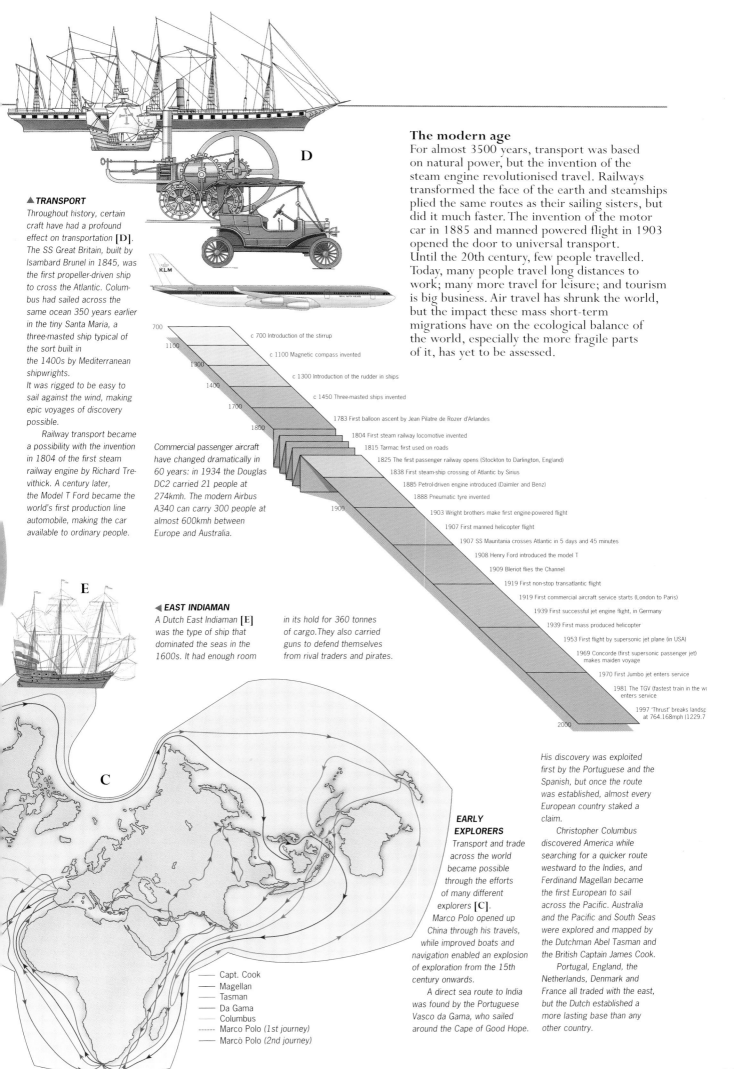

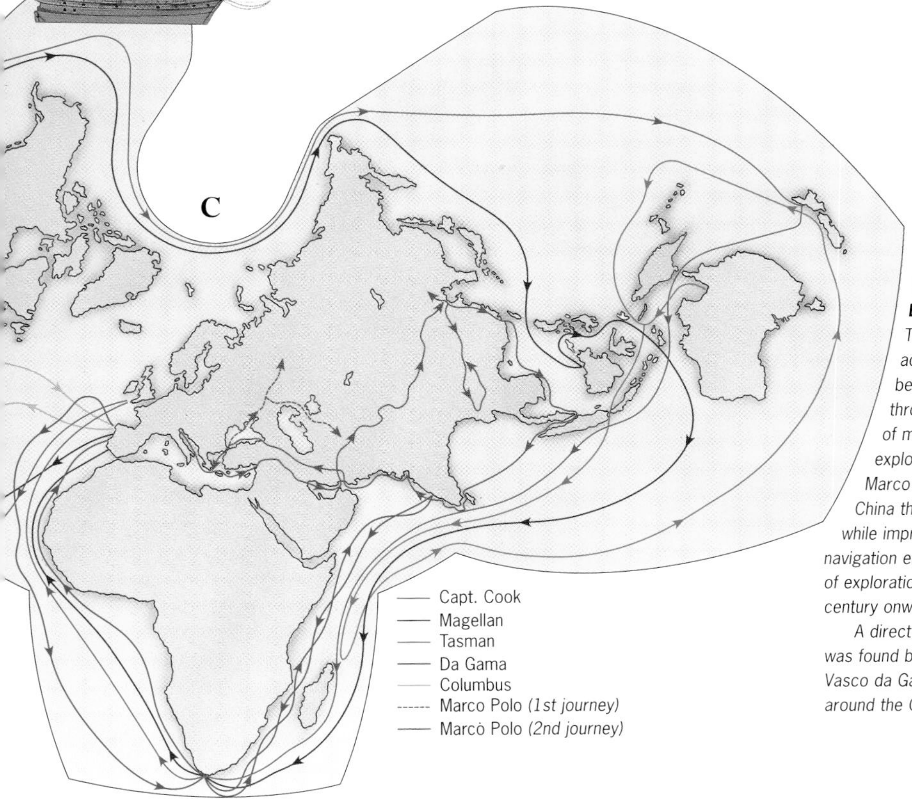

EARLY EXPLORERS

Transport and trade across the world became possible through the efforts of many different explorers [C].

Marco Polo opened up China through his travels, while improved boats and navigation enabled an explosion of exploration from the 15th century onwards.

A direct sea route to India was found by the Portuguese Vasco da Gama, who sailed around the Cape of Good Hope.

His discovery was exploited first by the Portuguese and the Spanish, but once the route was established, almost every European country staked a claim.

Christopher Columbus discovered America while searching for a quicker route westward to the Indies, and Ferdinand Magellan became the first European to sail across the Pacific. Australia and the Pacific and South Seas were explored and mapped by the Dutchman Abel Tasman and the British Captain James Cook.

Portugal, England, the Netherlands, Denmark and France all traded with the east, but the Dutch established a more lasting base than any other country.

—— Capt. Cook
—— Magellan
—— Tasman
—— Da Gama
—— Columbus
------ Marco Polo (1st journey)
—— Marco Polo (2nd journey)

THE LEGACY OF INDUSTRY

MODERN INDUSTRIAL SOCIETY PLACES GREAT DEMANDS on the Earth's natural resources and the environment, constantly increasing demand for materials and energy. Not only is our way of life diminishing our planet's resources rapidly, but industry often produces harmful by-products. One of the best-known examples is the hole in the ozone layer. Aerosol spray cans were invented in the 1950s, using chlorofluorocarbons (CFCs) as propellants. The harmful effect on the environment was only realised after the discovery of a hole forming in the ozone layer high above the Antarctic. Ozone exists mainly at high altitudes where it absorbs harmful ultra-violet light from the Sun – radiation so intense that it would render the Earth uninhabitable if it reached the surface unchecked. CFC molecules break down the ozone molecules, but remain unaltered themselves, so that one CFC molecule can destroy many ozone molecules. An international agreement has now banned the manufacture of CFCs, but it will be several more years before the expansion of the ozone hole comes to a halt.

Global greenhouse

Industrialisation and our increasingly energy-hungry society have lead to the production of high levels of carbon dioxide (CO^2). The major effect is to trap heat near the Earth's surface, and prevent its reflection into space. The average temperature of the planet may rise, melting some of the Polar ice-caps and raising sea levels, posing major problems for low-lying countries in the next century. First predictions suggested that the sea level would rise up to 60cm in the next century, compared to around 15cm this century.

Ironically, these predictions are now being revised downward because of a newly-discovered 'benefit' of a different industrial pollutant. Oxides of sulphur in the atmosphere, a by-product of coal burning, actually have a cooling effect on the Earth, but they create another major problem – acid rain. Many industrial processes produce oxides of sulphur and nitrogen, which rise high into the atmosphere and are carried over great distances by the wind. Acid rain forms when the molecules come into contact with water, falling on land up to 1000km away. It can slowly poison and kill entire forests and wipe out fish stocks in lakes.

The Scandinavian countries have been particularly affected by this problem – prevailing winds from heavily industrialised countries such as Britain blow the pollution towards them. Evergreen forests have been badly damaged as the acid rainfall not only acidifies the soil, but also increases the take-up of alkaline molecules, draining the soil even more. Nutrients are washed out of the acidified soil, and poisonous metals released. Because the acidity affects the soil first, the effects can spread through an entire forest before they start to show up in dying trees.

Water tables and rivers can be tainted either by leakage

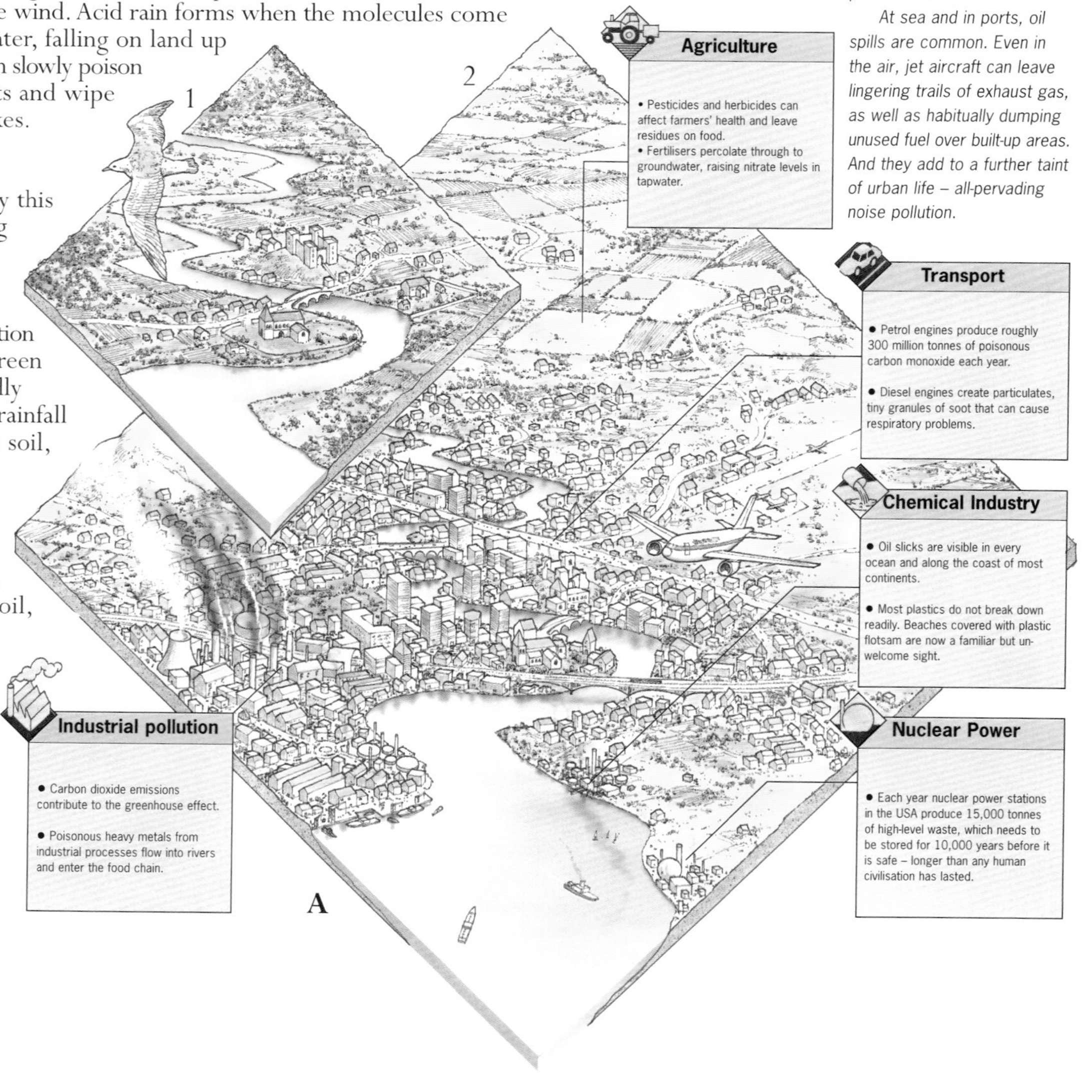

1
2
A
Agriculture
• Pesticides and herbicides can affect farmers' health and leave residues on food.
• Fertilisers percolate through to groundwater, raising nitrate levels in tapwater.
Transport
• Petrol engines produce roughly 300 million tonnes of poisonous carbon monoxide each year.
• Diesel engines create particulates, tiny granules of soot that can cause respiratory problems.
Chemical Industry
• Oil slicks are visible in every ocean and along the coast of most continents.
• Most plastics do not break down readily. Beaches covered with plastic flotsam are now a familiar but unwelcome sight.
Nuclear Power
• Each year nuclear power stations in the USA produce 15,000 tonnes of high-level waste, which needs to be stored for 10,000 years before it is safe – longer than any human civilisation has lasted.
Industrial pollution
• Carbon dioxide emissions contribute to the greenhouse effect.
• Poisonous heavy metals from industrial processes flow into rivers and enter the food chain.

▼***CAUSE AND EFFECT***
The effects of human activity on a landscape can be seen by examining the changes in a fictional town over 2 centuries of industrialisation **[A]**. *Where there was once a village on a riverbank [1] there is now an urban sprawl, suffering from pollution. This comes from many sources: industrial effluent and gas emissions; agricultural run-off of pesticides and fertilisers into the water course; exhaust emissions from road transport; the waste of the chemical and oil industries; and the possible radioactive poisoning of the environment from nuclear power stations.*

At sea and in ports, oil spills are common. Even in the air, jet aircraft can leave lingering trails of exhaust gas, as well as habitually dumping unused fuel over built-up areas. And they add to a further taint of urban life – all-pervading noise pollution.

▲ *Smoke pours out of an industrial complex and pollutes the atmosphere. Governments across the globe have brought in legislation in an attempt to control them but there is little success, especially in Asia.*

▶ ***THE GREENHOUSE EFFECT***
Carbon dioxide (CO^2), makes up only 0.035% of the Earth's atmosphere but is an important component as it traps the heat of the Sun in the greenhouse effect **[B]**. *Of incoming sunlight, 25% is reflected back into space by gases in the upper atmosphere* [1]. *A further 25% of the radiation is reflected back or absorbed by clouds* [2]. *Roughly 5% is immediately reflected by the Earth's surface* [3], *leaving 45% which is absorbed. The sunlight enters the atmosphere as relatively short wavelength ultraviolet and visible radiation, to which CO^2 is transparent. It is re-emitted by the Earth as longer wavelength infrared radiation, which CO^2 does absorb. This means that only 12% of the re-emitted radiation escapes into space* [4] *but 88% is reflected back to the ground, conserving the planet's heat* [5]. *The graph* **[C]** *shows how the average surface temperature of the Earth has been increasing over the last few years* **[D]**, *an effect that some scientists attribute to the increasing amount of CO^2 in the atmosphere due to the burning of fossil fuels. The warming may simply be part of a natural cycle, and could be countered by the cooling effects of other pollutants.*

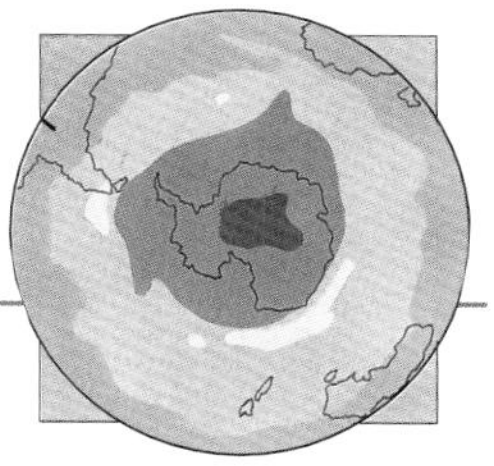

▲ ***THE OZONE HOLE***
In 1985 it was discovered that the level of protective ozone in the stratosphere above Antarctica had dropped dramatically. This 'hole' was caused by refrigerants called CFCs, whose production has now been banned.

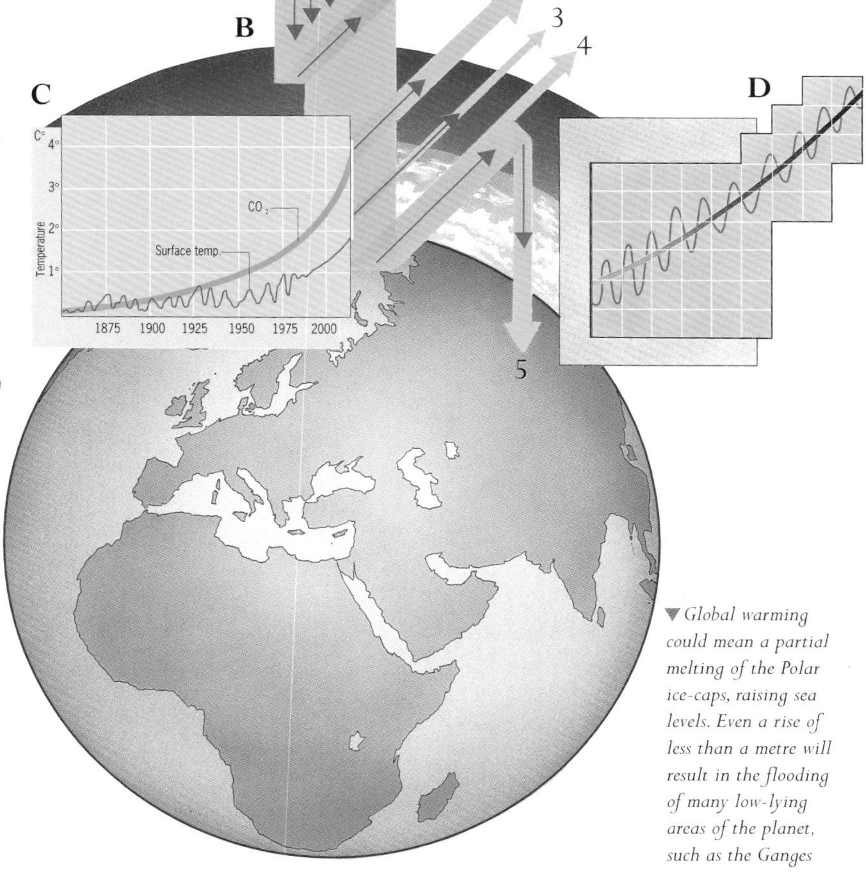

▼ *Global warming could mean a partial melting of the Polar ice-caps, raising sea levels. Even a rise of less than a metre will result in the flooding of many low-lying areas of the planet, such as the Ganges delta in Bangladesh.*

from industrial sites, or by 'run-off' of pesticides and fertilisers from agricultural land. Ground water is particularly vulnerable. In some places rainwater soaks into the ground and collects in underground reservoirs called aquifers. Aquifers provide a large proportion of water supplies, but can easily absorb agricultural chemicals, sewage or industrial waste soaking into the ground. Once polluted, they are difficult to clean up.

Not all ecological problems are caused by heavy industry. Across the world, deserts are spreading, not just because of changing climate, but because of the increasing needs of farmers who depend on the land that borders them. Constant grazing and cropping without ever giving the soil a chance to recover saps it of nutrients and moisture. Winds then blow away the topsoil, leaving an arid, infertile wasteland, which in turn prevents cloud formation and rain in the area. The deforestation of the rainforests also leaves topsoil which can only be farmed for a short time before becoming exhausted.

A hopeful future

We are still discovering many of the side-effects of modern industry. But recognising the problems is the first step towards solving them through methods such as recycling and the development of alternative energy sources and manufacturing processes.

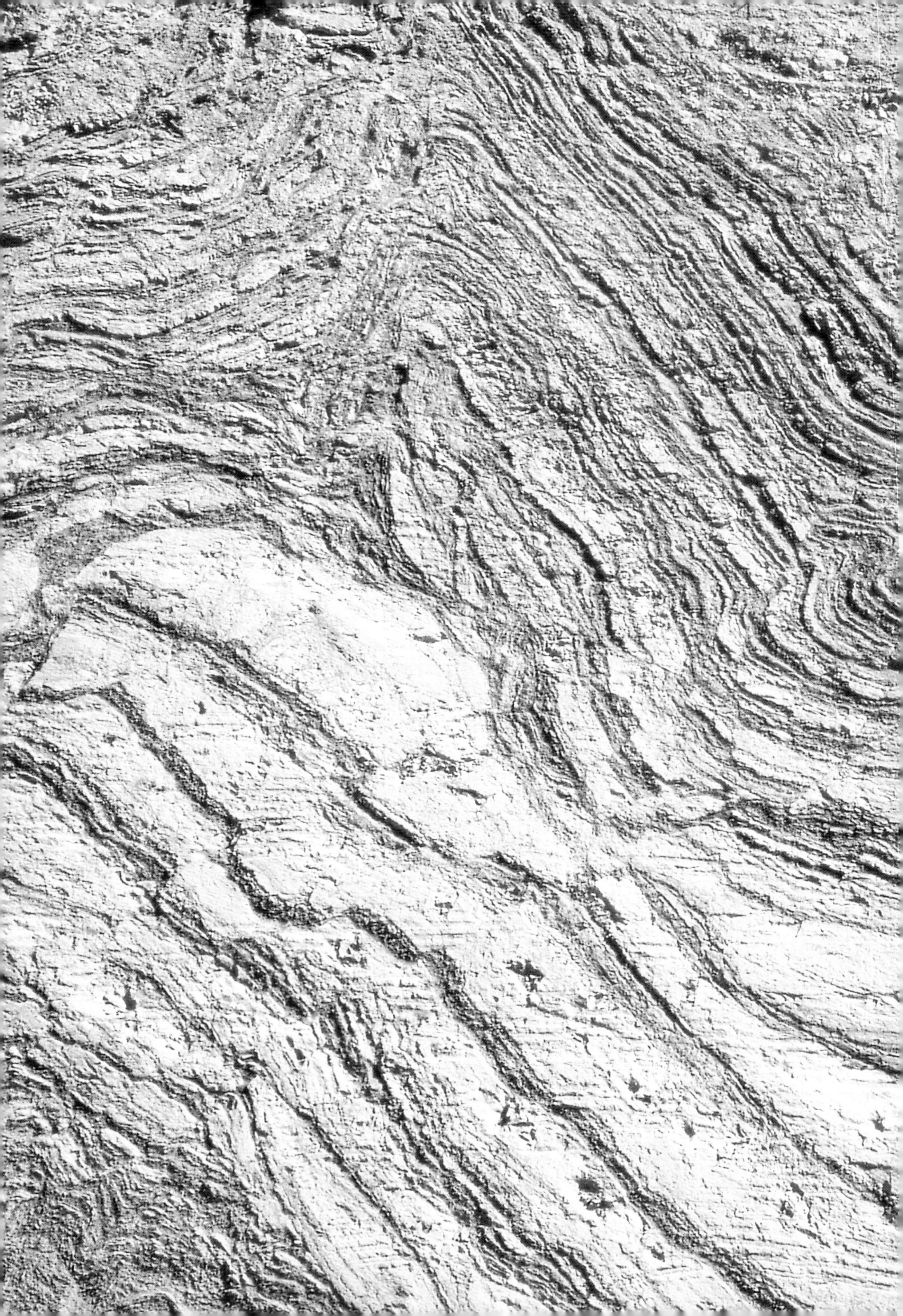

THE BRITISH ISLES
in maps

KEY TO MAP SYMBOLS

Political Regions

UNITED KINGDOM	country
SCOTLAND	nation or principality
━━━━━━━	international boundary
━━━━━━━	national boundary

Communications

══════	motorway
────────	main road
────────	other road
────────	main railway
────────	other railway
✈	major airport
✈	other airport

Hydrographic Features

～～～	river
～～～	canal
⬭	lake, reservoir

Each page also features a guide to relief colours

Cities, Towns & Capitals

■ **LONDON**	over 3 million
■ **DUBLIN**	1 – 3 million
■ **SHEFFIELD**	500 000 – 1 million
⦿ **Swansea**	100 000 – 500 000
● Guildford	50 000 – 100 000
○ Cashel	20 000 – 50 000
· Dalbeattie	under 20 000
LONDON	country capital
Belfast	national capital
⬭	urban area

Cultural Features

⌇DARTMOOR⌇	National Park
.∴ *Stonehenge*	ancient site or ruin
▪▪▪▪▪▪▪▪▪	ancient wall

Topographic Features

Lochnagar ▲1155	elevation above sea level (in metres)
▾2	elevation of land below sea level (in metres)

British Isles: Political

- Great Britain comprises England, Scotland and Wales, and is the largest island in Europe.
- The United Kingdom of Great Britain and Ireland was formed in 1801, when Great Britain and the island of Ireland were united by Act of Parliament.
- The United Kingdom of Great Britain and Northern Ireland and the Republic of Ireland both came into being in 1921, when Ireland was partitioned. Northern Ireland, which remained within the Union, comprises six of the former counties of the former Irish province of Ulster. The Republic of Ireland is that part of Ireland which left the Union, and comprises most (about four fifths) of the island's territory.
- The Channel Islands (comprising Jersey, Guernsey, Alderney and Sark) and the Isle of Man are not part of the United Kingdom; they are direct dependencies of the Crown.
- In May 1999, the devolution of government in Scotland and Wales led to the formation of a Scottish Parliament (based in Edinburgh) and a Welsh Assembly (based in Cardiff), giving the two much greater autonomy.
- Ever since Partition in Ireland, bitter conflicts have divided the community. Years of lengthy negotiations aimed at establishing a political settlement to these culminated on 10 May 1998, in the signing of the Good Friday Agreement. On 2 December 1999, the major step towards full implementation of this agreement was finally taken, with the devolution of government in Northern Ireland.

ENGLAND

1 Barnsley
2 Bath & NE Somerset
3 Birmingham
4 Blackburn with Darwen
5 Bolton
6 Bournemouth
7 Bracknell Forest
8 Bradford
9 Bristol
10 Bury
11 Calderdale
12 Coventry
13 Darlington
14 Derby
15 Doncaster
16 Dudley
17 Gateshead
18 Halton
19 Kirklees
20 Knowsley
21 Leicester
22 Liverpool
23 Luton
24 Manchester
25 Medway
26 Milton Keynes
27 Newcastle
28 North Somerset
29 Nottingham
30 Oldham
31 Poole
32 Portsmouth
33 Reading
34 Rochdale
35 Rotherham
36 Rutland
37 Salford
38 Sandwell
39 Sefton
40 Sheffield
41 Slough
42 Solihull
43 Southampton
44 South Gloucestershire
45 St Helens
46 Stockport
47 Stockton-on-Tees
48 Stoke-on-Trent
49 Swindon
50 Tameside
51 Telford & Wrekin
52 Thurrock
53 Trafford
54 Wakefield
55 Walsall
56 Warrington
57 Wigan
58 Windsor & Maidenhead
59 Wolverhampton

SCOTLAND

1 City of Edinburgh
2 Clackmannan
3 East Dunbartonshire
4 East Lothian
5 East Renfrewshire
6 Falkirk
7 Glasgow City
8 Inverclyde
9 Midlothian
10 North Ayrshire
11 North Lanarkshire
12 Renfrewshire
13 West Dunbartonshire
14 West Lothian

NORTHERN IRELAND

1 Antrim
2 Ards
3 Ballymena
4 Ballymoney
5 Banbridge
6 Belfast
7 Carrickfergus
8 Castlereagh
9 Coleraine
10 Cookstown
11 Craigavon
12 Derry
13 Dungannon
14 Larne
15 Limavady
16 Lisburn
17 Magherafelt
18 Moyle
19 Newtownabbey
20 North Down

WALES

1 Blaenau Gwent
2 Bridgend
3 Caerphilly
4 Cardiff
5 City & County of Swansea
6 Denbighshire
7 Flintshire
8 Merthyr Tydfil
9 Monmouthshire
10 Neath Port Talbot
11 Newport
12 Rhondda Cynon Taff
13 The Vale of Glamorgan
14 Torfaen
15 Wrexham

Administrative boundaries are not shown within London. There are currently 33 London boroughs which will be joined, in April 2000, by an elected London-wide assembly called the Greater London Authority (GLA). The GLA, headed by an elected mayor, will not replace any of the functions of the borough councils, but will take responsibility for strategic planning and economic development for London as a whole.

Scale 1 : 1 750 000

20 40 60 80 100 km

20 40 60 miles

Ireland

Northern Ireland • Republic of Ireland

A
10° W
B
9°
C
8°
D
7°
E
6°
F
1
2
3
4
5
55°
54°
53°
52°
37
38
ATLANTIC OCEAN
North Channel
IRISH SEA
Celtic Sea
UNITED KINGDOM
NORTHERN IRELAND
REPUBLIC OF IRELAND
Ulster
Connaught
Munster
Leinster
DUBLIN (BAILE ÁTHA CLIATH)
Belfast
Londonderry
Malin Head
Inishtrahull
Inishowen
Tory
Tory Sound
Bloody Foreland
Dunfanaghy
Derryveagh Mts.
GLENVEAGH
Aran
Dungloe
Gweebarra Bay
Letterkenny
Buncrana
Moville
Lough Foyle
Portrush
Rathlin
Fair Head
Coleraine
Ballycastle
Ballymoney
Cushendall
Garren Pt
Limavady
Dungiven
Bann
Antrim Hills
Blue Stack Mts.
Ballybofey
Lifford
Strabane
Sperrin Mts.
Maghera
Ballymena
Larne
Island Magee
Rossan Point
Killybegs
Newtownstewart
Magherafelt
Randalstown
Ballyclare
Antrim
Whitehead
Carrickfergus
Glengormley
Bangor
Holywood
Newtownabbey
Donegal
Donegal Bay
Omagh
Cookstown
Lough Neagh
Newtownards
Comber
Ards Pen.
Ballyshannon
Lower Lough Erne
Belleek
Irvinestown
Dungannon
Ballygawley
Lisburn
Carryduff
Strangford Lough
Inishmurray
Grange
Sligo Bay
Manorhamilton
Enniskillen
Craigavon
Lurgan
Portadown
Dromore
Ballynahinch
Portaferry
Armagh
Tandragee
Banbridge
Downpatrick
Erris Head
Downpatrick Head
Killala Bay
Belmullet
Sligo
Collooney
Lisnaskea
Upper Lough Erne
Clones
Monaghan
Rathfriland
Castlewellan
Bangor Erris
Ballina
Blacksod Bay
Nephin Beg Mts.
Lough Conn
Achill Head
Achill
Newtownbutler
Lough Allen
Newry
Newcastle
Mourne Mts.
Dundrum Bay
Castleblayney
Warrenpoint
Rostrevor
Kilkeel
Corraun Peninsula
Charlestown
Boyle
Carrick-on-Shannon
Swinford
Newport
Castlebar
Clew Bay
Clare
Ballaghaderreen
Cavan
Dundalk
Carrickmacross
Dundalk Bay
Westport
Inishturk
Lough Carra
Ballyhaunis
Castlerea
Strokestown
Virginia
Ardee
Inishbofin
Inishark
Lough Mask
Claremorris
Longford
Granard
Lough Sheelin
Clogher Head
Kells
Slane
Drogheda
Ballinrobe
Maumturk Mts.
Lough Derravaragh
Roscommon
Julianstown
Clifden
CONNEMARA
Navan
Balbriggan
Tuam
Ballygar
Lough Owel
Boyne
Slyne Head
Lough Corrib
Lough Ree
Mullingar
Oughterard
Suck
Lough Ennell
Athlone
Dunshaughlin
Lambay
Moate
Kinnegad
Royal Canal
Swords
Malahide
Claregalway
Gorumna
Galway
Ballinasloe
Oranmore
Kilbeggan
Grand Canal
Lucan
Liffey
Inishmore
Galway Bay
Tullamore
Bog of Allen
Rathcoole
Dublin Bay
Dalkey
Dún Laoghaire
Loughrea
Shannon
Clogh an
Kilcormac
Inishmaan
Aran Islands
Naas
Bray
Kildare
The Burren
Inisheer
Gort
Slieve Aughty Mts.
Birr
Slieve Bloom Mts.
Mountmellick
Monasterevin
Blessington Lakes
Wicklow Mts.
WICKLOW MOUNTAINS
Ennistymon
Borrisokane
Lough Derg
Mountrath
Port Laoise
Roscrea
Nore
Castletown
Athy
Liscannor Bay
926
Lugnaquilla
Wicklow
Wicklow Head
Rathdrum
Ennis
Nenagh
Abbeyleix
Durrow
Carlow
Templemore
Bagenalstown
Tullow
Kilkee
Silvermine Mts.
Arklow
Limerick
Kilrush
Thurles
Barrow
Kilkenny
Mouth of the Shannon
Loop Head
Tarbert
Adare
Slieveardagh Hills
Gorey
Rathkeale
Golden Vale
Listowel
Cashel
Callan
Cahore Point
Newcastle West
Tipperary
Thomastown
Enniscorthy
Abbeyfeale
Slaney
Tralee Bay
Rath Luirc
Cahir
New Ross
950
Brandon Mt.
Tralee
Clonmel
Carrick-on-Suir
Wexford
Castleisland
Suir
Wexford Harbour
Dingle
Mitchelstown
Waterford
Rosslare Harbour
Dingle Bay
Killorglin
Lough Leane
Killarney
Mallow
Blackwater
Fermoy
Tallowbridge
Carnsore Point
Saltee Islands
1040
Macgillycuddy's Reeks
Boggeragh Mts.
Dungarvan
Dungarvan Harbour
Hook Head
Cahersiveen
KILLARNEY
Kenmare
Macroom
Lee
Cork
Youghal
Douglas
Ballincollig
Youghal Bay
Skelligs Bay
Kenmare River
Caha Mts.
Cobh
Cork Harbour
Dursey
Bantry Bay
Bantry
Kinsale
Bear I.
Clonakilty
Kinsale Harbour
Dunmanus Bay
Schull
Old Head of Kinsale
Clonakilty Bay
Mizen Head
Roaringwater
Sherkin Island
Cape Clear
Clear Island

metres	feet
1000	3280
500	1640
200	656
100	328
0	0

feet	metres
164	50
328	100
656	200
3280	1000
6560	2000

- ■ over 3 million
- ▣ 1 – 3 million
- ▩ 500 000 – 1 million
- ● 100 000 – 500 000
- • 50 000 – 100 000
- ○ 20 000 – 50 000
- · under 20 000
- country capital underline
- state or province capital underline
- urban area

Scale 1 : 1 750 000

0 20 40 60 80 100 km

0 20 40 60 miles

SHETLAND ISLANDS
Haroldswick
Herma Ness
Unst
Fetlar
Out Skerries
Whalsay
Mid Yell
Yell
Yell Sound
North Roe
449
Ronas Hill
Hillswick
Brae
Lerwick
Bressay
Isle of Noss
Mousa
Sumburgh
Sumburgh Head
Mainland
St. Magnus Bay
Muckle Roe
Papa Stour
West Burra
Foula
Fair Isle
ORKNEY ISLANDS
North Ronaldsay
Sanday
Stronsay
Papa Westray
Westray
The North Sound
Eday
Shapinsay
Kirkwall
Rousay
Mainland
Twatt
Stromness
Scapa Flow
Hoy
South Ronaldsay
Pentland Firth
Stroma
Duncansby Head
John o' Groats
Dunnet Head
Thurso
Sinclair's Bay
Wick
Lybster
Halkirk
Caithness
Helmsdale
Kinbrace
Brora
Strathy
Strathy Point
Bettyhill
Tongue
Tongue Bay
962
Ben Klibreck
Loch Eriboll
927
Ben Hope
Lairg
Loch Shin
Durness
Cape Wrath
998
Ben More Assynt
Elphin
Lochinver
Scourie
Eddrachillis Bay
Enard Bay
Ullapool
Loch Broom
Gruinard Bay
Dornoch
Dornoch Firth
Tarbat Ness
Tain
Easter Ross
Invergordon
1046
Ben Wyvis
Dingwall
Muir of Ord
Black Isle
Moray Firth
Inverness
Nairn
Forres
Lossiemouth
Elgin
Spey Bay
Buckie
Cullen
Banff
Macduff
Fraserburgh
Kinnaird Head
Peterhead
Buchan
Mintlaw
Turriff
Ellon
Oldmeldrum
Aberdeen
Girdle Ness
Inverurie
Kintore
Keith
Huntly
Rhynie
Charlestown of Aberlour
Strath Spey
Grantown-on-Spey
Aviemore
1309
Ben Macdui
Cairngorm Mts.
Braemar
Ballater
Aboyne
Banchory
Dee
Stonehaven
Inverbervie
Laurencekirk
Brechin
Montrose
1155
Lochnagar
Cray
Grampian Mountains
Pitlochry
Badenoch
Newtonmore
Kingussie
941
Carn Ban
Monadhliath Mts.
Tomatin
Loch Ness
Glen More
Drumnadrochit
Fort Augustus
Laggan
Loch Ericht
1148
Ben Alder
Spean Bridge
1343
Ben Nevis
Fort William
Loch Lochy
Glen Affric
North West Highlands
1108
Sgurr Mor
Achnasheen
Strathcarron
Loch Maree
Wester Ross
Kinlochewe
Gairloch
Kyle of Lochalsh
Shiel Bridge
Glenfinnan
Loch Shiel
Loch Morar
Mallaig
Acharacle
Sound of Arisaig
Point of Ardnamurchan
Eigg
Muck
Rum
Canna
Soay
Sound of Sleat
Broadford
Scalpay
Raasay
Inner Sound
Sound of Raasay
Rona
Skye
Portree
Sligachan
Cuillin Hills
Uig
Dunvegan
Loch Snizort
The Minch
Shiant Islands
Little Minch
Sea of the Hebrides
INNER HEBRIDES
OUTER HEBRIDES
Butt of Lewis
Port Nis
Stornoway
Barabhas
Lewis
Baile Ailein
North Harris
Tarbert
South Harris
Scalpay
Leverburgh
Sound of Harris
Taransay
Scarp
Gallan Head
Flannan Islands
Pabbay
Berneray
Lochmaddy
North Uist
Cairinis
Ronay
Monach Islands
Benbecula
Wick
South Uist
Lochboisdale
Eriskay
Sound of Barra
Barra
Castlebay
Vatersay
Sandray
Mingulay
ATLANTIC OCEAN
Sule Skerry
Stack Skerry
Rona
Sula Sgeir

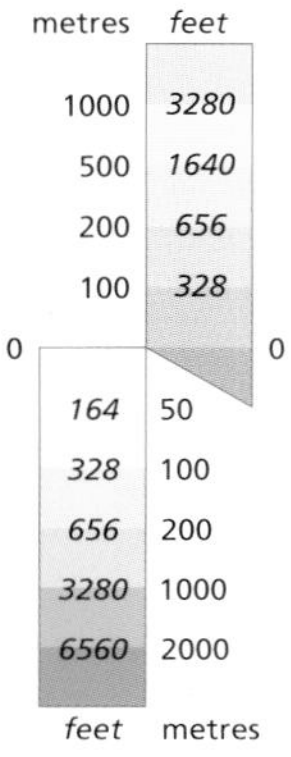

metres feet
1000 3280
500 1640
200 656
100 328
0 0
164 50
328 100
656 200
3280 1000
6560 2000
feet metres

Great Britain: North

Isle of Man • Northern England • Scotland

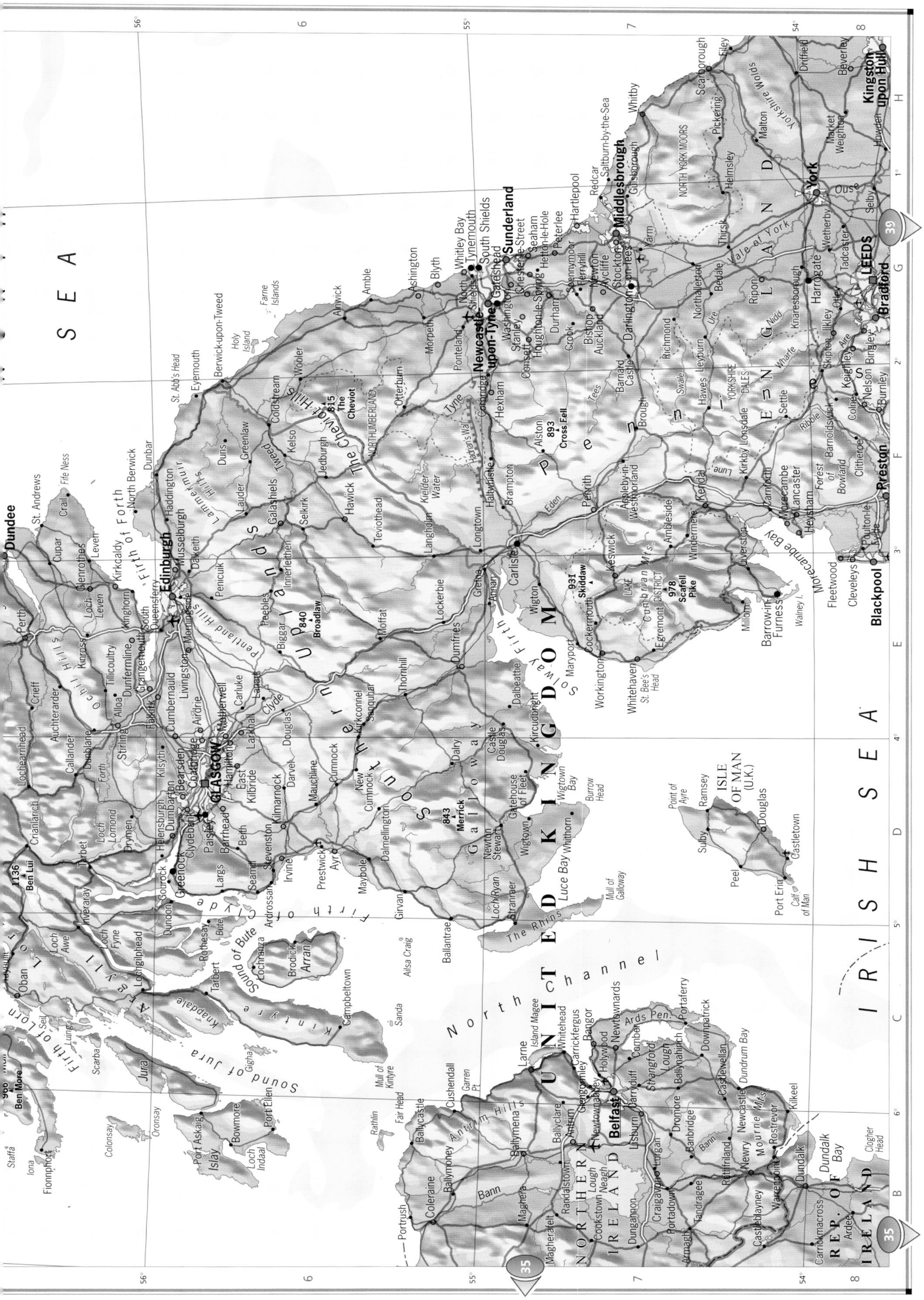

■ over 3 million
● 50 000 – 100 000
country capital underline
▣ 1 – 3 million
○ 20 000 – 50 000
state or province capital underline
▪ 500 000 – 1 million
• under 20 000
urban area
● 100 000 – 500 000

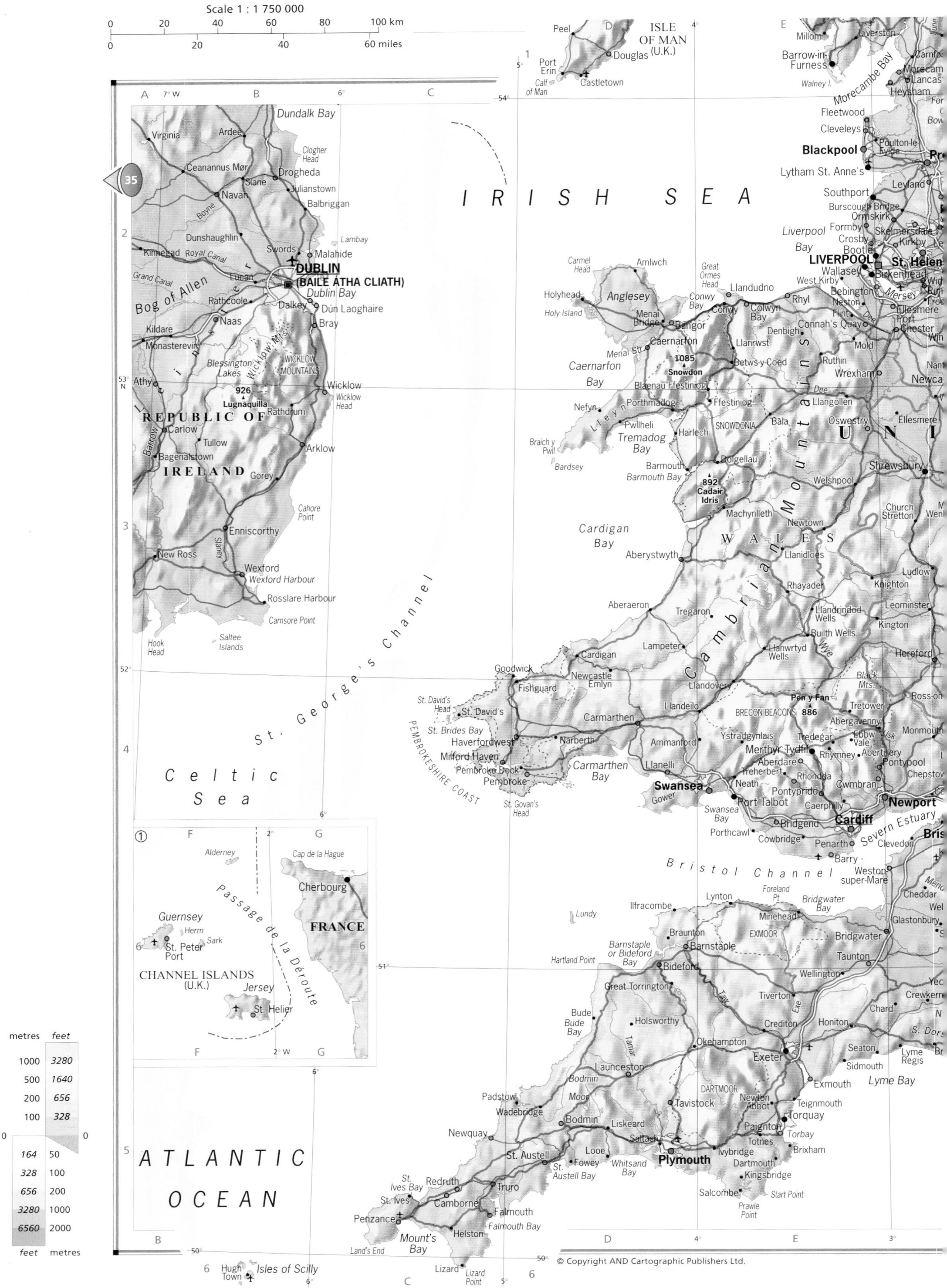
Scale 1 : 1 750 000
0 20 40 60 80 100 km
0 20 40 60 miles
IRISH SEA
ISLE OF MAN (U.K.)
Peel
Douglas
Port Erin
Calf of Man
Castletown
REPUBLIC OF IRELAND
Dundalk Bay
Virginia
Ardee
Clogher Head
Ceanannus Mør
Drogheda
Slane
Julianstown
Navan
Balbriggan
Boyne
Dunshaughlin
Lambay
Kinnegad
Royal Canal
Swords
Malahide
DUBLIN
(BAILE ÁTHA CLIATH)
Dublin Bay
Grand Canal
Lucan
Bog of Allen
Rathcoole
Dalkey
Dún Laoghaire
Bray
Naas
Kildare
Monasterevin
Wicklow Mts.
Blessington Lakes
WICKLOW MOUNTAINS
Leinster
Athy
Wicklow
Wicklow Head
926
Lugnaquilla
Rathdrum
Carlow
Tullow
Barrow
Arklow
Bagenalstown
Gorey
Cahore Point
Enniscorthy
Slaney
New Ross
Wexford
Wexford Harbour
Rosslare Harbour
Carnsore Point
Hook Head
Saltee Islands
St. George's Channel
Celtic Sea
ATLANTIC OCEAN
Anglesey
Carmel Head
Amlwch
Holyhead
Holy Island
Menai Bridge
Bangor
Great Ormes Head
Llandudno
Conwy Bay
Conwy
Colwyn Bay
Rhyl
Caernarfon
Menai Str.
1085
Snowdon
Llanrwst
Betws-y-Coed
Denbigh
Caernarfon Bay
Blaenau Ffestiniog
Nefyn
Porthmadog
Ffestiniog
Lleyn
Pwllheli
Tremadog Bay
Harlech
SNOWDONIA
Bala
Braich y Pwll
Bardsey
Barmouth
Barmouth Bay
Dolgellau
892
Cadair Idris
Machynlleth
Cardigan Bay
Aberystwyth
WALES
Cambrian Mountains
Newtown
Llanidloes
Rhayader
Aberaeron
Tregaron
Llandrindod Wells
Builth Wells
Lampeter
Llanwrtyd Wells
Wye
Cardigan
Goodwick
Newcastle Emlyn
Fishguard
Llandovery
St. David's Head
St. David's
St. Brides Bay
Haverfordwest
Milford Haven
Pembroke Dock
Pembroke
PEMBROKESHIRE COAST
St. Govan's Head
Narberth
Carmarthen
Carmarthen Bay
Llandeilo
Ammanford
Llanelli
Swansea
Gower
Swansea Bay
Pen y Fan
886
BRECON BEACONS
Black Mts.
Ystradgynlais
Merthyr Tydfil
Tredegar
Ebbw Vale
Abergavenny
Aberdare
Rhymney
Abertillery
Treherbert
Rhondda
Pontypool
Neath
Pontypridd
Cwmbran
Port Talbot
Caerphilly
Bridgend
Cardiff
Newport
Porthcawl
Cowbridge
Penarth
Barry
Severn Estuary
Bristol Channel
Lundy
Ilfracombe
Lynton
Foreland Pt
Minehead
EXMOOR
Braunton
Barnstaple
Barnstaple or Bideford Bay
Bideford
Hartland Point
Great Torrington
Taw
Bude
Bude Bay
Holsworthy
Tamar
Okehampton
Launceston
Bodmin Moor
DARTMOOR
Tavistock
Padstow
Wadebridge
Bodmin
Liskeard
Newquay
Saltash
Plymouth
Looe
St. Austell
Fowey
St. Austell Bay
Whitsand Bay
Truro
St. Ives Bay
St. Ives
Redruth
Camborne
Penzance
Falmouth
Falmouth Bay
Helston
Mount's Bay
Land's End
Lizard
Lizard Point
Isles of Scilly
Hugh Town
Ivybridge
Dartmouth
Kingsbridge
Salcombe
Start Point
Prawle Point
Totnes
Paignton
Torbay
Brixham
Torquay
Teignmouth
Newton Abbot
Exeter
Exmouth
Exe
Crediton
Tiverton
Honiton
Seaton
Sidmouth
Lyme Regis
Lyme Bay
Wellington
Taunton
Bridgwater
Bridgwater Bay
Weston-super-Mare
Cheddar
Glastonbury
Chard
Crewkerne
Millom
Ulverston
Barrow-in-Furness
Walney I.
Morecambe Bay
Morecambe
Lancaster
Heysham
Fleetwood
Cleveleys
Blackpool
Poulton-le-Fylde
Lytham St. Anne's
Southport
Leyland
Burscough Bridge
Ormskirk
Formby
Skelmersdale
Liverpool Bay
Crosby
Kirkby
Bootle
LIVERPOOL
St. Helens
Wallasey
Birkenhead
West Kirby
Bebington
Mersey
Neston
Flint
Ellesmere Port
Connah's Quay
Dee
Chester
Mold
Ruthin
Wrexham
Llangollen
Oswestry
Ellesmere
Shrewsbury
Welshpool
Church Stretton
Ludlow
Knighton
Leominster
Kington
Hereford
Ross-on-Wye
Monmouth
Tretower
Usk
Chepstow
Clevedon
UNITED KINGDOM
CHANNEL ISLANDS (U.K.)
Alderney
Passage de la Déroute
Cap de la Hague
Cherbourg
FRANCE
Guernsey
Herm
Sark
St. Peter Port
Jersey
St. Helier
metres feet
1000 3280
500 1640
200 656
100 328
0 0
164 50
328 100
656 200
3280 1000
6560 2000
feet metres
© Copyright AND Cartographic Publishers Ltd.

Great Britain: South

Channel Islands • Southern England • Wales

 over 3 million
1 – 3 million
500 000 – 1 million
100 000 – 500 000
50 000 – 100 000
20 000 – 50 000
under 20 000
country capital underline
state or province capital underline
urban area

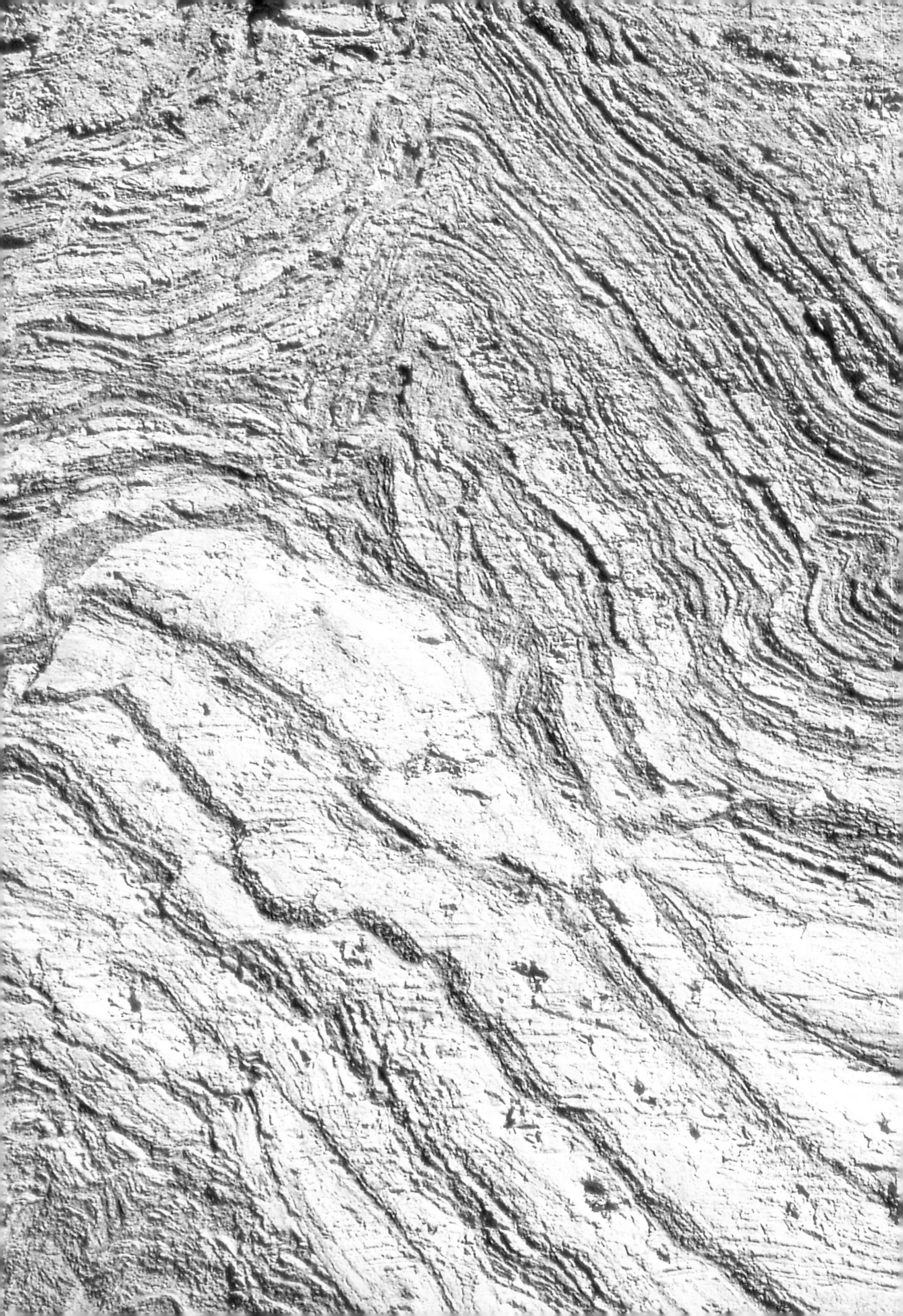

THE WORLD
in maps

KEY TO MAP SYMBOLS

Political Regions

CANADA	country
ONTARIO	state or province
━━━━━━	international boundary
────────	state or province boundary
─ · ─ · ─ · ─	undefined/disputed boundary or ceasefire/demarcation line

Communications

──────	motorway
──────	main road
─ ─ ─ ─	other road or track
──────	railway
✈	international airport

Hydrographic Features

～～～	river, canal
┈┈┈	seasonal river
Niagara Falls Kariba Dam	waterfall, dam
⬭	lake, seasonal lake
⬭	salt lake, seasonal salt lake
⬭	ice cap or glacier

Cities, Towns & Capitals

■ **CHICAGO**	over 3 million
■ **HAMBURG**	1 – 3 million
◉ **Bulawayo**	250 000 – 1 million
● Antofogasta	100 000 – 250 000
○ Ajaccio	25 000 – 100 000
· Indian Springs	under 25 000
LONDON	country capital
Columbia	state or province capital
⬭	urban area

Cultural Features

∴ Persepolis	ancient site or ruin
■■■■■■■■■■■■	ancient wall

Topographic Features

Mount Ziel ▲1510	elevation above sea level (in metres)
▾133	elevation of land below sea level (in metres)
✕ **Khyber Pass** 1080	mountain pass (height in metres)

Each page also features a guide to relief colours

Equatorial Scale 1 : 112 000 000

0 1000 2000 3000 4000 km

0 1000 2000 miles

150°
120°
90°
60°
30°
0°
ARCTIC OCEAN
Ellesmere Island
GREENLAND
(Denmark)
Greenland Sea
Baffin Bay
Baffin Island
Victoria Island
Beaufort Sea
Arctic Circle
Yukon
ALASKA
(U.S.)
Mackenzie
Anchorage
Nuuk
(Godthåb)
ICELAND
Reykjavik
Norwegi
Sea
Hudson
Bay
Bering
Sea
Gulf of
Alaska
CANADA
ROCKY MOUNTAINS
Edmonton
Calgary
Winnipeg
Lake Superior
Vancouver
Seattle
Missouri
Lake Huron
Lake Michigan
St Lawrence
Québec
Montréal
Ottawa
Toronto
Chicago
Detroit
Denver
New York
Philadelphia
Washington D.C.
UNITED STATES
Kansas City
San Francisco
Los Angeles
San Diego
Phoenix
Dallas
Atlanta
Mississippi
Houston
New Orleans
Rio Grande
Bermuda
(U.K.)
ATLANTIC
OCEAN
Monterrey
MEXICO
Gulf of
Mexico
THE BAHAMAS
Tropic of Cancer
HAWAII
(U.S.)
La Habana
CUBA
Guadalajara
Ciudad de México
DOMINICAN REP
HAITI
Santo Domingo
PUERTO RICO (U.S.)
ANTIGUA & BARBUDA
JAMAICA
ST KITTS-NEVIS
DOMINICA
BELIZE
HONDURAS
Caribbean Sea
ST LUCIA
Guatemala
GUATEMALA
ST VINCENT & THE GRENADINES
BARBADOS
EL SALVADOR
NICARAGUA
GRENADA
Managua
COSTA RICA
San José
Panamá
Caracas
TRINIDAD & TOBAGO
PANAMA
VENEZUELA
Georgetown
GUYANA
SURINAM
FRENCH GUIANA (Fr.)
Bogotá
COLOMBIA
Islas Galápagos
(Ecuador)
Quito
ECUADOR
PACIFIC
OCEAN
Equator
Amazon
Belém
Fortaleza
Manaus
Iquitos
KIRIBATI
BRAZIL
Recife
PERU
Lima
Salvador
La Paz
BOLIVIA
Brasília
Arequipa
Sucre
French Polynesia
PARAGUAY
Belo Horizonte
Tropic of Capricorn
Rio de Janeiro
São Paulo
Asunción
Pitcairn Is.
(U.K.)
Curitiba
Porto Alegre
Córdoba
Santiago
CHILE
URUGUAY
Buenos Aires
Montevideo
ARGENTINA
Falkland Islands
(U.K.)
South Georgia
(U.K.)
Punta Arenas
South Sandwich Islands
(U.K.)
Antarctic Circle
Bellinghausen
Sea
Weddell Sea
Ross Sea
Açores
(Portugal)
Madeira
(Portugal)
Islas Canarias
(Spain)
REPUBLIC OF IRELAND
Dublin
UNITED KINGDOM
London
PORTUGAL
Lisboa
SPAIN
Madrid
ANDORRA
Rabat
Casablanca
MOROCCO
WESTERN SAHARA
(Morocco)
MAURITANIA
MALI
Nouakchott
CAPE VERDE
Dakar
THE GAMBIA
Banjul
Bamako
GUINEA-BISSAU
Bissau
GUINEA
Conakry
Freetown
SIERRA LEONE
Monrovia
LIBERIA
IVORY COAST
Yamoussoukro
GHANA
Accra
Niger

Mt. Everest, China/Nepal : 8,848 m or 29,029 ft

Arica, Chile : 0.08 cm or 0.03 in

Nile, Egypt : 6,690 km or 4,160 mi

Dead Sea, Israel/Jordan : 400 m or 1312 ft

Mawsynram, India : 1187.2 cm or 467.4 in

Caspian Sea : 371,000 km² or 143,240 sq mi

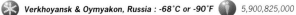

Verkhoyansk & Oymyakon, Russia : -68°C or -90°F

Al Aziziyah, Libya : 58°C or 136°F

5,900,825,000

43 per km² or 112 per sq mi

136,268,000 km² or 52,614,000 sq mi

192

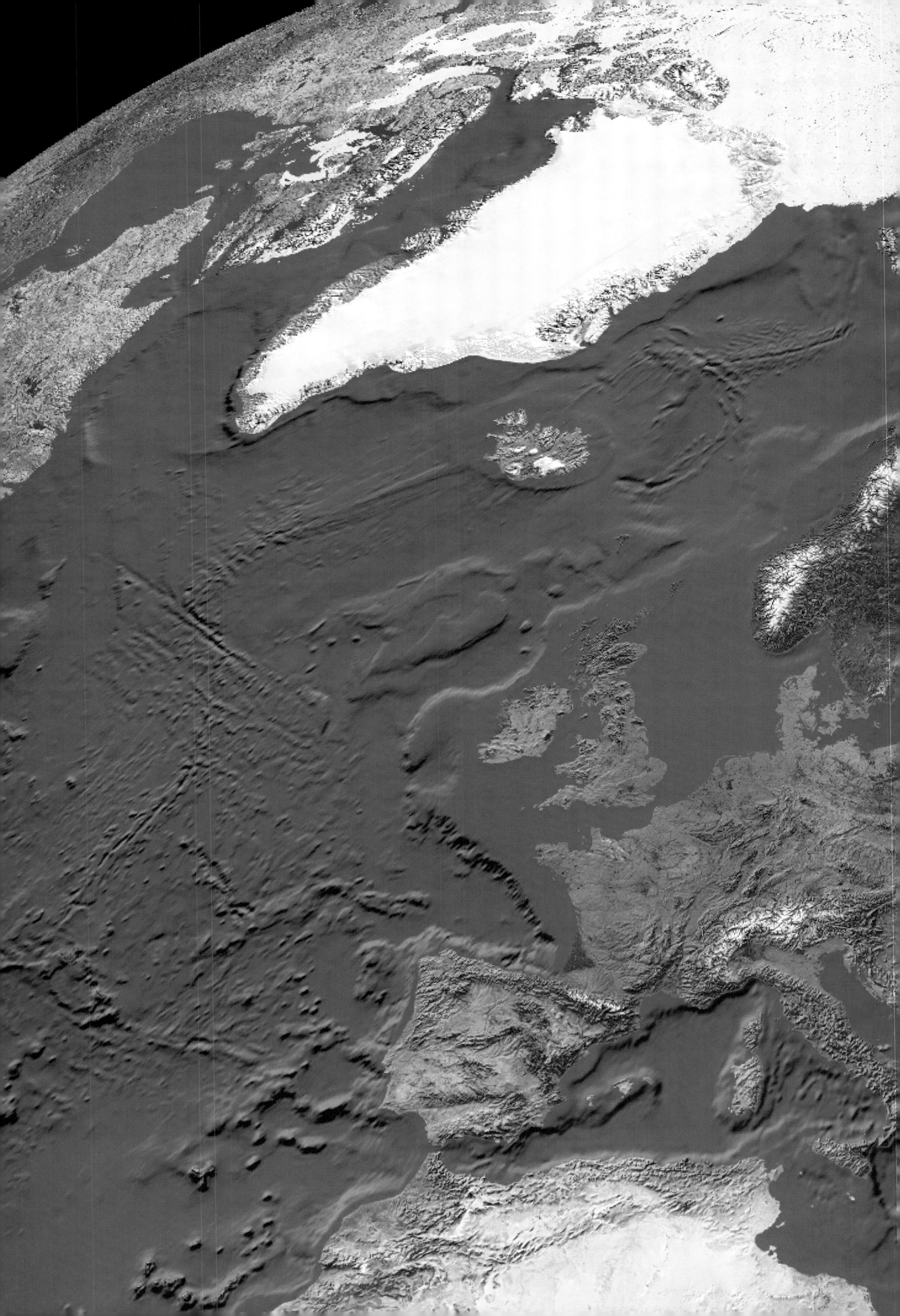

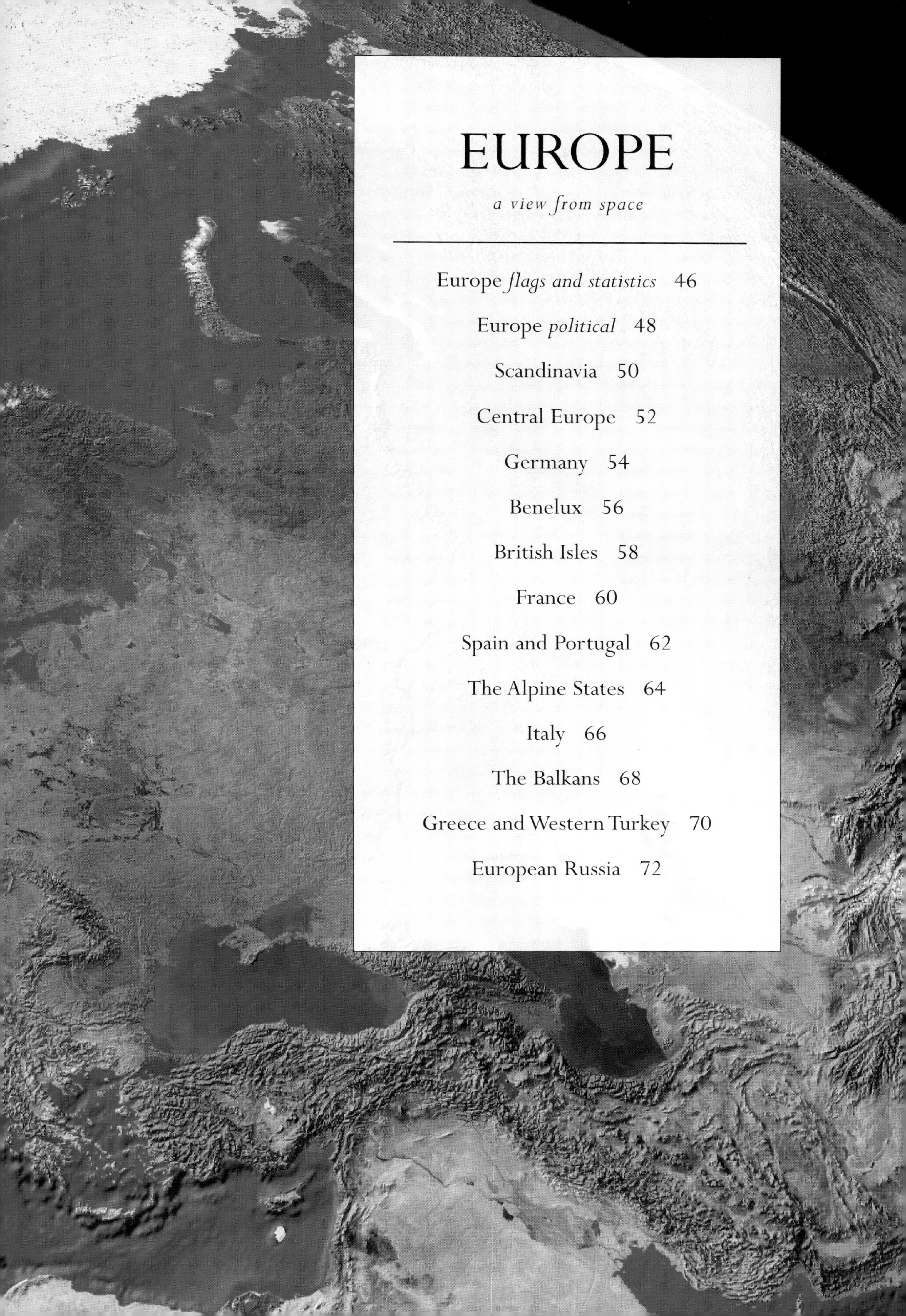

EUROPE

a view from space

Europe *flags and statistics* 46

Europe *political* 48

Scandinavia 50

Central Europe 52

Germany 54

Benelux 56

British Isles 58

France 60

Spain and Portugal 62

The Alpine States 64

Italy 66

The Balkans 68

Greece and Western Turkey 70

European Russia 72

EUROPE

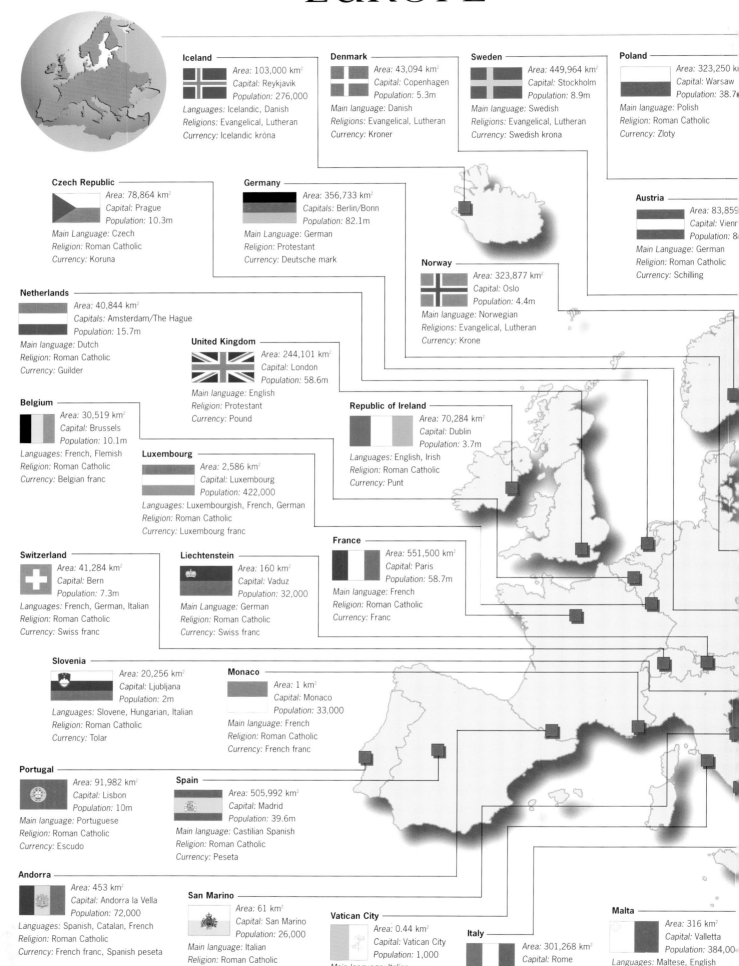

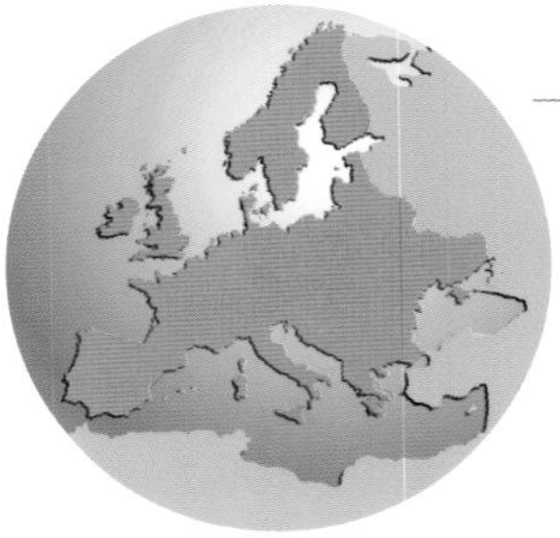

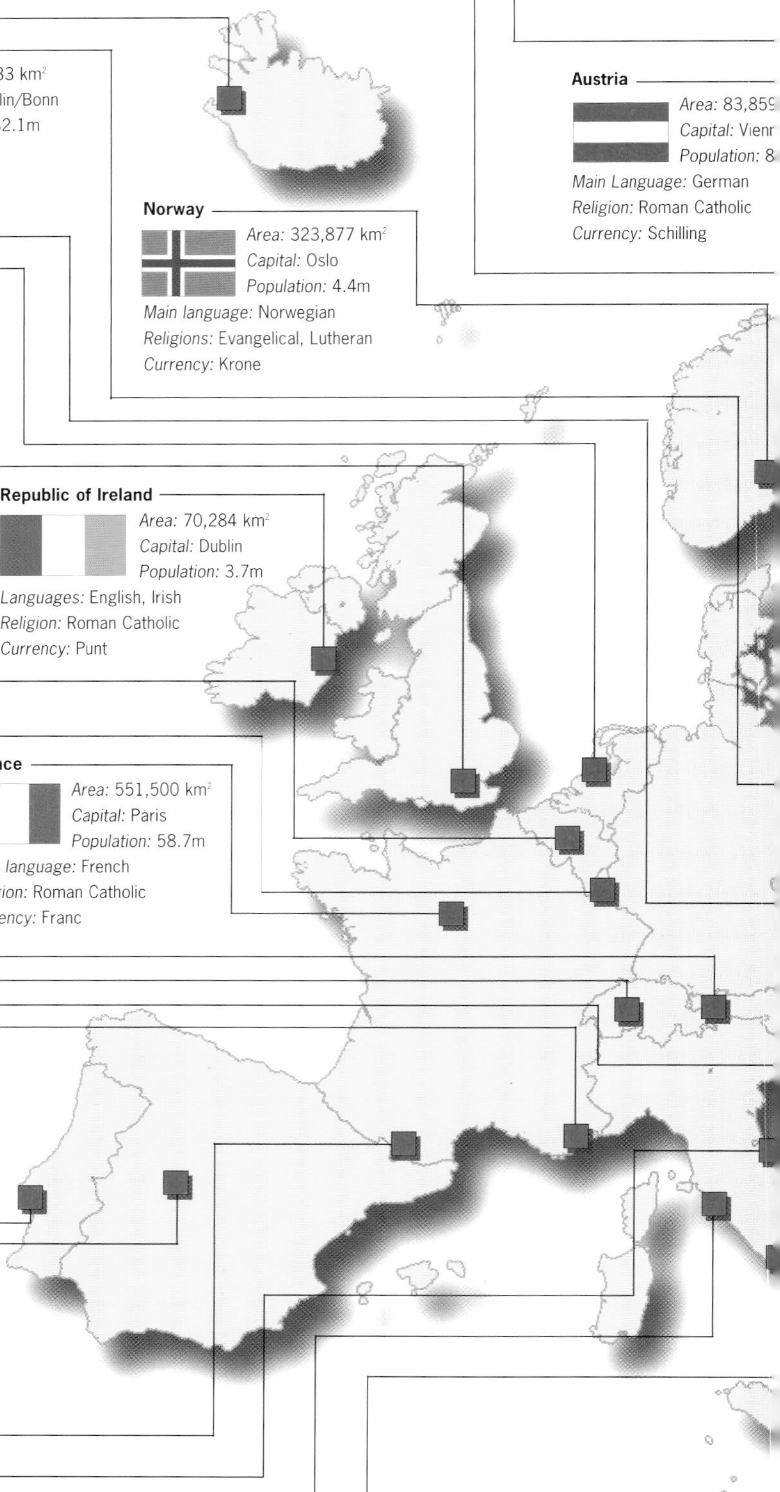

Iceland
Area: 103,000 km²
Capital: Reykjavik
Population: 276,000
Languages: Icelandic, Danish
Religions: Evangelical, Lutheran
Currency: Icelandic króna

Denmark
Area: 43,094 km²
Capital: Copenhagen
Population: 5.3m
Main language: Danish
Religions: Evangelical, Lutheran
Currency: Kroner

Sweden
Area: 449,964 km²
Capital: Stockholm
Population: 8.9m
Main language: Swedish
Religions: Evangelical, Lutheran
Currency: Swedish krona

Poland
Area: 323,250 k
Capital: Warsaw
Population: 38.7
Main language: Polish
Religion: Roman Catholic
Currency: Zloty

Czech Republic
Area: 78,864 km²
Capital: Prague
Population: 10.3m
Main Language: Czech
Religion: Roman Catholic
Currency: Koruna

Germany
Area: 356,733 km²
Capitals: Berlin/Bonn
Population: 82.1m
Main Language: German
Religion: Protestant
Currency: Deutsche mark

Austria
Area: 83,85
Capital: Vienr
Population: 8
Main Language: German
Religion: Roman Catholic
Currency: Schilling

Norway
Area: 323,877 km²
Capital: Oslo
Population: 4.4m
Main language: Norwegian
Religions: Evangelical, Lutheran
Currency: Krone

Netherlands
Area: 40,844 km²
Capitals: Amsterdam/The Hague
Population: 15.7m
Main language: Dutch
Religion: Roman Catholic
Currency: Guilder

United Kingdom
Area: 244,101 km²
Capital: London
Population: 58.6m
Main language: English
Religion: Protestant
Currency: Pound

Belgium
Area: 30,519 km²
Capital: Brussels
Population: 10.1m
Languages: French, Flemish
Religion: Roman Catholic
Currency: Belgian franc

Republic of Ireland
Area: 70,284 km²
Capital: Dublin
Population: 3.7m
Languages: English, Irish
Religion: Roman Catholic
Currency: Punt

Luxembourg
Area: 2,586 km²
Capital: Luxembourg
Population: 422,000
Languages: Luxembourgish, French, German
Religion: Roman Catholic
Currency: Luxembourg franc

France
Area: 551,500 km²
Capital: Paris
Population: 58.7m
Main language: French
Religion: Roman Catholic
Currency: Franc

Switzerland
Area: 41,284 km²
Capital: Bern
Population: 7.3m
Languages: French, German, Italian
Religion: Roman Catholic
Currency: Swiss franc

Liechtenstein
Area: 160 km²
Capital: Vaduz
Population: 32,000
Main Language: German
Religion: Roman Catholic
Currency: Swiss franc

Slovenia
Area: 20,256 km²
Capital: Ljubljana
Population: 2m
Languages: Slovene, Hungarian, Italian
Religion: Roman Catholic
Currency: Tolar

Monaco
Area: 1 km²
Capital: Monaco
Population: 33,000
Main language: French
Religion: Roman Catholic
Currency: French franc

Portugal
Area: 91,982 km²
Capital: Lisbon
Population: 10m
Main language: Portuguese
Religion: Roman Catholic
Currency: Escudo

Spain
Area: 505,992 km²
Capital: Madrid
Population: 39.6m
Main language: Castilian Spanish
Religion: Roman Catholic
Currency: Peseta

Andorra
Area: 453 km²
Capital: Andorra la Vella
Population: 72,000
Languages: Spanish, Catalan, French
Religion: Roman Catholic
Currency: French franc, Spanish peseta

San Marino
Area: 61 km²
Capital: San Marino
Population: 26,000
Main language: Italian
Religion: Roman Catholic
Currency: San Marino & Italian lira

Vatican City
Area: 0.44 km²
Capital: Vatican City
Population: 1,000
Main language: Italian
Religion: Roman Catholic
Currency: Italian lira

Italy
Area: 301,268 km²
Capital: Rome
Population: 57.4m
Main language: Italian
Religion: Roman Catholic
Currency: Lira

Malta
Area: 316 km²
Capital: Valletta
Population: 384,00
Languages: Maltese, English
Religion: Roman Catholic
Currency: Maltese lira

ALTHOUGH IT IS THE second smallest continent, Europe has a wide variety of climates and terrain, from tundra in the far north to the warm, dry Mediterranean. The northern plain is fertile and rich in oil, coal and gas. A curve of mountain ranges, including the Alps, divides north from south.

via

Area: 64,600 km²
Capital: Riga
Population: 2.4m
guages: Latvian, Russian
igions: Evangelical, Lutheran
rency: Lats

Finland

Area: 338,145 km²
Capital: Helsinki
Population: 5.2m
Languages: Finnish, Swedish
Religions: Evangelical, Lutheran
Currency: Markka

Estonia

Area: 45,100 km²
Capital: Tallinn
Population: 1.4m
Languages: Estonian, Russian
Religions: Evangelical, Lutheran
Currency: Kroon

GROSS NATIONAL PRODUCT PER CAPITA (US$)

5 highest		5 lowest	
Luxembourg	45,440	Yugoslavia	1,400
Switzerland	44,430	Bulgaria	1,140
Norway	36,090	Macedonia	1,090
Liechtenstein	33,500	Ukraine	1,040
Denmark	32,500	Moldova	540

POPULATION DENSITY (per km²)

5 highest		5 lowest	
Monaco	33,000	Sweden	20
Vatican City	2,273	Finland	15
Malta	1,215	Norway	14
San Marino	426	Slovenia	10
Netherlands	384	Iceland	3

LIFE EXPECTANCY (years)

5 highest		5 lowest	
San Marino	81	Hungary	69
Iceland	79	Ukraine	69
Monaco	79	Estonia	69
Andorra	78	Latvia	68
Greece	78	Moldova	68

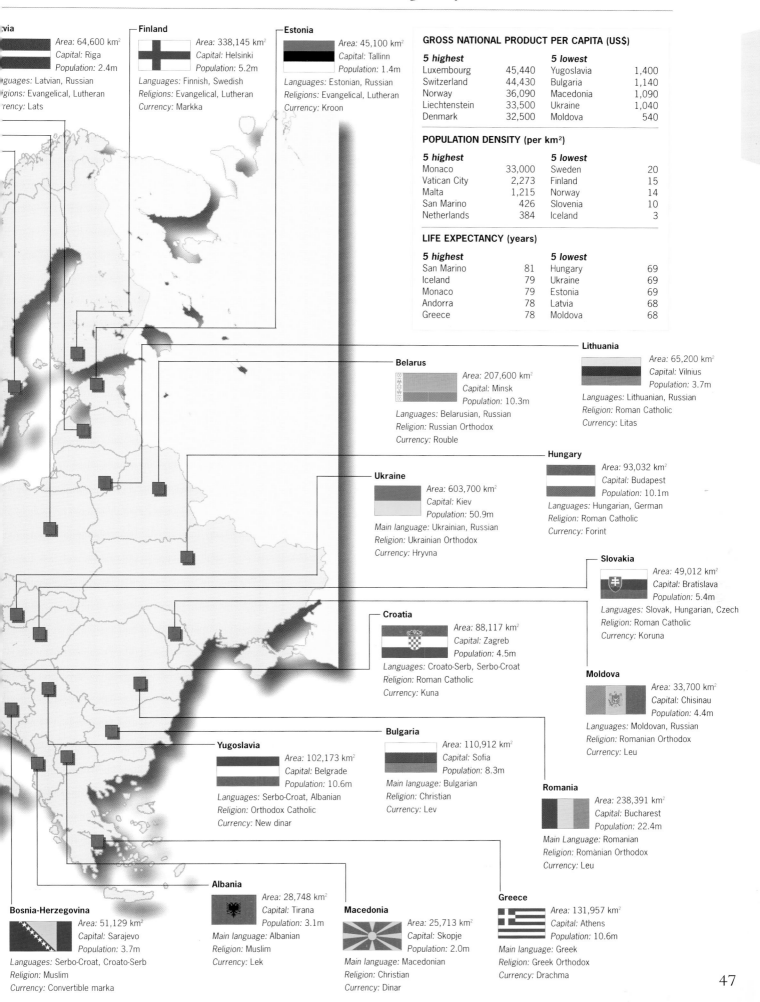

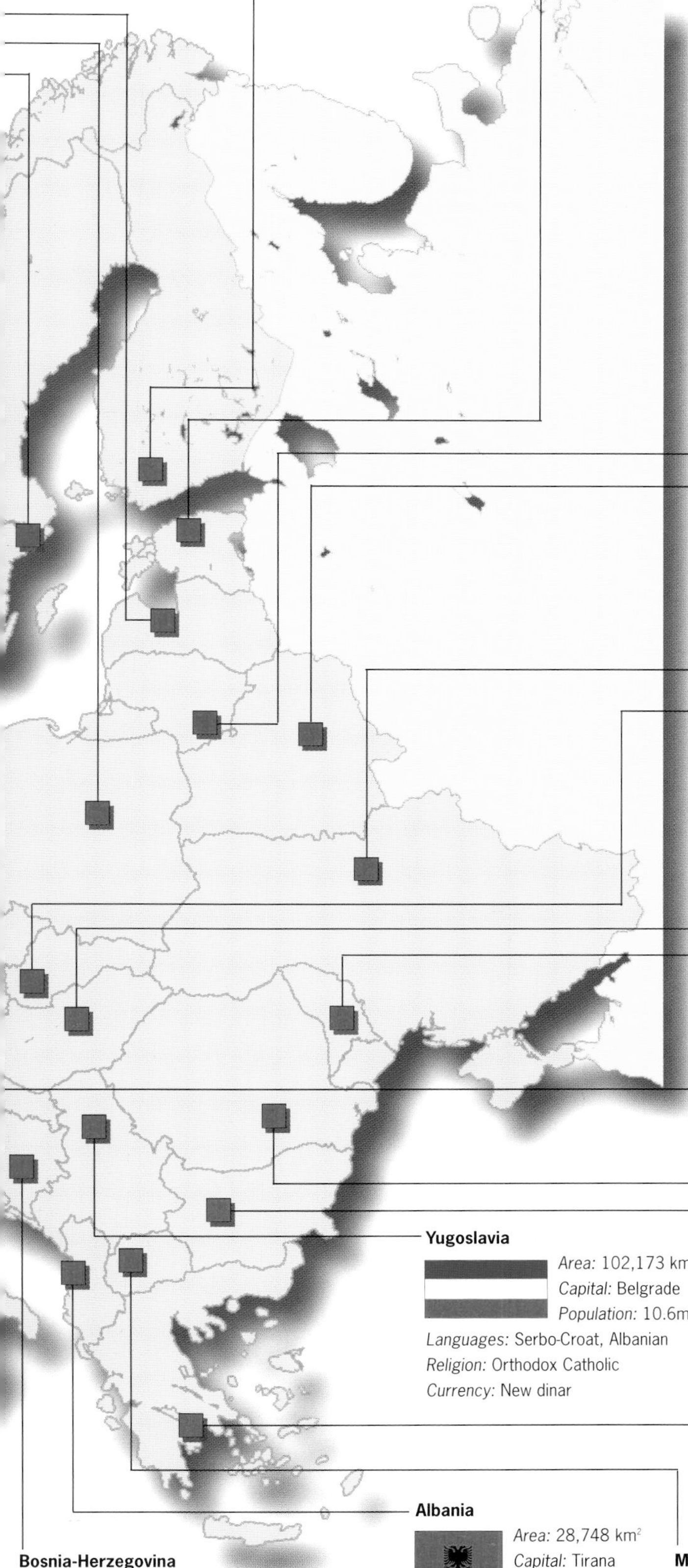

Lithuania

Area: 65,200 km²
Capital: Vilnius
Population: 3.7m
Languages: Lithuanian, Russian
Religion: Roman Catholic
Currency: Litas

Belarus

Area: 207,600 km²
Capital: Minsk
Population: 10.3m
Languages: Belarusian, Russian
Religion: Russian Orthodox
Currency: Rouble

Hungary

Area: 93,032 km²
Capital: Budapest
Population: 10.1m
Languages: Hungarian, German
Religion: Roman Catholic
Currency: Forint

Ukraine

Area: 603,700 km²
Capital: Kiev
Population: 50.9m
Main language: Ukrainian, Russian
Religion: Ukrainian Orthodox
Currency: Hryvna

Slovakia

Area: 49,012 km²
Capital: Bratislava
Population: 5.4m
Languages: Slovak, Hungarian, Czech
Religion: Roman Catholic
Currency: Koruna

Croatia

Area: 88,117 km²
Capital: Zagreb
Population: 4.5m
Languages: Croato-Serb, Serbo-Croat
Religion: Roman Catholic
Currency: Kuna

Moldova

Area: 33,700 km²
Capital: Chisinau
Population: 4.4m
Languages: Moldovan, Russian
Religion: Romanian Orthodox
Currency: Leu

Bulgaria

Area: 110,912 km²
Capital: Sofia
Population: 8.3m
Main language: Bulgarian
Religion: Christian
Currency: Lev

Yugoslavia

Area: 102,173 km²
Capital: Belgrade
Population: 10.6m
Languages: Serbo-Croat, Albanian
Religion: Orthodox Catholic
Currency: New dinar

Romania

Area: 238,391 km²
Capital: Bucharest
Population: 22.4m
Main Language: Romanian
Religion: Romànian Orthodox
Currency: Leu

Albania

Area: 28,748 km²
Capital: Tirana
Population: 3.1m
Main language: Albanian
Religion: Muslim
Currency: Lek

Bosnia-Herzegovina

Area: 51,129 km²
Capital: Sarajevo
Population: 3.7m
Languages: Serbo-Croat, Croato-Serb
Religion: Muslim
Currency: Convertible marka

Macedonia

Area: 25,713 km²
Capital: Skopje
Population: 2.0m
Main language: Macedonian
Religion: Christian
Currency: Dinar

Greece

Area: 131,957 km²
Capital: Athens
Population: 10.6m
Main language: Greek
Religion: Greek Orthodox
Currency: Drachma

Scale 1 : 20 200 000

0 250 500 750 1000 km

0 100 200 300 400 500 miles

ICELAND
Reykjavik
Arctic Circle
Norwegian Sea
Faeroes (Denmark)
Rockall
Shetland Is. (U.K.)
Outer Hebrides
Orkney Is.
SCOTLAND
Glasgow
Edinburgh
NORTHERN IRELAND
Belfast
REP. OF IRELAND
DUBLIN (BAILE ÁTHA CLIATH)
UNITED KINGDOM
WALES
BIRMINGHAM
ENGLAND
Cardiff
Plymouth
LONDON
English Channel
Channel Islands
North Sea
ATLANTIC OCEAN
NORWAY
SWEDEN
Tromsø
Trondheim
Bergen
Stavanger
Oslo
Sundsvall
Gulf of Bothnia
Stockholm
Vänern
Göteborg
Gotland
Baltic Sea
DENMARK
Århus
København (Copenhagen)
Bornholm
Gdańsk
RUSSIA
Kaliningrad
LIT
Amsterdam
's-Gravenhage (The Hague)
NETHERLANDS
Bruxelles (Brussels)
BELGIUM
Luxembourg
LUXEMBOURG
HAMBURG
Hannover
BERLIN
GERMANY
Bonn
Frankfurt
Elbe
Ems
Rhine
Wisła
WARSZAWA (WARSAW)
POLAND
Odra (Oder)
Vistula
PRAHA (PRAGUE)
CZECH REP.
Seine
PARIS
Loire
FRANCE
Strasbourg
MÜNCHEN (MUNICH)
Danube
WIEN (VIENNA)
SLOVAKIA
Bratislava
BUDAPEST
HUNGARY
Bay of Biscay
Cabo Fisterra
Bordeaux
Lyon
Massif Central
Rhône
Bern
SWITZERLAND
Vaduz
LIECHTENSTEIN
AUSTRIA
4808 Mt. Blanc
Alps
SLOVENIA
Ljubljana
Zagreb
CROATIA
LISBOA (LISBON)
PORTUGAL
Tajo
MADRID
SPAIN
Ebro
Pyrenees
Andorra la Vella
ANDORRA
Marseille
Genova (Genoa)
MILANO (MILAN)
SAN MARINO
MONACO
BOSNIA-HERZEGOVINA
Sarajevo
BEOGRAD (BELGRADE)
YUGOSLAVIA
SOFIYA (SOFIA)
Skopje
MACEDONIA
Cabo de São Vicente
BARCELONA
Corse (Corsica) (France)
Ajaccio
VATICAN CITY
ROMA (ROME)
ITALY
Appennino
Adriatic Sea
Tiranë (Tirana)
ALBANIA
Valencia
Islas Baleares (Balearic Islands)
Menorca
Mallorca
Eivissa
Sardegna (Sardinia) (Italy)
NAPOLI (NAPLES)
Taranto
Strait of Gibraltar
Gibraltar (U.K.)
Ceuta (Spain)
RABAT
Melilla (Spain)
Mediterranean Sea
Cagliari
Tyrrhenian Sea
Kerkyra (Corfu)
GREECE
ALGER (ALGIERS)
Palermo
Mte. Etna 3340
Sicilia (Sicily)
Ionian Sea
Tunis
Valletta
MALTA
AFRICA
Tarābulus (Tripoli)
Banghāzī

Elbrus, Russia : 5,642 m or 18,510 ft

Astrakhan, Russia : 16.3 cm or 6.4 in

Volga, Russia : 3,531 km or 2,194 mi

Caspian Sea : 29 m or 84 ft

Crkvica, Bosnia-Herzegovina : 465 cm or 183 in

Caspian Sea : 371,000 km² or 143,240 sq mi

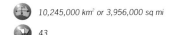

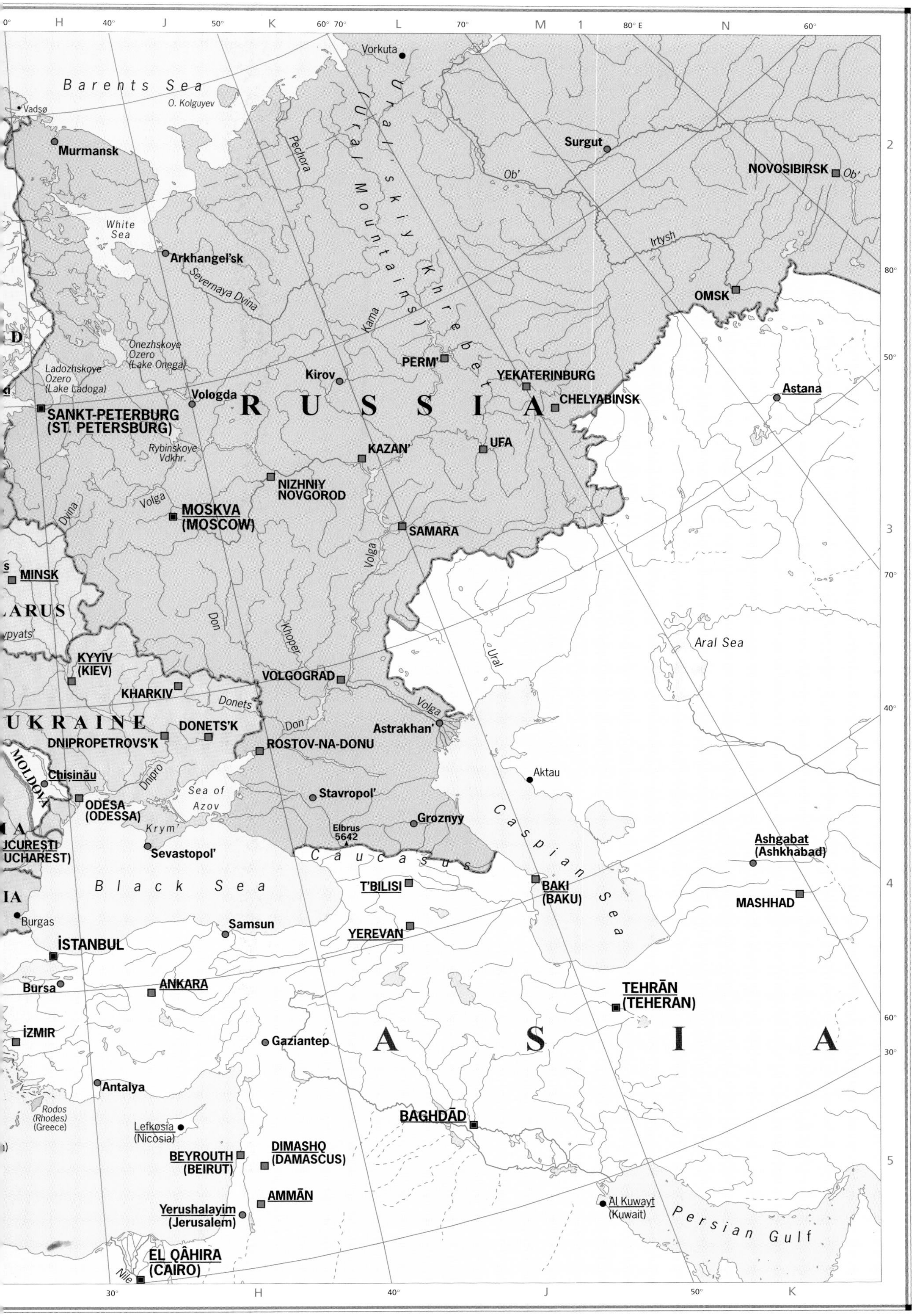
H
J
K
L
M
N
Barents Sea
O. Kolguyev
Vadsø
Murmansk
White Sea
Arkhangel'sk
Severnaya Dvina
Pechora
Vorkuta
Ural'skiy Khrebet (Ural Mountains)
Kama
Surgut
Ob'
NOVOSIBIRSK
Irtysh
OMSK
Onezhskoye Ozero (Lake Onega)
Ladozhskoye Ozero (Lake Ladoga)
Vologda
Kirov
PERM'
YEKATERINBURG
CHELYABINSK
RUSSIA
Astana
SANKT-PETERBURG (ST. PETERSBURG)
Rybinskoye Vdkhr.
KAZAN'
UFA
NIZHNIY NOVGOROD
Volga
Dvina
MOSKVA (MOSCOW)
SAMARA
MINSK
Don
Khoper
Ural
Aral Sea
KYYIV (KIEV)
KHARKIV
VOLGOGRAD
Donets
UKRAINE
DONETS'K
DNIPROPETROVS'K
ROSTOV-NA-DONU
Astrakhan'
MOLDOVA
Chişinău
Dnipro
Sea of Azov
ODESA (ODESSA)
Stavropol'
Aktau
Krym'
Elbrus 5642
Groznyy
Caucasus
Caspian Sea
Sevastopol'
Ashgabat (Ashkhabad)
Black Sea
T'BILISI
BAKI (BAKU)
MASHHAD
Burgas
Samsun
YEREVAN
İSTANBUL
Bursa
ANKARA
TEHRĀN (TEHERAN)
İZMIR
Gaziantep
ASIA
Antalya
Rodos (Rhodes) (Greece)
Lefkosia (Nicosia)
BAGHDĀD
BEYROUTH (BEIRUT)
DIMASHQ (DAMASCUS)
AMMĀN
Al Kuwayt (Kuwait)
Persian Gulf
Yerushalayim (Jerusalem)
EL QÂHIRA (CAIRO)
Nile
2
3
4
5
30°
40°
50°
60°
70°
80°

Ust'-Shchugor, Russia : -55 °C or -67 °F

Seville, Spain : 50 °C or 122 °F

699,644,000

68 per km² or 177 per sq mi

10,245,000 km² or 3,956,000 sq mi

43

Scale 1 : 5 800 000

0 100 200 300 km

0 50 100 150 miles

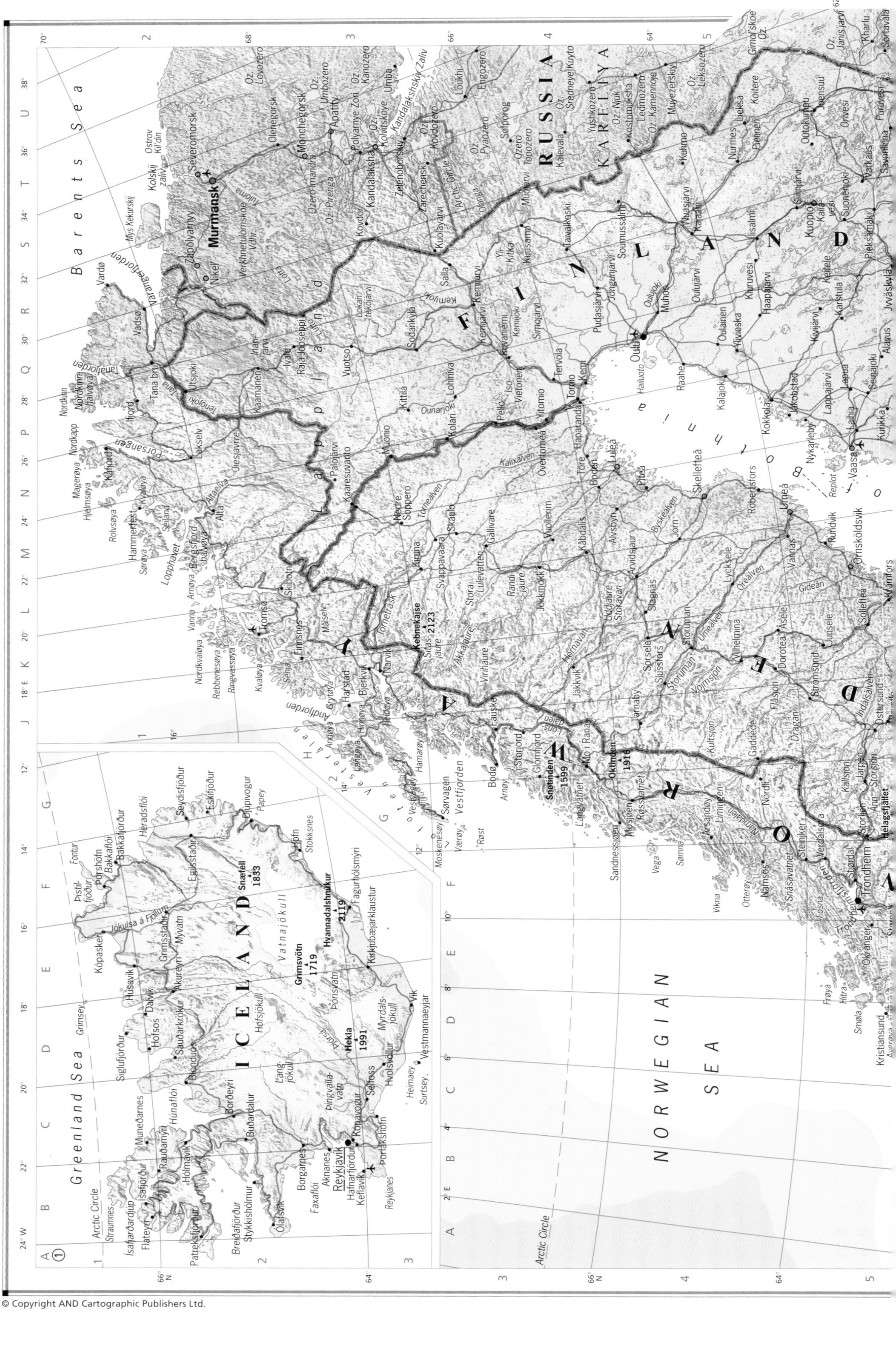

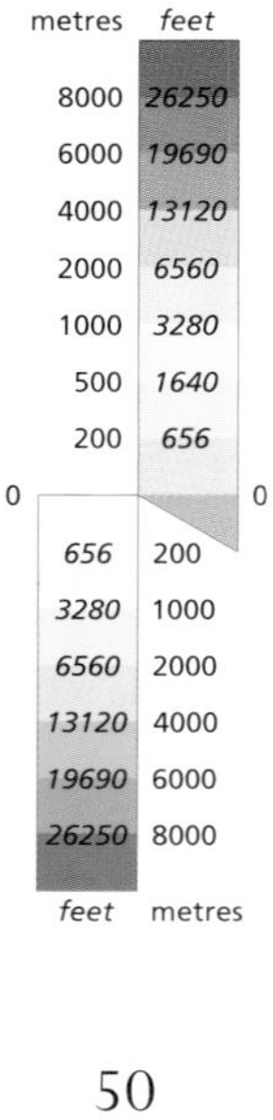

metres feet
8000 26250
6000 19690
4000 13120
2000 6560
1000 3280
500 1640
200 656
0 0
656 200
3280 1000
6560 2000
13120 4000
19690 6000
26250 8000
feet metres

Scandinavia

Denmark • Estonia • Finland • Iceland
Latvia • Lithuania • Norway • Sweden

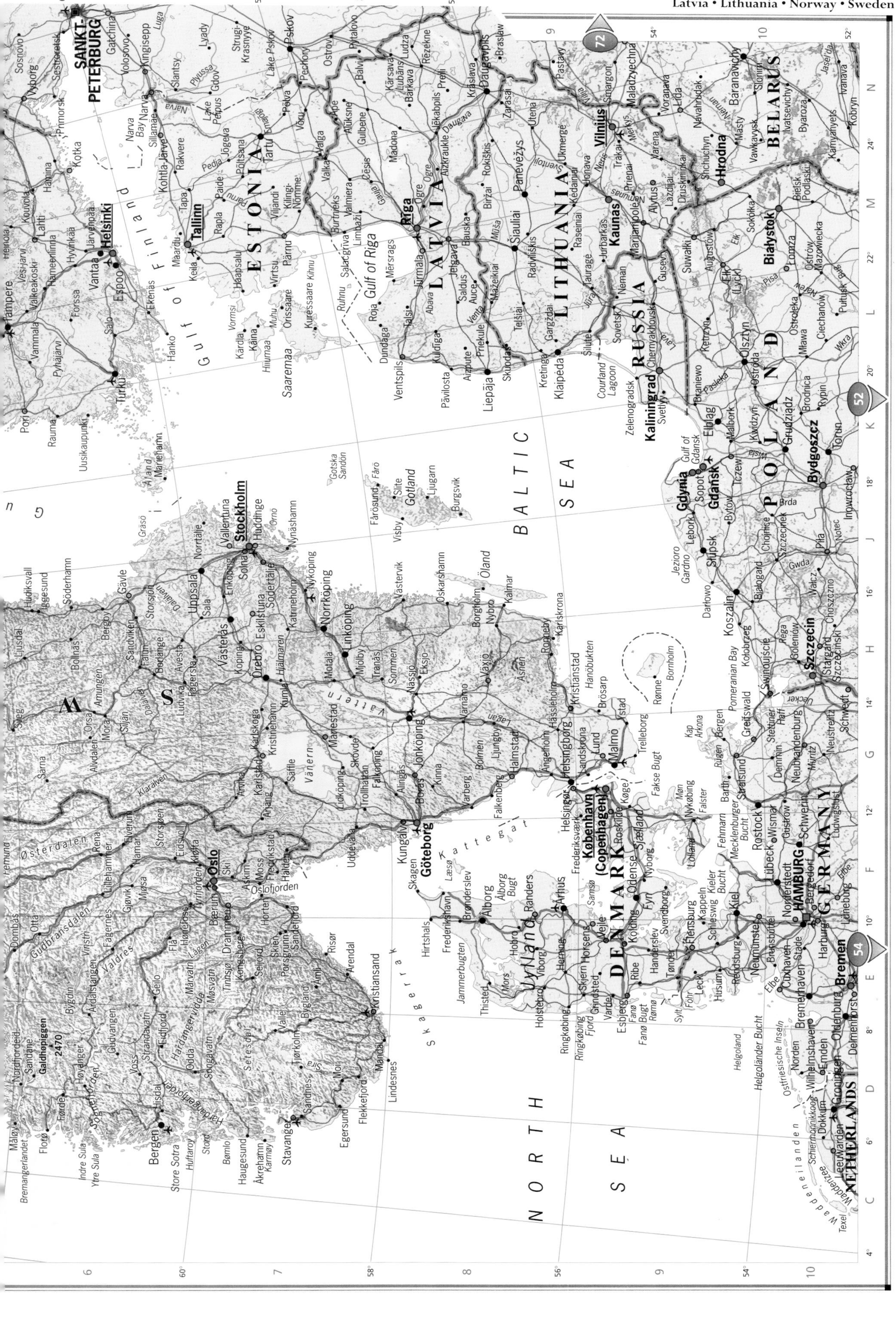

■ over 3 million
■ 1 – 3 million
● 250 000 – 1 million
● 100 000 – 250 000
○ 25 000 – 100 000
• under 25 000
—— country capital underline

Scale 1 : 3 450 000

0 50 100 150 km

0 25 50 75 miles

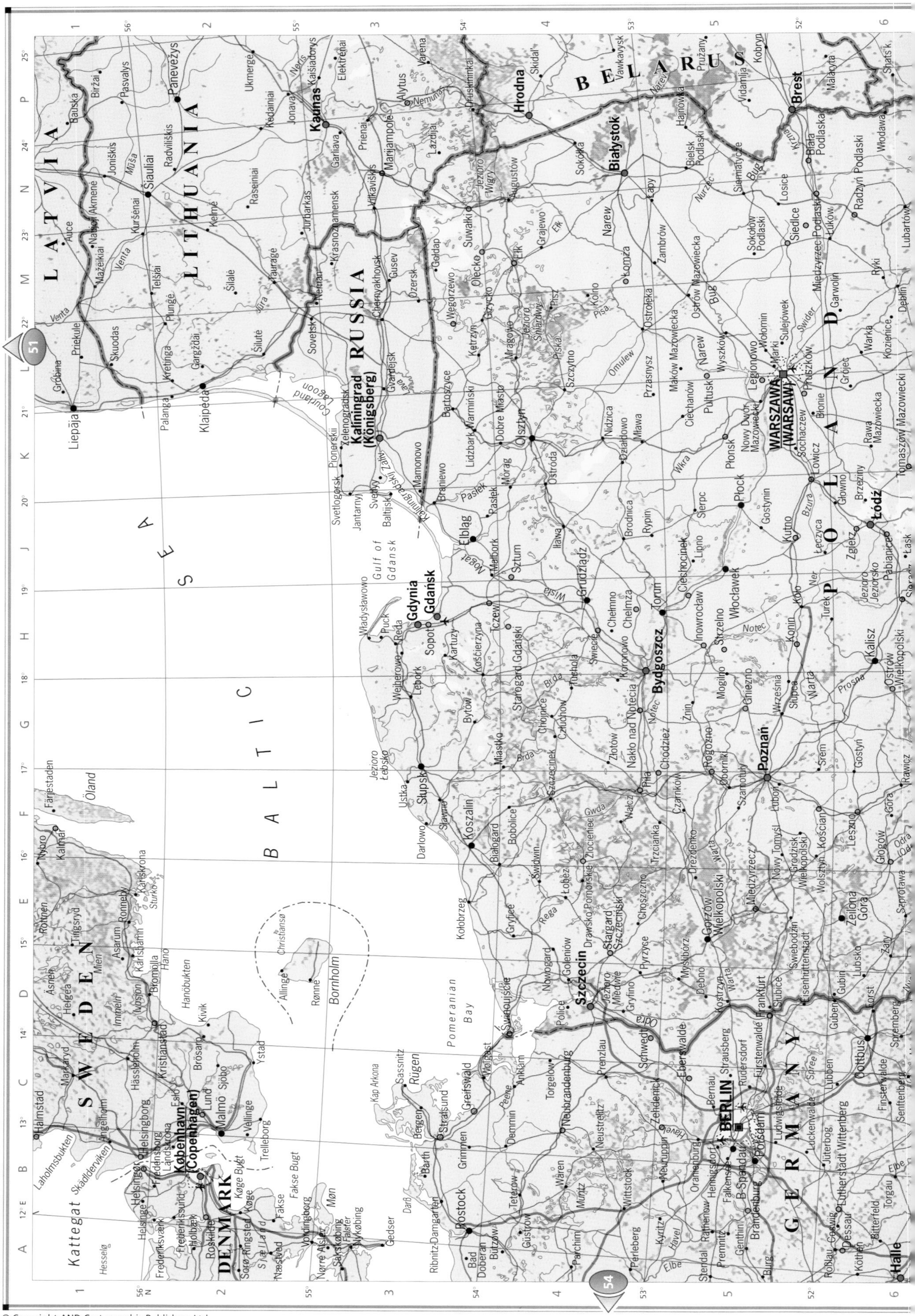

metres	feet
8000	26250
6000	19690
4000	13120
2000	6560
1000	3280
500	1640
200	656
0	0
200	656
1000	3280
2000	6560
4000	13120
6000	19690
8000	26250
metres	feet

Czech Republic • Hungary • Poland • Slovakia

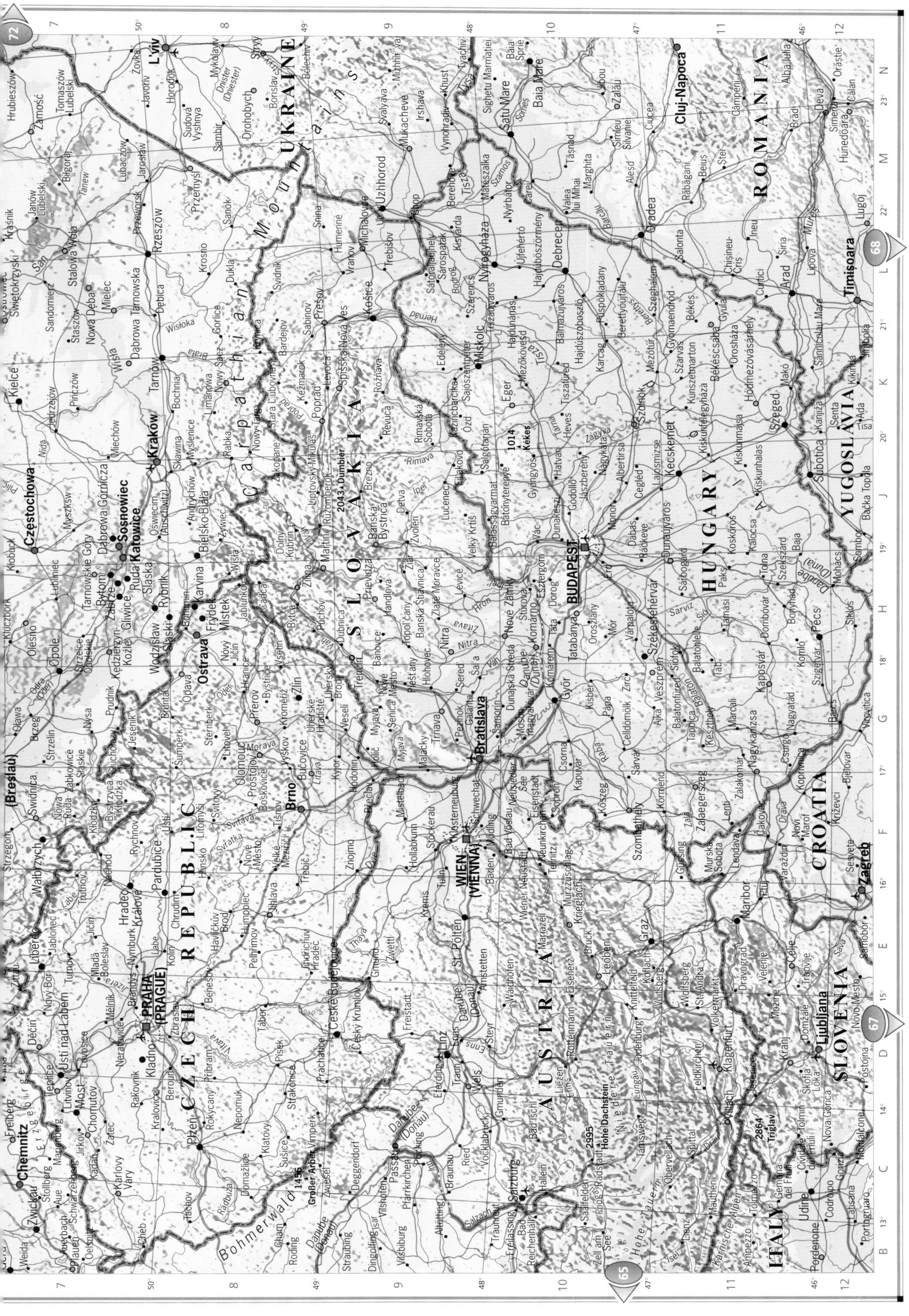

■ over 3 million	● 100 000 – 250 000	country capital underline
■ 1 – 3 million	○ 25 000 – 100 000	urban area
● 250 000 – 1 million	• under 25 000	

Scale 1 : 2 600 000

0 50 100 150 km

0 25 50 75 miles

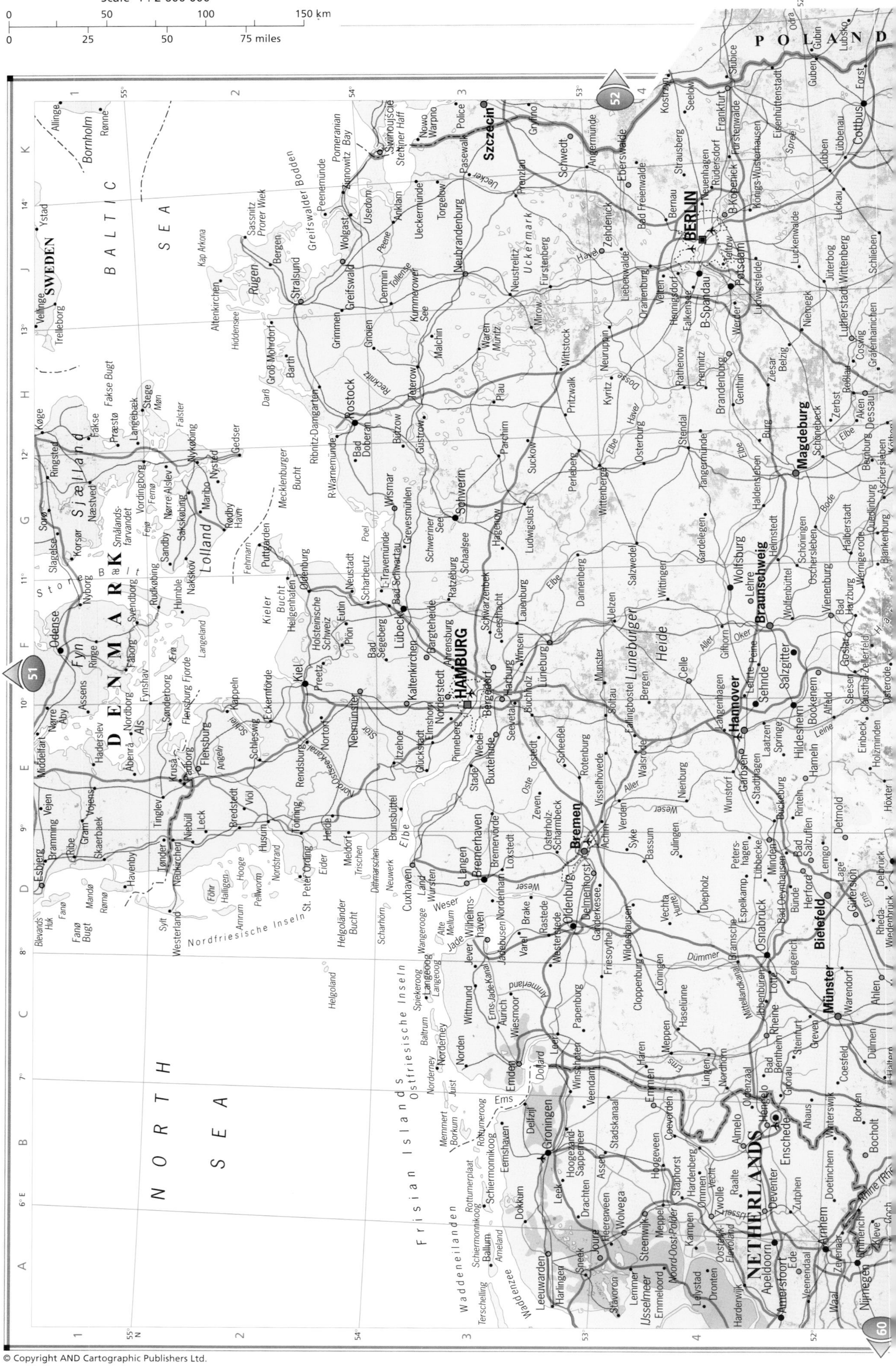

metres	feet
8000	26250
6000	19690
4000	13120
2000	6560
1000	3280
500	1640
200	656
0	0
656	200
3280	1000
6560	2000
13120	4000
19690	6000
26250	8000
feet	metres

Germany

Germany • Luxembourg

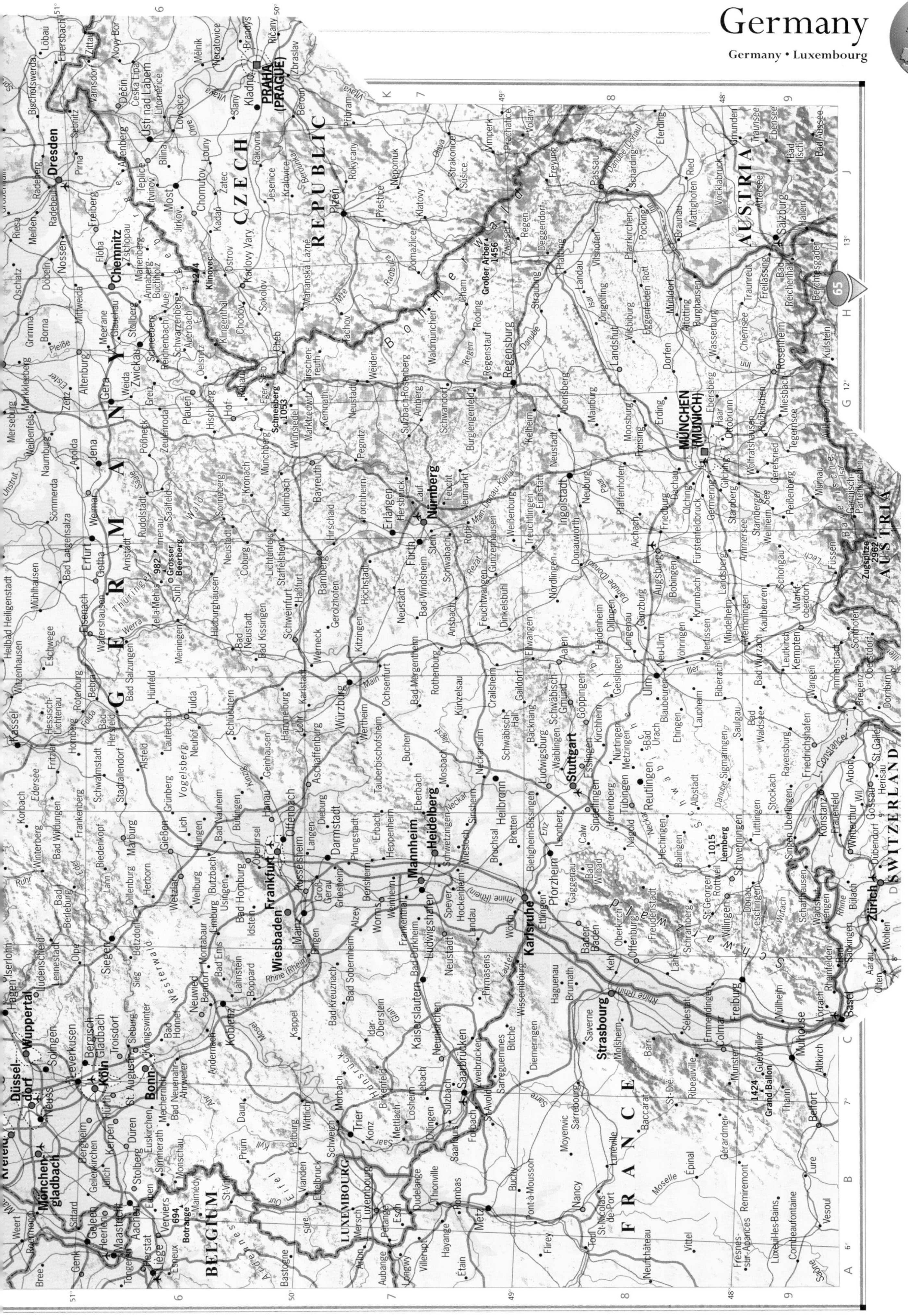

- ■ over 3 million
- ■ 1 – 3 million
- ● 250 000 – 1 million
- ● 100 000 – 250 000
- ○ 25 000 – 100 000
- • under 25 000
- country capital underline
- urban area

Scale 1 : 2 300 000

0 50 100 150 km

0 25 50 75 miles

metres	feet
8000	26250
6000	19690
4000	13120
2000	6560
1000	3280
500	1640
200	656
0	0
656	200
3280	1000
6560	2000
13120	4000
19690	6000
26250	8000
feet	metres

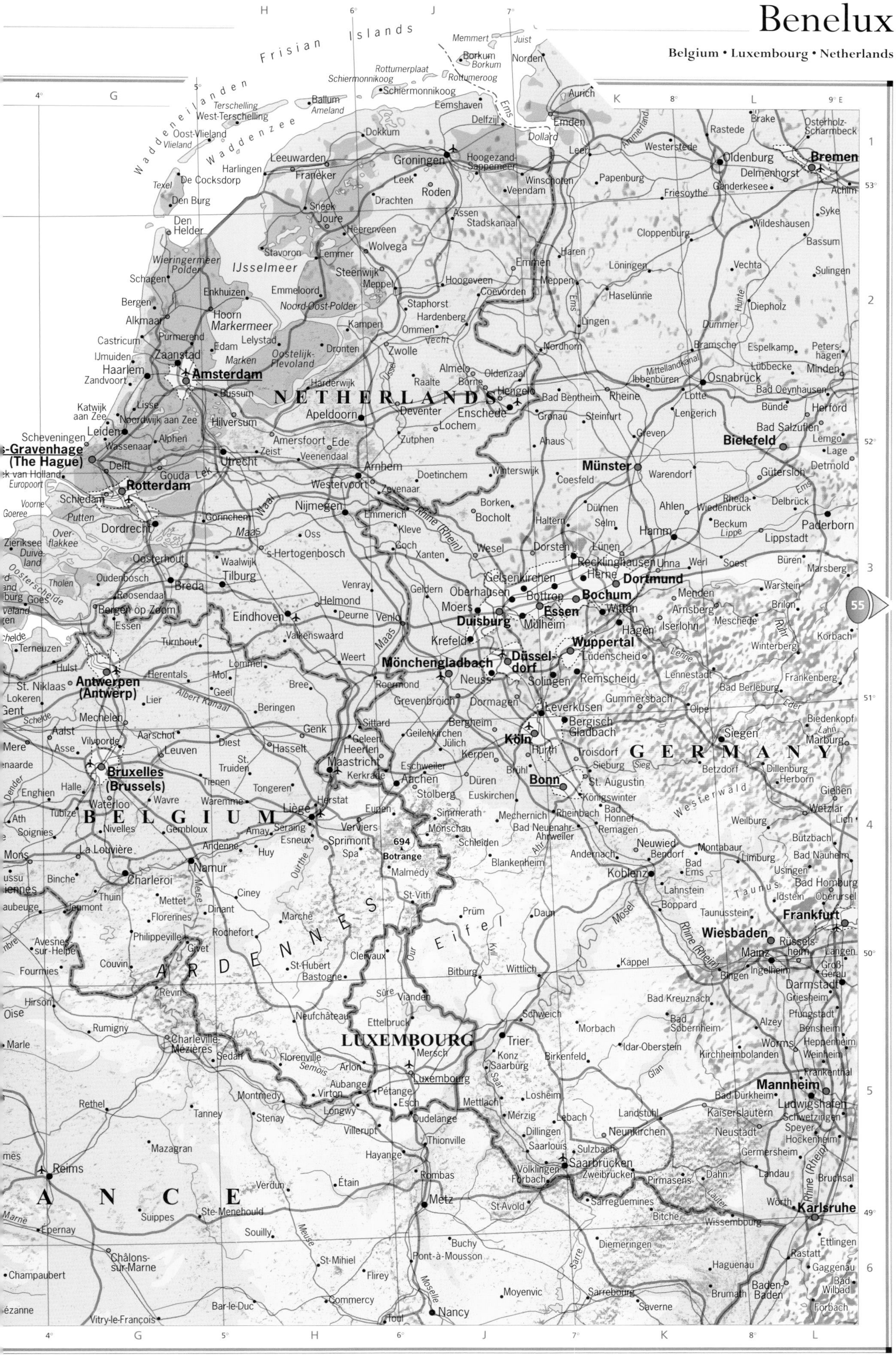

■ over 3 million
■ 1 – 3 million
● 250 000 – 1 million
● 100 000 – 250 000
○ 25 000 – 100 000
• under 25 000
country capital underline
urban area

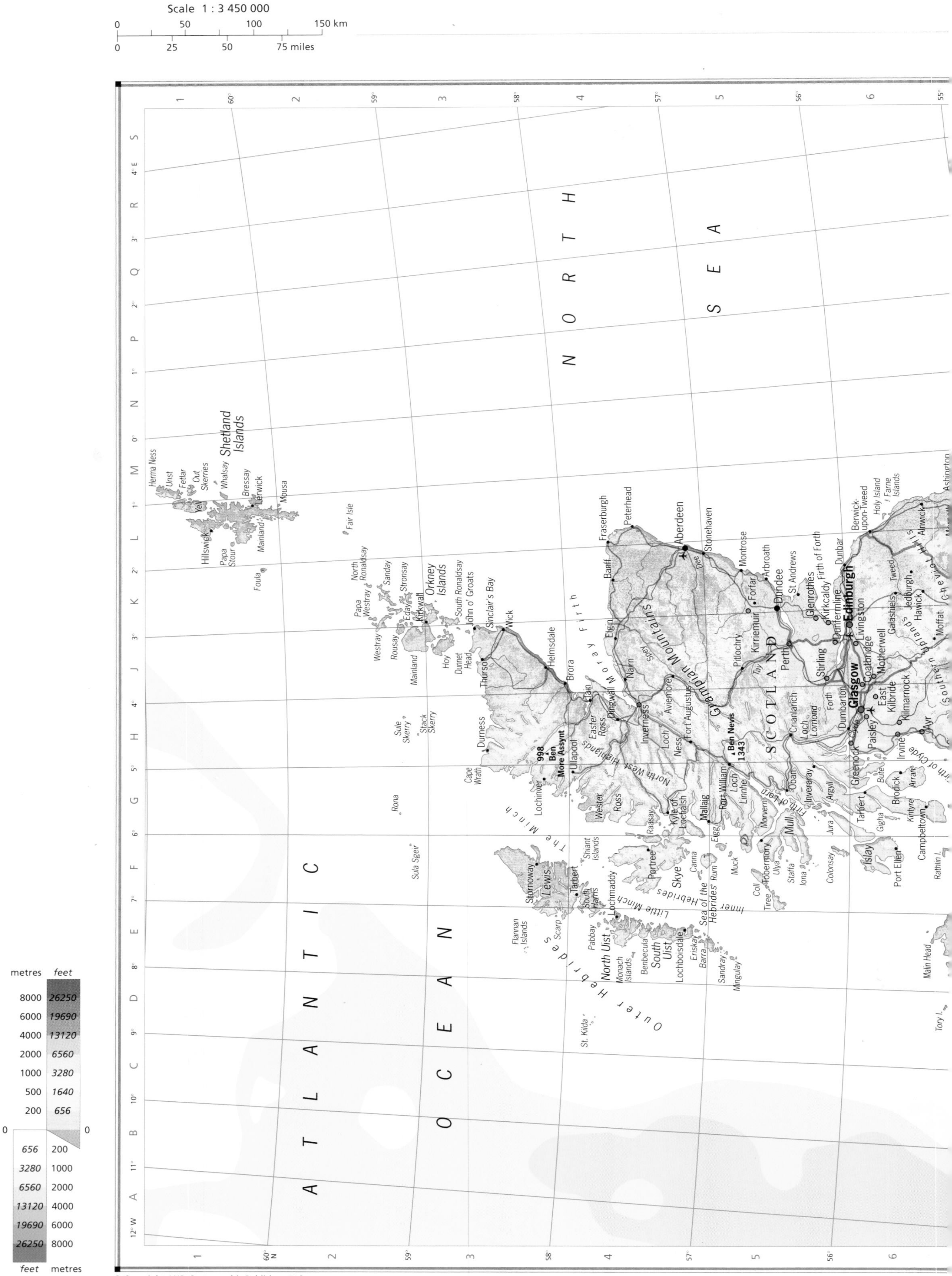

Scale 1 : 3 450 000

```
0 50 100 150 km
0 25 50 75 miles
```

metres	feet
8000	26250
6000	19690
4000	13120
2000	6560
1000	3280
500	1640
200	656
0	0

feet	metres
656	200
3280	1000
6560	2000
13120	4000
19690	6000
26250	8000

ATLANTIC OCEAN

NORTH SEA

Shetland Islands

Orkney Islands

Outer Hebrides

SCOTLAND

Grampian Mountains

North West Highlands

The Minch

Little Minch

Sea of the Hebrides

Inner Hebrides

Herma Ness
Unst
Yell
Fetlar
Out Skerries
Whalsay
Bressay
Lerwick
Mousa
Hillswick
Papa Stour
Mainland
Foula
Fair Isle

Westray
Papa Westray
North Ronaldsay
Sanday
Rousay
Stronsay
Eday
Mainland
Kirkwall
South Ronaldsay
Hoy
John o' Groats
Dunnet Head
Sinclair's Bay
Wick

Sule Skerry
Stack Skerry
Rona
Sula Sgeir

Durness
Cape Wrath
Thurso
Helmsdale
Brora

Lochinver
998 Ben More Assynt
Ullapool
Tain
Dingwall
Easter Ross
Inverness
Nairn
Elgin
Spey
Loch Ness
Aviemore
Fort Augustus
Wester Ross

Banff
Fraserburgh
Peterhead
Aberdeen
Stonehaven
Montrose
Arbroath
Forfar
Dundee
St Andrews

Stornoway
Lewis
Tarbert
Harris
Flannan Islands
Scarp
Pabbay
North Uist
Monach Islands
Benbecula
South Uist
Lochmaddy
Eriskay
Lochboisdale
Barra
Sandray
Mingulay

St. Kilda

Shiant Islands
Portree
Raasay
Skye
Canna
Rum
Eigg
Muck
Coll
Tiree
Staffa
Iona
Ulva
Mull
Colonsay
Mallaig
Kyle of Lochalsh
Ben Nevis 1343
Fort William
Loch Linnhe
Morvern
Oban
Firth of Lorn
Jura
Islay
Port Ellen
Gigha
Kintyre
Campbeltown
Rathlin I.
Malin Head
Tory I.

Pitlochry
Kirriemuir
Glenrothes
Kirkcaldy
Firth of Forth
Dunfermline
Dunbar
Perth
Tay
Stirling
Forth
Livingston
EDINBURGH
Galashiels
Jedburgh
Hawick
Berwick-upon-Tweed
Holy Island
Farne Islands
Alnwick
Ashington
Tweed
Moffat
Southern Uplands
Loch Lomond
Cranlarich
Inveraray
Argyll
Tarbert
Bute
Brodick
Arran
GLASGOW
Dumbarton
Paisley
Greenock
Coatbridge
Motherwell
East Kilbride
Kilmarnock
Irvine
Ayr
Firth of Clyde

Dee

58

© Copyright AND Cartographic Publishers Ltd.

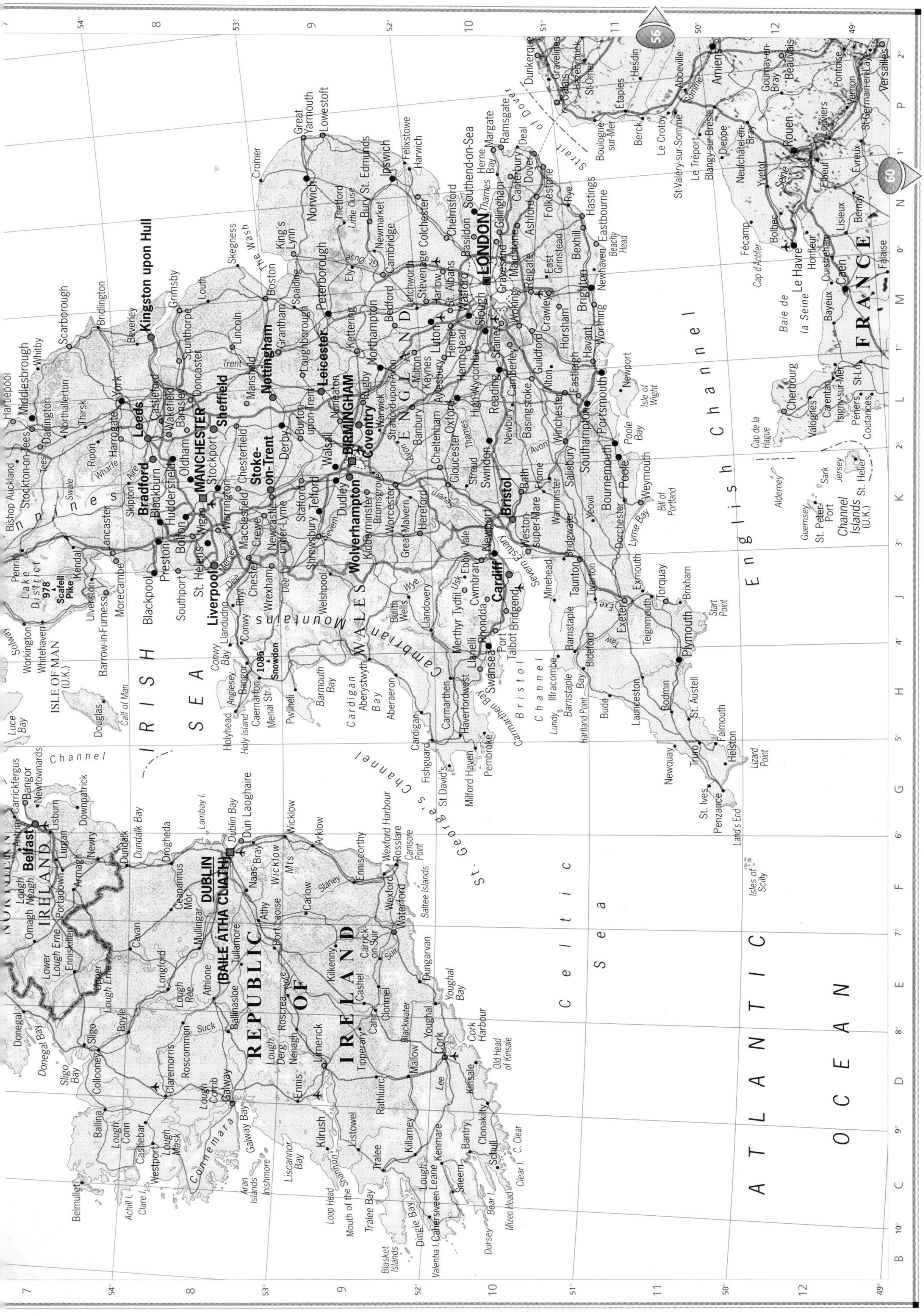

■ over 3 million
■ 1 – 3 million
● 250 000 – 1 million
● 100 000 – 250 000
○ 25 000 – 100 000
• under 25 000

country capital underline
state or province capital underline
urban area

Scale 1 : 3 450 000

0 50 100 150 km

0 25 50 75 miles

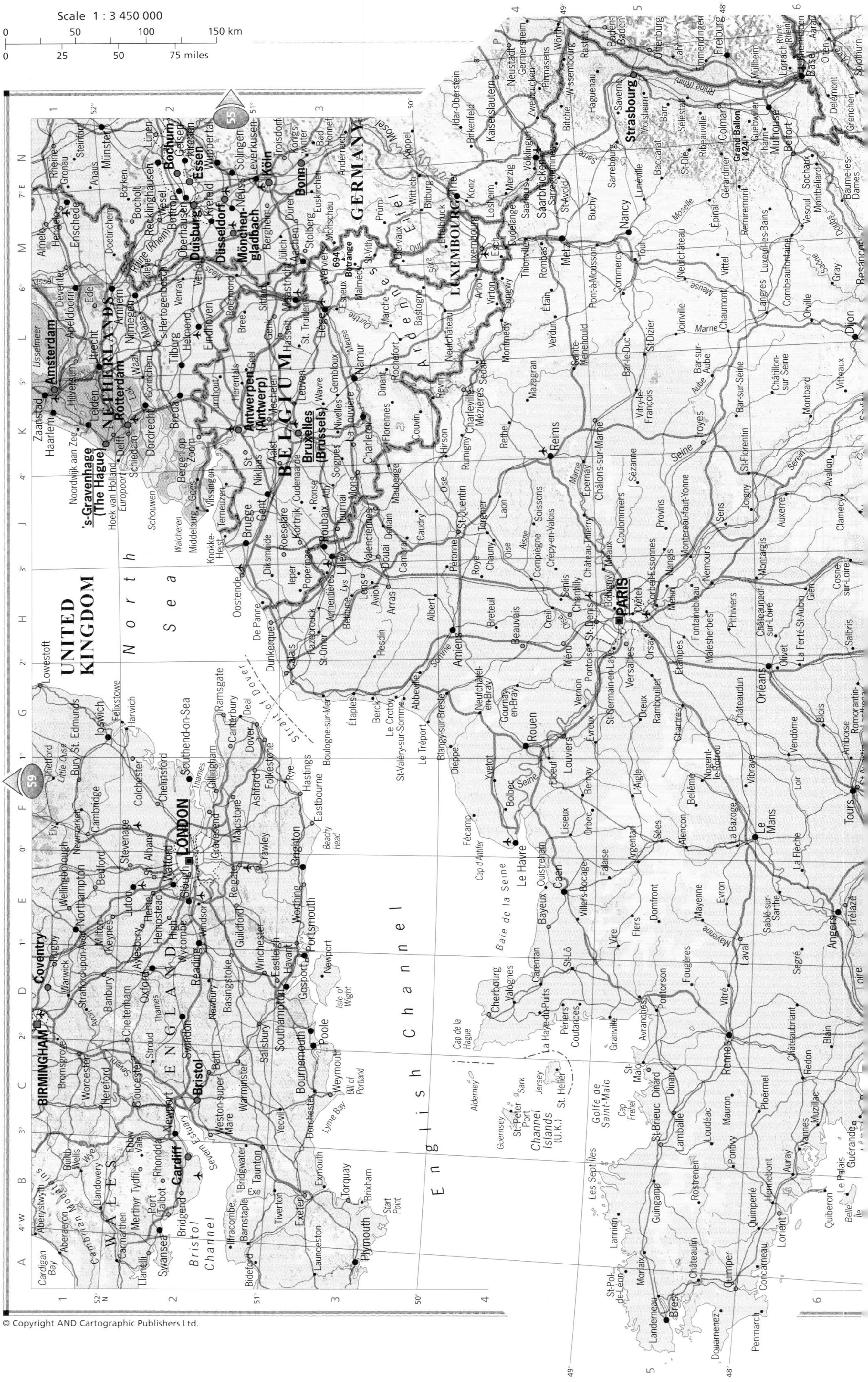

metres	feet
8000	26250
6000	19690
4000	13120
2000	6560
1000	3280
500	1640
200	656
0	0
656	200
3280	1000
6560	2000
13120	4000
19690	6000
26250	8000
feet	metres

France

Andorra • Channel Islands • France • Monaco

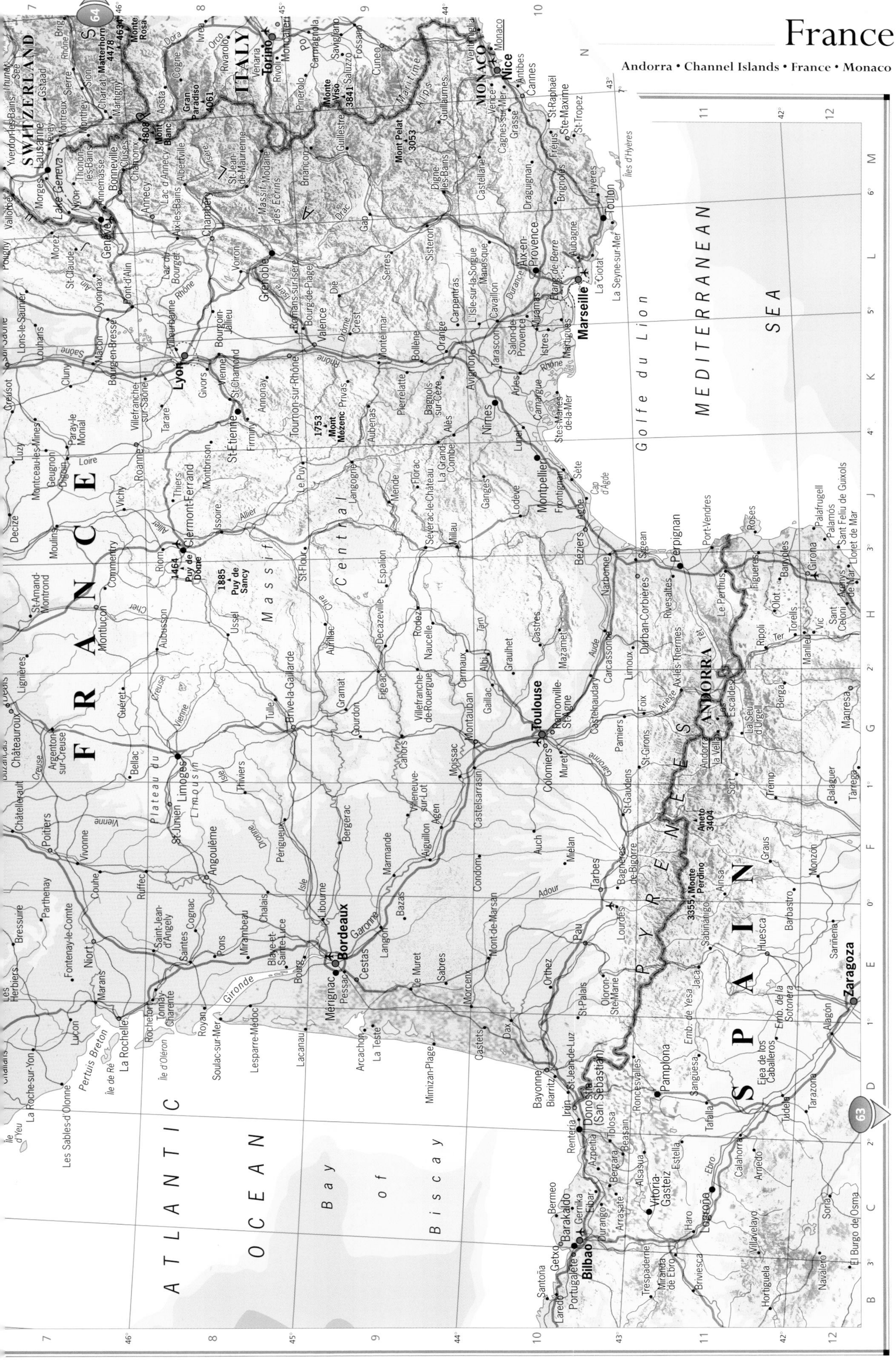

■ over 3 million	● 100 000 – 250 000
■ 1 – 3 million	○ 25 000 – 100 000
● 250 000 – 1 million	• under 25 000

country capital underline

state or province capital underline

urban area

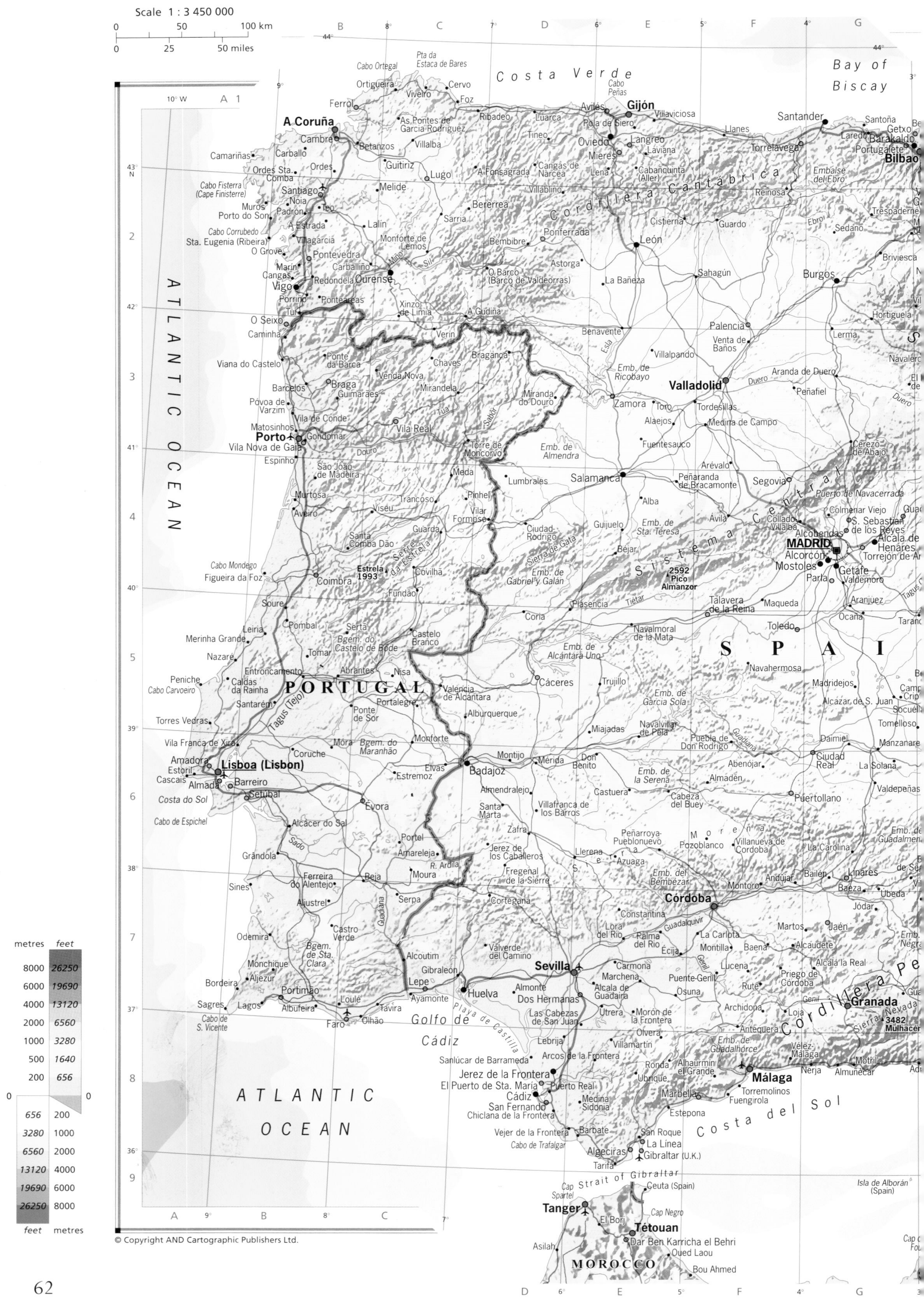
Scale 1 : 3 450 000
0 50 100 km
0 25 50 miles
Bay of Biscay
Costa Verde
ATLANTIC OCEAN
PORTUGAL
SPAIN
MOROCCO
Cordillera Cantábrica
Sistema Central
Sierra Morena
Cordillera Penibética
Sierra Nevada
Sierra de Gata
Serra da Estrela
Golfo de Cádiz
Playa de Castilla
Costa del Sol
Costa do Sol
Strait of Gibraltar
Cabo Ortegal
Pta da Estaca de Bares
Cabo Peñas
Cabo Fisterra (Cape Finisterre)
Cabo Corrubedo
Cabo Mondego
Cabo Carvoeiro
Cabo de Espichel
Cabo de S. Vicente
Cabo de Trafalgar
Cap Spartel
Cap Negro
Isla de Alborán (Spain)
A Coruña
Ferrol
Ortigueira
Viveiro
Cervo
Foz
Ribadeo
Luarca
Avilés
Gijón
Villaviciosa
Oviedo
Pola de Siero
Langreo
Mieres
Santander
Torrelavega
Llanes
Santoña
Laredo
Getxo
Barakaldo
Portugalete
Bilbao
Reinosa
Embalse del Ebro
Cambre
Carballo
Camariñas
Betanzos
As Pontes de García Rodríguez
Villalba
Guitiriz
Lugo
Ordes
Santiago
Melide
Noia
Padrón
Muros
Porto do Son
A Estrada
Vilagarcia
Sta. Eugenia (Ribeira)
O Grove
Pontevedra
Marín
Cangas
Vigo
Redondela
Porriño
Ponteareas
Tui
O Seixo
Caminha
Lalín
Carballiño
Ourense
Monforte de Lemos
Sarria
Becerreá
A Fonsagrada
Cangas de Narcea
Villablino
Tineo
Ponferrada
Bembibre
O Barco (Barco de Valdeorras)
Astorga
León
La Bañeza
Cistierna
Guardo
Sahagún
Burgos
Palencia
Venta de Baños
Benavente
Villalpando
Valladolid
Zamora
Toro
Tordesillas
Medina de Campo
Aranda de Duero
Peñafiel
Lerma
Xinzo de Limia
A Gudiña
Verín
Chaves
Bragança
Ponte da Barca
Braga
Guimarães
Venda Nova
Mirandela
Miranda do Douro
Viana do Castelo
Barcelos
Póvoa de Varzim
Vila de Conde
Matosinhos
Porto
Gondomar
Vila Nova de Gaia
Espinho
Vila Real
Torre de Moncorvo
São João de Madeira
Murtosa
Aveiro
Meda
Trancoso
Pinhel
Viseu
Vilar Formoso
Guarda
Santa Comba Dão
Estrela 1993
Covilhã
Coimbra
Figueira da Foz
Fundão
Soure
Pombal
Sertã
Leiria
Marinha Grande
Nazaré
Tomar
Castelo Branco
Entroncamento
Abrantes
Nisa
Peniche
Caldas da Rainha
Santarém
Torres Vedras
Vila Franca de Xira
Amadora
Estoril
Cascais
Lisboa (Lisbon)
Almada
Barreiro
Setúbal
Portalegre
Ponte de Sor
Coruche
Mora
Monforte
Elvas
Estremoz
Évora
Alcácer do Sal
Grândola
Sines
Ferreira do Alentejo
Beja
Portel
Amareleja
Moura
Serpa
Aljustrel
Castro Verde
Odemira
Monchique
Aljezur
Bordeira
Sagres
Lagos
Portimão
Albufeira
Loulé
Faro
Olhão
Tavira
Alcoutim
Gibraleón
Lepe
Ayamonte
Huelva
Salamanca
Lumbrales
Alba
Peñaranda de Bracamonte
Arévalo
Segovia
Ciudad-Rodrigo
Guijuelo
Béjar
Ávila
2592 Pico Almanzor
Plasencia
Coria
Talavera de la Reina
Maqueda
Toledo
Aranjuez
Ocaña
MADRID
Alcobendas
Alcorcón
Mostoles
Getafe
Parla
Valdemoro
Alcalá de Henares
Torrejón de Ar
Colmenar Viejo
S. Sebastián de los Reyes
Collado Villalba
Puerto de Navacerrada
Cerezo de Abajo
Fuentesauco
Alaejos
Navalmoral de la Mata
Cáceres
Trujillo
Valencia de Alcántara
Alburquerque
Miajadas
Navahermosa
Puebla de Don Rodrigo
Madridejos
Alcázar de S. Juan
Tomelloso
Daimiel
Manzanares
Ciudad Real
La Solana
Valdepeñas
Puertollano
Almadén
Abenójar
Badajoz
Montijo
Mérida
Don Benito
Almendralejo
Santa Marta
Villafranca de los Barros
Castuera
Cabeza del Buey
Zafra
Jerez de los Caballeros
Fregenal de la Sierre
Llerena
Azuaga
Peñarroya-Pueblonuevo
Pozoblanco
Villanueva de Cordoba
La Carolina
Andújar
Bailén
Linares
Baeza
Úbeda
Jódar
Martos
Jaén
Alcaudete
Alcalá la Real
Córdoba
Montoro
Constantina
Lora del Río
Palma del Río
Écija
La Carlota
Montilla
Baena
Lucena
Priego de Córdoba
Rute
Puente-Genil
Osuna
Cortegana
Valverde del Camino
Sevilla
Carmona
Marchena
Almonte
Dos Hermanas
Alcalá de Guadaira
Utrera
Morón de la Frontera
Las Cabezas de San Juan
Lebrija
Villamartín
Olvera
Arcos de la Frontera
Sanlúcar de Barrameda
Jerez de la Frontera
El Puerto de Sta. María
Puerto Real
Cádiz
San Fernando
Chiclana de la Frontera
Medina Sidonia
Vejer de la Frontera
Barbate
Algeciras
Tarifa
San Roque
La Línea
Gibraltar (U.K.)
Ronda
Ubrique
Alhaurín el Grande
Antequera
Archidona
Loja
Granada
3482 Mulhacén
Vélez-Málaga
Málaga
Torremolinos
Fuengirola
Marbella
Estepona
Nerja
Motril
Almuñécar
Ceuta (Spain)
Tanger
El Borj
Tétouan
Dar Ben Karricha el Behri
Oued Laou
Bou Ahmed
Asilah
Miño
Sil
Douro
Duero
Tua
Sabor
Esla
Tajus (Tejo)
Tiétar
Guadiana
Sado
Guadalquivir
Genil
Ebro
Emb. de Ricobayo
Emb. de Almendra
Emb. de Sta. Teresa
Emb. de Gabriel y Galán
Emb. de Alcántara Uno
Emb. de García Sola
Emb. de la Serena
Emb. del Bembézar
Emb. de Guadalhorce
Bgem. do Castelo de Bode
Bgem. do Maranhão
Bgem. de Sta. Clara
R. Ardila
metres feet
8000 26250
6000 19690
4000 13120
2000 6560
1000 3280
500 1640
200 656
0 0
656 200
3280 1000
6560 2000
13120 4000
19690 6000
26250 8000
feet metres

FRANCE
61
Bayonne
Biarritz
Orthez
Irún
St-Jean-de-Luz
St-Palais
Pau
Tarbes
Muret
Castelnaudary
Béziers
Agde
Sète
Cap d'Agde
Carcassonne
Narbonne
Golfe du Lion
Donostia
(San Sebastián)
Rentería
Azpeitia
Tolosa
Beasain
Oloron-Ste-Marie
Lourdes
Bagnères-de-Bigorre
St-Gaudens
Pamiers
Limoux
Sigean
St-Girons
Foix
Rivesaltes
Perpignan
Ax-les-Thermes
Port-Vendres
Le Perthus
Roncesvalles
Alsasua
Pamplona
P Y R E N E E S
Estella
Emb. de Yesa
Jaca
Sangüesa
Sabiñánigo
3355 Monte Perdino
Aneto 3404
ANDORRA
Andorra la Vella
Les Escaldes
Sort
La Seu d'Urgell
Roses
Figueres
Banyoles
Olot
Ripoll
Tafalla
Calahorra
Arnedo
Ejea de los Caballeros
Tudela
Emb. de la Sotonera
Huesca
Graus
Tremp
Berga
Torelló
Manlleu
Vic
Girona
Palafrugell
Palamós
Costa Brava
Barbastro
Monzón
Tarazona
Alagón
Sariñena
Balaguer
Manresa
Sant Celoni
Sant Feliu de Guixols
Lloret de Mar
Arenys de Mar
Granollers
Mataró
Zaragoza
Lleida
Tàrrega
Igualada
Terrassa
Sabadell
Badalona
BARCELONA
Torrelapaja
El Burgo de Ebro
Fraga
Cinca
Ebro
Montblanc
Vilafranca del Penedès
Sant Boi
El Prat de Llobregat
Gavà
Vilanova y la Geltrú
Sitges
Valls
Reus
Tarragona
Cambrils
Calatayud
Azaila
Caspe
Daroca
Alcañiz
Gandesa
Costa Dorada
Molina de Aragón
Calamocha
Montalbán
Tortosa
Cabo Tortosa
Monreal del Campo
Guadalope
Amposta
Sant Carlos de la Ràpita
Morella
Vinaròs
Benicarló
Sierra de Gúdar
Teruel
Torreblanca
Cuenca
Barracas
Onda
Vila-real
Castelló de la Plana
Borriana
La Vall d'Uixo
Islas Columbretes
Islas Baleares
(Balearic Islands)
Ciutadella
Menorca
Mahón
Pollença
Cap de Formentor
Sóller
Sa Pobla
Inca
Arta
Palma
Manacor
Sa Dragonera
Llucmajor
Santanyí
Mallorca
Cap de ses Salines
Cabrera
Emb. de Contreras
Utiel
Requena
Motilla del Palancar
Burjassot
Paterna
Valencia
Torrent
Sagunt
Golfo de Valencia
Cofrentes
Júcar
Carlet
Algemes
Alzira
Cullera
Xàtiva
Gandia
Oliva
Dénia
Xàbia
Cabo de la Nao
Albacete
Chinchilla de Monte-Aragón
Almansa
Ontinyent
Alcoi
Eivissa (Ibiza)
San Juan Bautista
San Antonio Abad
Formentera
Yecla
Villena
Hellín
Jumilla
Elda
Benidorm
La Vila Joiosa
Novelda
Aspe
Alicante
Cieza
Crevillent
Elch
Santa Pola
Costa Blanca
Caravaca de la Cruz
Molina de Segura
Orihuela
Alcantarilla
Murcia
Torrevieja
Zarzadilla de Totana
Alhama de Murcia
Torre-Pacheco
La Union
Cabo de Palos
Lorca
Cartagena
Golfo de Mazarrón
Huercal-Overa
Águilas
Albox
Vera
Carboneras
Almería
Cabo de Gata
Mediterranean Sea
ALGER
(ALGIERS)
Dellys
Ain Taya
Tizi Ouzou
Thenia
Rouiba
Bou Ismail
Larba
Lakhdaria
Cherchell
Boufarik
Boghni
Gouraya
Hadjout
Blida
Bouira
Ténès
Médéa
Aïn Bessem
Miliana
Beni Slimane
Sour el Ghozlane
Bouzghaïa
Khemis Miliana
Berrouaghia
Ech Chélif
Atlas Mountains
ALGERIA
Aïn-Tédélès
Chélif
Bou Kadir
Theniet el Had
Ksar el Boukhari
Aïn el Hadjel
Mostaganem
Arzew
Bordj Bounaam
Mers el Kébir
Gdyel
Relizane
Bougzoul
Oran
113
Mohammadia
Cap Figalo
Oued Tlélat
El Amria
Sig
Hammam Bou Hadjar
Mascara
Beni Saf
Aïn Témouchent

■ over 3 million
■ 1 – 3 million
● 250 000 – 1 million
● 100 000 – 250 000
○ 25 000 – 100 000
• under 25 000
country capital underline
urban area

Scale 1 : 2 600 000

0 50 100 150 km

0 25 50 75 miles

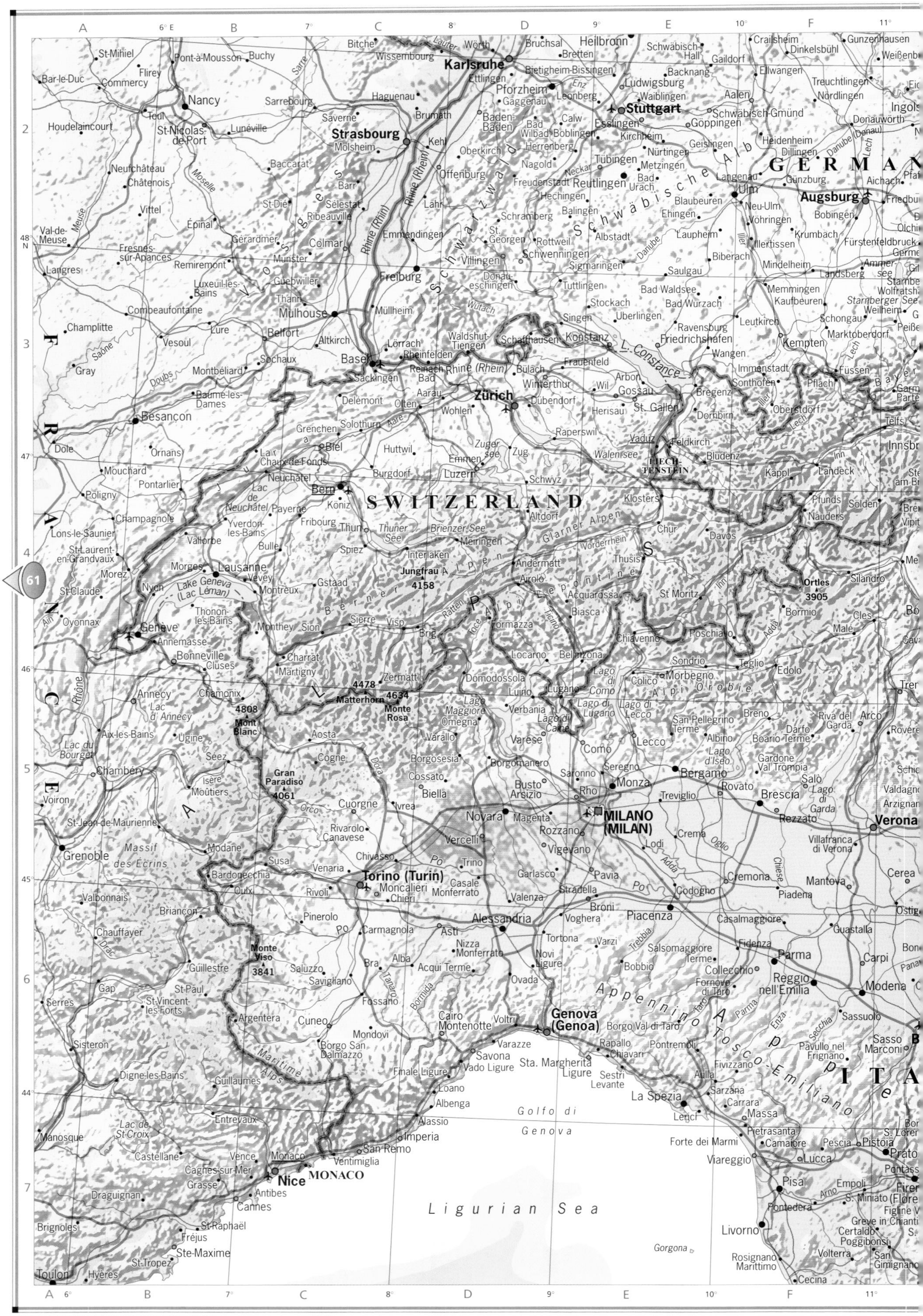

metres feet
8000 26250
6000 19690
4000 13120
2000 6560
1000 3280
500 1640
200 656
0 0
656 200
3280 1000
6560 2000
13120 4000
19690 6000
26250 8000
feet metres

The Alpine States

Austria • Liechtenstein • Slovenia • Switzerland

over 3 million
1 – 3 million
250 000 – 1 million
100 000 – 250 000
25 000 – 100 000
under 25 000
country capital underline
urban area

Scale 1 : 3 450 000

0 50 100 150 km

0 25 50 75 miles

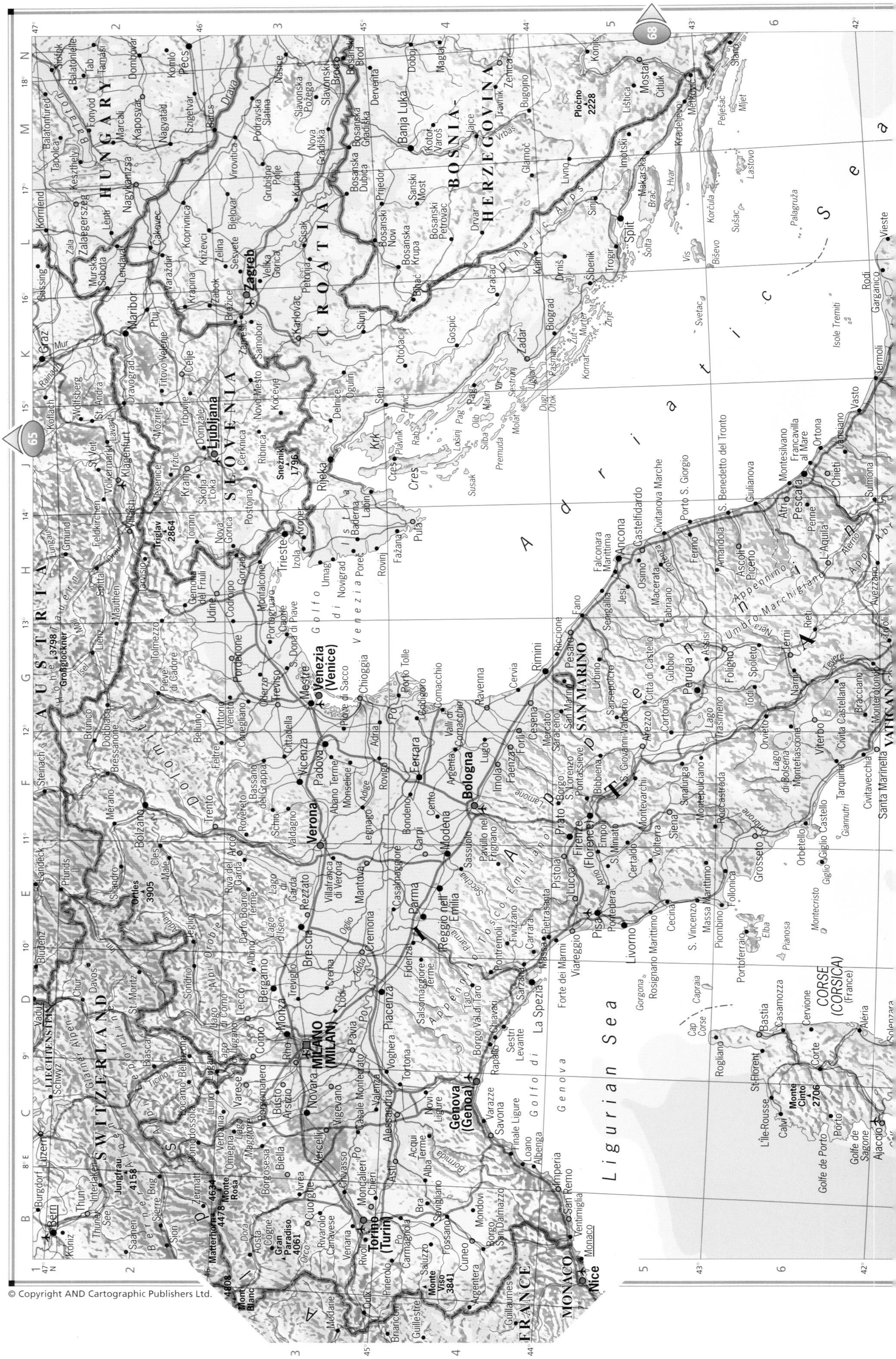

metres	feet
8000	26250
6000	19690
4000	13120
2000	6560
1000	3280
500	1640
200	656
0	0
656	200
3280	1000
6560	2000
13120	4000
19690	6000
26250	8000
feet	metres

Italy

Corsica • Malta • San Marino • Vatican City

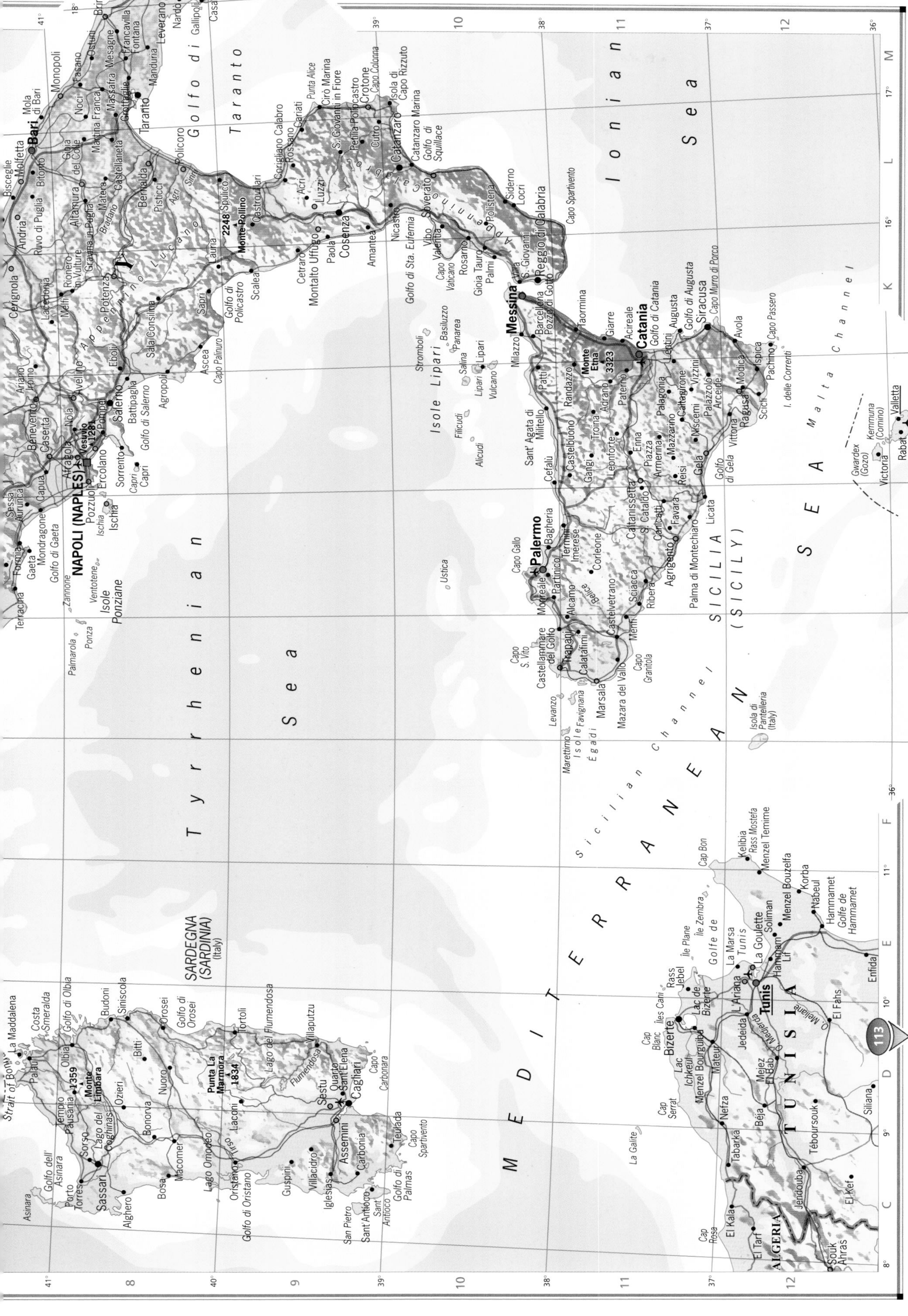

■ over 3 million
■ 1 – 3 million
● 250 000 – 1 million
● 100 000 – 250 000
○ 25 000 – 100 000
• under 25 000
country capital underline
urban area

Scale 1 : 3 450 000

0 50 100 150 km

0 25 50 75 miles

metres feet

8000 26250
6000 19690
4000 13120
2000 6560
1000 3280
500 1640
200 656
0 0
656 200
3280 1000
6560 2000
13120 4000
19690 6000
26250 8000

feet metres

The Balkans

Bosnia-Herzegovina • Bulgaria
Croatia • Moldova • Romania • Yugoslavia

■ over 3 million
■ 1 – 3 million
● 250 000 – 1 million
● 100 000 – 250 000
○ 25 000 – 100 000
• under 25 000

country capital underline
state or province capital underline
urban area

Scale 1 : 3 450 000

0 50 100 150 km

0 25 50 75 miles

metres	feet
8000	26250
6000	19690
4000	13120
2000	6560
1000	3280
500	1640
200	656
0	0
200	656
1000	3280
2000	6560
4000	13120
6000	19690
8000	26250

■ over 3 million
■ 1 – 3 million
● 250 000 – 1 million
● 100 000 – 250 000
○ 25 000 – 100 000
• under 25 000
country capital underline
state or province capital underline
urban area

Scale 1 : 10 400 000

0 200 400 600 km

0 100 200 300 miles

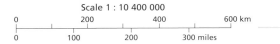

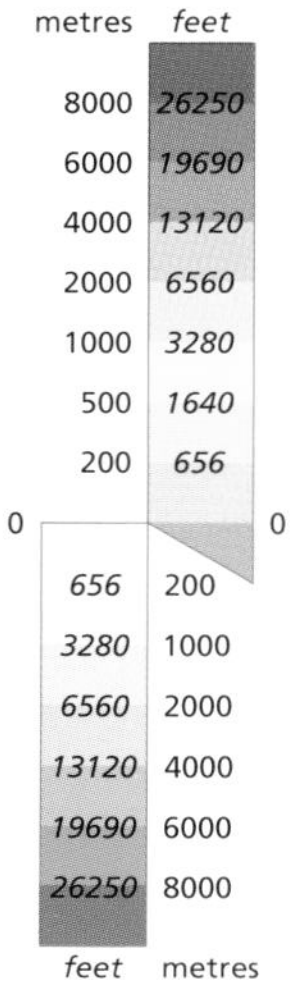

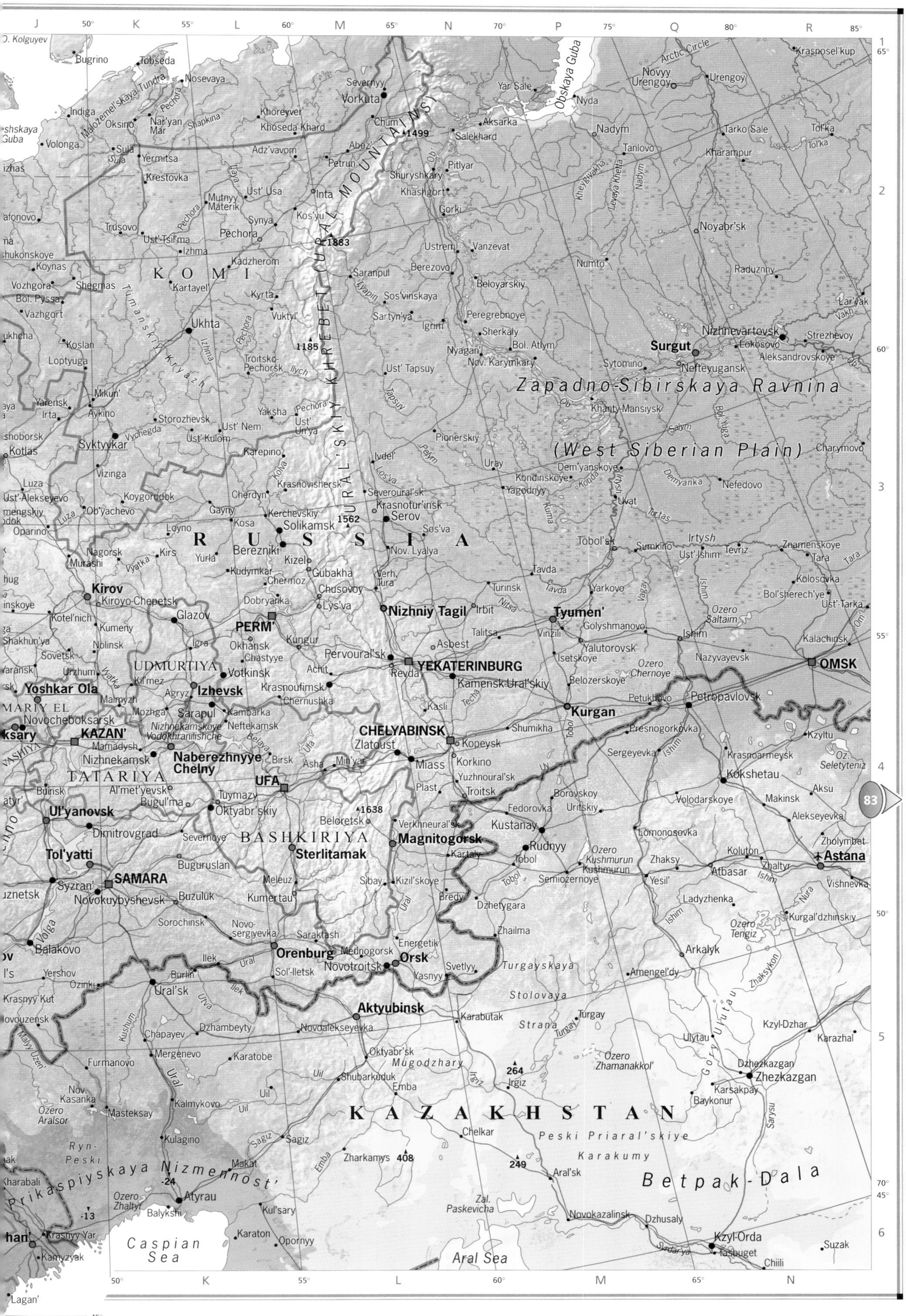

J
K
L
M
N
P
Q
R
50°
55°
60°
65°
70°
75°
80°
85°
1
2
3
4
5
6
O. Kolguyev
Bugrino
Tobseda
Nosevaya
Malozemel'skaya Tundra
Pechora
Indiga
Oksino
Nar'yan Mar
Shapkina
Khoreyver
Khoseda Khard
Vorkuta
Severnyy
Chum
1499
Aksarka
Salekhard
Yar Sale
Obskaya Guba
Nyda
Arctic Circle
Novyy Urengoy
Urengoy
Krasnosel'kup
Volonga
Sula
Yermitsa
Krestovka
Adz'vavom
Abez'
Petrun
Pitlyar
Shuryshkary
Khashgort
Gorki
Nadym
Tanlovo
Tarko Sale
Tol'ka
Kharampur
Ust' Usa
Inta
Mutnyy Materik
Synya
Kos'yu
Pechora
Trusovo
Ust'-Tsil'ma
Izhma
1883
URAL MOUNTAINS
Noyabr'sk
Ustrem
Vanzevat
Numto
Raduzhnyy
Koynas
Kadzherom
K O M I
Kartayel'
Saranpul
Berezovo
Beloyarskiy
Vozhgora
Shegmas
Bol. Pyssa
Vazhgort
Kyrta
Vuktyl'
Sos'vinskaya
Sartyn'ya
Igrim
Peregrebnoye
Sherkaly
Ukhta
Timanskiy Kryazh
Koslan
Loptyuga
1185
Troitsko-Pechorsk
Nyagan'
Bol. Atlym
Nov. Karymkary
Ust' Tapsuy
Surgut
Nizhnevartovsk
Lokosovo
Strezhevoy
Aleksandrovskoye
Sytomino
Nefteyugansk
Zapadno-Sibirskaya Ravnina
(West Siberian Plain)
Khanty-Mansiysk
Ural'skiy Khrebet
Mikun'
Yarensk
Aykino
Irta
Storozhevsk
Yaksha
Ust' Nem
Ust' Kulom
Ust' Un'ya
Syktyvkar
Kotlas
Pionerskiy
Charymovo
Karepino
Ivdel'
Uray
Dem'yanskoye
Kondinskoye
Yagodnyy
Nefedovo
Vizinga
Luza
Ust'-Alekseyevo
Koygorodok
Ob'yachevo
Krasnovishersk
Cherdyn'
Severoural'sk
Krasnotur'insk
Serov
Gayny
Kerchevskiy
1562
Solikamsk
Sos'va
Uvat
Oparino
Loyno
Kosa
R U S S I A
Berezniki
Nov. Lyalya
Tobol'sk
Sumkino
Irtysh
Ust'-Ishim
Tevriz
Znamenskoye
Tara
Nagorsk
Murashi
Kirs
Yurla
Kizel
Kudymkar
Gubakha
Chermoz
Chusovoy
Verh. Tura
Tavda
Turinsk
Yarkovo
Kolosovka
Bol'sherech'ye
Ust'-Tarka
Kirov
Kiroyo-Chepetsk
Kotel'nich
Glazov
Dobryanka
PERM'
Lys'va
Nizhniy Tagil
Irbit
Tyumen'
Ozero Saltaim
Kumeny
Nolinsk
Okhansk
Kungur
Talitsa
Golyshmanovo
Vinzili
Ishim
Kalachinsk
Sovetsk
UDMURTIYA
Chastyye
Pervoural'sk
Asbest
Yalutorovsk
Nazyvayevsk
OMSK
Urzhum
Kil'mez
Votkinsk
Achit
Revda
YEKATERINBURG
Isetskoye
Ozero Chernoye
Yoshkar Ola
MARIY EL
Agryz
Izhevsk
Krasnoufimsk
Kamensk-Ural'skiy
Belozerskoye
Petukhovo
Petropavlovsk
Malmyzh
Chernushka
Novocheboksarsk
Mozhga
Sarapul
Kambarka
Kasli
Kurgan
KAZAN'
Neftekamsk
Nizhnekamskoye Vodokhranilishche
CHELYABINSK
Shumikha
Presnogor'kovka
Kzyltu
Mamadysh
Nizhnekamsk
Naberezhnyye Chelny
Birsk
Asha
Zlatoust
Min'yar
Miass
Kopeysk
Korkino
Sergeyevka
Krasnoarmeysk
Oz. Seletyteniz
TATARIYA
UFA
Yuzhnoural'sk
Troitsk
Plast
Kokshetau
Aksu
Buinsk
Al'met'yevsk
Bugul'ma
Tuymazy
Oktyabr'skiy
Borovskoy
Uritskiy
Volodarskoye
Makinsk
Ul'yanovsk
1638
Beloretsk
Fedorovka
Kustanay
Lomonosovka
Alekseyevka
Dimitrovgrad
Severnoye
BASHKIRIYA
Verkhneural'sk
Magnitogorsk
Rudnyy
Ozero Kushmurun
Kushmurun
Zholymbet
Tol'yatti
Sterlitamak
Kartaly
Tobol
Zhaksy
Koluton
Astana
Buguruslan
Atbasar
Zhaltyr
Syzran'
SAMARA
Meleuz
Sibay
Kizil'skoye
Semiozernoye
Yesil'
Vishnevka
Novokuybyshevsk
Buzuluk
Kumertau
Bredy
Dzhetygara
Ladyzhenka
Kurgal'dzhinskiy
Sorochinsk
Novo-sergiyevka
Saraktash
Zhailma
Ozero Tengiz
Balakovo
Orenburg
Mednogorsk
Energetik
Orsk
Arkalyk
Ershov
Ilek
Ural
Sol'-Iletsk
Novotroitsk
Svetlyy
Yasnyy
Turgayskaya
Stolovaya
Strana
Amengel'dy
Zhaksykon
Ozinki
Burlin
Ural'sk
Krasnyy Kut
Aktyubinsk
Karabutak
Turgay
Chapayev
Dzhambeyty
Novoalekseyevka
Ulytau
Kzyl-Dzhar
Karazhal
Mergenevo
Karatobe
Oktyabr'sk
Mugodzhary
Ozero Zhamanakkol'
Dzhezkazgan
Zhezkazgan
Furmanovo
264
Irgiz
Shubarkuduk
Emba
Karsakpay
Baykonur
Nov. Kasanka
Ozero Aralsor
Masteksay
Kalmykovo
Uil
K A Z A K H S T A N
Sarysu
Ryn-Peski
Kulagino
Sagiz
Chelkar
Peski Priaral'skiye Karakumy
Prikaspiyskaya Nizmennost'
Makat
-24
Zharkamys
408
249
Aral'sk
Betpak-Dala
Ozero Zhaltyr
Atyrau
-13
Balykshi
Kul'sary
Zal. Paskevicha
Novokazalinsk
Dzhusaly
Krasnyy Yar
Karaton
Opornyy
Kzyl-Orda
Suzak
Kamyzyak
Caspian Sea
Aral Sea
Tasbuget
Syrdar'ya
Chiili
83
Lagan'
45°

- ■ over 3 million
- ■ 1 – 3 million
- ● 250 000 – 1 million
- ● 100 000 – 250 000
- ○ 25 000 – 100 000
- • under 25 000
- country capital underline
- state or province capital underline

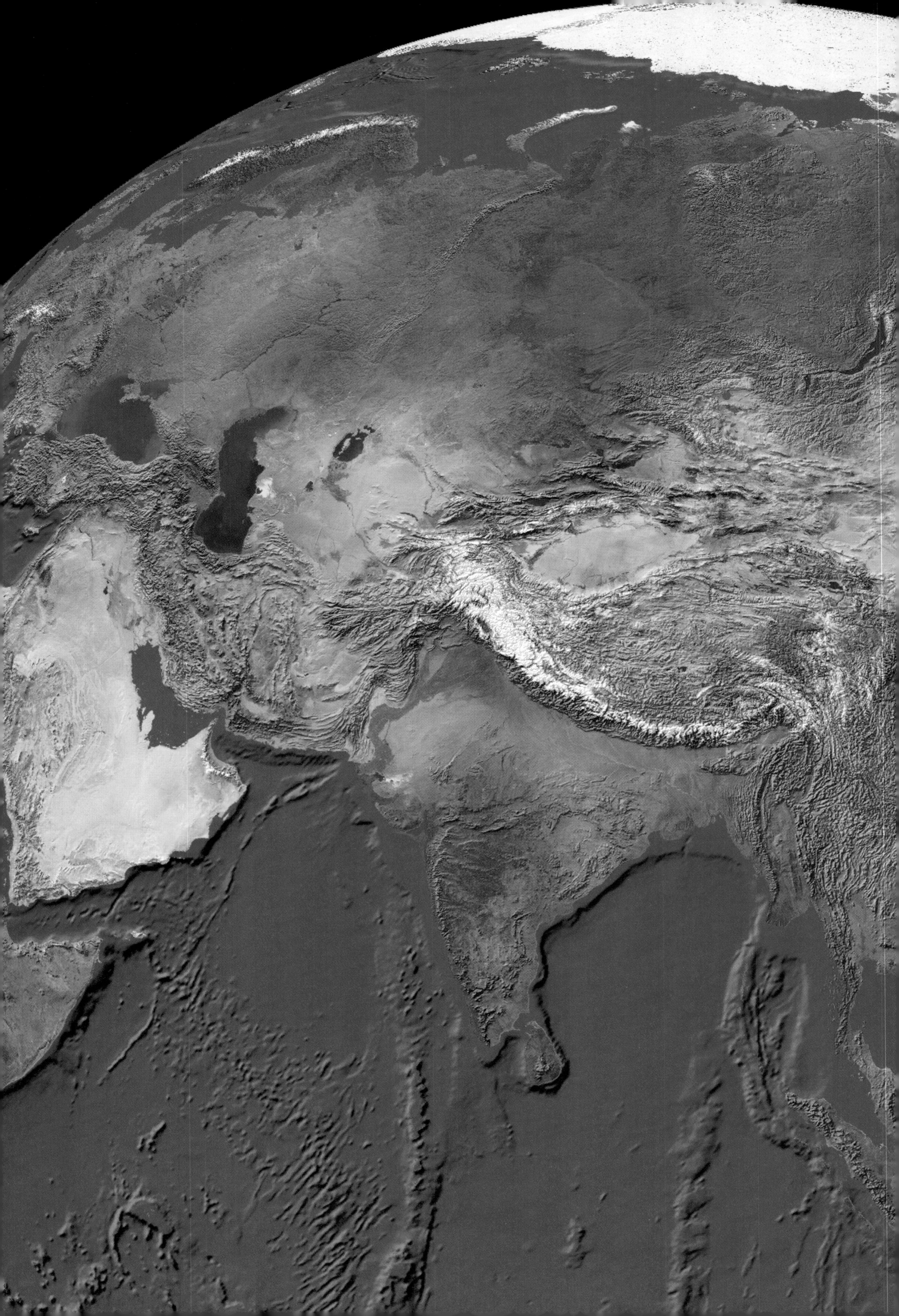

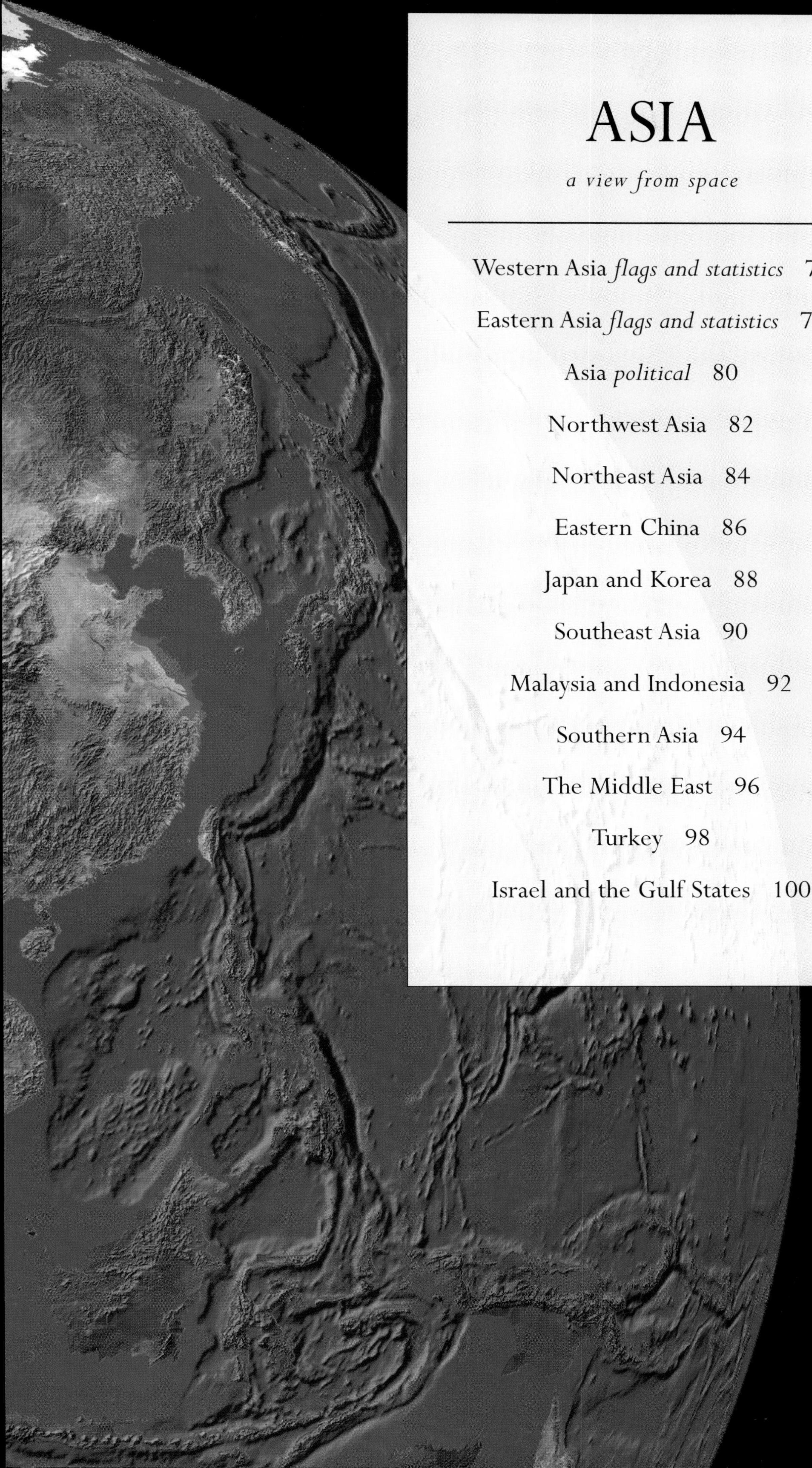

ASIA

a view from space

Western Asia *flags and statistics* 76

Eastern Asia *flags and statistics* 78

Asia *political* 80

Northwest Asia 82

Northeast Asia 84

Eastern China 86

Japan and Korea 88

Southeast Asia 90

Malaysia and Indonesia 92

Southern Asia 94

The Middle East 96

Turkey 98

Israel and the Gulf States 100

WESTERN ASIA

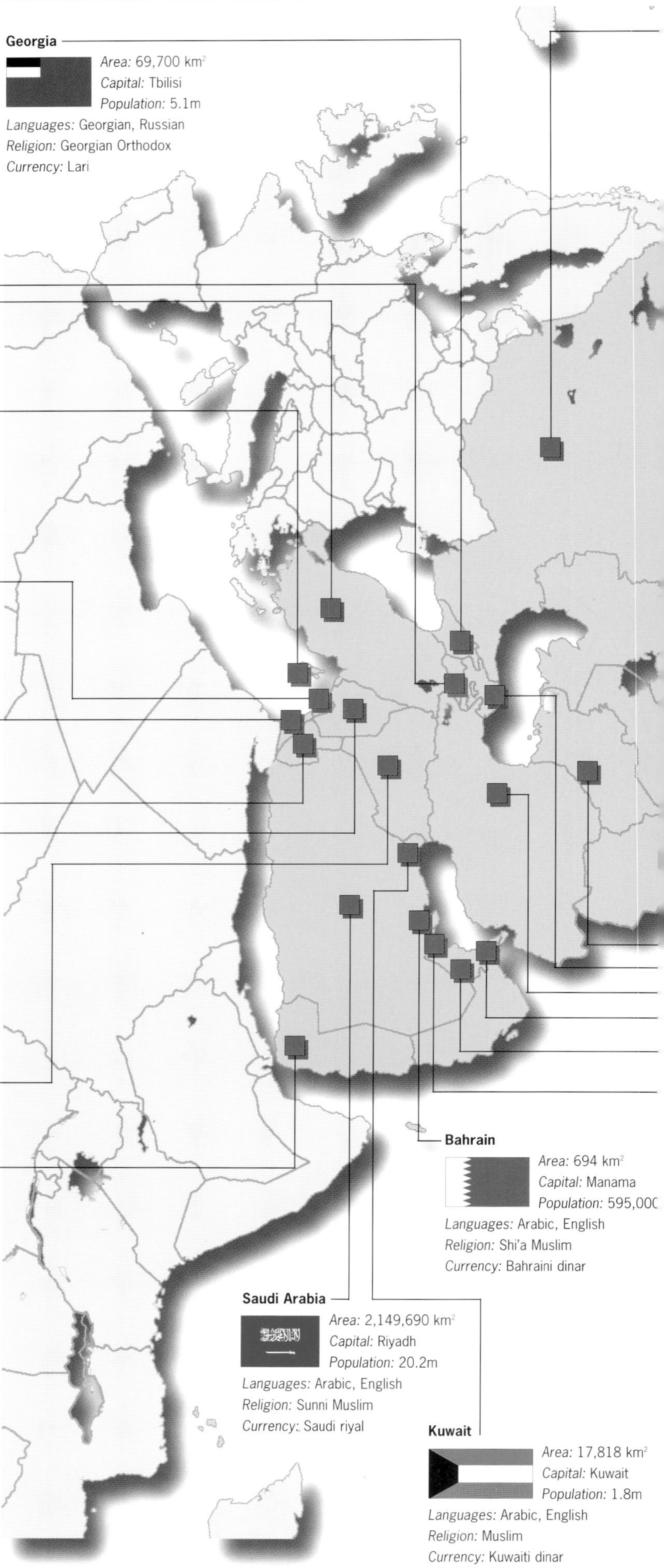

Georgia

Area: 69,700 km²
Capital: Tbilisi
Population: 5.1m
Languages: Georgian, Russian
Religion: Georgian Orthodox
Currency: Lari

Armenia

Area: 29,800 km²
Capital: Yerevan
Population: 3.5m
Languages: Armenian, Russian
Religion: Armenian Apostolic
Currency: Dram

Turkey

Area: 774,815 km²
Capital: Ankara
Population: 64.5m
Main language: Turkish
Religion: Muslim
Currency: Turkish lira

Cyprus

Area: 9,251 km²
Capital: Nicosia
Population: 771,000
Languages: Greek, Turkish
Religions: Greek Orthodox, Muslim
Currency: Cyprus pound

Lebanon

Area: 10,400 km²
Capital: Beirut
Population: 3.2m
Languages: Arabic, French, English
Religion: Muslim
Currency: Lebanese pound

Israel

Area: 21,056 km²
Capital: Jerusalem
Population: 7.0m
Languages: Hebrew, Arabic
Religion: Jewish
Currency: Shekel

Jordan

Area: 97,740 km²
Capital: Amman
Population: 6.3m
Languages: Arabic, English, French
Religion: Muslim
Currency: Jordanian dinar

Syria

Area: 185,180 km²
Capital: Damascus
Population: 15.3m
Languages: Arabic, Kurdish, Turkish
Religion: Sunni Muslim
Currency: Syrian pound

Iraq

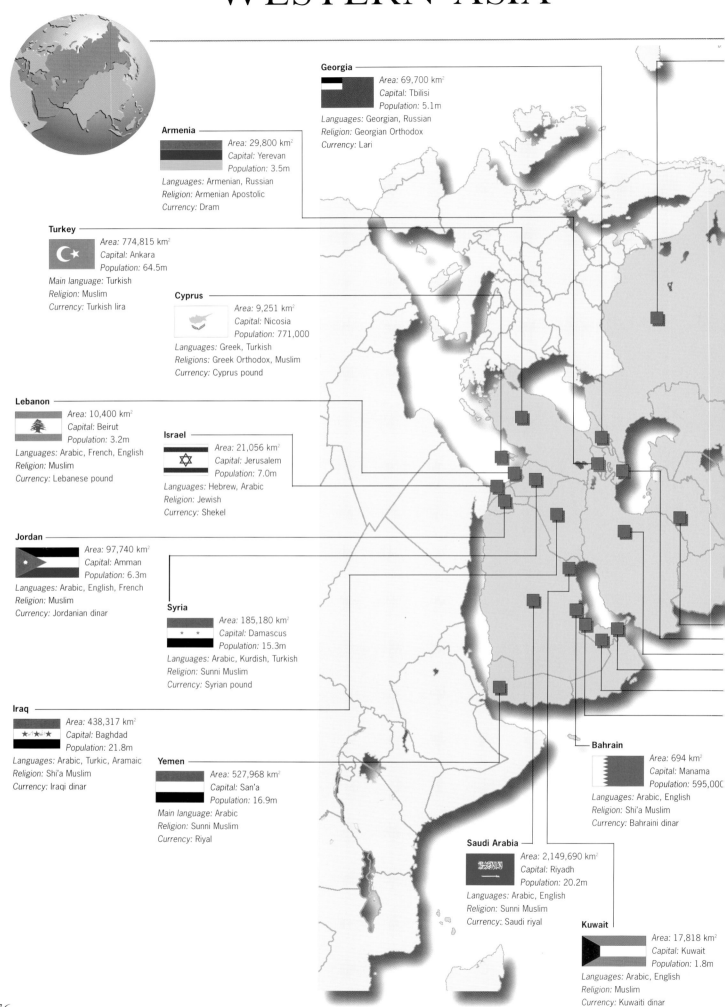

Area: 438,317 km²
Capital: Baghdad
Population: 21.8m
Languages: Arabic, Turkic, Aramaic
Religion: Shi'a Muslim
Currency: Iraqi dinar

Yemen

Area: 527,968 km²
Capital: San'a
Population: 16.9m
Main language: Arabic
Religion: Sunni Muslim
Currency: Riyal

Bahrain

Area: 694 km²
Capital: Manama
Population: 595,000
Languages: Arabic, English
Religion: Shi'a Muslim
Currency: Bahraini dinar

Saudi Arabia

Area: 2,149,690 km²
Capital: Riyadh
Population: 20.2m
Languages: Arabic, English
Religion: Sunni Muslim
Currency: Saudi riyal

Kuwait

Area: 17,818 km²
Capital: Kuwait
Population: 1.8m
Languages: Arabic, English
Religion: Muslim
Currency: Kuwaiti dinar

MUCH OF THIS REGION is dry, arid desert, or rugged mountains and plateaux, and cultivation largely depends on irrigation techniques. It also has some of the world's richest oil fields. Most of the population is clustered around the coastal regions, and is torn by long-term religious and ethnic strife.

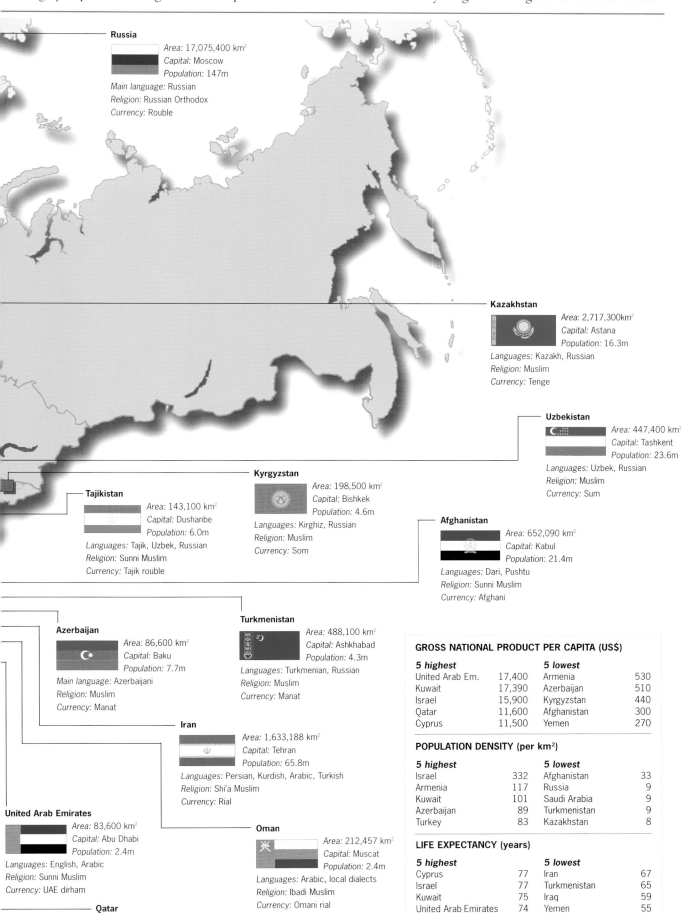

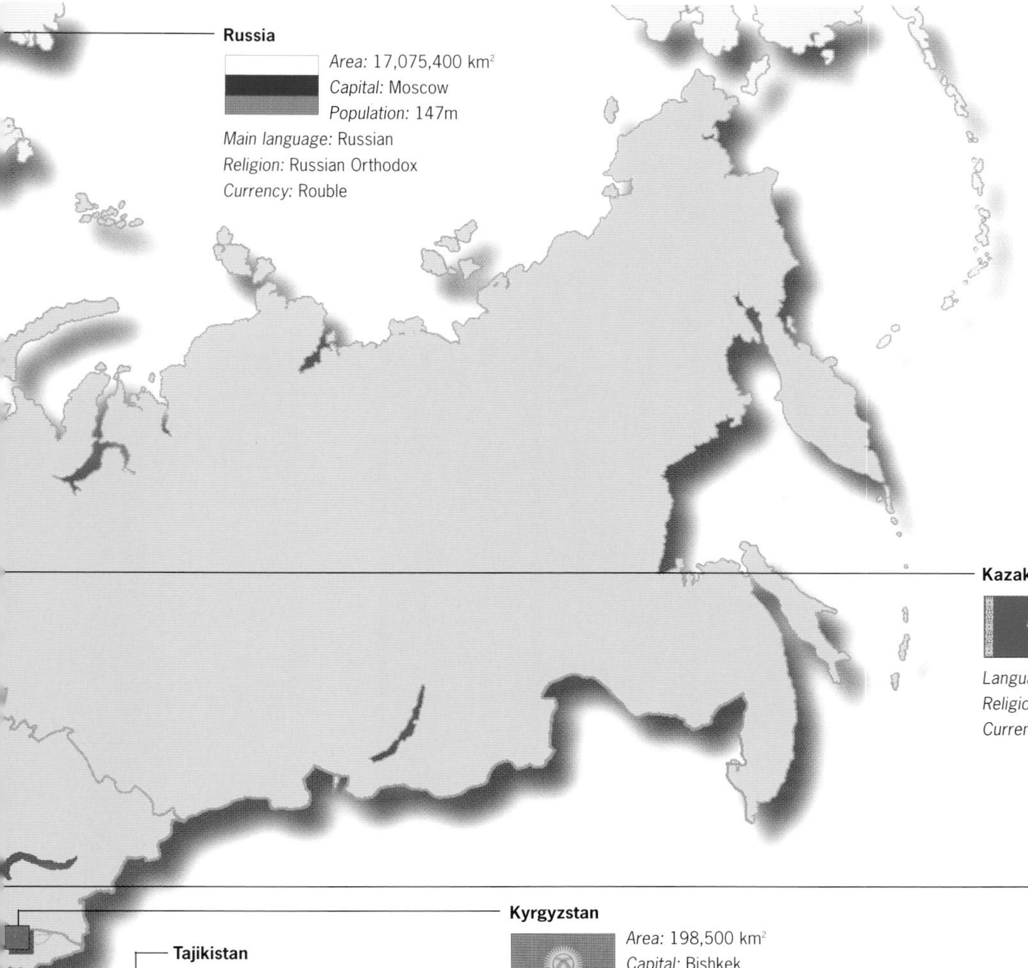

Russia

Area: 17,075,400 km²
Capital: Moscow
Population: 147m
Main language: Russian
Religion: Russian Orthodox
Currency: Rouble

Kazakhstan

Area: 2,717,300km²
Capital: Astana
Population: 16.3m
Languages: Kazakh, Russian
Religion: Muslim
Currency: Tenge

Uzbekistan

Area: 447,400 km²
Capital: Tashkent
Population: 23.6m
Languages: Uzbek, Russian
Religion: Muslim
Currency: Sum

Kyrgyzstan

Area: 198,500 km²
Capital: Bishkek
Population: 4.6m
Languages: Kirghiz, Russian
Religion: Muslim
Currency: Som

Tajikistan

Area: 143,100 km²
Capital: Dushanbe
Population: 6.0m
Languages: Tajik, Uzbek, Russian
Religion: Sunni Muslim
Currency: Tajik rouble

Afghanistan

Area: 652,090 km²
Capital: Kabul
Population: 21.4m
Languages: Dari, Pushtu
Religion: Sunni Muslim
Currency: Afghani

Turkmenistan

Area: 488,100 km²
Capital: Ashkhabad
Population: 4.3m
Languages: Turkmenian, Russian
Religion: Muslim
Currency: Manat

Azerbaijan

Area: 86,600 km²
Capital: Baku
Population: 7.7m
Main language: Azerbaijani
Religion: Muslim
Currency: Manat

Iran

Area: 1,633,188 km²
Capital: Tehran
Population: 65.8m
Languages: Persian, Kurdish, Arabic, Turkish
Religion: Shi'a Muslim
Currency: Rial

United Arab Emirates

Area: 83,600 km²
Capital: Abu Dhabi
Population: 2.4m
Languages: English, Arabic
Religion: Sunni Muslim
Currency: UAE dirham

Oman

Area: 212,457 km²
Capital: Muscat
Population: 2.4m
Languages: Arabic, local dialects
Religion: Ibadi Muslim
Currency: Omani rial

Qatar

Area: 11,000 km²
Capital: Doha
Population: 579,000
Languages: Arabic, English
Religion: Sunni Muslim
Currency: Qatar riyal

GROSS NATIONAL PRODUCT PER CAPITA (US$)

5 highest		*5 lowest*	
United Arab Em.	17,400	Armenia	530
Kuwait	17,390	Azerbaijan	510
Israel	15,900	Kyrgyzstan	440
Qatar	11,600	Afghanistan	300
Cyprus	11,500	Yemen	270

POPULATION DENSITY (per km²)

5 highest		*5 lowest*	
Israel	332	Afghanistan	33
Armenia	117	Russia	9
Kuwait	101	Saudi Arabia	9
Azerbaijan	89	Turkmenistan	9
Turkey	83	Kazakhstan	8

LIFE EXPECTANCY (years)

5 highest		*5 lowest*	
Cyprus	77	Iran	67
Israel	77	Turkmenistan	65
Kuwait	75	Iraq	59
United Arab Emirates	74	Yemen	55
Georgia	73	Afghanistan	43

EASTERN ASIA

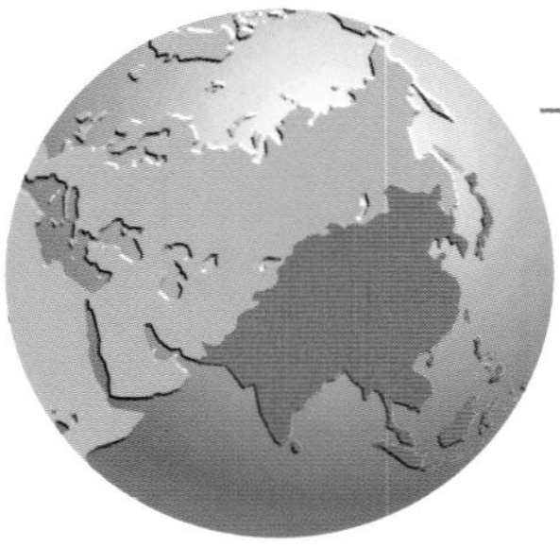

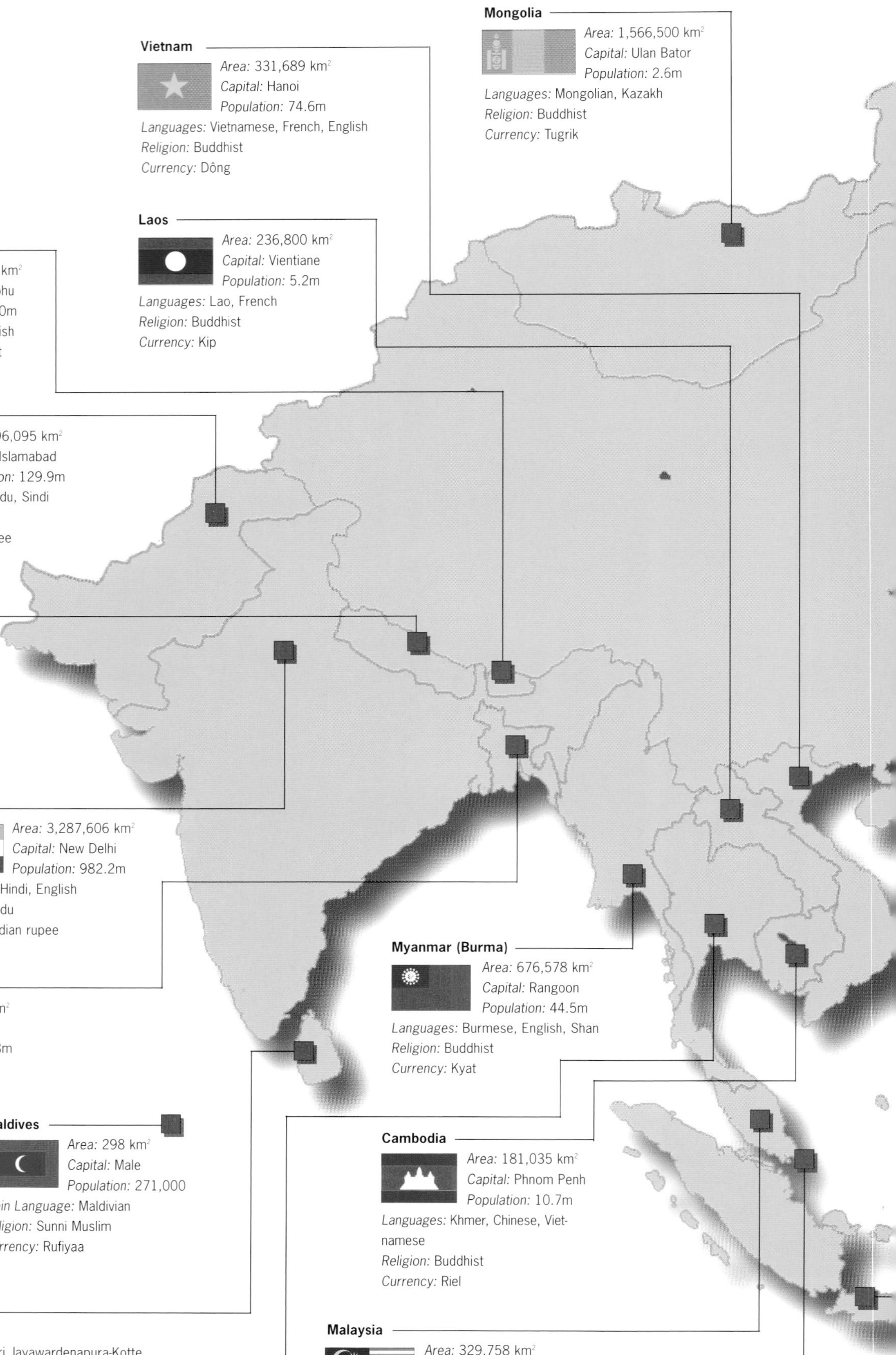

Vietnam

Area: 331,689 km²
Capital: Hanoi
Population: 74.6m
Languages: Vietnamese, French, English
Religion: Buddhist
Currency: Dông

Mongolia

Area: 1,566,500 km²
Capital: Ulan Bator
Population: 2.6m
Languages: Mongolian, Kazakh
Religion: Buddhist
Currency: Tugrik

Laos

Area: 236,800 km²
Capital: Vientiane
Population: 5.2m
Languages: Lao, French
Religion: Buddhist
Currency: Kip

Bhutan

Area: 47,000 km²
Capital: Thimphu
Population: 2.0m
Languages: Dzongkha, English
Religion: Mahayana Buddhist
Currency: Ngultrum

Pakistan

Area: 796,095 km²
Capital: Islamabad
Population: 129.9m
Languages: Punjabi, Urdu, Sindi
Religion: Sunni Muslim
Currency: Pakistan rupee

Nepal

Area: 147,181 km²
Capital: Kathmandu
Population: 22.8m
Main language: Nepali
Religion: Hindu
Currency: Nepalese rupee

India

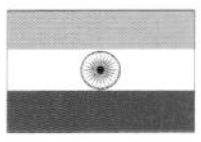

Area: 3,287,606 km²
Capital: New Delhi
Population: 982.2m
Languages: Hindi, English
Religion: Hindu
Currency: Indian rupee

Myanmar (Burma)

Area: 676,578 km²
Capital: Rangoon
Population: 44.5m
Languages: Burmese, English, Shan
Religion: Buddhist
Currency: Kyat

Bangladesh

Area: 143,998 km²
Capital: Dhaka
Population: 124.8m
Languages: Bengali, English
Religion: Muslim
Currency: Taka

Maldives

Area: 298 km²
Capital: Male
Population: 271,000
Main Language: Maldivian
Religion: Sunni Muslim
Currency: Rufiyaa

Cambodia

Area: 181,035 km²
Capital: Phnom Penh
Population: 10.7m
Languages: Khmer, Chinese, Vietnamese
Religion: Buddhist
Currency: Riel

Sri Lanka

Area: 65,610 km²
Capitals: Colombo/Sri Jayawardenapura-Kotte
Population: 18.5m
Languages: Sinhala, Tamil, English
Religion: Buddhist
Currency: Sri Lankan rupee

Malaysia

Area: 329,758 km²
Capital: Kuala Lumpur
Population: 21.4m
Languages: Malay, English
Religion: Muslim
Currency: Malaysian dollar

Thailand

Area: 513,115 km²
Capital: Bangkok
Population: 60.3m
Languages: Thai, Chinese, Malay
Religion: Buddhist
Currency: Baht

Singapore

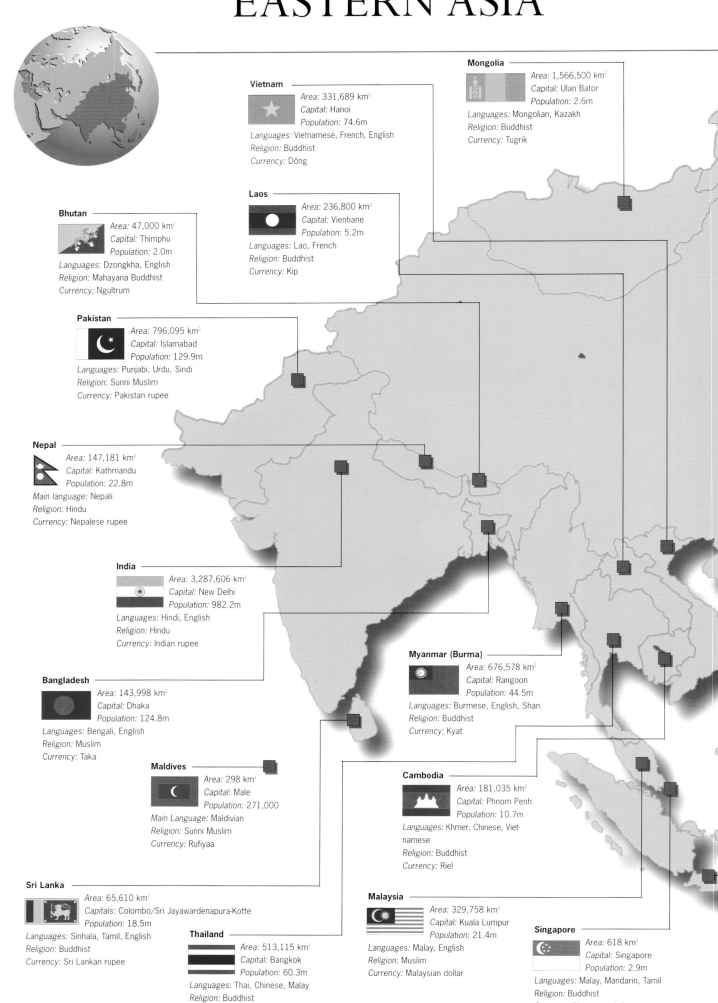

Area: 618 km²
Capital: Singapore
Population: 2.9m
Languages: Malay, Mandarin, Tamil
Religion: Buddhist
Currency: Singapore dollar

THIS STRETCHES FROM THE DENSELY populated subcontinent of India, dominated in the north by the Himalayas, to the mountainous regions of the southeast, covered in tropical rainforests, the frozen wastes of Siberia, China, with one-fifth of the world population, Japan and the Central Asian republics.

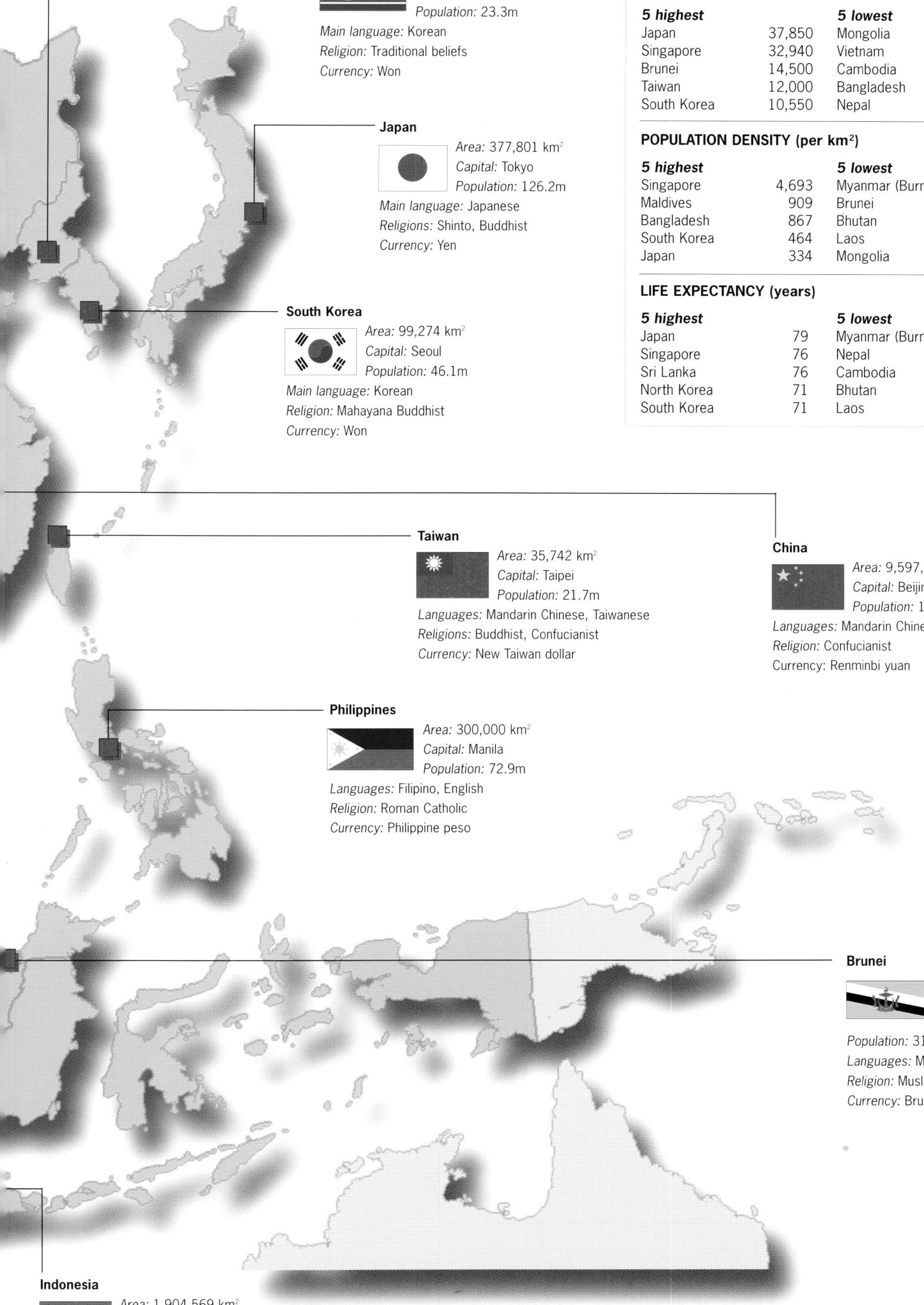

North Korea

Area: 120,538 km²
Capital: Pyongyang
Population: 23.3m
Main language: Korean
Religion: Traditional beliefs
Currency: Won

Japan

Area: 377,801 km²
Capital: Tokyo
Population: 126.2m
Main language: Japanese
Religions: Shinto, Buddhist
Currency: Yen

South Korea

Area: 99,274 km²
Capital: Seoul
Population: 46.1m
Main language: Korean
Religion: Mahayana Buddhist
Currency: Won

GROSS NATIONAL PRODUCT PER CAPITA (US$)

5 highest		*5 lowest*	
Japan	37,850	Mongolia	390
Singapore	32,940	Vietnam	320
Brunei	14,500	Cambodia	300
Taiwan	12,000	Bangladesh	270
South Korea	10,550	Nepal	210

POPULATION DENSITY (per km²)

5 highest		*5 lowest*	
Singapore	4,693	Myanmar (Burma)	66
Maldives	909	Brunei	55
Bangladesh	867	Bhutan	42
South Korea	464	Laos	22
Japan	334	Mongolia	2

LIFE EXPECTANCY (years)

5 highest		*5 lowest*	
Japan	79	Myanmar (Burma)	58
Singapore	76	Nepal	55
Sri Lanka	76	Cambodia	52
North Korea	71	Bhutan	51
South Korea	71	Laos	51

Taiwan

Area: 35,742 km²
Capital: Taipei
Population: 21.7m
Languages: Mandarin Chinese, Taiwanese
Religions: Buddhist, Confucianist
Currency: New Taiwan dollar

China

Area: 9,597,006 km²
Capital: Beijing
Population: 1,241m
Languages: Mandarin Chinese, Cantonese
Religion: Confucianist
Currency: Renminbi yuan

Philippines

Area: 300,000 km²
Capital: Manila
Population: 72.9m
Languages: Filipino, English
Religion: Roman Catholic
Currency: Philippine peso

Brunei

Area: 5,765 km²
Capital: Bandar Seri Begawan
Population: 315,000
Languages: Malay, English
Religion: Muslim
Currency: Brunei dollar

Indonesia

Area: 1,904,569 km²
Capital: Jakarta
Population: 207.2m
Languages: Bahasa Indonesian, Dutch
Religion: Muslim
Currency: Rupiah

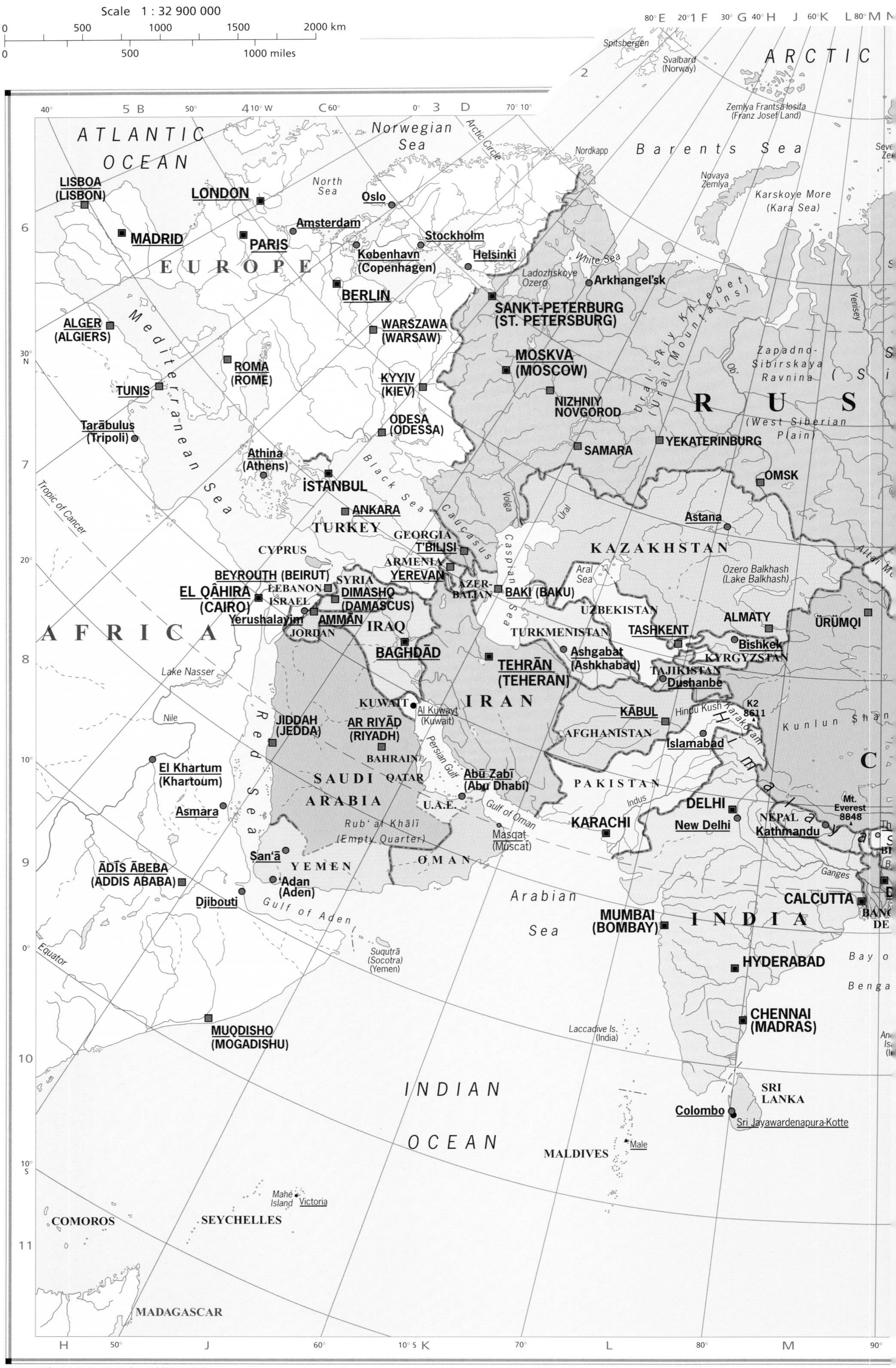
Scale 1 : 32 900 000
0 500 1000 1500 2000 km
0 500 1000 miles
ATLANTIC OCEAN
Norwegian Sea
North Sea
Arctic Circle
Spitsbergen
Svalbard (Norway)
ARCTIC
Zemlya Frantsa-Iosifa (Franz Josef Land)
Nordkapp
Barents Sea
Novaya Zemlya
Karskoye More (Kara Sea)
LISBOA (LISBON)
LONDON
Oslo
MADRID
PARIS
Amsterdam
Stockholm
København (Copenhagen)
Helsinki
EUROPE
BERLIN
White Sea
Ladozhskoye Ozero
Arkhangel'sk
SANKT-PETERBURG (ST. PETERSBURG)
Ural'skiy Khrebet (Ural Mountains)
ALGER (ALGIERS)
Mediterranean Sea
WARSZAWA (WARSAW)
ROMA (ROME)
MOSKVA (MOSCOW)
Zapadno-Sibirskaya Ravnina (West Siberian Plain)
Ob'
Yenisey
TUNIS
KYYIV (KIEV)
NIZHNIY NOVGOROD
RUS
Tarābulus (Tripoli)
ODESA (ODESSA)
SAMARA
YEKATERINBURG
Athina (Athens)
Black Sea
İSTANBUL
OMSK
Tropic of Cancer
ANKARA
Volga
Ural
Caucasus
Astana
TURKEY
GEORGIA
T'BILISI
KAZAKHSTAN
CYPRUS
ARMENIA
YEREVAN
Caspian Sea
Aral Sea
Ozero Balkhash (Lake Balkhash)
Altai
BEYROUTH (BEIRUT)
LEBANON
SYRIA
AZER-BAIJAN
BAKI (BAKU)
EL QÂHIRA (CAIRO)
ISRAEL
DIMASHQ (DAMASCUS)
UZBEKISTAN
Yerushalayim
AMMĀN
IRAQ
TASHKENT
ALMATY
ÜRÜMQI
AFRICA
JORDAN
TURKMENISTAN
Bishkek
BAGHDĀD
Ashgabat (Ashkhabad)
KYRGYZSTAN
Lake Nasser
TEHRĀN (TEHERAN)
TAJIKISTAN
Dushanbe
KUWAIT
Al Kuwayt (Kuwait)
IRAN
K2 8611
Nile
Red Sea
JIDDAH (JEDDA)
AR RIYĀD (RIYADH)
KĀBUL
Hindu Kush
Karakoram
Kunlun Shan
AFGHANISTAN
Islamabad
Persian Gulf
BAHRAIN
Himalaya
El Khartum (Khartoum)
SAUDI ARABIA
QATAR
Abū Zabī (Abu Dhabi)
PAKISTAN
C
Mt. Everest 8848
Asmara
U.A.E.
Gulf of Oman
Indus
DELHI
New Delhi
NEPAL
Kathmandu
Rub' al Khālī (Empty Quarter)
KARACHI
Masqat (Muscat)
San'ā
OMAN
YEMEN
Ganges
ĀDĪS ĀBEBA (ADDIS ABABA)
'Adan (Aden)
Arabian Sea
CALCUTTA
Djibouti
Gulf of Aden
MUMBAI (BOMBAY)
INDIA
Equator
Suqutrā (Socotra) (Yemen)
HYDERABAD
Bay of Bengal
CHENNAI (MADRAS)
MUQDISHO (MOGADISHU)
Laccadive Is. (India)
SRI LANKA
INDIAN OCEAN
Colombo
Sri Jayawardenapura-Kotte
MALDIVES
Male
Mahé Island
Victoria
COMOROS
SEYCHELLES
MADAGASCAR

Mt. Everest, China/Nepal : 8,848 m or 29,029 ft

Dead Sea, Israel/Jordan : 400 m or 1312 ft

Aden, Yemen : 4.6 cm or 1.8 in

Mawsynram, India : 1187.2 cm 467.4 in

Yangtze, China : 5,980 km or 3,720 mi

Aral Sea, Kazakhstan : 62,000 km² or 23,940 sq mi

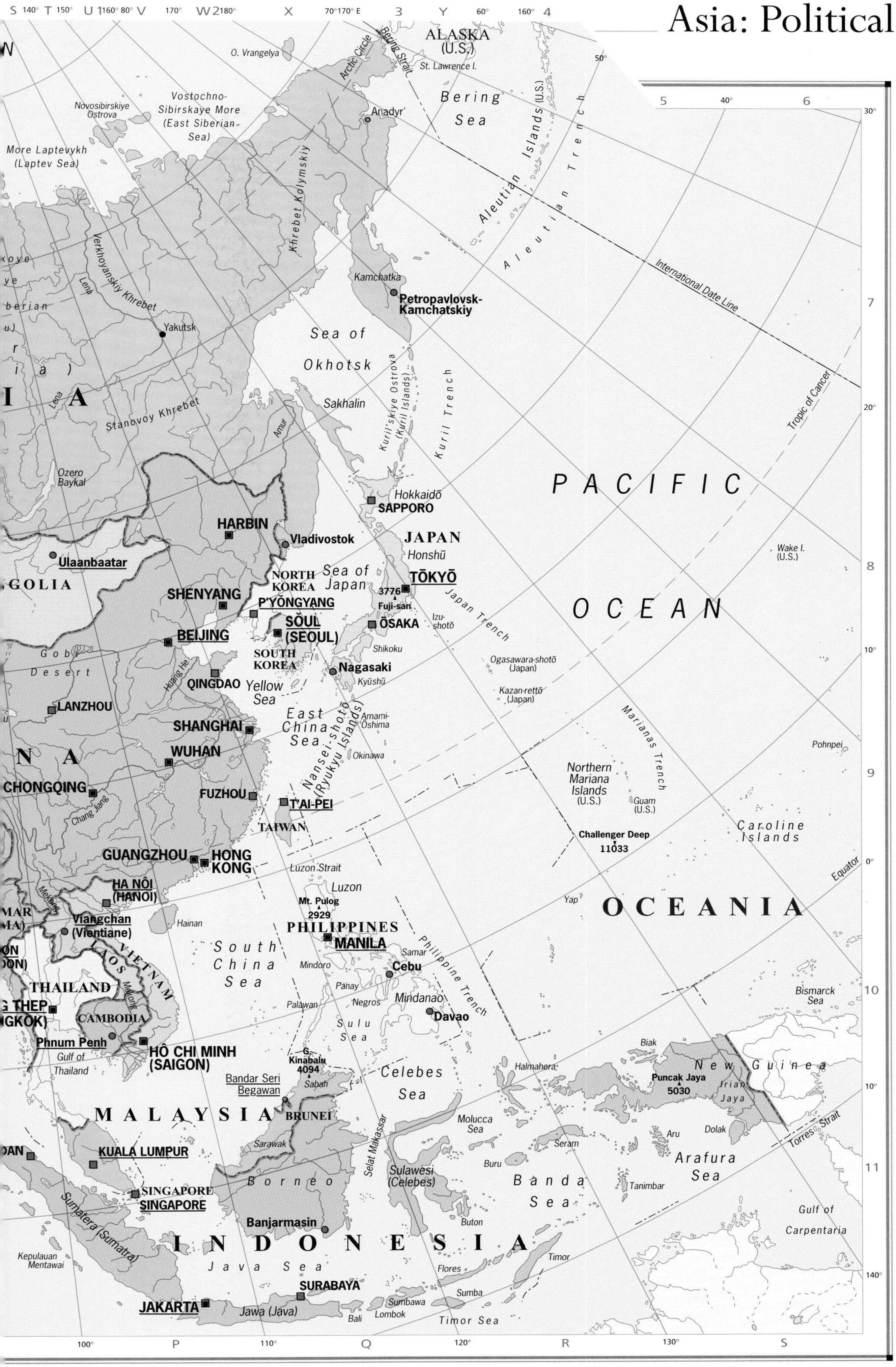
ALASKA (U.S.)
O. Vrangelya
St. Lawrence I.
Bering Strait
Arctic Circle
Anadyr'
Bering Sea
Aleutian Islands (U.S.)
Aleutian Trench
International Date Line
Novosibirskiye Ostrova
Vostochno-Sibirskaye More (East Siberian Sea)
More Laptevykh (Laptev Sea)
Khrebet Kolymskiy
Verkhoyanskiy Khrebet
Lena
Yakutsk
Kamchatka
Petropavlovsk-Kamchatskiy
Sea of Okhotsk
Kuril'skiye Ostrova (Kuril Islands)
Kuril Trench
Sakhalin
Stanovoy Khrebet
Amur
Ozero Baykal
Tropic of Cancer
PACIFIC OCEAN
Hokkaidō
SAPPORO
JAPAN
Honshū
HARBIN
Vladivostok
Ulaanbaatar
MONGOLIA
NORTH KOREA
Sea of Japan
TŌKYŌ
3776 Fuji-san
SHENYANG
P'YŎNGYANG
SŎUL (SEOUL)
ŌSAKA
Izu-shotō
Japan Trench
BEIJING
Gobi Desert
SOUTH KOREA
Shikoku
Nagasaki
Kyūshū
Ogasawara-shotō (Japan)
Kazan-rettō (Japan)
Wake I. (U.S.)
Huang He
QINGDAO
Yellow Sea
LANZHOU
SHANGHAI
East China Sea
Nansei-shotō (Ryukyu Islands)
Amami-Ōshima
Okinawa
Marianas Trench
WUHAN
CHONGQING
Chang Jiang
FUZHOU
T'AI-PEI
TAIWAN
Northern Mariana Islands (U.S.)
Guam (U.S.)
Challenger Deep 11033
Caroline Islands
Pohnpei
GUANGZHOU
HONG KONG
Luzon Strait
Luzon
HA NÔI (HANOI)
Mt. Pulog 2929
PHILIPPINES
MANILA
Yap
OCEANIA
Equator
Hainan
Viangchan (Vientiane)
LAOS
VIETNAM
South China Sea
Mindoro
Samar
Cebu
Philippine Trench
THAILAND
Panay
Negros
Mindanao
Davao
Palawan
Sulu Sea
Bismarck Sea
CAMBODIA
Phnum Penh
HÔ CHI MINH (SAIGON)
Gulf of Thailand
G. Kinabalu 4094
Sabah
Celebes Sea
Halmahera
Biak
Puncak Jaya 5030
New Guinea
Irian Jaya
Bandar Seri Begawan
BRUNEI
MALAYSIA
Molucca Sea
Aru
Dolak
Torres Strait
KUALA LUMPUR
Sarawak
Selat Makassar
Seram
Buru
Sulawesi (Celebes)
Banda Sea
Tanimbar
Arafura Sea
SINGAPORE
Borneo
Sumatera (Sumatra)
Banjarmasin
Buton
Gulf of Carpentaria
INDONESIA
Kepulauan Mentawai
Java Sea
Timor
Flores
SURABAYA
Sumba
JAKARTA
Jawa (Java)
Sumbawa
Bali
Lombok
Timor Sea

Verkhoyansk & Oymyakon, Russia : -68 °C or -90 °F | 3,614,371,000 | 44,493,000 km² or 17,179,000 sq mi

Tirat Tsevi, Israel : 54 °C or 129 °F | 81 per km² or 210 per sq mi | 48

Scale 1 : 13 800 000

0 200 400 600 km

0 100 200 300 miles

metres	feet
8000	26250
6000	19690
4000	13120
2000	6560
1000	3280
500	1640
200	656
0	0
200	656
1000	3280
2000	6560
4000	13120
6000	19690
8000	26250
metres	feet

■ over 3 million
■ 1 – 3 million
● 250 000 – 1 million
● 100 000 – 250 000
○ 25 000 – 100 000
• under 25 000
country capital underline
state or province capital underline

Northwest Asia

Kazakhstan • Kyrgyzstan • Central Russia
Tajikistan • Turkmenistan • Uzbekistan

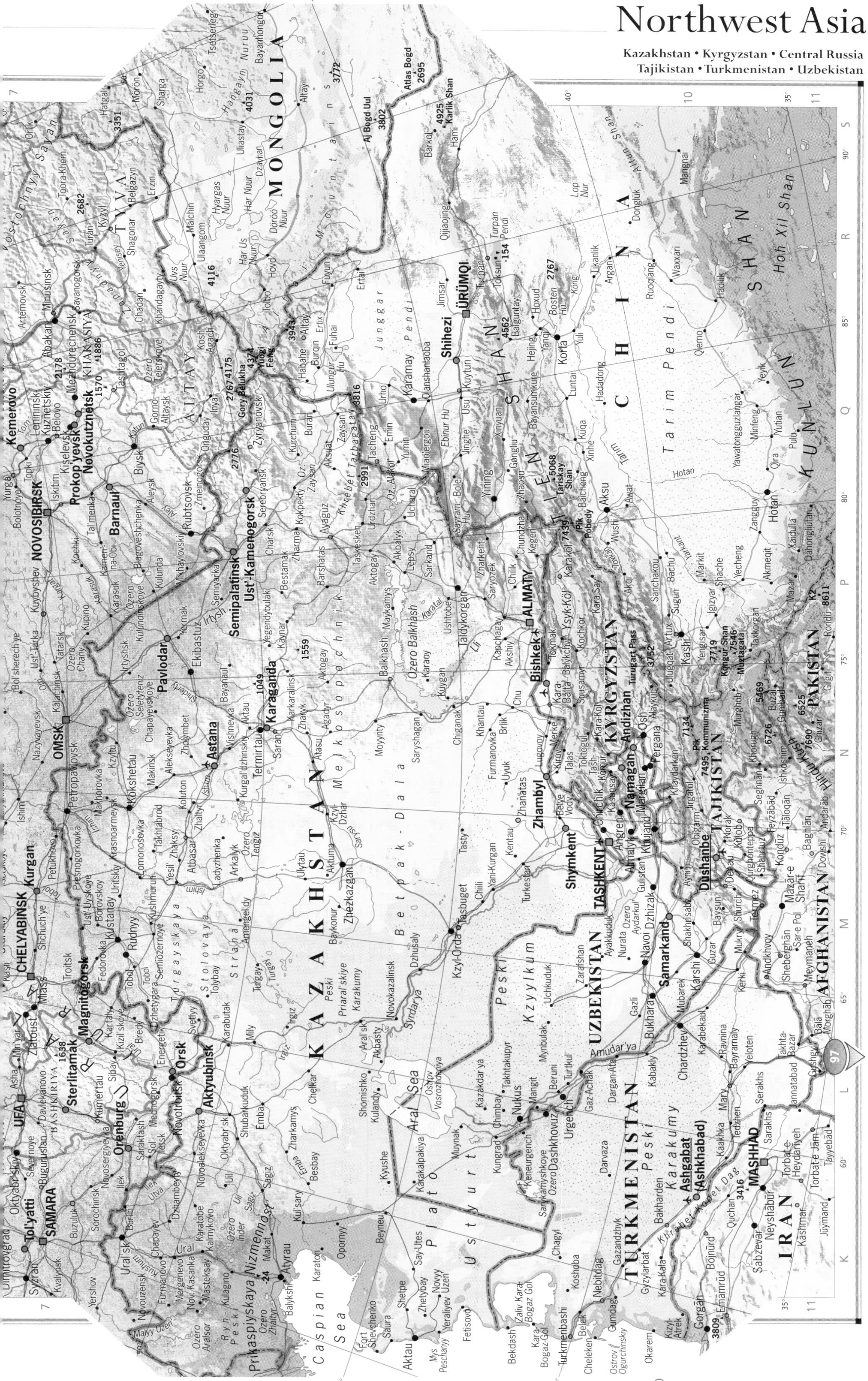

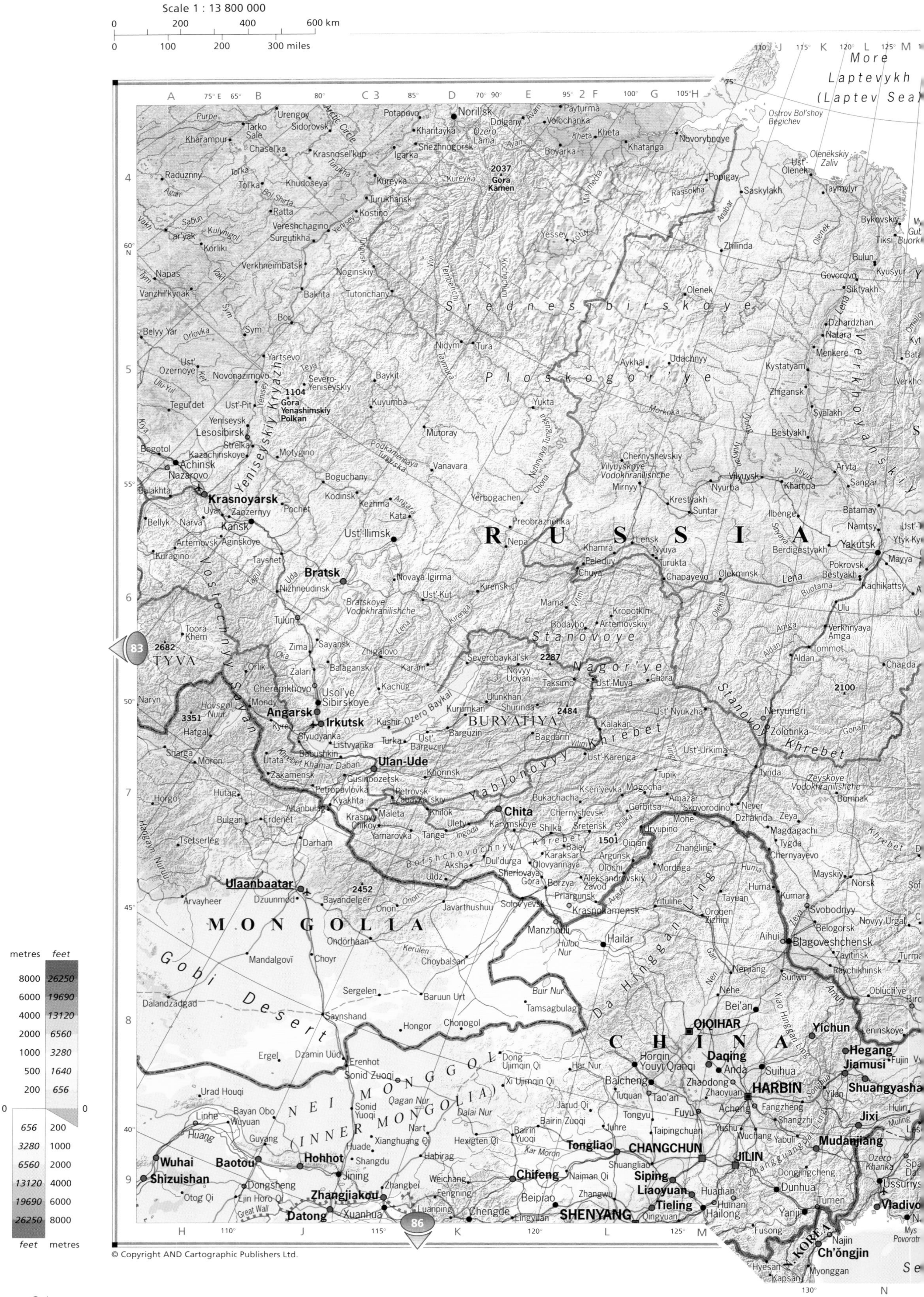
Scale 1 : 13 800 000
0 200 400 600 km
0 100 200 300 miles
More Laptevykh (Laptev Sea)
Ostrov Bol'shoy Begichev
Olenekskiy Zaliv
Norilsk
Dudinka
Urengoy
Tarko Sale
Kharampur
Igarka
Turukhansk
Khatanga
Popigay
Saskylakh
Zhilinda
Olenek
Sredne-Sibirskoye Ploskogor'ye
Verkhoyanskiy Khrebet
Udachnyy
Mirnyy
Vilyuysk
Yakutsk
Tura
Yenisey
Lesosibirsk
Yeniseysk
Achinsk
Nazarovo
Krasnoyarsk
Kansk
Bratsk
Ust'-Ilimsk
Bratskoye Vodokhranilishche
Tulun
Angarsk
Irkutsk
Usol'ye Sibirskoye
Vostochnyy Sayan
TYVA
Ozero Baykal
Severobaykal'sk
Stanovoye Nagor'ye
BURYATIYA
Ulan-Ude
Yablonovyy Khrebet
Chita
Stanovoy Khrebet
Neryungri
Tynda
Zeyskoye Vodokhranilishche
Skovorodino
Blagoveshchensk
R U S S I A
M O N G O L I A
Ulaanbaatar
Gobi Desert
Choybalsan
Sayshand
Dalandzadgad
Erenhot
Manzhouli
Hailar
Da Hinggan Ling
Xiao Hinggan Ling
C H I N A
QIQIHAR
Daqing
HARBIN
Yichun
Hegang
Jiamusi
Shuangyashan
Jixi
Mudanjiang
Jilin
CHANGCHUN
Siping
Liaoyuan
Tieling
SHENYANG
Tongliao
Chifeng
Chengde
NEI MONGGOL (INNER MONGOLIA)
Hohhot
Baotou
Wuhai
Shizuishan
Jining
Zhangjiakou
Datong
Great Wall
N. KOREA
Ch'ŏngjin
Vladivostok
Ussuriysk
83
86
metres feet
8000 26250
6000 19690
4000 13120
2000 6560
1000 3280
500 1640
200 656
0 0
656 200
3280 1000
6560 2000
13120 4000
19690 6000
26250 8000
feet metres

Northeast Asia

Mongolia • Eastern Russia

Q
R
S
T
U
V
W
X
Y 2
Z
AA 3
BB
145°
150°
155°
160°
165°
170°
175° E
180°
175° W
170°
165° W
65°
60°
55°
50°
45°
40°
4
5
6
7
8
9
Sibirskiye Ostrova
(New Siberia Islands)
Ostrov Novaya Sibir'
Ostrov Bol. Lyakhovskiy
Vostochno-Sibirskoye More
(East Siberian Sea)
Ostrov Vrangelya
Proliv Longa
Chukchi Sea
Arctic Circle
Bering Strait
Mys Dezhneva
Diomede Islands
King Island
ALASKA
(U.S.)
Enurmino
Uelen
Vankarem
Lavrentiya
Val'karay
Polyarnyy
Uvargin
Chukotskiy Poluostrov
Providenlya
Gambell
St. Lawrence Island
Mys Shelagskiy
1810
Chukotskiy Khrebet
Ostrov Ayon
Pevek
Palyavaam
Egvekinot
Zaliv Kresta
Nunligram
Ostrova Medvezh'i
Chaunskaya Guba
Mal. Baranikha
Ust' Chaun
Uel'kal
Anadyrskiy Zaliv
Mys Lopatka
Russoye Ust'ye
Tabor
Stanovaya
Ambarchik
1775
Bol. Osinovaya
Chokurdakh
Vstrechnyy
Bilibino
1504
Anadyrskaya
Ugol'nyye Kopi
Anadyr'
Cherskiy
Kolymskaya
Kolymskoye
Anyuysk
Nizmennost'
Beringovskiy
St. Matthew Island
Ozero Ozhogino
Ozhogino
Kolymskaya Nizmennost'
Chimchememel'
Otrozhnyy
1651
Mys Navarin
Markovo
Meynypil'gyno
Druzhina
Belaya Gora
Bur-Khaybyt
Sredenekolymsk
1465
Khatyrka
Suordakh
Yukagirskoye Ploskogor'ye
Shcherbakovo
Ayanka
Penzhina
2562
Gora Ledyanaya
Bering Sea
Khonuu
Yugo-Tala
Ugol'naya Zyryanka
Zyryanka
Dzhigudzhak
Mikino
Ust' Penzhino
Tylkhoy
Achayvayam
Gora Pobeda
3147
Khrebet Cherskogo
Adycha
Ust'-Nera
El'ginskiy
Artyk
1374
Dukat
Seymchan
Omsukchan
Gizhiga
Nayakhan
Penzhinskiy Khrebet
Koryakskiy Khrebet
Pakhachi
Olyutorskiy
Mys Olyutorskiy
Olyutorskiy Zaliv
Tilichiki
Korf
Khudzhakh
Tomtor
Susuman
Debin
Orotukan
Strelka
Pik Aborigen
2586
Talaya
Penzhinskaya Guba
Gizhiginskaya Guba
Il'pyrskiy
Mys Govena
Karaginskiy Zaliv
Ossora
Ostrov Karaginskiy
Khrebet Suntar Khayata
2959
Ust'-omchug
Atka
Ugulan
Zaliv Shelikhova
Palana
Kolyma
Kolymskiy Khrebet
1385
Palatka
Yamsk
Mys Tolstoy
Magadan
Talon
Okurchan
Mys Alevina
Arka
Okhotsk
Ulya
Maya
Mys Enkan
Ayan
Dzhugdzhur
Mys Yuzhnyy
Ust'-Khayryuzovo
Mys Sivuchiy
Komandorskiye Ostrova
Nikol'skoye
Ostrov Beringa
Ostrov Mednyy
Aleutian Islands
(U.S.)
Attu Island
Buldir Island
Cape Wrangell
Agattu Island
Klyuchi
Ust'-Kamchatsk
4750
Klyuchevskaya Sopka
Kamchatskiy Zaliv
KAMCHATKA
Atlasovo
Ust'-Sopochnoye
Sredinnyy Khrebet
Mil'kovo
Kronotskiy Zaliv
3456
Yelizovo
Petropavlovsk-Kamchatskiy
Shantarskiye Ostrova
Ostrov Bol. Shantar
Mys Elizavety
Poluostrov Shmidta
Okha
Sakhalinskiy Zaliv
Litke
Mago
Bol. Vlas'evo
Takht
Nikolayevsk-na-Amure
Oktyabr'skiy
Sea of Okhotsk
Ozernovskiy
Mys Lopatka
Ostrov Shumshu
Ostrov Atlasova
Severo-Kuril'sk
Ostrov Paramushir
Bogorodskoye
Lazarev
Nogliki
Sofiysk
De-Kastri
Ostrov Onekotan
1609
Komsomol'sk-na-Amure
Aleksandrov-Sakhalinskiy
Sakhalin
Proliv Tatarskiy
Gurskoye
Smirnykh
Poronaysk
Ostrov Shiashkotan
Kuril'skiye Ostrova
(Kuril Islands)
Shakhtërsk
Uglegorsk
Zaliv Terpeniya
Mys Terpeniya
Vanino
2078
Makarov
Ostrov Rasshua
PACIFIC
OCEAN
Ostrov Simushir
Tomari
Dolinsk
Nel'ma
Chekhov
Yuzhno-Sakhalinsk
Kholmsk
Korsakov
Ostrov Urup
Svetlaya
Zaliv Aniva
Mys Kril'on
Mys Aniva
Kuril'sk
La Pérouse Strait
Rebun-tō
Rishiri-tō
Wakkanai
Ostrov Iturup
Shiretoko-misaki
Monbetsu
Ostrov Kunashir
Shikotan-tō
Habomai-shoto
Asahikawa
2290
Kitami
Takikawa
Asahi-dake
Nemuro
Pristan'
Otaru
Obihiro
Kushiro
SAPPORO
Tomakomai
Hokkaidō
Oshamambe
Hiroo
Okushiri-tō
Muroran
Erimo-misaki
Esan-misaki
Hakodate
Mutsu
Tsugaru-kaikyō
JAPAN
P
140°
Q
145°
R 150°
S
155°
T
160°
U

over 3 million

1 – 3 million

250 000 – 1 million

100 000 – 250 000

25 000 – 100 000

under 25 000

country capital underline

state or province capital underline

Scale 1 : 11 600 000

0 200 400 600 km

0 100 200 300 miles

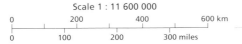

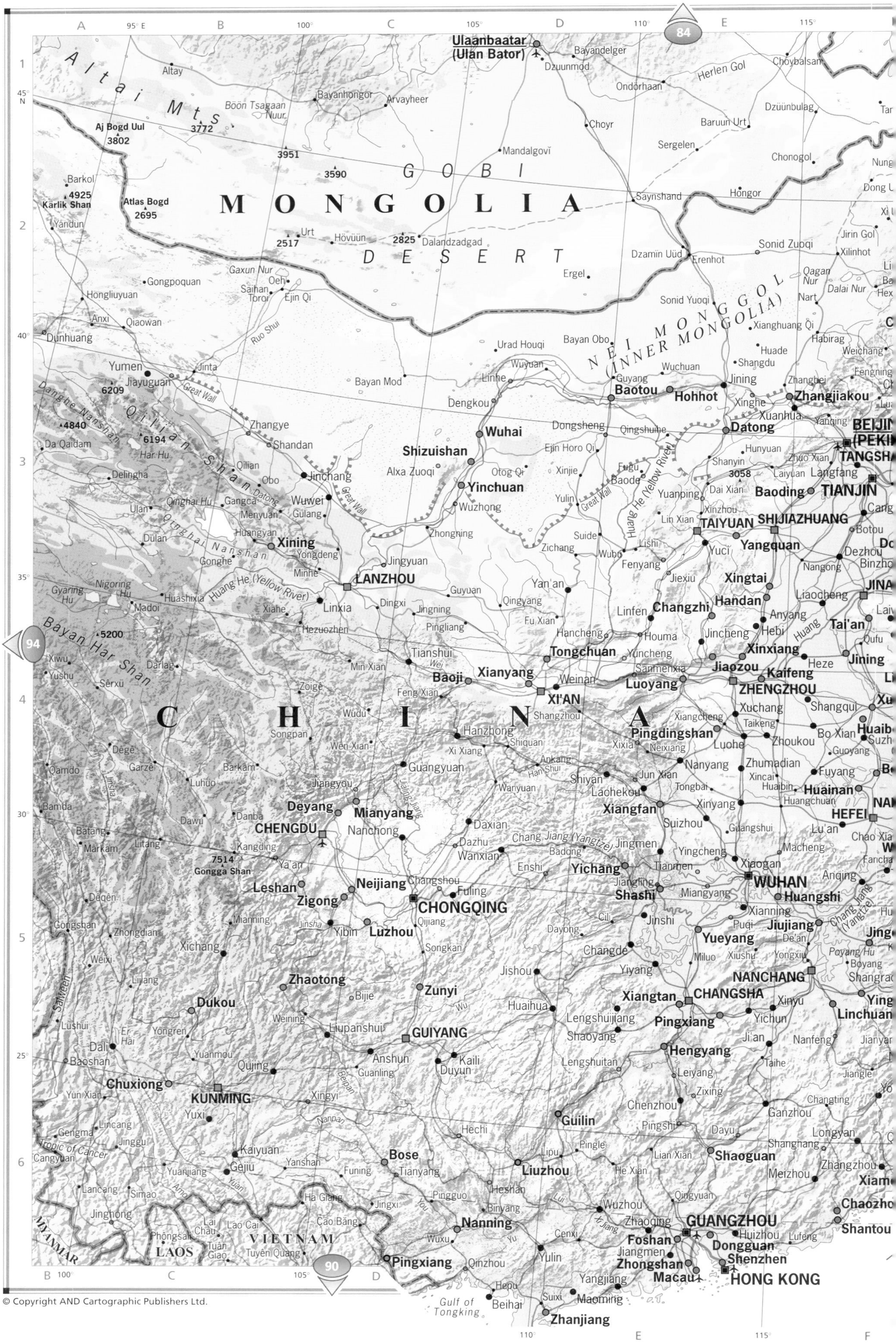

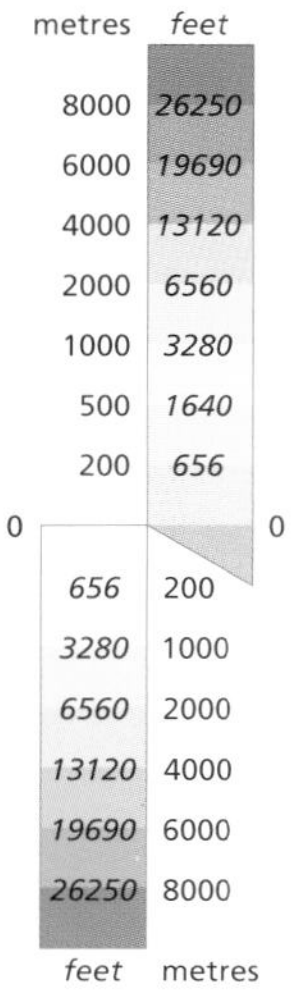

Eastern China

Eastern China • Japan
North Korea • South Korea • Taiwan

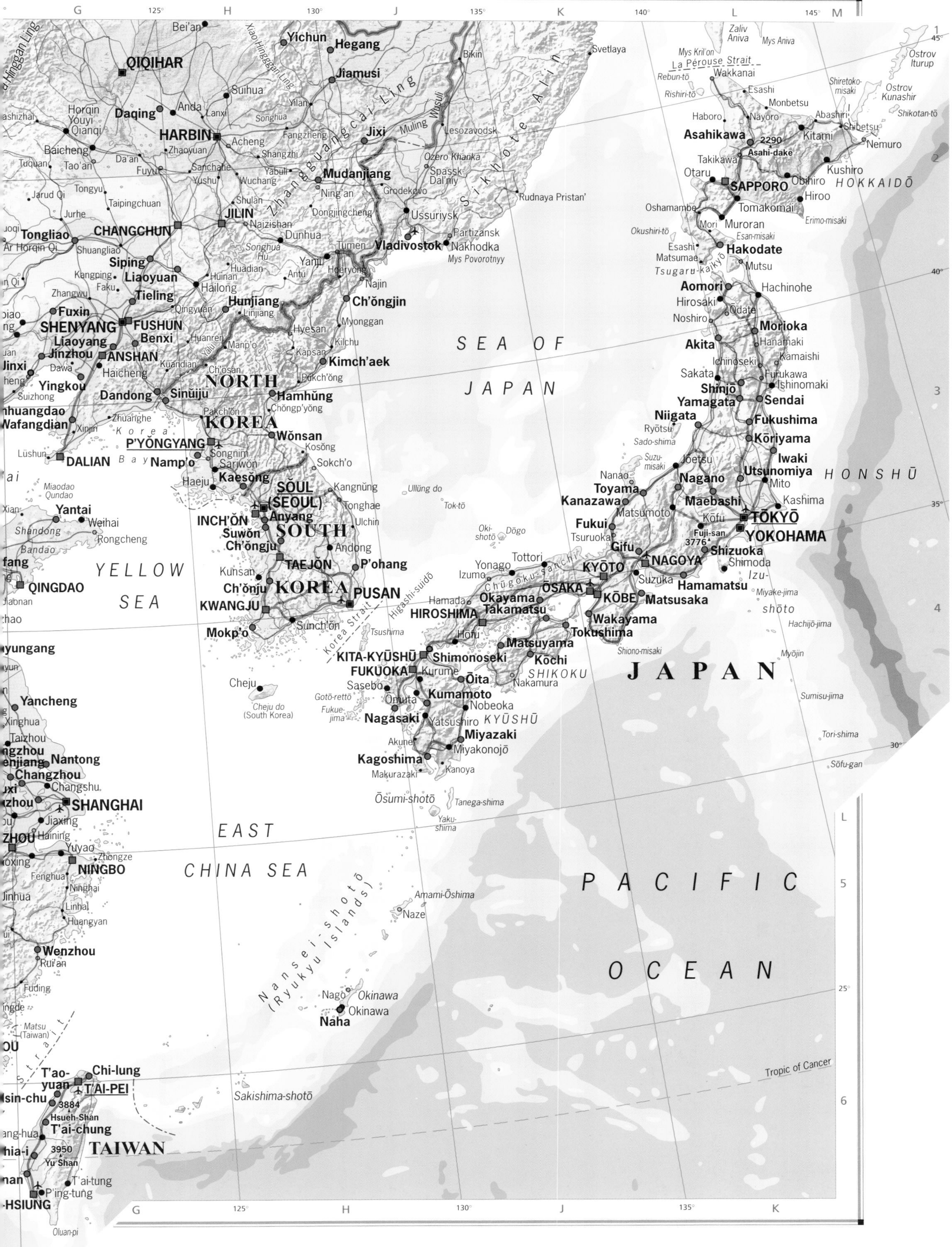

- ■ over 3 million
- ■ 1 – 3 million
- ● 250 000 – 1 million
- ● 100 000 – 250 000
- ○ 25 000 – 100 000
- • under 25 000
- —— country capital underline

Scale 1 : 5 800 000

0 100 200 300 km

0 50 100 150 miles

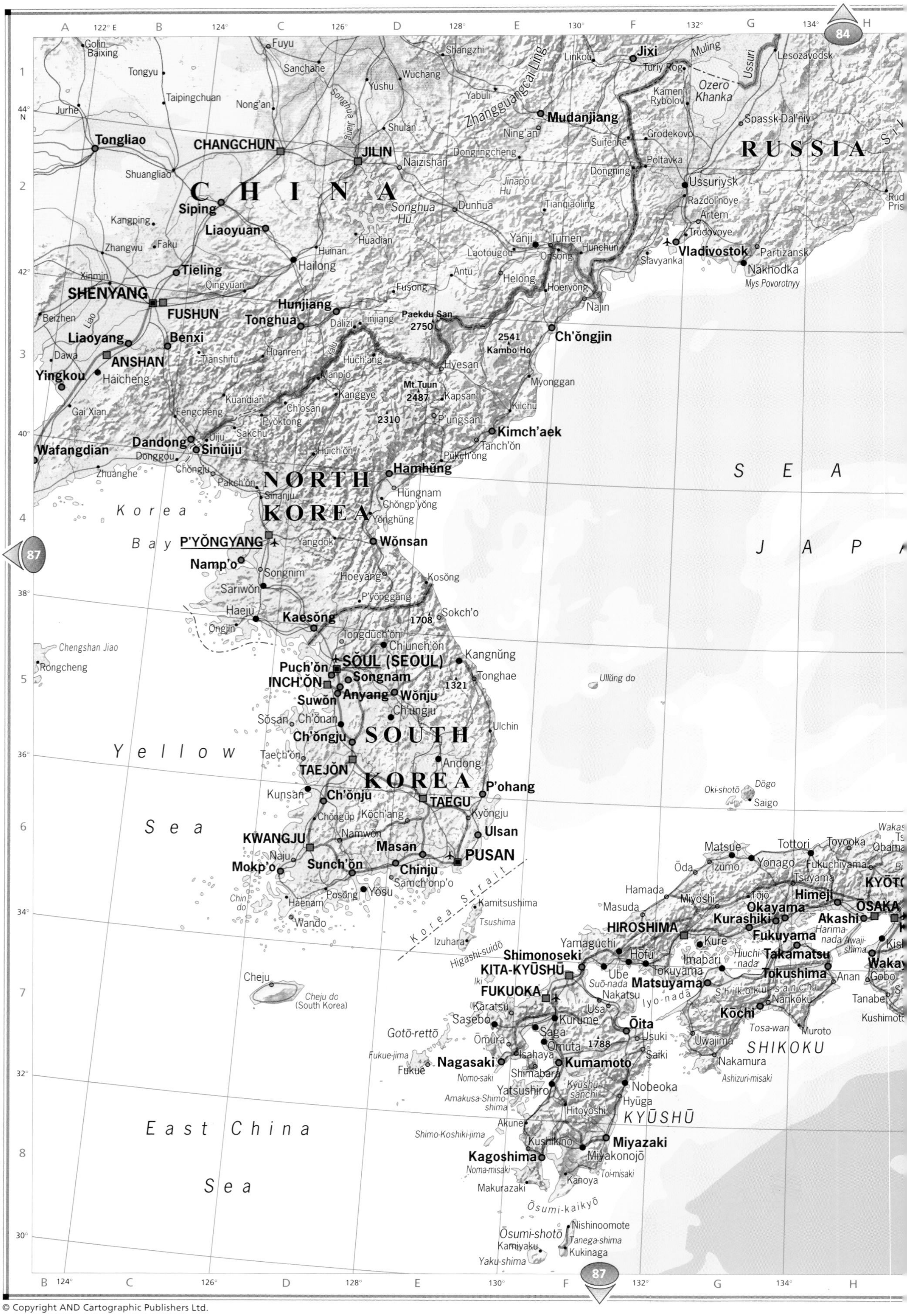

CHINA
RUSSIA
NORTH KOREA
SOUTH KOREA
Korea Bay
Yellow Sea
East China Sea
SEA OF JAPAN
Korea Strait
P'YŎNGYANG
SŎUL (SEOUL)
CHANGCHUN
SHENYANG
JILIN
FUSHUN
ANSHAN
Tongliao
Siping
Liaoyuan
Tieling
Hunjiang
Tonghua
Benxi
Liaoyang
Yingkou
Haicheng
Dandong
Sinŭiju
Wafangdian
Mudanjiang
Jixi
Ussuriysk
Vladivostok
Nakhodka
Ch'ŏngjin
Kimch'aek
Hamhŭng
Wŏnsan
Namp'o
Sariwŏn
Haeju
Kaesŏng
Kangnŭng
Puch'ŏn
INCH'ŎN
Songnam
Suwŏn
Anyang
Wŏnju
Ch'ŏngju
Ch'ŏnan
TAEJŎN
Andong
P'ohang
Ch'ŏnju
Kunsan
TAEGU
Ulsan
PUSAN
Masan
Chinju
KWANGJU
Mokp'o
Sunch'ŏn
Yŏsu
Cheju
Cheju do (South Korea)
Paekdu San 2750
Ullŭng do
Tsushima
Oki-shotō
SHIKOKU
KYŪSHŪ
HIROSHIMA
KITA-KYŪSHŪ
FUKUOKA
Shimonoseki
Nagasaki
Kumamoto
Kagoshima
Miyazaki
Ōita
Matsuyama
Kōchi
Takamatsu
Tokushima
Okayama
Kurashiki
Fukuyama
Himeji
Akashi
ŌSAKA
KYŌTO
Matsue
Tottori
Yonago
Ōsumi-shotō
Yaku-shima
Tanega-shima
Gotō-rettō

metres feet

metres	feet
8000	26250
6000	19690
4000	13120
2000	6560
1000	3280
500	1640
200	656
0	0
656	200
3280	1000
6560	2000
13120	4000
19690	6000
26250	8000

feet metres

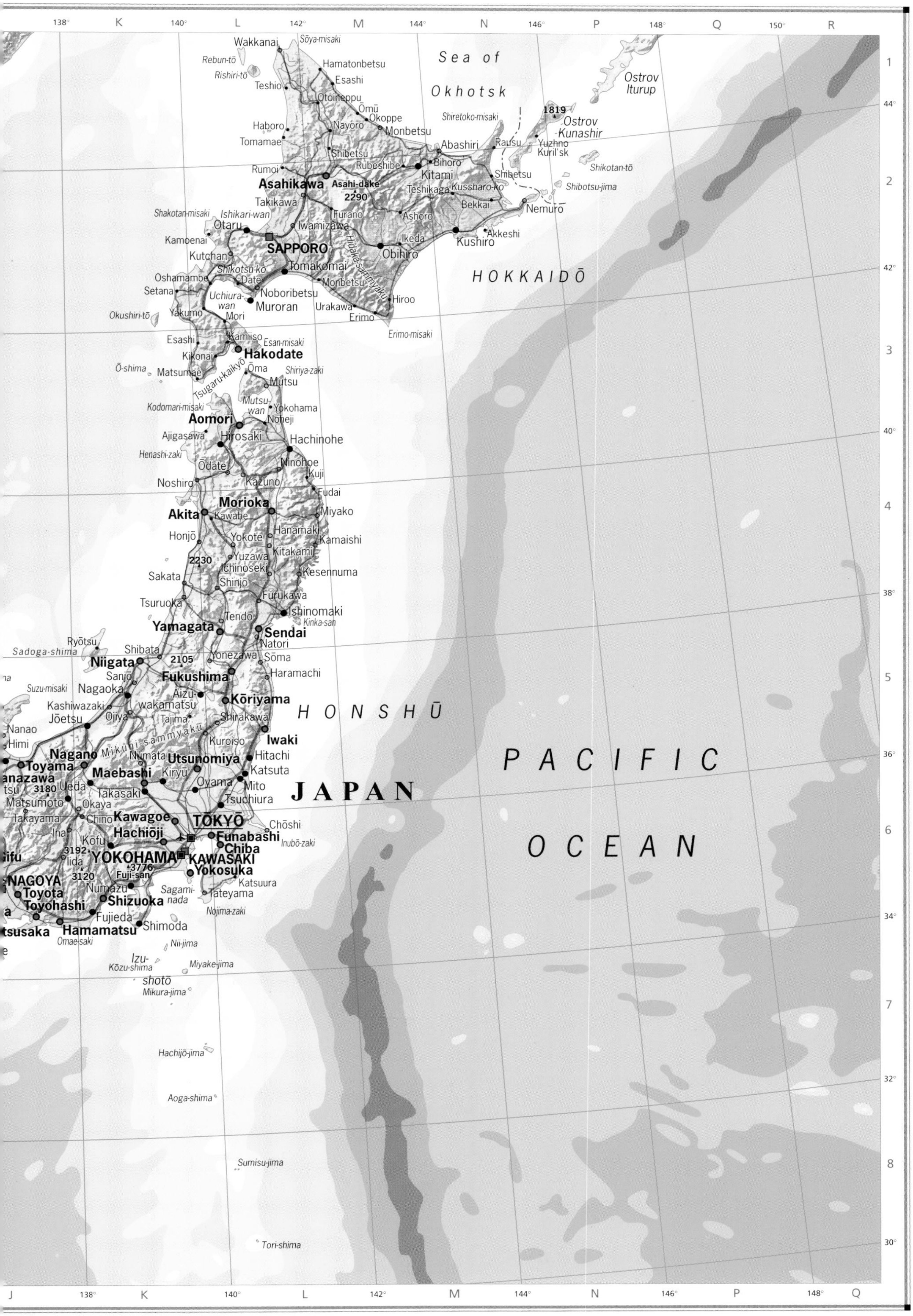

Japan • North Korea • South Korea

■ over 3 million	● 100 000 – 250 000	—— country capital underline
■ 1 – 3 million	○ 25 000 – 100 000	
● 250 000 – 1 million	• under 25 000	

Scale 1 : 11 600 000

0   200   400   600 km
0   100   200   300 miles

BHUTAN
Tashigang
Hápoli
Barpeta
Goalpara
Nagaon
Guwahati
Shillong
Dimapur
Sylhet
Silchar
Bhairab
Bazar
Agartala
Aizawl
Tropic of Cancer
Comilla
Karnafuli
Feni
Reservoir
CHITTAGONG
Rangamati
BANGLADESH
Cox's
Bazar
Teknaf
Sittwe
Paletwa 3053
Mt. Victoria
Kyaukpyu
Ramree Island
Cheduba Island
Sandoway
Kyeintali

Dibrugarh
Tinsukia
Itanagar
Brahmaputra
Jorhat
Golaghat
Nagaon
Kohima
Imphal
Mawlaik
Haka
Kalemyo
Kalewa
Kanbalu
Monywa
Mabein
Shwebo
Mogok
MANDALAY
Amarapura
Kyaukse
Myingyan
Chauk
Mong Yai
Meiktila
Kunhing
Magwe
Minbu
Taungdwingyi
Wan Hsa-la
Sinbaungwe
Lewe
Loikaw
Taungup
Pyè
Zigon
Letpadan
Henzada
Pathein
Insein
Myaungmya
**YANGON
(RANGOON)**
Cape
Negrais
Bogale
Labutta
Mouths of
the Irrawaddy

INDIA
Pangin
Zayu
Tazungdam
Gongshan
Dégén
Putao
Tabong
Maingkwan
Myitkyina
Mogaung
Hopin
Bhamo
Katha
Wandingzhen
Mong Yu
Hsweni
Lashio
Mong Kung
Kengtung
Muang
Sing
Muang
Xai
Chiang
Rai
Mae Hong Son
Chiang Mai
Siri
Kit
Dam
Lampang
Nan
Mae Sariang
Uttaradit

**MYANMAR
(BURMA)**

95° E
Zhongdian
Weixi
Lijiang
Lushui
Dali
Baoshan
Yun Xian
Lincang
Gengma
Cangyuan
Simao
Jinghong
Lancang
Mong Yai
Louang
Namtha
Phôngsali
Ban
Ban
Louangphrabang
Xiangkhoang
Viangchan
(Vientiane)
Chiang
Khan
Loei
Nong Khai
Udon Thani
Sakhon Nakhon
Chum
Phae
Khon Kaen
Roi Et
Khemmarat

100°
Xichang
Dukou
Weining
Liupanshui
Yuanmou
KUNMING
Chuxiong
Qujing
Kaiyuan
Gejiu
Yuanjiang
Lai
Chau
Tuan Giao
Son La
Mộc Chau
Xam Nua
Muang
Khoua
Tuyên Quang
Thai Nguyen
Việt Tri
**HA NỘI
(HANOI)**
Hòn Gai
HAI PHONG
Ninh Binh
Nam Dinh
Thanh Hoa
Vinh
Ha Tinh
Đông Hôi
Muang
Khammouan
Muang
Phin
Savannakhet
Mukdahan
Ban
M. Khôngxédôn

C
Zunyi
Wu
GUIYANG
Anshun
Duyun
Kaili
Bijie
Huaihua
Nanpan
You
Nanning
Wuxu
Qinzhou
Bose
Heshan
Hechi
Pingguo
Binyang
Pingxiang
Cao Bằng
Lang Son
Tiên Yen
Gulf of
Tongking
Dongfang
Hôi An
Da Nẵng
Quang Tri
Huê

LAOS
Mekong
Mae Nam Mun

THAILAND
Sara Buri
Ayutthaya
**KRUNG THEP
(BANGKOK)**
Rat Buri
Phet
Buri
Samut Songkhram
Bight
of
Bangkok
Pattaya
Rayong
Chanthaburi
Ban Hua Hin
Ko Chang
Prachuap Khiri Khan
Bang Saphan Yai
Chumphon
Kawthaung
Ranong
Takua Pa
Surat Thani
Ko Samui
Krabi
Nakhon Si Thammarat
Phuket
Thung Song
Phatthalung
Trang
Thale
Luang
Songkhla
Ban Hat Yai
Pattani
Satun
Langkawi
Narathiwat
Kangar
Yala
Kota Bharu
Alor Setar
Ban Betong
Sungei Petani
Gerik
Kuala Kerai
George Town
G. Korbu
Kuala Terengganu
Pinang
2182
Taiping
Dungun
Kemasik
MALA
Ipoh
Kuala Lipis
Malay
Kuantan
Peninsula
Bentong
Temerloh
KUALA LUMPUR
Seremban
Melaka
Segamat
Mersing
Muar
Keluang
Batu Pahat
Johor Bahru
SINGAPORE
SINGAPORE

Phitsanulok
Phichit
Chaiyaphum
Nakhon
Sawan
Chainat
**Nakhon
Ratchasima**
Surin
Det Udom
Ubon
Ratchathani
Pakxé
Suwannaphum
M. Khôngxédôn
Attapu
Virôchey
Stoeng Treng
Kon
Tum
Play Cu
Qui Nh
VIETNAM
Quang Ng
Sisôphôn
Siĕmréab
Bătdâmbâng
Tônlé Sap
Phumĭ Sâmraông M. Khôn
CAMBODIA
Kâmpóng Chhnăng
Krông Kaôh Kŏng
Phnum Penh
Kâmpôt
Sihanoukville
Dao Phu Quôc
Long Xuyên
Rach Gia
Cân Tho
Bac Liêu
Ca Mau
Nam Can
Côn Son
Mouths of
the Mekong
Kâmpóng Cham
Kra Khmau
Tay Ninh
Chon Thanh
Biên Hoa
**HÔ CHI MINH
(SAIGON)**
My Tho
Vung Tau
Da Lat
Bao Lôc
**Buôn Mê
Thuôt**
Phan Rar
Nha T
Cam R
Ninh Ho
Phan Thiêt
Tuy Ho

Bay of
Bengal

Gulf of
Martaban

Preparis North Channel

Preparis South Channel

Preparis Island

Coco Channel

Coco Island

North Andaman

Andaman Islands
(India)

Middle Andaman

Ritchie's
Archipelago

South Andaman
Port Blair

Duncan Passage

Little Andaman

Ten Degree Channel

Car Nicobar

Andaman

Sea

Katchall

Nicobar Islands
(India)

Little
Nicobar

Great
Nicobar

Távoy

Palaw

Mergui

Mergui

Archipelago

Bight

Gulf

of

Thailand

Sabang

Banda Aceh

Bireun

Lhokseumawe

Takengon

Langsa

Meulaboh

SUMATERA
(SUMATRA)

3145
Gunung Leuser

MEDAN

Tebingtinggi

Bagun Datuk

Sibigo

Danau Toba

Pematangsiantar

Prapat

OCEAN

Simeulue

Sinabang

Singkilbaru

Balige

Danau Toba

Bagansiapiapi

Kotapinang

Dumai

INDONESIA

Nias

Gunungsitoli

Sibolga

Barus

Balai

Duri

Strait of Malacca

INDIAN

Laut

Natuna Besar

Panarik

Kepulauan
Natuna

Jemaja

Kepulauan
Anambas

(Indonesia)

Subi Besar

Pemangkat

Sambas

Tanjung
Datu

Siluas

95° E

100°

105°

metres | feet
8000 | 26250
6000 | 19690
4000 | 13120
2000 | 6560
1000 | 3280
500 | 1640
200 | 656
0 | 0
656 | 200
3280 | 1000
6560 | 2000
13120 | 4000
19690 | 6000
26250 | 8000

feet | metres

95

92

© Copyright AND Cartographic Publishers Ltd.

A   B   C   D

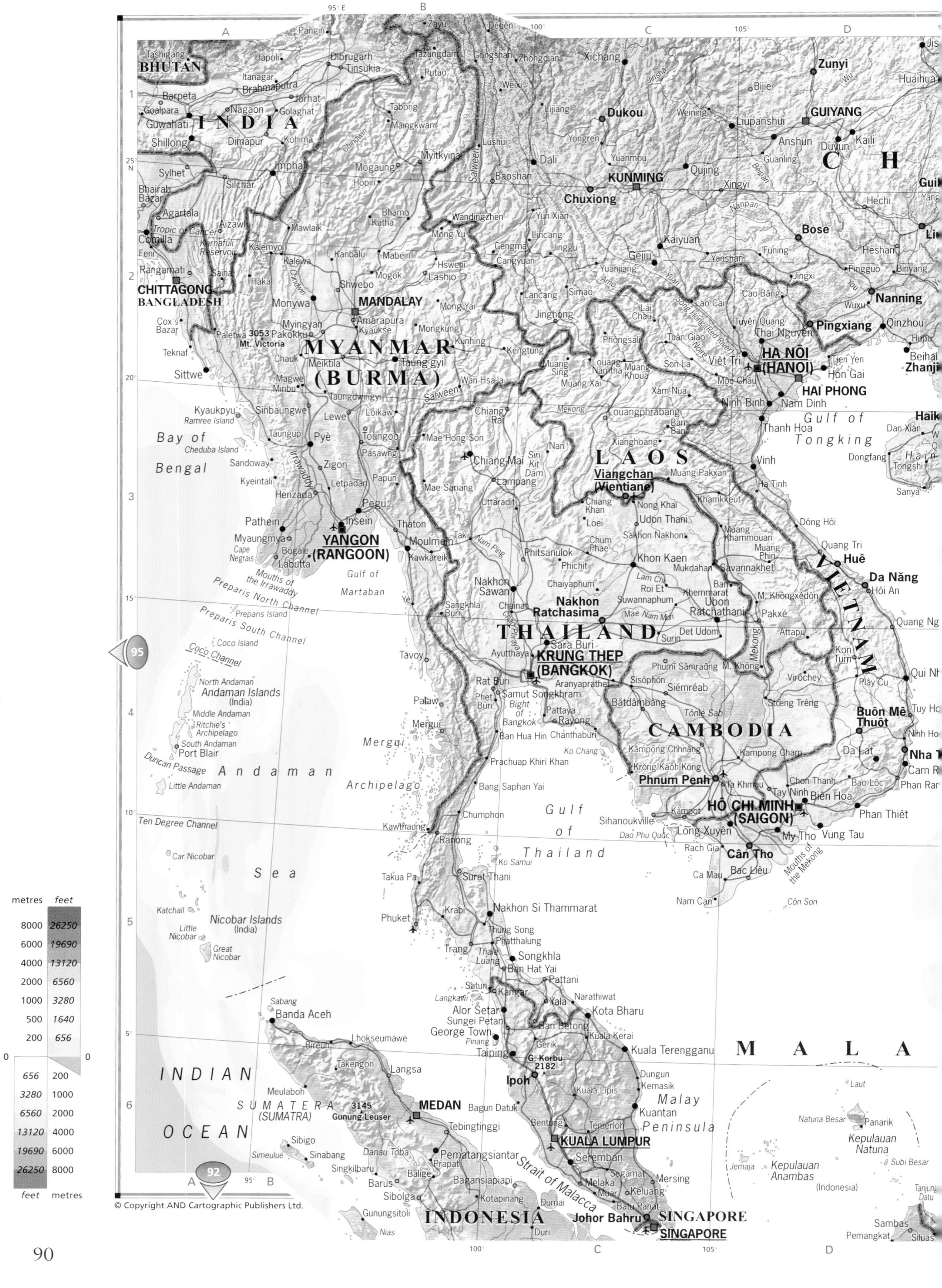

Southeast Asia

Cambodia • Laos • Myanmar (Burma)
Philippines • Thailand • Vietnam

E
115°
F
120°
G
125°
H
130°
J
1
2
3
4
5
6
25°
20°
15°
10°
5°
CHANGSHA
Xinyu
Yichun
Pingxiang
Linchuan
Shangrao
Pucheng
Wenzhou
Fuding
Hengyang
Ji'an
Taihe
Jiangle
Nanping
Ningde
Leiyang
Zixing
Chenzhou
Ganzhou
Changting
Yong'an
Matsu (Taiwan)
FUZHOU
Putian
Longyan
Quanzhou
Shaoguan
Meizhou
Zhangzhou
Chinmen (Taiwan)
Xiamen
Qingyuan
Chaozhou
Shantou
GUANGZHOU
Huizhou
Lufeng
Shanwei
Dongguan
Foshan
Jiangmen
Shenzhen
Zhongshan
Macau
HONG KONG
Yangjiang
Taiwan Strait
T'ao-yuan
Chi-lung
T'AI-PEI
Hsin-chu
3884
Hsueh-Shan
T'ai-chung
Chang-hua
Chia-i
3950
Yu Shan
TAIWAN
T'ai-nan
T'ai-tung
KAO-HSIUNG
P'ing-tung
Oluan-pi
EAST CHINA SEA
Nansei-shotō (Ryukyu Islands)
Nago
Okinawa
Naha
JAPAN
Sakishima-shotō
Tropic of Cancer
Luzon Strait
Batan Islands
Basco
Dongsha Qundao (Pratas) (China)
PACIFIC OCEAN
Balintang Channel
Babuyan Islands
Bangui
Claveria
San Vicente
Laoag
Aparri
Kabugao
Lal-lo
Vigan
Bangued
Tuguegarao
Santa Cruz
Luzon
Palanan
San Fernando
Bontoc
Ilagan
Mt. Pulog
2929
Baguio
Santiago
Alaminos
Dagupan
Casiguran
Lingayen
San Carlos
Baler
Tarlac
Cabanatuan
Angeles
Gapan
Paracel Islands
SOUTH CHINA SEA
Olongapo
Polillo Is.
QUEZON CITY
MANILA
Calagua Is.
Pasig
San Pablo
Daet
Pandan
Nasugbu
Calauag
Catanduanes
Batangas
Lucena
Lopez
Naga
Boac
Virac
Mamburao
Calapan
Pascual
Legaspi
Mindoro
2488
Pinamalayan
Sorsogon
Mount Baco
Bulan
Catarman
Mindoro Strait
Masbate
Samar
Allen
San Pedro
Calbayog
Calamian Group
Coron
Nabas
Placer
Catbalogan
Borongan
Kalibo
Roxas
Tacloban
El Nido
Panay
Bogo
Ormoc
Iloilo
Bacolod
Leyte
San Jose de Buenavista
Cebu
Sogod
Libjo
Bago
Maasin
Dinagat
Spratly Islands
Roxas
Carcar
Cebu
Talibon
Bohol
Surigao
Dapa
Palawan
Cauayan
Bais
Tagbilaran
Madrid
Puerto Princesa
Negros
Dumaguete
Butuan
Tandag
Quezon
PHILIPPINES
Prosperidad
Dipolog
Cagayan de Oro
Brooke's Point
Manukan
2560
Iligan
Malaybalay
Bislig
Liloy
Mindanao
Tagum
Sulu Sea
Bugsuk
Balabac
Pagadian
Davao
Balabac Strait
Sibuco
Cotabato
Mati
Zamboanga
2954
Mt. Apo
Kudat
Moro Gulf
Isabela
Tacurong
Cape San Agustin
Polomolok
General Santos
Langkon
Kota Belud
4094
G. Kinabalu
Ranau
Basilan
Palimbang
Pangutaran Group
Jolo
Sandakan
Kota Kinabalu
Jolo
Glan
Sarangani Is.
SABAH
Beaufort
Lahad Datu
Tungku
Tawitawi
Sulu Archipelago
Kepulauan Nanusa
Bandar Seri Begawan
Bongao
Kepulauan Karkaralong
Beo
Seria
BRUNEI
Kalabakan
Semporna
Kepulauan Talaud
Gunung Mulu
2371
Bareo
Tawau
Celebes Sea
Sangir
Tahuna
INDONESIA
Kepulauan Sangir
Morotai
Tarakan
Bintulu
Belaga
2499
Tanjungselor
Daruba
Molucca Sea
SARAWAK
Tanjungredeb
93
INDONESIA
Kapit
2988
KALIMANTAN
Sepinang
Sangkulirang
Muarawahau

■ over 3 million	● 100 000 – 250 000	country capital underline
■ 1 – 3 million	○ 25 000 – 100 000	
● 250 000 – 1 million	• under 25 000	

Scale 1 : 11 600 000

0 200 400 600 km

0 100 200 300 miles

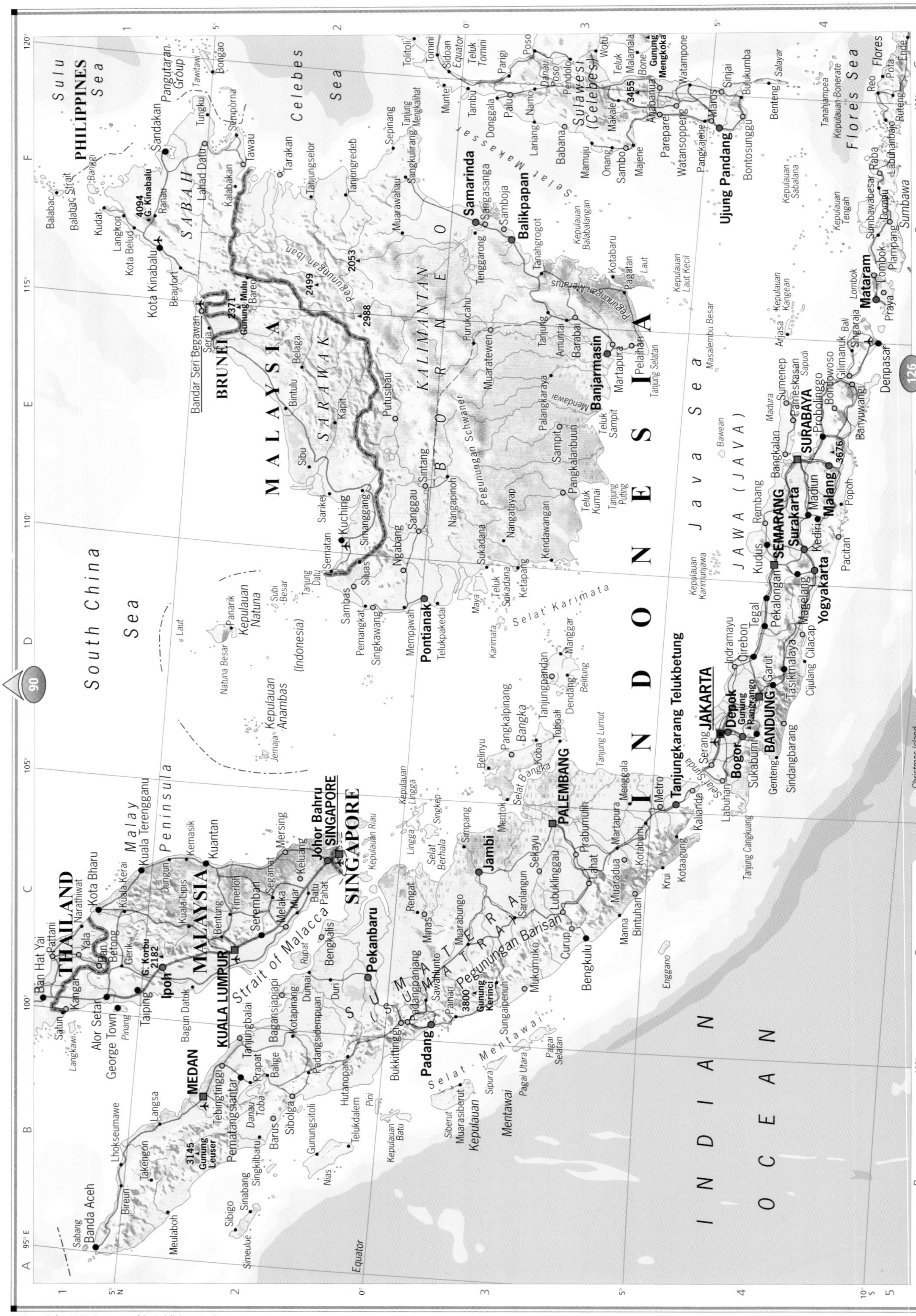

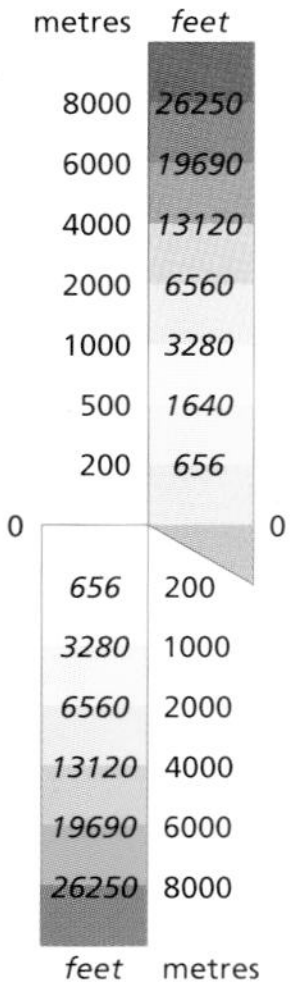

Malaysia and Indonesia

Brunei • Indonesia • Malaysia • Singapore

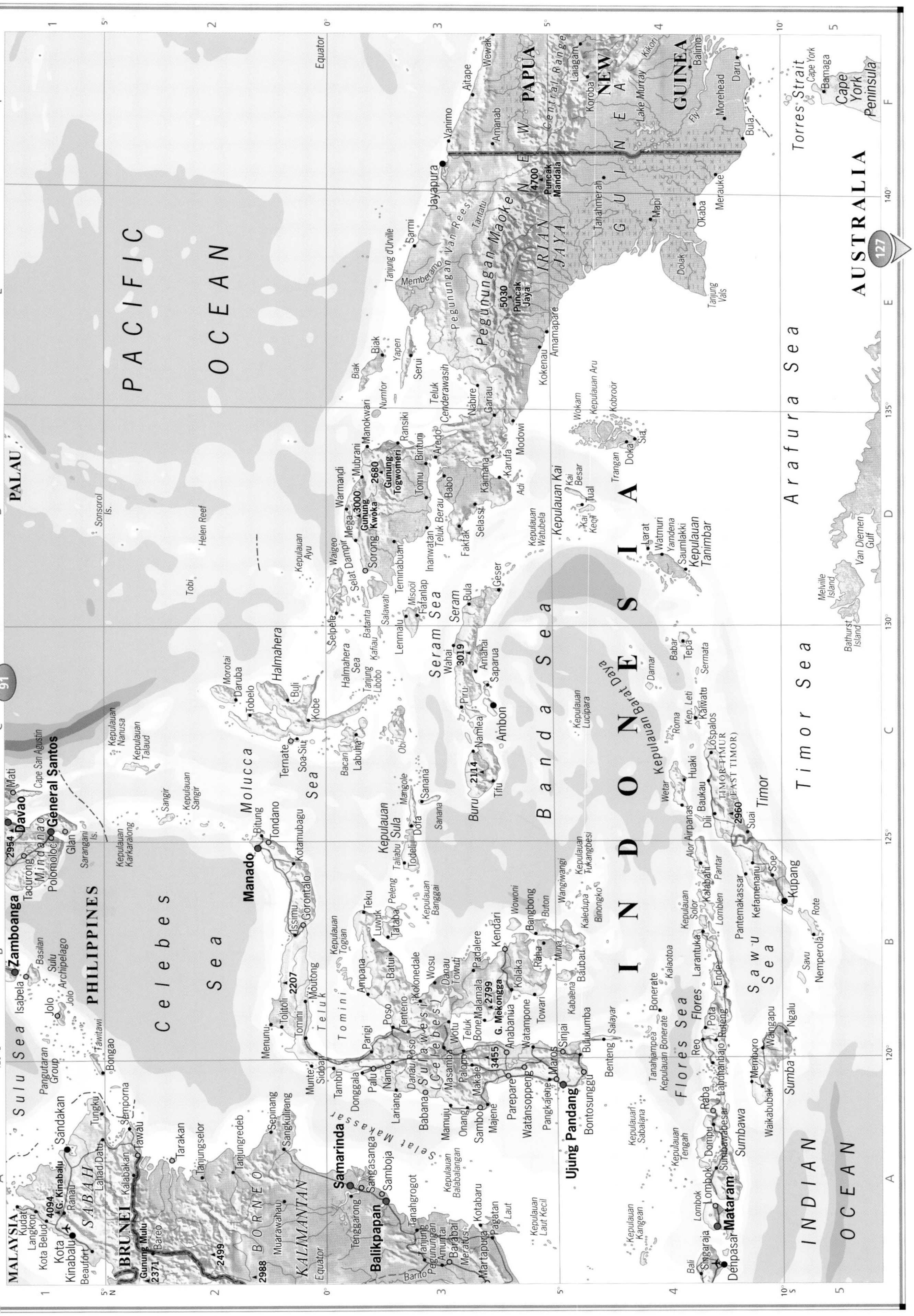

■ over 3 million	● 100 000 – 250 000
■ 1 – 3 million	○ 25 000 – 100 000
● 250 000 – 1 million	• under 25 000
—— country capital underline	

Scale 1 : 11 600 000

0 200 400 600 km

0 100 200 300 miles

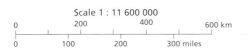

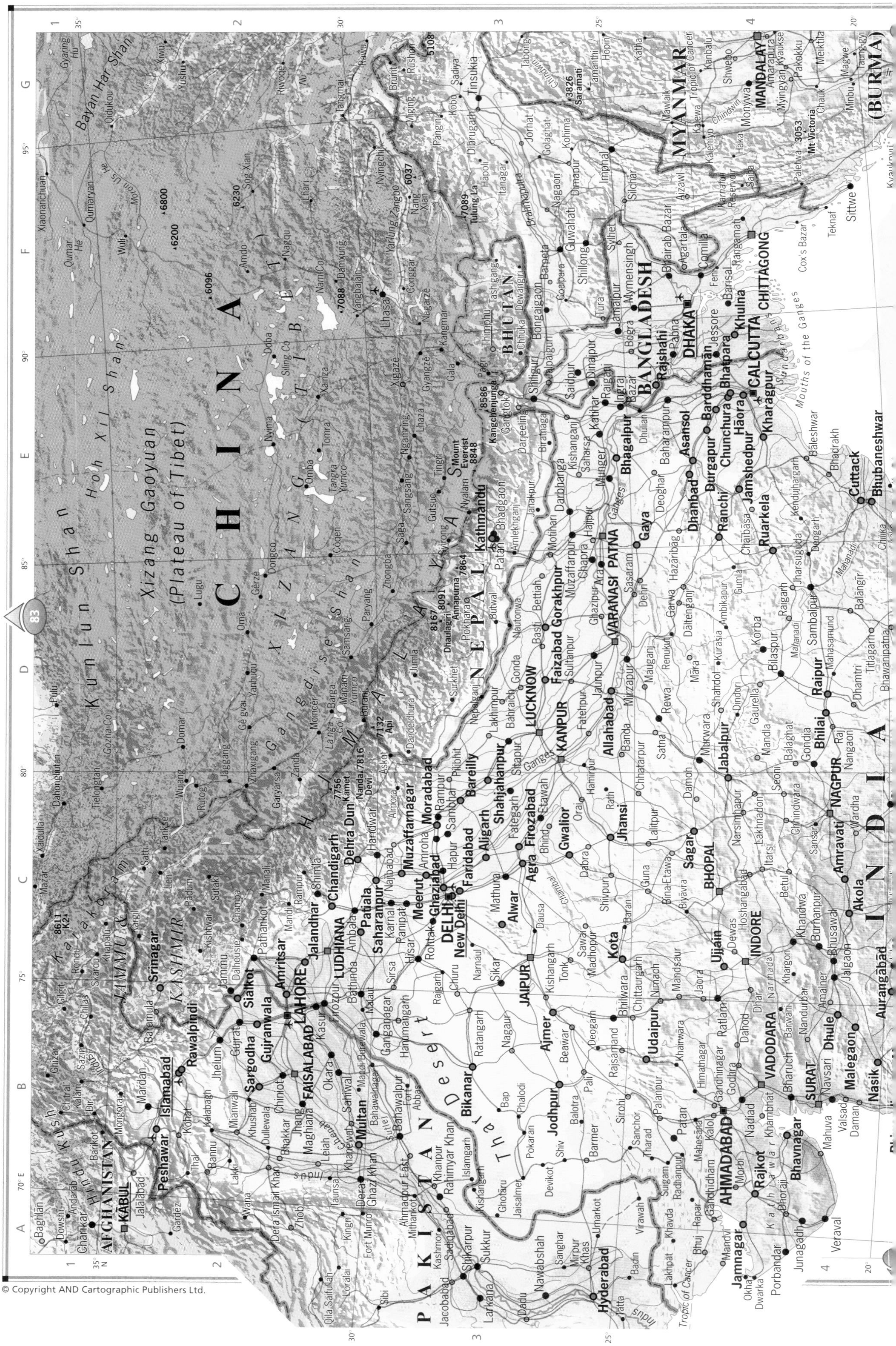

metres	feet
8000	26250
6000	19690
4000	13120
2000	6560
1000	3280
500	1640
200	656
0	0
656	200
3280	1000
6560	2000
13120	4000
19690	6000
26250	8000
feet	metres

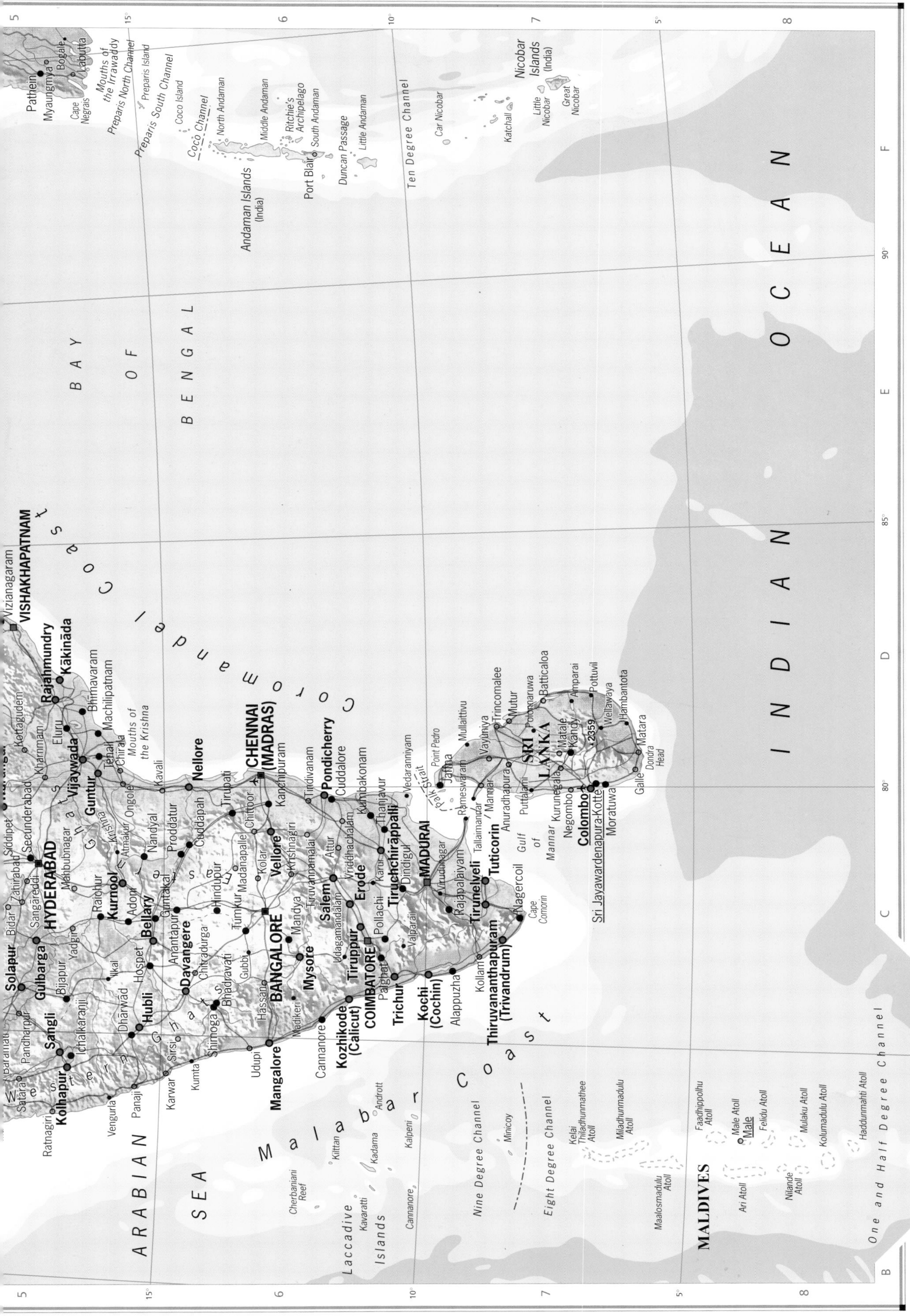

■ over 3 million
■ 1 – 3 million
● 250 000 – 1 million
• 100 000 – 250 000
○ 25 000 – 100 000
• under 25 000
—— country capital underline

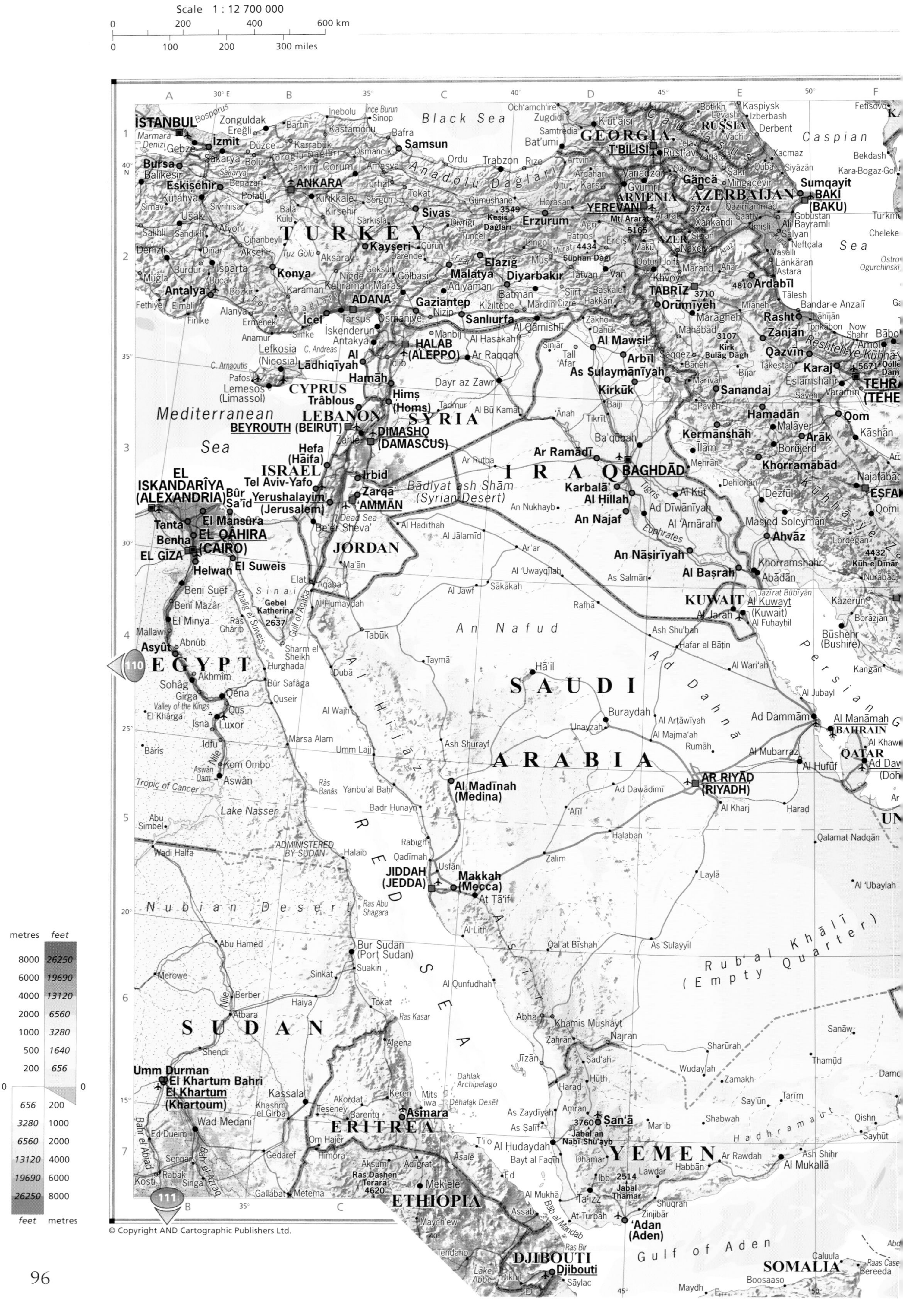
Scale 1 : 12 700 000
0 200 400 600 km
0 100 200 300 miles
Black Sea
Caspian Sea
Mediterranean Sea
Red Sea
Persian Gulf
Gulf of Aden
TURKEY
GEORGIA
ARMENIA
AZERBAIJAN
RUSSIA
CYPRUS
SYRIA
LEBANON
ISRAEL
JORDAN
IRAQ
KUWAIT
SAUDI ARABIA
BAHRAIN
QATAR
EGYPT
SUDAN
ERITREA
ETHIOPIA
DJIBOUTI
YEMEN
SOMALIA
İSTANBUL
ANKARA
T'BILISI
YEREVAN
BAKI (BAKU)
Lefkosia (Nicosia)
BEYROUTH (BEIRUT)
DIMASHQ (DAMASCUS)
HALAB (ALEPPO)
Yerushalayim (Jerusalem)
'AMMĀN
BAGHDĀD
Al Kuwayt (Kuwait)
AR RIYĀD (RIYADH)
Al Manāmah
EL QÂHIRA (CAIRO)
EL ISKANDARÎYA (ALEXANDRIA)
El Khartum
Asmara
San'ā
Djibouti
Makkah (Mecca)
Al Madīnah (Medina)
JIDDAH (JEDDA)
Tropic of Cancer
An Nafud
Ad Dahnā
Al Hijāz
Rub' al Khālī (Empty Quarter)
Nubian Desert
Bādiyat ash Shām (Syrian Desert)
Anadolu Dağları
Lake Nasser
Tigris
Euphrates
Nile
metres feet
8000 26250
6000 19690
4000 13120
2000 6560
1000 3280
500 1640
200 656
0 0
656 200
3280 1000
6560 2000
13120 4000
19690 6000
26250 8000
feet metres
110
111

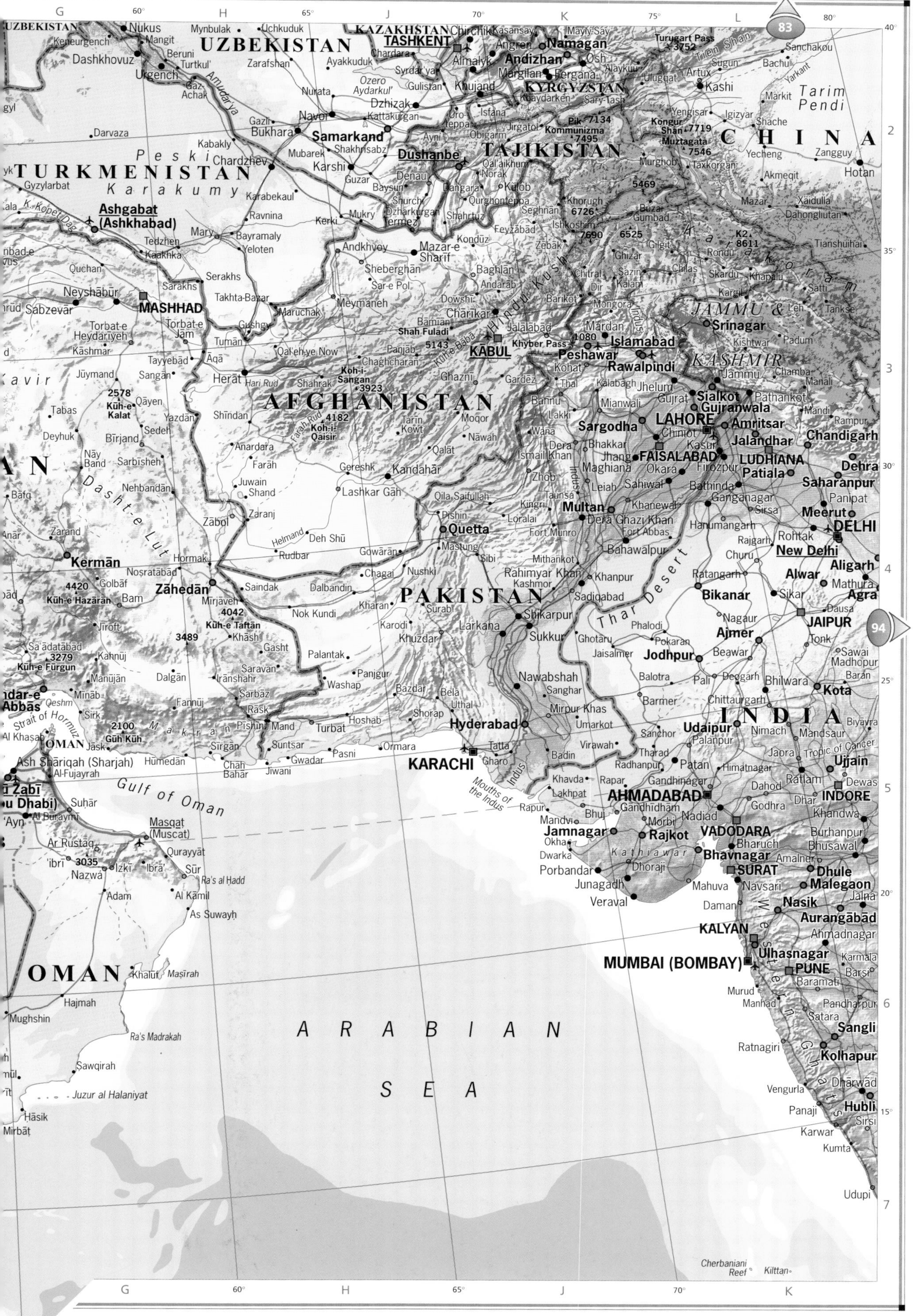

■ over 3 million
■ 1 – 3 million
● 250 000 – 1 million
• 100 000 – 250 000
○ 25 000 – 100 000
• under 25 000
—— country capital underline

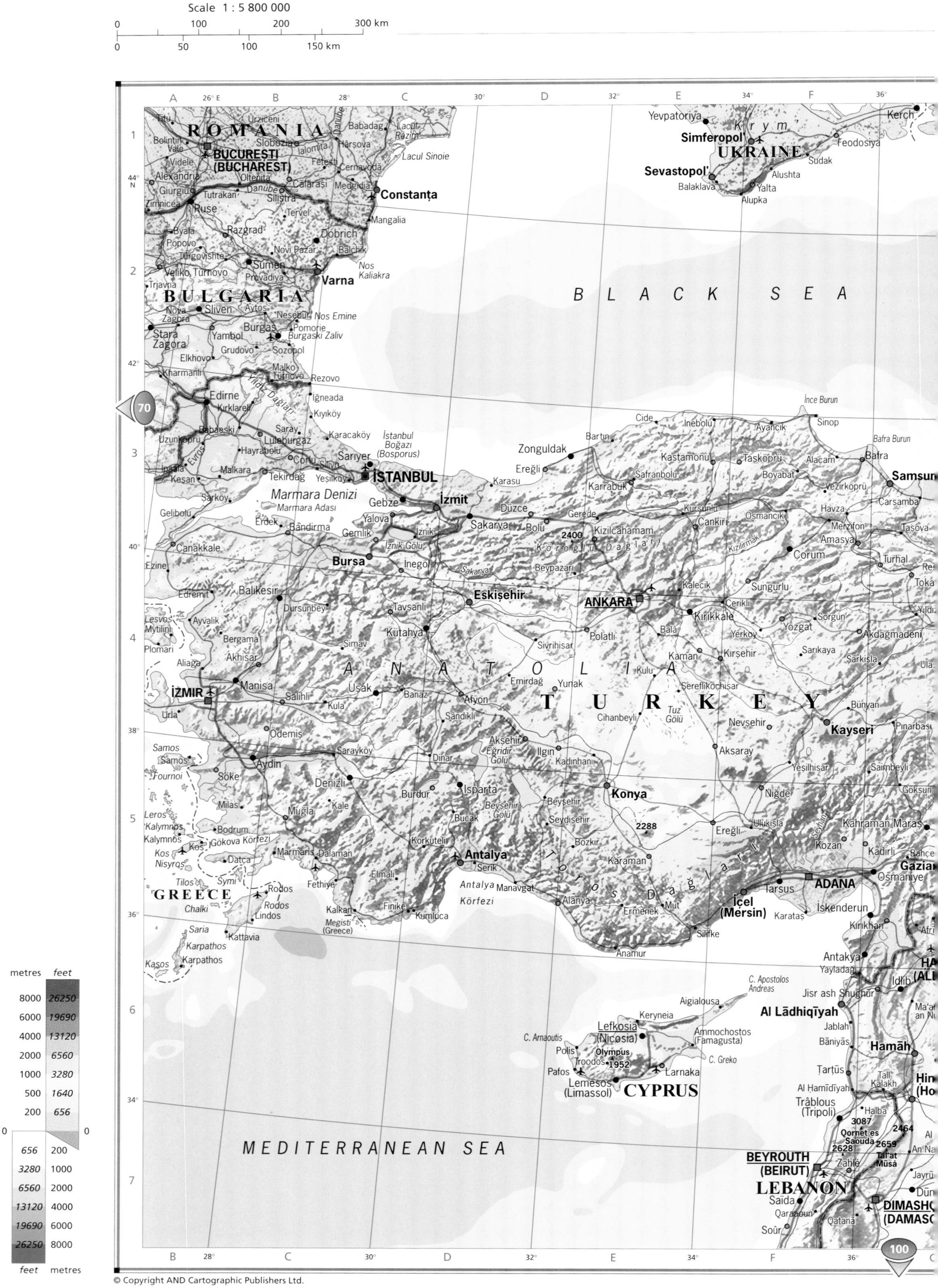

Scale 1 : 5 800 000
0 100 200 300 km
0 50 100 150 km
metres feet
8000 26250
6000 19690
4000 13120
2000 6560
1000 3280
500 1640
200 656
0 0
656 200
3280 1000
6560 2000
13120 4000
19690 6000
26250 8000
feet metres
ROMANIA
BUCUREŞTI (BUCHAREST)
Constanţa
UKRAINE
Krym
Simferopol'
Sevastopol'
Yevpatoriya
Kerch
Feodosiya
Yalta
BULGARIA
Varna
Burgas
Ruse
Dobrich
Stara Zagora
Sliven
BLACK SEA
Edirne
İSTANBUL
İstanbul Boğazı (Bosporus)
Marmara Denizi
İzmit
Bursa
Eskişehir
ANKARA
Zonguldak
Kastamonu
Samsun
Çorum
Amasya
Kayseri
Konya
Antalya
Adana
İçel (Mersin)
İskenderun
Antakya
İZMİR
Manisa
Aydın
Denizli
Uşak
Afyon
Kütahya
Balıkesir
Çanakkale
ANATOLIA
TURKEY
Toros Dağları
Tuz Gölü
GREECE
Rodos
Samos
Kos
Lesvos
Karpathos
CYPRUS
Lefkosia (Nicosia)
Lemesos (Limassol)
Larnaka
Pafos
Olympus 1952
Ammochostos (Famagusta)
Kyreneia
MEDITERRANEAN SEA
Al Lādhiqīyah
Ḩamāh
Trâblous (Tripoli)
BEYROUTH (BEIRUT)
LEBANON
DIMASHQ (DAMASCUS)
Saïda
Soûr
70
100

■ over 3 million	● 100 000 – 250 000	country capital underline
■ 1 – 3 million	◉ 25 000 – 100 000	state or province capital underline
◉ 250 000 – 1 million	• under 25 000	

Scale 1 : 2 850 000

0 50 100 150 km

0 25 50 75 miles

CYPRUS
Lapithos
Keryneia
Akanthou
Lefkosia (Nicosia)
Lefkonikon
Trikomon
C. Eleaia
Ammochostos Bay
Ammochostos (Famagusta)
Mesaoria Plain
Ceasefire line
Paralimni
Aya Napa
C. Greko
Dhekelia
Larnaka
Vasilikos
Lemesos (Limassol)
MEDITERRANEAN SEA
LEBANON
BEYROUTH (BEIRUT)
Trâblous (Tripoli)
Batroûn
Jbail
Joûnié
Aley
Zahlé
Baaqline
Saïda
Jezzine
Marjayoûn
Soûr
Bent Jbail
Enn Nâqoûra
Zgharta
Halba
Hermel
Qornet es Saouda
3087
2216
2628
Qartaba
Ba'albek
Jebel Liban
Jebel esh Sharqi
Tal 'at Mūsá 2659
Mt. Hermon 2814
SYRIA
Hamāh
Hims (Homs)
Tartūs
Bāniyās
Jablah
Al Qadmūs
Masyāf
Kafr Buhum
Ar Rastan
Burj Sāfitā
Tall Kalakh
Al Hamīdīyah
Khān Shaykhūn
Khirbat Isrīyah
As Sa'ān
Salamīyah
Furqlus
Tiyās
Bahrat Hims
Al Qusayr
Hisyah
Ghunthur
Al Qaryatayn
Al Burayj
Bi'r Bazīrī
An Nabk
Yabrūd
Sab' Ābār
Jayrūd
Al Qutayfah
Dumayr
Az Zabadānī
Dūmā
DIMASHQ (DAMASCUS)
Qatana
Burāq
Ghabāghib
Al Qunaytirah
As Sanamayn
GOLAN HEIGHTS
Nawá
Izra'
Shahbā'
Shaykh Miskīn
As Suwaydā'
1735
Jabal ad Durūz
Busrá ash Shām
Salkhad
Ghadīr Minqār
Bādiyat ash Shām (Syrian Desert)
Jab. an Nusayrīyah
1385
ISRAEL
Nahariyya
'Akko
Qiryat Motzkin
Hefa (Haifa)
Qiryat Ata
Karmiel
Zefat
Qiryat Shemona
Teverya
Sea of Galilee
Nazareth
Afula
Zikhron Ya'aqov
Hadera
Bet She'an
Netanya
Herzliyya
Tel Aviv-Yafo
Petah Tiqwa
Rishon le Ziyyon
Rehovot
Ramla
Ashdod
Ashqelon
Qiryat Gat
Yerushalayim (Jerusalem)
Bethlehem
Hebron
Sederot
Ofaqim
Be'er Sheva'
Dimona
Arad
Yatta
New Zohars
Sedom
Revivim
Negev
Sede Boqer
'En Hazeva
Mizpe Ramon
Qezi'ot
Har Saggi
1000
1006
Beer Menuha
Yotvata
Beer Ora
Elat
WEST BANK
Jenin
Tubas
Tulkarm
Nablus
Damiya
Ramallah
Jericho
GAZA STRIP
Gaza
Khān Yūnis
Rafah
Dead Sea
Jordan
JORDAN
'AMMAN
Irbid
Dar'a
Ramtha
Husn
Ajlun
1247
Jarash
Mafraq
Tisīyah
1234
Es Samrā
Zarqā'
Salt
Suweilih
Er Ruseifa
Sahāb
Nā'ūr
Suweima
Mādabā
Qasr el Kharana
El Azraq
Qasr el Azraq
Qā 'Azamān
1010
Dab'a
Dhībān
Khān az Zabīb
Al Hadīthah
Kāf
Al Qarqar
An Nabk
Wādī as Sirhān
'Ayn al Baida'
Qatrāna
Mazra
Karak
Manzil
Mazār
Safi
Tafila
Bāyir
Hāsā
J. el Atā'ita 1641
Jurf ed Darāwīsh
1082
Shaubak
'Unayzah
1615
Wādī Mūsā
Jebel Ithrīyat
El Jafr
Jebel Mubrāk 1727
Ma'ān
Gharandal
Naqb Ashtar
Jebel el Batrā 1555
El Quweira
Ram
J. Bāqir 1592
J. Ram 1754
'Aqaba
Gulf of Aqaba
1520
Ar Ramlah
Al Mudawwara
SAUDI ARABIA
At Tubayq
1224 Ath Thāyat
EGYPT
SINAI
Sabkhet el Bardawil
El 'Arish
Sadût
El Mazâr
Yammit
Abu Aweigila
G. Halâl 892
El Quseima
Bîr Hasana
Bîr Gifgâfa
1094
G. Yi'allaq
El Kuntilla
Nakhl
El Thamad
1030
Gebel el Tîh
1080
Râs el Nafas
Bîr Tâba
98
111
A B C D E
34° 35° 36° 37° 38°
35° N 34° 33° 32° 31° 30°
1 2 3 4 5 6 7

metres	feet
8000	26250
6000	19690
4000	13120
2000	6560
1000	3280
500	1640
200	656
0	0
200	656
1000	3280
2000	6560
4000	13120
6000	19690
8000	26250
metres	feet

Scale 1 : 5 800 000

0 100 200 300 km
0 50 100 150 km

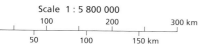

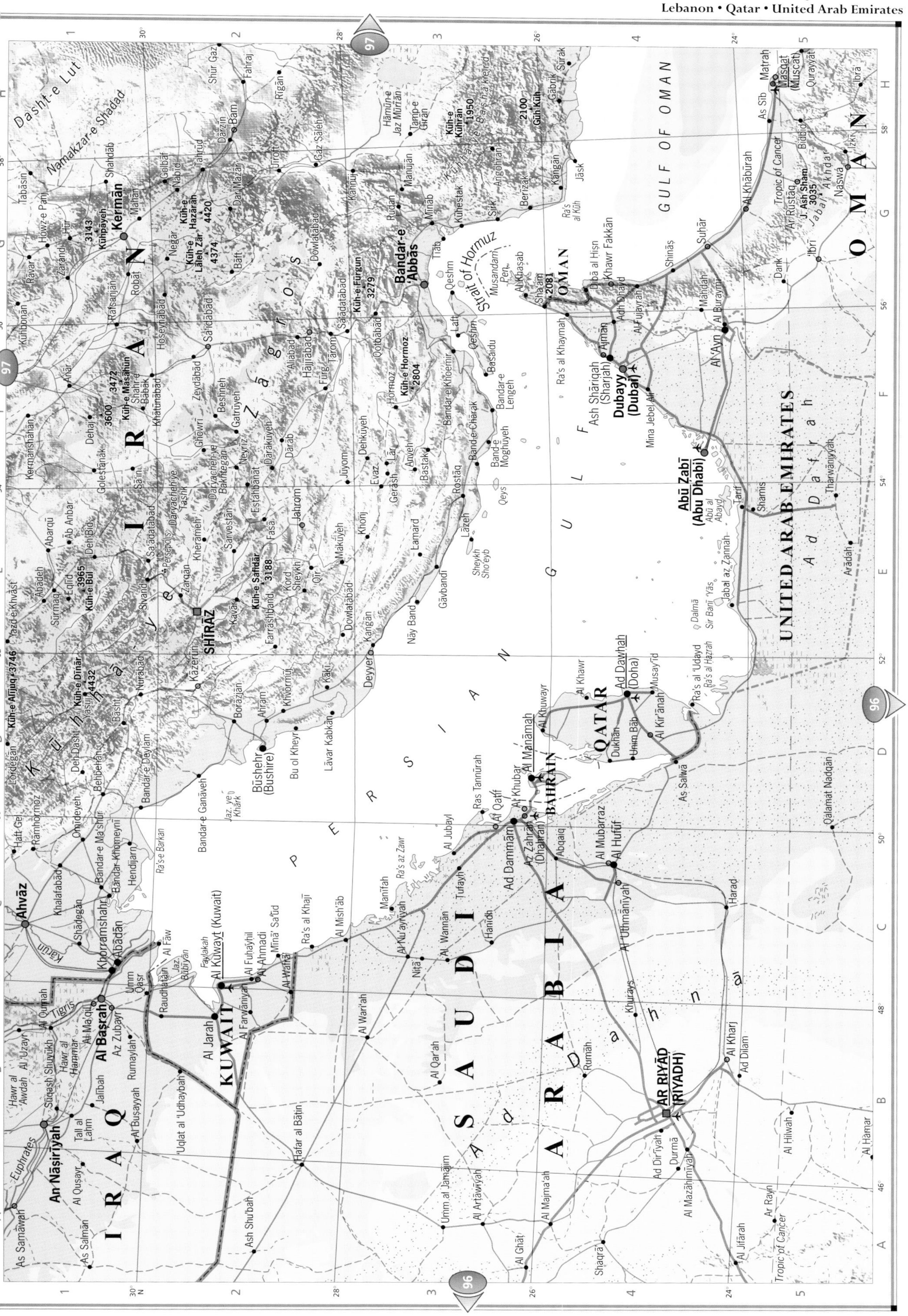

■ over 3 million	● 100 000 – 250 000	country capital underline
■ 1 – 3 million	○ 25 000 – 100 000	urban area
● 250 000 – 1 million	• under 25 000	

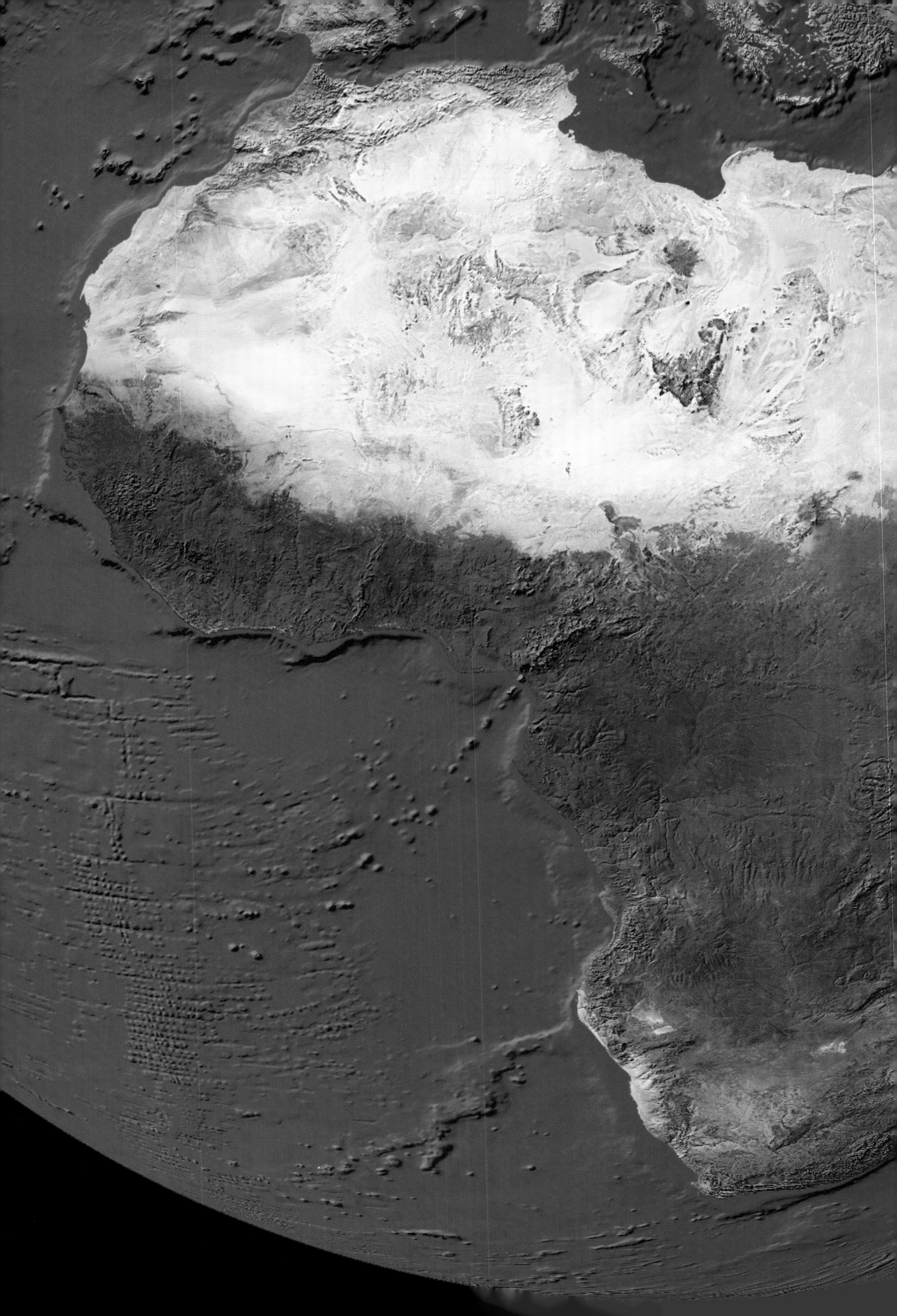

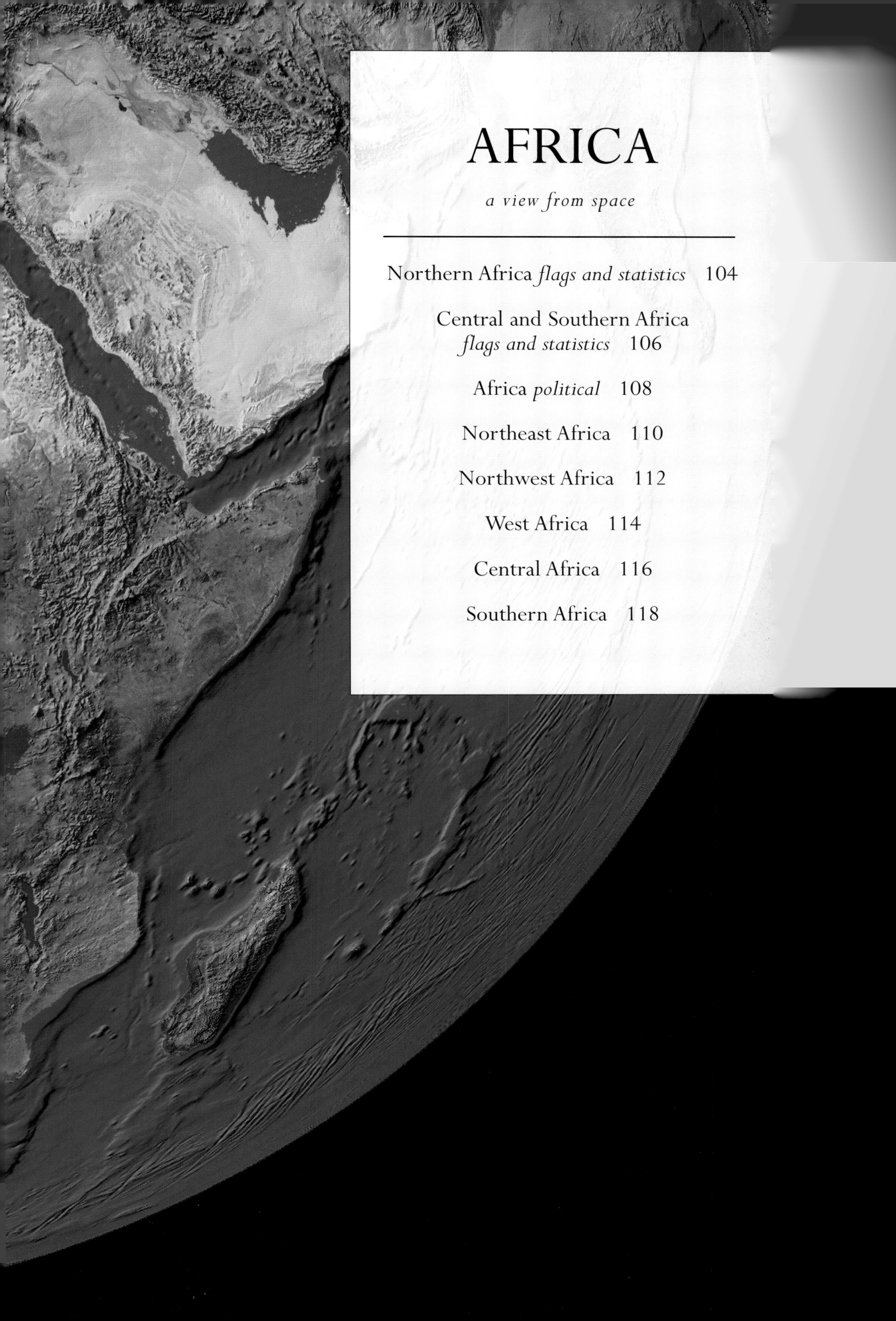

AFRICA

a view from space

Northern Africa *flags and statistics* 104

Central and Southern Africa *flags and statistics* 106

Africa *political* 108

Northeast Africa 110

Northwest Africa 112

West Africa 114

Central Africa 116

Southern Africa 118

NORTHERN AFRICA

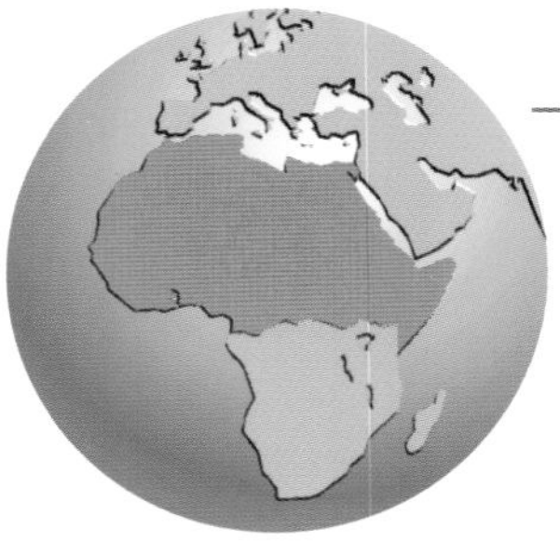

Morocco
Area: 446,550 km²
Capital: Rabat
Population: 27.4m
Languages: Arabic, Berber
Religion: Muslim
Currency: Dirham

Algeria
Area: 2,381,741 km²
Capital: Algiers
Population: 30.1m
Languages: Arabic, Berber, French
Religion: Muslim
Currency: Algerian dinar

Tunisia
Area: 163,610 km
Capital: Tunis
Population: 9.3m
Languages: Arabic, French, Engli
Religion: Muslim
Currency: Tunisian dinar

Mali
Area: 1,240,192 km²
Capital: Bamako
Population: 10.7m
Languages: French, local dialects
Religion: Muslim
Currency: Franc CFA

Burkina
Area: 274,000 km²
Capital: Ouagadougou
Population: 11.3m
Main language: French
Religion: Traditional beliefs
Currency: Franc CFA

Niger
Area: 1,267,000 km²
Capital: Niamey
Population: 10.1m
Languages: French, Hausa
Religion: Muslim
Currency: Franc CFA

Cape Verde
Area: 4,033 km²
Capital: Praia
Population: 408,000
Languages: Portuguese, Creole
Religion: Roman Catholic
Currency: Cape Verde escudo

Mauritania
Area: 1,025,520 km²
Capital: Nouakchott
Population: 2.5m
Languages: Arabic, Pulaar, French
Religion: Muslim
Currency: Ouguiya

Senegal
Area: 196,722 km²
Capital: Dakar
Population: 9.0m
Languages: French, local dialects
Religion: Muslim
Currency: Franc CFA

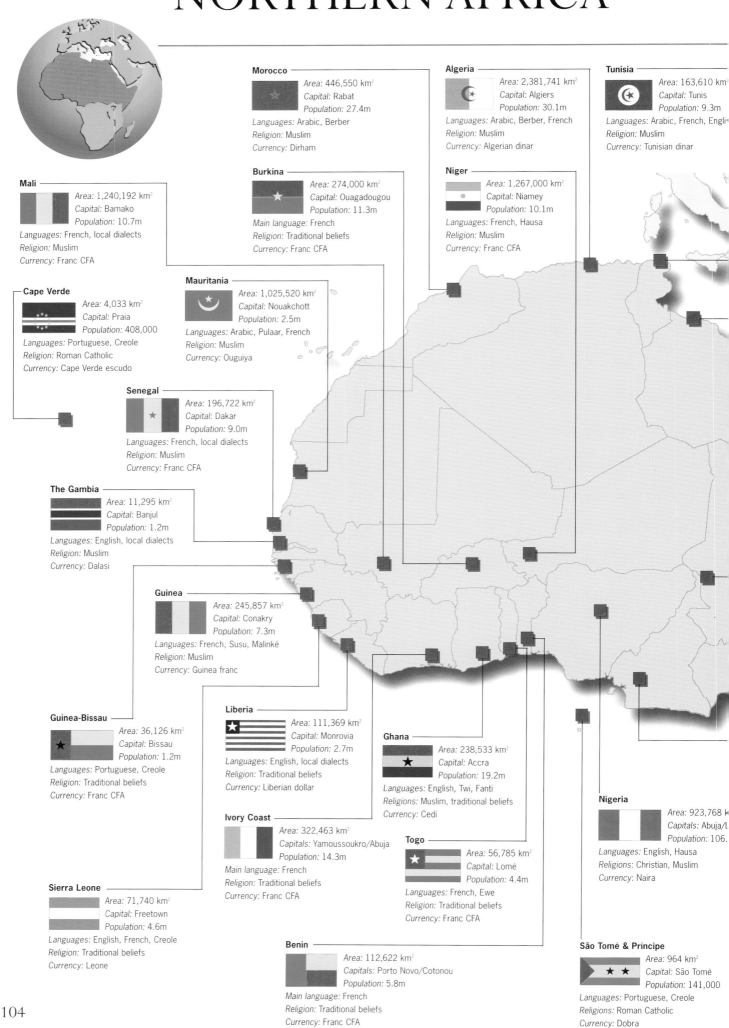

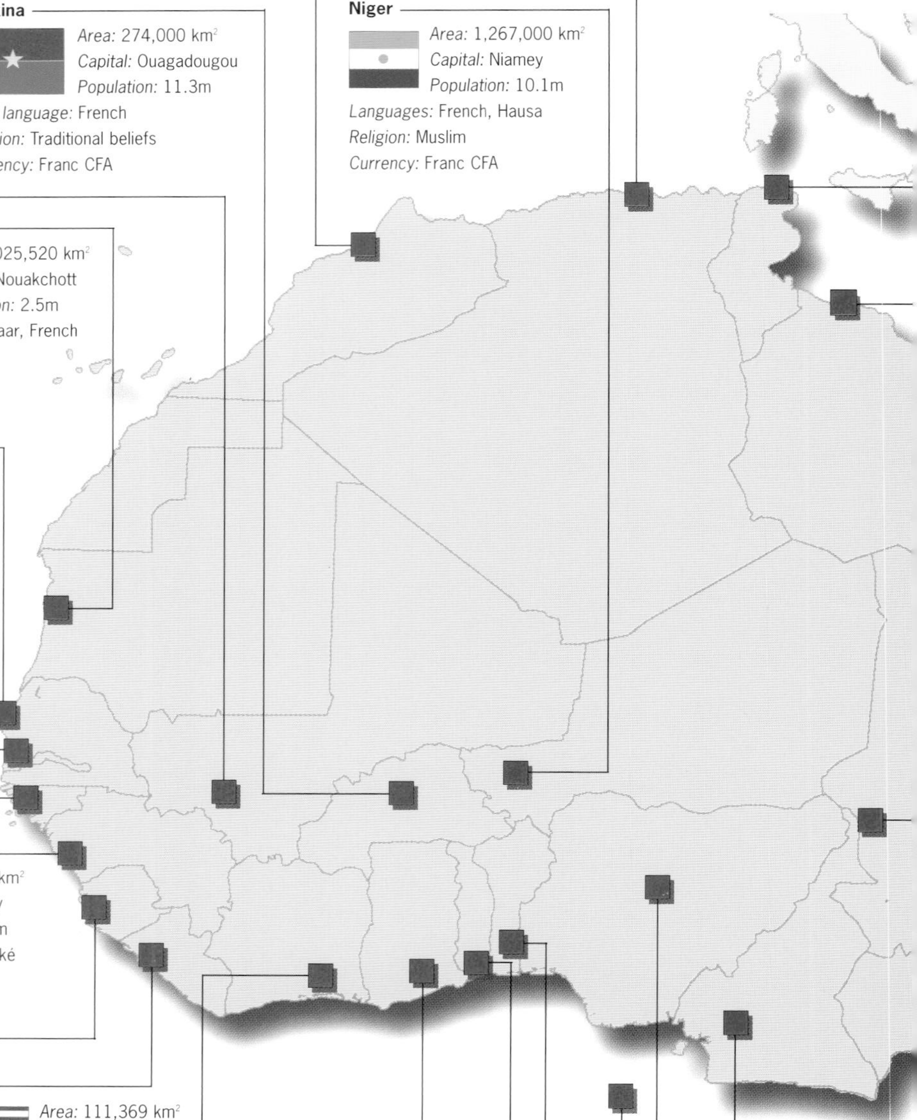

The Gambia
Area: 11,295 km²
Capital: Banjul
Population: 1.2m
Languages: English, local dialects
Religion: Muslim
Currency: Dalasi

Guinea
Area: 245,857 km²
Capital: Conakry
Population: 7.3m
Languages: French, Susu, Malinké
Religion: Muslim
Currency: Guinea franc

Guinea-Bissau
Area: 36,126 km²
Capital: Bissau
Population: 1.2m
Languages: Portuguese, Creole
Religion: Traditional beliefs
Currency: Franc CFA

Liberia
Area: 111,369 km²
Capital: Monrovia
Population: 2.7m
Languages: English, local dialects
Religion: Traditional beliefs
Currency: Liberian dollar

Ghana
Area: 238,533 km²
Capital: Accra
Population: 19.2m
Languages: English, Twi, Fanti
Religions: Muslim, traditional beliefs
Currency: Cedi

Nigeria
Area: 923,768 k
Capitals: Abuja/L
Population: 106.
Languages: English, Hausa
Religions: Christian, Muslim
Currency: Naira

Ivory Coast
Area: 322,463 km²
Capitals: Yamoussoukro/Abuja
Population: 14.3m
Main language: French
Religion: Traditional beliefs
Currency: Franc CFA

Togo
Area: 56,785 km²
Capital: Lomé
Population: 4.4m
Languages: French, Ewe
Religion: Traditional beliefs
Currency: Franc CFA

Sierra Leone
Area: 71,740 km²
Capital: Freetown
Population: 4.6m
Languages: English, French, Creole
Religion: Traditional beliefs
Currency: Leone

Benin
Area: 112,622 km²
Capitals: Porto Novo/Cotonou
Population: 5.8m
Main language: French
Religion: Traditional beliefs
Currency: Franc CFA

São Tomé & Príncipe
Area: 964 km²
Capital: São Tomé
Population: 141,000
Languages: Portuguese, Creole
Religions: Roman Catholic
Currency: Dobra

NORTHERN AFRICA IS DOMINATED by the Sahara desert and the beginnings of the Great Rift Valley in the east, while to the west and south of the region are tropical grasslands and rainforest, rich in minerals. The population covers a wide variety of peoples with their own distinctive cultures.

Libya

Area: 1,759,540 km²
Capital: Tripoli
Population: 5.3m
Main language: Arabic
Religion: Muslim
Currency: Libyan dinar

Egypt

Area: 1,001,449 km²
Capital: Cairo
Population: 66.0m
Main language: Arabic
Religion: Muslim
Currency: Egyptian pound

Sudan

Area: 2,505,813 km²
Capital: Khartoum
Population: 28.3m
Languages: Arabic, English
Religion: Muslim
Currency: Sudanese dinar

Eritrea

Area: 117,600 km²
Capital: Asmara
Population: 3.6m
Languages: English, Arabic
Religions: Coptic Christian, Muslim
Currency: Nakfa

Chad

Area: 1,284,000 km²
Capital: Ndjamena
Population: 7.3m
Languages: Arabic, French, Sara
Religion: Muslim
Currency: Franc CFA

Djibouti

Area: 23,200 km²
Capital: Djibouti
Population: 623,000
Languages: Arabic, French
Religion: Christian
Currency: Djibouti franc

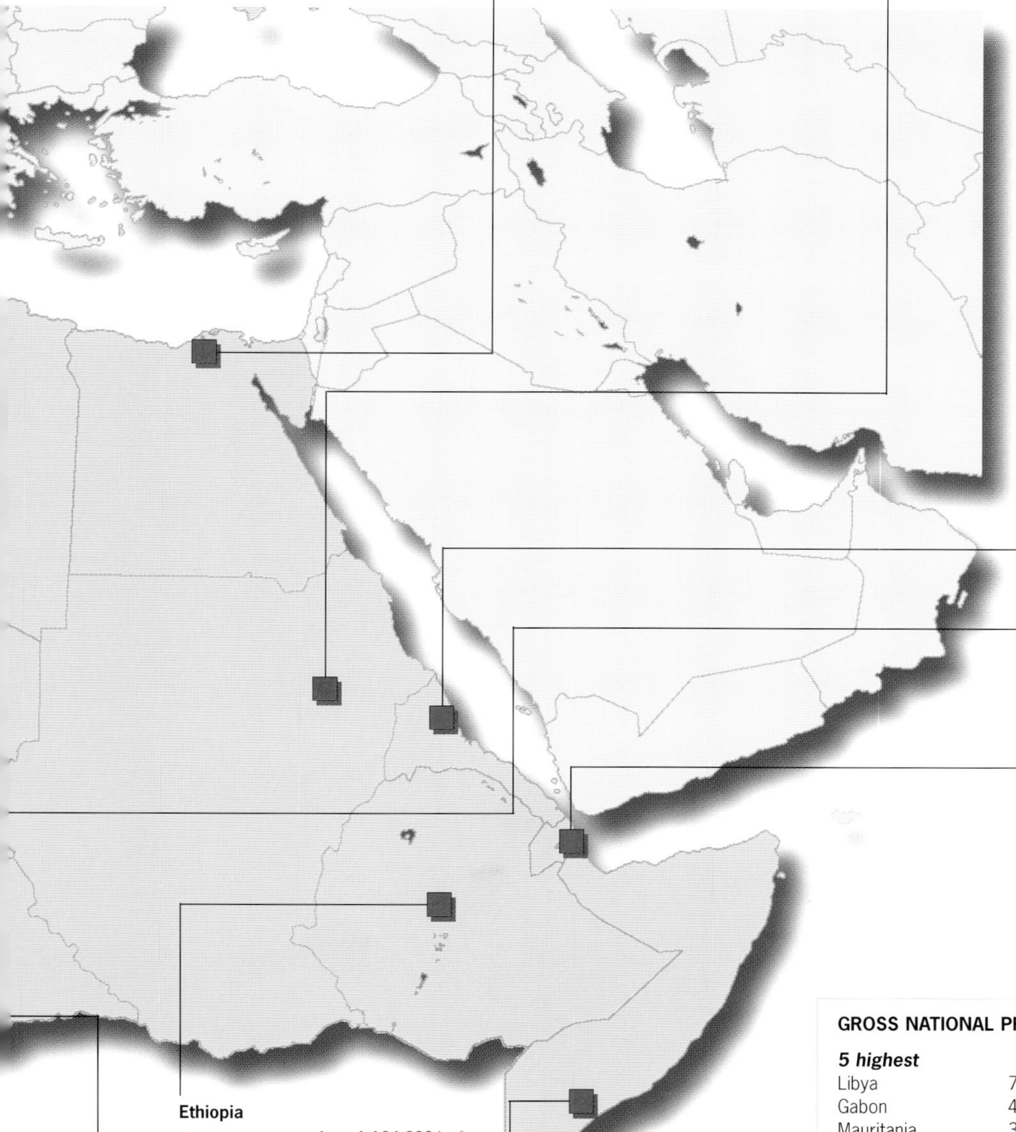

Ethiopia

Area: 1,104,300 km²
Capital: Addis Ababa
Population: 59.6m
Main language: Amharic
Religions: Muslim, Christian
Currency: Ethiopian birr

Central African Republic

Area: 622,984 km²
Capital: Bangui
Population: 3.5m
Languages: French, Sango
Religions: Christian, traditional beliefs
Currency: Franc CFA

Cameroon

Area: 475,442 km²
Capital: Yaoundé
Population: 14.3m
Languages: English, French
Religion: Traditional beliefs
Currency: Franc CFA

Somalia

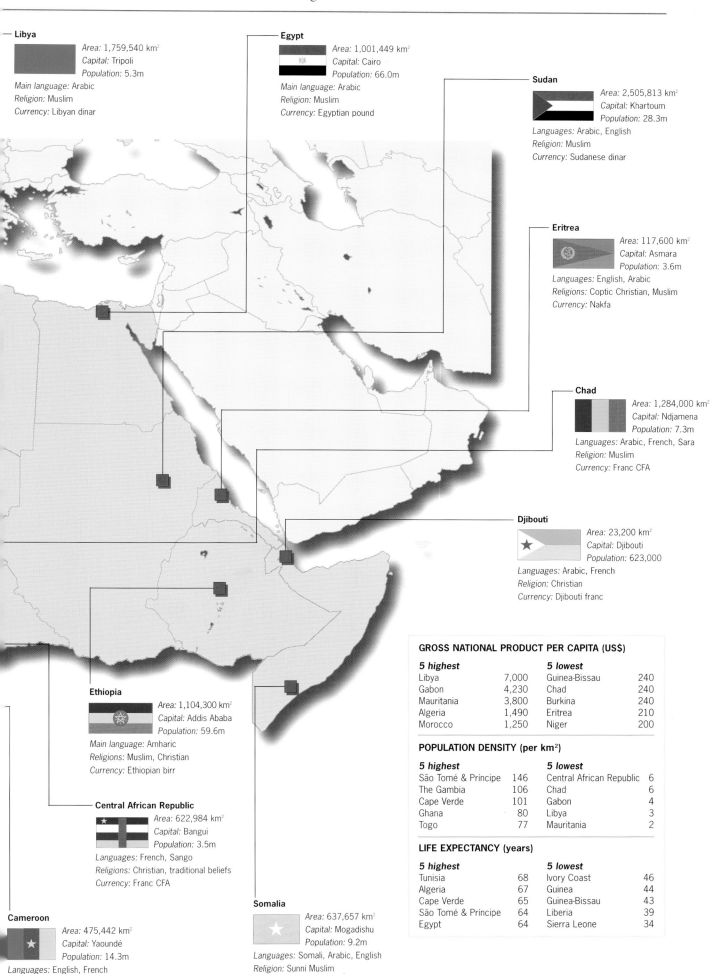

Area: 637,657 km²
Capital: Mogadishu
Population: 9.2m
Languages: Somali, Arabic, English
Religion: Sunni Muslim
Currency: Somali shilling

GROSS NATIONAL PRODUCT PER CAPITA (US$)

5 highest		***5 lowest***	
Libya	7,000	Guinea-Bissau	240
Gabon	4,230	Chad	240
Mauritania	3,800	Burkina	240
Algeria	1,490	Eritrea	210
Morocco	1,250	Niger	200

POPULATION DENSITY (per km²)

5 highest		***5 lowest***	
São Tomé & Príncipe	146	Central African Republic	6
The Gambia	106	Chad	6
Cape Verde	101	Gabon	4
Ghana	80	Libya	3
Togo	77	Mauritania	2

LIFE EXPECTANCY (years)

5 highest		***5 lowest***	
Tunisia	68	Ivory Coast	46
Algeria	67	Guinea	44
Cape Verde	65	Guinea-Bissau	43
São Tomé & Príncipe	64	Liberia	39
Egypt	64	Sierra Leone	34

CENTRAL AND SOUTHERN AFRICA

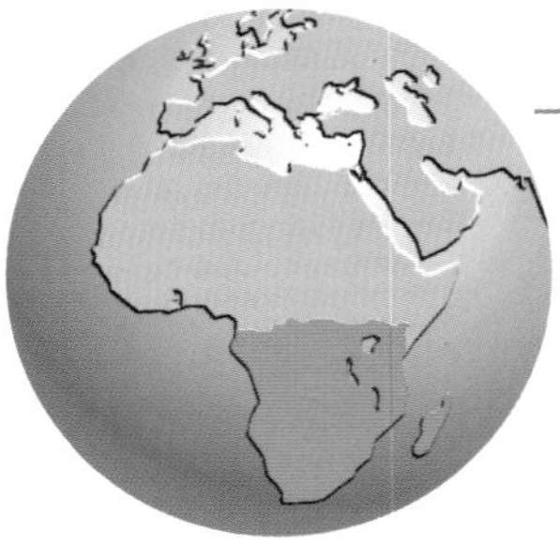

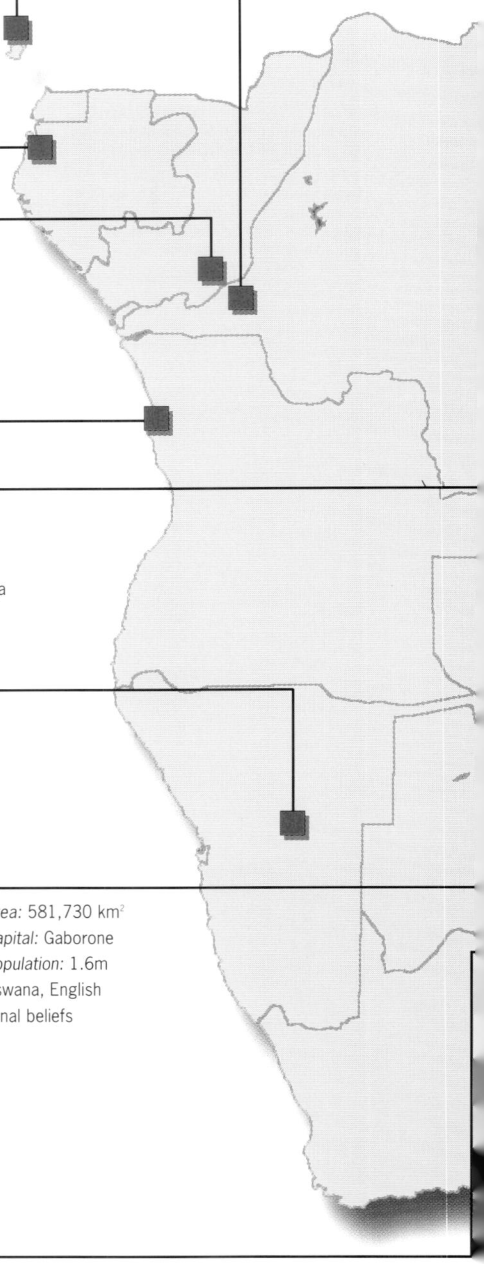

Democratic Republic of Congo

Area: 2,344,869 km²
Capital: Kinshasa
Population: 49.1m
Languages: Swahili, Lingala, French
Religions: Christian, traditional beliefs
Currency: Congolese franc

Equatorial Guinea

Area: 28,051 km²
Capital: Malabo
Population: 431,000
Languages: French, Spanish
Religion: Roman Catholic
Currency: Franc CFA

Gabon

Area: 267,668 km²
Capital: Libreville
Population: 1.2m
Languages: French, Fang, Eshira
Religion: Roman Catholic
Currency: Franc CFA

Congo

Area: 342,000 km²
Capital: Brazzaville
Population: 2.8m
Languages: French, Lingala, Kikongo
Religion: Roman Catholic
Currency: Franc CFA

Angola

Area: 1,246,700 km²
Capital: Luanda
Population: 12.1m
Main language: Portuguese
Religions: Roman Catholic, Protestant
Currency: Readjusted kwanza

Zambia

Area: 752,618 km²
Capital: Lusaka
Population: 8.8m
Languages: English, Nyanja, Tonga
Religion: Christian
Currency: Kwacha

Namibia

Area: 824,292 km²
Capital: Windhoek
Population: 1.7m
Languages: English, Afrikaans, German
Religion: Christian
Currency: Namibian dollar

Botswana

Area: 581,730 km²
Capital: Gaborone
Population: 1.6m
Languages: Setswana, English
Religion: Traditional beliefs
Currency: Pula

GROSS NATIONAL PRODUCT PER CAPITA (US$)

5 highest		***5 lowest***	
Seychelles	6,880	Rwanda	210
Mauritius	3,800	Tanzania	210
South Africa	3,400	Dem. Rep. of Congo	110
Botswana	3,260	Ethiopia	110
Namibia	2,220	Mozambique	90

POPULATION DENSITY (per km²)

5 highest		***5 lowest***	
Mauritius	539	Angola	10
Comoros	294	Lesotho	7
Rwanda	251	Botswana	3
Burundi	234	South Africa	3
Malawi	87	Namibia	2

LIFE EXPECTANCY (years)

5 highest		***5 lowest***	
Seychelles	71	Mozambique	46
Mauritius	70	Comoros	45
South Africa	63	Malawi	42
Lesotho	58	Uganda	41
Swaziland	58	Rwanda	23

South Africa

Area: 1,221,037 km²
Capitals: Pretoria/Cape Town
Population: 39m
Languages: English, Afrikaans, Zulu
Religion: Protestant
Currency: Rand

Lesotho

Area: 30,355 km²
Capital: Maseru
Population: 2m
Languages: Sesotho, English
Religion: Roman Catholic
Currency: Loti

CENTRAL AFRICA HAS A BELT of tropical rainforest across the Equator, while further south are tropical grasslands which support livestock. The extreme south is very fertile, with a Mediterranean climate. The region is also rich in minerals. There is a wide diversity of population and cultures.

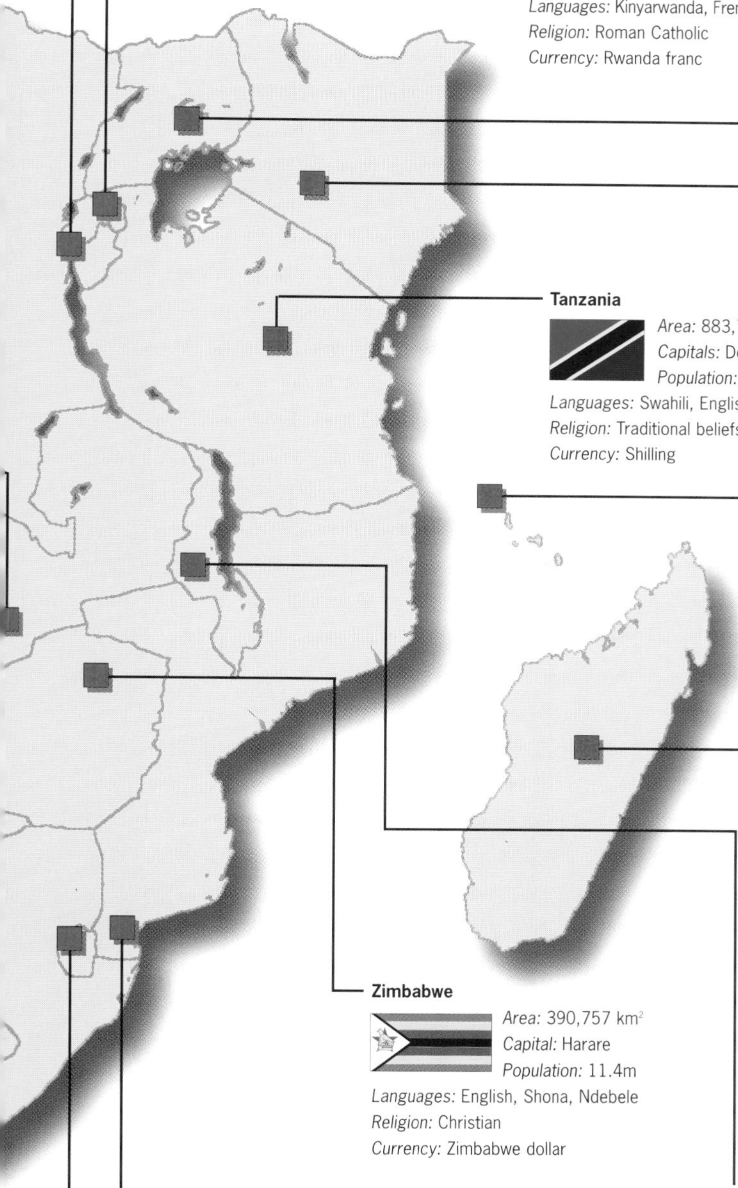

Burundi

Area: 27,834 km²
Capital: Bujumbura
Population: 6.5m
Languages: Kirundi, French, Kishwahili
Religion: Roman Catholic
Currency: Burundi franc

Uganda

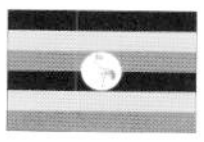

Area: 241,038 km²
Capital: Kampala
Population: 20.6m
Languages: English, Swahili
Religions: Roman Catholic, Protestant
Currency: Uganda shilling

Rwanda

Area: 26,338 km²
Capital: Kigali
Population: 6.6m
Languages: Kinyarwanda, French, English
Religion: Roman Catholic
Currency: Rwanda franc

Kenya

Area: 580,367 km²
Capital: Nairobi
Population: 29.0m
Languages: English, Swahili
Religions: Roman Catholic, Protestant
Currency: Kenyan shilling

Tanzania

Area: 883,749 km²
Capitals: Dodoma/Dar es Salaam
Population: 32.1m
Languages: Swahili, English
Religion: Traditional beliefs
Currency: Shilling

Comoros

Area: 2,235 km²
Capital: Moroni
Population: 658,000
Languages: French, Arabic, Comoran
Religion: Muslim
Currency: Comoran franc

Seychelles

Area: 455 km²
Capital: Victoria
Population: 76,000
Languages: French, English, Creole
Religion: Roman Catholic
Currency: Seychelles rupee

Madagascar

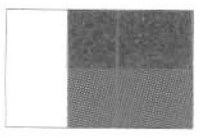

Area: 587,041 km²
Capital: Antananarivo
Population: 15.1m
Languages: Malagasy, French
Religion: Traditional beliefs
Currency: Malagasy franc

Zimbabwe

Area: 390,757 km²
Capital: Harare
Population: 11.4m
Languages: English, Shona, Ndebele
Religion: Christian
Currency: Zimbabwe dollar

Malawi

Area: 118,484 km²
Capital: Lilongwe
Population: 10.3m
Languages: Chichewa, English
Religions: Protestant, Catholic
Currency: Kwacha

Mauritius

Area: 2,040 km²
Capital: Port Louis
Population: 1.1m
Languages: Creole, French, English
Religion: Hindu
Currency: Mauritius rupee

Swaziland

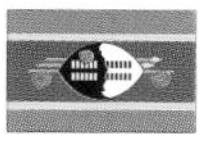

Area: 17,364 km²
Capitals: Mbabane/Lobamba
Population: 952,000
Languages: SiSwati, English
Religion: Protestant
Currency: Lilangeni

Mozambique

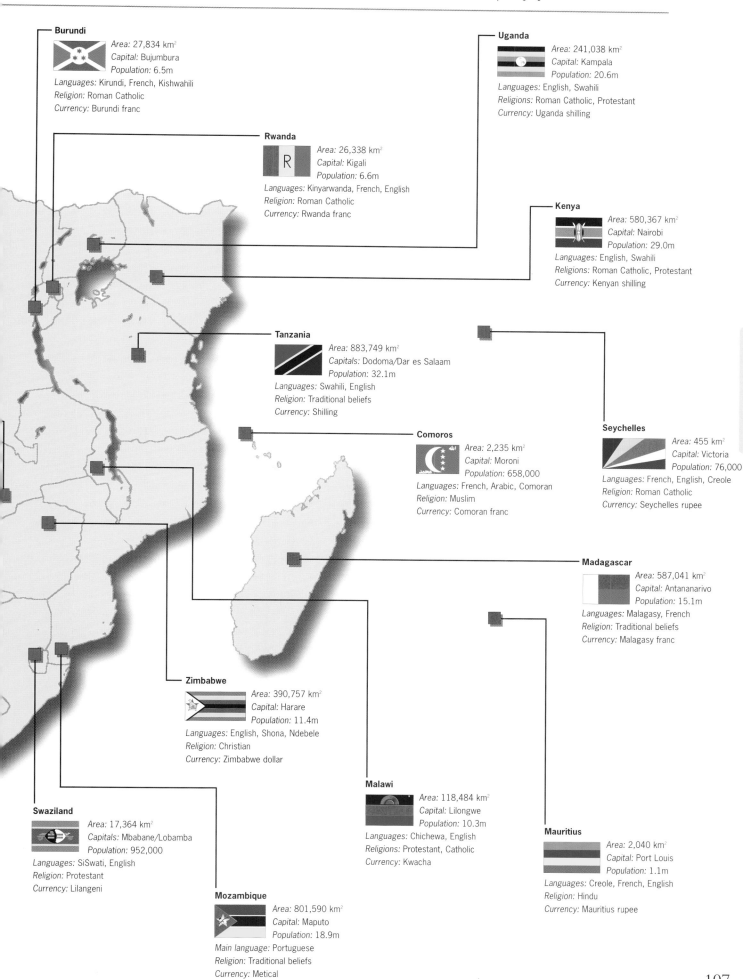

Area: 801,590 km²
Capital: Maputo
Population: 18.9m
Main language: Portuguese
Religion: Traditional beliefs
Currency: Metical

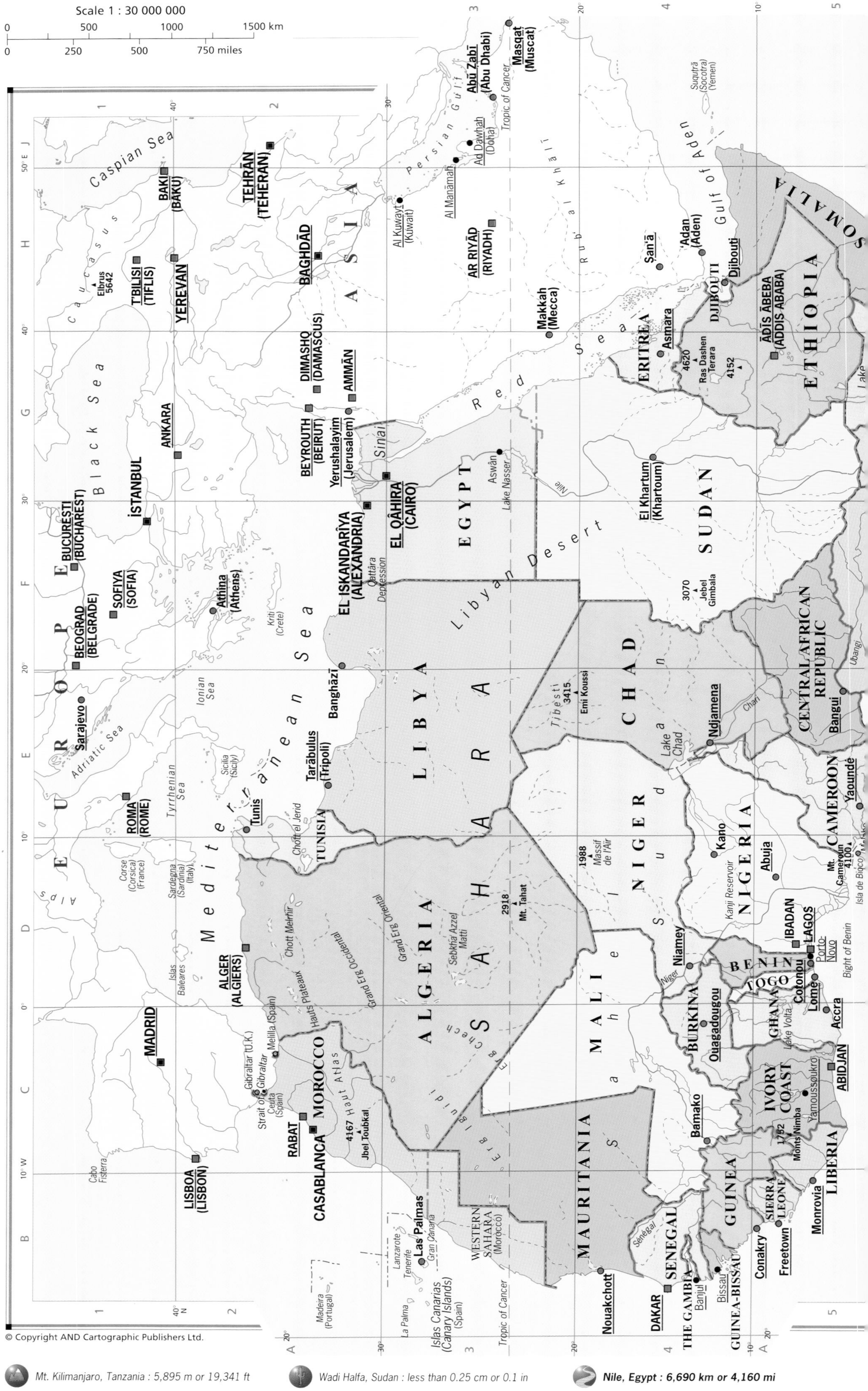

Mt. Kilimanjaro, Tanzania : 5,895 m or 19,341 ft

Wadi Halfa, Sudan : less than 0.25 cm or 0.1 in

Nile, Egypt : 6,690 km or 4,160 mi

Lake Assal, Djibouti : 156 m or 512 ft

Debundscha, Cameroon : 1029 cm or 405 in

Lake Victoria, East Africa : 62,940 km² or 24,300 sq mi

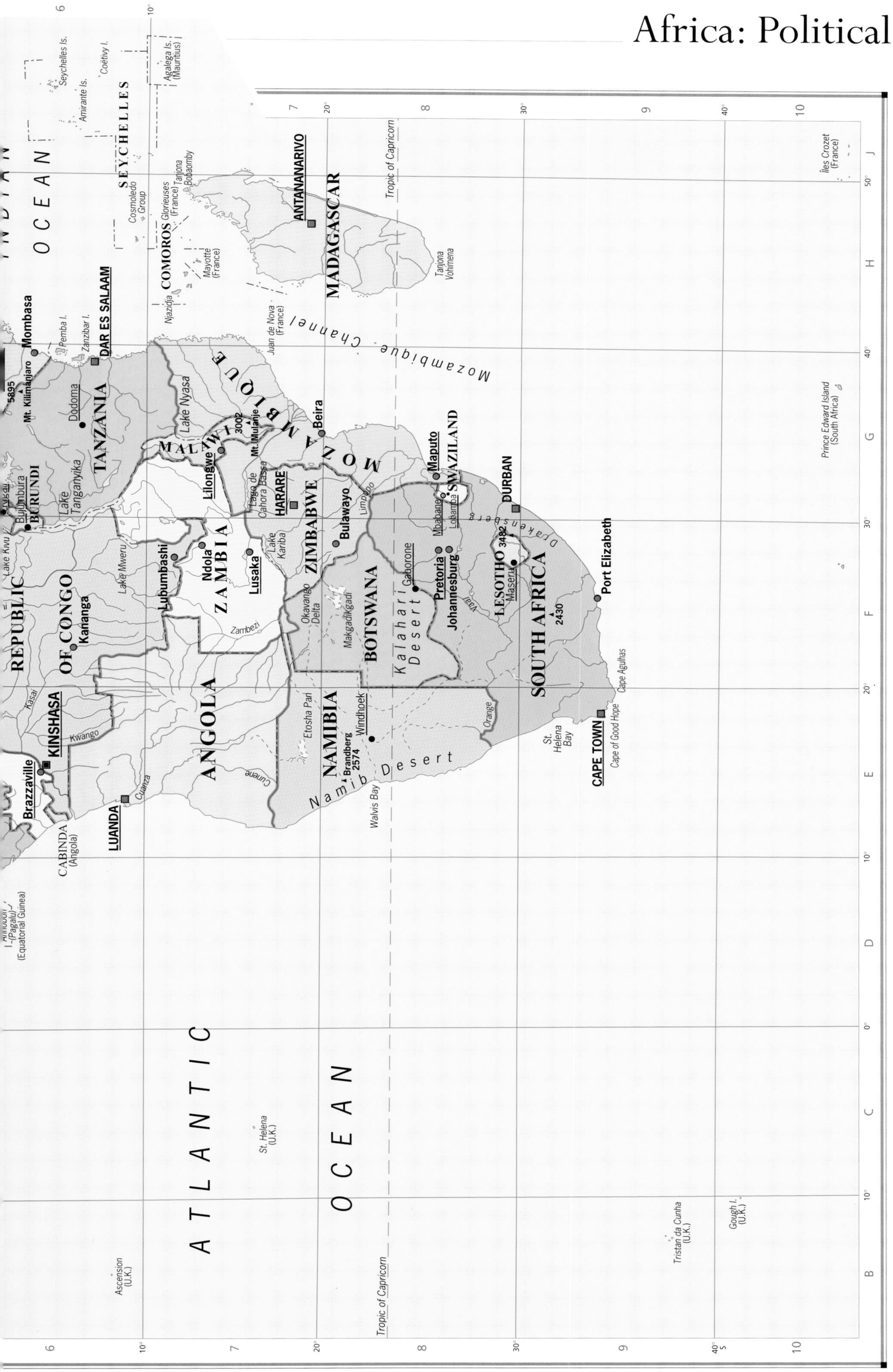
INDIAN OCEAN
ATLANTIC OCEAN
SEYCHELLES
Seychelles Is.
Amirante Is.
Coëtivy I.
Agalega Is. (Mauritius)
Cosmoledo Group
Glorieuses (France)
Tanjona Bobaomby
COMOROS
Njazidja
Mayotte (France)
MADAGASCAR
ANTANANARIVO
Tanjona Vohimena
Juan de Nova (France)
Mozambique Channel
Mombasa
Pemba I.
Zanzibar I.
DAR ES SALAAM
5895
Mt. Kilimanjaro
Dodoma
TANZANIA
Lake Tanganyika
BURUNDI
Bujumbura
Lake Kivu
REPUBLIC OF CONGO
Kananga
Kasai
KINSHASA
Kwango
Brazzaville
CABINDA (Angola)
LUANDA
Cuanza
ANGOLA
Cunene
Lake Mweru
Lubumbashi
Ndola
ZAMBIA
Lusaka
Zambezi
Lake Nyasa
MALAWI
Lilongwe
3002
Mt. Mulanje
MOZAMBIQUE
Beira
Lago de Cahora Bassa
HARARE
Lake Kariba
ZIMBABWE
Bulawayo
Limpopo
Maputo
Mbabane
Lobamba
SWAZILAND
DURBAN
Drakensberg
3482
LESOTHO
Maseru
SOUTH AFRICA
2430
Port Elizabeth
Pretoria
Johannesburg
Vaal
Gaborone
Kalahari Desert
BOTSWANA
Okavango Delta
Makgadikgadi
Etosha Pan
NAMIBIA
Windhoek
Brandberg 2574
Namib Desert
Walvis Bay
Orange
St. Helena Bay
CAPE TOWN
Cape of Good Hope
Cape Agulhas
Tropic of Capricorn
Prince Edward Island (South Africa)
Îles Crozet (France)
St. Helena (U.K.)
Ascension (U.K.)
Tristan da Cunha (U.K.)
Gough I. (U.K.)
(Pagalu) (Equatorial Guinea)

Ifrane, Morocco : -24 °C or -11 °F

Al Aziziyah, Libya : 58 °C or 136 °F

748,927,000

25 per km² or 64 per sq mi

30,293,000 km² or 11,696,000 sq mi

53

Scale 1 : 11 600 000

0 200 400 600 km

0 100 200 300 miles

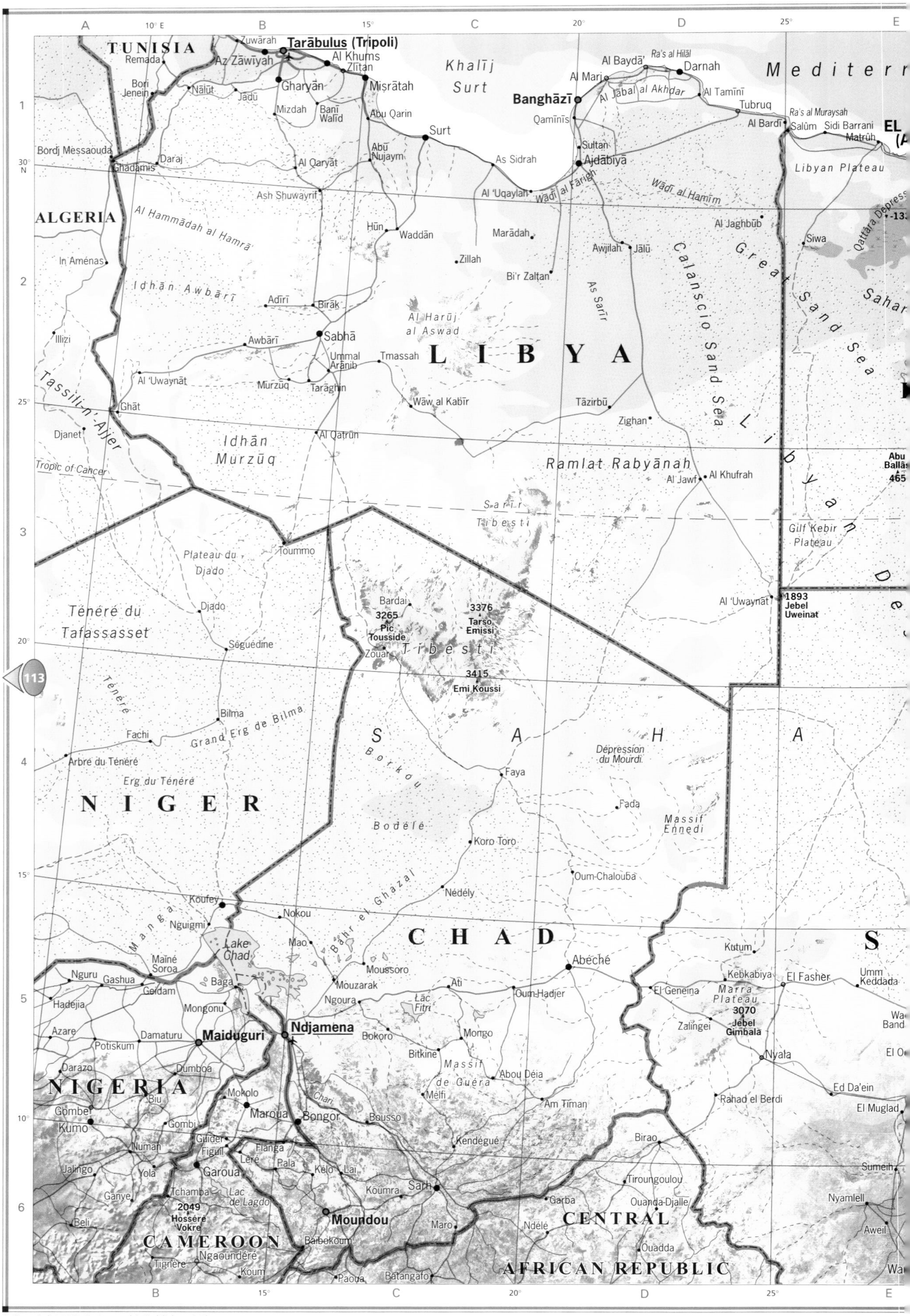

113

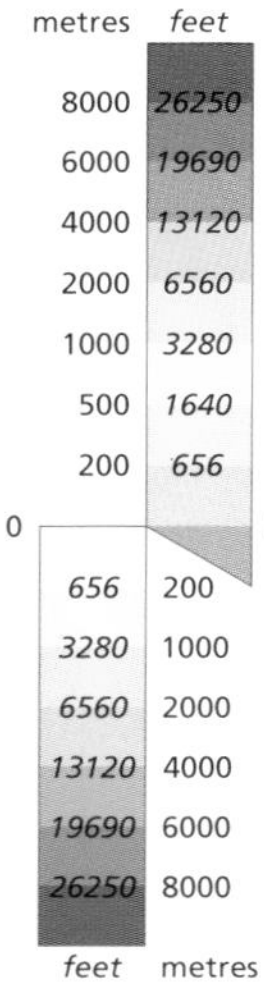

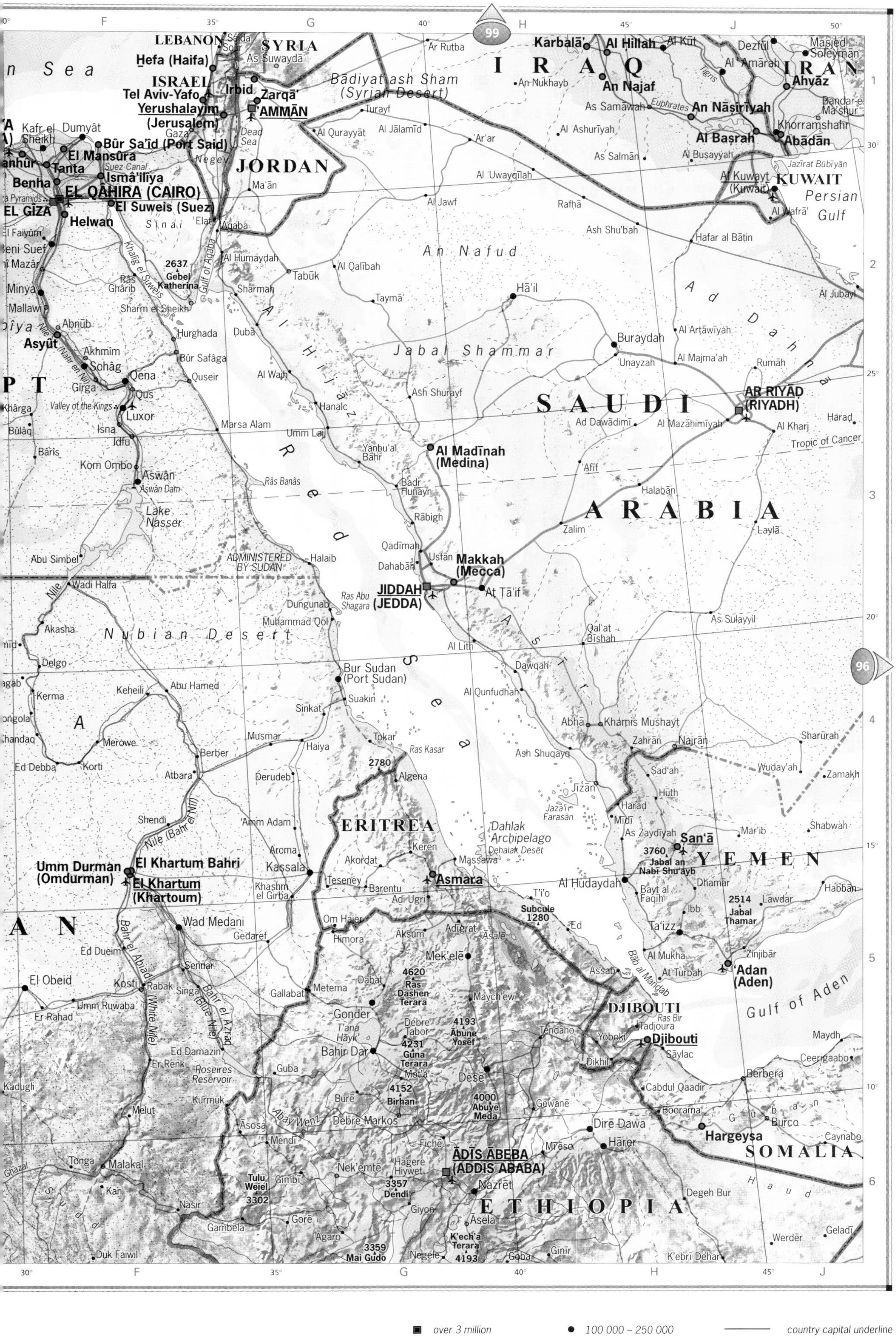

■ over 3 million	● 100 000 – 250 000	country capital underline
■ 1 – 3 million	○ 25 000 – 100 000	
● 250 000 – 1 million	• under 25 000	

Scale 1 : 11 600 000

0 200 400 600 km

0 100 200 300 miles

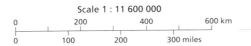

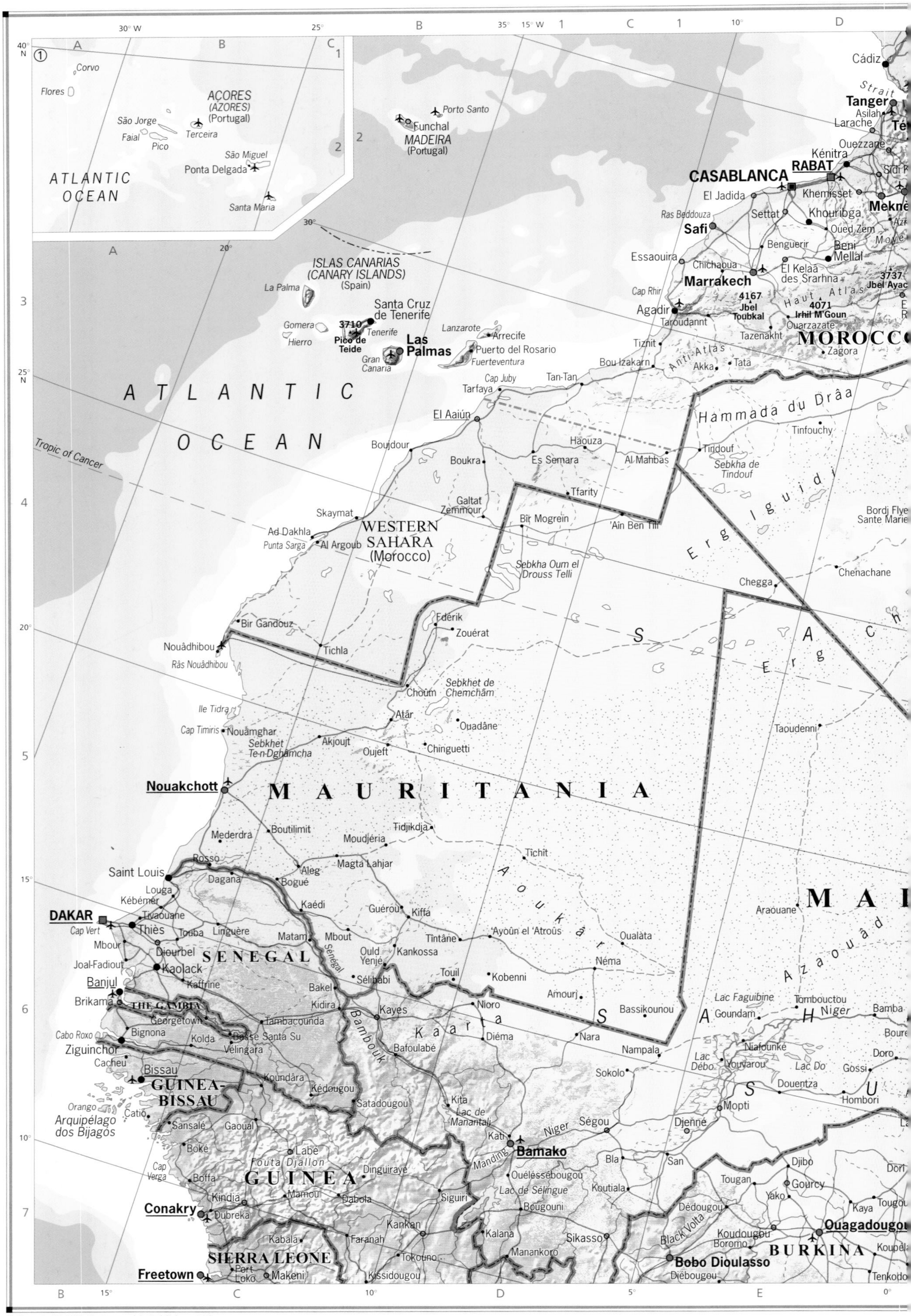

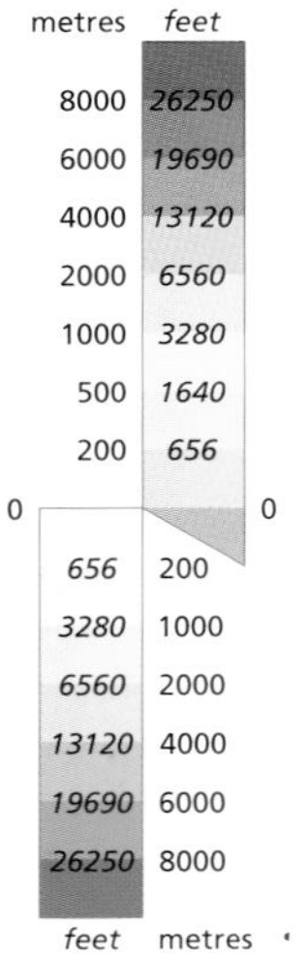

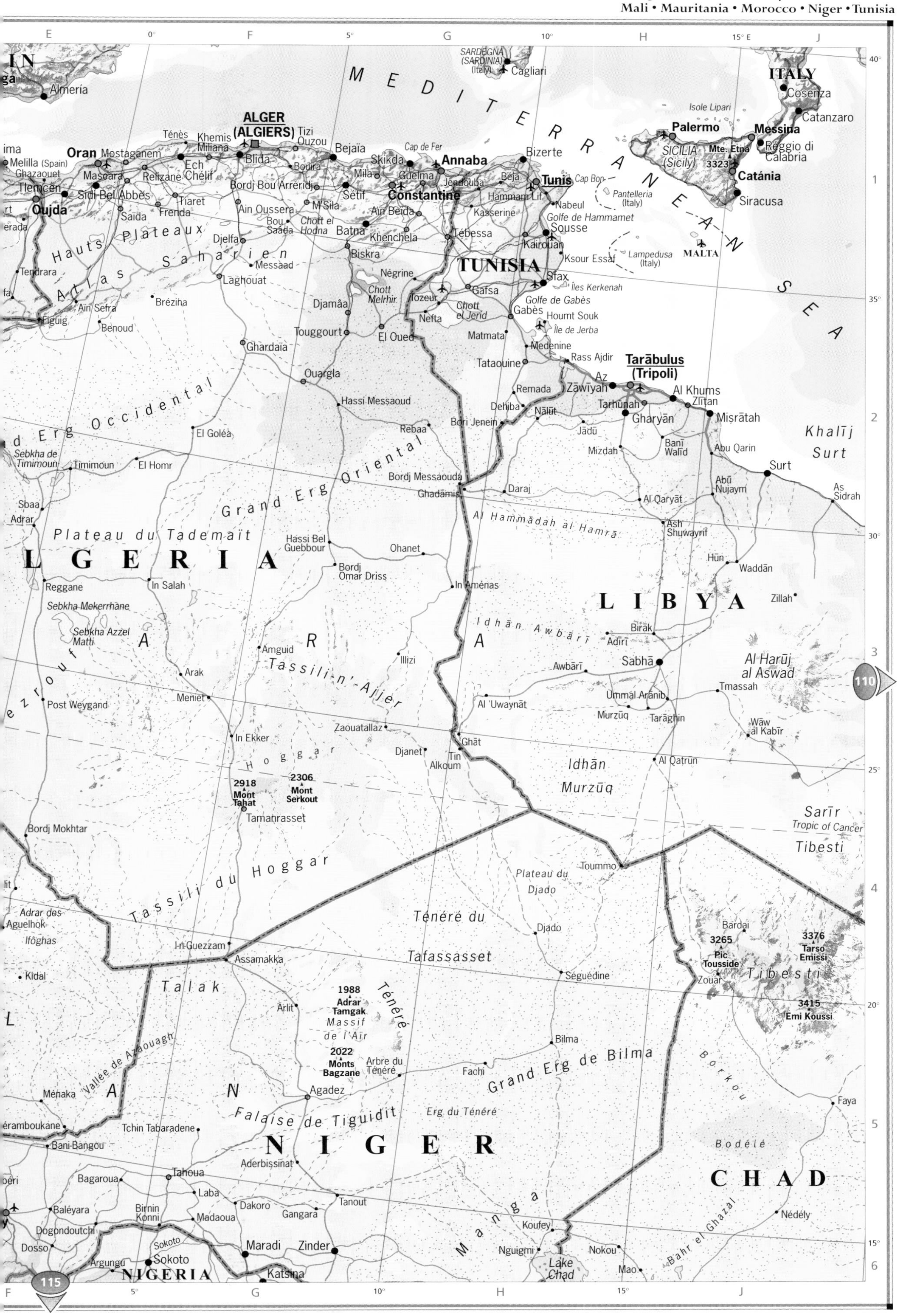

■ over 3 million
■ 1 – 3 million
● 250 000 – 1 million
• 100 000 – 250 000
○ 25 000 – 100 000
• under 25 000
——— country capital underline

Scale 1 : 11 600 000

0 200 400 600 km

0 100 200 300 miles

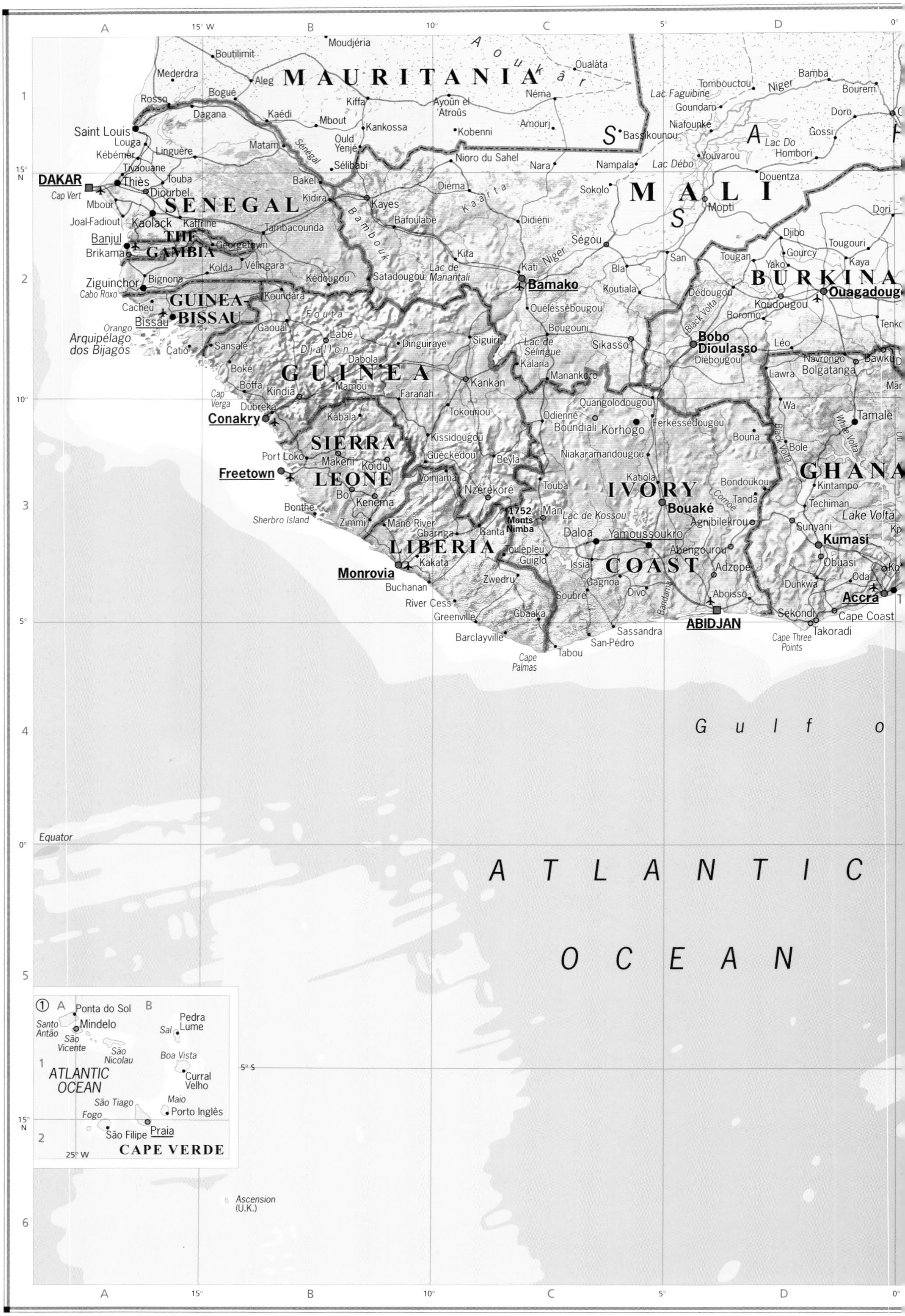

A
B
C
D
15° W
10°
5°
0°
1
2
3
4
5
6
15° N
10°
5°
0°
5°
Moudjéria
Boutilimit
Mederdra
Aleg
MAURITANIA
Aoukâr
Oualâta
Bogué
Rosso
Dagana
Kaédi
Kiffa
Mbout
Ayoûn el Atroûs
Néma
Kankossa
Kobenni
Amourj
Saint Louis
Louga
Kébémer
Linguère
Matam
Sénégal
Ould Yenjé
Sélibabi
Nioro du Sahel
Nara
Tivaouane
DAKAR
Cap Vert
Thiès
Touba
Diourbel
Mbour
SENEGAL
Bakel
Kidira
Diéma
Kaarta
Kayes
Joal-Fadiout
Kaolack
Kaffrine
Bafoulabé
Didiéni
Banjul
THE GAMBIA
Tambacounda
Brikama
Georgetown
Bambouk
Kita
Ségou
Kolda
Vélingara
Ziguinchor
Bignona
Cabo Roxo
Kédougou
Satadougou
Lac de Manantali
Kati
Niger
Bamako
Cacheu
Bissau
GUINEA-BISSAU
Koundara
Fouta
Orango
Arquipélago dos Bijagós
Catió
Gaoual
Labé
Djallon
Sansalé
Dabola
Dinguiraye
Siguiri
Boké
Boffa
GUINEA
Mamou
Kindia
Cap Verga
Dubreka
Faranah
Kankan
Conakry
Kabala
Tokounou
Kissidougou
SIERRA
Port Loko
Makeni
Koidu
Guéckédou
Beyla
Freetown
LEONE
Voinjama
Bo
Kenema
Nzérékoré
Bonthe
Sherbro Island
Zimmi
Mano River
Gbarnga
1752 Monts Nimba
Santa
Man
LIBERIA
Kakata
Monrovia
Buchanan
River Cess
Greenville
Barclayville
Cape Palmas
Zwedru
Toulepleu
Guiglo
Gbaaka
Tabou
Tombouctou
Lac Faguibine
Goundam
Niger
Bamba
Bourem
Niafounké
Bassikounou
Gossi
Doro
Lac Do
Hombori
Youvarou
Nampala
Lac Débo
Douentza
Sokolo
MALI
Mopti
Dori
Djibo
Tougouri
San
Tougan
Yako
Gourcy
Kaya
Bla
Koutiala
BURKINA
Dédougou
Ouagadougou
Koudougou
Ouélessébougou
Boromo
Black Volta
Bougouni
Lac de Sélingue
Kalana
Sikasso
Bobo Dioulasso
Diébougou
Léo
Tenko
Manankoro
Navrongo
Bolgatanga
Bawku
Lawra
Quangolodougou
Odienné
Boundiali
Korhogo
Ferkessédougou
Wa
Tamale
White Volta
Bouna
Bole
Niakaramandougou
Katiola
Bondoukou
GHANA
Touba
IVORY
Kintampo
Comoé
Tanda
Techiman
Lac de Kossou
Bouaké
Agnibilekrou
Lake Volta
Sunyani
Daloa
Yamoussoukro
Kumasi
Abengourou
COAST
Issia
Gagnoa
Adzopé
Obuasi
Divo
Dunkwa
Soubré
Bandama
Aboisso
Accra
ABIDJAN
Sekondi
Cape Coast
Sassandra
San-Pédro
Cape Three Points
Takoradi
Gulf o
Equator
ATLANTIC
OCEAN
① A Ponta do Sol B
Santo Antão
Mindelo
São Vicente
Sal
Pedra Lume
São Nicolau
Boa Vista
1
ATLANTIC OCEAN
Curral Velho
Maio
São Tiago
Porto Inglês
Fogo
Praia
São Filipe
2
25° W
CAPE VERDE
Ascension (U.K.)

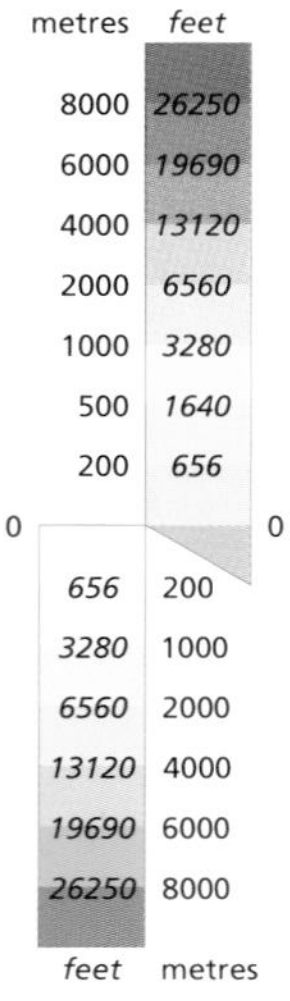

metres
feet
8000
26250
6000
19690
4000
13120
2000
6560
1000
3280
500
1640
200
656
0
0
656
200
3280
1000
6560
2000
13120
4000
19690
6000
26250
8000
feet
metres

West Africa

Benin • Burkina • Cameroon • Cape Verde • Congo • Equatorial Guinea • Gabon • The Gambia • Ghana
Guinea • Guinea-Bissau • Ivory Coast • Liberia • Nigeria • São Tomé & Príncipe • Senegal • Sierra Leone • Togo

■ over 3 million
■ 1 – 3 million
● 250 000 – 1 million
● 100 000 – 250 000
○ 25 000 – 100 000
• under 25 000
country capital underline
state or province capital underline

Scale 1 : 11 600 000

0 200 400 600 km

0 100 200 300 miles

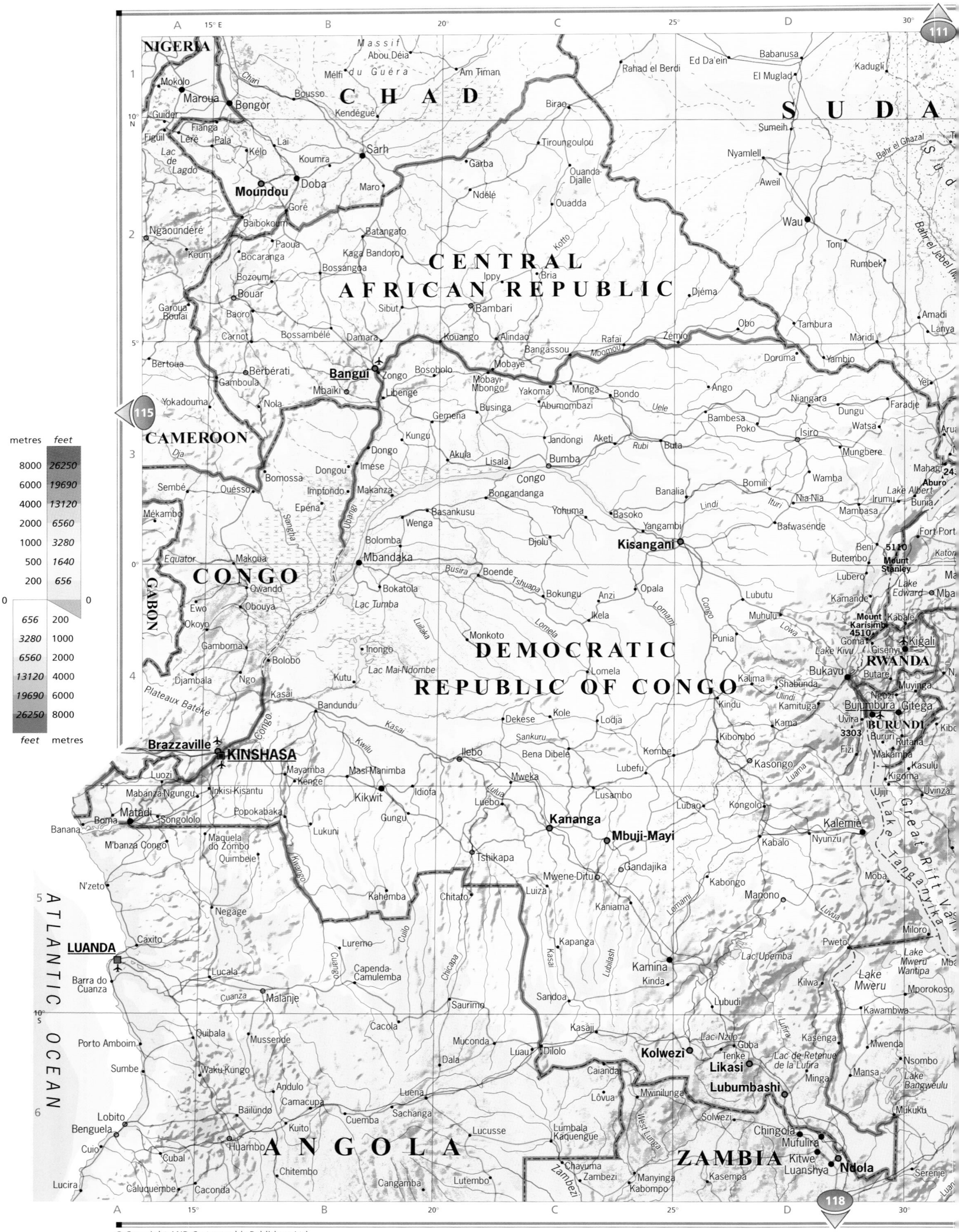

Central Africa

Angola • Burundi • Central African Republic • Democratic Republic of Congo
Djibouti • Ethiopia • Kenya • Rwanda • Somalia • Tanzania • Uganda

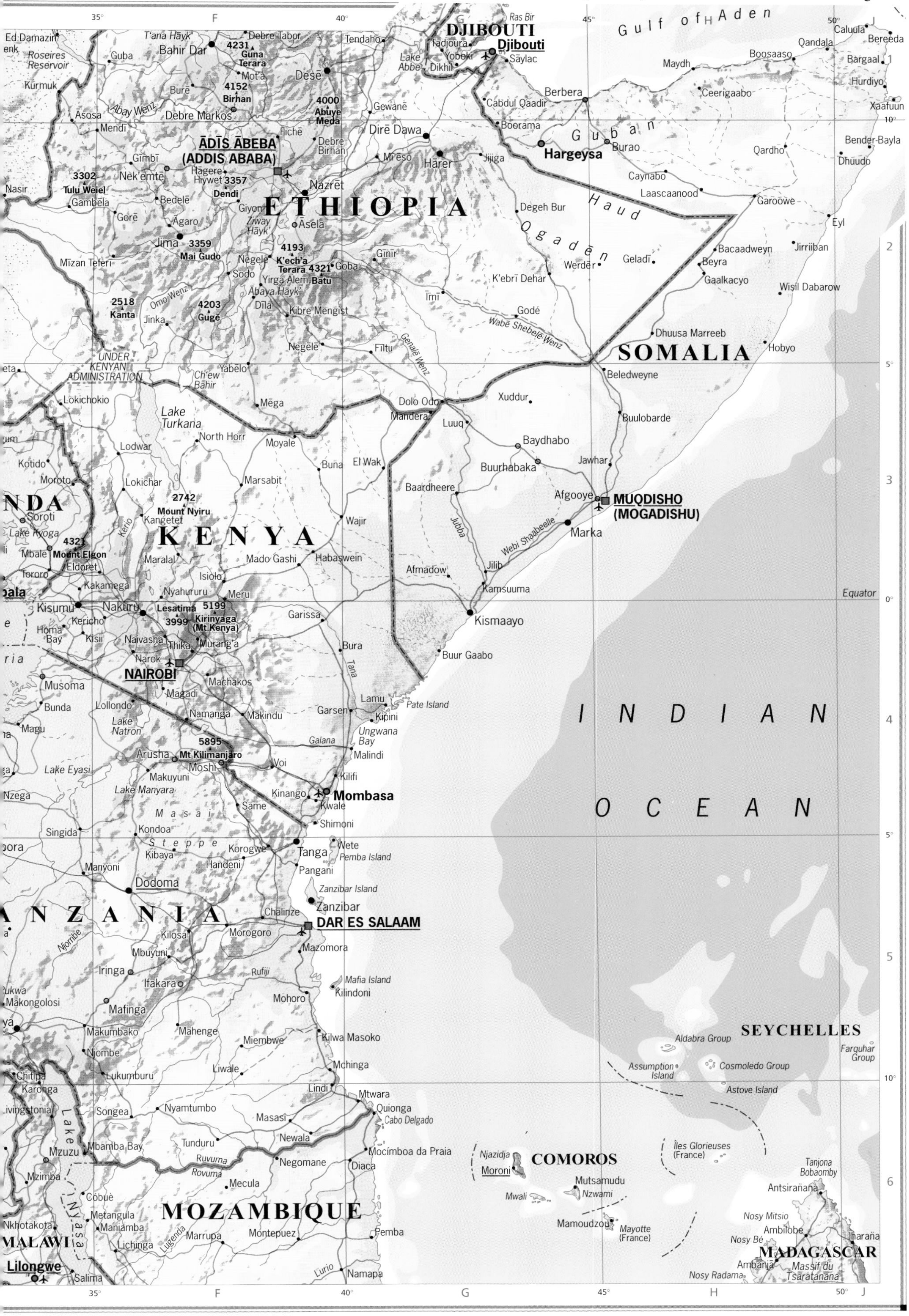

■ over 3 million	● 100 000 – 250 000
■ 1 – 3 million	○ 25 000 – 100 000
● 250 000 – 1 million	• under 25 000
——— country capital underline	

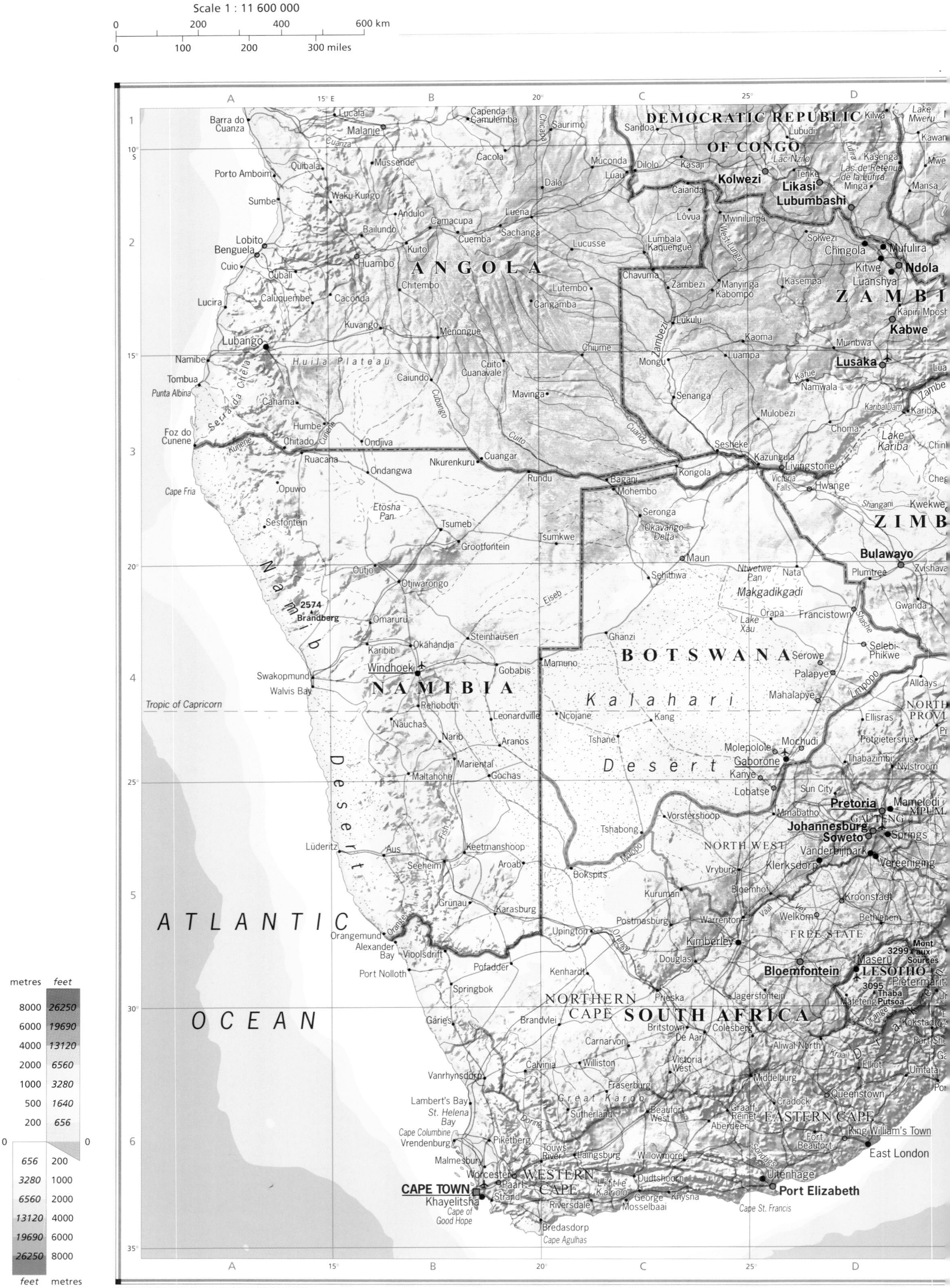

Scale 1 : 11 600 000

```
 0 200 400 600 km
 ├────┬────┬────┬────┬────┬────┤
 0 100 200 300 miles
```

| A | 15° E | B | 20° | C | 25° | D |

DEMOCRATIC REPUBLIC
OF CONGO

Barra do Cuanza
Lucala
Malanje
Capenda-Camulemba
Chicapa
Saurimo
Sandoa
Kilwa
Lake Mweru
Kawan

Porto Amboim
Quibala
Mussende
Cacola
Muconda
Dilolo
Kasaji
Lac Nzilo
Kaseng
Lac de Retenue de la Lufira
Mwe
Minga
Mansa

Sumbe
Waku-Kungo
Andulo
Camacupa
Luena
Luau
Caianda
Kolwezi
Tenke
Likasi
Lubumbashi

Lobito
Benguela
Cuio
Cubali
Huambo
Bailundo
Kuito
Cuemba
Sachanga
Lucusse
Lumbala Kaquengue
Mwinilunga
Sokwezi
Chingola
Mufulira

Lucira
Caluquembe
Caconda
Chitembo
ANGOLA
Cangamba
Chavuma
Zambezi
Manyinga
Kabompo
Kitwe
Luanshya
Ndola
ZAMBI

Lubango
Namibe
Kuvango
Menongue
Chiume
Mongu
Kaoma
Luampa
Mumbwa
Kapiri Mposh
Kabwe

Tombua
Punta Albina
Huila Plateau
Caiundo
Cuito Cuanavale
Mavinga
Senanga
Kafue
Namwala
Lusaka
Lua

Foz do Cunene
Cahama
Humbe
Cuangar
Cuito
Sesheke
Mulobezi
Choma
Lake Kariba
KaribaDam
Kariba
Chin

Cape Fria
Chitado
Ondjiva
Ruacana
Ondangwa
Nkurenkuru
Rundu
Bagani
Kongola
Kazungula
Livingstone
Victoria Falls
Hwange
Shangani
Kwekwe

Opuwo
Sesfontein
Etosha Pan
Tsumeb
Grootfontein
Tsumkwe
Mohembo
Seronga
Okavango Delta
ZIMB

Outjo
Otjiwarongo
Eiseb
Maun
Sehithwa
Ntwetwe Pan
Nata
Plumtree
Bulawayo
Zvishan

2574 Brandberg
Omaruru
Ghanzi
Makgadikgadi
Lake Xau
Orapa
Francistown
Selebi-Phikwe
Gwanda
Alldays

Karibib
Okahandja
Steinhausen
Mamuno
BOTSWANA
Serowe
NORTH PROVI

Swakopmund
Walvis Bay
Windhoek
Gobabis
Palapye
Mahalapye
Limpopo

Tropic of Capricorn
Rehoboth
NAMIBIA
Leonardville
Ncojane
Kang
Kalahari
Molepolole
Mochudi
Potgietersrus
Nylstroom

Nauchas
Narib
Aranos
Tshane
Desert
Gaborone
Kanye
Thabazimbi
Sun City
Pretoria
Mamelodi
MPUM

Mariental
Gochas
Lobatse
Mmabatho
GAUTENG
Johannesburg
Soweto
Springs

Maltahöhe
Vorstershoop
NORTH WEST
Vanderbijlpark
Vereeniging

Lüderitz
Aus
Keetmanshoop
Tshabong
Vryburg
Klerksdorp
Kroonstad
Bethlehem

Seeheim
Aroab
Bokspits
Kuruman
Bloemhof
Welkom
FREE STATE

Grünau
Karasburg
Postmasburg
Warrenton
Maseru
Mont aux Sources 3299

Orangemund
Alexander Bay
Vioolsdrift
Pofadder
Upington
Douglas
Kimberley
Bloemfontein
LESOTHO
Pietermarit
3095 Thaba

Port Nolloth
Kenhardt
Prieska
Jagersfontein
Maseru
Mafeteng Putsoa
Kokstad

A T L A N T I C
Springbok
NORTHERN CAPE
Brandvlei
Britstown
De Aar
Colesberg
Aliwal North
Queenstown
Port Sh

Gäries
Carnarvon
Victoria West
SOUTH AFRICA
Middelburg
Elliot
Umtata

O C E A N
Vanrhynsdorp
Calvinia
Williston
Fraserburg
Beaufort West
Cradock
Graaff-Reinet
Aberdeen
King William's Town

Lambert's Bay
St. Helena Bay
Sutherland
Great Karoo
Doring
Fort Beaufort
East London

Cape Columbine
Vrendenburg
Piketberg
Touws River
Laingsburg
Willowmore
Uitenhage
Port Elizabeth

Malmesbury
Worcester
WESTERN CAPE
Little Karoo
Dudtshoorn
George
Knysna

CAPE TOWN
Paarl
Strand
Riversdale
Mosselbaai
Cape St. Francis

Khayelitsha
Cape of Good Hope
Bredasdorp
Cape Agulhas

metres	feet
8000	26250
6000	19690
4000	13120
2000	6560
1000	3280
500	1640
200	656
0	0

feet	metres
656	200
3280	1000
6560	2000
13120	4000
19690	6000
26250	8000

| A | 15° | B | 20° | C | 25° | D |

© Copyright AND Cartographic Publishers Ltd.

Botswana • Comoros • Lesotho • Madagascar • Malawi • Mauritius
Mozambique • Namibia • Seychelles • South Africa • Swaziland • Zambia • Zimbabwe

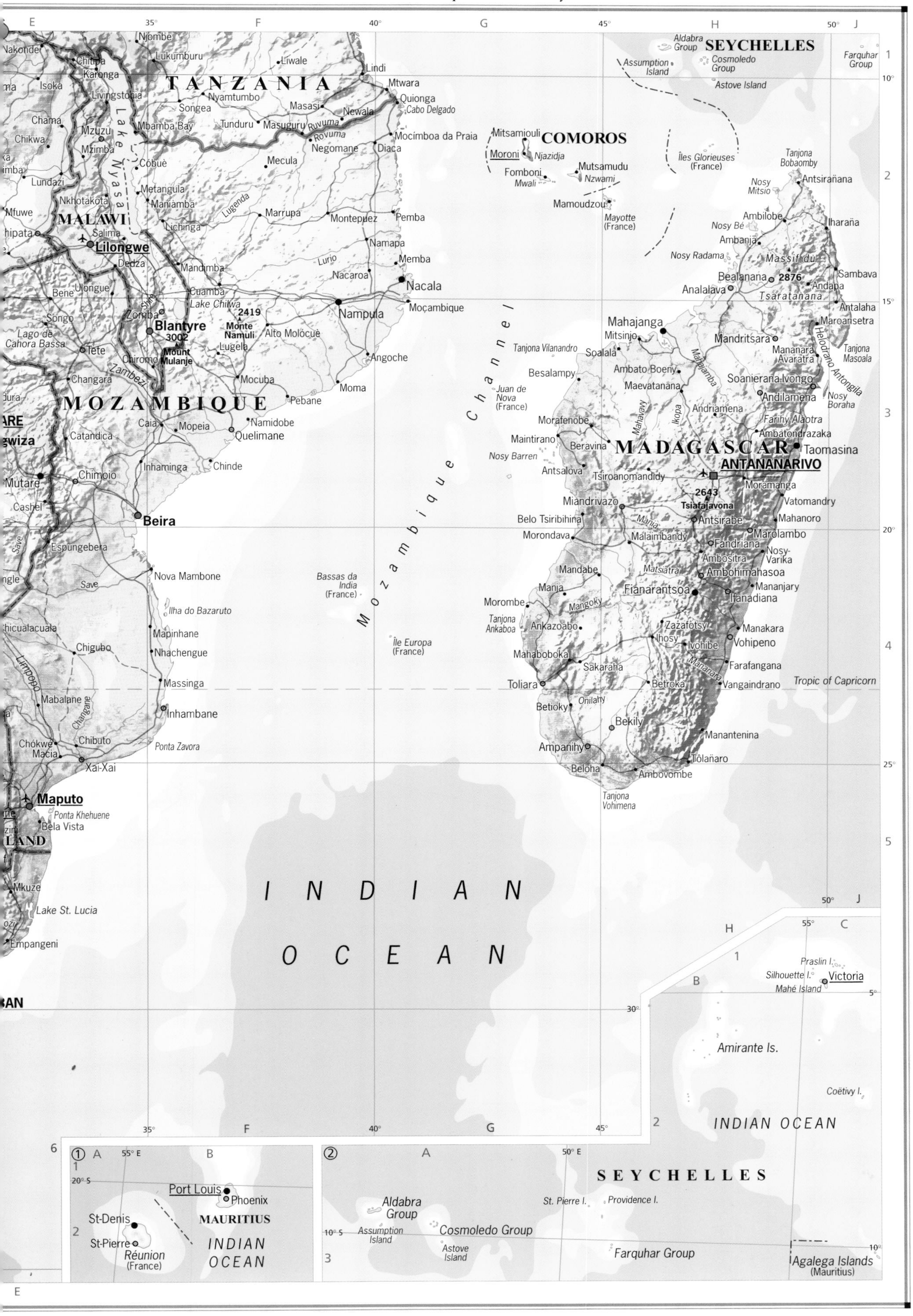

TANZANIA
Njombe
Lukumburu
Liwale
Lindi
Mtwara
Quionga
Cabo Delgado
Nyamtumbo
Songea
Masasi
Newala
Tunduru
Masuguru
Ruvuma
Negomane
Diaca
Mocímboa da Praia
Chitipa
Karonga
Isoka
Livingstonia
Chama
Chikwa
Mzuzu
Mzimba
Mbamba Bay
Lake Nyasa
Cóbuè
Mecula
Lundazi
Metangula
Maniamba
Nkhotakota
Mfuwe
MALAWI
Salima
Lilongwe
Lichinga
Lugenda
Marrupa
Montepuez
Pemba
Namapa
Memba
Lurio
Nacaroa
Nacala
Dedza
Mandimba
Bene
Ulongue
Cuamba
Lake Chilwa
2419
Monte Namuli
Alto Molócuè
Nampula
Moçambique
Songo
Zomba
Shire
Blantyre
3002
Mount Mulanje
Lugela
Lago de Cahora Bassa
Tete
Chiromo
Angoche
Changara
Zambezi
Mocuba
Moma
Pebane
MOZAMBIQUE
Caia
Mopeia
Namidobe
Quelimane
Catandica
Inhaminga
Chinde
Mutare
Chimoio
Beira
Espungebera
Save
Nova Mambone
Ilha do Bazaruto
Mapinhane
Nhachengue
Chigubo
Limpopo
Massinga
Mabalane
Changane
Inhambane
Chókwè
Chibuto
Macia
Xai-Xai
Ponta Zavora
Maputo
Ponta Khehuene
Bela Vista
Mkuze
Lake St. Lucia
Empangeni
Mozambique Channel
Tanjona Vilanandro
Juan de Nova (France)
Bassas da India (France)
Île Europa (France)
SEYCHELLES
Aldabra Group
Assumption Island
Cosmoledo Group
Astove Island
Farquhar Group
COMOROS
Mitsamiouli
Moroni
Njazidja
Fomboni
Mwali
Mutsamudu
Nzwani
Mamoudzou
Mayotte (France)
Îles Glorieuses (France)
Tanjona Bobaomby
Antsirañana
Nosy Mitsio
Ambilobe
Iharaña
Nosy Be
Ambanja
Nosy Radama
Massif du Tsaratanana
2876
Sambava
Bealanana
Andapa
Analalava
Antalaha
Maroantsetra
Mahajanga
Mitsinjo
Mandritsara
Helodrano Antongila
Tanjona Masoala
Soalala
Mahajamba
Mananara Avaratra
Besalampy
Ambato Boeny
Maevatanana
Soanierana-Ivongo
Andilamena
Nosy Boraha
Mahavavy
Ikopa
Andriamena
Morafenobe
Fenoarivo Atsinanana
Ambatondrazaka
Maintirano
Beravina
MADAGASCAR
Toamasina
Nosy Barren
ANTANANARIVO
Antsalova
Tsiroanomandidy
Moramanga
Miandrivazo
2643
Tsiafajavona
Vatomandry
Belo Tsiribihina
Antsirabe
Mahanoro
Morondava
Mania
Malaimbandy
Marolambo
Fandriana
Ambositra
Nosy-Varika
Mandabe
Matsiatra
Ambohimahasoa
Manja
Fianarantsoa
Mananjary
Ifanadiana
Morombe
Mangoky
Tanjona Ankaboa
Ankazoabo
Zazafotsy
Ihosy
Ivohibe
Manakara
Vohipeno
Mahaboboka
Sakaraha
Farafangana
Toliara
Betroka
Vangaindrano
Tropic of Capricorn
Betioky
Onilahy
Bekily
Manantenina
Ampanihy
Tôlañaro
Beloha
Ambovombe
Tanjona Vohimena
INDIAN OCEAN
Praslin I.
Silhouette I.
Victoria
Mahé Island
Amirante Is.
Coëtivy I.
INDIAN OCEAN
Port Louis
Phoenix
MAURITIUS
St-Denis
St-Pierre
Réunion (France)
INDIAN OCEAN
SEYCHELLES
St. Pierre I.
Providence I.
Aldabra Group
Assumption Island
Cosmoledo Group
Astove Island
Farquhar Group
Agalega Islands (Mauritius)

■ over 3 million
■ 1 – 3 million
● 250 000 – 1 million
● 100 000 – 250 000
○ 25 000 – 100 000
• under 25 000
country capital underline
state or province capital underline

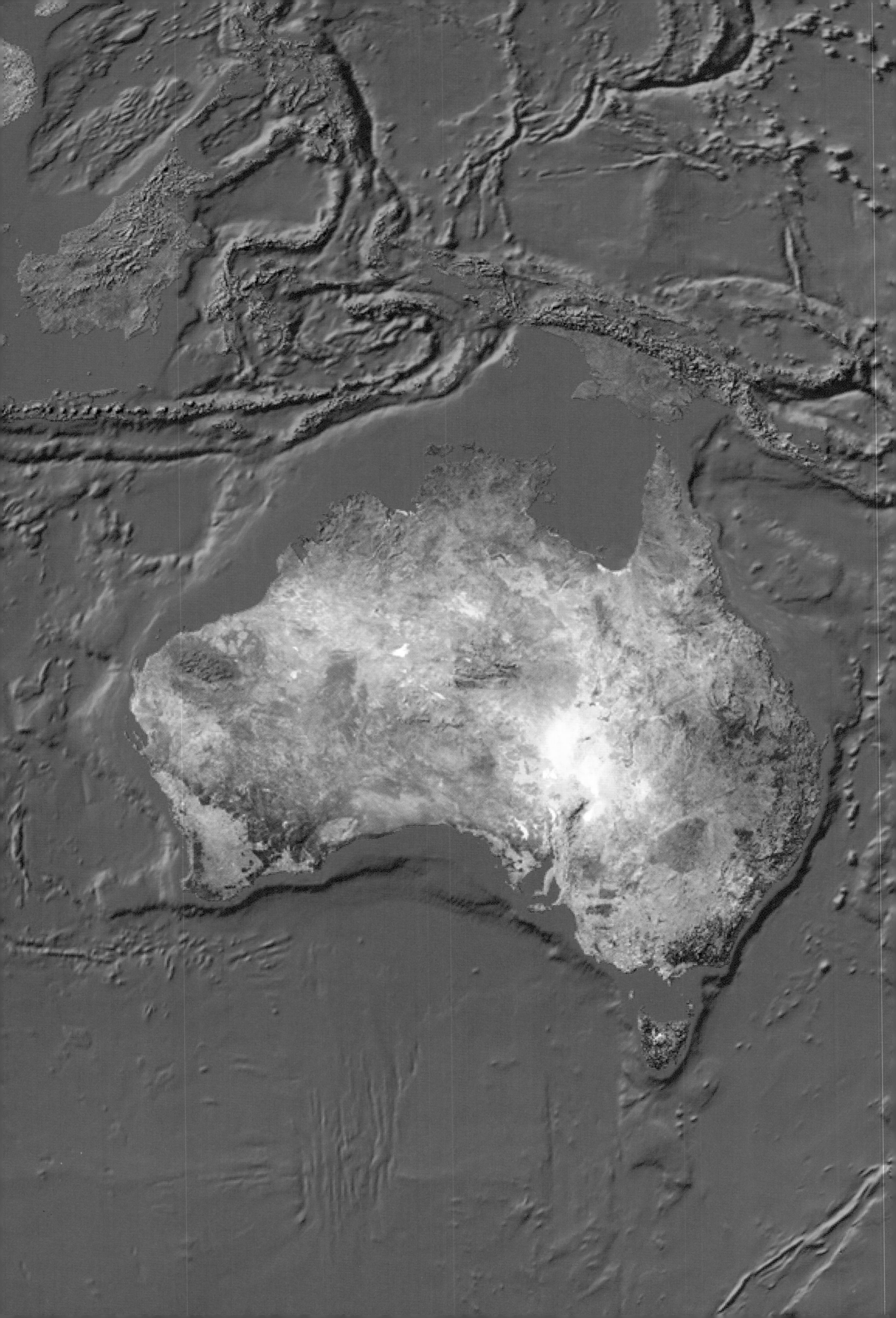

OCEANIA

a view from space

OCEANIA

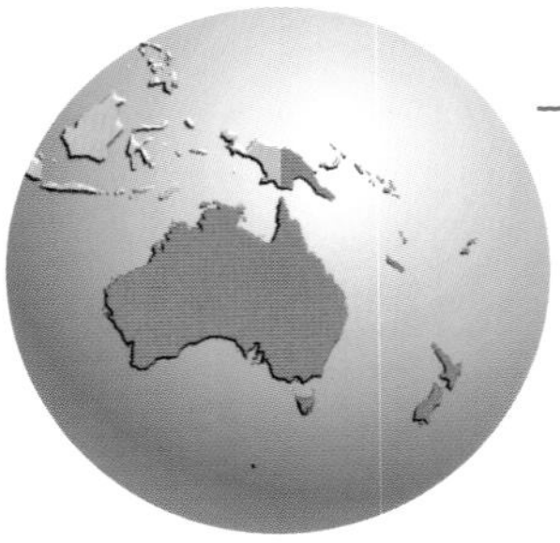

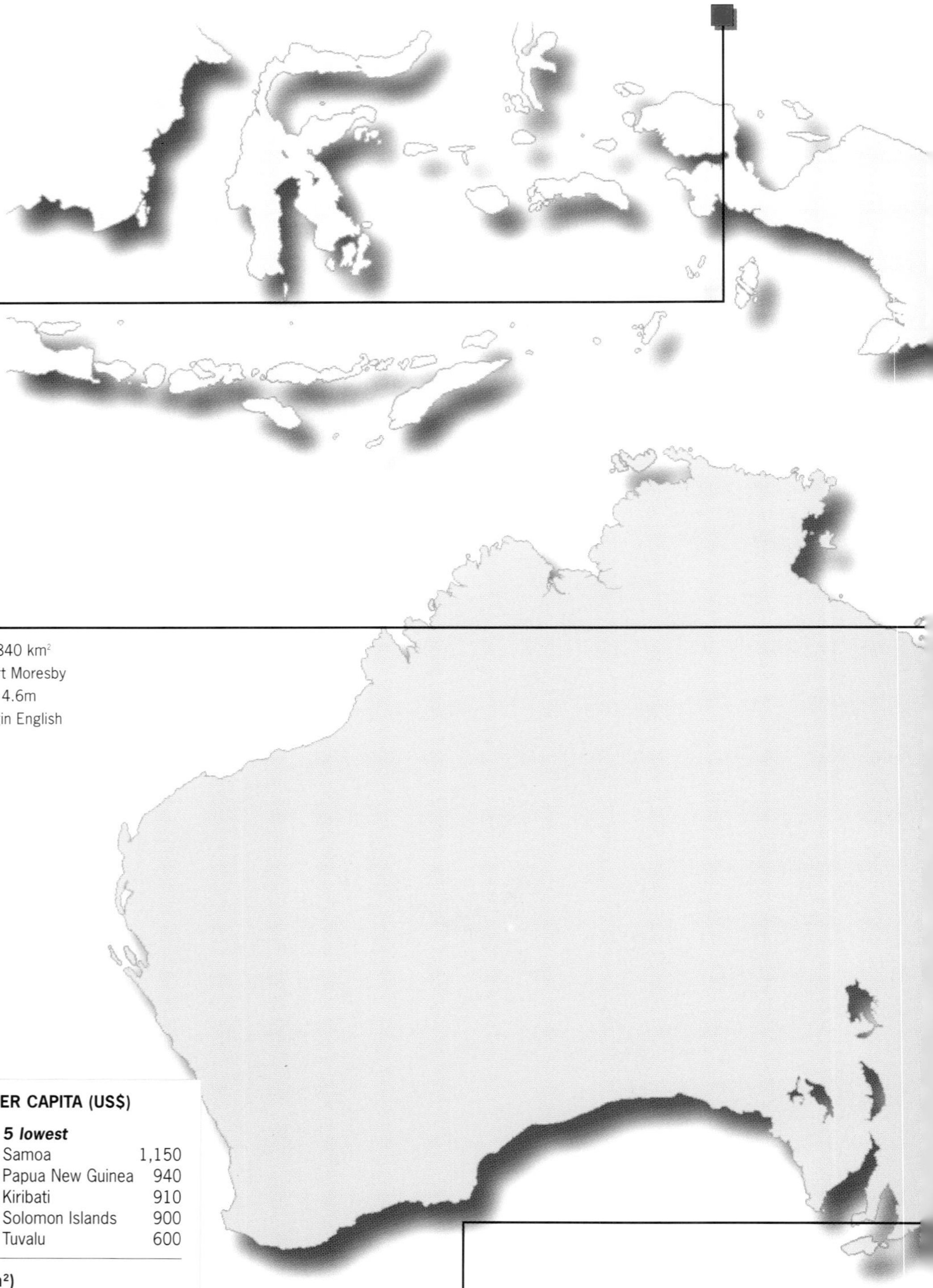

Palau

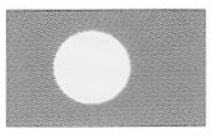

Area: 459 km²
Capital: Koror
Population: 19,000
Languages: Palauan, English
Religion: Christian
Currency: US dollar

Papua New Guinea

Area: 462,840 km²
Capital: Port Moresby
Population: 4.6m
Languages: English, Pidgin English
Religion: Christian
Currency: Kina

GROSS NATIONAL PRODUCT PER CAPITA (US$)

5 highest		*5 lowest*	
Australia	20,540	Samoa	1,150
New Zealand	16,480	Papua New Guinea	940
Nauru	10,000	Kiribati	910
Fiji	2,470	Solomon Islands	900
Palau	2,260	Tuvalu	600

POPULATION DENSITY (per km²)

5 highest		*5 lowest*	
Nauru	524	Vanuatu	15
Tuvalu	423	Solomon Islands	14
Marshall Islands	331	New Zealand	14
Fed. States of Micronesia	162	Papua New Guinea	10
Tonga	127	Australia	2

LIFE EXPECTANCY (years)

5 highest		*5 lowest*	
Australia	78	Nauru	67
New Zealand	76	Vanuatu	65
Fiji	71	Marshall Islands	63
Palau	69	Kiribati	60
Samoa	68	Papua New Guinea	56

Australia

Area: 7,741,260 km²
Capital: Canberra
Population: 19m
Main language: English
Religion: Protestant
Currency: Australian dollar

AUSTRALIA IS FLAT, DRY, and rich in minerals. The sparse population lives mainly in the coastal lowlands. New Zealand is temperate and rugged while Papua New Guinea is covered in tropical rainforest. The rest of Oceania comprises three main groups of volcanic, coral islands scattered across the Pacific.

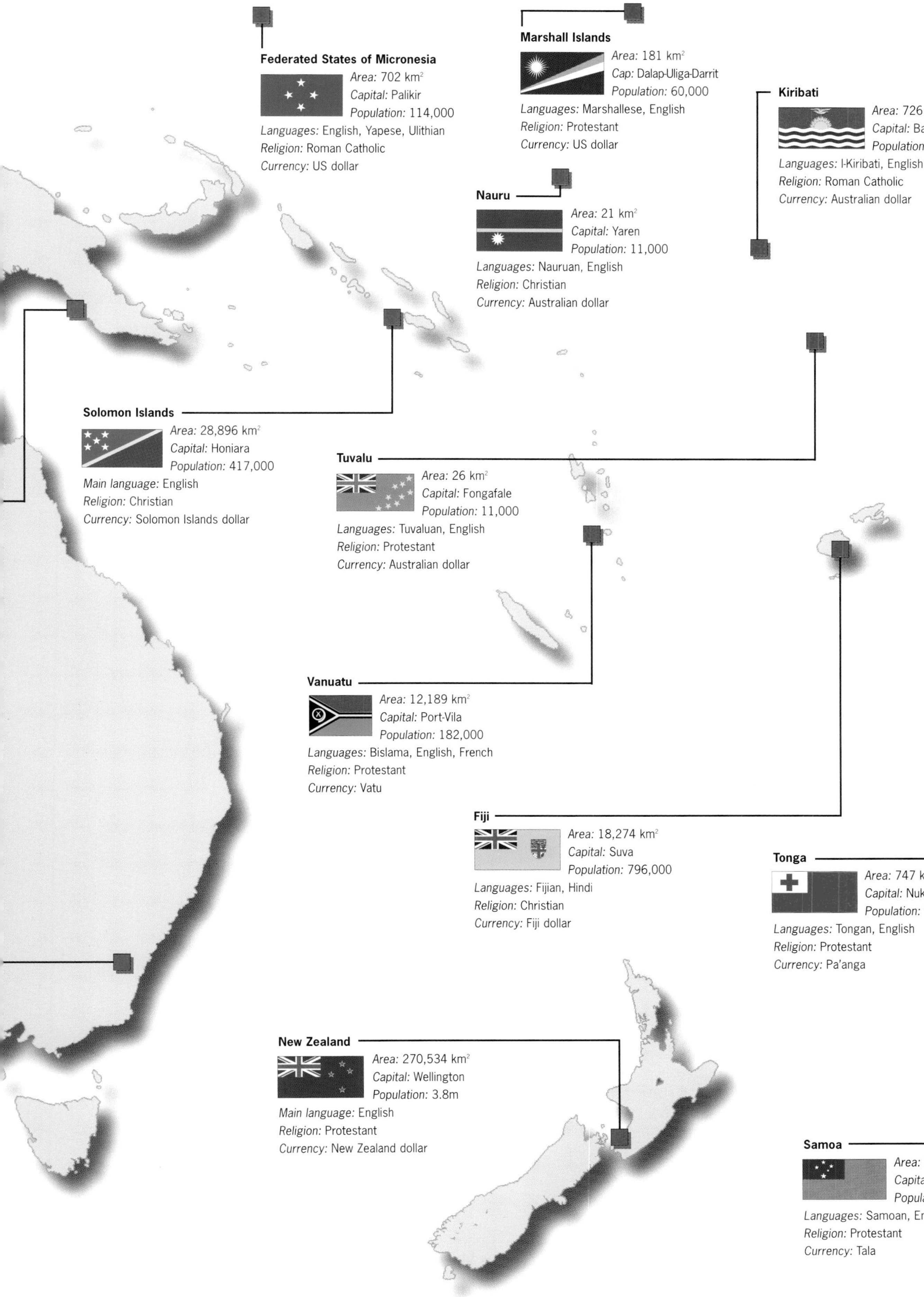

Federated States of Micronesia

Area: 702 km²
Capital: Palikir
Population: 114,000
Languages: English, Yapese, Ulithian
Religion: Roman Catholic
Currency: US dollar

Marshall Islands

Area: 181 km²
Cap: Dalap-Uliga-Darrit
Population: 60,000
Languages: Marshallese, English
Religion: Protestant
Currency: US dollar

Kiribati

Area: 726 km²
Capital: Bairiki
Population: 81,000
Languages: I-Kiribati, English
Religion: Roman Catholic
Currency: Australian dollar

Nauru

Area: 21 km²
Capital: Yaren
Population: 11,000
Languages: Nauruan, English
Religion: Christian
Currency: Australian dollar

Solomon Islands

Area: 28,896 km²
Capital: Honiara
Population: 417,000
Main language: English
Religion: Christian
Currency: Solomon Islands dollar

Tuvalu

Area: 26 km²
Capital: Fongafale
Population: 11,000
Languages: Tuvaluan, English
Religion: Protestant
Currency: Australian dollar

Vanuatu

Area: 12,189 km²
Capital: Port-Vila
Population: 182,000
Languages: Bislama, English, French
Religion: Protestant
Currency: Vatu

Fiji

Area: 18,274 km²
Capital: Suva
Population: 796,000
Languages: Fijian, Hindi
Religion: Christian
Currency: Fiji dollar

Tonga

Area: 747 km²
Capital: Nuku'alofa
Population: 98,000
Languages: Tongan, English
Religion: Protestant
Currency: Pa'anga

New Zealand

Area: 270,534 km²
Capital: Wellington
Population: 3.8m
Main language: English
Religion: Protestant
Currency: New Zealand dollar

Samoa

Area: 2,831 km²
Capital: Apia
Population: 174,000
Languages: Samoan, English
Religion: Protestant
Currency: Tala

Scale 1 : 40 500 000

0 500 1000 1500 2000 km

0 250 500 750 1000 miles

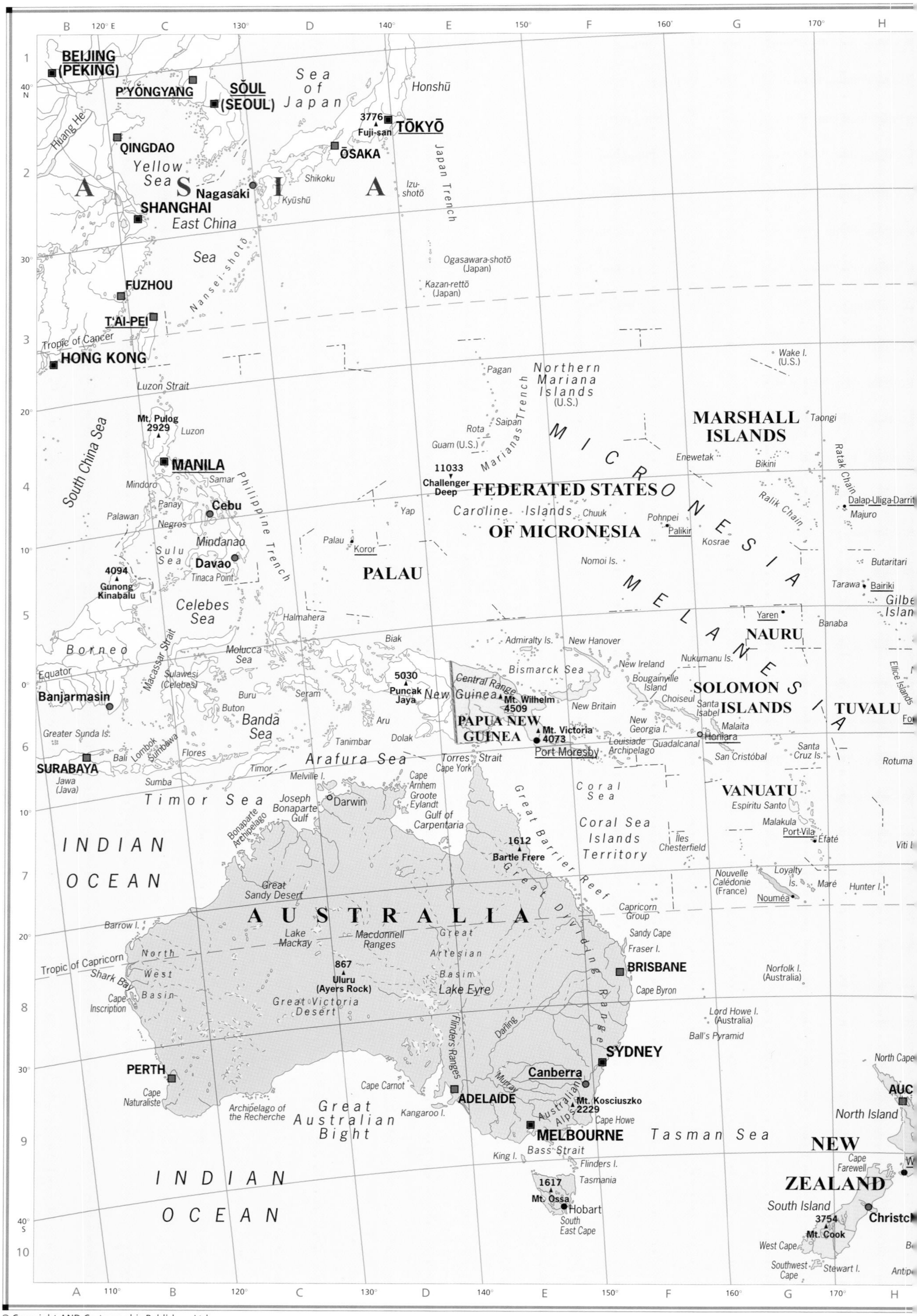

Mt. Wilhelm, Papua New Guinea : 4,509 m or 14,793 ft

Mulka, Australia : 10.3 cm or 4.05 in

Murray-Darling, Australia : 3,750 km^2 or 2,330 sq mi

Lake Eyre, Australia : 15 m or 49 ft

Mt. Waialeale, Hawaii : 1168 cm or 460 in

Lake Eyre, Australia : 8,800 km^2 or 3,400 sq mi

Charlotte Pass, Australia : -23 °C or -9.4 °F

Cloncurry, Australia : 53 °C or 128 °F

29,642,000

3.3 per km² or 8.6 per sq mi

8,945,000 km² or 3,454,000 sq mi

14

Scale 1 : 13 800 000

0 200 400 600 km

0 100 200 300 miles

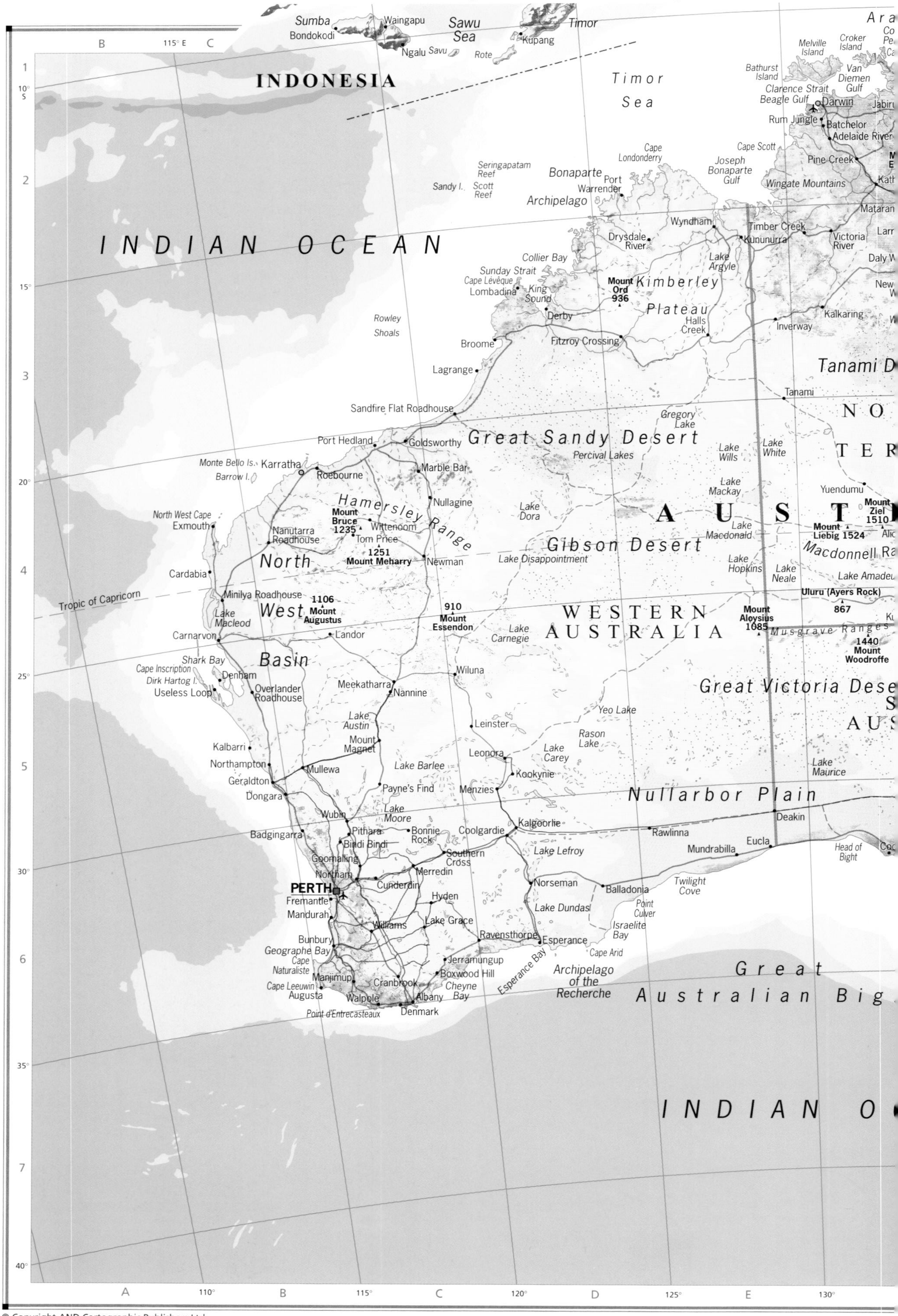

INDONESIA
Sumba
Waingapu
Bondokodi
Ngalu
Sawu Sea
Sawu
Rote
Kupang
Timor
Timor Sea
Melville Island
Croker Island
Bathurst Island
Van Diemen Gulf
Clarence Strait
Beagle Gulf
Darwin
Rum Jungle
Batchelor
Adelaide River
Cape Scott
Pine Creek
Joseph Bonaparte Gulf
Wingate Mountains
Cape Londonderry
Seringapatam Reef
Sandy I.
Scott Reef
Bonaparte Archipelago
Port Warrender
Wyndham
Timber Creek
Kununurra
Victoria River
Drysdale River
INDIAN OCEAN
Collier Bay
Sunday Strait
Cape Lévêque
Lombadina
King Sound
Derby
Mount Ord 936
Kimberley Plateau
Lake Argyle
Halls Creek
Inverway
Kalkaring
Rowley Shoals
Broome
Fitzroy Crossing
Lagrange
Tanami
Sandfire Flat Roadhouse
Gregory Lake
Port Hedland
Goldsworthy
Great Sandy Desert
Percival Lakes
Lake Wills
Lake White
Monte Bello Is.
Barrow I.
Karratha
Roebourne
Marble Bar
Lake Mackay
Yuendumu
Nullagine
Hamersley Range
Mount Bruce 1235
Wittenoom
Tom Price
1251 Mount Meharry
Newman
North West Cape
Exmouth
Nanutarra Roadhouse
Lake Dora
Gibson Desert
Lake Disappointment
Lake Macdonald
Mount Liebig 1524
Mount Ziel 1510
Macdonnell Ra
Lake Hopkins
Lake Neale
Lake Amadeus
Cardabia
Tropic of Capricorn
Minilya Roadhouse
1106 Mount Augustus
910 Mount Essendon
Uluru (Ayers Rock) 867
North West Basin
Lake Macleod
Carnarvon
Landor
Lake Carnegie
WESTERN AUSTRALIA
AUST
Mount Aloysius 1085
Musgrave Ranges
1440 Mount Woodroffe
Shark Bay
Cape Inscription
Dirk Hartog I.
Denham
Useless Loop
Overlander Roadhouse
Meekatharra
Nannine
Wiluna
Great Victoria Desert
Lake Austin
Yeo Lake
Leinster
Rason Lake
Mount Magnet
Kalbarri
Northampton
Mullewa
Geraldton
Dongara
Lake Barlee
Payne's Find
Leonora
Lake Carey
Kookynie
Menzies
Lake Maurice
Nullarbor Plain
Deakin
Wubin
Pithara
Lake Moore
Bonnie Rock
Coolgardie
Kalgoorlie
Rawlinna
Badgingarra
Bindi Bindi
Goomalling
Southern Cross
Lake Lefroy
Mundrabilla
Eucla
Head of Bight
Northam
Merredin
PERTH
Cunderdin
Fremantle
Mandurah
Hyden
Norseman
Balladonia
Twilight Cove
Williams
Lake Grace
Lake Dundas
Point Culver
Israelite Bay
Bunbury
Geographe Bay
Cape Naturaliste
Ravensthorpe
Esperance
Cape Arid
Jerramungup
Manjimup
Boxwood Hill
Esperance Bay
Archipelago of the Recherche
Cape Leeuwin
Augusta
Cranbrook
Cheyne Bay
Walpole
Albany
Denmark
Point d'Entrecasteaux
Great Australian Bight
INDIAN OCEAN

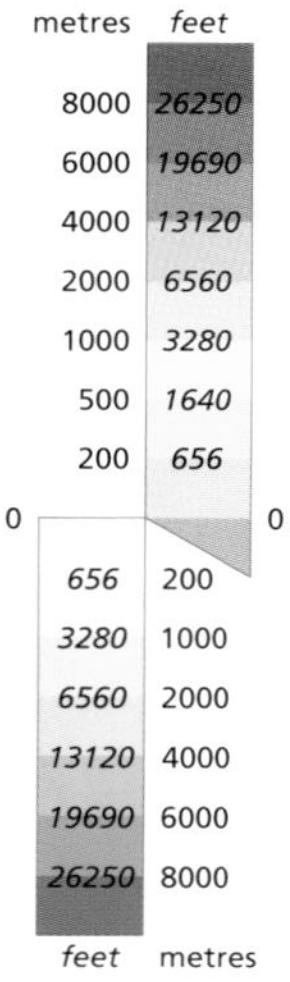

metres feet
8000 26250
6000 19690
4000 13120
2000 6560
1000 3280
500 1640
200 656
0 0
656 200
3280 1000
6560 2000
13120 4000
19690 6000
26250 8000
feet metres

■ over 3 million

■ 1 – 3 million

● 250 000 – 1 million

● 100 000 – 250 000

○ 25 000 – 100 000

• under 25 000

country capital underline

state or province capital underline

93
G
140°
H
145°
J
150°
K
155°
L
1
2
3
4
5
6
7
8
10°
15°
20°
25°
30°
35°
40°
160°
M
Mulgrave I.
Moa (Banks Island)
Torres Strait
Prince of Wales Island
Cape York
Bamaga
Somerset
Port Moresby
PAPUA NEW GUINEA
Alotau
D'Entrecasteaux Islands
Louisiade Archipelago
Cape Wessel
Wessel Islands
Cape Arnhem
Nhulunbuy
Cape Grenville
Duifken Point
Weipa
Albatross Bay
Aurukun
Cape York Peninsula
Cape Direction
Princess Charlotte Bay
CORAL SEA ISLANDS
CORAL SEA
TERRITORY
(Australia)
Bickerton Island
Groote Eylandt
Gulf of Carpentaria
Numbulwar
Coen
Silver Plains
Cape Melville
Osprey Reef
Shark Reef
Sir Edward Pellew Group
Kowanyama
Laura
Cape Flattery
Cooktown
Bougainville Reef
Holmes Reefs
Diane Bank
Wellesley Islands
Dunbar
Mornington I.
Bentinck I.
Cape Crawford
Port Douglas
Cairns
Mareeba
Willis Group
Magdelaine Cays
Herald Cays
Diamond Islets
Karumba
Burketown
Normanton
1612 Mount Bartle Frere
Innisfail
Mount Garnet
Flinders Reefs
Turtle I.
Tregosse Islets
Malay Reef
Croydon
Georgetown
Lorraine
Forsayth
GREAT BARRIER REEF
Ingham
Halifax Bay
Greenvale
Mutarnee
Townsville
PACIFIC OCEAN
Camooweal
Ayr
Bowen
The Whitsundays
Charters Towers
Proserpine
Repulse Bay
Mount Isa
Cloncurry
Lake Nash
Richmond
Hughenden
Dalrymple Lake
Mackay
McKinlay
Sarina
QUEENSLAND
Swain Reefs
Tobermorey
Nebo
Broad Sound
Winton
Clairview
Boulia
Muttaburra
Townshend I.
GREAT DIVIDING RANGE
Clermont
Great Artesian Basin
Longreach
Barcaldine
Jericho
Emerald
Blackwater
Yeppoon
Rockhampton
Curtis I.
Capricorn Group
Simpson Desert
Cato I.
Tropic of Capricorn
Blackall
Springsure
Gladstone
Jundah
Yaraka
Tambo
Biloela
Banana
Bundaberg
Birdsville
Betoota
Windorah
Sandy Cape
Lake Yamma Yamma
Eidsvold
Hervey Bay
Fraser I.
Augathella
Taroom
Maryborough
Lake Eyre Basin
Sturt Stony Desert
Charleville
Gayndah
Gympie
Quilpie
Roma
Muckadilla
Miles
Kingaroy
Caloundra
Tirari Desert
Glenmorgan
Moreton I.
Lake Eyre North
Grey Range
Thargomindah
St George
Moonie
Dalby
BRISBANE
Toowoomba
North Stradbroke I.
Cunnamulla
Beenleigh
Mount Roberts 1387
Surfers Paradise
Gold Coast
Lake Eyre South
Lake Blanche
Hungerford
Dirranbandi
Bungunya
Goondiwindi
Boggabilla
Casino
Cape Byron
Ballina
Marree
Lake Callabonna
Tibbooburra
Wanaaring
Enngonia
Tenterfield
Moree
Brewarrina
Leigh Creek
Bourke
Walgett
Glen Innes
Grafton
Glendambo
Lake Torrens
Lake Frome
White Cliffs
Louth
Narrabi
Armidale
Round Mountain 1608
Coffs Harbour
Pimba
Flinders Ranges
Darling
Coolabah
Gunnedah
Hawker
Broken Hill
Wilcannia
NEW SOUTH WALES
Cobar
Coonabarabran
Black Sugarloaf 1494
Nyngan
Tamworth
Quirindi
Port Augusta
Menindee
Gilgandra
Port Macquarie
Whyalla
Orroroo
Dubbo
Taree
Lord Howe I.
Kyancutta
Ivanhoe
Roto
Condobolin
Ball's Pyramid
Eyre Pen.
Port Pirie
Pooncarie
Singleton
Cowell
Burra
Murray River
Orange
1274
Cessnock
Newcastle
Morgan
Wentworth
Goolgowi
Marsden
Bathurst
Lithgow
Spencer Gulf
Gawler
Renmark
Murray Basin
Balranald
Cowra
1204
Katoomba
SYDNEY
ADELAIDE
Hay
Cootamundra
Murray Bridge
Inneston
Victor Harbor
Swan Hill
Narrandera
Wollongong
Investigator Strait
Tailem Bend
Ouyen
Wagga Wagga
Canberra
Nowra
Cape Borda
Kingscote
Kangaroo I.
Hopetoun
Big Desert
Deniliquin
Finley
Tumut
A.C.T.
Border Town
Albury
Batemans Bay
Lacepede Bay
VICTORIA
Little Desert
Shepparton
Cape Jaffa
2229 Mount Kosciuszko
Cooma
Robe
Horsham
Seymour
Mount Bogong 1986
Omeo
Bombala
Hamilton
Ballarat
Yea
Eden
Mount Gambier
MELBOURNE
Portland
Geelong
Bairnsdale
Cape Howe
Cape Nelson
Warrnambool
Morwell
Sale
Korumburra
Apollo Bay
Walkerville
Port Albert
Wilson's Promontory
South East Point
King Island
Currie
Bass Strait
Flinders I.
Furneaux Group
Whitemark
Cape Grim
Stanley
Cape Barren I.
Burnie
George Town
Banks Strait
TASMAN SEA
TASMANIA
Devonport
Launceston
1617 Mount Ossa
Queenstown
Swansea
Cape Forestier
Lake Gordon
Hobart
Port Arthur
Dover
Storm Bay
South West Cape
South East Cape
A.C.T. = Australian Capital Territory
128

Scale 1 : 4 650 000

0 100 200 km

0 50 100 miles

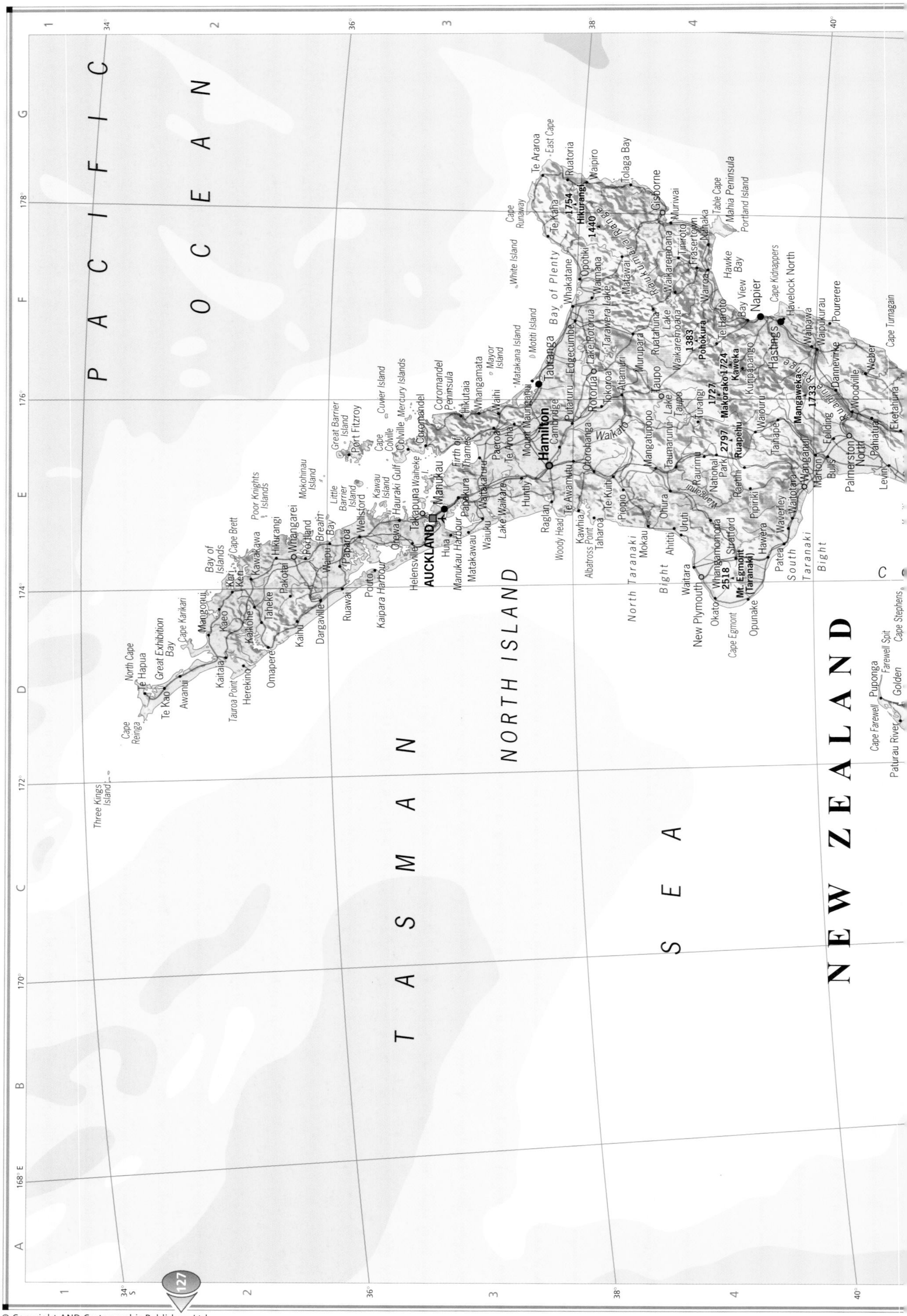

PACIFIC OCEAN
TASMAN SEA
NORTH ISLAND
NEW ZEALAND
AUCKLAND
Hamilton
Tauranga
Rotorua
Taupo
Napier
Hastings
Gisborne
New Plymouth
Whangarei
Wanganui
Palmerston North
Bay of Plenty
Hawke Bay
North Taranaki Bight
South Taranaki Bight
Mt. Egmont (Taranaki)
Ruapehu
2797
Three Kings Islands
Cape Reinga
North Cape
Great Barrier Island
Coromandel Peninsula
East Cape

metres	feet
8000	*26250*
6000	*19690*
4000	*13120*
2000	*6560*
1000	*3280*
500	*1640*
200	*656*
0	0
656	200
3280	1000
6560	2000
13120	4000
19690	6000
26250	8000
feet	metres

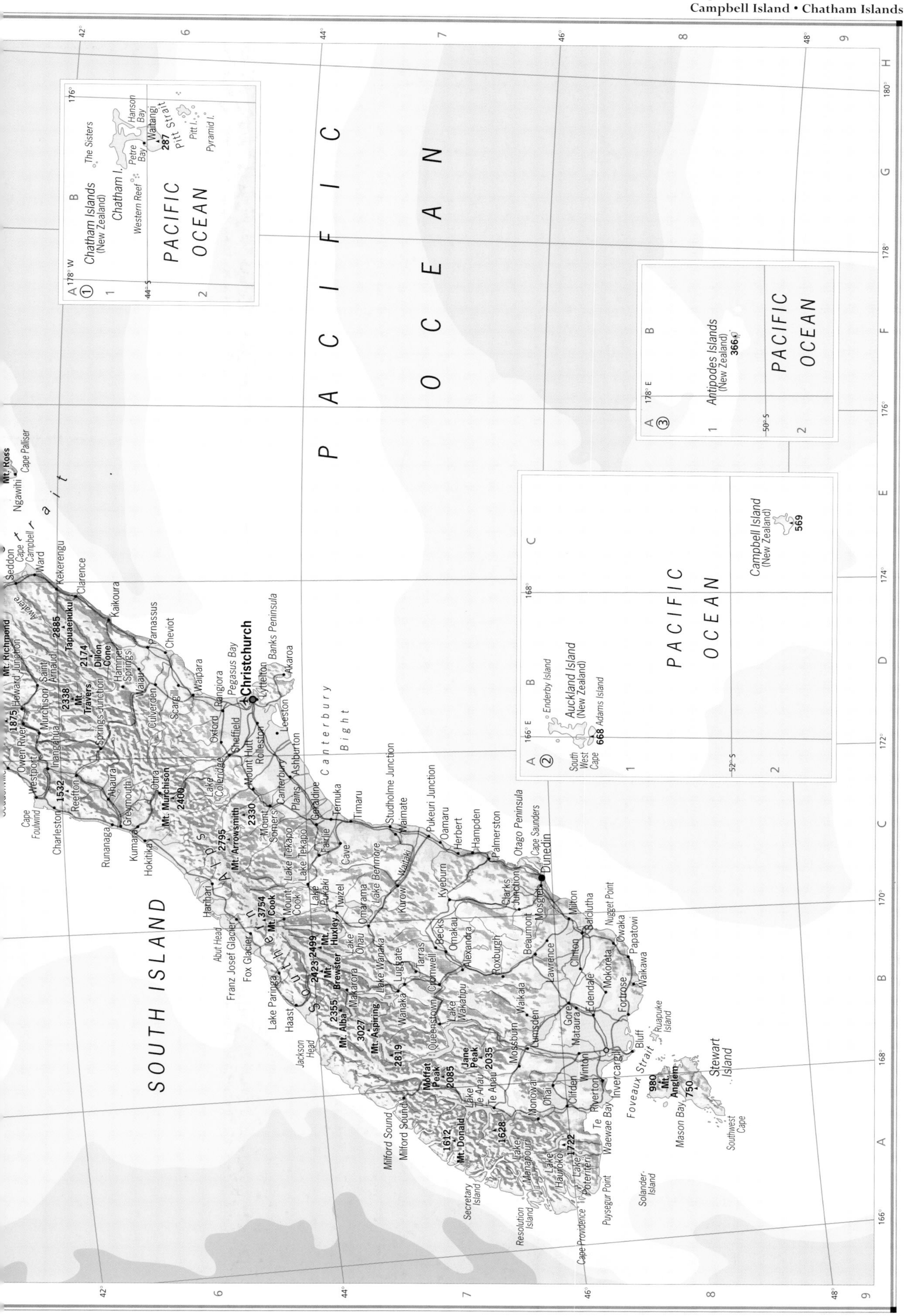

■	over 3 million	●	100 000 – 250 000	——	country capital underline
■	1 – 3 million	○	25 000 – 100 000		
●	250 000 – 1 million	·	under 25 000		

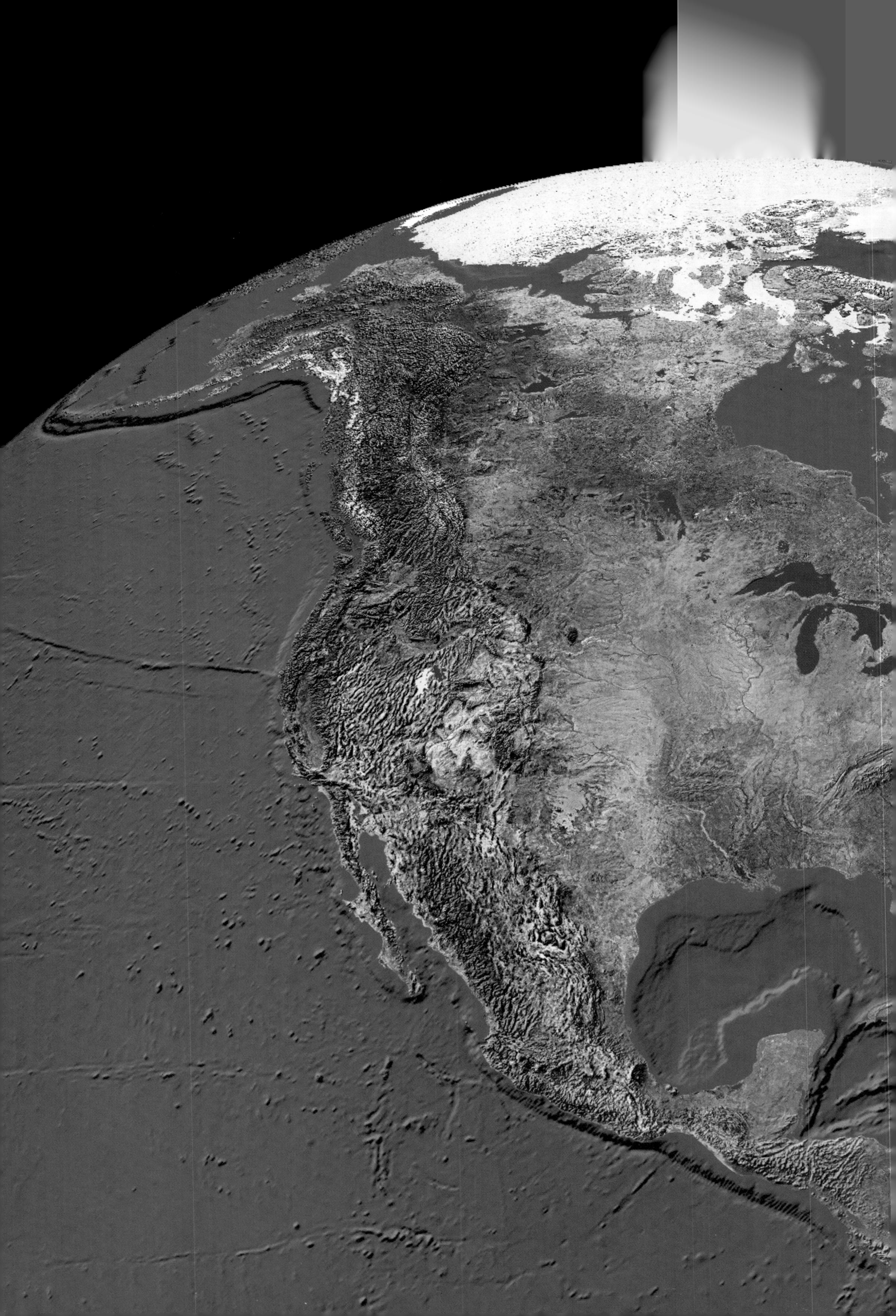

NORTH AMERICA

a view from space

North America *flags and statistics* 132

North America *political* 134

Canada 136

United States 138

Northwest United States 140

Northeast United States 142

Southeast United States 144

Southwest United States 146

Central America and the Caribbean 148

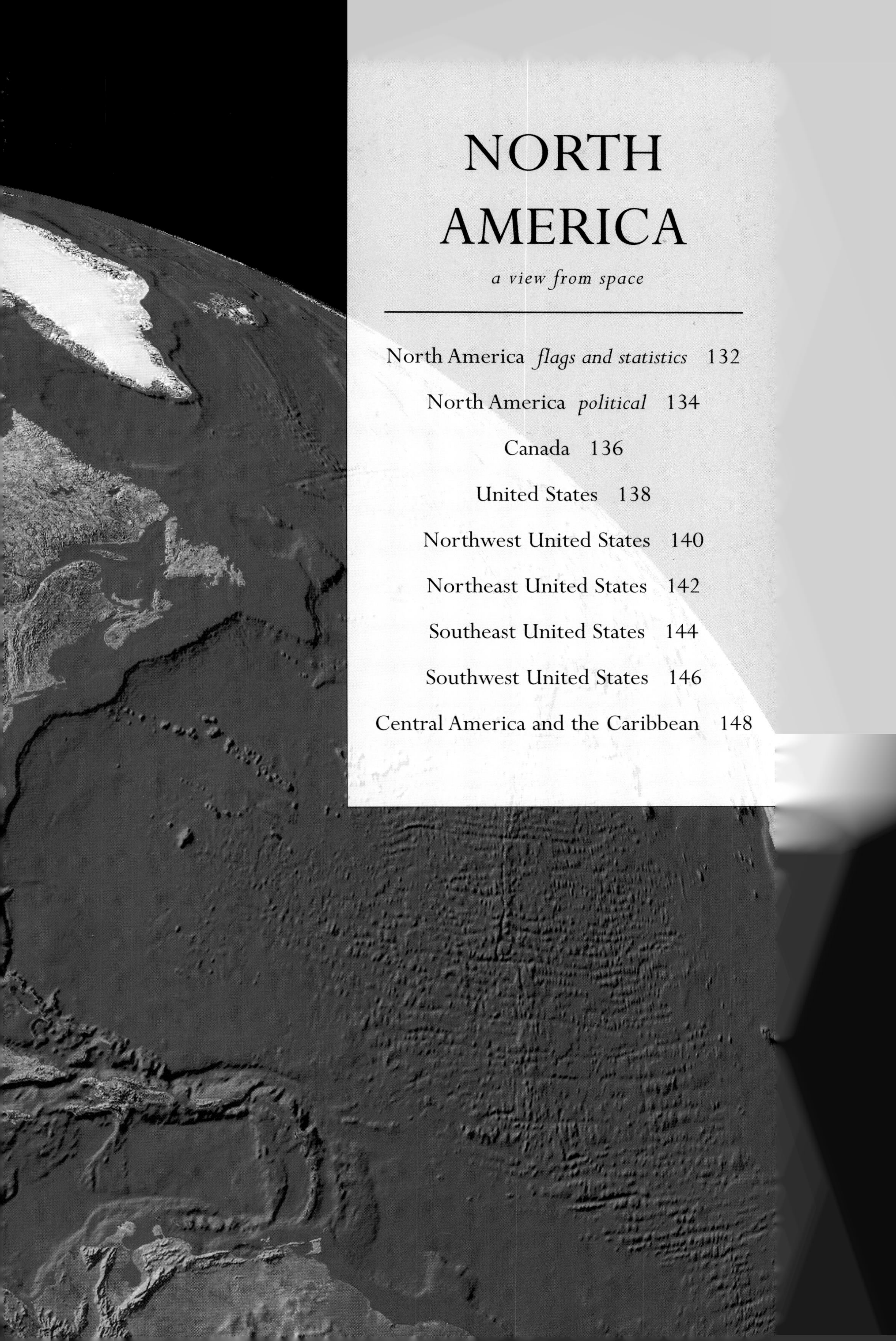

NORTH AMERICA

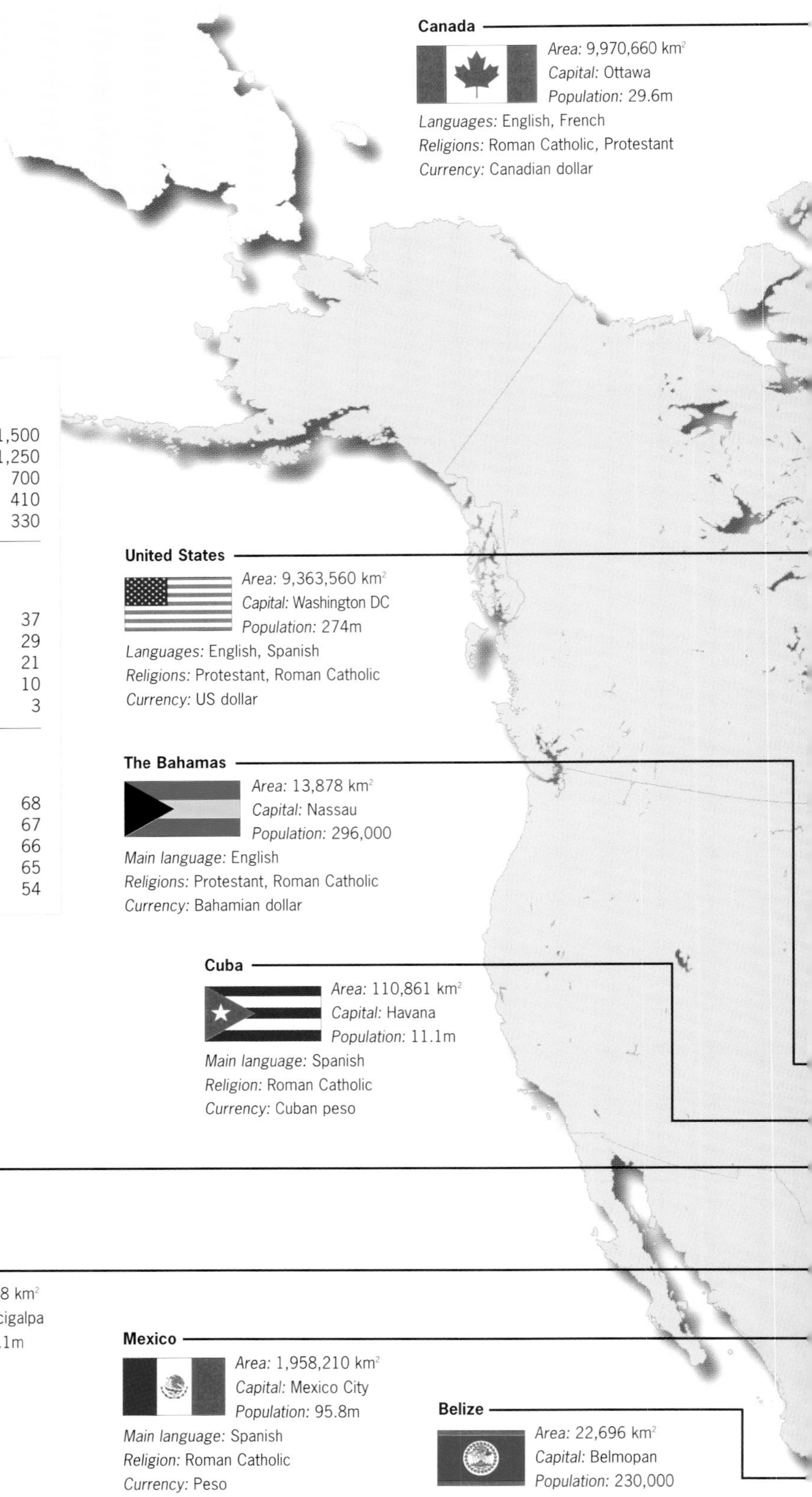

GROSS NATIONAL PRODUCT PER CAPITA (US$)

5 highest		***5 lowest***	
United States	28,740	Guatemala	1,500
Canada	19,290	Cuba	1,250
The Bahamas	11,940	Honduras	700
Barbados	6,560	Nicaragua	410
St Kitts & Nevis	6,160	Haiti	330

POPULATION DENSITY (per km²)

5 highest		***5 lowest***	
Barbados	623	Panama	37
St Vincent & the Grenadines	289	United States	29
Haiti	288	The Bahamas	21
El Salvador	285	Belize	10
Trinidad & Tobago	253	Canada	3

LIFE EXPECTANCY (years)

5 highest		***5 lowest***	
Canada	78	El Salvador	68
Dominica	77	St Kitts & Nevis	67
Barbados	76	Nicaragua	66
Costa Rica	76	Guatemala	65
United States	76	Haiti	54

Canada

Area: 9,970,660 km²
Capital: Ottawa
Population: 29.6m
Languages: English, French
Religions: Roman Catholic, Protestant
Currency: Canadian dollar

United States

Area: 9,363,560 km²
Capital: Washington DC
Population: 274m
Languages: English, Spanish
Religions: Protestant, Roman Catholic
Currency: US dollar

The Bahamas

Area: 13,878 km²
Capital: Nassau
Population: 296,000
Main language: English
Religions: Protestant, Roman Catholic
Currency: Bahamian dollar

Cuba

Area: 110,861 km²
Capital: Havana
Population: 11.1m
Main language: Spanish
Religion: Roman Catholic
Currency: Cuban peso

Jamaica

Area: 10,990 km²
Capital: Kingston
Population: 2.5m
Languages: English, Creole
Religion: Christian
Currency: Jamaican dollar

Honduras

Area: 112,088 km²
Capital: Tegucigalpa
Population: 6.1m
Languages: Spanish, English
Religion: Roman Catholic
Currency: Lempira

Mexico

Area: 1,958,210 km²
Capital: Mexico City
Population: 95.8m
Main language: Spanish
Religion: Roman Catholic
Currency: Peso

Belize

Area: 22,696 km²
Capital: Belmopan
Population: 230,000
Languages: English, Spanish
Religion: Christian
Currency: Belize dollar

Guatemala

Area: 108,889 km²
Capital: Guatemala City
Population: 10.8m
Main language: Spanish
Religion: Christian
Currency: Quetzal

El Salvador

Area: 21,041 km²
Capital: San Salvador
Population: 6.0m
Main language: Spanish
Religion: Roman Catholic
Currency: El Salvador colón

Nicaragua

Area: 130,000 km²
Capital: Managua
Population: 4.8m
Languages: Spanish, English
Religion: Roman Catholic
Currency: Córdoba

MUCH OF NORTH AMERICA lies between the Rockies and the Appalachians and is rich in minerals and oil. Population and industry is mostly concentrated in the temperate northeast. Central America and the Caribbean is mountainous and volcanic, with a tropical climate.

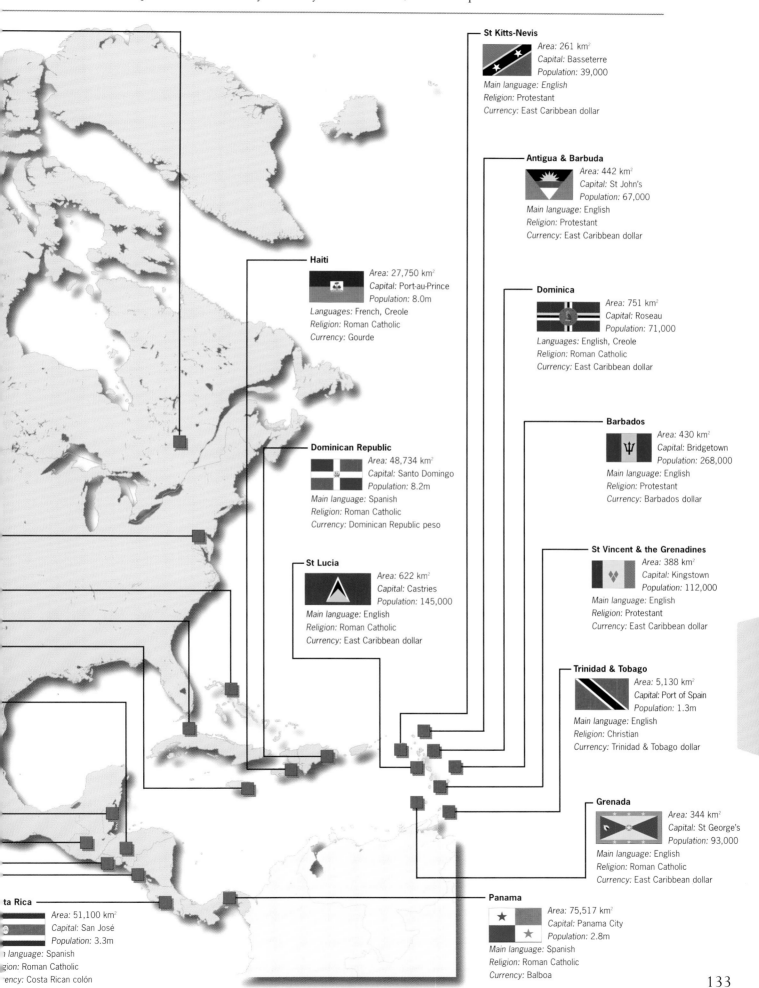

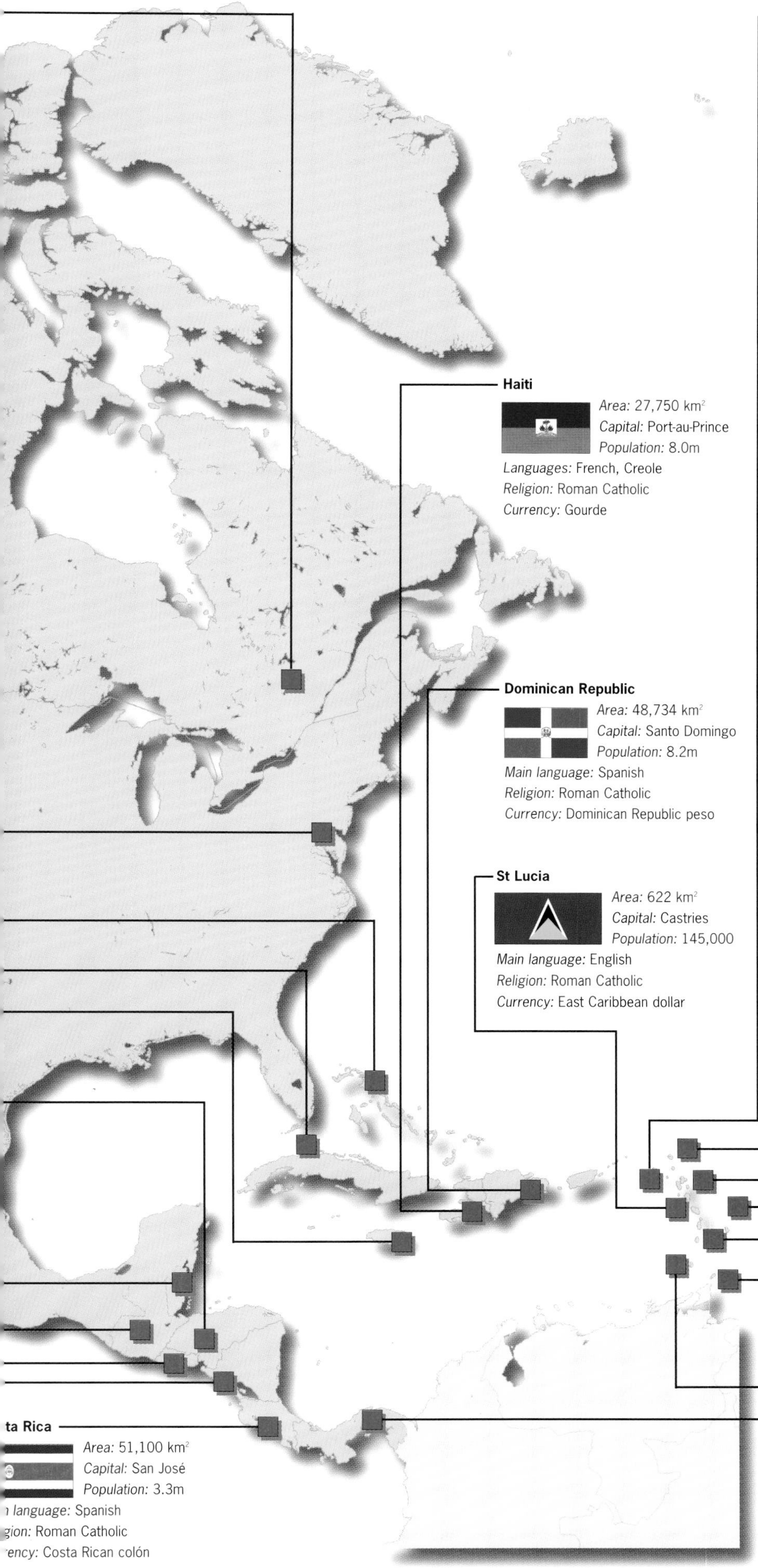

St Kitts-Nevis
Area: 261 km^2
Capital: Basseterre
Population: 39,000
Main language: English
Religion: Protestant
Currency: East Caribbean dollar

Antigua & Barbuda
Area: 442 km^2
Capital: St John's
Population: 67,000
Main language: English
Religion: Protestant
Currency: East Caribbean dollar

Haiti
Area: 27,750 km^2
Capital: Port-au-Prince
Population: 8.0m
Languages: French, Creole
Religion: Roman Catholic
Currency: Gourde

Dominica
Area: 751 km^2
Capital: Roseau
Population: 71,000
Languages: English, Creole
Religion: Roman Catholic
Currency: East Caribbean dollar

Barbados
Area: 430 km^2
Capital: Bridgetown
Population: 268,000
Main language: English
Religion: Protestant
Currency: Barbados dollar

Dominican Republic
Area: 48,734 km^2
Capital: Santo Domingo
Population: 8.2m
Main language: Spanish
Religion: Roman Catholic
Currency: Dominican Republic peso

St Vincent & the Grenadines
Area: 388 km^2
Capital: Kingstown
Population: 112,000
Main language: English
Religion: Protestant
Currency: East Caribbean dollar

St Lucia
Area: 622 km^2
Capital: Castries
Population: 145,000
Main language: English
Religion: Roman Catholic
Currency: East Caribbean dollar

Trinidad & Tobago
Area: 5,130 km^2
Capital: Port of Spain
Population: 1.3m
Main language: English
Religion: Christian
Currency: Trinidad & Tobago dollar

Grenada
Area: 344 km^2
Capital: St George's
Population: 93,000
Main language: English
Religion: Roman Catholic
Currency: East Caribbean dollar

ta Rica
Area: 51,100 km^2
Capital: San José
Population: 3.3m
ı language: Spanish
gion: Roman Catholic
ency: Costa Rican colón

Panama
Area: 75,517 km^2
Capital: Panama City
Population: 2.8m
Main language: Spanish
Religion: Roman Catholic
Currency: Balboa

Scale 1 : 34 700 000

0 500 1000 1500 2000 km

0 500 1000 miles

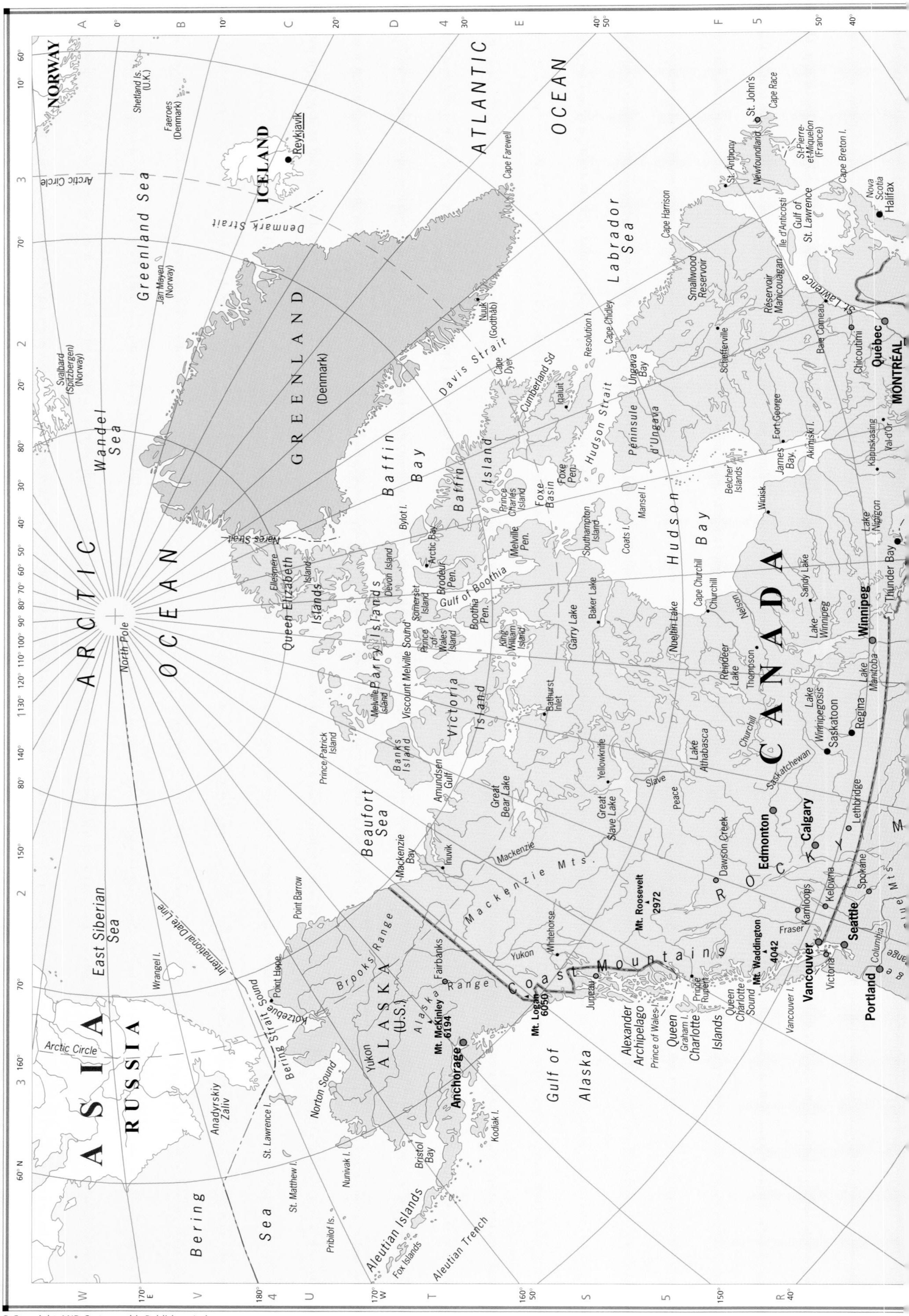

ARCTIC
OCEAN
North Pole
ATLANTIC
OCEAN
NORWAY
Shetland Is. (U.K.)
Faeroes (Denmark)
ICELAND
Reykjavik
Arctic Circle
Greenland Sea
Denmark Strait
Jan Mayen (Norway)
Svalbard (Spitsbergen) (Norway)
Wandel Sea
GREENLAND (Denmark)
Cape Farewell
Nuuk (Godthåb)
Davis Strait
Baffin Bay
Labrador Sea
Cape Harrison
Nares Strait
Ellesmere Island
Queen Elizabeth Islands
Parry Islands
Devon Island
Bylot I.
Baffin Island
Cape Dyer
Cumberland Sd
Iqaluit
Resolution I.
Cape Chidley
Ungava Bay
Hudson Strait
Péninsule d'Ungava
Foxe Pen.
Foxe Basin
Prince Charles Island
Arctic Bay
Brodeur Pen.
Melville Pen.
Somerset Island
Gulf of Boothia
Boothia Pen.
Prince of Wales Island
King William Island
Southampton Island
Coats I.
Mansel I.
Hudson Bay
Belcher Islands
James Bay
Akimiski I.
Fort George
Winisk
Cape Churchill
Churchill
Baker Lake
Garry Lake
Nueltin Lake
Reindeer Lake
Thompson
Nelson
Viscount Melville Sound
Melville Island
Victoria Island
Banks Island
Prince Patrick Island
Amundsen Gulf
Bathurst Inlet
Beaufort Sea
Mackenzie Bay
Inuvik
Great Bear Lake
Great Slave Lake
Yellowknife
Slave
Peace
Lake Athabasca
Churchill
Saskatchewan
CANADA
Lake Winnipegosis
Lake Winnipeg
Lake Manitoba
Sandy Lake
Winnipeg
Saskatoon
Regina
Lethbridge
Edmonton
Calgary
Dawson Creek
Mackenzie
Mackenzie Mts.
Mt. Roosevelt 2972
Mt. Waddington 4042
ROCKY Mts
Kamloops
Kelowna
Spokane
Fraser
Vancouver
Victoria
Vancouver I.
Seattle
Columbia
Portland
Queen Charlotte Sound
Queen Charlotte Islands
Graham I.
Prince Rupert
Prince of Wales I.
Alexander Archipelago
Juneau
Coast Mountains
Whitehorse
Yukon
Mt. Logan 6050
Gulf of Alaska
Kodiak I.
Anchorage
Mt. McKinley 6194
Alaska Range
Fairbanks
ALASKA (U.S.)
Brooks Range
Yukon
Point Barrow
Point Hope
Kotzebue Sound
Bering Strait
Norton Sound
Nunivak I.
St. Lawrence I.
St. Matthew I.
Pribilof Is.
Bristol Bay
Aleutian Islands
Fox Islands
Aleutian Trench
Bering Sea
Anadyrskiy Zaliv
ASIA
RUSSIA
Wrangel I.
East Siberian Sea
International Date Line
Arctic Circle
Smallwood Reservoir
Schefferville
Reservoir Manicouagan
Baie Comeau
Chicoutimi
Québec
MONTRÉAL
St. Lawrence
Île d'Anticosti
Gulf of St. Lawrence
St. Anthony
Newfoundland
St. John's
Cape Race
St-Pierre-et-Miquelon (France)
Cape Breton I.
Nova Scotia
Halifax
Kapuskasing
Val-d'Or
Lake Nipigon
Thunder Bay

Mt. McKinley, Alaska : 6,194 m or 20,322 ft

Death Valley, USA : 86 m or 282 ft

Bateques, Mexico : 3.0 cm or 1.2 in

Henderson Lake, Canada : 650 cm or 256 in

Mississippi-Missouri, USA : 6,020 km or 3,740 mi

Lake Superior, USA/Canada : 82,260 km² or 31,760 sq mi

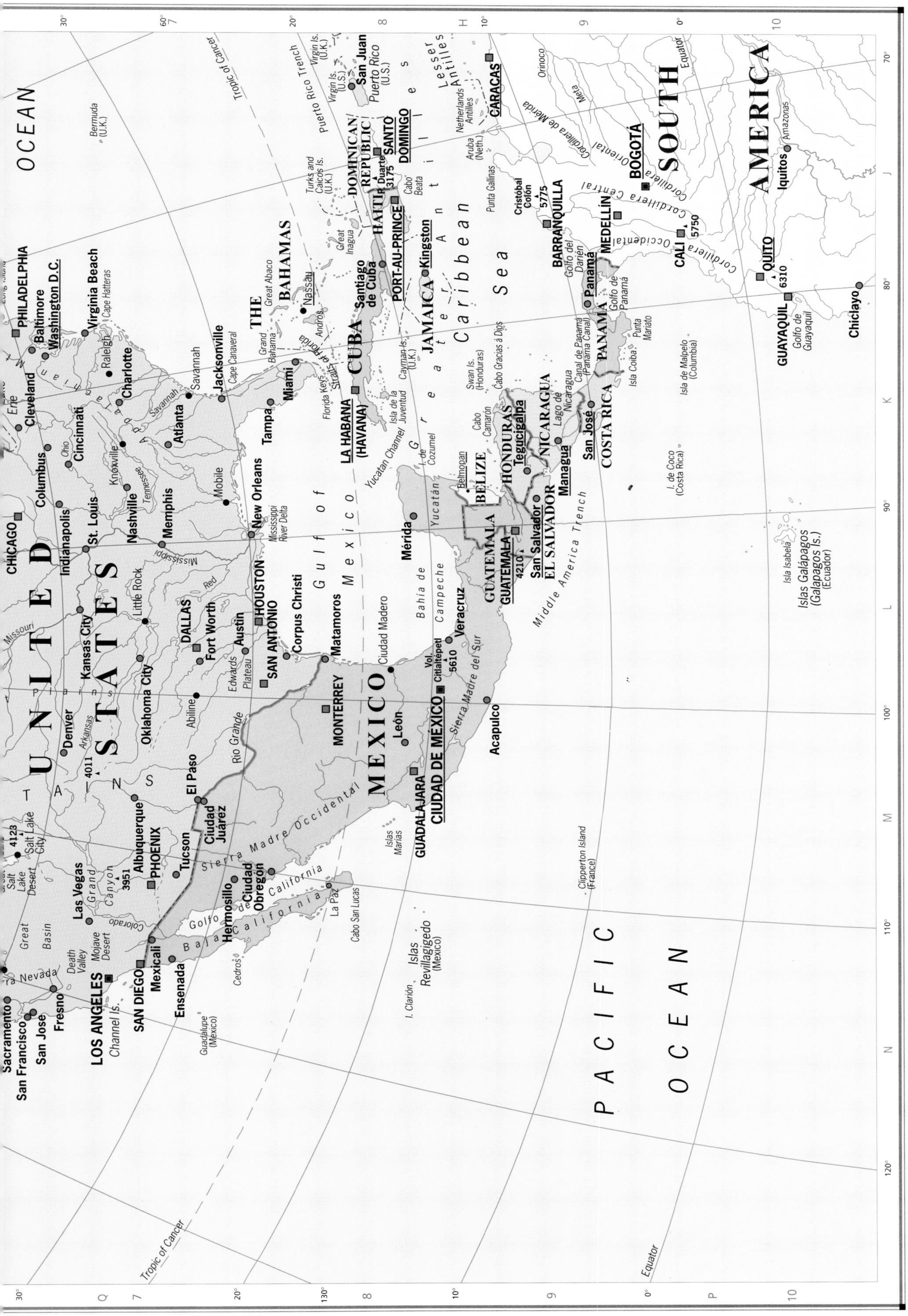

Northice, Greenland : -66 °C or -87 °F	Death Valley, USA : 57 °C or 134 °F
475,525,000	19 per km² or 50 per sq mi
24,454,000 km² or 9,442,000 sq mi	23

Scale 1 : 13 800 000

0 200 400 600 km

0 100 200 300 miles

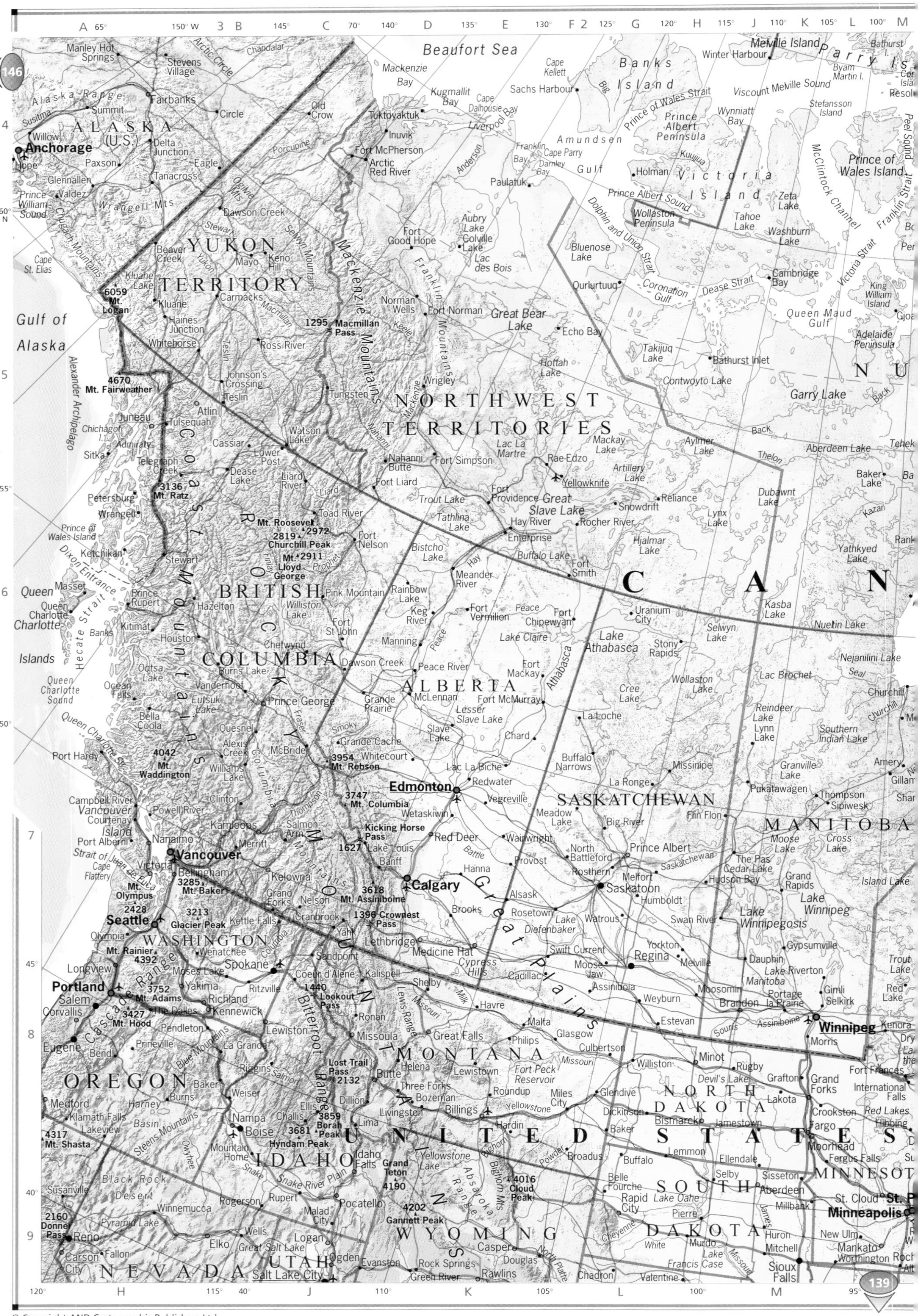

metres | feet
8000 | 26250
6000 | 19690
4000 | 13120
2000 | 6560
1000 | 3280
500 | 1640
200 | 656
0 | 0
656 | 200
3280 | 1000
6560 | 2000
13120 | 4000
19690 | 6000
26250 | 8000
feet | metres

■ over 3 million
■ 1 – 3 million
● 250 000 – 1 million
● 100 000 – 250 000
○ 25 000 – 100 000
• under 25 000
country capital underline
state or province capital underline

Canada

Greenland • St. Pierre & Miquelon

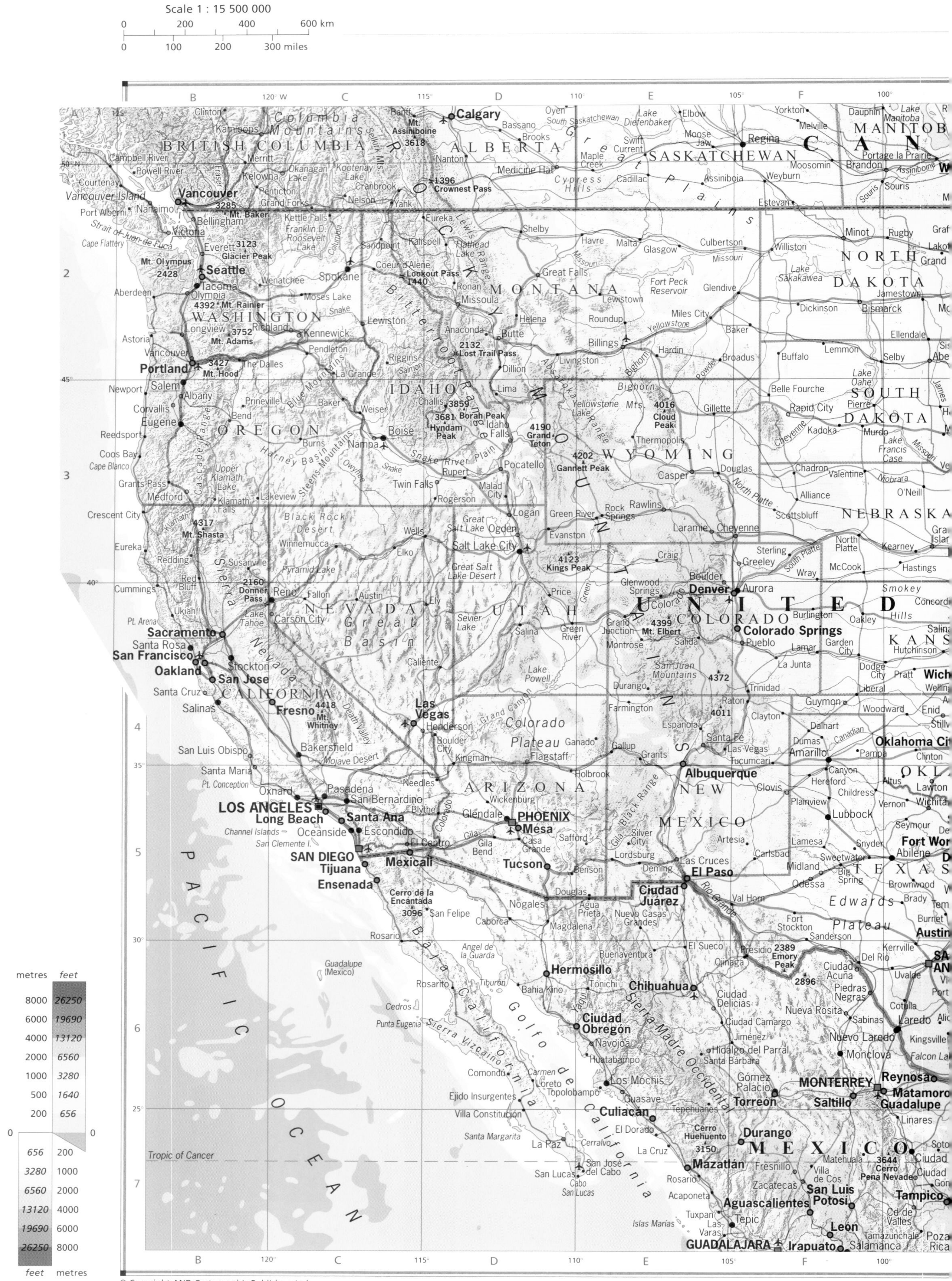

Scale 1 : 15 500 000
0 200 400 600 km
0 100 200 300 miles
metres feet
8000 26250
6000 19690
4000 13120
2000 6560
1000 3280
500 1640
200 656
0
656 200
3280 1000
6560 2000
13120 4000
19690 6000
26250 8000
feet metres
B C D E F
120° W 115° 110° 105° 100°
2 3 4 5 6 7
50° N 45° 40° 35° 30° 25°
BRITISH COLUMBIA
Columbia Mountains
Calgary
ALBERTA
SASKATCHEWAN
Regina
MANITOBA
CANADA
Vancouver Island
Vancouver
3285 Mt. Baker
Strait of Juan de Fuca
Victoria
Cape Flattery
3123 Glacier Peak
Mt. Olympus 2428
Seattle
Tacoma
Olympia
4392 Mt. Rainier
WASHINGTON
Spokane
3752 Mt. Adams
Portland
3427 Mt. Hood
1396 Crownest Pass
Lookout Pass 1440
2132 Lost Trail Pass
MONTANA
Great Falls
Missoula
Helena
Butte
Billings
Bitterroot Range
Great Plains
NORTH DAKOTA
Bismarck
SOUTH DAKOTA
Rapid City
Pierre
OREGON
Salem
Eugene
Medford
Cascade Range
Upper Klamath Lake
4317 Mt. Shasta
IDAHO
Boise
3859 Borah Peak
3681 Hyndam Peak
4190 Grand Teton
4202 Gannett Peak
Snake River Plain
Pocatello
Idaho Falls
Twin Falls
WYOMING
Casper
Cheyenne
Laramie
Rock Springs
Rawlins
NEBRASKA
North Platte
Scottsbluff
Black Rock Desert
Great Salt Lake
Great Salt Lake Desert
Salt Lake City
Ogden
Logan
Provo
4123 Kings Peak
UTAH
NEVADA
Great Basin
Reno
Carson City
Lake Tahoe
2160 Donner Pass
Sierra Nevada
Sacramento
San Francisco
Oakland
San Jose
Stockton
Fresno
4418 Mt. Whitney
Death Valley
Las Vegas
CALIFORNIA
Bakersfield
Mojave Desert
LOS ANGELES
Long Beach
Santa Ana
San Bernardino
Pasadena
SAN DIEGO
Tijuana
Ensenada
Mexicali
Channel Islands
San Clemente I.
Pt. Conception
Pt. Arena
COLORADO
Denver
Aurora
Boulder
4399 Mt. Elbert
Colorado Springs
Pueblo
San Juan Mountains
4372
KANSAS
Grand Junction
ARIZONA
PHOENIX
Mesa
Tucson
Flagstaff
Colorado Plateau
Grand Canyon
Lake Powell
NEW MEXICO
Albuquerque
Santa Fe
Las Cruces
El Paso
Ciudad Juárez
4011
OKLAHOMA
Oklahoma City
TEXAS
Amarillo
Lubbock
Abilene
Fort Worth
Midland
Odessa
Edwards Plateau
San Antonio
Austin
Rio Grande
2389 Emory Peak
2896
UNITED STATES
MEXICO
Hermosillo
Chihuahua
Ciudad Obregón
Sierra Madre Occidental
Baja California
Golfo de California
3096 Cerro de la Encantada
Culiacán
Mazatlán
Durango
3150 Cerro Huehuento
Torreón
Saltillo
MONTERREY
Monclova
Nuevo Laredo
Laredo
Reynosa
Matamoros
3644 Cerro Peña Nevada
San Luis Potosí
Aguascalientes
Zacatecas
Tampico
León
GUADALAJARA
Irapuato
Tepic
Islas Marías
La Paz
San José del Cabo
Cabo San Lucas
Tropic of Cancer
Guadalupe (Mexico)
PACIFIC OCEAN

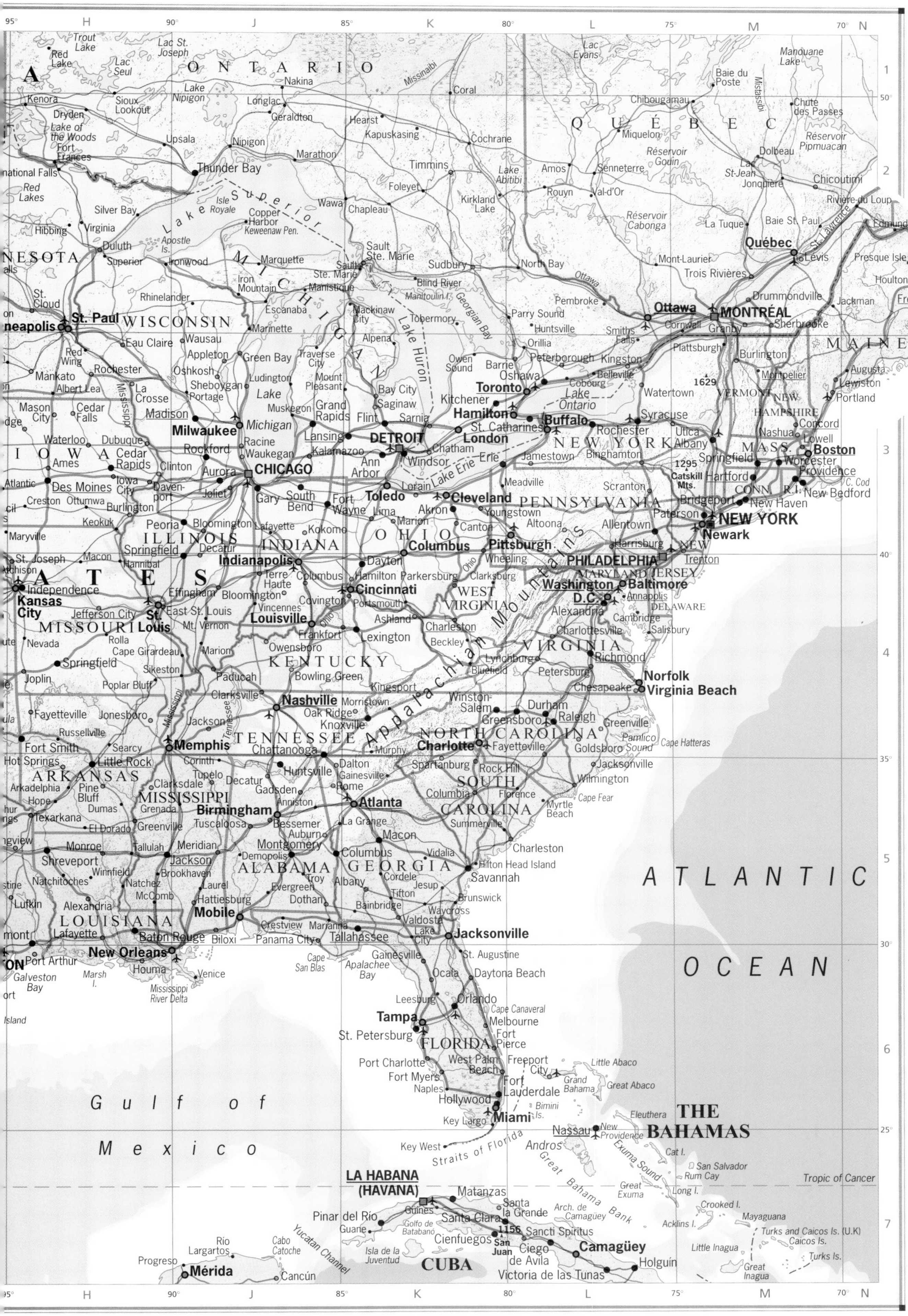

■ over 3 million	● 100 000 – 250 000		country capital underline
■ 1 – 3 million	○ 25 000 – 100 000		state or province capital underline
● 250 000 – 1 million	• under 25 000		

Scale 1 : 7 200 000

0 100 200 300 km

0 50 100 150 miles

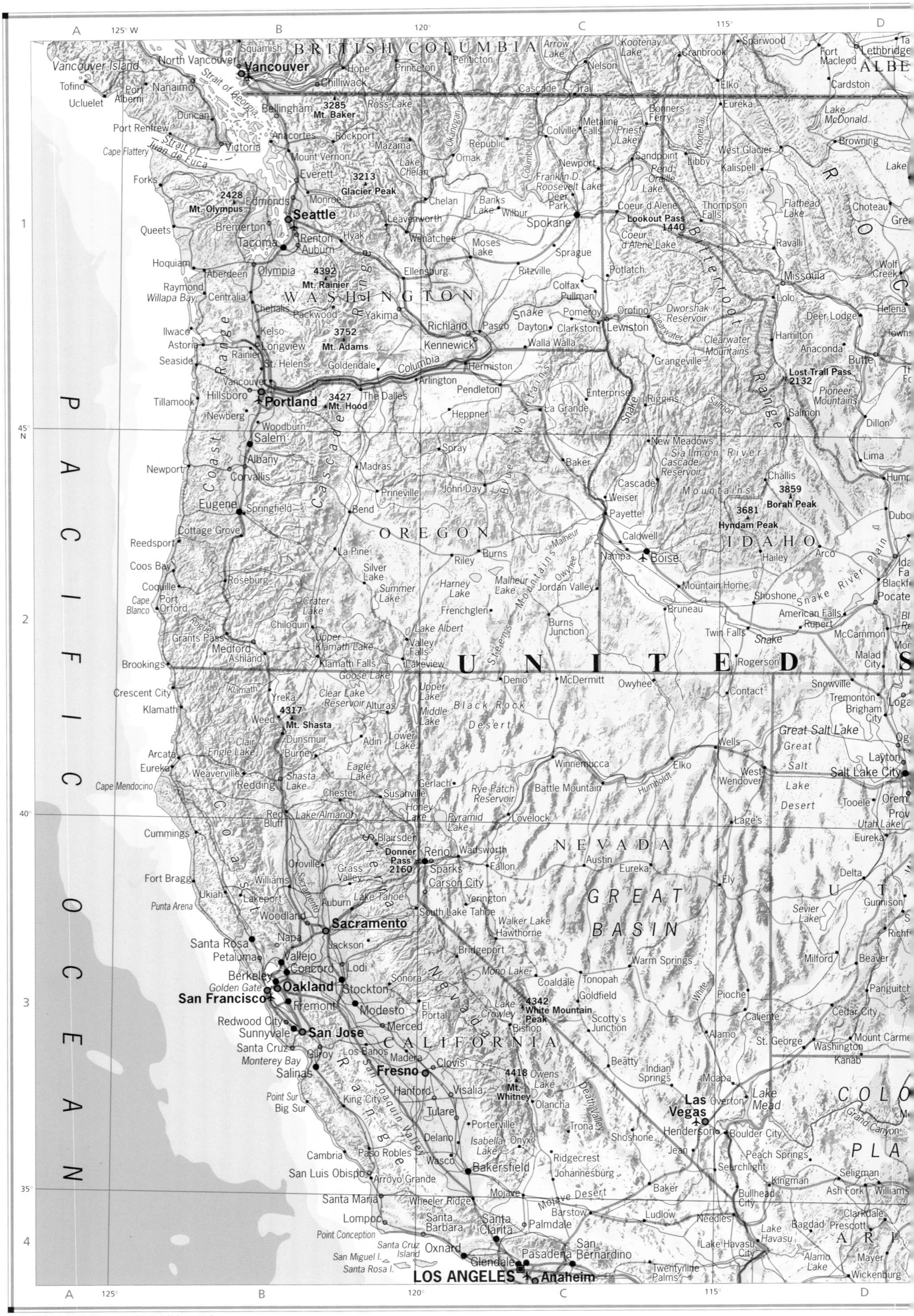

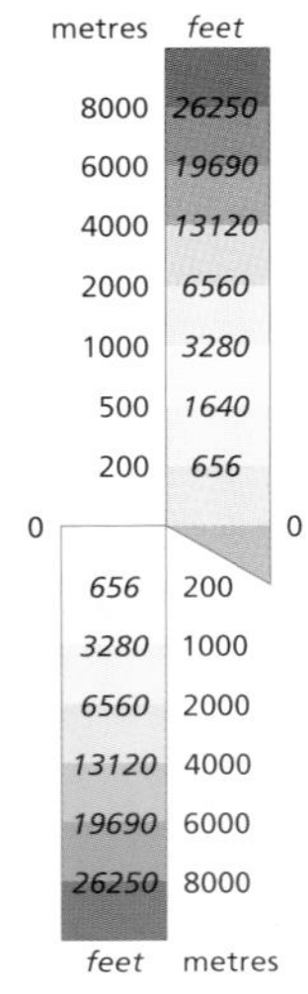

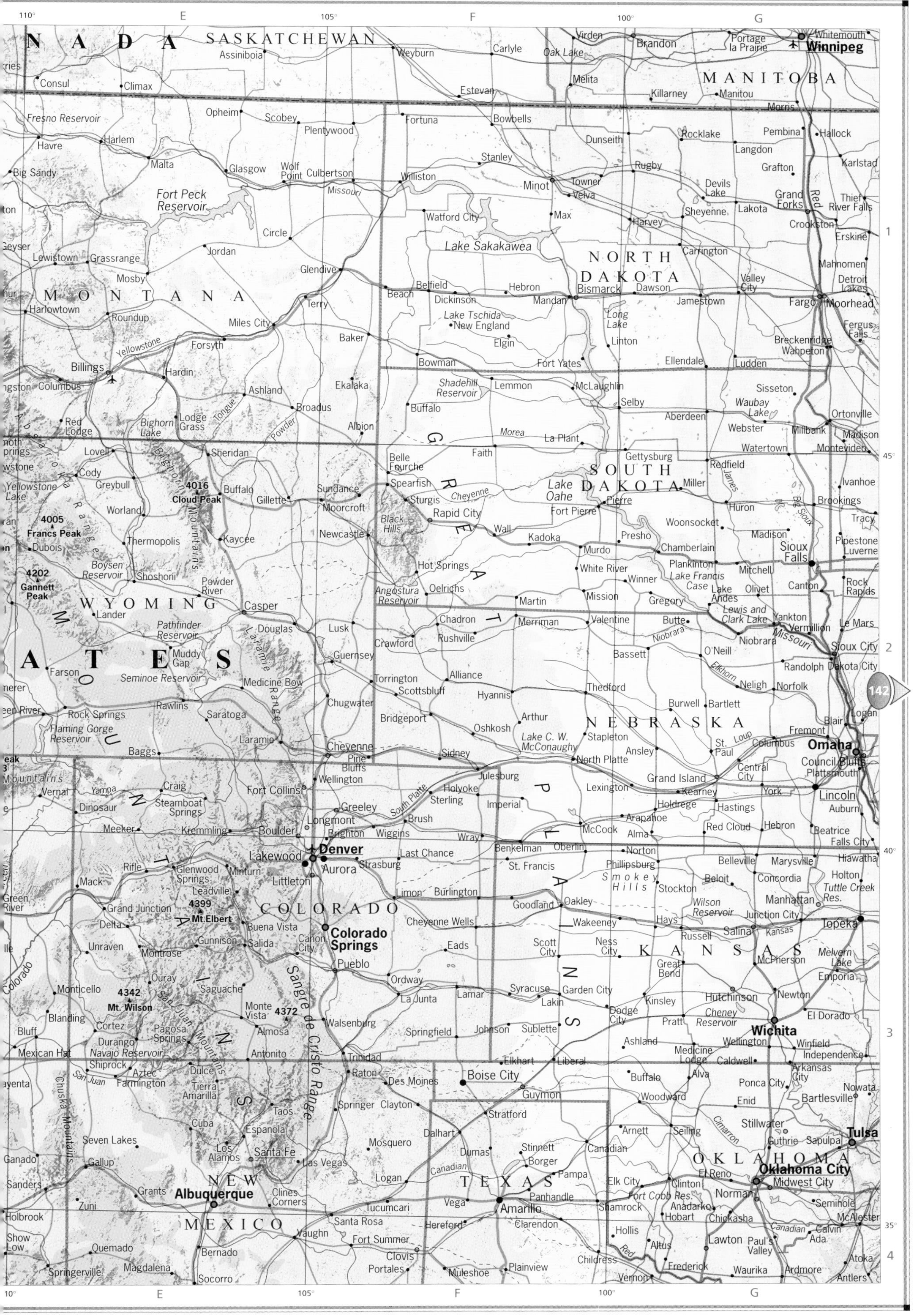

■ over 3 million
■ 1 – 3 million
● 250 000 – 1 million
● 100 000 – 250 000
○ 25 000 – 100 000
• under 25 000
country capital underline
state or province capital underline

Scale 1 : 7 200 000

0 100 200 300 km

0 50 100 150 miles

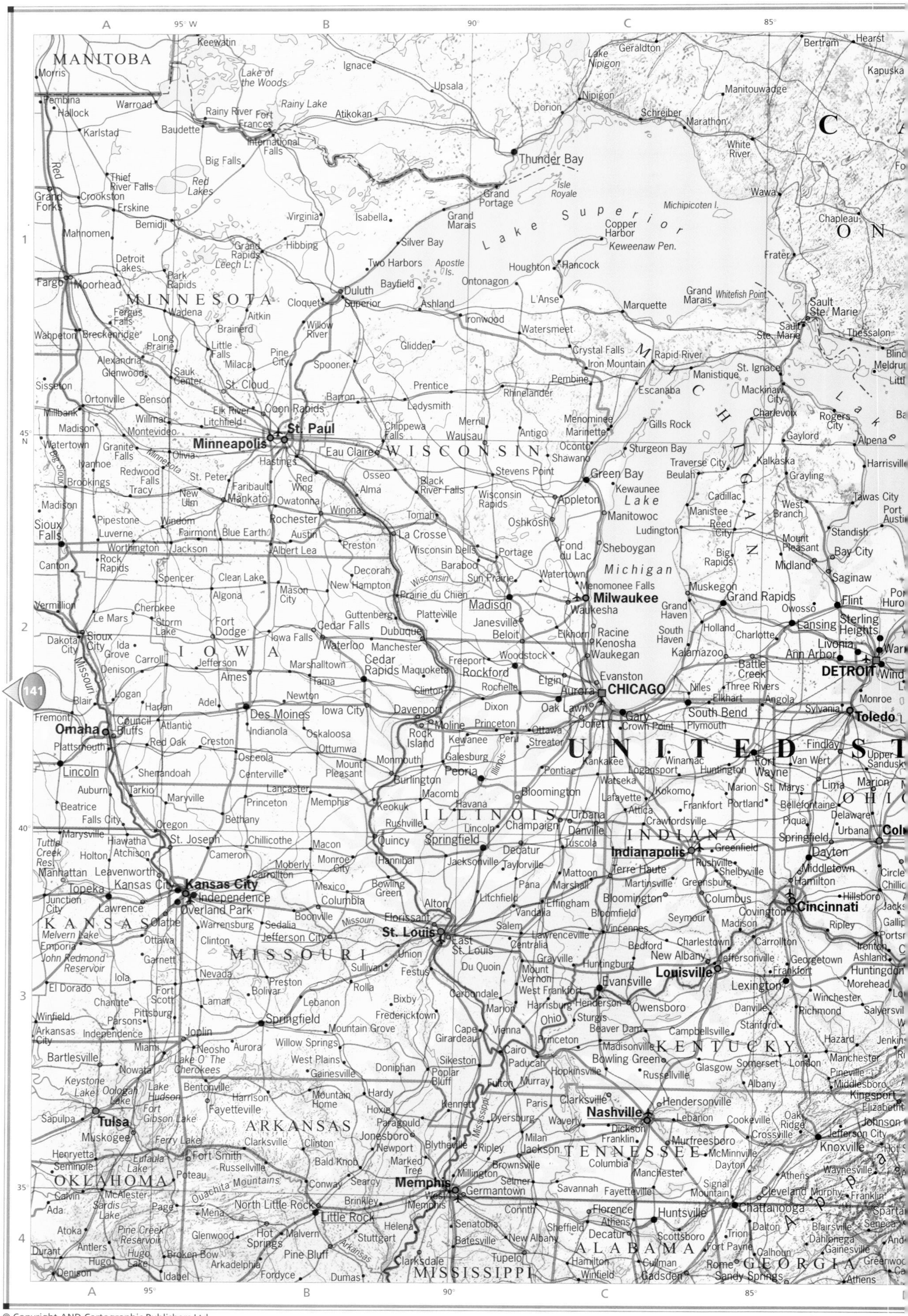

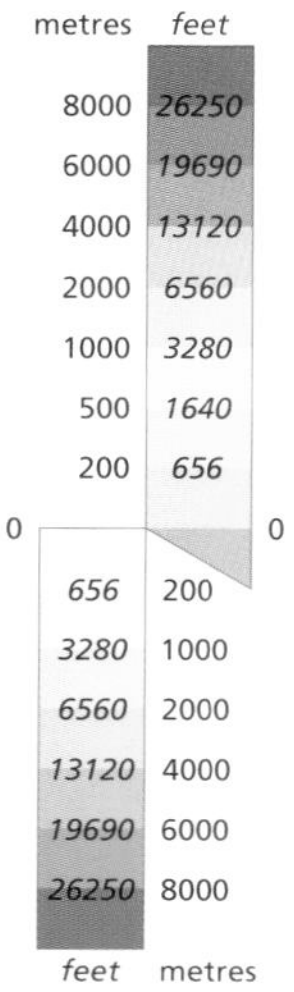

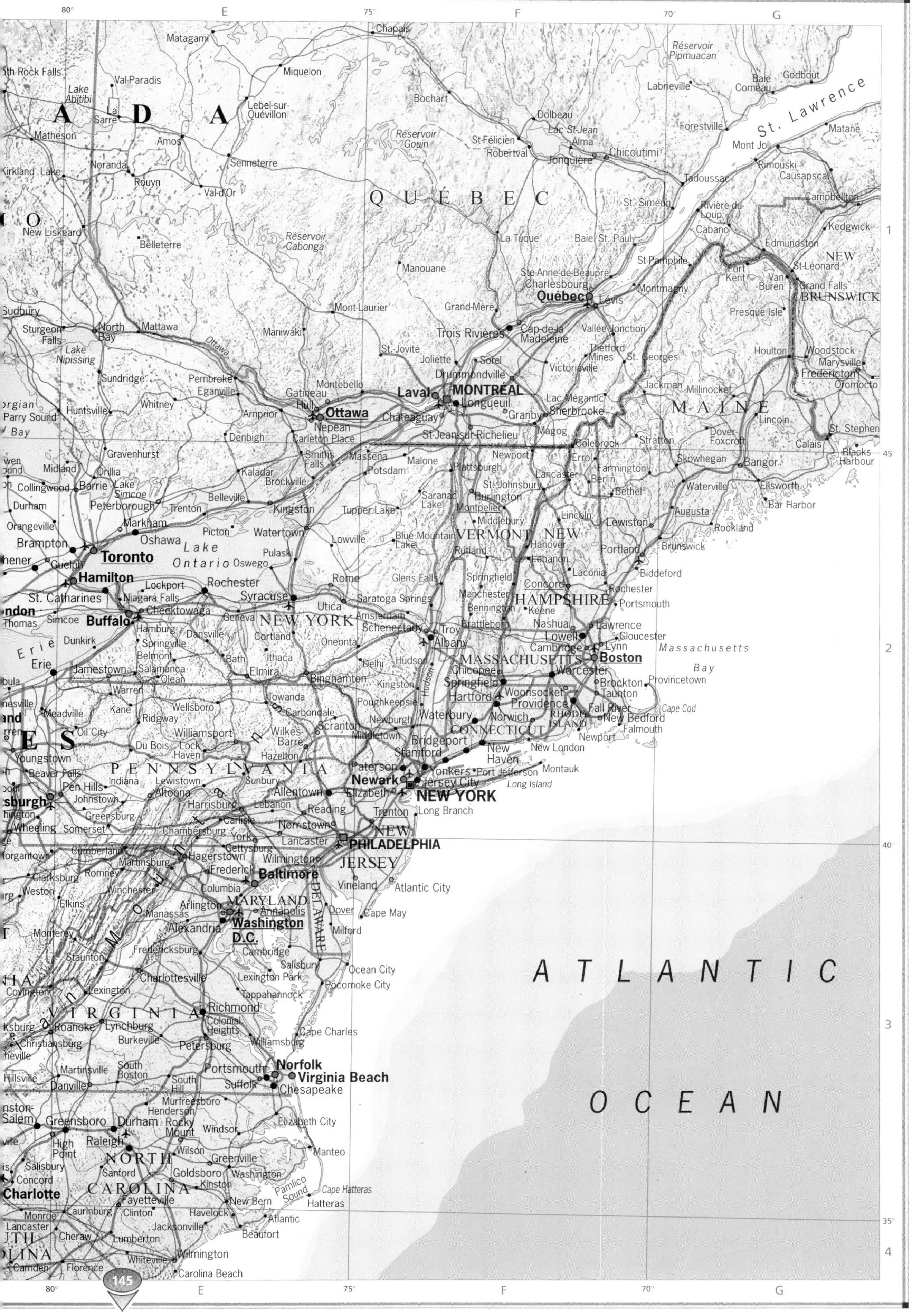

Connecticut • Delaware • District of Columbia • Illinois • Indiana • Iowa • Maine • Maryland • Massachusetts • Michigan
Minnesota • New Hampshire • New Jersey • New York • Ohio • Pennsylvania • Rhode Island • Vermont • West Virginia • Wisconsin

■ over 3 million	● 100 000 – 250 000	—— country capital underline
◼ 1 – 3 million	○ 25 000 – 100 000	—— state or province capital underline
● 250 000 – 1 million	• under 25 000	

Scale 1 : 7 200 000

0 100 200 300 km

0 50 100 150 miles

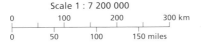

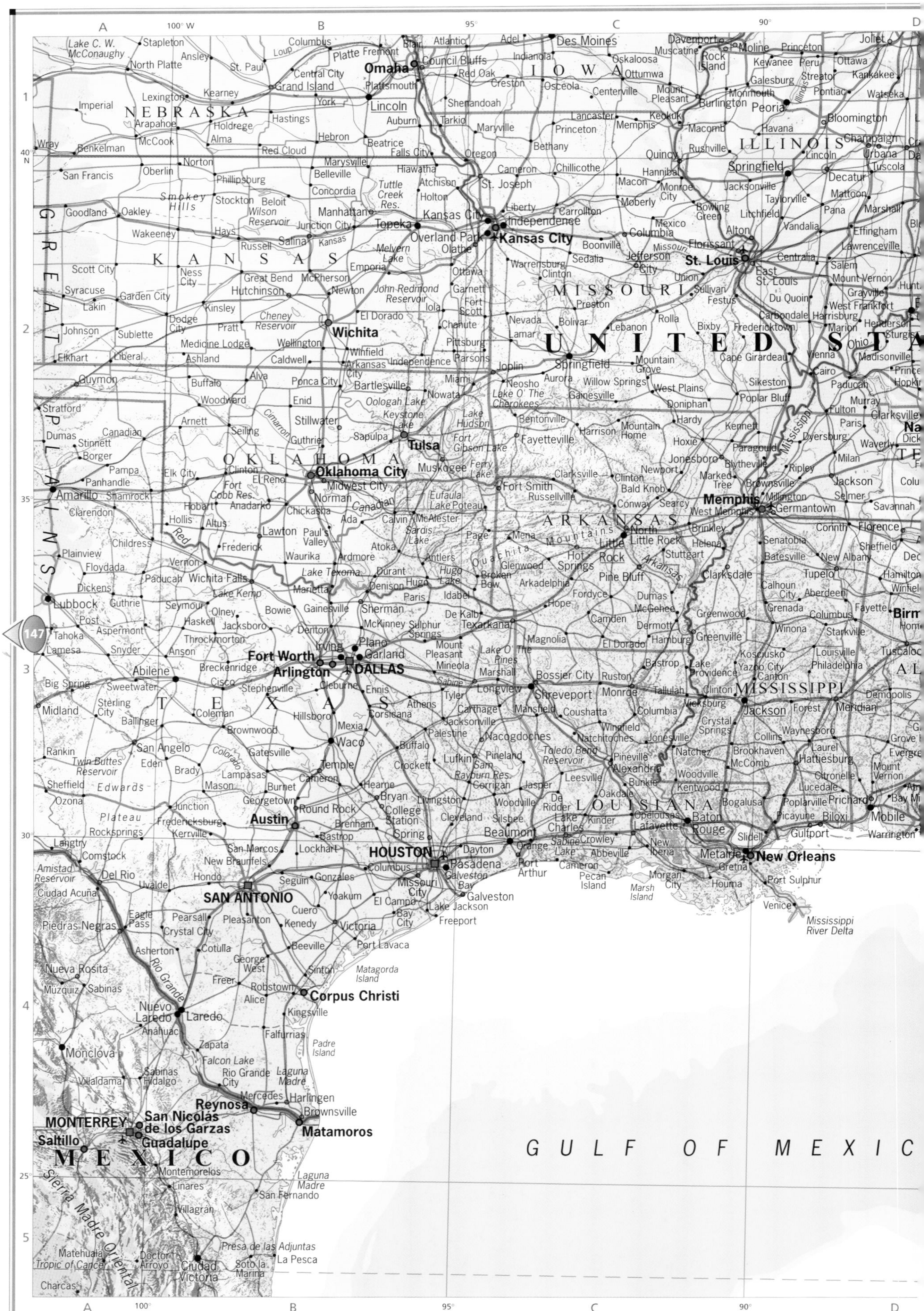

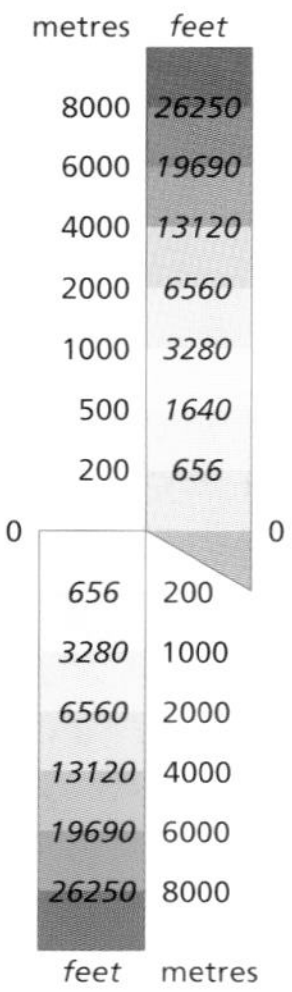

Southeast United States

Alabama • Arkansas • The Bahamas • Florida • Georgia • Kentucky • Louisiana
Mississippi • Missouri • North Carolina • South Carolina • Tennessee • Texas • Virginia

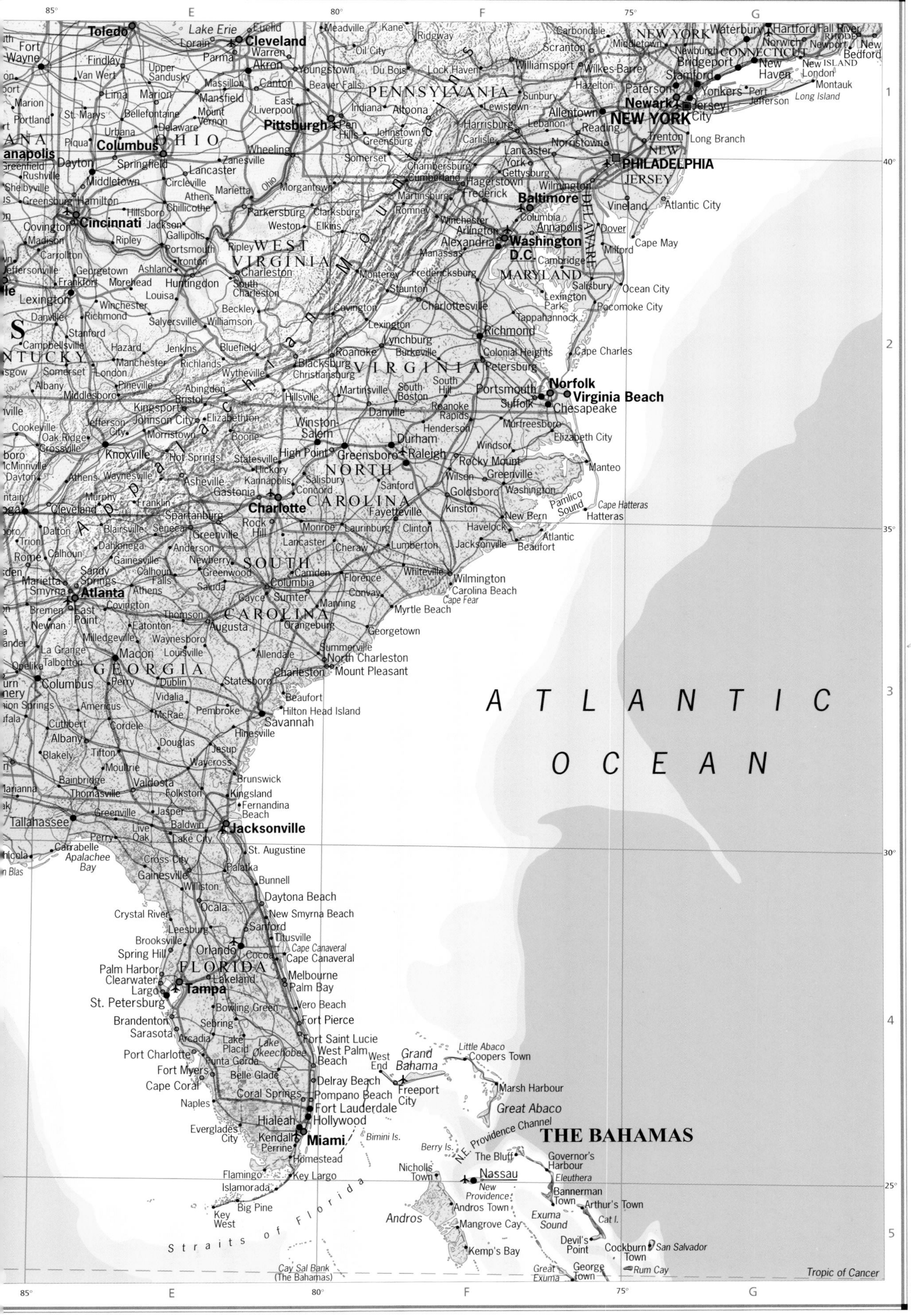

■ over 3 million	● 100 000 – 250 000	country capital underline
■ 1 – 3 million	◉ 25 000 – 100 000	state or province capital underline
● 250 000 – 1 million	• under 25 000	

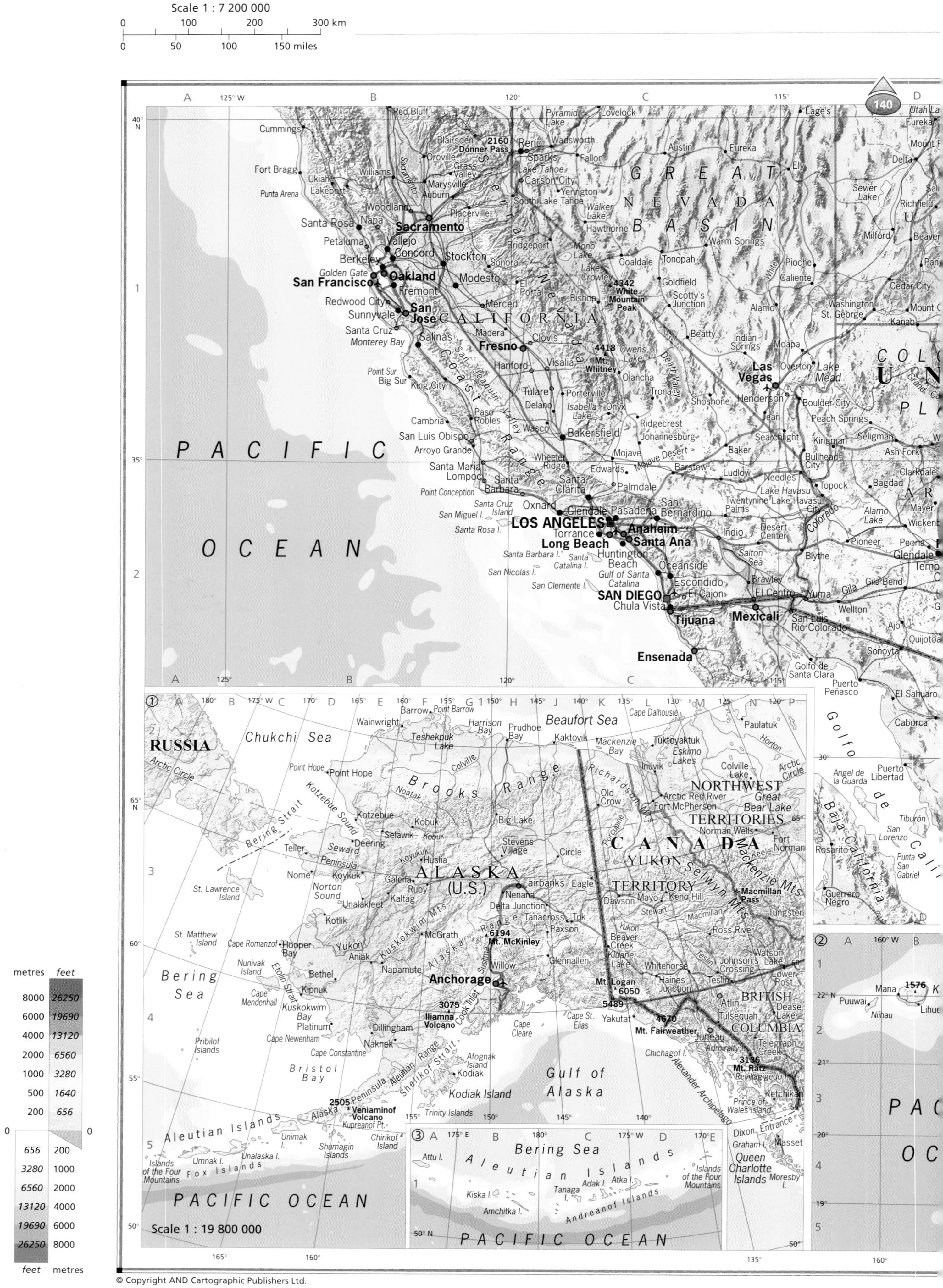

Scale 1 : 7 200 000
0 100 200 300 km
0 50 100 150 miles
140
PACIFIC OCEAN
GREAT BASIN
NEVADA
CALIFORNIA
Sierra Nevada
Coast Ranges
San Joaquin Valley
Mojave Desert
Death Valley
Sacramento
San Francisco
Oakland
San Jose
Fresno
Bakersfield
LOS ANGELES
Long Beach
Anaheim
Santa Ana
SAN DIEGO
Tijuana
Mexicali
Ensenada
Las Vegas
Reno
Lake Tahoe
Carson City
Stockton
Modesto
4418 Mt. Whitney
4342 White Mountain Peak
2160 Donner Pass
Golfo de California
Baja California
① Beaufort Sea
Chukchi Sea
RUSSIA
ALASKA (U.S.)
CANADA
YUKON TERRITORY
NORTHWEST TERRITORIES
BRITISH COLUMBIA
Brooks Range
Alaska Range
Bering Strait
Bering Sea
Gulf of Alaska
Anchorage
Fairbanks
6194 Mt. McKinley
Mt. Logan 6050
Aleutian Islands
PACIFIC OCEAN
Scale 1 : 19 800 000
② PACIFIC OCEAN
③ Bering Sea
Aleutian Islands
PACIFIC OCEAN
metres feet
8000 26250
6000 19690
4000 13120
2000 6560
1000 3280
500 1640
200 656
0 0
656 200
3280 1000
6560 2000
13120 4000
19690 6000
26250 8000
feet metres

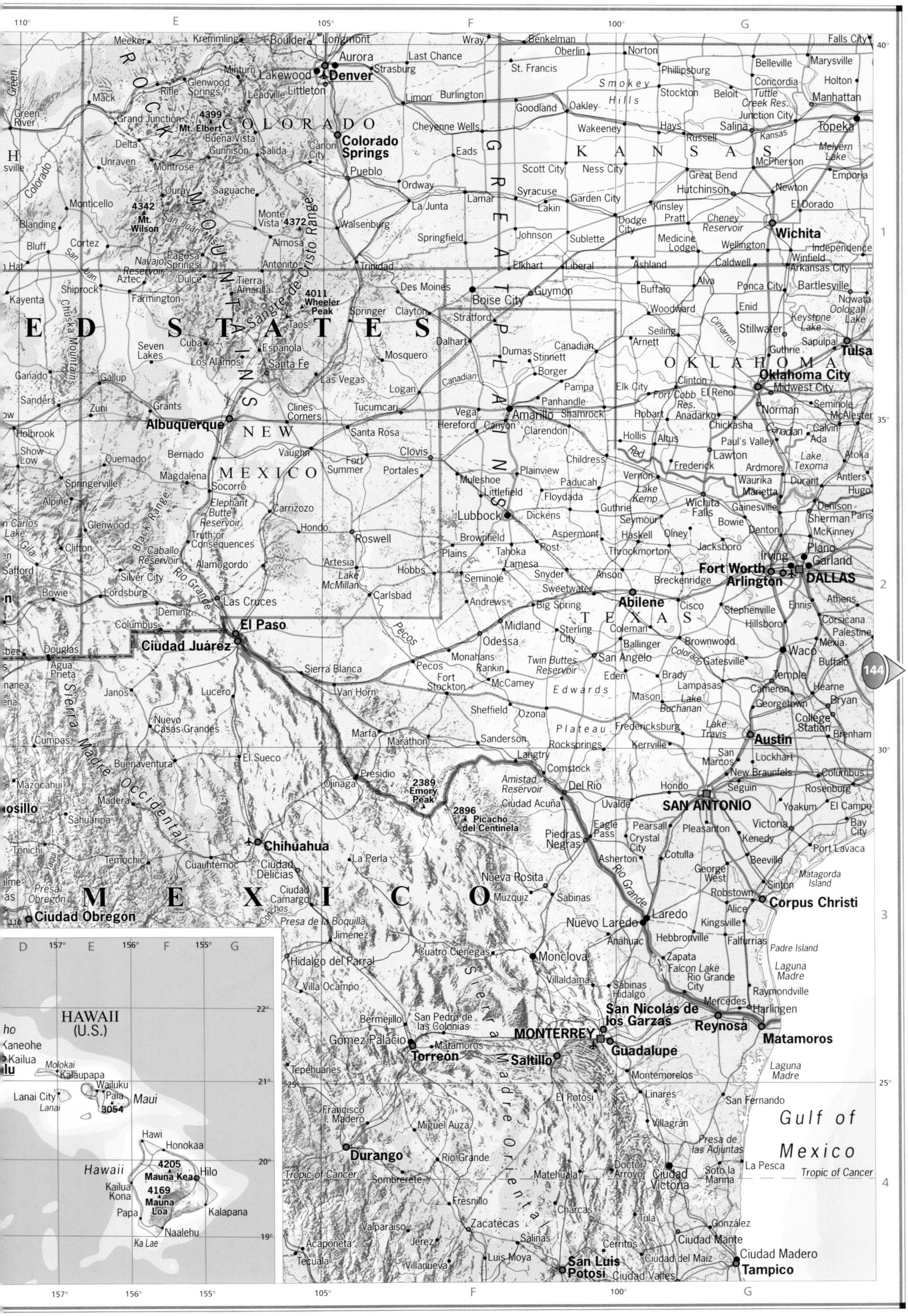

■ over 3 million
■ 1 – 3 million
● 250 000 – 1 million
● 100 000 – 250 000
○ 25 000 – 100 000
• under 25 000
country capital underline
state or province capital underline

Scale 1 : 16 100 000

0 200 400 600 km

0 100 200 300 miles

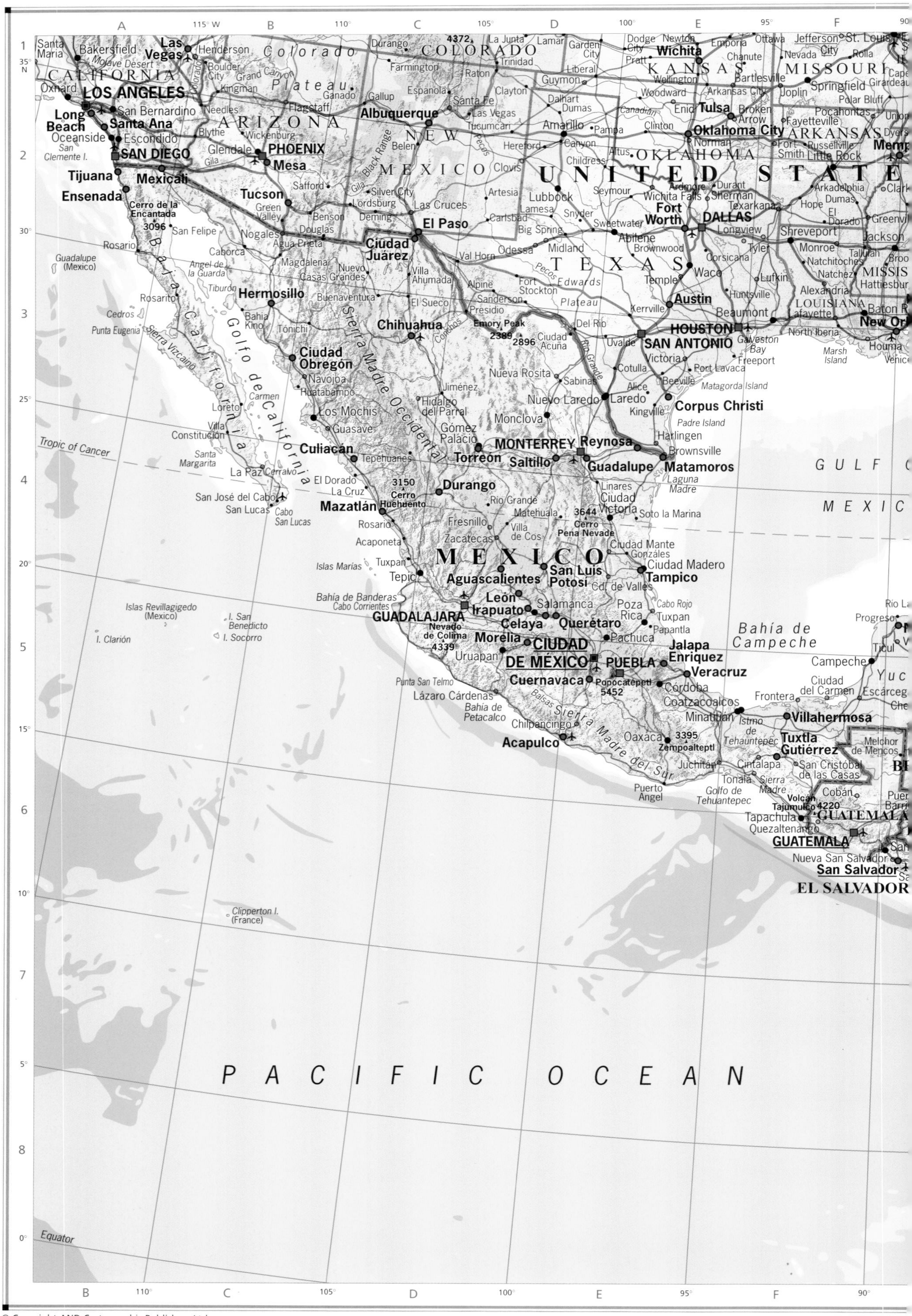

metres feet

metres	feet
8000	26250
6000	19690
4000	13120
2000	6560
1000	3280
500	1640
200	656
0	0
656	200
3280	1000
6560	2000
13120	4000
19690	6000
26250	8000

feet metres

Central America and the Caribbean

**Belize • Caribbean Islands • Costa Rica • El Salvador
Guatemala • Honduras • Nicaragua • Panama**

■ over 3 million
■ 1 – 3 million
● 250 000 – 1 million
● 100 000 – 250 000
○ 25 000 – 100 000
• under 25 000
country capital underline
state or province capital underline

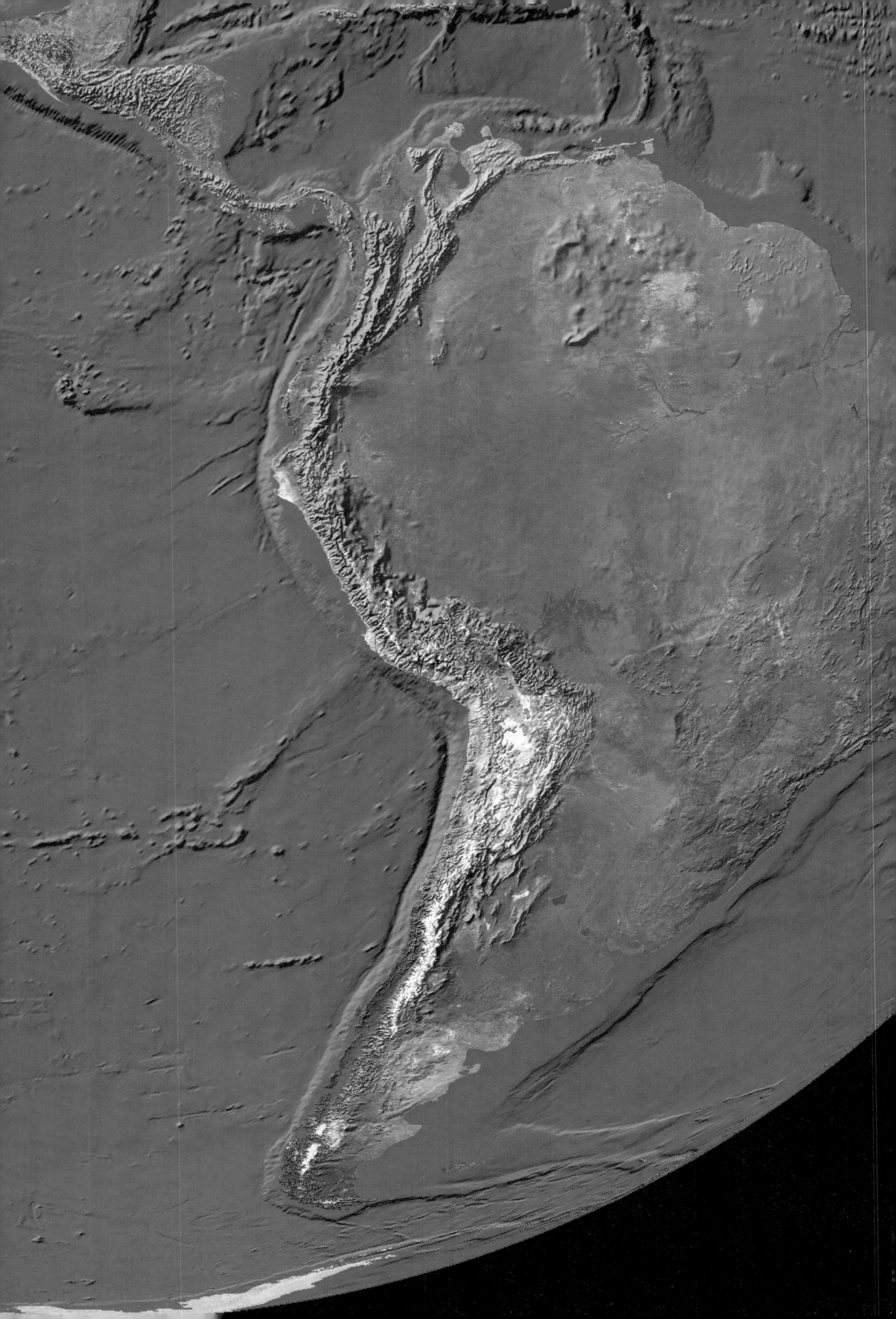

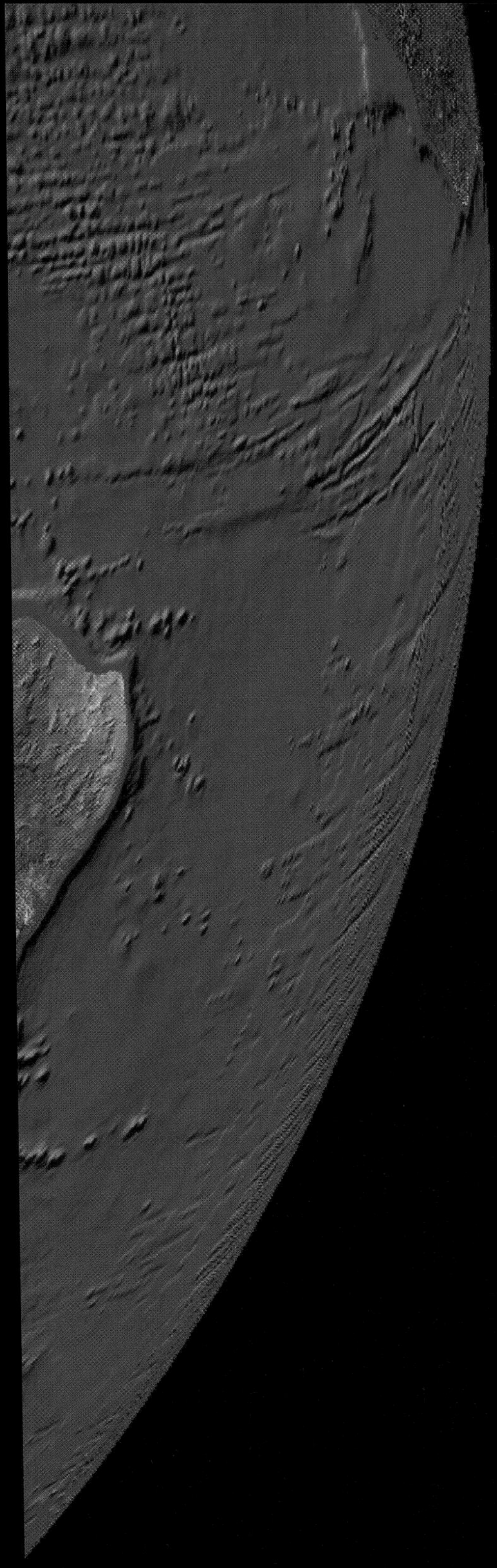

SOUTH AMERICA

a view from space

South America *flags and statistics* 152

South America *political* 154

Northern South America 156

Southern South America 158

SOUTH AMERICA

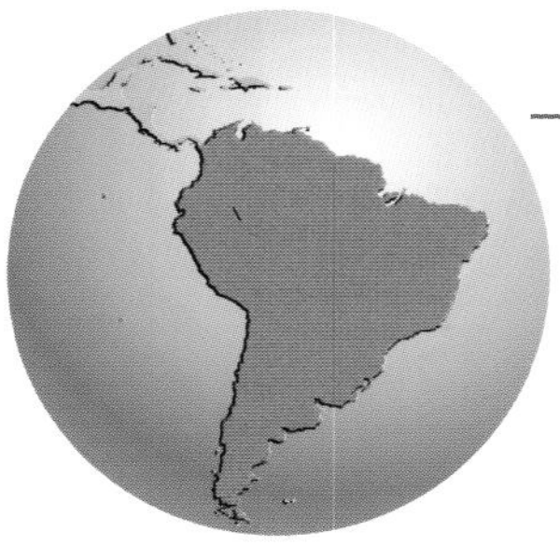

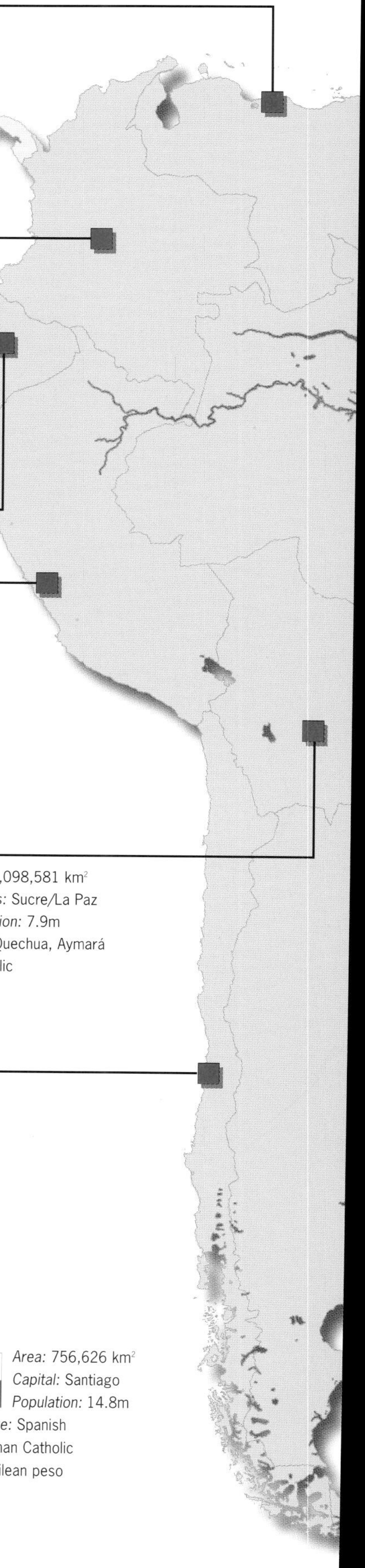

Venezuela

Area: 912,050 km²
Capital: Caracas
Population: 23.2m
Main language: Spanish
Religion: Roman Catholic
Currency: Bolivar

Colombia

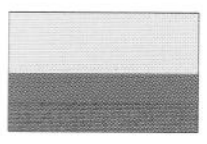

Area: 1,138,914 km²
Capital: Bogotá
Population: 40.8m
Main language: Spanish
Religion: Roman Catholic
Currency: Colombian peso

Ecuador

Area: 283,561 km²
Capital: Quito
Population: 12.2m
Languages: Spanish, Quechua
Religion: Roman Catholic
Currency: Sucre

Peru

Area: 1,285,216 km²
Capital: Lima
Population: 24.8m
Languages: Spanish, Quechua, Aymará
Religion: Roman Catholic
Currency: New Sol

Bolivia

Area: 1,098,581 km²
Capitals: Sucre/La Paz
Population: 7.9m
Languages: Spanish, Quechua, Aymará
Religion: Roman Catholic
Currency: Boliviano

GROSS NATIONAL PRODUCT PER CAPITA (US$)

5 highest		*5 lowest*	
Argentina	8,570	Paraguay	2,010
Uruguay	6,020	Ecuador	1,590
Chile	5,020	Surinam	1,240
Brazil	4,720	Bolivia	950
Venezuela	3,450	Guyana	800

POPULATION DENSITY (per km²)

5 highest		*5 lowest*	
Ecuador	43	Argentina	13
Colombia	36	Paraguay	13
Venezuela	25	Bolivia	7
Brazil	19	Surinam	4
Peru	19	Guyana	4

LIFE EXPECTANCY (years)

5 highest		*5 lowest*	
Chile	75	Ecuador	69
Argentina	72	Paraguay	69
Uruguay	72	Brazil	66
Venezuela	72	Guyana	63
Colombia	70	Bolivia	59

Chile

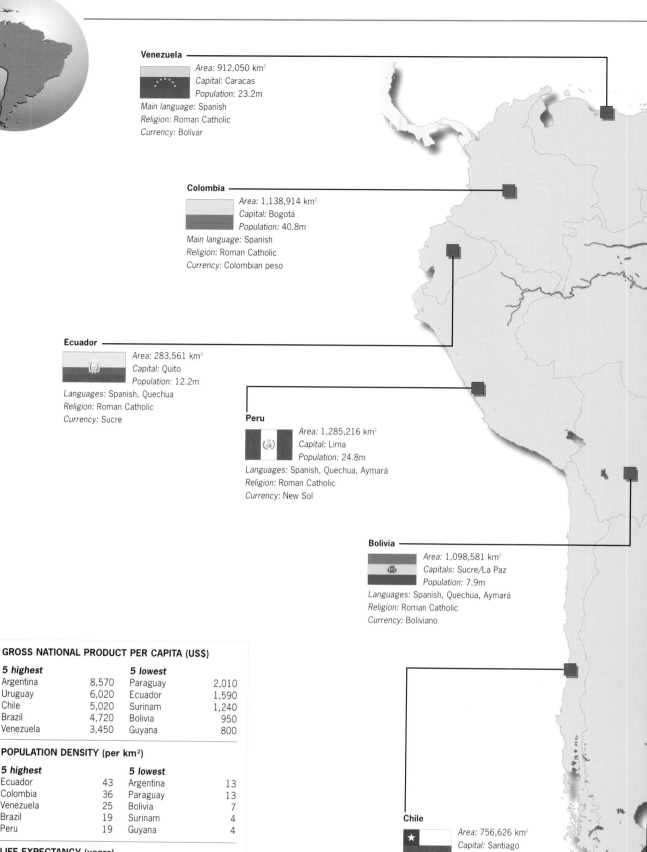

Area: 756,626 km²
Capital: Santiago
Population: 14.8m
Main language: Spanish
Religion: Roman Catholic
Currency: Chilean peso

THE FOURTH LARGEST continent in the world contains the Amazon rainforest and the Andes mountain chain. It has massive mineral resources. Most of the population, concentrated in the coastal regions, is of mixed European and Amerindian descent. Spanish is the most widely-spoken language.

Guyana

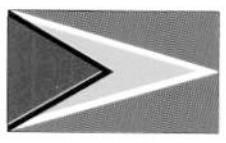

Area: 214,967 km^2
Capital: Georgetown
Population: 850,000
Languages: English, Creole
Religions: Christian, Hindu
Currency: Guyana dollar

Surinam

Area: 163,265 km^2
Capital: Paramaribo
Population: 414,000
Languages: Dutch, Sranang Togo
Religions: Christian, Hindu
Currency: Surinam guilder

Paraguay

Area: 406,752 km^2
Capital: Asuncion
Population: 5.2m
Languages: Spanish, Guaraní
Religion: Roman Catholic
Currency: Guaraní

Brazil

Area: 8,547,443 km^2
Capital: Brasilia
Population: 165.9m
Main language: Portuguese
Religion: Christian
Currency: Real

Uruguay

Area: 177,414 km^2
Capital: Montevideo
Population: 3.3m
Main language: Spanish
Religion: Roman Catholic
Currency: New Uruguayan peso

Argentina

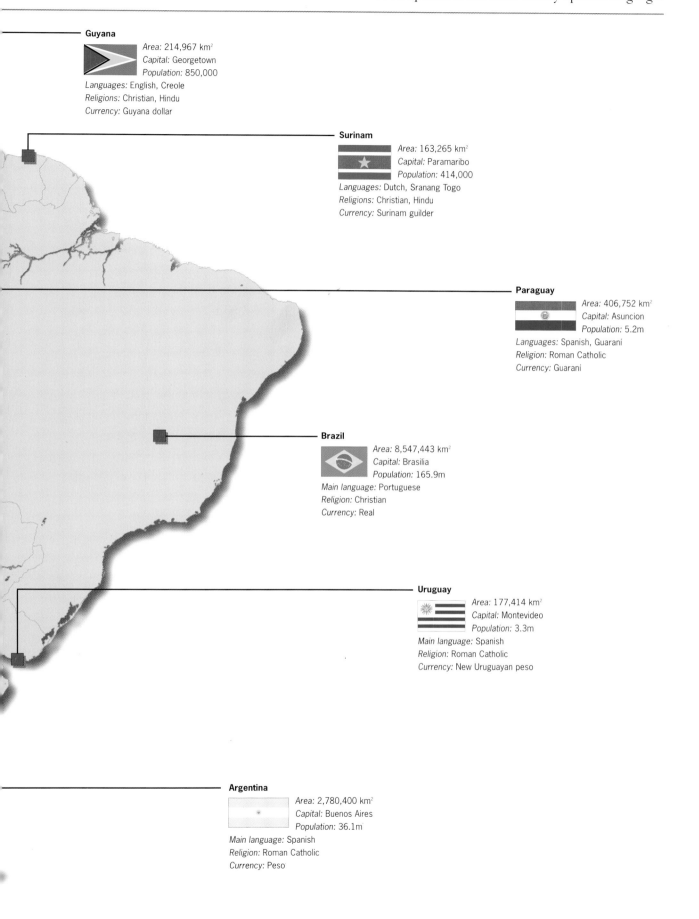

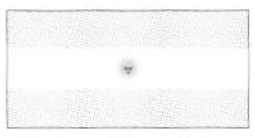

Area: 2,780,400 km^2
Capital: Buenos Aires
Population: 36.1m
Main language: Spanish
Religion: Roman Catholic
Currency: Peso

Scale 1 : 28 000 000

0 500 1000 1500 km

0 250 500 750 miles

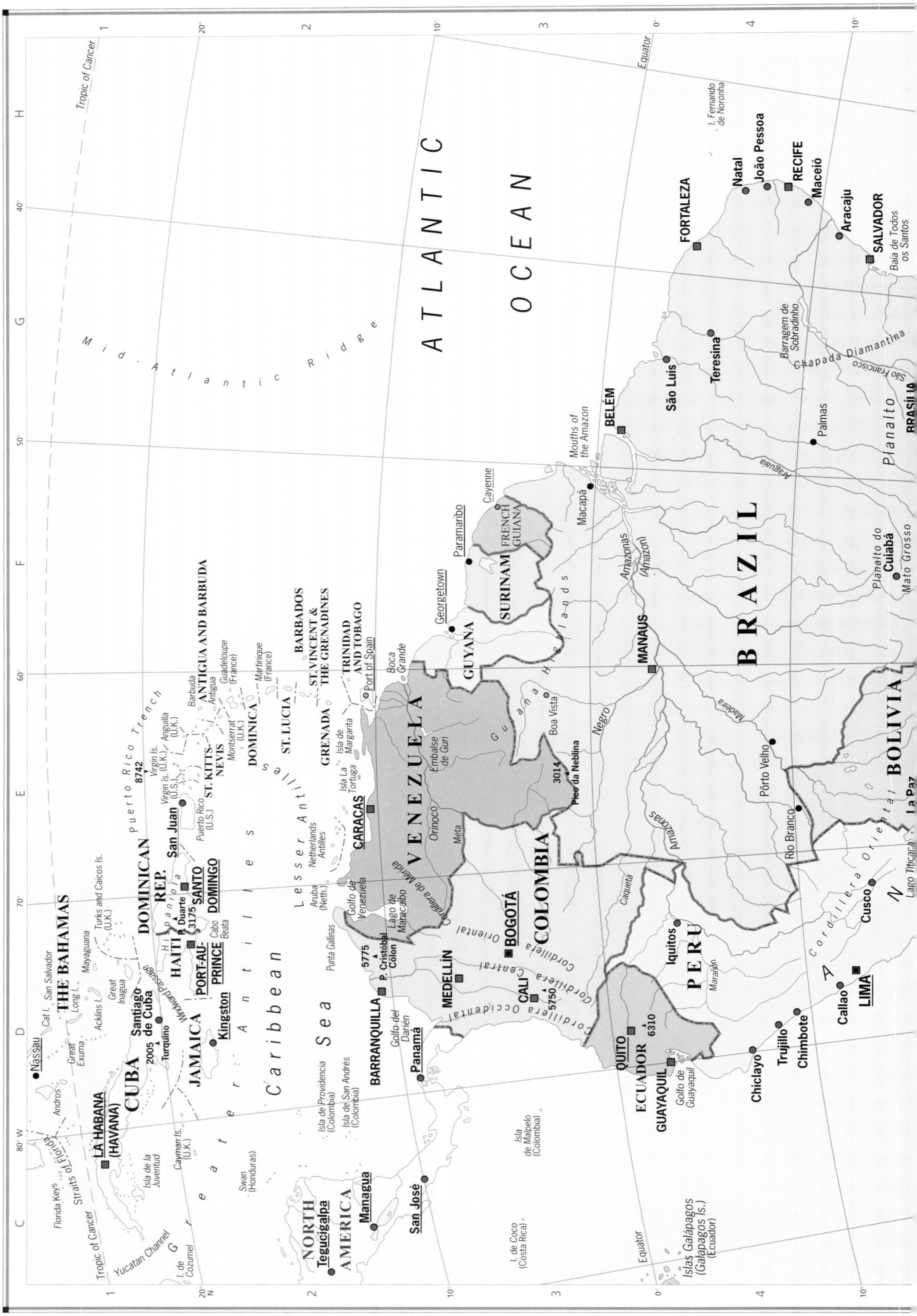

ATLANTIC
OCEAN
Mid-Atlantic Ridge
Tropic of Cancer
Equator
Caribbean Sea
Greater Antilles
Lesser Antilles
Puerto Rico Trench
THE BAHAMAS
Nassau
CUBA
LA HABANA (HAVANA)
Santiago de Cuba
JAMAICA
Kingston
HAITI
PORT-AU-PRINCE
DOMINICAN REP.
SANTO DOMINGO
San Juan
ANTIGUA AND BARBUDA
ST. KITTS-NEVIS
DOMINICA
ST. LUCIA
BARBADOS
ST. VINCENT & THE GRENADINES
GRENADA
TRINIDAD AND TOBAGO
Port of Spain
NORTH AMERICA
Tegucigalpa
Managua
San José
Panamá
BARRANQUILLA
VENEZUELA
CARACAS
Lago de Maracaibo
Orinoco
COLOMBIA
BOGOTÁ
MEDELLÍN
CALI
ECUADOR
QUITO
GUAYAQUIL
PERU
LIMA
Callao
Trujillo
Chimbote
Chiclayo
Iquitos
Cusco
GUYANA
Georgetown
SURINAM
Paramaribo
FRENCH GUIANA
Cayenne
BRAZIL
MANAUS
BELÉM
Macapá
Mouths of the Amazon
Amazonas (Amazon)
São Luís
Teresina
FORTALEZA
Natal
João Pessoa
RECIFE
Maceió
Aracaju
SALVADOR
Palmas
Cuiabá
Pôrto Velho
Rio Branco
Boa Vista
BOLIVIA
Islas Galápagos (Galapagos Is.) (Ecuador)

Aconcagua, Argentina : 6,960 m or 22,835 ft

Península Valdés, Argentina : 40 m or 131 ft

Arica, Chile : 0.08 cm or 0.03 in

Quibdo, Colombia : 899 cm or 354 in

Amazon-Ucayali, Brazil : 6,570 km or 4,080 mi

Lake Maracaibo, Venezuela : 13,010 km^2 or 5,020 sq mi

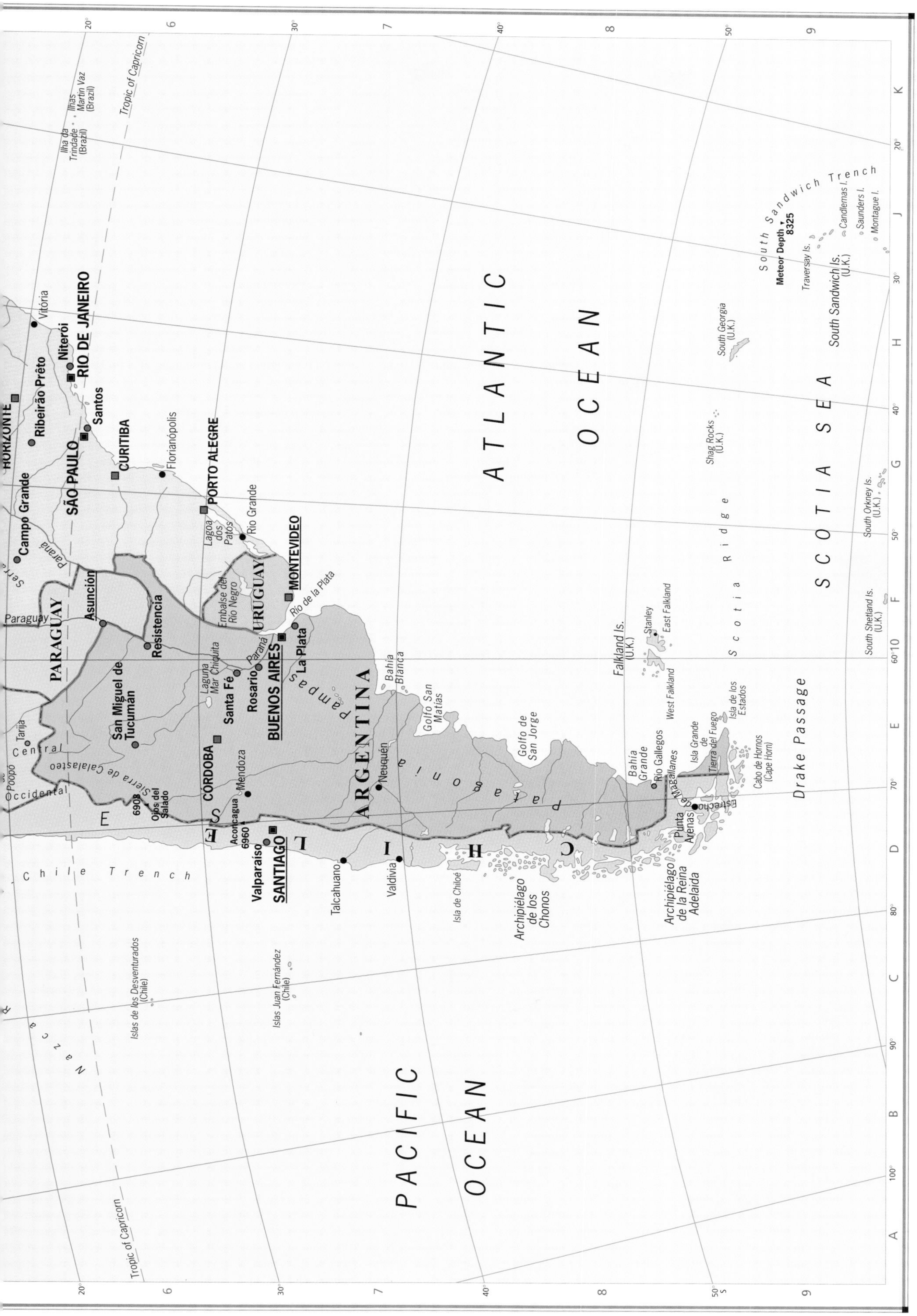
ATLANTIC OCEAN
PACIFIC OCEAN
SCOTIA SEA
Scotia Ridge
Drake Passage
South Sandwich Trench
Meteor Depth 8325
Chile Trench
Nazca
Tropic of Capricorn
ARGENTINA
CHILE
PARAGUAY
URUGUAY
BUENOS AIRES
MONTEVIDEO
SANTIAGO
Asunción
RIO DE JANEIRO
SÃO PAULO
PORTO ALEGRE
CURITIBA
CÓRDOBA
HORIZONTE
Vitória
Niterói
Ribeirão Prêto
Santos
Florianópolis
Campo Grande
Rio Grande
Lagoa dos Patos
Embalse del Río Negro
Río de la Plata
La Plata
Rosario
Santa Fé
Paraná
Laguna Mar Chiquita
Resistencia
San Miguel de Tucumán
Mendoza
Aconcagua 6960
Ojos del Salado 6908
Valparaíso
Talcahuano
Valdivia
Neuquén
Bahía Blanca
Golfo San Matías
Golfo de San Jorge
Pampas
Patagonia
Río Gallegos
Bahía Grande
Estrecho de Magallanes
Punta Arenas
Isla Grande de Tierra del Fuego
Isla de los Estados
Cabo de Hornos (Cape Horn)
Isla de Chiloé
Archipiélago de los Chonos
Archipiélago de la Reina Adelaida
Falkland Is. (U.K.)
Stanley
East Falkland
West Falkland
South Georgia (U.K.)
Shag Rocks (U.K.)
South Orkney Is. (U.K.)
South Shetland Is. (U.K.)
South Sandwich Is. (U.K.)
Traversay Is.
Candlemas I.
Saunders I.
Montague I.
Ilha da Trindade (Brazil)
Ilhas Martin Vaz (Brazil)
Islas de los Desventurados (Chile)
Islas Juan Fernández (Chile)
Tarija
Poopó
Central
Occidental
Sierra de Calalaste
Paraguay
Paraná
Serra

Sarmiento, Argentina : -33 °C or -27 °F

Rivadavia, Argentina : 49 °C or 120 °F

335,716,000

19 per km² or 49 per sq mi

17,838,000 km² or 6,887,000 sq mi

12

Scale 1 : 16 100 000

0 200 400 600 km

0 100 200 300 miles

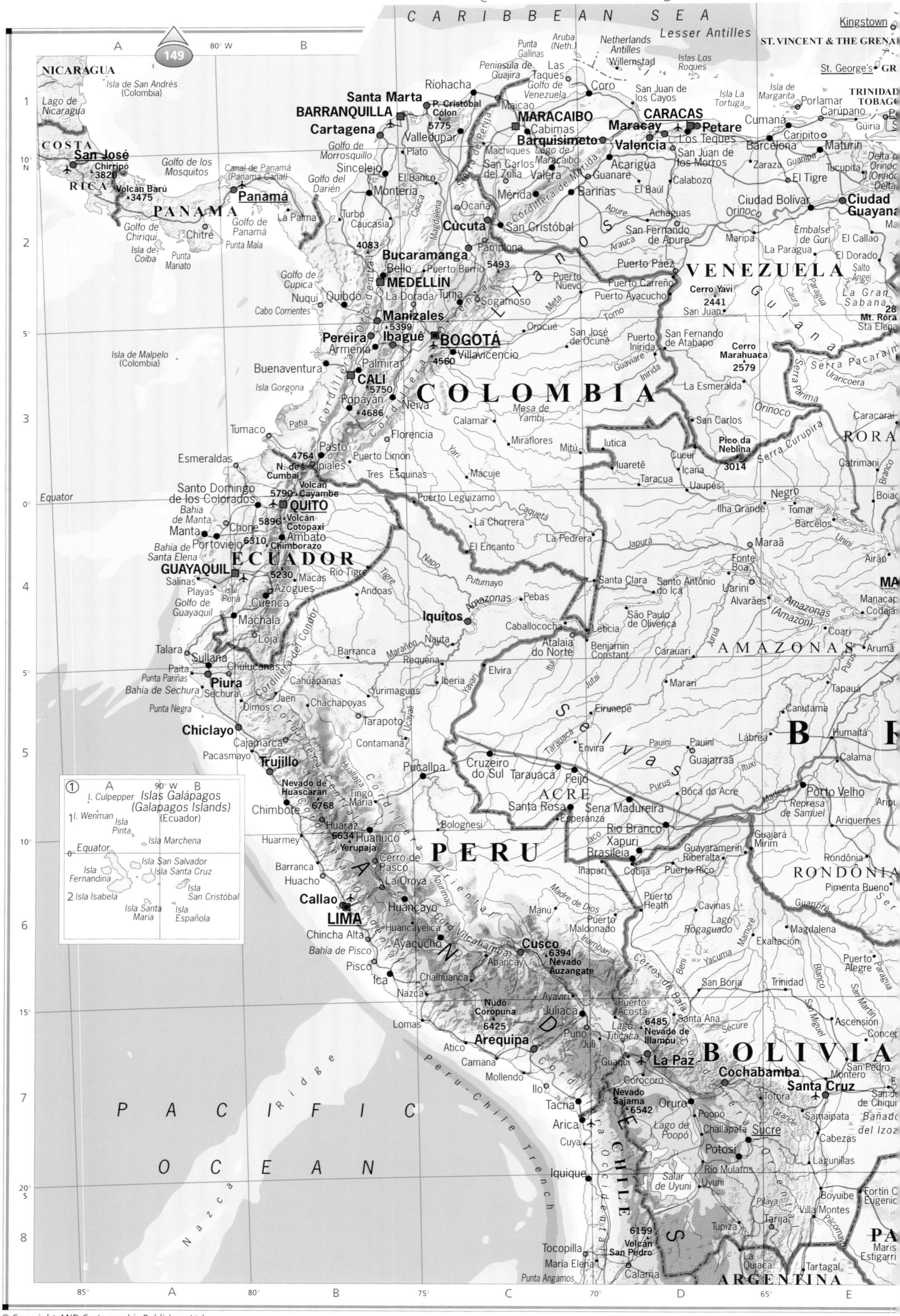
CARIBBEAN SEA
PACIFIC OCEAN
Lesser Antilles
Netherlands Antilles
Aruba (Neth.)
Kingstown
ST. VINCENT & THE GRENADINES
St. George's
TRINIDAD & TOBAGO
NICARAGUA
COSTA RICA
PANAMA
COLOMBIA
VENEZUELA
ECUADOR
PERU
BOLIVIA
CHILE
ARGENTINA
AMAZONAS
RONDÔNIA
ACRE
Isla de San Andrés (Colombia)
Lago de Nicaragua
San José
Chirripó 3820
Volcán Barú 3475
Golfo de los Mosquitos
Canal de Panamá (Panama Canal)
Panamá
Golfo de Panamá
Golfo de Chiriquí
Chitré
Isla de Coiba
Punta Mariato
Punta Mala
Golfo del Darién
Santa Marta
BARRANQUILLA
Cartagena
Golfo de Morrosquillo
Sincelejo
Montería
Valledupar
Riohacha
Península de Guajira
Punta Gallinas
MARACAIBO
Cabimas
Lago de Maracaibo
Barquisimeto
Valencia
Maracay
CARACAS
Petare
Los Teques
Coro
Willemstad
Barcelona
Cumaná
Maturín
Ciudad Bolívar
Ciudad Guayana
San Fernando de Apure
Barinas
Mérida
Cordillera de Mérida
San Cristóbal
Cúcuta
Bucaramanga
MEDELLÍN
Manizales
Pereira
Armenia
Ibagué
BOGOTÁ
Villavicencio
CALI
Palmira
Buenaventura
Popayán
Neiva
Pasto
Tumaco
Florencia
Isla de Malpelo (Colombia)
Isla Gorgona
Cabo Corrientes
Quibdó
Llanos
Orinoco
Guiana Highlands
Pico da Neblina 3014
Cerro Marahuaca 2579
Cerro Yavi 2441
Mitú
Esmeraldas
Equator
QUITO
Volcán Cayambe 5790
Volcán Cotopaxi 5896
Chimborazo 6310
Ambato
Manta
Portoviejo
GUAYAQUIL
Golfo de Guayaquil
Cuenca
Machala
Loja
Talara
Sullana
Piura
Chiclayo
Trujillo
Chimbote
Nevado de Huascarán 6768
Yerupajá 6634
Huánuco
Cerro de Pasco
Callao
LIMA
Huancayo
Ayacucho
Cusco
Nevado Auzangate 6394
Nudo Coropuna 6425
Arequipa
Juliaca
Puno
Lago Titicaca
Nevado de Illampu 6485
La Paz
Cochabamba
Santa Cruz
Oruro
Sucre
Potosí
Tacna
Arica
Iquique
Nevado Sajama 6542
Salar de Uyuni
Volcán San Pedro 6159
Tocopilla
Calama
Iquitos
Pucallpa
Cruzeiro do Sul
Rio Branco
Porto Velho
Manaus
Amazonas (Amazon)
Cordillera Occidental
Cordillera Oriental
Cordillera Central
Andes
Selvas
Peru-Chile Trench
Nazca Ridge
Islas Galápagos (Galapagos Islands) (Ecuador)
Isla Isabela
Isla Fernandina
Isla Santa Cruz
Isla San Cristóbal
Isla Santa María
Isla Española
Isla Marchena
Isla Pinta
Isla San Salvador
I. Culpepper
I. Wenman
149

metres	feet
8000	26250
6000	19690
4000	13120
2000	6560
1000	3280
500	1640
200	656
0	0
656	200
3280	1000
6560	2000
13120	4000
19690	6000
26250	8000
feet	metres

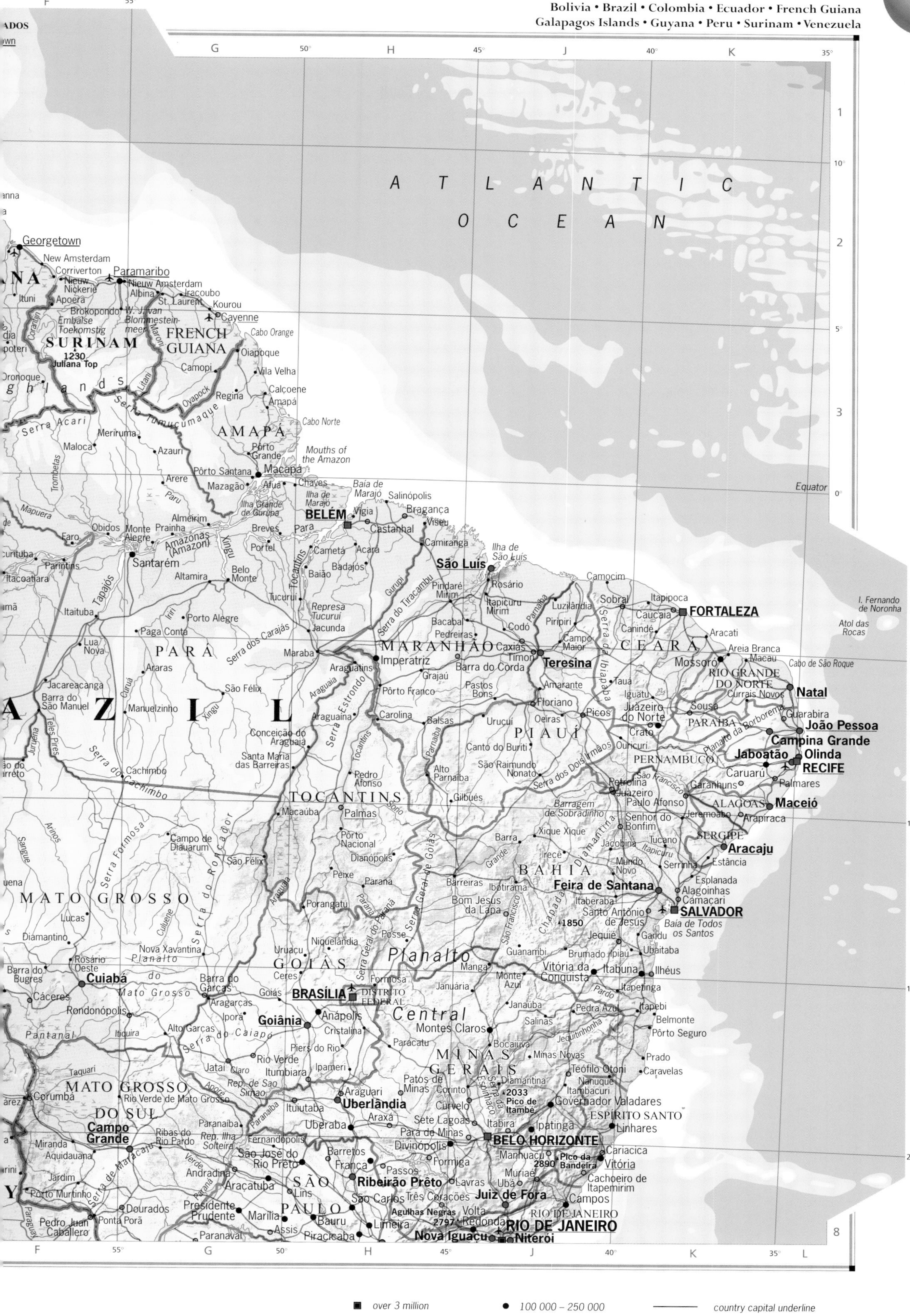

ATLANTIC OCEAN
Equator
SURINAM
FRENCH GUIANA
AMAPÁ
PARÁ
MARANHÃO
PIAUÍ
CEARÁ
RIO GRANDE DO NORTE
PARAÍBA
PERNAMBUCO
ALAGOAS
SERGIPE
BAHIA
TOCANTINS
GOIÁS
DISTRITO FEDERAL
MATO GROSSO
MATO GROSSO DO SUL
MINAS GERAIS
ESPÍRITO SANTO
SÃO PAULO
RIO DE JANEIRO
BRAZIL
Georgetown
Paramaribo
Cayenne
Macapá
BELÉM
São Luís
Teresina
FORTALEZA
Natal
João Pessoa
Campina Grande
RECIFE
Olinda
Jaboatão
Maceió
Aracaju
SALVADOR
Feira de Santana
BRASÍLIA
Goiânia
Cuiabá
Campo Grande
Uberlândia
Ribeirão Prêto
BELO HORIZONTE
Vitória
Juiz de Fora
RIO DE JANEIRO
Niterói
Nova Iguaçu
Santarém
Imperatriz
Planalto Central
Pantanal
Mouths of the Amazon
Ilha de Marajó
Cabo Orange
Cabo Norte
Cabo de São Roque
I. Fernando de Noronha
Atol das Rocas
Baía de Todos os Santos
1230 Juliana Top
2033 Pico de Itambé
2890 Pico da Bandeira
2797 Agulhas Negras
1850

■ over 3 million
■ 1 – 3 million
● 250 000 – 1 million
● 100 000 – 250 000
○ 25 000 – 100 000
• under 25 000
country capital underline
state or province capital underline

Scale 1 : 16 100 000

0 200 400 600 km

0 100 200 300 miles

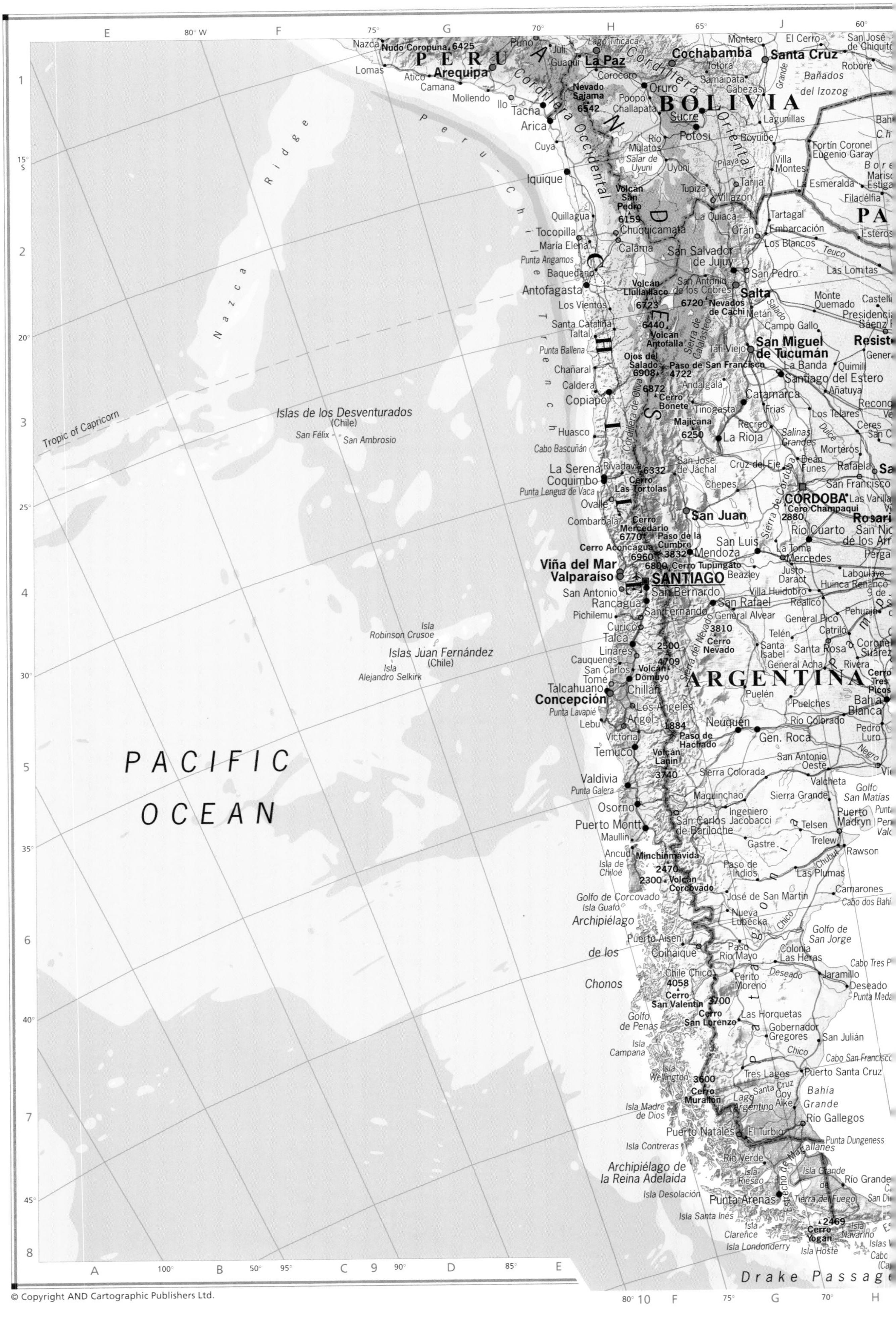

PACIFIC OCEAN
Tropic of Capricorn
Nazca Ridge
Peru-Chile Trench
Islas de los Desventurados (Chile)
San Félix
San Ambrosio
Isla Robinson Crusoe
Islas Juan Fernández (Chile)
Isla Alejandro Selkirk
PERU
BOLIVIA
CHILE
ARGENTINA
ANDES
Cordillera Occidental
Cordillera Oriental
Lago Titicaca
Nazca
Nudo Coropuna 6425
Lomas
Atico
Arequipa
Camana
Mollendo
Ilo
Puno
Juli
Guaqui
La Paz
Corocoro
Nevado Sajama 6542
Tacna
Arica
Cochabamba
Santa Cruz
Montero
El Cerro
San José de Chiquitos
Roboré
Bañados del Izozog
Totora
Samaipata
Cabezas
Oruro
Poopó
Challapata
Sucre
Potosí
Lagunillas
Rio Mulatos
Salar de Uyuni
Uyuni
Boyuibe
Cuya
Iquique
Volcán San Pedro 6159
Tupiza
Tarija
Villazón
Villa Montes
Fortín Coronel Eugenio Garay
La Esmeralda
Filadelfia
Quillagua
Tocopilla
María Elena
Punta Angamos
Chuquicamata
Calama
La Quiaca
Orán
Tartagal
Embarcación
Los Blancos
Teuco
Baquedano
Antofagasta
San Salvador de Jujuy
San Pedro
Las Lomitas
Volcán Llullaillaco 6723
San Antonio de los Cobres
Salta
Nevados de Cachi 6720
Los Vientos
Santa Catalina
Taltal
6440
Volcán Antofalla
Metán
Monte Quemado
Campo Gallo
Punta Ballena
Ojos del Salado 6908
Paso de San Francisco 4722
Tafí Viejo
San Miguel de Tucumán
La Banda
Santiago del Estero
Añatuya
Chañaral
Caldera
Copiapó
6872
Andalgalá
Cerro Bonete
Tinogasta
Catamarca
Frias
Los Telares
Majicana 6250
La Rioja
Recreo
Salinas Grandes
Dulce
Huasco
Cabo Bascuñán
La Serena
Coquimbo
Punta Lengua de Vaca
Rivadavia
6332
Cerro Las Tórtolas
San José de Jáchal
Chepes
Cruz del Eje
Dean Funes
Rafaela
San Francisco
Ovalle
Combarbalá
Cerro Mercedario 6770
San Juan
Córdoba
Cerro Champaquí 2880
Río Cuarto
Cerro Aconcagua 6960
Paso de la Cumbre 3832
Mendoza
San Luis
La Toma
Mercedes
Viña del Mar
Valparaíso
6800 Cerro Tupungato
SANTIAGO
Justo Daract
Beazley
San Antonio
Rancagua
San Bernardo
Villa Huidobro
San Rafael
Realicó
Pichilemu
San Fernando
General Alvear
Curicó
Talca
3810
Cerro Nevado
General Pico
Catriló
Linares
2500
Telén
Santa Isabel
Santa Rosa
Cauquenes
San Carlos
4709
Volcán Domuyo
General Acha
Rivera
Tomé
Talcahuano
Concepción
Chillán
Puelén
Punta Lavapié
Lebu
Los Ángeles
Angol
1884
Neuquén
Puelches
Río Colorado
Bahía Blanca
Victoria
Paso de Hachado
Gen. Roca
Temuco
Volcán Lanín 3740
San Antonio Oeste
Sierra Colorada
Valdivia
Punta Galera
Valcheta
Osorno
Maquinchao
Sierra Grande
Golfo San Matías
Puerto Montt
Maullín
San Carlos de Bariloche
Ingeniero Jacobacci
Telsen
Puerto Madryn
Trelew
Gastre
Rawson
Ancud
Isla de Chiloé
Minchinmávida
2470
2300
Volcán Corcovado
Paso de Indios
Las Plumas
Chubut
Camarones
Golfo de Corcovado
Isla Guafo
José de San Martín
Archipiélago de los Chonos
Nueva Lubecka
Chico
Golfo de San Jorge
Puerto Aisén
Coihaique
Río Mayo
Colonia Las Heras
Chile Chico
4058
Cerro San Valentín
Perito Moreno
Deseado
Jaramillo
Puerto Deseado
3700
Cerro San Lorenzo
Las Horquetas
Golfo de Penas
Gobernador Gregores
San Julián
Isla Campana
Isla Wellington
3600
Cerro Murallón
Tres Lagos
Puerto Santa Cruz
Lago Argentino
Santa Cruz
Coyle
Bahía Grande
Isla Madre de Dios
Río Gallegos
Puerto Natales
El Turbio
Punta Dungeness
Isla Contreras
Archipiélago de la Reina Adelaida
Río Verde
Isla Riesco
Estrecho de Magallanes
Isla Grande de Tierra del Fuego
Río Grande
Isla Desolación
Punta Arenas
Isla Santa Inés
Isla Clarence
Isla Londonderry
2469
Cerro Yogan
Isla Navarino
Isla Hoste
Drake Passage

metres	feet
8000	26250
6000	19690
4000	13120
2000	6560
1000	3280
500	1640
200	656
0	0
656	200
3280	1000
6560	2000
13120	4000
19690	6000
26250	8000
feet	metres

Southern South America

Argentina • Chile • Falkland Islands • Paraguay • Uruguay

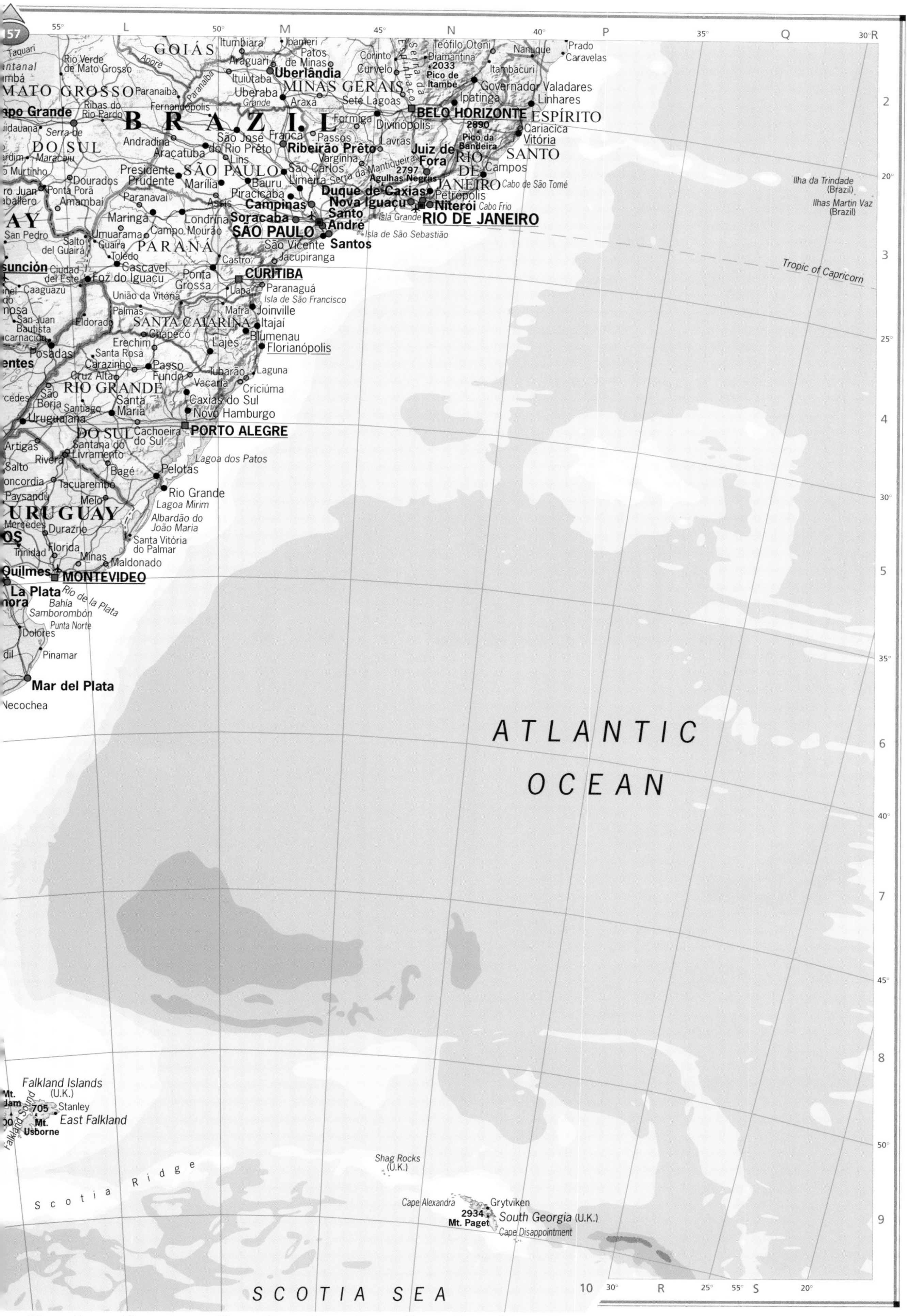

157
GOIÁS
MATO GROSSO
Campo Grande
DO SUL
BRAZIL
MINAS GERAIS
ESPÍRITO
SANTO
RIO DE JANEIRO
SÃO PAULO
PARANÁ
SANTA CATARINA
RIO GRANDE
DO SUL
URUGUAY
Uberlândia
Uberaba
Araxá
Sete Lagoas
BELO HORIZONTE
Divinópolis
Formiga
Teófilo Otoni
Diamantina
Pico de Itambé
2033
Governador Valadares
Ipatinga
Linhares
Cariacica
Vitória
Juiz de Fora
Pico da Bandeira
2890
Campos
Cabo de São Tomé
Agulhas Negras
2797
Ribeirão Prêto
São José do Rio Prêto
Araçatuba
Presidente Prudente
Marília
Bauru
São Carlos
Limeira
Piracicaba
Campinas
Sorocaba
Santo André
SÃO PAULO
Santos
São Vicente
Isla de São Sebastião
Duque de Caxias
Nova Iguaçu
Niterói
Petrópolis
Cabo Frio
Isla Grande
RIO DE JANEIRO
Maringá
Londrina
Campo Mourão
Umuarama
Paranavaí
Dourados
Ponta Porã
Amambaí
Salto del Guairá
Guaíra
Toledo
Cascavel
Ciudad del Este
Foz do Iguaçu
Ponta Grossa
CURITIBA
Paranaguá
Isla de São Francisco
Castro
Jacupiranga
União da Vitória
Palmas
Mafra
Joinville
Itajaí
Blumenau
Florianópolis
Chapecó
Erechim
Lajes
Eldorado
San Juan Bautista
Posadas
Santa Rosa
Carazinho
Passo Fundo
Cruz Alta
Tubarão
Laguna
Vacaria
Criciúma
Caxias do Sul
Novo Hamburgo
São Borja
Santiago
Santa Maria
Uruguaiana
Cachoeira do Sul
PORTO ALEGRE
Santana do Livramento
Artigas
Rivera
Salto
Bagé
Pelotas
Lagoa dos Patos
Rio Grande
Lagoa Mirim
Albardão do João Maria
Santa Vitória do Palmar
Tacuarembó
Paysandú
Melo
Mercedes
Durazno
Trinidad
Florida
Minas
Maldonado
Quilmes
MONTEVIDEO
La Plata
Río de la Plata
Bahía Samborombón
Punta Norte
Dolores
Pinamar
Mar del Plata
Necochea
Ilha da Trindade (Brazil)
Ilhas Martin Vaz (Brazil)
Tropic of Capricorn
ATLANTIC
OCEAN
Falkland Islands (U.K.)
Stanley
705
Mt. Usborne
East Falkland
Falkland Sound
Scotia Ridge
Shag Rocks (U.K.)
Cape Alexandra
Grytviken
2934
Mt. Paget
South Georgia (U.K.)
Cape Disappointment
SCOTIA SEA

■ over 3 million	● 100 000 – 250 000	——— country capital underline
■ 1 – 3 million	○ 25 000 – 100 000	——— state or province capital underline
● 250 000 – 1 million	• under 25 000	

Scale 1 : 50 700 000
0 500 1000 1500 2000 km
0 250 500 750 1000 miles

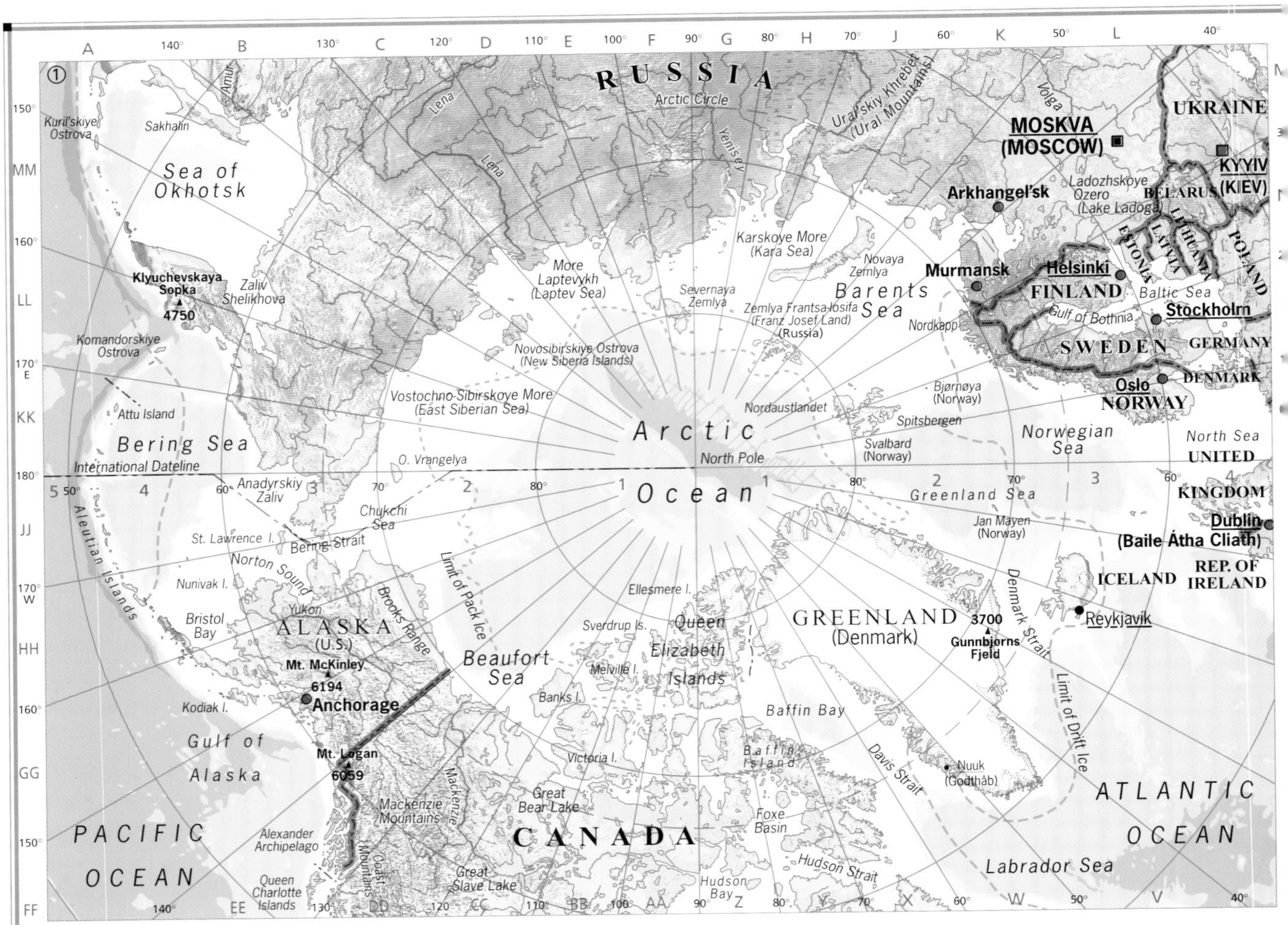
①
RUSSIA
Arctic Circle
UKRAINE
MOSKVA (MOSCOW)
KYYIV (KIEV)
BELARUS
Arkhangel'sk
Ladozhskoye Ozero (Lake Ladoga)
ESTONIA
LATVIA
LITHUANIA
POLAND
Ural'skiy Khrebet (Ural Mountains)
Volga
Yenisey
Lena
Amur
Kuril'skiye Ostrova
Sakhalin
Sea of Okhotsk
Karskoye More (Kara Sea)
Novaya Zemlya
Murmansk
Helsinki
FINLAND
Baltic Sea
Stockholm
Gulf of Bothnia
SWEDEN
GERMANY
DENMARK
Oslo
NORWAY
Barents Sea
Nordkapp
Zemlya Frantsa-Iosifa (Franz Josef Land) (Russia)
Severnaya Zemlya
More Laptevykh (Laptev Sea)
Klyuchevskaya Sopka 4750
Zaliv Shelikhova
Komandorskiye Ostrova
Novosibirskiye Ostrova (New Siberia Islands)
Vostochno-Sibirskoye More (East Siberian Sea)
Attu Island
Bering Sea
International Dateline
O. Vrangelya
Arctic Ocean
North Pole
Nordaustlandet
Bjørnøya (Norway)
Spitsbergen
Svalbard (Norway)
Norwegian Sea
North Sea
UNITED KINGDOM
Dublin (Baile Átha Cliath)
REP. OF IRELAND
Anadyrskiy Zaliv
Chukchi Sea
Greenland Sea
Jan Mayen (Norway)
ICELAND
Reykjavík
Aleutian Islands
St. Lawrence I.
Bering Strait
Norton Sound
Nunivak I.
Yukon
Bristol Bay
ALASKA (U.S.)
Brooks Range
Limit of Pack Ice
Ellesmere I.
Sverdrup Is.
Queen Elizabeth Islands
GREENLAND (Denmark)
3700 Gunnbjørns Fjeld
Denmark Strait
Limit of Drift Ice
Mt. McKinley 6194
Anchorage
Beaufort Sea
Melville I.
Banks I.
Baffin Bay
Kodiak I.
Gulf of Alaska
Mt. Logan 6059
Victoria I.
Baffin Island
Davis Strait
Nuuk (Godthåb)
ATLANTIC OCEAN
Mackenzie Mountains
Mackenzie
Great Bear Lake
CANADA
Foxe Basin
PACIFIC OCEAN
Alexander Archipelago
Queen Charlotte Islands
Coast Mountains
Great Slave Lake
Hudson Bay
Hudson Strait
Labrador Sea

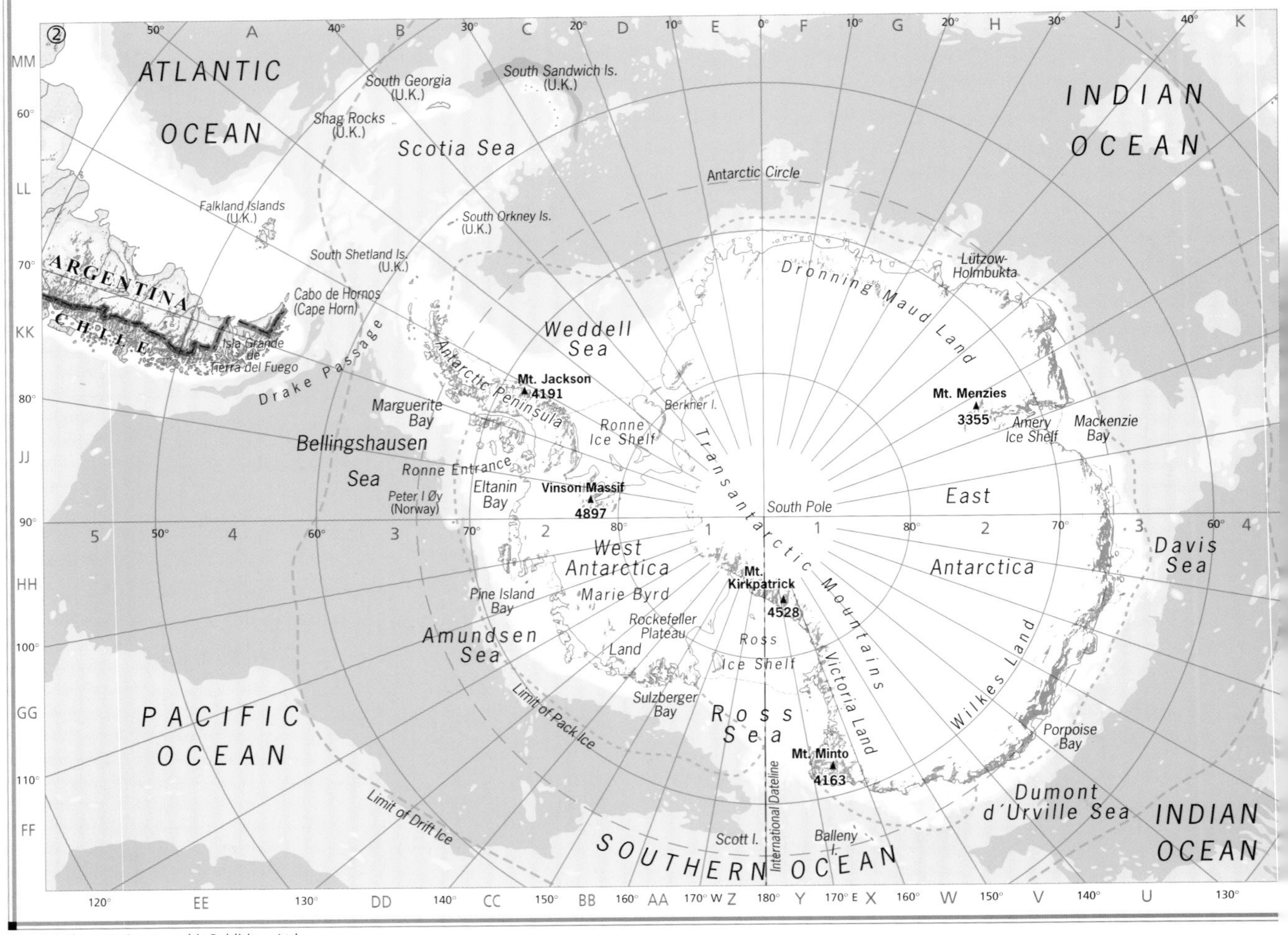
②
ATLANTIC OCEAN
South Georgia (U.K.)
South Sandwich Is. (U.K.)
Shag Rocks (U.K.)
Scotia Sea
INDIAN OCEAN
Antarctic Circle
Falkland Islands (U.K.)
South Orkney Is. (U.K.)
South Shetland Is. (U.K.)
ARGENTINA
CHILE
Cabo de Hornos (Cape Horn)
Isla Grande de Tierra del Fuego
Drake Passage
Dronning Maud Land
Lützow-Holmbukta
Weddell Sea
Antarctic Peninsula
Mt. Jackson 4191
Marguerite Bay
Berkner I.
Ronne Ice Shelf
Mt. Menzies 3355
Amery Ice Shelf
Mackenzie Bay
Bellingshausen Sea
Ronne Entrance
Peter I Øy (Norway)
Eltanin Bay
Vinson Massif 4897
Transantarctic Mountains
South Pole
East Antarctica
Davis Sea
West Antarctica
Marie Byrd Land
Pine Island Bay
Mt. Kirkpatrick 4528
Rockefeller Plateau
Amundsen Sea
Ross Ice Shelf
Victoria Land
Wilkes Land
Limit of Pack Ice
Sulzberger Bay
Ross Sea
PACIFIC OCEAN
Mt. Minto 4163
Porpoise Bay
Limit of Drift Ice
Dumont d'Urville Sea
International Dateline
Scott I.
Balleny Is.
SOUTHERN OCEAN

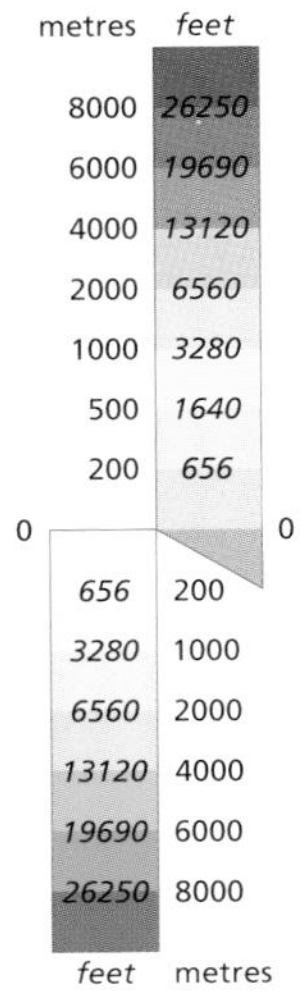
metres feet
8000 26250
6000 19690
4000 13120
2000 6560
1000 3280
500 1640
200 656
0 0
656 200
3280 1000
6560 2000
13120 4000
19690 6000
26250 8000
feet metres

- ■ over 3 million
- ■ 1 – 3 million
- ● 250 000 – 1 million
- ● 100 000 – 250 000
- ○ 25 000 – 100 000
- • under 25 000
- ——— country capital underline

Index

How to use the index

This is an alphabetically arranged index of the places and features that can be found on the maps in this atlas. Each name is generally indexed to the largest scale map on which it appears. If that map covers a double page, the name will always be indexed by the left-hand page number.

Names composed of two or more words are alphabetised as if they were one word.

All names appear in full in the index, except for 'St.' and 'Ste.', which although abbreviated, are indexed as though spelled in full.

Where two or more places have the same name, they can be distinguished from each other by the country or province name which immediately follows the entry. These names are indexed in the alphabetical order of the country or province.

Alternative names, such as English translations, can also be found in the index and are cross-referenced to the map form by the '=' sign. In these cases the names also appear in brackets on the maps.

Settlements are indexed to the position of the symbol, all other features are indexed to the position of the name on the map.

Abbreviations used in this index are explained in the list opposite.

Finding a name on the map

Each index entry contains the name, followed by a symbol indicating the feature type (for example, settlement, river), a page reference and a grid reference:

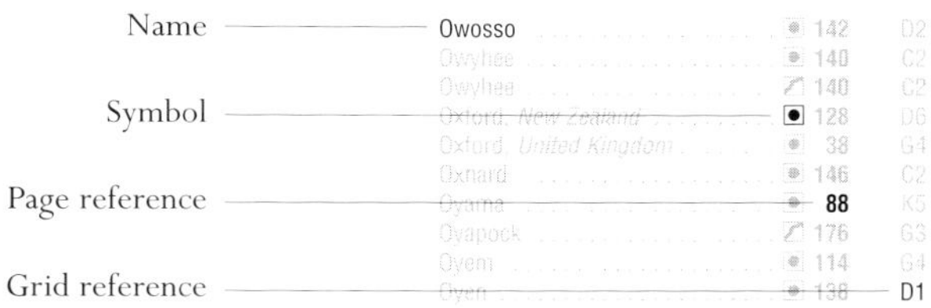

The grid reference locates a place or feature within a rectangle formed by the network of lines of longitude and latitude. A name can be found by referring to the red letters and numbers placed around the maps. First find the letter, which appears along the top and bottom of the map, and then the number, down the sides. The name will be found within the rectangle uniquely defined by that letter and number. A number in brackets preceding the grid reference indicates that the name is to be found within an inset map.

Abbreviations

Ak.	Alaska
Al.	Alabama
Ariz.	Arizona
Ark.	Arkansas
B.C.	British Columbia
Calif.	California
Colo.	Colorado
Conn.	Connecticut
Del.	Delaware
Dem. Rep. of Congo	Democratic Republic of Congo
Eng.	England
Fla.	Florida
Ga.	Georgia
Ia.	Iowa
Id.	Idaho
Ill.	Illinois
Ind.	Indiana
Kans.	Kansas
Ky.	Kentucky
La.	Louisiana
Man.	Manitoba
Mass.	Massachusetts
Md.	Maryland
Me.	Maine
M.G.	Mato Grosso
Mich.	Michigan
Minn.	Minnesota
Miss.	Mississippi
Mo.	Missouri
Mont.	Montana
N.B.	New Brunswick
N.C.	North Carolina
N.D.	North Dakota
Nebr.	Nebraska
Nev.	Nevada
Nfld.	Newfoundland
N.H.	New Hampshire
N. Ire.	Northern Ireland
N.J.	New Jersey
N. Mex.	New Mexico
N.W.T.	Northwest Territories
N.Y.	New York
Oh.	Ohio
Okla.	Oklahoma
Ont.	Ontario
Oreg.	Oregon
Orkney Is.	Orkney Islands
Pa.	Pennsylvania
R.G.S.	Rio Grande do Sul
R.I.	Rhode Island
S.C.	South Carolina
Scot.	Scotland
S.D.	South Dakota
Shetland Is.	Shetland Islands
Tenn.	Tennessee
Tex.	Texas
Ut.	Utah
Va.	Virginia
Vt.	Vermont
Wash.	Washington
Wis.	Wisconsin
W. Va.	West Virginia
Wyo.	Wyoming
Y.T.	Yukon Territory

Symbols

- Continent name
- Country name
- State or province name
- Country capital
- State or province capital
- Settlement
- Mountain, volcano, peak
- Mountain range
- Physical region or feature
- River, canal
- Lake, salt lake
- Gulf, strait, bay
- Sea, ocean
- Cape, point
- Island or island group, rocky or coral reef
- Place of interest
- National park or other protected area
- Historical or cultural region

Glossary

This is an alphabetically arranged glossary of the geographical terms used on the maps and in this index. The first column shows the map form, the second the language of origin and the third the English translation.

A

açude	Portuguese	reservoir
adası	Turkish	island
akra	Greek	peninsula
alpen	German	mountains
alpes	French	mountains
alpi	Italian	mountains
älven	Swedish	river
archipiélago	Spanish	archipelago
arquipélago	Portuguese	archipelago

B

bab	Arabic	strait
bahía	Spanish	bay
bahir, bahr	Arabic	bay, lake, river
baia	Portuguese	bay
baie	French	bay
baja	Spanish	lower
bandar	Arabic, Somalian, Malay, Persian	harbour, port
baraji	Turkish	dam
barragem	Portuguese	reservoir
ben	Gaelic	mountain
Berg(e)	German	mountain(s)
boğazı	Turkish	strait
Bucht	German	bay
buḩayrat	Arabic	lake
burnu, burun	Turkish	cape

C

cabo	Spanish	cape
canal	French, Spanish	canal, channel
canale	Italian	canal, channel
cerro	Spanish	mountain
chott	Arabic	marsh, salt lake
co	Tibetan	lake
collines	French	hills
cordillera	Spanish	range

D

dağ(ı)	Turkish	mountain
dağlar(ı)	Turkish	mountains
danau	Indonesian	lake
daryacheh	Persian	lake
dasht	Persian	desert
djebel	Arabic	mountain(s)
-do	Korean	island

E

embalse	Spanish	reservoir
erg	Arabic	sandy desert
estrecho	Spanish	strait

F

feng	Chinese	mountain
-fjördur	Icelandic	fjord
-flói	Icelandic	bay

G

Gebirge	German	range
golfe	French	bay, gulf
golfo	Italian, Portuguese, Spanish	bay, gulf
göl, gölü	Turkish	lake
gora	Russian	mountain
gory	Russian	mountains
gunong	Malay	mountain
gunung	Indonesian	mountain

H

hai	Chinese	lake, sea
hāmūn	Persian	lake, marsh
hawr	Arabic	lake
hu	Chinese	lake, reservoir

I

île(s)	French	island(s)
ilha(s)	Portuguese	island(s)
isla(s)	Spanish	island(s)

J

jabal	Arabic	mountain(s)
-järvi	Finnish	lake
jaza'īr	Arabic	islands
jazīrat	Arabic	island
jbel	Arabic	mountain
jebel	Arabic	mountain
jezero	Serbo-Croatian	lake
jezioro	Polish	lake
jiang	Chinese	river
-jima	Japanese	island
-joki	Finnish	river
-jökull	Icelandic	glacier

K

kepulauan	Indonesian	islands
khrebet	Russian	mountain range
-ko	Japanese	lake
kolpos	Greek	bay, gulf
körfezi	Turkish	bay, gulf
kryazh	Russian	ridge
kūh(ha)	Persian	mountain(s)

L

lac	French	lake
lacul	Romanian	lake
lago	Italian, Portuguese, Spanish	lake
lagoa	Portuguese	lagoon
laguna	Spanish	lagoon, lake
limni	Greek	lake
ling	Chinese	mountain(s), peak
liqeni	Albanian	lake
loch, lough	Gaelic	lake

M

massif	French	mountains
-meer	Dutch	lake, sea
mont	French	mount
monte	Italian, Portuguese, Spanish	mount
montes	Portuguese, Spanish	mountains
monts	French	mountains
muntii	Romanian	mountains
mys	Russian	cape

N

nafud	Arabic	desert
nevado	Spanish	snow-capped mountain
nuruu	Mongolian	mountains
nuur	Mongolian	lake

O

ostrov(a)	Russian	island(s)
ozero	Russian	lake

P

pegunungan	Indonesian	mountains
pelagos	Greek	sea
pendi	Chinese	basin
pesky	Russian	sandy desert
pic	French	peak
pico	Portuguese, Spanish	peak
planalto	Portuguese	plateau
planina	Bulgarian	mountains
poluostrov	Russian	peninsula
puerto	Spanish	harbour, port
puncak	Indonesian	peak
punta	Italian, Spanish	point
puy	French	peak

Q

qundao	Chinese	archipelago

R

ras, râs, ra's	Arabic	cape
represa	Portuguese	dam, reservoir
-rettō	Japanese	archipelago
rio	Portuguese	river
río	Spanish	river

S

sahra	Arabic	desert
salar	Spanish	salt flat
-san	Japanese, Korean	mountain
-sanmaek	Korean	mountains
sebkha	Arabic	salt flat
sebkhet	Arabic	salt marsh
See	German	lake
serra	Portuguese	range
severnaya, severo-	Russian	northern
shan	Chinese	mountain(s)
-shima	Japanese	island
-shotō	Japanese	islands
sierra	Spanish	range

T

tanjona	Malagasy	cape
tanjung	Indonesian	cape
teluk	Indonesian	bay, gulf
ténéré	Berber	desert
-tō	Japanese	island

V

vârful	Romanian	mountain
-vesi	Finnish	lake
vodokhranilishche	Russian	reservoir
volcán	Spanish	volcano

W

wādī	Arabic	watercourse
Wald	German	forest

Z

-zaki	Japanese	cape
zaliv	Russian	bay, gulf

A

Aachen 56 J4
Aalen 54 F8
Aalst 56 G4
Aarau 64 D3
Aare 64 C3
Aarschot 56 G4
Aba 114 F3
Abādān 101 C1
Ābādeh 101 E1
Abadla 112 E2
Abaji 114 F3
Abakaliki 114 F3
Abakan 82 S7
Āb Anbar 101 E1
Abancay 156 C6
Abano Terme 64 G5
Abarqū 101 E1
Abashiri 88 N1
Abava 50 M8
Ābaya Hāyk' 116 F2
Abay Wenz 110 G5
Abbeville, *France* 56 D4
Abbeville, *United States* 144 C4
Abbeyfeale 35 B4
Abbeyleix 35 D4
Abd al Kūrī 96 F7
Abéché 110 D5
Abengourou 114 D3
Abenójar 62 F6
Åbenrå 54 E1
Abensberg 54 G8
Abeokuta 114 E3
Aberaeron 38 D3
Aberdare 38 E4
Aberdeen, *South Africa* 118 C6
Aberdeen, *United Kingdom* 36 F4
Aberdeen, *Miss., United States* 144 D3
Aberdeen, *S.D., United States* 140 G1
Aberdeen, *Wash., United States* 140 B1
Aberdeen Lake 136 M4
Aberfeldy 36 E5
Abergavenny 38 E4
Abertillery 38 E4
Aberystwyth 38 D3
Abez' 72 M1
Abhā 110 H4
Abhar 98 N5
Abidjan 114 D3
Abilene 146 G2
Abiline 134 M6
Abingdon, *United Kingdom* 38 G4
Abingdon, *United States* 144 E2
Abnūb 110 F2
Aboisso 114 D3
Abomey 114 E3
Abong Mbang 114 G4
Abou Déia 110 C5
Aboyne 36 F4
Abqaiq 101 C4
Abrantes 62 B5
Abrud 68 L3
Absaroka Range 140 E1
Abū al Abayḑ 101 E4
Abu Aweigîla 100 B6
Abu Ballâs 110 E3
Abu Dhabi = Abū Ẓabī 101 F4
Abu Hamed 110 F4
Abuja 114 F3
Abumombazi 116 C3
Ābune Yosēf 110 G5
Abū Nujaym 110 C1
Abu Qarin 110 C1
Aburo 116 E3
Abu Simbel 110 F3
Abut Head 128 B6
Abuye Meda 116 F1
Abū Ẓabī 101 F4
Abv Nujaym 112 J2
Acaponeta 138 E7
Acapulco 148 E5
Acará 156 H4
Acarigua 156 D2
Accra 114 D3
Accrington 38 F2
Achaguas 148 L7
Achayvayam 84 W4
Acheng 86 H1
Achenkirch 64 G3
Achen See 64 G3
Achill 35 A3
Achill Head 35 A3
Achim 54 E3
Achinsk 82 S6
Achit 72 L3
Achnasheen 36 C4
Aci Göl 70 M7
A Cihanbeyli 70 Q6
Acireale 66 K11
Acklins Island 148 K4
Aconcagua 154 D7
Açores 112 (1)B2
A Coruña 62 B1
Acquarossa 64 D4
Acqui Terme 64 D6
Acre 156 C5
Acri 66 L9
Ada 144 B3
Ada 52 K12
Adak Island 146 (3)C1
Adam 96 G5
Adamas 70 G8
Adams Island 128 (2)B1
'Adan 96 E7
Adana 98 F5
Adare 35 C4
Adda 64 E5
Ad Dafrah 101 E5
Ad Dahnā 101 B3
Ad Dakhla 112 B4
Ad Dammām 101 D3
Ad Dawādimī 96 D5
Ad Dawḩah 101 D4
Ad Dilam 101 B5
Ad Dir'īyah 101 B4
Addis Ababa = Ādīs Ābeba 116 F2
Ad Dīwānīyah 96 D3
Adel 142 B2
Adelaide 126 G6
Adelaide Peninsula 136 M3
Adelaide River 126 F2
Aden = Adan 96 E7
Aderbissinat 114 F1
Adh Dhayd 101 F4
Adi 93 D3
Adige 64 G5
Adīgrat 110 G5
Adilabad 94 C5
Adin 140 B2
Adīrī 110 B2
Ādīs Ābeba 116 F2
Adi Ugri 110 G5
Adıyaman 96 C2
Adjud 68 Q3
Adler 98 H2
Admiralty Island 136 E5
Admiralty Islands 124 E6
Adoni 94 C5
Adour 60 F10
Adra 62 H8
Adrano 66 J11
Adrar 112 E3
Adrar des Ifôghas 112 F5
Adrar Tamgak 112 G5
Adria 64 H5
Adriatic Sea 66 H4
Adwick le Street 38 G2
Adycha 84 P3
Adygeya 98 J1
Adygeysk 98 H1
Adzopé 114 D3
Adz'vavom 72 L1
Aegean Sea 70 H5
A Estrada 62 B2
Afghanistan 96 H3
Afgooye 116 H3
'Afif 110 H3
Afikpo 114 F3
Afmadow 116 G3
Afognak Island 146 (1)G4
A Fonsagrada 62 C1
Afragola 66 J8
'Afrīn 98 G5
Afuá 156 G4
'Afula 100 C4
Afyon 70 N6
Agadez 112 G5
Agadir 112 D2
Agadyr' 82 N8
Agalega Islands 108 J7
Agan 84 B4
Āgaro 116 F2
Agartala 94 F4
Agathonisi 70 J7
Agattu Island 84 W6
Ağcabädi 98 M3
Agde 60 J10
Agen 60 F9
Agia Triada 70 D7
Ağin 98 H4
Aginskoye 82 S6
Agiokampos 70 E5
Agios Efstratios 70 H5
Agios Georgios 70 F7
Agios Nikolaos 70 H9
Agnibilekrou 114 D3
Agnita 68 M4
Agra 94 C3
Agrakhanskiy Poluostrov 98 M2
Agri 66 L8
Ağri 98 K4
Agrigento 66 H11
Agrinio 70 D6
Agropoli 66 K8
Agryz 72 K3
Ağsu 98 N3
Agua Prieta 146 E2
Aguascalientes 148 D4
A Gudiña 62 C2
Aguelhok 112 F5
Águilas 62 J7
Agulhas Negras 156 H8
Ağva 70 M3
Ahar 98 M4
Ahaura 128 C6
Ahaus 56 K2
Ahititi 128 E4
Ahlen 56 K3
Ahmadabad 94 B4
Ahmadnagar 94 B5
Ahmadpur East 94 B3
Ahr 54 B6
Ahram 101 D2
Ahrensburg 54 F3
Ahvāz 96 E3
Aichach 54 G8
Aigialousa 98 F6
Aigina 70 F7
Aigina 70 F7
Aigio 70 E6
Aigosthena 70 F6
Aiguillon 60 F9
Aihui 84 M6
Ailsa Craig 36 C6
Aim 84 N5
Ain 60 L7
Aïn Beïda 112 G1
'Aïn Ben Tili 112 D3
Aïn Bessem 62 P8
Aïn el Hadjel 62 P9
Ain Oussera 112 F1
Ainsa 62 L2
Aïn Sefra 112 E2
Ain Taya 62 P8
Aïn-Tédélès 62 L8
Aïn Témouchent 62 J9
Airão 156 E4
Airdrie 36 E6
Aire 38 G2
Air Force Island 136 S3
Airolo 64 D4
Airpanas 93 C4
Aisne 56 F5
Aitape 93 F3
Aitkin 142 B1
Aitutaki 124 K7
Aiud 68 L3
Aix-en-Provence 60 L10
Aix-les-Bains 60 L8
Aizawl 94 F4
Aizkraukle 50 N8
Aizpute 50 L8
Aizu-wakamatsu 88 K5
Ajaccio 66 C7
Aj Bogd Uul 86 B2
Ajdābiyā 110 D1
Ajigasawa 88 L3
Ajka 52 G10
Ajlun 100 C4
Ajmān 101 F4
Ajmer 94 B3
Ajo 146 D2
Akanthou 100 A1
Akaroa 128 D6
Akasha 110 F3
Akashi 88 H6
Akbalyk 82 P8
Akbasty 82 L8
Akçakale 98 H5
Akçakoca 70 P3
Akdağmadeni 98 F4
Aken 54 H5
Aketi 116 C3
Akhalk'alak'i 98 K3
Akhisar 70 K6
Akhmîm 110 F2
Akhty 98 M3
Akimiski Island 136 Q6
Akita 88 L4
Akjoujt 112 C5
Akka 112 D3
Akkajaure 50 J3
Akkeshi 88 N2
'Akko 100 C4
Akmeqit 96 L2
Aknanes 50 (1)B2
Akobo 116 E2
Akola 94 C4
Akonolinga 114 G4
Akordat 110 G4
Akpatok Island 136 T4
Akqi 82 P9
Akra Drepano 70 G5
Akra Sounio 70 F7
Akra Spatha 70 F9
Akra Trypiti 70 G9
Åkrehamn 50 C7
Akron 142 D2
Aksaray 98 E4
Aksarka 82 M4
Akşehir 70 P6
Akseki 70 P7
Aksha 84 J6
Akshiy 82 P9
Aksu 82 Q9
Aksuat 82 Q8
Āksum 110 G5
Aktau, *Kazakhstan* 48 K3
Aktau, *Kazakhstan* 82 N7
Aktogay, *Kazakhstan* 82 N8
Aktogay, *Kazakhstan* 82 P8
Aktuma 82 M8
Aktyubinsk 72 L4
Akula 116 C3
Akulivik 136 R4
Akune 88 F8
Akure 114 F3
Akureyri 50 (1)E2
Akwanga 114 F3
Alabama 144 D3
Alaçam 98 F3
Alaejos 62 E3
Alagoas 156 K5
Alagoinhas 156 K6
Alagón 62 J3
Al Ahmadi 101 C2
Al 'Amārah 96 E3
Alaminos 90 F3
Alamo 140 C3
Alamogordo 146 E2
Alamo Lake 146 D2
Åland 50 K6
Alanya 98 E5
Alappuzha 94 C7
Al Argoub 112 B4
Al Artāwīyah 96 E4
Alaşehir 70 L6
Al 'Ashurīyah 110 H1
Alaska 146 (1)F2
Alaska Peninsula 146 (1)E4
Alaska Range 146 (1)G3
Alassio 64 D6
Alatri 66 H7
Alatyr' 72 J4
Alaverdi 98 L3
Alavus 50 M5
Alaykuu 82 N9
Al 'Ayn 101 F4
Alazeya 84 S2
Alba, *Italy* 64 D6
Alba, *Spain* 62 E4
Albacete 62 J5
Alba Iulia 68 L3
Albania 70 B3
Albany 136 Q6
Albany, *Australia* 126 C6
Albany, *Ga., United States* 144 E3
Albany, *Ky., United States* 144 E2
Albany, *N.Y., United States* 142 F2
Albany, *Oreg., United States* 140 B2
Albardão do João Maria 158 L4
Al Bardī 110 D1
Al Başrah 96 E3
Albatross Bay 126 H2
Albatross Point 128 E4
Al Bayḑā' 110 D1
Albenga 64 D6
Albert 56 E4
Alberta 136 H6
Albertirsa 52 J10
Albert Kanaal 56 G3
Albert Lea 142 B2
Albert Nile 116 E3
Albertville 60 M8
Albi 60 H10
Albina 156 G2
Albino 64 E5
Albion 140 F1
Ålborg 50 E8
Ålborg Bugt 50 F8
Albox 62 H7
Albstadt 54 E8
Albufeira 62 B7
Āl Bū Kamāl 98 J6
Albuquerque 146 E1
Al Burayj 100 D2
Al Buraymī 96 G5
Alburquerque 62 D5
Albury 126 J7
Al Buşayyah 101 B1
Alcácer do Sal 62 B6
Alcala de Guadaira 62 E7
Alcala de Henares 62 G4
Alcalá la Real 62 G7
Alcamo 66 G11
Alcañiz 62 K3
Alcantarilla 62 J7
Alcaraz 62 H6
Alcaudete 62 F7
Alcazar de San Juan 62 G5
Alcobendas 62 G4
Alcoi 62 K6
Alcolea del Pinar 62 H3
Alcorcón 62 G4
Alcoutim 62 C7
Aldabra Group 118 (2)A2
Aldan 84 M5
Aldan 84 N5
Aldeburgh 38 K3
Alderley Edge 38 F2
Alderney 38 (1)F6
Aldershot 38 H4
Aleg 112 C5
Aleksandrov-Sakhalinskiy 84 Q6
Aleksandrovskiy Zavod 84 K6
Aleksandrovskoye 72 Q2
Alekseyevka 82 N7
Aleksinac 68 J6
Alençon 60 F5
Aleppo = Ḩalab 98 G5
Aléria 66 D6
Alès 60 K9
Aleşd 52 M10
Alessandria 64 D6
Ålesund 50 D5
Aleutian Islands 146 (3)B1
Aleutian Range 146 (1)F4
Aleutian Trench 80 W5
Alexander Archipelago 146 (1)K4
Alexander Bay 118 B5
Alexander City 144 D3
Alexandra 128 B7
Alexandreia 70 E4
Alexandria = El Iskandarîya, *Egypt* 110 E1
Alexandria, *Romania* 68 N6
Alexandria, *La., United States* 144 C3
Alexandria, *Minn., United States* 142 A1
Alexandria, *Va., United States* 142 E3
Alexandroupoli 70 H4
Alexis Creek 136 G6
'Āley 100 C3
Aley 82 Q7
Aleysk 82 Q7
Al Farwānīyah 101 B2
Al Fāw 101 C2
Alfeld 54 E5
Alföld 68 H2
Alfonsine 64 H6
Alfreton 38 G2
Al Fuḩayḩīl 101 C2
Al-Fujayrah 101 G4
Algeciras 62 E8
Algemes 62 K5
Algena 110 G4
Alger 112 F1
Algeria 112 E3
Al Ghāţ 101 A3
Al Ghayḑah 96 F6
Alghero 66 C8
Algiers = Alger 112 F1
Algona 142 B2
Al Hadīthah 100 E5
Alhama de Murcia 62 J7
Al Ḩamar 101 B5
Al Ḩamīdīyah 100 C2
Al Ḩammādah al Ḩamrā' 112 G3
Al Harūj al Aswad 110 C2
Al Ḩasakah 98 J5
Alhaurmín el Grande 62 F8
Al Ḩijāz 110 G2
Al Ḩillah 96 D3
Al Ḩilwah 101 B5
Al Hoceima 112 E1
Al Ḩudaydah 110 H5
Al Hufūf 101 C4
Al Ḩumayḑah 96 C4
Aliabad 101 F2
Aliağa 70 J6
Aliakmonas 70 E4
Āli Bayramlı 98 N4
Alicante 62 K6
Alice 144 B4
Alice Springs 126 F4
Alicudi 66 J10
Aligarh 94 C3
Alindao 116 C2

Alingås 50 G8
Alisos 146 D2
Aliwal North 118 D6
Al Jabal al Akhḑar 110 D1
Al Jaghbūb 110 D2
Al Jālamīd 110 G1
Al Jarah 101 B2
Al Jawf, *Libya* 110 D3
Al Jawf, *Saudi Arabia* 110 G2
Aljezur 62 B7
Al Jifārah 101 A5
Al Jubayl 101 C3
Aljustrel 62 B7
Al Kāmil 96 G5
Al Khābūrah 101 G5
Al Khālis 98 L7
Al Kharj 101 B4
Al Khaşab 101 G3
Al Khawr 101 D4
Al Khubar 101 D3
Al Khufrah 110 D3
Al Khums 112 H2
Al Khuwayr 101 D3
Al Kir'ānah 101 D4
Alkmaar 56 G2
Al Kūt 96 E3
Al Kuwayt 101 C2
Al Lādhiqīyah 98 F6
Allahabad 94 D3
Allakh-Yun' 84 P4
Alldays 118 D4
Allen 90 G4
Allendale 144 E3
Allentown 142 E2
Aller 54 E4
Aller = Cabañaquinta 62 E1
Alliance 140 F2
Allier 60 J8
Allinge 52 D2
Al Lith 110 H3
Alloa 36 E5
Alma, *Canada* 142 F1
Alma, *Nebr., United States* 140 G2
Alma, *Wis., United States* 142 B2
Almada 62 A6
Almadén 62 F6
Al Madīnah 110 G3
Al Mahbas 112 D3
Al Majma'ah 96 E4
Almalyk 82 M9
Al Manāmah 101 D3
Almansa 62 J6
Al Ma'qil 101 B1
Al Marj 110 D1
Almaty 82 P9
Al Mawşil 98 K5
Al Mazāḩimīyah 101 B4
Almazán 62 H3
Almeirim 156 G4
Almelo 56 J2
Almendralejo 62 D6
Almería 62 H8
Al'met'yevsk 82 J7
Almiros 70 E5
Al Mish'āb 101 C2
Almonte 62 D7
Almora 94 C3
Almosa 140 E3
Al Mubarraz 101 C4
Al Mudawwara 100 D7
Al Mukallā 96 E7
Al Mukhā 110 H5
Almuñécar 62 G8
Al Muqdādīyah 98 L7
Al Nu'ayrīyah 101 C3
Alnwick 36 G6
Alonnisos 70 F5
Alor 93 B4
Alor Setar 90 C5
Alotau 126 K2
Alpena 142 D1
Alphen 56 G2
Alpi Lepontine 64 D4
Alpine 146 E2
Alpi Orobie 64 E4
Alps 64 B5
Al Qadmūs 100 D1
Al Qalībah 110 G2
Al Qāmishlī 98 J5
Al Qar'ah 101 B3
Al Qarqar 100 E5
Al Qaryāt 110 B1
Al Qaryatayn 100 E2
Al Qaţif 101 C3
Al Qaţrūn 110 B3
Al Qunayţirah 100 C3
Al Qunfudhah 110 H4
Al Qurayyāt 110 G1
Al Qurnah 101 B1
Al 'Quşayr, *Iraq* 101 A1
Al 'Quşayr, *Syria* 100 D2
Al Quţayfah 100 D3
Als 54 E1
Alsask 136 K6
Alsasua 62 H2
Alsfeld 54 E6
Alston 36 F7
Alta 50 M2
Altaelva 50 M2
Altai Mountains 86 A1
Al Tamīnī 110 D1
Altamira 156 G4
Altamura 66 L8
Altanbulag 84 H6
Altay 82 R7
Altay, *China* 82 R8
Altay, *Mongolia* 86 B1
Altdorf 64 D4
Alte Mellum 54 D3
Altenberg 54 J6
Altenburg 54 H6
Altenkirchen 54 J2
Altkirch 64 C3
Alto Garças 156 G7
Alto Molócuè 118 F3
Alton, *United Kingdom* 38 H4
Alton, *United States* 142 B3
Altoona 142 E2
Alto Parnaiba 156 H5
Altötting 64 H2
Altun Shan 82 S10
Alturas 140 B2
Altus 144 B3
Al 'Ubaylah 96 F5
Alūksne 50 P8
Alupka 98 E1
Al 'Uqaylah 110 C1
Alushta 98 F1
Al 'Uthmānīyah 101 C4
Al 'Uwaynāt, *Libya* 110 B2
Al 'Uwaynāt, *Libya* 110 D3
Al 'Uwayqīlah 110 H1
Al 'Uzayr 101 B1
Alva 144 B2
Alvarães 156 E4
Älvdalen 50 H6
Älvsbyn 50 L4
Al Wafrā' 101 B2
Al Wajh 110 G2
Al Wannān 101 C3
Alwar 94 C3
Al Wari'ah 101 B3
Alxa Zouqi 86 D3
Alytus 52 P3
Alzey 54 D7
Alzira 62 K5
Amadi 116 E2
Amādīyah 98 K5
Amadjuak Lake 136 S4
Amadora 62 A6
Amahai 93 C3
Amakusa-Shimo-shima 88 E7
Amaliada 70 D7
Amalner 94 C4
Amamapare 93 E3
Amambaí 158 K3
Amami-Ōshima 80 S7
Amanab 93 F3
Amandola 66 H6
Amantea 66 L9
Amapá 156 G3
Amapá 156 G3
Amarante 156 J5
Amarapura 90 B2
Amareleja 62 C6
Amarillo 146 F1
Amasya 98 F3
Amay 56 H4
Amazar 84 L6
Amazon = Amazonas 154 F4
Amazonas 156 D4
Amazonas 156 E4
Ambala 94 C2
Ambanjā 118 H2
Ambarchik 84 U3
Ambato 156 B4
Ambato Boeny 118 H3
Ambatondrazaka 118 H3
Amberg 54 G7
Ambikapur 94 D4
Ambilobe 118 H2
Amble 36 G6
Ambleside 36 F7
Ambohimahasoa 118 H4
Amboise 60 G6
Ambon 93 C3
Ambositra 118 H4
Ambovombe 118 H5
Amchitka Island 146 (3)B1
Amderma 82 L4
Amdo 94 F2
Ameland 56 H1
Amengel'dy 82 M7
American Falls 140 D2
American Samoa 124 J7
Americus 144 E3
Amersfoort 56 H2
Amery 136 N5
Amery Ice Shelf 160 (2)M2
Ames 142 B2
Amesbury 38 G4
Amfilochia 70 D6
Amfissa 70 E6
Amga 84 N4
Amga 84 L5
Amguid 112 G3
Amgun' 84 P6
Amherst 136 U7
Amiens 56 E5
Amirante Islands 118 (2)B2
Amistad Reservoir 146 F3
Amlekhganj 94 D3
Åmli 50 E7
Amlwch 38 D2
'Amm Adam 110 G4
'Ammān 100 C5
Ammanford 38 E4
Ammerland 56 K1
Ammersee 64 F2
Ammochostos 98 E6
Ammochostos Bay 100 A1
Amo 90 C2
Amol 96 F2
Amorgos 70 H8
Amos 142 E1
Amourj 112 D5
Ampana 93 B3
Ampanihy 118 G4
Amparai 94 D7
Ampezzo 64 H4
Amposta 62 L4
Amrān 96 D6
Amravati 94 C4
Amritsar 94 B2
Amroha 94 C3
Amrum 54 D2
Amsterdam, *Netherlands* 56 G2
Amsterdam, *United States* 142 F2
Amstetten 64 K2
Am Timan 110 D5
Amudar'ya 82 L9
Amundsen Gulf 136 G2
Amundsen Sea 160 (2)GG3
Amungen 50 H6
Amuntai 92 F3
Amur 84 P6
Amursk 84 P6
Amvrakikos Kolpos 70 C6
Anabanua 93 B3
Anabar 84 J2
Anaconda 140 D1
Anacortes 140 B1
Anadarko 140 G3
Anadolu Dağları 98 H3
Anadyr' 84 X4
Anadyrskaya Nizmennost' 84 X3
Anadyrskiy Zaliv 84 Y3
Anafi 70 H8
'Ānah 98 J6
Anaheilt 36 C5
Anaheim 146 C2
Anáhuac 146 F3
Analalava 118 H2
Anamur 98 E5
Anan 88 H7
Anantapur 94 C6
Anan'yiv 68 T2
Anapa 98 G1
Anápolis 156 H7
Anār 101 F1
Anārak 96 F3
Anardara 96 H3
Anatolia 70 M6
Añatuya 158 J4
Anchorage 146 (1)H3
Ancona 66 H5
Ancud 158 G7
Anda 86 H1
Andalgalá 158 H4
Åndalsnes 50 D5
Andalusia 144 D3
Andaman Islands 90 A4
Andaman Sea 90 A4
Andapa 118 H2
Andarāb 96 J2
Andenne 56 H4
Andéramboukane 114 E1
Andermatt 64 D4
Andernach 56 K4
Anderson 136 F3
Anderson 144 E3
Andes 154 D5
Andfjorden 50 J2
Andilamena 118 H3
Andipsara 70 H6
Andizhan 82 N9
Andkhvoy 96 J2
Andoas 156 B4
Andong 88 E5
Andorra 62 L2
Andorra la Vella 62 M2
Andover 38 G4
Andøya 50 H2
Andradina 158 L3
Andreanof Islands 146 (3)C1
Andrews 146 F2
Andria 66 L7
Andriamena 118 H3
Andros 70 G7
Andros, *Greece* 70 G7
Andros, *The Bahamas* 144 F5
Andros Town 144 F5
Andrott 94 B6
Andrychów 52 J8
Andûjar 62 F6
Andulo 118 B2
Aneto 62 L2
Angara 84 G5
Angarsk 84 G6
Ånge 50 H5
Angel de la Guarda 146 D3
Angeles 90 G3
Ängelholm 50 G8
Angeln 54 E2
Angermünde 54 K4
Angern 64 M2
Angers 60 E6
Anglesey 38 D2
Angmagssalik = Tasiilaq 136 Z3
Ango 116 D3
Angoche 118 F3
Angohrān 101 G3
Angol 158 G6
Angola 108 E7
Angola 142 D2
Angostura Reservoir 140 F2
Angoulême 60 F8
Angren 82 M9
Anguilla 148 M5
Aniak 146 (1)F3
Anina 68 J4
Aniyaman 98 H5
Ankang 86 D4
Ankara 98 E4
Ankazoabo 118 G4
Anklam 54 J3
Ankpa 114 F3
Ånn 50 G5
Anna 72 H4
Annaba 112 G1
Annaberg-Buchholz 54 H6
An Nabk, *Saudi Arabia* 100 E5
An Nabk, *Syria* 100 D2
An Nafud 110 G2
An Nāirīyah 96 E3
An Najaf 96 D3
Annan 36 E7
Annapolis 142 E3
Annapurna 94 D3
Ann Arbor 142 D2
An Nāşirīyah 110 J1
Annecy 64 B5
Annemasse 64 B4
Anniston 144 D3
Annobón 114 F5
Annonay 60 K8
An Nukhayb 96 D3
Anqing 86 F4
Ansbach 54 F7
Anshan 88 B3
Anshun 86 D5
Ansley 140 G2
Anson 144 B3
Ansongo 112 F5
Antakya 98 G5
Antalaha 118 J2
Antalya 70 N8
Antalya Körfezi 70 N8
Antananarivo 118 H3
Antarctic Peninsula 160 (2)LL3
Antequera 62 F7
Anti-Atlas 112 D3
Antibes 64 C7
Antigo 142 C1
Antigua 148 M5
Antigua and Barbuda 148 M5
Antikythira 70 F9
Antiparos 70 G7
Antipaxoi 70 C5
Antipayuta 82 P4
Antipodes Islands 128 (3)A1
Antlers 144 B3
Antofagasta 158 G3
Antonito 140 E3
Antrim 35 E2
Antrim Hills 35 E2
Antropovo 72 H3
Antsalova 118 G3
Antsirabe 118 H3
Antsirañana 118 H2
Antu 88 E2
Antwerp = Antwerpen 56 G3
Antwerpen 56 G3
Anuradhapura 94 D7
Anveh 101 F3
Anxi 86 B2
Anyang, *China* 86 E3
Anyang, *South Korea* 88 D5
Anyuysk 84 U3
Anzhero-Sudzhensk 82 R6
Anzi 116 C4
Anzio 66 G7
Aoga-shima 88 K7
Aomori 88 L3
Aosta 64 C5
Aoukâr 112 C5
Aoukoukar 114 C1
Apalachee Bay 144 E4
Apalachicola 144 D4
Aparri 90 G3
Apatin 68 F4
Apatity 72 F1
Ape 50 P8
Apeldoorn 56 H2
Api 94 D2
Apia 124 J7
Apoera 156 F2
Apolda 54 G5
Apollo Bay 126 H7
Aporé 156 G7
Apostle Islands 142 B1
Apoteri 156 F3
Appalachian Mountains 144 E3
Appennino 66 G5
Appennino Abruzzese 66 H6
Appennino Calabro 66 K10
Appennino Lucano 66 K8
Appennino Tosco-Emiliano 64 E6
Appennino Umbro-Marchigiano 66 H6
Appleby-in-Westmorland 36 F7
Appleton 142 C2
Aprilia 66 G7
Apure 156 D2
Apurimac 156 C6
Āqā 96 H3
'Aqaba 100 C7
Aquidauana 156 F8
Ara 94 D3
Arabian Sea 96 H6
Aracaju 156 K6
Aracati 156 K4
Araçatuba 156 G8
Aracuca 148 L7
Arad 68 J3
Arādah 96 F5
Arafura Sea 93 D5
Aragarças 156 G7
Araguaia 154 F4
Araguaína 156 H5
Araguari 156 H7
Araguatins 156 H5
Arak 112 F3
Arāk 96 E3
Aral Sea 82 K8
Aral'sk 72 M5
Aran 35 C1
Aranda de Duero 62 G3
Aranđjelovac 68 H5
Aran Islands 35 B3
Aranjuez 62 G4
Aranos 118 B4
Aranyaprathet 90 C4
Araouane 112 E5
Arapahoe 140 G2
Arapiraca 156 K5
'Ar'ar 96 D3
Araras 156 G5
Ararat 98 L4
Arauca 156 D2
Araxá 156 H7
Araz 98 L4
Arbīl 98 K5
Arbon 64 E3
Arbre du Ténéré 112 G5
Arbroath 36 F5
Arcachon 60 D9
Arcadia 144 E4
Arcata 140 B2
Archidona 62 F7
Archipelago of the Recherche 126 D6
Archipel de la Société 124 L7
Archipel des Tuamotu 124 M7
Archipiélago de Camagüey 148 J4
Archipiélago de la Reina Adelaida 158 F9

Archipiélago de los Chonos 158 F7
Arco, *Italy* 64 F5
Arco, *United States* 140 D2
Arcos de la Frontera 62 E8
Arctic Bay 136 P2
Arctic Ocean 160 (1)A1
Arctic Red River 136 E3
Arda 70 H3
Ardabīl 98 N4
Ardahan 98 K3
Årdalstangen 50 D6
Ardas 70 J3
Ardatov 72 J4
Ardee 35 E3
Ardennes 56 G4
Ardestān 96 F3
Ardila 62 C6
Ardmore 138 G5
Ardrossan 36 D6
Ards Peninsula 35 F2
Aredo 93 D3
Areia Branca 156 K5
Arendal 50 E7
Arenys de Mar 62 N3
Areopoli 70 E8
Arequipa 156 C7
Arere 156 G4
Arévalo 62 F3
Arezzo 66 F5
Argan 82 R9
Argenta 64 G6
Argentan 56 B6
Argentera 64 B6
Argentina 158 H6
Argenton-sur-Creuse 60 G7
Argeș 68 N5
Argolikos Kolpos 70 E7
Argos 70 E7
Argos Orestiko 70 D4
Argostoli 70 C6
Argun' 84 K6
Argungu 114 E2
Argunsk 84 L6
Argyll 36 C5
Ar Horqin Qi 86 G2
Århus 50 F8
Ariano Irpino 66 K7
Ari Atoll 94 B8
Arica 156 C7
Ariège 60 G11
Arihge 62 M2
Arinos 156 F6
Aripuanã 156 E5
Aripuanã 156 E5
Ariquemes 156 E5
Arizona 146 D2
Arjäng 50 G7
Arjasa 92 F4
Arka 84 Q5
Arkadak 72 H4
Arkadelphia 144 C3
Arkalyk 82 M7
Arkansas 144 C3
Arkansas 144 C3
Arkansas City 144 B2
Arkhalts'ikhe 98 K3
Arkhangel'sk 72 H2
Arkhipelag Nordenshel'da 82 R2
Arklow 35 E4
Arkoudi 70 C6
Arles 60 K10
Arlington, *Oreg., United States* 140 B1
Arlington, *Tex., United States* 144 B3
Arlington, *Va., United States* 142 E3
Arlit 112 G5
Arlon 56 H4
Armagh 35 E2
Armavir 98 J1
Armenia 156 B3
Armenia 98 K3
Armentières 56 E4
Armidale 126 K6
Armstrong 136 P6
Armyans'k 72 F5
Arnedo 62 H2
Arnett 144 B2
Arnhem 56 H3
Arnhem Land 126 F2
Arno 64 F7
Arnold 38 G2
Arnøy 50 G3
Arnøya 50 L1
Arnprior 142 E1
Arnsberg 56 L3
Arnstadt 54 F6
Aroab 118 B5
Arolsen 54 E5
Aroma 110 G4
Arorae 124 H6
Arquipélago dos Bijagós 114 A2
Ar Ramādī 96 D3
Ar Ramlah 100 C7
Arran 36 C6
Ar Raqqah 98 H6
Arras 56 E4
Arrasate 62 H1
Ar Rastan 100 D2
Ar Rawḍah 96 E7
Ar Rayn 101 A5
Arrecife 112 C3
Ar Riyāḍ 96 E5
Arrow Lake 140 C1
Arroyo Grande 146 B1
Ar Ruṣāfah 98 H6
Ar Rustāq 96 G5
Ar Ruṭba 96 D3
Ar Ruways 96 F5
Årsandøy 50 G4
Arta, *Greece* 70 C5
Arta, *Mallorca* 62 P5
Artem 88 G2
Artemovsk 82 S7
Artemovskiy 84 K5
Artesia 146 F2
Arthur 140 F2
Arthur's Town 144 F5
Artigas 158 K5
Artillery Lake 136 J4
Artsyz 68 S4
Artux 82 P10
Artvin 98 J3
Artyk 84 Q4
Aru 124 D6
Arua 116 E3
Aruba 148 K6
Arumã 156 E4
Arusha 116 F4
Arvayheer 86 C1
Arviat 136 N4
Arvidsjaur 50 K4
Arvika 50 G7
Ary 82 Y3
Aryta 84 M4
Arzamas 72 H3
Arzew 62 K9
Arzignano 64 G5
Asahi-dake 88 M2
Asahikawa 88 M2
Āsalē 110 G5
Asansol 94 E4
Asarum 52 D1
Asbest 72 M3
Ascea 66 K8
Ascension 108 B6
Ascensión 156 E7
Aschaffenburg 54 E7
Aschersleben 54 G5
Ascoli Piceno 66 H6
Åsela 116 F2
Åsele 50 J4
Asenovgrad 70 G3
Asha 72 L3
Ashbourne, *Republic of Ireland* 35 E3
Ashbourne, *Eng., United Kingdom* 38 G2
Ashburton 128 C6
Ashby-de-la-Zouch 38 G3
Ashdod 100 B5
Asherton 144 B4
Asheville 142 D3
Ashford 38 J4
Ash Fork 146 D1
Ashgabat 96 G2
Ashington 36 G6
Ashizuri-misaki 88 G7
Ashkhabad = Ashgabat 96 G2
Ashland, *Kans., United States* 140 G3
Ashland, *Ky., United States* 142 D3
Ashland, *Mont., United States* 140 E1
Ashland, *Oreg., United States* 140 B2
Ashland, *Wis., United States* 142 B1
Ashoro 88 M2
Ashqelon 100 B5
Ash Shadādah 98 J5
Ash Shāriqah 101 F4
Ash Sharqāt 98 K6
Ash Shiḥr 96 E7
Ash Shu'bah 101 A2
Ash Shuqayq 110 H4
Ash Shurayf 110 G2
Ash Shuwayrif 112 H3
Ashtabula 142 D2
Ashton-under-Lyne 38 F2
Ashuanipi 136 T6
Ashuanipi Lake 136 T6
Asia 124 B2
Āsika 94 D5
Asilah 112 D1
Asinara 66 C7
Asino 82 R6
Asīr 110 H3
Aşkale 98 J4
Askim 50 F7
Askot 94 D3
Asmara 110 G4
Åsnen 50 H8
Āsosa 116 E1
Aspang Markt 64 M3
Aspe 62 K6
Aspermont 146 F2
As Pontes de Garcia Rodriguez 62 C1
As Sa'an 100 E1
Assab 110 H5
As Ṣalīf 96 D6
As Salmān 96 E3
As Salwā 101 D4
Assamakka 112 G5
As Samāwah 110 J1
Aş Şanamayn 100 D3
As Sarīr 110 D2
Asse 56 G4
Assemini 66 C9
Assen 56 J2
Assens 54 E1
As Sīb 101 H5
As Sidrah 110 C1
Assiniboia 136 K7
Assiniboine 136 M7
Assis 158 L3
Assisi 66 G5
As Sukhnah 98 H6
As Sulaymānīyah 98 L6
As Sulayyil 96 E5
Assumption Island 116 H5
As Suwaydā' 100 D4
As Suwayh 96 G5
Astakida 70 J9
Astana 82 N7
Astara 96 E2
Asti 64 D6
Astorga 62 D2
Astoria 140 B1
Astove Island 116 H6
Astrakhan' 72 J5
Astypalaia 70 J8
Asunción 158 K4
Aswân 110 F3
Aswân Dam 110 F3
Asyût 110 F2
As Zaydīyah 110 H4
Ata 124 J8
Atafu 124 J6
Atakpamé 114 E3
Atalaia do Norte 156 C4
Atâr 112 C4
Atasu 82 N8
Atbara 110 F4
Atbasar 72 N4
Atchison 144 B2
Aterno 66 H6
Ath 56 F4
Athabasca 136 J5
Athens = Athina 70 F7
Athens, *Al., United States* 144 D3
Athens, *Ga., United States* 144 E3
Athens, *Oh., United States* 144 E2
Athens, *Tenn., United States* 144 E2
Athens, *Tex., United States* 144 B3
Athina 70 F7
Athlone 35 D3
Ath Thāyat 100 D7
Athy 35 E4
Ati 110 C5
Atiamuri 128 F4
Atico 156 C7
Atikokan 142 B1
Atka 84 S4
Atka Island 146 (3)C1
Atlanta 144 E3
Atlantic, *Ia., United States* 144 B1
Atlantic, *N.C., United States* 144 F3
Atlantic City 142 F3
Atlantic Ocean 48 C3
Atlas Bogd 86 B2
Atlas Mountains 62 N9
Atlasovo 84 T5
Atlas Saharien 112 E2
Atlin 136 E5
Atmakur 94 C5
Atmore 144 D3
Atoka 144 B3
Atokos 70 C6
Atol das Rocas 156 L4
Atri 66 H6
Aṭ Ṭā'if 96 D5
Attapu 90 D4
Attawapiskat 136 Q6
Attersee 64 J3
Attica 142 C2
Attleborough 38 K3
Attu Island 146 (3)A1
Attu Island 160 (1)KK4
Attur 94 C6
At Turbah 110 H5
Atyrau 72 K5
Aubagne 60 L10
Aubange 56 H5
Aube 60 K5
Aubenas 60 K9
Aubry Lake 136 F3
Auburn, *Al., United States* 144 D3
Auburn, *Calif., United States* 140 B3
Auburn, *Nebr., United States* 140 G2
Auburn, *Wash., United States* 140 B1
Aubusson 60 H8
Auce 52 M1
Auch 60 F10
Auchi 114 F3
Auchterarder 36 E5
Auckland 128 E3
Auckland Island 128 (2)B1
Aude 60 H10
Aue 54 H6
Auerbach 54 H6
Augathella 126 J5
Augsburg 64 F2
Augusta, *Australia* 126 C6
Augusta, *Italy* 66 K11
Augusta, *Ga., United States* 144 E3
Augusta, *Me., United States* 142 G2
Augustów 52 M4
Aulla 64 E6
Aurangābād 94 C5
Auray 60 C6
Aurich 56 K1
Aurillac 60 H9
Aurora, *Colo., United States* 140 F3
Aurora, *Ill., United States* 142 C2
Aurora, *Mo., United States* 144 C2
Aurukun 126 H2
Aus 118 B5
Auschwitz = Oświęcim 52 J7
Austin, *Minn., United States* 142 B2
Austin, *Nev., United States* 140 C3
Austin, *Tex., United States* 144 B3
Australia 126 E4
Australian Alps 124 E9
Australian Capital Territory 126 J7
Austria 64 J3
Autun 60 K7
Auxerre 60 J6
Auxonne 60 L6
Avallon 60 J6
Avam 84 E2
Āvārsin 98 M4
Aveiro 62 B4
Avellino 66 J8
Averøya 50 D5
Avesnes-sur-Helpe 56 F4
Avesta 50 J6
Avezzano 66 H6
Aviemore 36 E4
Avignon 60 K10
Ávila 62 F4
Avilés 62 E1
Avion 56 E4
Avola 66 K12
Avon, *Eng., United Kingdom* 38 G3
Avon, *Eng., United Kingdom* 38 G4
Avonmouth 38 F4
Avranches 60 D5
Avrig 68 M4
Awaji-shima 88 H6
Awanui 128 D2
Awat 82 Q9
Awatere 128 D5
Awbārī 110 B2
Aweil 116 D2
Awjilah 110 D2
Awka 114 F3
Ax-les-Thermes 60 G11
Ayacucho 156 C6
Ayaguz 82 Q8
Ayakkuduk 82 M9
Ayamonte 62 C7
Ayan 84 P5
Ayan 84 E3
Aya Napa 100 A2
Ayancık 98 F3
Ayanka 84 V4
Ayaviri 156 C6
Aydin 98 B5
Aydıncık 70 R8
Ayers Rock = Uluru 126 F5
Aykhal 84 J3
Aykino 82 H5
Aylesbury 38 H4
Aylmer Lake 136 K4
Aylsham 38 K3
'Ayn al Baida' 100 D5
Ayní 82 M10
Ayni 96 J2
Ayn 'Isá 98 H5
Ayoûn el 'Atroûs 112 D5
Ayr, *Australia* 126 J3
Ayr, *United Kingdom* 36 D6
Aytos 68 Q7
Ayutthaya 90 C4
Ayvalik 70 J5
Azaila 62 K3
Azaouâd 112 E5
Āzarān 98 M5
Azare 114 G2
Azauri 156 G3
A'zāz 98 G5
Azdavay 70 R3
Azerbaijan 98 M3
Aziza 62 H3
Azogues 156 B4
Azores = Açores 112 (1)B2
Azov 72 G5
Azpeitia 62 H1
Azrou 112 D2
Aztec 140 E3
Azuaga 62 E6
Azul 158 K6
Az Zabadānī 100 D3
Aẓ Ẓahrān 101 D3
Az Zāwīyah 110 B1
Az Zubayr 101 B1

B

Ba'albek 100 D2
Baaqline 100 C3
Baardheere 116 G3
Babadag 68 R5
Babaeski 70 K3
Bāb al Mandab 96 D7
Babana 93 A3
Babanusa 116 D1
Babar 93 C4
Babayevo 72 G3
Babayurt 98 M2
Babo 93 D3
Bābol 96 F2
Babruysk 72 E4
Babura 114 F2
Babushkin 84 H6
Babuyan Islands 90 G3
Bacaadweyn 116 H2
Bacabal 156 J4
Bacan 93 C3
Bacău 68 P3
Baccarat 64 B2
Bachu 96 L2
Back 136 M3
Bačka Palanka 68 G4
Bačka Topola 68 G4
Backnang 64 E2
Bac Liêu 90 D5
Bacolod 90 G4
Badajós 156 H4
Badajoz 62 D6
Bad al Milḥ 98 K7
Badalona 62 N3
Bad Ausee 64 J3
Bad Bentheim 56 K2
Bad Berleburg 54 D5
Bad Doberan 54 G2
Bad Dürkheim 54 D7
Bad Ems 56 K4
Baden 52 F9
Baden-Baden 64 D2
Badenoch 36 D5
Baderna 66 H3
Bad Freienwalde 54 K4
Badgastein 64 J3
Badgingarra 126 C6
Bad Harzburg 54 F5
Bad Hersfeld 54 E6
Bad Homburg 54 D6
Bad Honnef 56 K4
Badin 94 A4
Bad Ischl 64 J3
Bādiyat ash Shām 100 D4
Bad Kissingen 54 F6
Bad Kreuznach 56 K5
Bad Langensalza 54 F5
Bad Lauterberg 54 F5
Bad Liebenwerda 54 J5
Bad Mergentheim 54 E7
Bad Nauheim 54 D6
Bad Neuenahr-Ahrweiler 56 K4
Bad Neustadt 54 F6
Bad Oeynhausen 54 D4
Badong 86 E4
Bad Reichenhall 64 H3
Badr Ḥunayn 110 G3
Bad Säckingen 54 C9
Bad Salzuflen 54 D4
Bad Salzungen 54 F6
Bad Schwartau 54 F3
Bad Segeberg 54 F3

Bad Sobernheim	56	K5
Bad Urach	64	E2
Bad Vöslau	68	D2
Bad Waldsee	64	E3
Bad Wilbad	64	D2
Bad Wildungen	54	E5
Bad Windsheim	54	F7
Bad Wurzach	64	E3
Baena	62	F7
Bærum	50	F7
Baeza	62	G6
Baffin Bay	134	J2
Baffin Island	136	R2
Bafia	114	G4
Bafoulabé	114	B2
Bafoussam	114	G3
Bāfq	96	G3
Bafra	98	F3
Bafra Burun	98	G3
Bāft	101	G2
Bafwasende	116	D3
Baga	110	B5
Bagani	118	C3
Bagansiapiapi	92	C2
Bagaroua	114	E2
Bagdad	146	D2
Bagdarin	84	J6
Bagé	158	L5
Bagenalstown	35	E4
Baggs	140	E2
Baghdād	96	D3
Bagheria	66	H10
Baghlān	96	J2
Bagnères-de-Bigorre	60	F10
Bagno di Romagna	64	G7
Bagnols-sur-Cèze	60	K9
Bago	90	G4
Baguio	90	G3
Bagun Datuk	92	C2
Baharampur	94	E4
Bahawalnagar	94	B3
Bahawalpur	94	B3
Bahçe	98	G5
Bahia	156	J6
Bahía Blanca	158	J6
Bahía Blanca	158	J6
Bahía de Banderas	148	C4
Bahía de Campeche	148	F4
Bahía de Manta	156	A4
Bahía de Petacalco	148	D5
Bahía de Pisco	156	B6
Bahía de Santa Elena	156	A4
Bahía de Sechura	156	A5
Bahía Grande	158	H9
Bahía Kino	138	D6
Bahía Negra	158	K3
Bahía Samborombón	158	K6
Bahir Dar	110	G5
Bahraich	94	D3
Bahrain	101	D4
Baḥrat Ḥimş	100	D2
Bahr el Abiad	110	F5
Bahr el Azraq	110	F5
Bahr el Ghazal	110	C5
Bahr el Ghazal	116	D2
Bahr el Jebe	116	E2
Bahr el Nîl = Nile	110	F4
Baia	68	R5
Baía de Marajó	156	H4
Baía de Todos os Santos	156	K6
Baía do Bengo	114	G6
Baia Mare	68	L2
Baião	156	H4
Baia Sprie	68	L2
Baïbokoum	116	B2
Baicheng, *China*	82	Q9
Baicheng, *China*	86	G1
Baie Comeau	142	G1
Baie de la Seine	56	B5
Baie de la Somme	56	D4
Baie du Poste	136	S6
Baie St. Paul	142	F1
Baiji	98	K6
Baile Ailein	36	B2
Baile Átha Cliath = Dublin	35	E3
Băilești	62	G6
Bailleul	56	E4
Bailundo	118	B2
Bainbridge	144	E3
Bairiki	124	H5
Bairin Yuoqi	86	F2
Bairin Zuoqi	86	F2
Bairnsdale	126	J7
Bais	90	G5
Baja	68	F3
Baja California	138	C5
Bajram Curri	70	B2
Bakchar	82	Q6
Bakel	114	B2
Baker	124	J5
Baker, *Calif., United States*	140	C3
Baker, *Mont., United States*	140	F1
Baker, *Oreg., United States*	140	C2
Baker Lake	136	M4
Baker Lake	136	N4
Bakersfield	146	C1
Bakewell	38	G2
Bakharden	82	K10
Bakhta	84	D4
Baki	96	E1
Bakkafjörður	50	(1)F1
Bakkaflói	50	(1)F1
Baku = Baki	96	E1
Bala	38	E3
Balâ	98	E4
Balabac	90	F5
Balabac	90	F5
Balabac Strait	90	F5
Balagansk	84	G6
Balaghat	94	D4
Balaguer	62	L3
Balakhta	82	S6
Balaklava	98	E1
Balakovo	72	J4
Bālā Morghāb	82	L10
Bălan	68	N3
Balāngīr	94	D4
Balashov	72	H4
Balassagyarmat	68	G1
Balaton	68	E3
Balatonfüred	68	E3
Balatonlelle	68	E3
Balbina	156	F4
Balbriggan	35	E3
Balchik	98	C2
Balclutha	128	B8
Bald Knob	142	B3
Baldwin	144	E3
Balearic Islands = Islas Baleares	62	N5
Baler	90	G3
Bāleshwar	94	E4
Baley	84	K6
Baléyara	114	E2
Balguntay	82	R9
Bali	92	F4
Balige	92	B2
Balıkesir	70	K5
Balikpapan	92	F3
Balimo	93	F4
Balingen	64	D2
Balintang Channel	90	G3
Balkhash	82	N8
Ballachulish	36	C5
Balladonia	126	D6
Ballaghaderreen	35	C3
Ballantrae	36	C6
Ballarat	126	H7
Ballater	36	E4
Balleny Island	160	(2)Y3
Ballina, *Australia*	126	K5
Ballina, *Republic of Ireland*	35	B2
Ballinasloe	35	C3
Ballincollig	35	C5
Ballinger	146	G2
Ballinrobe	35	B3
Ballinskelligs Bay	35	A5
Ball's Pyramid	126	L6
Ballum	56	H1
Ballybofey	35	D2
Ballycastle	35	E1
Ballyclare	35	F2
Ballygar	35	C3
Ballygawley	35	D2
Ballyhaunis	35	C3
Ballymena	35	E2
Ballymoney	35	E1
Ballynahinch	35	F2
Ballyshannon	35	C2
Balmazújváros	68	J2
Balotra	94	B3
Balranald	126	H6
Balş	68	M5
Balsas	148	D5
Balsas	156	H5
Balta	68	S2
Bălți	68	Q2
Baltic Sea	50	J8
Baltijsk	52	J3
Baltimore	142	E3
Baltrum	54	C3
Balvi	50	P8
Balykchy	82	P9
Balykshi	72	K5
Bam	96	G4
Bamaga	126	H2
Bamako	114	C2
Bamba	112	E5
Bambari	116	C2
Bamberg	54	F7
Bambesa	116	D3
Bambouk	112	C6
Bambouk Kaarta	114	B2
Bamda	86	B4
Bamenda	114	G3
Bāmīān	96	J3
Banaba	124	G6
Bañados del Izozog	156	E7
Banalia	116	D3
Banana, *Australia*	126	K4
Banana, *Dem. Rep. of Congo*	116	A5
Banaz	70	M6
Ban Ban	90	C3
Ban Betong	92	C1
Banbridge	35	E2
Banbury	38	G3
Banchory	36	F4
Banda	94	D3
Banda Aceh	90	B5
Bandama	114	C3
Bandar-e 'Abbās	101	G3
Bandar-e Anzalī	96	E2
Bandar-e Deylam	101	D1
Bandar-e Ganāveh	101	D2
Bandar-e Khoemir	101	F3
Bandar-e Lengeh	101	F3
Bandar-e Ma'shur	101	C1
Bandar-e Torkeman	96	F2
Bandar Khomeynī	101	C1
Bandar Seri Begawan	92	E2
Banda Sea	93	C3
Band-e Chārak	101	F3
Band-e Moghūyeh	101	F3
Bandirma	70	K4
Bandundu	116	B4
Bandung	92	D4
Băneasa	68	Q5
Bāneh	98	L6
Banff, *Canada*	136	H6
Banff, *United Kingdom*	36	F4
Bangalore	94	C6
Bangangté	114	G3
Bangassou	116	C3
Bangbong	93	B3
Banggi	92	F1
Banghāzī	110	D1
Bangka	92	D3
Bangkalan	92	E4
Bangkok = Krung Thep	90	C4
Bangladesh	94	E4
Bangor, *N. Ire., United Kingdom*	35	F2
Bangor, *Wales, United Kingdom*	38	D2
Bangor, *United States*	142	G2
Bangor Erris	35	B2
Bang Saphan Yai	90	B4
Bangued	90	G3
Bangui, *Central African Republic*	116	B3
Bangui, *Philippines*	90	G3
Ban Hat Yai	90	C5
Ban Hua Hin	90	B4
Bani-Bangou	114	E1
Banī Walīd	112	H2
Bāniyās	98	F6
Banja Luka	68	E5
Banjarmasin	92	E3
Banjul	114	A2
Ban Khemmarat	90	D3
Banks Island = Moa, *Australia*	126	H2
Banks Island, *B.C., Canada*	136	E6
Banks Island, *N.W.T., Canada*	136	G2
Banks Lake	140	C1
Banks Peninsula	128	D6
Banks Strait	126	J8
Bann, *N. Ire., United Kingdom*	35	E2
Bann, *N. Ire., United Kingdom*	35	E2
Bannerman Town	144	F5
Bannu	94	B2
Bánovce	52	H9
Banská	52	J9
Banská Štiavnica	52	H9
Bansko	70	F3
Bantry	35	B5
Bantry Bay	35	B5
Banyo	114	G3
Banyoles	62	N2
Banyuwangi	92	E4
Baode	86	E3
Baoding	86	F3
Baoji	86	D4
Bao Lôc	90	D4
Baoro	116	B2
Baoshan	90	B1
Baotou	86	E2
Baoying	86	F4
Bap	94	B3
Bapaume	56	E4
Ba'qūbah	96	D3
Baquedano	158	H3
Bar	68	G7
Barabai	92	F3
Barabhas	36	E2
Baraboo	142	C2
Barakaldo	62	H1
Baramati	94	B5
Baramula	94	B2
Baran	94	C3
Baranavichy	72	E4
Baraolt	68	N3
Barbados	156	F1
Barbastro	62	L2
Barbate	62	E8
Barbuda	148	M5
Barcaldine	126	J4
Barcău	68	K2
Barcellona Pozzo di Gotto	66	K10
Barcelona, *Spain*	62	N3
Barcelona, *Venezuela*	148	M6
Barcelos, *Brazil*	156	E4
Barcelos, *Spain*	62	B3
Barclayville	114	C4
Barco de Valdeorras = O Barco	62	D2
Barcs	68	E4
Bardā	98	M3
Bardai	110	C3
Barddhamān	94	E4
Bardejov	52	L8
Bardonecchia	64	B5
Bardsey	38	D3
Bareilly	94	C3
Barentin	56	C5
Barents Sea	82	E3
Barentu	110	G4
Bareo	92	F2
Barga	94	D2
Bargaal	116	J1
Bargteheide	54	F3
Barguzin	84	H6
Bar Harbor	142	G2
Bari	66	L7
Barikot	94	B1
Barinas	156	C2
Bārīs	110	F3
Barisal	94	F4
Barito	93	A3
Barkam	86	C4
Barkava	50	P8
Barkly Tableland	126	F3
Barkol	82	S9
Bârlad	68	Q3
Bârlad	68	Q3
Bar-le-Duc	56	H6
Barletta	66	L7
Barmer	94	B3
Barmouth	38	D3
Barmouth Bay	38	D3
Barnard Castle	36	G7
Barnaul	82	Q7
Barnet	38	H4
Barnoldswick	38	F2
Barnsley	38	G2
Barnstaple	38	D4
Barnstaple Bay	38	D4
Barpeta	94	F3
Barquisimeto	156	D1
Barr	64	C2
Barra, *Brazil*	156	J6
Barra, *United Kingdom*	36	A4
Barracão do Barreto	156	G5
Barracas	62	K5
Barra do Bugres	156	F7
Barra do Corda	156	H5
Barra do Cuanza	116	A5
Barra do Garças	156	G7
Barra do São Manuel	156	G5
Barragem de Santa Clara	62	B7
Barragem de Sobradinho	156	J5
Barragem do Castelo de Bode	62	B5
Barragem do Maranhão	62	C6
Barranca, *Peru*	156	B4
Barranca, *Peru*	156	B6
Barranquilla	148	K6
Barreiras	156	H6
Barreiro	62	A6
Barretos	156	H8
Barrhead	36	D6
Barrie	142	E2
Barron	142	B1
Barrow	146	(1)F1
Barrow	35	E4
Barrow Creek	126	F4
Barrow-in-Furness	36	E7
Barrow Island	126	B4
Barrow Strait	136	N2
Barry	38	E4
Barshatas	82	P8
Barsi	94	C5
Barstow	146	C2
Bar-sur-Aube	60	K5
Bar-sur-Seine	60	K5
Barth	54	H2
Bartın	98	E3
Bartle Frere	124	E7
Bartlesville	144	B2
Bartlett	140	G2
Barton-upon-Humber	38	H2
Bartoszyce	52	K3
Barus	92	B2
Baruun Urt	86	E1
Barwani	94	B4
Barysaw	72	E4
Basaidu	101	F3
Basankusu	116	B3
Basarabeasca	68	R3
Basarabi	68	R5
Basca	66	C2
Basco	90	G2
Basel	64	C3
Bashkiriya	72	K4
Bāsht	101	D1
Basilan	93	B1
Basildon	38	J4
Basiluzzo	66	K10
Basingstoke	38	G4
Başkale	98	K4
Basoko	116	C3
Bassano	138	D1
Bassano del Grappa	64	G5
Bassar	114	E3
Bassas da India	118	F4
Basse Santa Su	112	C6
Basse Terre	148	M5
Bassett	140	G2
Bassikounou	112	D5
Bass Strait	126	H7
Bassum	54	D4
Bastak	101	F3
Bastānābād	98	M5
Basti	94	D3
Bastia	66	D6
Bastogne	56	H4
Bastrop, *La., United States*	144	C3
Bastrop, *Tex., United States*	144	B3
Bata	114	F4
Batagay	84	N3
Batagay-Alyta	84	N3
Batak	70	G3
Batamay	84	M4
Batang	86	B5
Batangas	90	G4
Batan Islands	90	G2
Batanta	93	C3
Batchelor	126	F2
Batemans Bay	126	K7
Batesville	144	D3
Bath, *United Kingdom*	38	F4
Bath, *United States*	142	E2
Bathinda	94	B2
Bathurst, *Australia*	126	J6
Bathurst, *Canada*	136	T7
Bathurst Inlet	136	K3
Bathurst Island, *Australia*	126	E2
Bathurst Island, *Canada*	136	M1
Batman	96	D2
Batna	112	G1
Baton Rouge	144	C3
Bátonyterenye	68	G2
Batouri	114	G4
Batroûn	100	C2
Batticaloa	94	D7
Battipaglia	66	J8
Battle	136	J6
Battle	38	J5
Battle Creek	142	C2
Battle Harbour	136	V6
Battle Mountain	140	C2
Batu	116	F2
Batui	93	B3
Bat'umi	98	J3
Batu Pahat	92	C2
Baturino	82	R6
Baubau	93	B4
Bauchi	114	F2
Baudette	142	B1
Baukau	93	C4
Baume-les-Dames	60	M6
Bauru	158	M3
Bauska	50	N8
Bautzen	52	D6
Bawean	92	E4
Bawiti	110	E2
Bawku	114	D2
Bayamo	148	J4
Bayanaul	82	P7
Bayandelger	84	H7
Bayan Har Shan	86	B4
Bayanhongor	86	C1
Bayan Mod	86	C2
Bayan Obo	86	D2
Bayansumküre	82	Q9
Bayburt	98	J3
Bay City, *Mich., United States*	142	D2
Bay City, *Tex., United States*	144	B4
Baydhabo	116	G3
Bayerische Alpen	64	G3
Bayeux	56	B5

Bayfield 142 B1
Bayindir 70 K6
Bāyir 100 D6
Baykit 82 T5
Baykonur 82 M8
Bay Minette 144 D3
Bay of Bengal 94 E5
Bay of Biscay 60 C9
Bay of Fundy 136 T8
Bay of Islands 128 E2
Bay of Plenty 128 F3
Bayonne 60 D10
Bayramaly 96 H2
Bayramiç 70 J5
Bayreuth 54 G7
Baysun 96 J2
Bayt al Faqīh 110 H5
Bay View 128 F4
Baza 62 H7
Bazas 60 E9
Bazdar 96 J4
Beach 140 F1
Beachy Head 38 J5
Beaconsfield 38 H4
Beagle Gulf 126 E2
Bealanana 118 H2
Bear Island = Bjørnøya, *Norway* 82 B3
Bear Island, *Republic of Ireland* 35 B5
Bear Lake 140 D2
Bearsden 36 D6
Beasain 62 H1
Beas de Segura 62 H6
Beatrice 144 B1
Beatty 146 C1
Beaufort, *Malaysia* 92 F1
Beaufort, *N.C., United States* 144 F3
Beaufort, *S.C., United States* 144 E3
Beaufort Sea 134 Q2
Beaufort West 118 C6
Beaumont, *New Zealand* 128 B7
Beaumont, *United States* 144 C3
Beaune 60 K6
Beauvais 56 E5
Beaver 140 D3
Beaver Creek 146 (1)J3
Beaver Dam 142 C3
Beaver Falls 142 D2
Beawar 94 B3
Beazley 158 H5
Bebington 38 E2
Bebra 54 E6
Beccles 38 K3
Bečej 68 H4
Béchar 112 E2
Beckley 144 E2
Becks 128 B7
Beckum 56 L3
Beclean 68 M2
Bedale 36 G7
Bedelē 116 F2
Bedford, *United Kingdom* 38 H3
Bedford, *United States* 144 D2
Bedworth 38 G3
Beenleigh 126 K5
Beer Menuha 100 C6
Beer Ora 100 C7
Be'ér Sheva' 100 B5
Beeston 38 G3
Beeville 144 B4
Behbehān 101 D1
Bei'an 84 M7
Beihai 90 D2
Beijing 86 F3
Beipan 86 D5
Beipiao 86 G2
Beira 118 E3
Beirut = Beyrouth 100 C3
Beith 36 D6
Beiuş 68 K3
Beizhen 88 A3
Béja 112 G1
Bejaïa 112 G1
Béjar 62 E4
Bekdash 96 F1
Békés 52 L11
Békéscsaba 68 J3
Bekily 118 H4
Bekkai 88 N2
Bela 96 J4
Bela Crkva 68 J5
Belaga 92 E2
Belarus 48 G2
Bela Vista 118 E5
Belaya 72 K3
Belaya Gora 84 R3
Bełchatów 52 J6
Belcher Islands 136 Q5
Beledweyne 116 H3
Belek 82 J10
Belém 156 H4
Belen 148 C2
Belfast 35 F2
Belfield 140 F1
Belfort 64 B3
Belgazyn 82 T7
Belgium 56 G4
Belgorod 72 G4
Belgrade = Beograd 68 H5
Beli 114 G3
Belice 66 H11
Beli Manastir 68 F4
Belinyu 92 D3
Belitung 92 D3
Belize 148 G5
Belize 148 G5
Bellac 60 G7
Bella Coola 136 F6
Bellary 94 C5
Belleek 35 C2
Bellefontaine 142 D2
Belle Fourche 140 F2
Belle Glade 144 E4
Belle Île 60 B6
Belle Isle 136 V6
Bellême 60 F5
Belleterre 142 E1
Belleville, *Canada* 142 E2
Belleville, *United States* 144 B2
Bellingham 140 B1
Bellingshausen Sea 160 (2)JJ4
Bellinzona 64 E4
Bello 156 B2
Belluno 64 H4
Bellyk 84 E6
Belmont 142 E2
Belmonte, *Brazil* 156 K7
Belmonte, *Spain* 62 H5
Belmopan 148 G5
Belmullet 35 B2
Belogorsk 84 M6
Belogradchik 68 K6
Beloha 118 H5
Belo Horizonte 156 J7
Beloit, *Kans., United States* 144 B2
Beloit, *Wis., United States* 142 C2
Belo Monte 156 G4
Belomorsk 72 F2
Belorechensk 98 H1
Beloretsk 72 L4
Belo Tsiribihina 118 G3
Belovo 82 R7
Beloyarskiy 82 M5
Beloye More 72 G1
Belozersk 72 G2
Belozerskoye 72 N3
Belper 38 G2
Belye Vody 82 M9
Belyy Yar 82 Q6
Belzig 54 H4
Bembibre 62 D2
Bemidji 142 A1
Bena Dibele 116 C4
Ben Alder 36 D5
Benavente 62 E3
Benbecula 36 A4
Bend 140 B2
Bender-Bayla 116 J2
Bendorf 56 K4
Bene 118 E3
Benešov 52 D8
Benevento 66 J7
Bengbu 86 F4
Bengkalis 92 C2
Bengkulu 92 C3
Benguela 118 A2
Benguerir 112 D2
Benha 110 F1
Ben Hope 36 D3
Beni 116 D3
Beni 156 D6
Beni Abbès 112 E2
Benicarló 62 L4
Benidorm 62 K6
Benī Mazār 110 F2
Beni Mellal 112 D2
Benin 114 E2
Benin City 114 F3
Beni Saf 62 J9
Beni Slimane 62 P8
Beni Suef 110 F2
Benito Juaréz 158 K6
Benjamin Constant 156 D4
Benkelman 140 F2
Ben Klibreck 36 D3
Benkovac 64 L6
Ben Lawers 36 D5
Ben Lui 36 D5
Ben Macdui 36 E4
Ben More 36 B5
Ben More Assynt 36 D3
Ben Nevis 36 D5
Bennington 142 F2
Benoud 112 F2
Bensheim 54 D7
Benson, *Ariz., United States* 146 D2
Benson, *Minn., United States* 138 G2
Benteng 93 B4
Bentinck Island 126 G3
Bent Jbail 100 C3
Bentley 38 G2
Bentonville 144 C2
Bentung 92 C2
Benue 114 G3
Ben Wyvis 36 D4
Benxi 86 G2
Beo 90 H6
Beograd 68 H5
Bepazarı 98 D3
Berat 70 B4
Beravina 118 H3
Berber 110 F4
Berbera 110 H5
Berbérati 116 B3
Berchtesgaden 64 J3
Berck 56 D4
Berdigestyakh 84 M4
Berdyans'k 72 G5
Berdychiv 72 E5
Bereeda 116 J1
Berehove 68 K1
Bererreá 62 C2
Berettyóújfalu 68 J2
Berettys 52 L10
Bereznik 72 H2
Berezniki 72 L3
Berezovo 72 N2
Berezovyy 84 P6
Berga 62 M2
Bergama 70 K5
Bergamo 64 E5
Bergara 62 H1
Bergby 50 J6
Bergedorf 54 F3
Bergen, *Germany* 54 J2
Bergen, *Germany* 54 E4
Bergen, *Netherlands* 56 G2
Bergen, *Norway* 50 C6
Bergen op Zoom 56 G3
Bergerac 60 F9
Bergheim 56 J4
Bergisch Gladbach 54 C6
Bergsfjordhalvøya 50 L1
Beringen 56 H3
Beringovskiy 84 X4
Bering Sea 146 (1)C4
Bering Strait 146 (1)C2
Berīzak 101 G3
Berkeley 146 B1
Berkner Island 160 (2)A2
Berkovitsa 68 L6
Berlin, *Germany* 54 J4
Berlin, *United States* 142 F2
Bermejillo 146 F3
Bermejo 158 K4
Bermeo 62 H1
Bermuda 134 H6
Bern 64 C4
Bernado 146 E2
Bernalda 66 L8
Bernau 54 J4
Bernay 56 C5
Bernburg 54 G5
Berner Alpen 64 C4
Berneray 36 A4
Beroun 52 D8
Berounka 54 J7
Berovo 70 E3
Berrouaghia 62 N8
Berry Islands 144 F4
Bertoua 114 G4
Bertram 142 D1
Beruni 82 L9
Berwick-upon-Tweed 36 F6
Besalampy 118 G3
Besançon 60 M6
Besbay 82 K8
Beshneh 101 F2
Bessemer 144 D3
Bestamak 82 P8
Bestuzhevo 72 H2
Bestyakh, *Russia* 84 L3
Bestyakh, *Russia* 84 M4
Betanzos 62 B1
Bětdâmbâng 90 C4
Bethany 142 B2
Bethel, *Ak., United States* 146 (1)E3
Bethel, *Pa., United States* 142 F2
Bethlehem, *Israel* 100 C5
Bethlehem, *South Africa* 118 D5
Béthune 56 E4
Betioky 118 G4
Betoota 126 H5
Betpak-Dala 82 M8
Betroka 118 H4
Bet-She'an 100 C4
Bettiah 94 D3
Bettyhill 36 D3
Betul 94 C4
Betws-y-Coed 38 E2
Betzdorf 54 C6
Beulah 142 C2
Beverley 38 H2
Beverungen 54 E5
Bexhill 38 J5
Bey Dağlari 70 M8
Beykoz 70 M3
Beyla 114 C3
Beyneu 82 J8
Beypazarı 70 P4
Beyra 116 H2
Beyrouth 100 C3
Beyşehir 70 P7
Beyşehir Gölü 70 P7
Bezhetsk 72 G3
Béziers 60 J10
Bhadgaon 94 E3
Bhadrakh 94 E4
Bhadravati 94 C6
Bhagalpur 94 E3
Bhairab Bazar 94 F4
Bhakkar 94 B2
Bhamo 90 B2
Bharuch 94 B4
Bhatpara 94 E4
Bhavnagar 94 B4
Bhawanipatna 94 D5
Bhilai 94 D4
Bhilwara 94 B3
Bhīmavaram 94 D5
Bhind 94 C3
Bhiwandi 94 B5
Bhopal 94 C4
Bhubaneshwar 94 E4
Bhuj 94 A4
Bhusawal 94 C4
Bhutan 94 E3
Biak 93 E3
Biak 93 E3
Biała 52 K8
Biała Podlaska 52 N5
Białogard 52 F3
Białystok 52 N4
Biarritz 60 D10
Biasca 64 D4
Bibbiena 64 G7
Biberach 64 E2
Bicaz 68 P3
Bicester 38 G4
Bickerton Island 126 G2
Bicske 68 F2
Bida 114 F3
Bidar 94 C5
Bidbid 101 H5
Biddeford 142 F2
Bideford 38 D4
Bideford Bay = Barnstaple Bay 38 D4
Biedenkopf 54 D6
Biel 64 C3
Bielefeld 54 D4
Biella 64 D5
Bielsko-Biała 52 J8
Bielsk Podlaski 52 N5
Biên Hoa 90 D4
Bietigheim-Bissingen 64 E2
Big 136 G2
Biga 70 K4
Bigadiç 70 L5
Big Desert 126 H7
Big Falls 142 B1
Biggar 36 E6
Biggleswade 38 H3
Bighorn 138 E2
Bighorn Lake 140 E1
Bighorn Mountains 140 E2
Bight of Bangkok 90 C4
Bight of Benin 114 E3
Bight of Biafra 114 F4
Big Lake 146 (1)H2
Bignona 112 B6
Big Pine 144 E5
Big Rapids 142 C2
Big River 136 K6
Big Sandy 140 D1
Big Sioux 140 G2
Big Spring 146 F2
Big Sur 146 B1
Big Trout Lake 136 P6
Bihać 64 L6
Bihoro 88 N2
Bijapur 94 C5
Bījār 98 M6
Bijeljina 68 G5
Bijelo Polje 68 G6
Bijie 86 D5
Bikanar 94 B3
Bikin 84 N7
Bikini 124 G4
Bilaspur 94 D4
Biläsuvar 98 N4
Bila Tserkva 72 F5
Bilbao 62 H1
Bileća 68 F7
Bilecik 70 M4
Bilečko Jezero 68 F7
Biled 68 H4
Biłgoraj 52 M7
Bilhorod-Dnistrovs'kyy 72 F5
Bilibino 84 V3
Bilina 54 J6
Billericay 38 J4
Billings 140 D1
Billingshurst 38 H4
Bill of Portland 38 F5
Bilma 110 B4
Biloela 126 K4
Biloxi 144 D3
Bimini Islands 144 F4
Bina-Etawa 94 C4
Binche 56 G4
Bindi Bindi 126 C6
Bindura 118 E3
Bingen 54 C7
Binghamton 142 E2
Bingley 38 G2
Bingöl 98 J4
Binongko 93 B4
Bintuhan 92 C3
Bintulu 92 E2
Bintuni 93 D3
Binyang 90 D2
Binzhou 86 F3
Biograd 64 L7
Birāk 112 H3
Birao 110 D5
Biratnagar 94 E3
Bi'r Bazīrī 100 E2
Birdsville 126 G5
Bireun 92 B1
Bir Gandouz 112 B4
Bîr Gifgâfa 100 A6
Birhan 110 G5
Bîr Hasana 100 A6
Birjand 96 G3
Birkenfeld 56 K5
Birkenhead 38 E2
Birmingham, *United Kingdom* 38 G3
Birmingham, *United States* 144 D3
Bîr Mogreïn 112 C3
Birnie 124 J6
Birnin-Gwari 114 F2
Birnin Kebbi 114 E2
Birnin Konni 114 F2
Birnin Kudu 114 F2
Birobidzhan 84 N7
Birr 35 D3
Birsk 72 L3
Bîr Tâba 100 B7
Biržai 52 P1
Bi'r Zalṭan 110 C2
Bisbee 146 E2
Bisceglie 66 L7
Bischofshofen 64 J3
Bischofswerda 52 D6
Biševo 66 L6
Bishkek 82 N9
Bishop 140 C3
Bishop Auckland 36 G7
Bishop's Cleeve 38 F4
Bishop's Stortford 38 J4
Biskra 112 G2
Bislig 90 H5
Bismarck 138 F2
Bismarck Sea 124 E6
Bissau 112 B6
Bistcho Lake 136 H5
Bistrița 68 M2
Bistrița 68 P3
Bitburg 56 J5
Bitche 54 C7
Bitkine 110 C5
Bitlis 98 K4
Bitola 70 D3
Bitonto 66 L7
Bitterfeld 54 H5
Bitterroot Range 140 C1
Bitti 66 D8
Bitung 93 C2
Biu 114 G2
Biwa-ko 88 H6
Bixby 142 B3
Biyävra 94 C4
Biysk 82 R7
Bizerte 112 G1
Bjelovar 68 D4

Name	Page	Grid
Bjerkvik	50	J2
Bjørnøya	82	B3
B-Köpenick	54	J4
Bla	114	C2
Blaby	38	G3
Blackburn	38	F2
Blackfoot	140	D2
Blackfoot Reservoir	140	D2
Black Hills	140	F2
Black Isle	36	D4
Black Mountains	38	E3
Blackpool	38	E2
Black Range	146	E2
Black River Falls	142	B2
Black Rock Desert	140	C2
Blacksburg	142	D3
Black Sea	98	D2
Blacks Harbour	142	G1
Blacksod Bay	35	A2
Black Sugarloaf	126	K6
Black Volta	114	D3
Blackwater	126	J4
Blackwater	35	C4
Blaenau Ffestiniog	38	E3
Blagodarnyy	98	K1
Blagoevgrad	70	F3
Blagoveshchenka	82	P7
Blagoveshchensk	84	M6
Blain	60	D6
Blair	142	A2
Blairgowrie	36	E5
Blairsden	140	B3
Blairsville	144	E3
Blaj	68	L3
Blakely	144	E3
Blanco	156	E6
Blandford Forum	38	F5
Blanding	146	E1
Blangy-sur-Bresle	56	D5
Blankenberge	56	F3
Blankenburg	54	F5
Blankenheim	56	J4
Blantyre	118	F3
Blasket Islands	35	A4
Blaubeuren	64	E2
Blaye-et-Sainte-Luce	60	E8
Bled	64	K4
Blenheim	128	D5
Blessington Lakes	35	E3
Bletchley	38	H3
Blevands Huk	54	D1
Blida	112	F1
Blind River	138	K2
Bloemfontein	118	D5
Bloemhof	118	D5
Blois	60	G6
Blönduós	50	(1)C2
Błonie	52	K5
Bloody Foreland	35	C1
Bloomfield	144	D2
Bloomington, *Ill., United States*	142	C2
Bloomington, *Ind., United States*	142	C3
Bloxwich	38	F3
Bludenz	64	E3
Blue Earth	142	B2
Bluefield	142	D3
Bluefields	148	H6
Blue Mountain Lake	142	F2
Blue Mountains	140	C2
Blue Nile = Bahr el Azraq	110	F5
Bluenose Lake	136	H3
Blue Stack Mountains	35	C2
Bluff, *New Zealand*	128	B8
Bluff, *United States*	146	E1
Blumenau	158	M4
Blyth	36	G6
Blythe	146	D2
Blytheville	144	D2
Bo	114	B3
Boac	90	G4
Boa Vista, *Brazil*	156	E3
Boa Vista, *Cape Verde Islands*	114	(1)B1
Bobbili	94	D5
Bobbio	64	E6
Bobigny	56	E6
Bobingen	64	F2
Böblingen	64	E2
Bobo Dioulasso	114	D2
Bobolice	52	F4
Bobr	52	E6
Bobrov	72	H4
Bôca do Acre	156	D5
Boca Grande	148	M7
Boca Grande	154	E3
Bocaiúva	156	J7
Bocaranga	116	B2
Bochart	142	F1
Bochnia	52	K8
Bocholt	54	B5
Bochum	54	C5
Bockenem	54	F4
Bodaybo	84	J5
Bode	54	G4
Bodélé	110	C4
Boden	50	L4
Bodham	94	C5
Bodmin	38	D5
Bodmin Moor	38	D5
Bodø	50	H3
Bodrog	52	L9
Bodrum	70	K7
Boe	140	D2
Boende	116	C4
Boffa	114	B2
Bogale	90	B3
Bogalusa	144	D3
Boggabilla	126	K5
Boggeragh Mountains	35	C4
Boghni	62	P8
Bognor Regis	38	H5
Bogo	90	G4
Bog of Allen	35	E3
Bogor	92	D4
Bogorodskoye	84	Q6
Bogotá	156	C3
Bogotol	82	R6
Bogra	94	E4
Boguchany	84	F5
Bogué	112	C5
Bo Hai	86	F3
Bohmerwald	54	H7
Bohol	90	G5
Bohumin	52	H8
Boiaçu	156	E4
Boise	140	C2
Boise City	146	F1
Bojnürd	82	K10
Bokatola	116	B4
Boké	114	B2
Bokoro	114	H2
Bokspits	118	C5
Bokungu	116	C4
Bolbec	56	C5
Boldu	68	Q4
Bole, *China*	82	Q9
Bole, *Ghana*	114	D3
Bolechiv	52	N8
Bolesławiec	52	E6
Bolgatanga	114	D2
Bolhrad	68	R4
Bolintin-Vale	68	N5
Bolivar	142	B3
Bolivia	156	D7
Bollène	60	K9
Bollnäs	50	J6
Bolmen	50	G8
Bolnisi	98	L3
Bolobo	114	H5
Bologna	64	G6
Bolognesi	156	C5
Bolomba	114	H4
Bolotnoye	82	Q6
Bol'shaya Pyssa	72	J2
Bol'sherech'ye	72	P3
Bol'shezemel'skaya Tundra	82	J4
Bol Shirta	84	C4
Bolshoy Atlym	72	N2
Bol'shoy Osinovaya	84	W3
Bol'shoy Vlas'evo	84	Q6
Bolshoy Yuga	72	P2
Bolsover	38	G2
Bolton	38	F2
Bolu	98	D3
Bolvadin	70	P6
Bolzano	64	G4
Boma	114	G6
Bombala	126	J7
Bombay = Mumbai	94	B5
Bomili	116	D3
Bom Jesus da Lapa	156	J6
Bømlo	50	C7
Bomnak	84	M6
Bomossa	114	H4
Bonāb	98	M5
Bonaparte Archipelago	126	B2
Bonavista Bay	136	W7
Bondeno	64	G6
Bondo	116	C3
Bondokodi	126	C1
Bondoukou	114	D3
Bondowoso	92	E4
Bonerate	93	B4
Bongaigaon	94	F3
Bongandanga	116	C3
Bongao	93	A1
Bongor	114	H2
Bonifacio	66	D7
Bonn	54	C6
Bonners Ferry	140	C1
Bonneville	64	B4
Bonnie Rock	126	C6
Bonorva	66	C8
Bonthe	114	B3
Bontoc	90	G3
Bontosunggu	93	A4
Bonyhád	68	F3
Boone	142	D3
Boonville	144	C2
Boorama	116	G2
Boosaaso	116	H1
Boothia Peninsula	136	M2
Bootle	36	E7
Booué	114	G5
Boppard	54	C6
Bor, *Russia*	84	D4
Bor, *Sudan*	116	E2
Bor, *Turkey*	70	S7
Bor, *Yugoslavia*	68	K5
Borah Peak	140	C3
Borås	50	G8
Borāzjān	101	D2
Bordeaux	60	E9
Bordeira	62	B7
Borden Peninsula	136	Q2
Border Town	126	H7
Bordj Bou Arréridj	112	F1
Bordj Bounaam	62	M9
Bordj Flye Sante Marie	112	E3
Bordj Messaouda	112	G2
Bordj Mokhtar	112	F4
Bordj Omar Driss	112	G3
Borgarnes	50	(1)C2
Borger	146	F1
Borgholm	50	J8
Borgomanero	64	D5
Borgo San Dalmazzo	64	C6
Borgo San Lorenzo	64	G7
Borgosesia	64	D5
Borgo Val di Taro	64	E6
Bori Jenein	112	H2
Borislav	52	N8
Borisoglebsk	72	H4
Borjomi	98	K3
Borken	56	J3
Borkou	110	C4
Borkum	56	J1
Borkum	56	J1
Borlänge	50	H6
Bormida	64	D6
Bormio	64	F4
Borna	54	H5
Borne	56	J2
Borneo	92	E3
Bornholm	50	H9
Borodino	82	R5
Borodinskoye	50	Q6
Boromo	114	D2
Borongan	90	H4
Borovichi	72	F3
Borovskoy	72	M4
Borriana	62	K5
Borrisokane	35	C4
Borroloola	126	G3
Borşa	68	M2
Borshchiv	68	P1
Borshchovochnyy Khrebet	84	J7
Borðeyri	50	(1)C2
Borūjerd	96	E3
Borzya	84	K6
Bosa	66	C8
Bosanska Dubica	68	D4
Bosanska Gradiška	68	E4
Bosanska Kostajnica	64	M5
Bosanska Krupa	68	D5
Bosanski Brod	68	F4
Bosanski Novi	68	D4
Bosanski Petrovac	68	D5
Bosansko Grahovo	64	M6
Boşca	68	J4
Bose	90	D2
Bosilegrad	68	K7
Boskovice	52	F8
Bosna	68	F5
Bosnia-Herzegovina	68	E5
Bosobolo	116	B3
Bosporus = İstanbul Boğazı	70	M3
Bosporus	96	A1
Bossambélé	116	B2
Bossangoa	116	B2
Bossier City	144	C3
Bosten Hu	82	R9
Boston, *United Kingdom*	38	H3
Boston, *United States*	142	F2
Botevgrad	68	L7
Botlikh	96	E1
Botna	68	R3
Botoşani	68	P2
Botou	86	F3
Botrange	56	J4
Botswana	118	C4
Bottrop	56	J3
Bou Ahmed	62	F9
Bouaké	114	C3
Bouar	116	B2
Bouârfa	112	E2
Boufarik	62	N8
Bougainville Island	124	F6
Bougainville Reef	126	J3
Bougouni	114	C2
Bougzoul	62	N9
Bouira	112	F1
Bou Ismaïl	62	N8
Bou Izakarn	112	D3
Boujdour	112	C3
Bou Kadir	62	M8
Boukra	112	C3
Boulder	140	E2
Boulder City	146	D1
Boulia	126	G4
Boulogne-sur-Mer	56	D4
Bouna	114	D3
Boundiali	114	C3
Bounty Islands	124	H10
Bourem	112	E5
Bourg	60	E8
Bourg-de-Piage	60	L9
Bourg-en-Bresse	60	L7
Bourges	60	H6
Bourgoin-Jallieu	60	L8
Bourke	126	J6
Bourne	38	H3
Bournemouth	38	G5
Bou Saâda	112	F1
Bousso	110	C5
Boussu	56	F4
Boutilimit	112	C5
Bouzghaia	62	M8
Bowbells	140	F1
Bowen	126	J4
Bowie, *Ariz., United States*	146	E2
Bowie, *Tex., United States*	146	G2
Bowkan	98	M5
Bowling Green, *Fla., United States*	144	E4
Bowling Green, *Ky., United States*	144	D2
Bowling Green, *Mo., United States*	144	C2
Bowman	140	F1
Bowman Bay	136	R3
Bowmore	36	B6
Bo Xian	86	F4
Boxwood Hill	126	C6
Boyabat	98	F3
Boyang	86	F5
Boyarka	84	F2
Boyle	35	C3
Boyne	35	E3
Boysen Reservoir	140	E2
Boyuibe	158	J3
Bozcaada	70	H5
Boz Dağ	70	M7
Bozeman	140	D1
Bozkır	70	Q7
Bozoum	116	B2
Bozova	98	H5
Bozüyük	70	N5
Bra	64	C6
Brač	68	D6
Bracciano	66	G6
Bräcke	50	H5
Brackley	38	G3
Bracknell	38	H4
Brad	68	K3
Bradano	66	L8
Bradford	38	G2
Brady	144	B3
Brae	36	(1)G1
Braemar	36	E4
Braga	62	B3
Bragança, *Brazil*	156	H4
Bragança, *Portugal*	62	D3
Brahmapur	94	D5
Brahmaputra	94	F3
Braich y Pwll	38	D3
Brăila	68	Q4
Brainerd	142	B1
Braintree	38	J4
Brake	54	D3
Bramming	54	D1
Brampton	142	E2
Brampton	36	F7
Bramsche	54	D4
Branco	156	E3
Brandberg	118	A4
Brandenburg	54	H4
Brandenton	144	E4
Brandon	136	M7
Brandon Mountain	35	A4
Brandvlei	118	C5
Brandýs	52	D7
Braniewo	52	J3
Brasileia	156	D6
Brasília	156	H7
Braslaw	50	P9
Braşov	68	N4
Bratislava	52	G9
Bratsk	84	G5
Bratskoye Vodokhranilishche	84	G5
Brattleboro	142	F2
Braţul	68	R4
Bratunac	68	G5
Braunau	64	J2
Braunschweig	54	F4
Braunton	38	D4
Brawley	146	C2
Bray	35	E3
Brazil	154	F4
Brazzaville	116	B4
Brčko	68	F5
Brda	52	G4
Bream Bay	128	E2
Brechin	36	F5
Breckenridge	146	G2
Břeclav	52	F9
Brecon Beacons National Park	38	E4
Breda	56	G3
Bredasdorp	118	C6
Bredstedt	54	E2
Bredy	72	M4
Bree	56	H3
Bree	60	L2
Bregenz	64	E3
Breiðafjörður	50	(1)A2
Bremangerlandet	50	B6
Bremen, *Germany*	54	D3
Bremen, *United States*	144	D3
Bremerhaven	54	D3
Bremerton	140	B1
Bremervörde	54	E3
Brenham	144	B3
Brennero	64	G4
Breno	64	F5
Brentwood	38	J4
Brescia	64	F5
Breslau = Wrocław	52	G6
Bressanone	64	G4
Bressay	36	(1)H1
Bressuire	60	E7
Brest, *Belarus*	72	D4
Brest, *France*	60	A5
Breteuil	56	E5
Bretten	54	D7
Breves	156	G4
Brewarrina	126	J5
Brewton	144	D3
Brežice	68	C4
Brézina	112	F2
Brezno	52	J9
Bria	116	C2
Briançon	64	B6
Briceni	68	Q1
Bridgend	38	E4
Bridgeport, *Calif., United States*	146	C1
Bridgeport, *Conn., United States*	142	F2
Bridgeport, *Nebr., United States*	140	F2
Bridgetown	156	F1
Bridgewater	136	U8
Bridgnorth	38	F3
Bridgwater	38	E4
Bridgwater Bay	38	E4
Bridlington	38	H1
Bridport	38	F5
Brienzer See	64	D4
Brig	64	C4
Brigg	38	H2
Brigham City	140	D2
Brighouse	38	G2
Brighton, *United Kingdom*	38	H5
Brighton, *United States*	140	F3
Brignoles	64	B7
Brikama	114	A2
Brilon	54	D5
Brindisi	66	M8
Brinkley	144	C3
Brisbane	126	K5
Bristol, *United Kingdom*	38	F4
Bristol, *United States*	144	E2
Bristol Bay	146	(1)E4
Bristol Channel	38	E4
British Columbia	136	F5
Britstown	118	C6
Brive-la-Gaillarde	60	G8
Briviesca	62	G2
Brixham	38	E5
Brlik	82	N9
Brno	52	F8
Broadford	36	C4
Broadlaw	36	E6
Broad Sound	126	J4
Broadstairs	38	K4
Broadus	140	E1
Brockton	142	F2
Brockville	142	E2
Brod	68	J9
Brodeur Peninsula	136	P2
Brodick	36	C6

Brodnica 52 J4
Broken Arrow 148 E1
Broken Bow 144 C3
Broken Hill 126 H6
Brokopondo 156 F2
Bromley 38 J4
Bromölla 52 D1
Bromsgrove 38 F3
Brønderslev 50 E8
Broni 64 E5
Brooke's Point 90 F5
Brookhaven 144 C3
Brookings, *Oreg., United States* 140 B2
Brookings, *S.D., United States* 140 G2
Brooks 136 J6
Brooks Range 146 (1)F2
Brooksville 144 E4
Broome 126 D3
Brora 36 E3
Brösarp 50 H9
Brough 38 H2
Broughton Island 136 U3
Brovary 72 F4
Brownfield 146 F2
Brownhills 38 G3
Browning 140 D1
Brownsville, *Tenn., United States* 144 D2
Brownsville, *Tex., United States* 144 B4
Brownwood 144 B3
Bruchsal 54 D7
Bruck, *Austria* 64 L3
Bruck, *Austria* 64 M2
Bruck an der Mur 68 C2
Brugge 56 F3
Brühl 56 J4
Bruint 94 G3
Brumado 156 J6
Brumath 64 C2
Bruneau 140 C2
Brunei 92 E2
Brunflo 50 H5
Brunico 66 F2
Brunsbüttel 54 E3
Brunswick, *Ga., United States* 144 E3
Brunswick, *Me., United States* 142 G2
Bruntal 52 G8
Brush 140 F2
Brussels = Bruxelles 56 G4
Bruxelles 56 G4
Bryan 144 B3
Bryanka 82 S6
Bryansk 72 F4
Brzeg 52 G7
Brzeg Dolny 52 F6
Brzeziny 52 J6
B-Spandau 52 C5
Bubi 118 E4
Bucak 98 D5
Bucaramanga 156 C2
Buchan 36 F4
Buchanan 114 B3
Buchan Gulf 136 S2
Bucharest = București 68 P5
Buchen 54 E7
Buchholz 54 E3
Buchy 60 M5
Bückeburg 54 E4
Buckie 36 F4
Buckingham 38 H3
Bučovice 52 F8
București 68 P5
Budapest 68 G2
Bude 38 D5
Bude Bay 38 D5
Budennovsk 98 L1
Büdingen 54 E6
Budoni 66 D8
Budrio 64 G6
Budva 68 F7
Buenaventura, *Colombia* 156 B3
Buenaventura, *Mexico* 146 E3
Buena Vista 140 E3
Buenos Aires 158 K5
Buffalo, *Okla., United States* 144 B2
Buffalo, *N.Y., United States* 142 E2
Buffalo, *S.D., United States* 140 F1
Buffalo, *Tex., United States* 144 B3
Buffalo, *Wyo., United States* 140 E2
Buffalo Lake 136 J4
Buffalo Narrows 136 K5
Buftea 68 N5
Bug 52 L5
Bugojno 68 E5
Bugrino 82 H4
Bugsuk 90 F5
Bugul'ma 72 K4
Buguruslan 72 K4
Buḩayrat al Asad 98 H5
Buḩayrat ath Tharthār 98 K6
Buhuși 68 P3
Builth Wells 38 E3
Buinsk 72 J3
Buir Nuur 86 F1
Bujanovac 68 J7
Buje 64 J5
Bujumbura 116 D4
Bukachacha 84 K6
Bukavu 116 D4
Bukhara 96 H2
Bukkittinggi 92 C3
Bukoba 116 E4
Bula, *Indonesia* 93 D3
Bula, *Papua New Guinea* 93 F4
Bülach 64 D3
Bulan 90 G4
Bûlâq 110 F2
Bulawayo 118 D4
Buldir Island 84 X6
Bulgan 84 G7
Bulgaria 68 M7
Buli 93 C2
Bulle 64 C4
Bullhead City 146 D1
Bulls 128 E5
Bulukumba 93 B4
Bulun 84 M2
Bumba 116 C3
Bumbești Jiu 68 L4
Buna 116 F3
Bunbury 126 C6
Buncrana 35 D1
Bunda 116 E4
Bundaberg 126 K4
Bünde 54 D4
Bungunya 126 J5
Bunia 116 E3
Bunkie 144 C3
Bunnell 144 E4
Bünyan 98 F4
Bu ol Kheyr 101 D2
Buôn Mê Thuôt 90 D4
Buotama 84 M4
Bura 116 F4
Buran 82 R8
Buranj 94 D2
Burao 116 H2
Burāq 100 D3
Buraydah 96 D4
Burco 110 J6
Burdur 98 D5
Burdur Gölü 70 N7
Burē 110 G5
Büren 56 L3
Burg 54 G4
Burgas 68 Q7
Burgaski Zaliv 68 Q7
Burgdorf 64 C3
Burgess Hill 38 H5
Burghausen 64 H2
Burglengenfeld 54 H7
Burgos 62 G2
Burgsvik 50 K8
Burhaniye 70 K5
Burhanpur 94 C4
Burjassot 62 K5
Burj Sāfitā 100 D2
Burketown 126 G3
Burkeville 142 E3
Bur-Khaybyt 84 P3
Burkina 114 D2
Burlin 72 K4
Burlington, *Colo., United States* 146 F1
Burlington, *Ia., United States* 142 B2
Burlington, *Vt., United States* 142 F2
Burma = Myanmar 90 B2
Burnet 144 B3
Burney 140 B2
Burnie 126 J8
Burnley 38 F2
Burns 140 C2
Burns Junction 140 C2
Burns Lake 136 F6
Burqin 82 R8
Burra 126 G6
Burrel 70 C3
Burrow Head 36 D7
Bursa 70 M4
Bûr Safâga 110 F2
Bûr Sa'îd 110 F1
Burscough Bridge 38 F2
Bur Sudan 110 G4
Burtnieks 50 N8
Burton upon Trent 38 G3
Buru 93 C3
Burundi 116 D4
Bururi 116 D4
Burwell 140 G2
Bury 38 F2
Buryatiya 84 J6
Bury St. Edmunds 38 J3
Būshehr 101 D2
Bushey 38 H4
Bushire = Būshehr 101 D2
Businga 116 C3
Busira 116 C4
Buşrá ash Shām 100 D4
Bussum 56 H2
Busto Arsizio 64 D5
Buta 116 C3
Butare 116 D4
Butaritari 124 H5
Bute 36 C6
Butembo 116 D3
Buðardalur 50 (1)C2
Buton 93 B3
Butte, *Mont., United States* 140 D1
Butte, *Nebr., United States* 140 G2
Butt of Lewis 36 B3
Butuan 90 H5
Butwal 94 D3
Butzbach 54 D6
Bützow 54 G3
Buulobarde 116 H3
Buur Gaabo 116 G4
Buurhabaka 116 G3
Buxtehude 54 E3
Buxton 38 G2
Buy 72 H3
Buynaksk 98 M2
Büyükada 70 L4
Büyükçekmece 70 L4
Buzai Gumbad 96 K2
Buzançais 60 G7
Buzău 68 P4
Buzău 68 Q4
Buzuluk 72 K4
Byala, *Bulgaria* 68 N6
Byala, *Bulgaria* 68 Q7
Byala Slatina 68 L6
Byam Martin Island 136 L2
Byaroza 50 N10
Bydgoszcz 52 H4
Bygdin 50 D6
Bygland 50 D7
Bykovskiy 84 M2
Bylot Island 136 R2
Byskeälven 50 L4
Bystřice 52 G8
Bystrzyca Kłodzka 52 F7
Bytatay 84 N3
Bytča 52 H8
Bytom 52 H7
Bytów 52 G3
Bzura 52 J5

C

Caaguazú 158 K4
Caballococha 156 C5
Caballo Reservoir 146 E2
Cabañaquinta 62 E1
Cabanatuan 90 G3
Cabano 142 G1
Cabdul Qaadir 110 H5
Cabeza del Buey 62 E6
Cabezas 156 E7
Cabimas 156 C1
Cabinda 114 G6
Cabinda 114 G6
Cabo Bascuñán 158 G4
Cabo Beata 148 K5
Cabo Camarón 148 G5
Cabo Carvoeiro 62 A5
Cabo Catoche 148 G4
Cabo Corrientes, *Colombia* 156 B2
Cabo Corrientes, *Mexico* 148 C4
Cabo Corrubedo 62 A2
Cabo Cruz 148 J5
Cabo de Espichel 62 A6
Cabo de Gata 62 H8
Cabo de Hornos 158 H10
Cabo de la Nao 62 L6
Cabo Delgado 118 G2
Cabo de Palos 62 K7
Cabo de São Roque 156 K5
Cabo de Sao Tomé 158 N3
Cabo de São Vicente 62 A7
Cabo de Trafalgar 62 D8
Cabo dos Bahías 158 H8
Cabo Fisterra 62 A2
Cabo Frio 158 N3
Cabo Gracias á Dios 148 H6
Cabo Mondego 62 A4
Cabo Norte 156 H3
Cabo Orange 156 G3
Cabo Ortegal 62 B1
Cabo Peñas 62 E1
Caborca 146 D2
Cabo Rojo 148 E4
Cabo Roxo 114 A2
Cabo San Diego 158 H9
Cabo San Francisco de Paula 158 H8
Cabo San Juan 114 F4
Cabo San Lucas 138 D7
Cabo Santa Elena 148 J7
Cabo Tortosa 62 L4
Cabo Tres Puntas 158 H8
Cabot Strait 136 U7
Cabrera 62 N5
Čačak 68 H6
Cáceres, *Brazil* 156 F7
Cáceres, *Spain* 62 D5
Cacheu 114 A2
Cachimbo 156 G5
Cachoeira do Sul 158 L4
Cachoeiro de Itapemirim 156 J8
Cacola 118 B2
Caconda 118 B2
Čadca 52 H8
Cader Idris 38 E3
Cadillac, *Mich., United States* 142 C2
Cadillac, *Mont., United States* 138 E2
Cádiz 62 D8
Caen 56 B5
Caernarfon 38 D2
Caernarfon Bay 38 D2
Caerphilly 38 E4
Cagayan de Oro 90 G5
Cagli 64 H7
Cagliari 66 D9
Cagnes-sur-Mer 64 C7
Caguas 148 L5
Cahama 118 A3
Caha Mountains 35 B5
Caher 35 D4
Cahersiveen 35 A5
Cahors 60 G9
Cahuapanas 156 B5
Cahul 68 R4
Caia 118 F3
Caianda 118 C2
Caicos Islands 148 K4
Cairinis 36 A4
Cairngorm Mountains 36 E4
Cairns 126 J3
Cairo = El Qâhira, *Egypt* 110 F1
Cairo, *United States* 144 D2
Cairo Montenotte 64 D6
Caister-on-Sea 38 K3
Caithness 36 E3
Caiundo 118 B3
Cajamarca 156 B5
Čakovec 68 D3
Calabar 114 F3
Calabozo 156 D2
Calabro 66 L9
Calafat 68 K6
Calagua Islands 90 G4
Calahorra 62 J2
Calais 56 D4
Calama, *Brazil* 156 E5
Calama, *Peru* 158 H3
Calamar 156 C3
Calamian Group 90 F4
Calamocha 62 J4
Călan 68 L4
Calanscio Sand Sea 110 D2
Calapan 90 G4
Călărași, *Moldova* 68 R2
Călărași, *Romania* 68 Q5
Calatafim 66 G11
Calatayud 62 J3
Calauag 90 G4
Calbayog 90 G4
Calçoene 156 G3
Calcutta 94 E4
Caldas da Rainha 62 A5
Caldera 158 G4
Caldicot 38 F4
Caldwell, *Id., United States* 140 C2
Caldwell, *Kans., United States* 144 B2
Calf of Man 36 D7
Calgary 136 J6
Calhoun 144 E3
Calhoun City 144 D3
Calhoun Falls 144 E3
Cali 156 B3
Calicut = Kozhikode 94 C6
Caliente 140 D3
California 138 B4
Calilabad 98 N4
Callan 35 D4
Callander 36 D5
Callao 156 B6
Caloundra 126 K5
Caltagirone 66 J11
Caltanissetta 66 J11
Caluquembe 118 A2
Caluula 116 J1
Calvi 66 C6
Calvin 144 B3
Calvinia 118 B6
Calw 64 D2
Camaçari 156 K6
Camacupa 118 B2
Camagüey 148 J4
Camaiore 64 F7
Camana 156 C7
Camargue 60 K10
Camariñas 62 A1
Camarones 158 H7
Ca Mau 90 D5
Camberley 38 H4
Cambodia 90 C4
Camborne 38 C5
Cambrai 56 F4
Cambre 62 B1
Cambria 140 B3
Cambrian Mountains 38 E3
Cambridge, *New Zealand* 128 E3
Cambridge, *United Kingdom* 38 J3
Cambridge, *Md., United States* 142 E3
Cambridge, *Mass., United States* 142 F2
Cambridge, *Oh., United States* 142 D3
Cambridge Bay 136 K3
Cambrils 62 M3
Camden, *Ark., United States* 144 C3
Camden, *S.C., United States* 144 E3
Cameron, *La., United States* 144 C4
Cameron, *Mo., United States* 144 C2
Cameron, *Tex., United States* 144 B3
Cameroon 114 G3
Cametá 156 H4
Çamiçigölü 70 K7
Caminha 62 B3
Camiranga 156 H4
Camocim 156 J4
Camooweal 126 G3
Camopi 156 G3
Campbell Island 128 (2)C2
Campbell River 136 F7
Campbellsville 142 C3
Campbellton 142 G1
Campbeltown 36 C6
Campeche 148 F5
Câmpeni 68 L3
Câmpia Turzii 68 L3
Câmpina 68 N4
Campina Grande 156 L5
Campinas 158 M3
Campobasso 66 J7
Campo de Criptana 62 G5
Campo de Diauarum 156 G6
Campo Gallo 158 J4
Campo Grande 158 L3
Campo Maior 156 J4
Campo Mourão 158 L3
Campos 158 N3
Câmpulung 68 N4
Câmpulung Moldovenesc 68 N2
Cam Ranh 90 D4
Çan 70 K4
Canada 134 M4
Canadian 146 F1
Canadian 146 F1
Çanakkale 70 J4
Çanakkale Boğazı 70 J4
Canal de Panamá 148 J7
Cananea 146 D2
Canary Islands = Islas Canarias 112 A3
Cañaveras 62 H4
Canberra 126 J7
Cancún 148 G4
Çandarli Körfezi 70 J6
Candelaro 68 C8
Candlemas Island 154 J9
Cangamba 118 B2
Cangas 62 B2
Cangas de Narcea 62 D1
Cangyuan 90 B2
Cangzhou 86 F3
Canicattì 66 H11
Canindé 156 K4
Çankiri 98 E3
Canna 36 B4
Cannanore 94 C6
Cannanore 94 B6
Cannes 64 C7
Cannock 38 F3
Canon City 146 E1
Cantanduanes 90 G4
Canterbury 38 K4
Canterbury Bight 128 C7
Canterbury Plains 128 C6
Cân Tho 90 D5
Canto do Buriti 156 J5
Canton, *Miss., United States* 144 D3
Canton, *Oh., United States* 144 E1
Canton, *S.D., United States* 140 G2
Canumã 156 F4
Canumã 156 F5
Canutama 156 E5
Canvey Island 38 J4

Canyon	146	F1
Canyon Ferry Lake	140	D1
Cao Bǎng	90	D2
Caorle	64	H5
Cap Blanc	66	D11
Cap Bon	112	H1
Cap Corse	66	D5
Cap d'Agde	60	J10
Cap d'Antifer	56	C5
Cap de Fer	112	G1
Cap de Formentor	62	P5
Cap de la Hague	60	D4
Cap-de-la-Madeleine	142	F1
Cap de Nouvelle-France	136	S4
Cap de ses Salines	62	P5
Cap des Trois Fourches	62	H9
Cape Agulhas	118	C6
Cape Alexandra	158	P9
Cape Andreas	96	B2
Cape Apostolos Andreas	98	F6
Cape Arid	126	D6
Cape Arnaoutis	98	D6
Cape Arnhem	126	G2
Cape Barren Island	126	J8
Cape Bauld	136	V6
Cape Blanco	140	B2
Cape Borda	126	G7
Cape Breton Island	136	U7
Cape Brett	128	E2
Cape Byron	126	K5
Cape Campbell	128	E5
Cape Canaveral	144	E4
Cape Canaveral	144	E4
Cape Carnot	126	F6
Cape Charles	142	E3
Cape Chidley	136	U4
Cape Christian	136	T2
Cape Churchill	136	N5
Cape Clear	35	B5
Cape Cleare	146	(1)H4
Cape Coast	114	D3
Cape Cod	142	G2
Cape Columbine	118	B6
Cape Colville	128	E3
Cape Comorin	94	C7
Cape Constantine	146	(1)E4
Cape Coral	144	E4
Cape Crawford	126	G3
Cape Croker	126	F2
Cape Dalhousie	146	(1)L1
Cape Direction	126	H2
Cape Disappointment	158	P9
Cape Dominion	136	R3
Cape Dorchester	136	Q3
Cape Dorset	136	R4
Cape Dyer	136	U3
Cape Egmont	128	D4
Cape Eleaia	100	B1
Cape Farewell, *Greenland*	134	F4
Cape Farewell, *New Zealand*	128	D5
Cape Fear	144	F3
Cape Finisterre = Cabo Fisterra	62	A2
Cape Flattery, *Australia*	126	J2
Cape Flattery, *United States*	140	A1
Cape Forestier	126	J8
Cape Foulwind	128	C5
Cape Fria	118	A3
Cape Girardeau	142	C3
Cape Greko	98	F6
Cape Grenville	126	H2
Cape Grim	126	H8
Cape Harrison	136	V6
Cape Hatteras	144	F2
Cape Henrietta Maria	136	Q5
Cape Horn = Cabo de Hornos	158	H10
Cape Howe	126	K7
Cape Inscription	126	B5
Cape Jaffa	126	G7
Cape Karikari	128	D2
Cape Kellett	136	F2
Cape Kidnappers	128	F4
Cape Leeuwin	126	B6
Cape Lévêque	126	D3
Cape Londonderry	126	E2
Cape Lookout	148	J2
Cape May	142	F3
Cape Melville	126	H2
Cape Mendenhall	146	(1)D4
Cape Mendocino	140	A2
Cape Mercy	136	U4
Cape Meredith	158	J9
Cape Naturaliste	126	B6
Capenda-Camulemba	118	B1
Cape Negrais	90	A3
Cape Nelson	126	H7
Cape Newenham	146	(1)E4
Cape of Good Hope	118	B6
Cape Palliser	128	E5
Cape Palmas	114	C4
Cape Parry	136	G2
Cape Providence	128	A8
Cape Race	134	G5
Cape Ray	136	V7
Cape Reinga	128	D2
Cape Romanzof	146	(1)D3
Cape Runaway	128	G3
Cape Sable	136	T8
Cape St. Elias	146	(1)J4
Cape St. Francis	118	C6
Cape San Agustin	90	H5
Cape San Blas	144	D4
Cape Saunders	128	C7
Cape Scott	126	E1
Cape Stephens	128	D5
Cape Terawhiti	128	E5
Cape Three Points	114	D4
Cape Town	118	B6
Cape Turnagain	128	F5
Cape Verde	114	(1)B2
Cape Wessel	126	G2
Cape Wrangell	84	W6
Cape Wrath	36	D3
Cape York	126	H2
Cape York Peninsula	126	H2
Cap Figalo	62	J9
Cap Fréhel	60	C5
Cap Gris-Nez	56	D4
Cap-Haïtien	148	K5
Cap Juby	112	C3
Čapljina	68	E6
Cap Lopez	114	F5
Cap Negro	62	E9
Capo Carbonara	66	D10
Capo Colonna	66	M9
Capo Gallo	66	H10
Capo Granitola	66	G11
Capo Murro di Porco	66	K11
Capo Palinuro	66	J8
Capo Passero	66	K12
Capo Santa Maria di Leuca	66	N9
Capo San Vito	66	G10
Capo Spartivento, *Italy*	66	C10
Capo Spartivento, *Italy*	66	L11
Capo Vaticano	66	K10
Capraia	66	D5
Cap Rhir	112	C2
Capri	66	J8
Capri	66	J8
Capricorn Group	126	K4
Cap Rosa	66	C11
Cap Serrat	66	D11
Cap Spartel	62	E9
Cap Timiris	112	B5
Capua	66	J7
Cap Verga	114	B2
Cap Vert	114	A2
Caquetá	156	C4
Caracal	68	M5
Caracarai	156	E3
Caracas	156	D1
Caransebeş	68	K4
Carauari	156	D4
Caravaca de la Cruz	62	J6
Caravelas	156	K7
Carazinho	158	L4
Carballiño	62	B2
Carballo	62	B1
Carbondale, *Ill., United States*	144	D2
Carbondale, *Pa., United States*	144	F1
Carboneras	62	J7
Carbonia	66	C9
Carcar	90	G4
Carcassonne	60	H10
Cardabia	126	B4
Cardiff	38	E4
Cardigan	38	D3
Cardigan Bay	38	D3
Cardston	140	D1
Carei	68	K2
Carentan	60	D4
Cariacica	158	N3
Cariati	66	L9
Caribbean Sea	148	J6
Caripito	156	E1
Carlet	62	K5
Carleton Place	142	E1
Carlisle, *United Kingdom*	36	F7
Carlisle, *United States*	142	E2
Carlow	35	E4
Carlsbad	146	F2
Carluke	36	E6
Carlyle	140	F1
Carmacks	136	D4
Carmagnola	64	C6
Carmarthen	38	D4
Carmarthen Bay	38	D4
Carmaux	60	H9
Carmel Head	38	D2
Carmen	148	B3
Carmona	62	E7
Carnarvon, *Australia*	126	B4
Carnarvon, *South Africa*	118	C6
Carn Bàn	36	D4
Carnforth	36	F7
Car Nicobar	94	F7
Carnot	116	B2
Carnsore Point	35	E4
Carolina	156	H5
Carolina Beach	144	F3
Caroline Island	124	L6
Caroline Islands	124	E5
Carpathian Mountains	52	J8
Carpații Meridionali	68	K4
Carpentras	60	L9
Carpi	64	F6
Carrabelle	144	E4
Carrara	64	F6
Carrickfergus	35	F2
Carrickmacross	35	E3
Carrick-on-Shannon	35	C3
Carrick-on-Suir	35	D4
Carrington	140	G1
Carrizozo	146	E2
Carroll	142	B2
Carrollton, *Ky., United States*	142	D3
Carrollton, *Mo., United States*	144	C1
Carryduff	35	F2
Çarşamba	98	G3
Carson City	140	C3
Cartagena, *Colombia*	156	B1
Cartagena, *Spain*	62	K7
Carthage	144	C3
Cartwright	136	V6
Caruarú	156	K5
Carúpano	156	E1
Casablanca	112	D2
Casa Grande	146	D2
Casale Monferrato	64	D5
Casalmaggiore	64	F6
Casamozza	66	D6
Casarano	66	N9
Cascade, *Id., United States*	140	C2
Cascade, *Mont., United States*	140	C1
Cascade Range	140	B2
Cascade Reservoir	140	C2
Cascais	62	A6
Cascavel	158	L3
Caserta	66	J7
Cashel, *Republic of Ireland*	35	D4
Cashel, *Zimbabwe*	118	E3
Casiguran	90	G3
Casino	126	K5
Ćasma	64	M5
Caspe	62	K3
Casper	140	E2
Caspian Sea	48	J3
Cassiar	136	F5
Cassino	66	H7
Castanhal	156	H4
Castelbuono	66	J11
Castèl di Sangro	66	J7
Castelfidardo	66	H5
Castellammare del Golfo	66	G10
Castellane	64	B7
Castellaneta	66	L8
Castelli	158	J4
Castelló de la Plana	62	K5
Castelnaudary	60	G10
Castelo Branco	62	C5
Castelsarrasin	60	G10
Castelvetrano	66	G11
Castets	60	D10
Castiglion Fiorentino	64	G7
Castlebar	35	B3
Castlebay	36	A5
Castleblayney	35	E2
Castle Douglas	36	E7
Castleford	38	G2
Castleisland	35	B4
Castle Point	128	F5
Castlerea	35	C3
Castletown, *Isle of Man*	36	D7
Castletown, *Republic of Ireland*	35	D4
Castlewellan	35	F2
Castres	60	H10
Castricum	56	G2
Castries	148	M6
Castro	158	M3
Castro Verde	62	B7
Castrovillari	66	L9
Castuera	62	E6
Çatak	98	K5
Catamarca	158	H4
Catandica	118	E3
Catania	66	K11
Catanzaro	66	L10
Catanzaro Marina	66	L10
Catarman	90	G4
Catbalogan	90	H4
Catió	114	A2
Cat Island	144	F5
Cat Lake	136	N6
Cato Island	126	L4
Catriló	158	J6
Catrimani	156	E3
Catskill Mountains	138	M3
Cattolica	64	H7
Cauayan	90	G5
Cauca	156	C2
Caucaia	156	K4
Caucasia	156	B2
Caucasus	98	K2
Caudry	56	F4
Cauquenes	158	G6
Caura	156	E2
Causapscal	142	G1
Căuşeni	68	S3
Cavaillon	60	L10
Cavalese	64	G4
Cavan	35	D3
Cavarzere	64	H5
Cave	128	C7
Cavinas	156	D6
Cavtat	68	F7
Caxias	156	J4
Caxias do Sul	158	L4
Caxito	114	G6
Çay	70	P6
Cayce	144	E3
Çaycuma	70	Q3
Cayenne	156	G3
Cayman Islands	148	H5
Caynabo	116	H2
Cayos Miskitos	148	H6
Cay Sal Bank	144	E5
Cazorla	62	H7
Ceará	156	J4
Cebu	90	G4
Cebu	90	G4
Cecina	64	F7
Cedar City	140	D3
Cedar Falls	142	B2
Cedar Lake	136	L6
Cedar Rapids	142	B2
Cedros	138	C6
Ceduna	126	F6
Ceerigaabo	116	H1
Cefalù	66	J10
Cegléd	68	G2
Celaya	148	D4
Celebes = Sulawesi	93	A3
Celebes Sea	93	B2
Celje	68	C3
Celldömölk	68	E2
Celle	54	F4
Celtic Sea	58	E10
Centerville	142	B2
Cento	64	G6
Central African Republic	116	C2
Central City	140	G2
Centralia, *Ill., United States*	142	C3
Centralia, *Wash., United States*	140	B1
Central Range	93	F3
Central Siberian Plateau = Srednesibirskoye Ploskogor'ye	80	N2
Cenxi	90	E2
Cerea	64	G5
Ceres, *Argentina*	158	J4
Ceres, *Brazil*	156	H7
Cerezo de Abajo	62	G3
Cerignola	66	K7
Çerikli	98	E4
Çerkes	70	Q4
Çerkezköy	70	K3
Cerknica	64	K5
Cernavodă	68	R5
Cero Champaqui	158	J5
Cerralvo	138	E7
Cërrik	70	C3
Cerritos	146	F4
Cerro Aconcagua	158	G5
Cerro Bonete	158	H4
Cerro de la Encantada	138	C5
Cerro de Pasco	156	B6
Cerro Huehuento	148	C4
Cerro Las Tórtolas	158	H5
Cerro Marahuaca	156	D3
Cerro Mercedario	158	G5
Cerro Murallón	158	G8
Cerro Nevado	158	H6
Cerro Pena Nevade	148	D4
Cerro San Lorenzo	158	G8
Cerro San Valentín	158	G8
Cerros de Bala	156	D6
Cerro Tres Picos	158	J6
Cerro Tupungato	158	H5
Cerro Yaví	156	D2
Cerro Yogan	158	H9
Certaldo	64	G7
Cervaro	66	K7
Cervia	64	H6
Cervionne	66	D6
Cervo	62	C1
Cesano	64	J7
Cesena	64	H6
Cesenatico	64	H6
Cēsis	50	N8
Česka Lípa	54	K6
České Budějovice	64	K2
Český Krumlov	64	K2
Çeşme	70	J6
Česna	64	M5
Cessnock	126	K6
Cestas	60	E9
Cetate	68	L5
Cetinje	68	F7
Cetraro	66	K9
Ceuta	112	D1
Cevizli	70	P7
Chachapoyas	156	B5
Chaco Boreal	158	K3
Chad	110	C5
Chadan	82	S7
Chadron	140	F2
Chagai	96	H4
Chagda	84	N5
Chaghcharān	96	J3
Chagyl	96	G1
Chāh Bahār	96	H4
Chāībāsa	94	E4
Chainat	90	C3
Chaiyaphum	90	C3
Chalais	60	F8
Chalhuanca	156	C6
Chalinze	116	F5
Chalki	70	K8
Chalkida	70	F6
Chalkidiki	70	F4
Challans	60	D7
Challapata	156	D7
Challenger Deep	124	E4
Challis	140	D2
Châlons-sur-Marne	56	G6
Chalon-sur-Saône	60	K7
Cham	54	H7
Chama	118	E2
Chamba	94	C2
Chambal	94	C3
Chamberlain	140	G2
Chambersburg	142	E3
Chambéry	64	A5
Chambly	56	E5
Chamonix	64	B5
Champagnole	64	A4
Champaign	142	C2
Champaubert	56	F6
Champlitte	64	A3
Chañaral	158	G4
Chandalar	136	B3
Chandeleur Islands	148	G3
Chandigarh	94	C2
Chandler	146	D2
Chandrapur	94	C5
Changane	118	E4
Changara	118	E3
Changchun	88	C2
Changde	86	E5
Chang-hua	86	G6
Chang Jiang	86	D4
Changsha	86	E5
Changshou	86	D5
Changshu	86	G4
Changting	86	F5
Changzhi	86	E3
Changzhou	86	F4
Chania	70	G9
Channel Islands	38	(1)F6
Channel Islands	138	C5
Channel-Port aux Basques	136	V7
Chanthaburi	90	C4
Chantilly	56	E5
Chanute	144	B2
Chao Phraya	90	C4
Chaouèn	112	D1
Chao Xian	86	F4
Chaoyang	86	G2
Chaozhou	86	F6
Chapada Diamantina	156	J6
Chapais	142	F1
Chapayev	72	K4
Chapayevo	84	K4
Chapayevskoye	82	N7
Chapecó	158	L4
Chapeltown	38	G2
Chapleau	142	D1
Chapra	94	D3
Chara	84	K5
Charcas	146	F4
Chard	136	J5
Chard	38	F5
Chardara	96	J1
Chardzhev	96	H2
Chari	110	C5
Chārīkār	96	J2

Charleroi	56	G4
Charlesbourg	142	F1
Charleston, *New Zealand*	128	C5
Charleston, *S.C., United States*	144	F3
Charleston, *W. Va., United States*	144	E2
Charlestown, *Republic of Ireland*	35	C3
Charlestown, *United States*	144	D2
Charlestown of Aberlour	36	E4
Charleville	126	J5
Charleville-Mézières	56	G5
Charlevoix	142	C1
Charlotte, *Mich., United States*	142	D2
Charlotte, *N.C., United States*	144	E2
Charlottesville	144	F2
Charlottetown	136	U7
Charlton Island	136	Q6
Charlton Kings	38	F4
Charrat	64	C4
Charsk	82	Q8
Charters Towers	126	J4
Chartres	60	G5
Charymovo	72	Q3
Chasel'ka	84	C3
Chastyye	72	K3
Châteaguay	142	F1
Châteaubriant	60	D6
Châteaudun	60	G5
Châteaulin	60	A5
Châteauneuf-sur-Loire	60	H6
Châteauroux	60	G7
Château-Thierry	56	F5
Châtellerault	60	F7
Châtenois	64	A2
Chatham, *Canada*	142	D2
Chatham, *United Kingdom*	38	J4
Chatham Island	128	(1)B1
Chatham Islands	128	(1)B1
Châtillon-sur Seine	60	K6
Chattanooga	138	J4
Chatteris	38	J3
Chauffayer	64	B6
Chauk	94	F4
Chaumont	60	L5
Chaunskaya Guba	84	V3
Chauny	56	F5
Chaves, *Brazil*	156	G4
Chaves, *Portugal*	62	C3
Chavuma	118	C2
Cheb	54	H6
Cheboksary	72	J3
Chechnya	98	L2
Cheddar	38	F4
Cheduba Island	94	F5
Cheektowaga	142	E2
Chegdomyn	84	N6
Chegga	112	D3
Chegutu	118	E3
Chehalis	140	B1
Cheju	88	D7
Cheju do	88	D7
Chekhov	84	Q7
Chelan	140	C1
Cheleken	96	F2
Chélif	62	L8
Chelkar	82	K8
Chełm	52	N6
Chełmno	52	H4
Chelmsford	38	J4
Chelmźa	52	H4
Cheltenham	38	F4
Chelyabinsk	72	M3
Chelyuskin	82	U2
Chemnitz	54	H6
Chenab	94	B2
Chenachane	112	E3
Cheney Reservoir	144	B2
Chengde	86	F2
Chengdu	86	C4
Chengshan Jiao	88	B5
Chennai	94	D6
Chenzhou	86	E5
Chepes	158	H5
Chepstow	38	F4
Cher	60	G6
Cheraw	144	F3
Cherbaniani Reef	94	B6
Cherbourg	60	D4
Cherchell	62	N8
Cherdyn	72	L2
Cheremkhovo	84	G6
Cherepovets	72	G3
Cherkasy	72	F5
Cherkessk	98	K1
Chermoz	72	L3
Chernihiv	72	F4
Chernivtsi	72	E5
Chernushka	72	L3
Chernyakhovsk	52	L3
Chernyayevo	84	M6
Chernyshevsk	84	K6
Chernyshevskiy	84	J4
Chernyye Zemli	72	J5
Cherokee	142	A2
Cherskiy	84	U3
Cherven Bryag	68	M6
Chervonohrad	72	D4
Chesapeake	144	F2
Cheshskaya Guba	72	J1
Cheshunt	38	H4
Chester, *United Kingdom*	38	F2
Chester, *Calif., United States*	140	B2
Chester, *Mont., United States*	140	D1
Chesterfield	38	G2
Chesterfield Inlet	136	N4
Chester-le-Street	36	G7
Chetumal	148	G5
Chetwynd	136	G5
Cheviot	128	D6
Ch'ew Bahir	116	F3
Cheyenne	140	F2
Cheyenne	140	F2
Cheyenne Wells	146	F1
Cheyne Bay	126	C6
Chhatarpur	94	C4
Chhindwara	94	C4
Chhuka	94	E3
Chia-i	86	G6
Chiang Khan	90	C3
Chiang-Mai	90	B3
Chiang Rai	90	B3
Chiavari	64	E6
Chiavenno	64	E4
Chiba	88	L6
Chibougamau	136	S6
Chibuto	118	E4
Chicago	142	C2
Chicapa	116	C5
Chichagof Island	146	(1)K4
Chichaoua	112	D2
Chichester	38	H5
Chickasha	144	B3
Chiclana de la Frontera	62	D8
Chiclayo	156	B5
Chico	158	H8
Chicopee	142	F2
Chicoutimi	136	S7
Chicualacuala	118	E4
Chiemsee	64	H3
Chieri	64	C5
Chiese	64	F5
Chieti	66	J6
Chifeng	86	F2
Chiganak	82	N8
Chigubo	118	E4
Chihuahua	146	E3
Chili	82	M9
Chikwa	118	E2
Chilas	94	B1
Childress	146	F2
Chile	154	D8
Chile Chico	158	G8
Chilik	82	P9
Chilika Lake	94	D4
Chillán	158	G6
Chillicothe, *Mo., United States*	142	B3
Chillicothe, *Oh., United States*	142	D3
Chilliwack	140	B1
Chiloquin	140	B2
Chilpancingo	148	E5
Chiltern Hills	38	H4
Chi-lung	86	G5
Chimbay	82	K9
Chimborazo	156	B4
Chimbote	156	B5
Chimchememel'	84	V3
Chimec	68	J1
Chimoio	118	E3
China	80	N6
Chincha Alta	156	B6
Chincilla de Monte-Aragón	62	J6
Chinde	118	F3
Chin do	88	C6
Chindwin	90	A2
Chingola	118	D2
Chinguetti	112	C4
Chinhoyi	118	E3
Chiniot	94	B2
Chinju	88	E6
Chinmen	90	F2
Chinnur	94	C5
Chino	88	K6
Chioggia	64	H5
Chios	70	J6
Chios	70	H6
Chipata	118	E2
Chippenham	38	F4
Chippewa Falls	142	B2
Chipping Norton	38	G4
Chipping Sodbury	38	F4
Chirala	94	D5
Chirchik	82	M9
Chirikof Island	146	(1)F5
Chiromo	118	F3
Chirpan	70	H2
Chirripo	148	H7
Chişinău	68	R2
Chişineu-Criş	68	J3
Chita	84	J6
Chitado	118	A3
Chitato	116	C5
Chitembo	118	B2
Chitipa	116	E5
Chitradurga	94	C6
Chitral	94	B1
Chitré	148	H7
Chittagong	94	F4
Chittaurgarh	94	B4
Chittoor	94	C6
Chitungwiza	118	E3
Chiume	118	C3
Chivasso	64	C5
Chizha	72	H1
Chodov	54	H6
Chodzież	52	F5
Choiseul	124	F6
Chojnice	52	G4
Chojnów	52	F6
Chokurdakh	84	R2
Chókwè	118	E4
Cholet	60	E6
Choma	118	D3
Chomutov	52	C7
Chona	84	H4
Chonan	88	D5
Chone	156	A4
Ch'ŏngjin	88	E3
Ch'ŏngju	88	D6
Chŏngju	88	C4
Chŏngp'yŏng	88	D4
Chongqing	80	P7
Chŏngŭp	88	D6
Ch'ŏnju	88	D5
Chonogol	86	F1
Chon Thanh	90	D4
Chop	52	M9
Chorley	38	F2
Chornobyl'	72	F4
Chornomors'ke	72	F5
Ch'osan	88	C3
Chōshi	88	L6
Choszczno	52	E4
Choteau	140	D1
Chott el Hodna	112	F1
Chott el Jerid	112	G2
Chott Melrhir	112	G2
Choûm	112	C4
Choybalsan	84	J7
Choyr	86	D1
Chre	60	H9
Christchurch, *New Zealand*	128	D6
Christchurch, *United Kingdom*	38	G5
Christiansburg	142	D3
Christiansø	52	E2
Christmas Island	92	D5
Chrudim	52	E8
Chrysi	70	H10
Chrysoupoli	68	M9
Chu	82	N9
Chubut	158	H7
Chugach Mountains	136	B4
Chūgoku-sanchi	86	J3
Chugwater	140	F2
Chukchi Sea	146	(1)C2
Chukotskiy Khrebet	84	W3
Chukotskiy Poluostrov	84	Z3
Chula Vista	146	C2
Chulucanas	156	A5
Chulym	82	R6
Chum	72	M1
Chumikan	84	P6
Chum Phae	90	C3
Chumphon	90	B4
Ch'unch'ŏn	88	D5
Chunchura	94	E4
Chundzha	82	P9
Ch'ungju	88	D5
Chuquicamata	158	H3
Chur	64	E4
Churapcha	84	N4
Churchill	136	N5
Churchill, *Man., Canada*	136	M5
Churchill, *Nfld., Canada*	136	U6
Churchill Falls	136	U6
Churchill Peak	136	F5
Church Stretton	38	F3
Churu	94	B3
Chuska Mountains	146	E1
Chusovoy	72	L3
Chute des Passes	136	S7
Chuuk	124	F5
Chuvashiya	72	J3
Chuxiong	90	C2
Chuya	84	J5
Ciadîr-Lunga	68	R3
Cide	98	E3
Ciechanów	52	K5
Ciechocinek	52	H5
Ciego de Avila	148	J4
Cienfuegos	148	H4
Cieza	62	J6
Cihanbeyli	98	E4
Cijulang	92	D4
Cilacap	92	D4
Cili	86	E5
Cimarron	144	B2
Cimişlia	68	R3
Cîmpeni	52	N11
Cinca	62	L3
Cincinnati	142	D3
Çine	70	L7
Ciney	56	H4
Cintalapa	148	F5
Circle, *Ak., United States*	146	(1)J2
Circle, *Mont., United States*	140	E1
Circleville	142	D3
Cirebon	92	D4
Cirencester	38	G4
Cirò Marina	66	M9
Cisco	144	B3
Cistierna	62	E2
Čitluk	68	E6
Citronelle	144	D3
Cittadella	64	G5
Città di Castello	64	H7
Ciucea	68	K3
Ciudad Acuña	146	F3
Ciudad Bolívar	156	E2
Ciudad Camargo	146	E3
Ciudad del Carmen	148	F5
Ciudad del Este	158	L4
Ciudad Delicias	146	E3
Ciudad del Maíz	146	G4
Ciudad de México	148	E5
Ciudad de Valles	148	E4
Ciudad Guayana	156	E2
Ciudad Juárez	146	E2
Ciudad Madero	146	G4
Ciudad Mante	148	E4
Ciudad Obregón	148	C3
Ciudad Real	62	G6
Ciudad-Rodrigo	62	D4
Ciudad Valles	146	G4
Ciudad Victoria	138	G7
Ciutadella	62	P4
Cividale del Friuli	64	J4
Civita Castellana	66	G6
Civitanova Marche	66	H5
Civitavecchia	66	F6
Cizre	98	K5
Clacton-on-Sea	38	K4
Clair Engle Lake	140	B2
Clairview	126	J4
Clamecy	60	J6
Clare	35	A3
Claregalway	35	C3
Claremorris	35	C3
Clarence	128	D6
Clarence Strait	126	E2
Clarendon	146	F2
Clarkdale	146	D2
Clarksburg	144	E2
Clarksdale	144	C3
Clarks Junction	128	C7
Clarkston	140	C1
Clarksville, *Ark., United States*	144	C2
Clarksville, *Tenn., United States*	144	D2
Claro	156	G7
Clausthal-Zellerfeld	54	F5
Claveria	90	G3
Clayton	146	F1
Clear Island	35	B5
Clear Lake	142	B2
Clear Lake Reservoir	140	B2
Clearwater	140	C1
Clearwater	144	E4
Clearwater Mountains	140	C1
Cleburne	144	B3
Cleethorpes	38	H2
Clermont, *Australia*	126	J4
Clermont, *France*	56	E5
Clermont-Ferrand	60	J8
Clervaux	56	J4
Cles	64	F4
Clevedon	38	F4
Cleveland, *Oh., United States*	142	D2
Cleveland, *Tenn., United States*	144	E2
Cleveland, *Tex., United States*	144	B3
Cleveleys	38	E2
Clew Bay	35	B3
Clifden, *New Zealand*	128	A7
Clifden, *Republic of Ireland*	35	A3
Clifton	146	E2
Climax	140	E1
Clines Corners	146	E2
Clinton, *Canada*	136	G6
Clinton, *New Zealand*	128	B8
Clinton, *Ark., United States*	142	B3
Clinton, *Ia., United States*	138	H3
Clinton, *Miss., United States*	144	C3
Clinton, *Mo., United States*	142	B3
Clinton, *N.C., United States*	144	F3
Clinton, *Okla., United States*	144	B2
Clipperton Island	148	C6
Clitheroe	38	F2
Cloghan	35	D3
Clogher Head	35	E3
Clonakilty	35	C5
Clonakilty Bay	35	C5
Cloncurry	126	H4
Clones	35	D2
Clones	35	D2
Clonmel	35	D4
Cloppenburg	54	D4
Cloquet	142	B1
Cloud Peak	140	E2
Clovis, *Calif., United States*	140	C3
Clovis, *N. Mex., United States*	146	F2
Cluj-Napoca	68	L3
Cluny	60	K7
Cluses	64	B4
Clyde	36	E6
Clydebank	36	D6
Clyde River	136	T2
Coaldale	140	C3
Coalville	38	G3
Coari	156	E4
Coast Mountains	136	E5
Coast Range	140	B3
Coatbridge	36	D6
Coats Island	136	Q4
Coatzacoalcos	148	F5
Cobalt	136	R7
Cobán	148	F5
Cobh	35	C5
Cobija	156	D6
Cobourg	138	L3
Cobourg Peninsula	126	F2
Cóbuè	118	E2
Coburg	54	F6
Cochabamba	156	D7
Cochin = Kochi	94	C7
Cochrane	142	D1
Cockburn Town	144	G5
Cockermouth	36	E7
Coco	148	H6
Cocoa	144	E4
Cocobeach	114	F4
Coco Channel	90	A4
Coco Island	90	A4
Codajás	156	E4
Codigoro	64	H6
Cod Island	136	U5
Codlea	68	N4
Codó	156	J4
Codogno	64	E5
Codroipo	64	J5
Cody	140	E2
Coen	126	H2
Coesfeld	54	C5
Coëtivy Island	108	J6
Coeur d'Alene	140	C1
Coeur d'Alene Lake	140	C1
Coevorden	56	J2
Coffs Harbour	126	K6
Cofrents	62	J5
Coggeshall	38	J4
Cognac	60	E8
Cogne	64	C5
Coiba	154	C3
Coihaique	158	G8
Coimbatore	94	C6
Coimbra	62	B4
Colchester	38	J4
Coldstream	36	F6
Colebrook	142	F1
Coleman	144	B3
Coleraine	35	E1
Colesberg	118	D6
Colfax	140	C1
Colibaşi	68	M5
Colico	64	E4
Coll	36	B5
Collado-Villalba	62	F4
Collecchio	64	F6
College Station	144	B3
Collier Bay	126	D3
Collingwood	142	E2
Collins	144	D3
Collooney	35	C2
Colmar	64	C2
Colmenar Viejo	62	G4
Colne	38	F2
Colombia	154	C3
Colombo	94	C7

Colomiers 60 G10
Colonia Las Heras 158 H8
Colonial Heights 142 E3
Colonsay 36 B5
Colorado 140 E3
Colorado, *Colo., United States* 146 E1
Colorado, *Tex., United States* 146 G2
Colorado Plateau 146 D1
Colorado Springs 140 F3
Columbia 140 C1
Columbia, *La., United States* 144 C3
Columbia, *Md., United States* 144 F2
Columbia, *Mo., United States* 144 C2
Columbia, *S.C., United States* 144 E3
Columbia, *Tenn., United States* 144 D2
Columbia Mountains 136 G6
Columbus, *Ga., United States* 144 E3
Columbus, *Ind., United States* 144 D2
Columbus, *Miss., United States* 144 D3
Columbus, *Mont., United States* 140 E1
Columbus, *Nebr., United States* 140 G2
Columbus, *N. Mex., United States* 146 E2
Columbus, *Oh., United States* 144 E1
Columbus, *Tex., United States* 144 B4
Colville 128 E3
Colville 146 (1)G2
Colville Lake 146 (1)M2
Colwyn Bay 38 E2
Comacchio 64 H6
Comănești 68 P3
Comarnic 68 N4
Combarbalá 158 G5
Combeaufontaine 60 M6
Comber 35 F2
Comilla 90 A2
Comino = Kemmuna 66 J12
Commentry 60 H7
Commercy 56 H6
Como 64 E5
Comoé 114 D3
Comondú 138 D6
Comoros 118 G2
Compiègne 56 E5
Comrat 68 R3
Comstock 146 F3
Conakry 114 B3
Concarneau 60 B6
Conceição do Araguaia 156 H5
Concepción, *Bolivia* 156 E7
Concepción, *Chile* 158 G6
Conches-en-Ouche 56 C6
Conchos 148 C3
Concord, *Calif., United States* 146 B1
Concord, *N.H., United States* 142 F2
Concord, *N.C., United States* 144 E2
Concordia, *Argentina* 158 K5
Concordia, *United States* 144 B2
Condé-sur-Noireau 56 B6
Condobolin 126 J6
Condom 60 F10
Conegliano 64 H5
Conggar 94 F3
Congleton 38 F2
Congo 108 E6
Congo 114 G5
Coningsby 38 H2
Conisbrough 38 G2
Connah's Quay 38 E2
Connaught 35 C3
Connecticut 142 F2
Connemara 35 B3
Connemara National Park 35 B3
Conrad 140 D1
Consett 36 G7
Côn Son 90 D5
Constanța 98 C1
Constantina 62 E7
Constantine 112 G1
Consul 140 E1
Contact 140 D2
Contamana 156 B5
Contwoyto Lake 136 J3
Convay 144 F3
Conway 144 C2
Conwy 38 E2
Conwy Bay 38 E2
Coober Pedy 126 F5
Cookeville 142 C3
Cook Inlet 146 (1)G4
Cook Islands 124 K7
Cookstown 35 E2
Cook Strait 128 E5
Cooktown 126 J3
Coolabah 126 J6
Coolgardie 126 D6
Cooma 126 J7
Coonabarabran 126 J6
Coon Rapids 142 B1
Coopers Town 144 F4
Coorabie 126 F6
Coos Bay 140 B2
Cootamundra 126 J6
Copenhagen = København 50 G9
Copertino 66 N8
Copiapó 158 G4
Copper Harbor 142 C1
Côqen 94 E2
Coquille 140 B2
Coquimbo 158 G4
Corabia 68 M6
Coral 138 K1
Coral Harbour 136 Q4
Coral Sea 126 K2
Coral Sea Islands Territory 126 J2
Coral Springs 144 E4
Corantijn 156 F3
Corbeil-Essonnes 60 H5
Corbigny 60 J6
Corbridge 36 F7
Corbu 68 R5
Corby 38 H3
Cordele 144 E3
Cordillera Cantábrica 62 D2
Cordillera Central 154 E5
Cordillera del Condor 156 B5
Cordillera de Mérida 154 D3
Cordillera de Oliva 158 G4
Cordillera Isabella 148 G6
Cordillera Occidental 154 E5
Cordillera Oriental 154 D5
Cordillera Penibética 62 F8
Cordillera Vilcabamba 156 C6
Córdoba, *Argentina* 158 J5
Córdoba, *Spain* 62 F7
Corfu = Kerkyra 70 B5
Coria 62 D5
Corinth 144 D3
Corinto 156 H7
Cork 35 C5
Cork Harbour 35 C5
Corleone 66 H11
Çorlu 70 K3
Corn Islands 154 C2
Cornwall 138 M2
Cornwallis Island 136 M2
Coro 156 D1
Corocoro 156 D7
Coromandel 128 E3
Coromandel Coast 94 D6
Coromandel Peninsula 128 E3
Coron 90 G4
Coronation Gulf 136 J3
Coronel Oviedo 158 K4
Coronel Pringles 158 J6
Coronel Suárez 158 J6
Corpus Christi 144 B4
Corraun Peninsula 35 B3
Corrientes 158 K4
Corrigan 144 C3
Corriverton 156 F2
Corse 66 D6
Corsham 38 F4
Corsica = Corse 66 D6
Corsicana 144 B3
Corte 66 D6
Cortegana 62 D7
Cortez 146 E1
Cortina d'Ampezzo 64 H4
Cortland 142 E2
Cortona 66 F5
Coruche 62 B6
Çorum 98 F3
Corumbá 156 F7
Corvallis 140 B2
Corvo 112 (1)A2
Cosenza 66 L9
Cosmoledo Group 118 (2)A2
Cosne-sur-Loire 60 H6
Cossato 64 D5
Costa Blanca 62 K7
Costa Brava 62 P3
Costa del Sol 62 F8
Costa de Mosquitos 148 H6
Costa Dorada 62 M4
Costa do Sol 62 A6
Costa Rica 148 G7
Costa Smeralda 66 D7
Costa Verde 62 D1
Costești 68 M5
Coswig 54 H5
Cotabato 90 G5
Cotonou 114 E3
Cotswold Hills 38 F4
Cottage Grove 140 B2
Cottbus 52 D6
Cotulla 144 B4
Couhe 60 F7
Coulommiers 56 F6
Council Bluffs 140 F2
Coupar Angus 36 E5
Courland Lagoon 52 L2
Courtacon 56 F6
Courtenay 138 B2
Coushatta 144 C3
Coutances 60 D4
Couvin 56 G4
Covasna 68 P4
Coventry 38 G3
Covilhã 62 C4
Covington, *Ga., United States* 144 E3
Covington, *Ky., United States* 144 E2
Covington, *Va., United States* 142 D3
Cowbridge 38 E4
Cowell 126 G6
Cowes 38 G5
Cowra 126 J6
Cox's Bazar 94 F4
Coy Aike 158 H9
Cradock 118 D6
Craig 140 E2
Craigavon 35 E2
Crail 36 F5
Crailsheim 54 F7
Craiova 68 L5
Cranbrook, *Australia* 126 C6
Cranbrook, *United States* 138 C2
Crater Lake 140 B2
Crato 156 K5
Crawford 140 F2
Crawfordsville 142 C2
Crawley 38 H4
Cray 36 E5
Crediton 38 E5
Cree Lake 136 K5
Creil 56 E5
Crema 64 E5
Cremona 64 F5
Crépy-en-Valois 56 E5
Cres 64 K6
Cres 64 K6
Crescent City 140 B2
Crest 60 L9
Creston 142 B2
Crestview 138 J5
Crestview 148 G2
Crete = Kriti 70 H10
Créteil 56 E6
Creuse 60 G7
Crevillent 62 K6
Crewe 38 F2
Crewkerne 38 F5
Crianlarich 36 D5
Criciúma 158 M4
Crieff 36 E5
Cristalina 156 H7
Cristóbal Colón 134 J8
Crna Gora 68 F7
Croatia 68 C4
Crockett 144 B3
Croker Island 126 F2
Cromer 38 K3
Cromwell 128 B7
Crook 36 G7
Crooked Island 148 K4
Crookston 138 G2
Crosby 38 H2
Cross City 144 E3
Cross Fell 36 F7
Cross Lake 136 M6
Crossville 142 C3
Crotone 66 M9
Crowborough 38 J4
Crowley 144 C3
Crownest Pass 138 D2
Crown Point 142 C2
Croydon 126 H3
Croydon 38 H4
Cruz Alta 158 L4
Cruz del Eje 158 J5
Cruzeiro do Sul 156 C5
Crvenka 68 G4
Crystal City 144 B4
Crystal Falls 142 C1
Crystal River 144 E4
Crystal Springs 144 C3
Csorna 68 E2
Csurgó 64 N4
Cuamba 118 F2
Cuando 118 C3
Cuangar 118 B3
Cuango 116 B5
Cuanza 116 B5
Cuatro Ciénegas 146 F3
Cuauhtémoc 146 E3
Cuba 140 E3
Cuba 148 H4
Cubal 116 A6
Cubali 118 A2
Cubango 118 B3
Çubuk 70 R4
Cucuí 156 D3
Cúcuta 156 C2
Cuddalore 94 C6
Cuddapah 94 C6
Cuemba 118 B2
Cuenca, *Ecuador* 156 B4
Cuenca, *Spain* 62 H4
Cuernavaca 148 E5
Cuero 144 B4
Cuiabá 156 F7
Cuillin Hills 36 B4
Cuilo 116 B5
Cuio 116 A6
Cuito 118 B3
Cuito Cuanavale 118 B3
Culbertson 140 E1
Culfa 98 L4
Culiacán 148 C4
Cullen 36 F4
Cullera 62 K5
Cullman 144 D3
Culpepper 156 (1)A1
Culuene 156 G6
Culverden 128 D6
Cumaná 156 E1
Cumberland 142 E3
Cumberland Peninsula 136 T3
Cumberland Sound 136 T3
Cumbernauld 36 E6
Cumbrian Mountains 36 E7
Cummings 140 B3
Cumnock 36 D6
Cumpas 146 E2
Çumra 70 Q7
Cunderdin 126 C6
Cunene 118 A3
Cuneo 64 C6
Cunnamulla 126 J5
Cuorgne 64 C5
Cupar 36 E5
Ćuprija 68 J6
Cure 60 J6
Curicó 158 G5
Curitiba 158 M4
Currais Novos 156 K5
Curral Velho 114 (1)B1
Currie 126 H7
Curtea de Argeș 68 M4
Curtici 68 J3
Curtis Island 126 K4
Curuá 156 G5
Curup 92 C3
Curuzú Cuatiá 158 K4
Curvelo 156 J7
Cusco 156 C6
Cushendall 35 E1
Cuthbert 144 E3
Cutro 66 L9
Cuttack 94 E4
Cuvier Island 128 E3
Cuxhaven 54 D3
Cuya 156 C7
Cuyuni 156 F2
Cwmbran 38 E4
Cyclades = Kyklades 70 G7
Cypress Hills 138 D2
Cyprus 98 E6
Czarnków 52 F5
Czech Republic 52 C8
Częstochowa 52 J7
Człuchow 52 G4

D

Da'an 86 G1
Daaquam 142 F1
Dab'a 100 D5
Dabas 68 G2
Dabat 110 G5
Dabola 114 B2
Dabra 94 C3
Dąbrowa Górnicza 52 J7
Dąbrowa Tarnowska 52 K7
Dăbuleni 68 M6
Dachau 64 G2
Dadu 94 A3
Daet 90 G4
Dagana 112 B5
Dagestan 98 M2
Dagupan 90 G3
Dahabān 110 G3
Da Hinggan Ling 86 G1
Dahlak Archipelago 110 H4
Dahlonega 144 E3
Dahn 56 K5
Dahod 94 B4
Dahongliutan 96 L2
Dahūk 98 K5
Daimiel 62 G5
Dai Xian 86 E3
Dakar 114 A2
Dakoro 114 F2
Dakota City 140 G2
Dakovica 68 H7
Dakovo 68 F4
Dala 116 C6
Dalai Nur 86 F2
Dalälven 50 H6
Dalaman 98 C5
Dalandzadgad 86 C2
Dalap-Uliga-Darrit 124 H5
Da Lat 90 D4
Dalbandin 96 H4
Dalbeattie 36 E7
Dalby 126 K5
Dalgān 96 G4
Dalhart 146 F1
Dalhousie 94 C2
Dali 90 C1
Dalian 86 G3
Dalizi 88 D3
Dalkeith 36 E6
Dalkey 35 E3
Dallas 144 B3
Dalmā 101 E4
Dalmellington 36 D6
Daloa 114 C3
Dalry 36 D6
Dalrymple Lake 126 J4
Dāltenganj 94 D4
Dalton 144 E3
Dalvík 50 (1)D2
Daly Waters 126 F3
Daman 94 B4
Damanhûr 110 F1
Damar 93 C4
Damara 114 H3
Damasak 114 G2
Damascus = Dimashq 100 D3
Damaturu 114 G2
Dāmiya 100 C4
Damoh 94 C4
Damqawt 96 F6
Damxung 94 F2
Danau Poso 93 A3
Danau Toba 92 B2
Danau Towuti 93 B3
Danba 86 C4
Dandeldhura 94 D3
Dandong 88 C3
Da Năng 90 D3
Daneți 68 M6
Dangara 96 J2
Danger Islands 124 K7
Danghe Nanshan 86 B3
Daniel 140 D1
Danilov 72 H3
Dank 101 G5
Dankov 72 G4
Dannenberg 54 G3
Dannevirke 128 F5
Dansville 142 E2
Danube 48 F3
Danville, *Ill., United States* 144 D1
Danville, *Ky., United States* 144 E2
Danville, *Va., United States* 144 F2
Dan Xian 90 D3
Dao Phu Quôc 90 C4
Dapa 90 H5
Dapaong 114 E2
Da Qaidam 86 B3
Daqing 84 M7
Dar'ā 100 D4
Dārāb 101 F2
Darabani 68 P1
Daraj 110 B1
Dārākūyeh 101 F2
Darazo 114 G2
Dar Ben Karricha el Behri 62 E9
Darbhanga 94 E3
Dardanelles = Çanakkale Boğazı 70 J4
Darende 98 G4
Dar es Salaam 116 F5
Darfo Boario Terme 64 F5
Dargan-Ata 82 L9
Dargaville 128 D2
Darham 84 H7
Darjeeling 94 E3
Darling 126 H6
Darlington 36 G7
Darłowo 50 J9
Dārmănești 68 P3
Dar Mazār 101 G2
Darmstadt 54 D7
Darnah 110 D1
Darnley Bay 136 G3
Daroca 62 J3
Darß 54 H2
Dartford 38 J4
Dartmoor National Park 38 E5
Dartmouth 136 U8
Dartmouth 38 E5
Daru 93 F4

Name	Pg	Ref	Name	Pg	Ref	Name	Pg	Ref	Name	Pg	Ref
Daruba	93	C2	Delray Beach	144	E4	Dieburg	54	D7	Dolores	158	K6
Daruvar	64	N5	Del Rio	146	F3	Diéma	114	C2	Dolphin and Union Strait	136	H3
Darvaza	82	K9	Delta, Colo., United States	140	E3	Diemel	54	E5	Domar	94	D2
Darvel	36	D6	Delta, Ut., United States	140	D3	Diemeringen	54	C8	Domažlice	54	H7
Darwen	38	F2	Delta del Orinoco	156	E2	Diepholz	54	D4	Dombås	50	E5
Darwin	126	F2	Delta Junction	146	(1)H3	Dieppe	56	D5	Dombóvár	68	E3
Daryacheh-ye Bakhtegan	101	E2	Deming	146	E2	Diest	56	H4	Domfront	60	E5
Daryācheh-ye Orūmīyeh	98	L5	Demirci	70	L5	Diffa	114	G2	Dominica	154	E2
Daryacheh-ye Tashk	101	E2	Demmin	54	J3	Digne-les-Bains	64	B6	Dominican Republic	154	D1
Dārzīn	101	H2	Democratic Republic of Congo	116	C4	Digoin	60	J7	Domodossola	64	D4
Dashizhai	86	G1	Demopolis	144	D3	Dijon	60	L6	Domokos	70	E5
Dashkhovuz	82	K9	Demyanka	72	P3	Dikhil	110	H5	Dompu	93	A4
Dasht-e Kavir	96	F3	Dem'yanskoye	72	N3	Dikili	70	J5	Domžale	64	K4
Dasht-e Lut	101	H1	Denain	56	F4	Diklosmta	98	L2	Don	48	H2
Datça	70	K8	Denau	96	J2	Diksmuide	56	E3	Donau = Danube	64	H2
Date	88	L2	Denbigh, Canada	142	E1	Dikson	82	Q3	Donaueschingen	64	D3
Datong	86	E2	Denbigh, United Kingdom	38	E2	Dikwa	114	G2	Donauwörth	54	F8
Datong	86	C3	Den Burg	56	G1	Dīla	116	F2	Don Benito	62	E6
Daugava	72	E3	Dendang	92	D3	Dili	93	C4	Doncaster	38	G2
Daugavpils	72	E3	Dender	56	F4	Dilijan	98	L3	Dondra Head	94	D7
Daun	56	J4	Dendi	116	F2	Dillenburg	54	D6	Donegal	35	C2
Dauphin	136	M6	Dengkou	86	D2	Dilling	110	E5	Donegal Bay	35	C2
Daura	114	F2	Denham	126	B5	Dillingen, Germany	54	F8	Donets	48	H3
Dausa	94	C3	Den Helder	56	G2	Dillingen, Germany	54	B7	Donets'k	72	G5
Dāvāci	98	N3	Dénia	62	L6	Dillingham	146	(1)F4	Dongara	126	B5
Davangere	94	C6	Deniliquin	126	H7	Dillon	138	D2	Dongco	94	D2
Davao	90	H5	Denio	140	C2	Dillon	140	D1	Dongfang	90	D3
Davenport	142	B2	Denison, Ia., United States	142	A2	Dillon Cone	128	D6	Donggala	93	A3
Daventry	38	G3	Denison, Tex., United States	144	B3	Dilolo	118	C2	Donggou	88	C4
David	148	H7	Denizli	98	C5	Dimapur	94	F3	Dongguan	90	E2
Davis Sea	160	(2)Q3	Denmark	126	C6	Dimashq	100	D3	Dông Hôi	90	D3
Davis Strait	136	V3	Denmark	48	E2	Dimitrovgrad, Bulgaria	68	N7	Dongjingcheng	88	E1
Davlekanovo	82	J7	Denmark Strait	134	D3	Dimitrovgrad, Russia	72	J4	Donglük	82	R10
Davos	64	E4	Denpasar	92	E4	Dimitrovgrad, Yugoslavia	68	K7	Dongning	88	F2
Dawa	86	G2	Denton	146	G2	Dîmona	100	C5	Dongo	114	H4
Dawqah, Oman	96	F6	Denton	38	F2	Dinagat	90	H4	Dongola	110	F4
Dawqah, Saudi Arabia	110	H4	D'Entrecasteaux Islands	126	K1	Dinajpur	94	E3	Dongou	114	H4
Dawson	146	(1)K3	Denver	140	F3	Dinan	60	C5	Dongsha Qundao	90	F2
Dawson Creek, B.C., Canada	136	G5	Deogarh, India	94	B3	Dinant	56	G4	Dongsheng	86	E3
Dawson Creek, Y.T., Canada	136	D4	Deogarh, India	94	D4	Dinar	98	D4	Dong Ujimqin Qi	86	F1
Dawu	86	C4	Deoghar	94	E4	Dinard	60	C5	Dongying	86	F3
Dax	60	D10	Déols	60	G7	Dinaric Alps	64	L6	Doniphan	144	C2
Daxian	86	D4	De Panne	56	E3	Dindigul	94	C6	Donji Vakuf	64	N6
Dayong	86	E5	Depok	92	D4	Dindori	94	D4	Donner Pass	140	B3
Dayr az Zawr	98	J6	Dépression du Mourdi	110	D4	Dingle	35	A4	Donostia	62	J1
Dayton, Oh., United States	142	D3	Deputatskiy	84	P3	Dingle Bay	35	A4	Donousa	70	H7
Dayton, Tenn., United States	142	C3	Dêqên	90	B1	Dingolfing	64	H2	Dora	64	C5
Dayton, Tex., United States	144	C4	Dera Ghazi Khan	96	K3	Dinguiraye	114	B2	Dorchester	38	F5
Dayton, Wash., United States	140	C1	Dera Ismail Khan	96	K3	Dingwall	36	D4	Dordrecht	56	G3
Daytona Beach	144	E4	Derbent	96	E1	Dingxi	86	C3	Dorfen	64	H2
Dayu	86	E5	Derby, Australia	126	D3	Dinkelsbühl	54	F7	Dori	114	D2
Dazhu	86	D4	Derby, United Kingdom	38	G3	Dinosaur	140	E2	Doring	118	B6
De Aar	118	C6	De Ridder	144	C3	Diomede Islands	84	AA3	Dorion	142	C1
Dead Sea	100	C5	Dermott	144	C3	Dioriga Kointhou	70	F7	Dorking	38	H4
Deakin	126	E6	Derryveagh Mountains	35	C1	Diourbel	112	B6	Dormagen	56	J3
Deal	38	K4	Dersingham	38	J3	Dipolog	90	G5	Dornbirn	64	E3
De'an	86	F5	Derudeb	110	G4	Dir	94	B1	Dornoch	36	D4
Deán Funes	158	J5	Derventa	68	E5	Dirē Dawa	116	G2	Dornoch Firth	36	D4
Dease Lake	146	(1)M4	Desborough	38	H3	Dirk Hartog Island	126	B5	Doro	114	D1
Dease Strait	136	J3	Desē	110	G5	Dirranbandi	126	J5	Dorog	52	H10
Death Valley	140	C3	Deseado	158	H8	Disko = Qeqertarsuatsiaq	136	V2	Dorohoi	68	P2
Deba Habe	114	G2	Deseado	158	H8	Disko Bugt = Qeqertarsuup Tunua	136	V3	Döröö Nuur	82	S8
Debar	70	C3	Desert Center	146	C2	Diss	38	K3	Dorotea	50	J4
Dębica	52	L7	Des Moines, Ia., United States	138	H3	Distrito Federal	156	H7	Dorsten	56	J3
Debin	84	S4	Des Moines, N. Mex., United States	146	F1	Dithmarschen	54	D2	Dortmund	54	C5
Dęblin	52	L6	Desna	72	F4	Divāndarreh	98	M6	Doruma	116	D3
Dębno	52	D5	Dessau	54	H5	Divinópolis	158	N3	Dos Hermanas	62	E7
Debre Birhan	116	F2	Desvres	56	D4	Divo	114	C3	Dosse	54	H4
Debrecen	68	J2	Deta	68	J4	Divriği	98	H4	Dosso	114	E2
Debre Markos	110	G5	Detmold	54	D5	Dixon	142	C2	Dothan	144	D3
Debrešte	70	D3	Detroit	138	K3	Dixon Entrance	146	(1)L5	Douai	56	F4
Debre Tabor	110	G5	Detroit Lakes	142	A1	Diyarbakir	98	J5	Douala	114	F4
Decatur, Al., United States	142	C4	Det Udom	90	C4	Dja	114	G4	Douarnenez	60	A5
Decatur, Ill., United States	142	C3	Detva	52	J9	Djado	112	H4	Doubs	64	B3
Decazeville	60	H9	Deurne	56	H3	Djamâa	112	G2	Douentza	114	C2
Deccan	94	C5	Deva	68	K4	Djambala	114	G5	Douglas, Isle of Man	36	D7
Děčín	52	D7	Deventer	56	J2	Djanet	112	G4	Douglas, Republic of Ireland	35	C5
Decize	60	J7	Devikot	94	B3	Djelfa	112	F2	Douglas, South Africa	118	C5
De Cocksdorp	56	G1	Devil's Lake	136	L7	Djéma	116	D2	Douglas, Scot., United Kingdom	36	E6
Decorah	142	B2	Devils Lake	140	G1	Djenné	112	E6	Douglas, Ariz., United States	146	E3
Dedoplis	98	M3	Devil's Point	144	F5	Djibo	114	D2	Douglas, Ga., United States	144	E3
Dédougou	114	D2	Devizes	38	G4	Djibouti	110	H5	Douglas, Wyo., United States	140	E2
Dedza	118	E2	Devnya	68	Q6	Djibouti	110	H5	Doullens	56	E4
Dee, Eng., United Kingdom	38	E2	Devon Island	136	P1	Djolu	116	C3	Dourados	158	L3
Dee, Scot., United Kingdom	36	F4	Devonport	126	J8	Djougou	114	E3	Douro	62	B3
Deering	146	(1)E2	Dewangiri	94	F3	Djúpivogur	50	(1)F2	Dover, Australia	126	J8
Deer Lake	136	V7	Dewas	94	C4	Dnestrovsc	68	S3	Dover, United Kingdom	38	K4
Deer Lodge	140	D1	Dewsbury	38	G2	Dnieper	72	F5	Dover, United States	144	F2
Deer Park	140	C1	Deyang	86	C4	Dniester	68	Q1	Dover-Foxcroft	142	G1
De Funiak Springs	144	D3	Deyhuk	96	G3	Dnipro	48	H3	Dowlatābād, Iran	101	E2
Dêgê	86	B4	Deyyer	101	E3	Dniprodzerzhyns'k	72	F5	Dowlatābād, Iran	101	G2
Degeh Bur	116	G2	Dezfūl	96	E3	Dnipropetrovs'k	72	F5	Downham Market	38	J3
Degema	114	F4	Dezhou	86	F3	Dnister	48	G3	Downpatrick	35	D2
Deggendorf	64	J2	Dhahran = Az Zahrān	101	D3	Dno	72	E3	Downpatrick Head	35	B2
Dehaj	101	F1	Dhaka	94	F4	Doba, Chad	116	B2	Dowshī	96	J2
Dehalak Desēt	96	D6	Dhamār	110	H5	Doba, China	94	E2	Drac	64	B6
Deh Bid	101	E1	Dhamtri	94	D4	Dobbiaco	64	H4	Drachten	56	J1
Deh-Dasht	101	D1	Dhanbad	94	E4	Döbeln	54	J5	Dragan	50	H4
Dehiba	112	H2	Dhar	94	C4	Döbern	54	K5	Drăgănești-Olt	68	M5
Dehk'üyeh	101	F3	Dhārwād	94	B5	Doboj	68	F5	Drăgășani	68	M5
Dehlonān	96	E3	Dhaulagiri	94	D3	Dobre Miasto	52	K4	Draguignan	64	B7
Dehra	96	L3	Dhekelia	100	A2	Dobrich	68	Q6	Drakensberg	118	D6
Dehra Dun	94	C2	Dhībān	100	C5	Dobryanka	72	L3	Drake Passage	158	G10
Dehri	94	D4	Dhoraji	94	B4	Doctor Arroyo	146	F4	Drama	70	G3
Deh Shū	96	H3	Dhule	94	B4	Dodecanese = Dodekanisos	70	J8	Drammen	50	F7
Deinze	56	F4	Dhulian	94	E4	Dodge City	140	F3	Drasenhofen	64	M2
Dej	68	L2	Dhuudo	116	J2	Dodoma	116	F5	Drau	64	J4
De Kalb	144	C3	Dhuusa Marreeb	116	H2	Doetinchem	56	J3	Drava	68	E4
De-Kastri	84	Q6	Dia	70	H9	Dofa	93	C3	Dravograd	66	K2
Dekese	116	C4	Diaca	116	G6	Doğanşehir	98	G4	Drawsko Pomorskie	52	E4
Delano	146	C1	Diamantina	156	H7	Dôgo	88	G5	Dresden	54	J5
Delaware	142	D2	Diamantino	156	F6	Dogondoutchi	114	E2	Dreux	56	D6
Delaware	144	F2	Diamond Islets	126	K3	Dogubeyazit	98	L4	Drezdenko	52	E5
Delbrück	54	D5	Diane Bank	126	J3	Doha = Ad Dawḥah	101	D4	Driffield	38	H2
Delémont	64	C3	Dianópolis	156	H6	Doka	93	D4	Drina	68	G5
Delfoi	70	E6	Dibā al Hisn	101	G4	Dokkum	54	H1	Driva	50	E5
Delft	56	G2	Dibbiena	66	F5	Dolak	93	E4	Drniš	68	D6
Delfzijl	56	J1	Dibrugarh	94	F3	Dolbeau	142	F1	Drobeta-Turnu Severin	68	K5
Delgo	110	F3	Dickens	146	F2	Dole	64	A3	Drochia	68	Q1
Delhi, India	94	C3	Dickinson	140	F1	Dolgany	84	E2	Drogheda	35	D2
Delhi, United States	142	F2	Dickson	144	D2	Dolgellau	38	E3	Drohobych	52	N8
Delingha	86	B3	Didcot	38	G4	Dolinsk	84	Q7	Droitwich	38	F3
Delitzsch	54	H5	Didiéni	114	C2	Dollard	54	C3	Dromore	35	D2
Dellys	62	P8	Didymoteicho	70	J3	Dolný Kubín	52	J8	Drôme	60	K9
Delmenhorst	54	D3	Die	60	L9	Dolomiti	64	G4	Dronfield	38	G2
Delnice	64	K5	Diébougou	114	D2	Dolo Odo	116	G3	Dronne	60	F8

Dronning Maud Land	160	(2)F2
Dronten	56	H2
Drummondville	142	F1
Drumnadrochit	36	D4
Druskininkai	50	M9
Druzhina	84	Q3
Drvar	68	D5
Dryanovo	68	N7
Dryden	138	H2
Drymen	36	D5
Drysdale River	126	E3
Dschang	114	G3
Ḍubā	110	G2
Dubai = Dubayy	101	F4
Dubăsari	68	S2
Dubawnt Lake	136	L4
Dubayy	101	F4
Dubbo	126	J6
Dübendorf	64	D3
Dublin, *Republic of Ireland*	35	E3
Dublin, *United States*	144	E3
Dublin Bay	35	E3
Dubna	72	G3
Dubnica	52	H9
Du Bois	142	E2
Dubois, *Id., United States*	140	D2
Dubois, *Wyo., United States*	140	E2
Dubovskoye	72	H5
Dubreka	114	B3
Dubrovnik	68	F7
Dubuque	142	B2
Duchesne	140	D2
Ducie Island	124	P8
Dudelange	56	J5
Duderstadt	54	F5
Dudinka	82	R4
Dudley	38	F3
Duero	62	F3
Dugi Otok	68	B6
Duifken Point	126	H2
Duisburg	56	J3
Duiveland	56	F3
Dukat	84	T4
Duk Faiwil	116	E2
Dukhān	101	D4
Dukla	52	L8
Dukou	86	C5
Dulan	86	B3
Dulce	146	E1
Dulce	158	J4
Dul'Durga	84	J6
Dullewala	94	B2
Dülmen	54	C5
Dulovo	68	Q6
Duluth	142	B1
Dūmā	100	D3
Dumaguete	90	G5
Dumai	92	C2
Dumas, *Ark., United States*	144	C3
Dumas, *Tex., United States*	140	F3
Ḍumayr	100	D3
Dumbarton	36	D6
Ďumbier	52	J9
Dumboa	114	G2
Dumfries	36	E6
Dümmer	54	D4
Dumont d'Urville Sea	160	(2)U3
Dumyât	110	F1
Duna = Danube	68	E2
Dunaj = Danube	52	G10
Dunajská Streda	68	E2
Dunakeszi	68	G2
Dunărea = Danube	68	K5
Dunaújváros	68	F3
Dunav = Danube	68	J5
Dunayivtsi	72	E5
Dunbar, *Australia*	126	H3
Dunbar, *United Kingdom*	38	K4
Dunblane	36	E5
Duncan	140	B1
Duncan Passage	90	A4
Duncansby Head	36	F3
Dundaga	50	M8
Dundalk	35	E2
Dundalk Bay	35	E3
Dundee, *South Africa*	118	E5
Dundee, *United Kingdom*	36	F5
Dundrum Bay	35	F2
Dunedin	128	C7
Dunfanaghy	35	D1
Dunfermline	36	E5
Dungannon	35	E2
Dungarvan	35	D4
Dungarvan Harbour	35	D4
Dungeness	38	J5
Dungiven	35	E2
Dungu	116	D3
Dungun	90	C6
Dungunab	110	G3
Dunhua	88	E2
Dunhuang	86	A2
Dunkeld	36	E5
Dunkerque	56	E3
Dunkirk	142	E2
Dunkwa	114	D3
Dun Laoghaire	35	E3
Dunmanus Bay	35	B5
Dunnet Head	36	E3
Dunoon	36	D6
Duns	36	F6
Dunseith	140	G1
Dunshaughlin	35	E3
Dunsmuir	140	B2
Dunstable	38	H4
Dunvegan	36	B4
Duque de Caxias	158	N3
Du Quoin	144	D2
Durance	60	L10
Durango, *Mexico*	146	F4
Durango, *Spain*	62	H1
Durango, *United States*	140	E3
Durankurak	68	R6
Durant	144	B3
Durazno	158	K5
Durban	118	E5
Durban-Corbières	60	H10
Düren	56	J4
Durgapur	94	E4
Durham, *Canada*	142	D2
Durham, *United Kingdom*	36	G7
Durham, *United States*	144	F2
Duri	92	C2
Durmā	101	B4
Durmanec	68	C3
Durmitor	68	G6
Durness	36	D3
Durrës	70	B3
Durrow	35	D4
Dursey	35	A5
Dursunbey	70	L5
D'Urville Island	128	D5
Dushanbe	96	J2
Düsseldorf	56	J3
Duvno	64	N7
Duyun	86	D5
Düzce	70	P4
Dvina	48	H2
Dvinskaya Guba	72	G1
Dwarka	94	A4
Dworshak Reservoir	140	C1
Dyat'kovo	72	F4
Dyersburg	144	D2
Dyje	64	M2
Dzamin Üüd	84	J8
Dzavhan	82	S8
Dzerzhinsk	72	H3
Dzhalinda	84	L6
Dzhambeyty	72	K4
Dzhankoy	72	F5
Dzhardzhan	84	L3
Dzharkurgan	96	J2
Dzhetygara	72	M4
Dzhezkazgan	72	N5
Dzhigudzhak	84	T4
Dzhizak	82	M9
Dzhusaly	72	M5
Działdowo	52	K4
Dzüünbulag	86	F1
Dzuunmod	86	D1

E

Eads	140	F3
Eagle	146	(1)J3
Eagle Lake	140	B2
Eagle Pass	146	F3
East Antarctica	160	(2)P2
Eastbourne	38	J5
East Cape	128	G3
East China Sea	86	H4
East Dereham	38	J3
Easter Island	124	Q8
Eastern Cape	118	D6
Eastern Ghats	94	C6
Easter Ross	36	D4
East Falkland	158	K9
East Grinstead	38	H4
East Kilbride	36	D6
Eastleigh	38	G5
East Liverpool	144	E1
East London	118	D6
Eastmain	136	R6
Eastmain	136	S6
East Point	144	E3
East Retford	38	H2
East St. Louis	142	B3
East Siberian Sea = Vostochno-Sibirskoye More	84	U2
Eatonton	144	E3
Eau Claire	142	B2
Ebbw Vale	38	E4
Ebensee	64	J3
Eberbach	54	D7
Ebersbach	52	D6
Ebersberg	64	G2
Eberswalde	54	J4
Ebinur Hu	82	Q9
Eboli	66	K8
Ebolowa	114	G4
Ebro	62	K3
Eceabat	70	J4
Ech Chélif	112	F1
Echinos	70	G3
Echo Bay	136	H3
Écija	62	E7
Eckernförde	54	E2
Ecuador	156	B4
Ed	110	H5
Edam	56	H2
Eday	36	F2
Ed Da'ein	110	E5
Ed Damazin	110	F5
Ed Debba	110	F4
Eddrachillis Bay	36	C3
Ed Dueim	110	F5
Ede, *Netherlands*	56	H2
Ede, *Nigeria*	114	E3
Edéa	114	G4
Edelény	52	K9
Eden	36	F7
Eden, *Australia*	126	J7
Eden, *United States*	146	G2
Edendale	128	B8
Eder	54	D5
Edersee	54	E5
Edessa	70	E4
Edgecumbe	128	F3
Edinburgh	36	E6
Edineț	68	Q1
Edirne	70	J3
Edmonds	140	B1
Edmonton	136	J6
Edmundson	138	N2
Edmundston	142	G1
Edolo	64	F4
Edremit	70	J5
Edremit Körfezi	70	H5
Edwards	146	C2
Edwards Plateau	146	F2
Eeklo	56	F3
Eemshaven	56	J1
Éfaté	124	G7
Eferding	52	D9
Effingham	144	D2
Eganville	142	E1
Eger	54	G6
Eger	68	H2
Egersund	50	D7
Eggenfelden	64	H2
Egilsstaðir	50	(1)F2
Egremont	36	E7
Eğridir	70	N7
Eğridir Gölü	70	N6
Egvekinot	84	Y3
Egypt	110	E2
Ehingen	64	E2
Eibar	62	H1
Eichstätt	64	G2
Eider	54	D2
Eidfjord	50	D6
Eidsvold	126	K5
Eidsvoll	50	F6
Eifel	56	J4
Eigg	36	B5
Eight Degree Channel	94	B7
Eilenburg	54	H5
Einbeck	54	E5
Eindhoven	56	H3
Eirunepé	156	D5
Eiseb	118	C4
Eisenach	54	F6
Eisenerz	64	K3
Eisenhüttenstadt	52	D5
Eisenstadt	64	M3
Eisleben	54	G5
Eivissa	62	M5
Eivissa	62	M6
Ejea de los Caballeros	62	J2
Ejido Insurgentes	138	D6
Ejin Horo Qi	86	D3
Ejin Qi	86	C2
Ejmiadzin	98	L3
Ekalaka	140	F1
Ekenäs	50	M7
Eketahuna	128	E5
Ekibastuz	82	P7
Ekimchan	84	N6
Ekonda	82	V4
Eksjo	50	H8
Ekwan	136	Q6
El Aaiún	112	C3
Elafonisos	70	E8
El 'Alamein	110	E1
El Amria	62	J9
El 'Arîsh	100	A5
Elat	100	B7
Elazığ	98	H4
El Azraq	100	D5
Elba	66	E6
El Banco	156	C2
Elbasan	70	C3
El Baúl	156	D2
Elbe	54	F3
Elbeuf	56	D5
Elbistan	98	G4
Elbląg	52	J3
El Borj	62	E9
Elbow	138	E1
Elbrus	98	K2
El Burgo de Ebro	62	K3
El Burgo de Osma	62	G3
El Cajon	146	C2
El Callao	156	E2
El Campo	144	B4
El Centro	146	C2
El Cerro	156	E7
Elch	62	K6
Elda	62	K6
El'dikan	84	P4
Eldorado	158	L4
El Dorado, *Mexico*	138	E7
El Dorado, *Ark., United States*	144	C3
El Dorado, *Kans., United States*	144	B2
El Dorado, *Venezuela*	156	E2
Eldoret	116	F3
Elefsina	70	F6
Elektrėnai	52	P3
El Encanto	156	C4
Elephant Butte Reservoir	146	E2
Eleuthera	138	L6
El Fahs	66	D12
El Faiyûm	110	F2
El Fasher	110	E5
El Geneina	110	D5
Elgin, *United Kingdom*	36	E4
Elgin, *Ill., United States*	142	C2
Elgin, *N.D., United States*	140	F1
El'ginskiy	84	Q4
El Gîza	110	F1
El Goléa	112	F2
El Homr	112	F3
El Iskandarîya	110	E1
Elista	72	H5
Elizabeth	142	F2
Elizabeth City	144	F2
Elizabethton	144	E2
El Jadida	112	D2
El Jafr	100	D6
El Jafr	100	D6
Elk	52	M4
Ełk	52	M4
El Kala	66	C12
Elk City	146	G1
El Kef	66	C12
El Kelaâ des Srarhna	112	D2
El Khandaq	110	F4
El Khârga	110	F2
Elkhart, *Ind., United States*	142	C2
Elkhart, *Kans., United States*	144	A2
El Khartum	110	F4
El Khartum Bahri	110	F4
Elkhorn	140	G2
Elkhorn	142	C2
Elkhovo	70	J2
Elkins	142	E3
Elko, *Canada*	140	C1
Elko, *United States*	140	C2
Elk River	142	B1
El Kuntilla	100	B7
Ellendale	138	G2
Ellensburg	140	B1
Ellesmere	38	F3
Ellesmere Island	134	K1
Ellesmere Port	38	F2
Ellice Islands	124	H6
Elliot	118	D6
Ellis	136	J8
Ellisras	118	D4
Elliston	126	F6
Ellon	36	F4
Ellsworth	142	G2
Ellwangen	64	F2
Elmadağ	70	R5
Elmali	70	M8
El Mansûra	110	F1
El Mazâr	100	A5
El Minya	110	F2
Elmira	142	E2
Elmshorn	54	E3
El Muglad	110	E5
El Nido	90	F4
El Obeid	110	F5
El Odaiya	110	E5
El Oued	112	G2
El Paso	146	E2
Elphin	36	C3
El Portal	146	C1
El Potosí	146	F4
El Prat de Llobregat	62	N3
El Puerto de Santa Maria	62	D8
El Qâhira	110	F1
El Qasr	110	E2
El Quseima	100	B6
El Quweira	100	C7
El Reno	144	B2
El Sahuaro	146	D2
El Salvador	148	F6
Elster	54	H5
Elsterwerda	54	J5
Elstree	38	H4
El Sueco	146	E3
El Suweis	110	F2
Eltanin Bay	160	(2)JJ2
El Tarf	66	C12
El Thamad	100	B7
El Tigre	156	E2
El Turbio	158	G9
Eluru	94	D5
Elvas	62	C6
Elverum	50	F6
Elvira	156	C5
El Wak	116	G3
Ely, *United Kingdom*	38	J3
Ely, *United States*	140	D3
Emajõgi	50	P7
Emāmrūd	96	F2
Emba	72	L5
Emba	72	L5
Embalse de Alarcon	62	H5
Embalse de Alcántara Uno	62	D5
Embalse de Almendra	62	D3
Embalse de Contreras	62	J5
Embalse de Gabriel y Galán	62	D4
Embalse de Garcia Sola	62	E5
Embalse de Guadalhorce	62	F8
Embalse de Guadalmena	62	G6
Embalse de Guri	156	E2
Embalse de la Serena	62	E6
Embalse de la Sotonera	62	K2
Embalse del Bembézar	62	E6
Embalse del Ebro	62	G1
Embalse del Rio Negro	154	F7
Embalse de Negratín	62	G7
Embalse de Ricobayo	62	E3
Embalse de Santa Teresa	62	E4
Embalse de Yesa	62	J2
Embalse Toekomstig	156	F3
Embarcación	158	J3
Emden	54	C3
Emerald	126	J4
Emi Koussi	110	C4
Emin	82	Q8
Emirdağ	70	P5
Emmeloord	56	H2
Emmen	56	J2
Emmendingen	64	C2
Emmerich	56	J3
Emory Peak	146	F3
Empalme	146	D3
Empangeni	118	E5
Empoli	64	F7
Emporia	144	B2
Empty Quarter = Rub' al Khālī	96	E6
Ems	56	J1
Ems-Jade-Kanal	54	C3
Enafors	72	B2
Encarnación	158	K4
Encs	68	J1
Ende	93	B4
Enderby Island	128	(2)B1
Energetik	72	L4
Enewetak	124	F4
Enez	70	J4
Enfida	66	E12
Enfield	38	H4
Engel's	72	J4
Enggano	92	C4
Enghien	56	G4
England	58	L9
English Channel	38	H5
Engozero	50	S4
'En Hazeva	100	C6
Enid	144	B2
Enkhuizen	56	H2
Enköping	50	J7
Enna	66	J11
En Nahud	110	E5
Enngonia	126	J5
Ennis, *Republic of Ireland*	35	C4
Ennis, *United States*	140	D1
Enniscorthy	35	E4
Enniskillen	35	D2
Ennistymon	35	B4

Enn Nâqoûra 100 C3
Enns 64 K2
Enns 64 K3
Enschede 56 J2
Ensenada 146 C2
Enshi 86 D4
Entebbe 116 E3
Enterprise 140 C1
Entrevaux 64 B7
Entroncamento 62 B5
Enugu 114 F3
Enurmino 84 Z3
Envira 156 C5
Enz 64 D2
Enza 64 F6
Epanomi 70 E4
Epéna 116 B3
Épernay 60 J4
Épinal 64 B2
Episkopi 70 Q10
Epsom 38 H4
Eqlid 101 E1
Equatorial Guinea 114 F4
Erbach 54 D7
Erçek 98 K4
Erciş 98 K4
Ercolano 66 J8
Érd 68 F2
Erdek 70 K4
Erdemli 70 S8
Erdenet 84 G7
Erding 64 G2
Erechim 158 L4
Ereğli, *Turkey* 98 D3
Ereğli, *Turkey* 98 F5
Ereikoussa 70 B5
Erenhot 86 E2
Erfurt 54 G6
Ergani 98 H4
Erg Chech 112 D4
Erg du Ténéré 112 H5
Ergel 86 D2
Erg Iguidi 112 D3
Er Hai 86 C5
Erie 142 D2
Erimo 88 M2
Erimo-misaki 88 M3
Eriskay 36 A4
Eritrea 110 G4
Erlangen 54 G7
Ermenek 98 E5
Ermoupoli 70 G7
Ernard Bay 36 C3
Erode 94 C6
Er Rachidia 112 E2
Er Rahad 110 F5
Er Renk 116 E1
Erris Head 35 A2
Errol 142 F2
Er Ruseifa 100 D4
Ersekë 70 C4
Erskine 142 A1
Ertai 82 S8
Ertix 82 R8
Erzgebirge 54 H6
Erzin 82 S7
Erzincan 98 H4
Erzurum 98 J4
Esan-misaki 88 L3
Esashi, *Japan* 88 L3
Esashi, *Japan* 88 M1
Esbjerg 50 E9
Escanaba 142 C1
Escárcega 148 F5
Esch 56 J5
Eschwege 54 F5
Eschweiler 56 J4
Escondido 146 C2
Eséka 114 G4
Eşfahān 96 F3
Eskifjöður 50 (1)G2
Eskilstuna 50 J7
Eskimo Lakes 146 (1)L2
Eskişehir 98 D4
Esla 62 E3
Eslāmābād e Gharb 98 M6
Eslamshahr 96 F2
Esler Dağ 70 M7
Eslö 52 C2
Esmeraldas 156 B3
Esneux 56 H4
Espalion 60 H9
Espanola, *Canada* 142 D1
Espanola, *United States* 140 E3
Espelkamp 54 D4
Esperance 126 D6
Esperance Bay 126 D6
Esperanza 156 C5
Espinho 62 B4
Espírito Santo 156 J7
Espíritu Santo 124 G7
Esplanada 156 K6
Espoo 50 N6
Espungebera 118 E4
Es Samrā 100 D4
Essaouira 112 D2
Es Semara 112 C3
Essen, *Belgium* 56 G3
Essen, *Germany* 56 K3
Essequibo 156 F2
Esslingen 64 E2
Eşţahbānāt 101 F2
Este 64 G5
Estella 62 H2
Estepona 62 E8
Esteros 158 J3
Estevan 138 F2
Estonia 50 M7
Estoril 62 A6
Estrecho de Le Maire 158 H10
Estrecho de Magallanes 158 G9
Estrela 62 C4
Estremoz 62 C6
Estuário do Rio Amazonaz 156 H3
Esztergom 68 F2
Étain 56 H5
Étampes 60 H5
Étang de Berre 60 L10
Étaples 56 D4
Etawah 94 C3
Ethiopia 108 G5
Etolin Strait 146 (1)D3
Etosha Pan 118 B3
Étretat 56 C5
Ettelbruck 54 B7
Ettlingen 54 D8
Eucla 126 E6
Euclid 142 D2
Eufala 144 D3
Eufaula Lake 144 B2
Eugene 140 B2
Eupen 54 B6
Euphrates = Fırat 98 H4
Eure 56 D6
Eureka, *Calif., United States* 140 B2
Eureka, *Mont., United States* 140 C1
Eureka, *Nev., United States* 146 C1
Eureka, *Ut., United States* 140 D3
Europoort 56 F3
Euskirchen 54 B6
Eutin 54 F2
Eutsuk Lake 136 F6
Evans Strait 136 Q4
Evanston, *Ill., United States* 142 C2
Evanston, *Wyo., United States* 140 D2
Evansville 144 D2
Evaz 101 F3
Everett 140 B1
Everglades City 144 E4
Evergreen 144 D3
Evesham 38 G3
Évora 62 C6
Évreux 56 D5
Evron 60 E5
Evros 70 J3
Evvoia 70 F6
Ewo 114 G5
Exaltación 156 D6
Exe 38 E5
Exeter 38 E5
Exmoor National Park 38 E4
Exmouth, *Australia* 126 B4
Exmouth, *United Kingdom* 38 E5
Exuma Sound 138 L7
Eyemouth 36 F6
Eyl 116 H2
Eyre Peninsula 126 G2
Ezine 70 J5

F

Faadippolu Atoll 94 B8
Fåborg 54 F1
Fabriano 64 H7
Fachi 112 H5
Fada 110 D4
Fada Ngourma 114 E2
Faenza 64 G6
Færingehavn = Kangerluarsoruseq 136 W4
Faeroes 48 D1
Fafanlap 93 D3
Făgăraş 68 M4
Fagernes 50 E6
Fagersta 50 H6
Făget 68 K4
Fagurhólsmýri 50 (1)E3
Fahraj 101 H2
Faial 112 (1)B2
Fairbanks 146 (1)H3
Fair Head 35 E1
Fair Isle 36 (1)G2
Fairlie 128 C7
Fairmont 142 B2
Faisalabad 94 B2
Faith 140 F1
Faizabad 94 D3
Fakenham 38 J3
Fakfak 93 D3
Fakse 54 H1
Fakse Bugt 50 G9
Faku 86 G2
Falaise 56 B6
Falaise de Tiguidit 112 G5
Falconara Marittima 64 J7
Falcon Lake 144 B4
Fălești 68 Q2
Falfurrias 144 B4
Falkenberg 50 G8
Falkensee 54 J4
Falkirk 36 E6
Falkland Islands 158 K9
Falkland Sound 158 J9
Falköping 50 G7
Fallingbostel 54 E4
Fallon 140 C3
Fall River 142 F2
Falls City 138 G3
Falmouth, *United Kingdom* 38 C5
Falmouth, *United States* 142 F2
Falmouth Bay 38 C5
Falster 54 H2
Fălticeni 68 P2
Falun 50 H6
Famagusta = Ammochostos 100 A1
Fanchang 86 F4
Fandriana 118 H4
Fangzheng 86 H1
Fannūj 96 G4
Fanø 54 D1
Fano 64 J7
Fanø Bugt 54 D1
Faradje 116 D3
Farafangana 118 H4
Farāh 96 H3
Farah Rud 96 H3
Faranah 114 B2
Fareham 38 G5
Farewell Spit 128 D5
Fargo 138 G2
Faribault 142 B2
Faridabad 94 C3
Farihy Alaotra 118 H3
Färjestaden 52 F1
Farmington, *Me., United States* 142 F2
Farmington, *N. Mex., United States* 146 E1
Farnborough 38 H4
Farne Islands 36 G6
Farnham 38 H4
Fårö 50 K8
Faro, *Brazil* 156 F4
Faro, *Portugal* 62 C7
Fårösund 50 K8
Farquhar Group 118 (2)B3
Farrāshband 101 E2
Farson 140 E2
Fasā 101 E2
Fasano 66 M8
Fategarh 94 C3
Fatehpur 94 D3
Făurei 68 Q4
Fauske 50 H3
Fauville-en-Caux 56 C5
Favara 66 H11
Faversham 38 J4
Favignana 66 G11
Faxaflói 50 (1)B2
Faya 110 C4
Fayette 144 D3
Fayetteville, *Ark., United States* 144 C2
Fayetteville, *N.C., United States* 142 E3
Fayetteville, *Tenn., United States* 144 D2
Faylakah 101 C2
Fažana 66 H4
Fdérik 112 C4
Featherston 128 E5
Fécamp 56 C5
Federated States of Micronesia 124 E5
Fedorovka 72 M4
Fehmarn 54 G2
Feijó 156 C5
Feilding 128 E5
Feira de Santana 156 K6
Feistritz 64 L3
Fejø 54 G2
Feldbach 64 L4
Feldkirch 64 E3
Feldkirchen 64 K4
Felidu Atoll 94 B8
Felixstowe 38 K4
Feltre 64 G4
Femø 54 G2
Femund 50 F5
Fengcheng 88 C3
Fenghua 86 G5
Fengning 86 F2
Feng Xian 86 D4
Feni 94 F4
Fenyang 86 E3
Feodosiya 98 F1
Feres 70 J4
Fergana 96 K1
Fergus Falls 138 G2
Ferkessédougou 114 C3
Ferlach 64 K4
Fermo 66 H5
Fermoy 35 C4
Fernandina Beach 144 E3
Fernandópolis 158 L3
Ferndown 38 G5
Ferrara 64 G6
Ferreira do Alentejo 62 B7
Ferrol 62 B1
Ferryhill 36 G7
Ferry Lake 144 C2
Fès 112 E2
Festus 142 B3
Fetești 68 Q5
Fethiye 70 M8
Fetisovo 96 F1
Fetlar 36 (1)H1
Feucht 54 G7
Feuchtwangen 54 F7
Feyzābād 96 K2
Ffestiniog 38 E3
Fianarantsoa 118 H4
Fianga 116 B2
Fichē 116 F2
Fidenza 64 F6
Fieni 68 N4
Fier 70 B4
Fife Ness 36 F5
Figari 66 D7
Figeac 60 G9
Figline Valdarno 64 G7
Figueira da Foz 62 B4
Figueres 62 N2
Figuig 112 E2
Figuil 114 G3
Fiji 124 H8
Filadélfia 158 J3
Fil'akovo 52 J9
Filey 36 H7
Filiaşi 68 L5
Filicudi 66 J10
Filtu 116 G2
Finale Ligure 64 D6
Findlay 142 D2
Fingoè 118 E3
Finike 70 N8
Finland 50 P3
Finlay 136 F5
Finley 126 J7
Finnsnes 50 K2
Finsterwalde 54 J5
Fionnphort 36 B5
Firat 98 H4
Firenze 64 G7
Firminy 60 K8
Firozabad 94 C3
Firozpur 94 B2
Firth of Clyde 36 D6
Firth of Forth 36 F5
Firth of Lorn 36 C5
Firth of Thames 128 E3
Fish 118 B5
Fisher Strait 136 Q4
Fishguard 38 D4
Fiskenæsset = Qeqertarsuatsiaat 136 W4
Fismes 56 F5
Fitzroy Crossing 126 E3
Fivizzano 64 F6
Fizi 116 D4
Flå 50 E6
Flamborough Head 38 H1
Flaming Gorge Reservoir 140 E2
Flamingo 144 E4
Flannan Islands 36 A3
Flåsjön 50 H4
Flateyri 50 (1)B1
Flathead Lake 140 D1
Flat Point 128 E5
Fleetwood 38 E2
Flekkefjord 50 D7
Flensburg 54 E2
Flensburg Fjorde 54 E2
Flers 56 B6
Flinders Island 126 J7
Flinders Ranges 126 G6
Flinders Reefs 126 J3
Flin Flon 136 L6
Flint, *United Kingdom* 38 E2
Flint, *United States* 142 D2
Flint Island 124 L7
Flirey 64 A2
Flöha 54 J6
Florac 60 J9
Florence = Firenze, *Italy* 64 G7
Florence, *Al., United States* 144 D3
Florence, *S.C., United States* 144 F3
Florencia 156 B3
Florennes 56 G4
Florenville 56 H5
Flores, *Azores* 112 (1)A2
Flores, *Indonesia* 93 B4
Flores Sea 93 A4
Florești 68 R2
Floriano 156 J5
Florianópolis 158 M4
Florida 144 E4
Florida 158 K5
Florida Keys 134 K7
Florina 70 D4
Florissant 142 B3
Florø 50 C6
Floydada 146 F2
Flumendosa 66 D9
Fly 93 F4
Foča 68 F6
Foça 70 J6
Focşani 68 Q4
Foggia 66 K7
Fogo 114 (1)B1
Fogo Island 136 W7
Fohnsdorf 64 K3
Föhr 54 D2
Foix 60 G11
Folegandros 70 G8
Foleyet 142 D1
Foligno 66 G6
Folkestone 38 K4
Folkston 144 E3
Follonica 66 E6
Fomboni 118 G2
Fond du Lac 142 C2
Fondi 66 H7
Fongafale 124 H6
Fontainebleau 60 H5
Fontana 66 M8
Fonte Boa 156 D4
Fontenay-le-Comte 60 E7
Fontur 50 (1)F1
Fonyód 66 M2
Forbach, *France* 56 J5
Forbach, *Germany* 56 L6
Forchheim 54 G7
Førde 50 C6
Fordingbridge 38 G5
Fordyce 144 C3
Foreland Point 38 E4
Forest, *Canada* 142 D2
Forest, *United States* 144 D3
Forest of Bowland 38 F2
Forest of Dean 38 F4
Forestville 142 G1
Forfar 36 F5
Forges-les-Eaux 56 D5
Forks 140 B1
Forli 64 H6
Formazza 64 D4
Formby 38 E2
Formentera 62 M6
Formia 66 H7
Formiga 158 M3
Formosa, *Brazil* 156 H7
Formosa, *Paraguay* 158 K4
Fornovo di Taro 64 F6
Forres 36 E4
Forsayth 126 H3
Forssa 50 M6
Forst 54 K5
Forsyth 140 E1
Fort Abbas 94 B3
Fortaleza 156 K4
Fort Augustus 36 D4
Fort Bayne 142 C4
Fort Beaufort 118 D6
Fort Benton 140 D1
Fort Bragg 146 B1
Fort Chipewyan 136 J5
Fort Cobb Reservoir 144 B2
Fort Collins 140 E2
Fort-de-France 148 M6
Fort Dodge 142 B2
Forte dei Marmi 64 F7
Fortezza 64 G4
Fort Frances 142 B1
Fort George 136 R6
Fort Gibson Lake 144 B2
Fort Good Hope 136 F3
Forth 36 D5
Fort Hope 136 P6
Fortín Coronel Eugenio Garay 158 J3
Fort Kent 142 G1

Fort Lauderdale 144 E4
Fort Liard 136 G4
Fort Mackay 136 J5
Fort Macleod 140 D1
Fort McMurray 136 J5
Fort McPherson 146 (1)L2
Fort Munro 96 J4
Fort Myers 144 E4
Fort Nelson 136 G5
Fort Norman 146 (1)M3
Fort Payne 144 D3
Fort Peck Reservoir 140 E1
Fort Pierce 144 E4
Fort Pierre 140 F2
Fort Portal 116 E3
Fort Providence 136 H4
Fortrose 128 B8
Fort Rupert 136 R6
Fort St. John 136 G5
Fort Saint Lucie 144 E4
Fort Scott 144 C2
Fort Severn 136 P5
Fort Shevchenko 82 J9
Fort Simpson 136 G4
Fort Smith, *Canada* 136 J4
Fort Smith, *United States* 144 C2
Fort Stockton 146 F2
Fort Summer 146 F2
Fortuna 140 F1
Fortune Bay 136 V7
Fortuneswell 38 F5
Fort Vermilion 136 H5
Fort Wayne 144 D1
Fort William 36 C5
Fort Worth 144 B3
Fort Yates 140 F1
Foshan 90 E2
Fosna 50 F5
Fossano 64 C6
Fossombrone 64 H7
Fougamou 114 G5
Fougères 60 D5
Foula 36 (1)F1
Foulness 38 K4
Foumban 114 G3
Fourmies 56 G4
Fournoi 70 J7
Fouta Djallon 114 B2
Foveaux Strait 128 A8
Fowey 38 D5
Foxe Basin 136 R3
Foxe Channel 136 R4
Foxe Peninsula 136 R4
Fox Glacier 128 B6
Fox Islands 146 (1)D5
Foz 62 C1
Foz do Cunene 118 A3
Foz do Iguaçu 158 L4
Fraga 62 L3
Franca 158 M3
Francavilla al Mare 66 J6
France 60 G7
Franceville 114 G5
Francisco I. Madero 146 F4
Francistown 118 D4
Francs Peak 140 E2
Franeker 56 H1
Frankenberg 54 D5
Frankenthal 54 D7
Frankfort, *Ind., United States* 144 D1
Frankfort, *Ky., United States* 144 E2
Frankfurt, *Germany* 54 K4
Frankfurt, *Germany* 54 D6
Franklin, *N.C., United States* 142 D3
Franklin, *Tenn., United States* 142 C3
Franklin Bay 136 F2
Franklin D. Roosevelt Lake 140 C1
Franklin Mountains 136 F3
Franklin Strait 136 M2
Franz Josef Glacier 128 C6
Franz Josef Land =
Zemlya Frantsa-Iosifa 82 J2
Fraser 136 G6
Fraserburg 118 C6
Fraserburgh 36 F4
Fraser Island 126 K5
Frasertown 128 F4
Frater 142 D1
Frauenfeld 64 D3
Fredensborg 52 B2
Frederick, *Md., United States* 142 E3
Frederick, *Okla., United States* 144 B3
Fredericksburg, *Tex., United States* 144 B3
Fredericksburg, *Va., United States* 142 E3
Fredericktown 142 B3
Fredericton 136 T7
Frederikshåb = Paamiut 136 X4
Frederikshavn 50 F8
Frederikssund 52 B2
Frederiksværk 50 G9
Fredrikstad 50 F7
Freeport, *Ill., United States* 142 C2
Freeport, *Tex., United States* 144 B4
Freeport City 144 F4
Freer 144 B4
Free State 118 D5
Freetown 114 B3
Fregenal de la Sierre 62 D6
Freiberg 54 J6
Freiburg 64 C3
Freilassing 64 H3
Freising 64 G2
Freistadt 64 K2
Fréjus 60 M10
Fremantle 126 C6
Fremont, *Calif., United States* 146 B1
Fremont, *Nebr., United States* 138 G3
Frenchglen 140 C2
French Guiana 156 G3
French Pass 128 D5
French Polynesia 124 L7
Frenda 112 F1
Fresnes-sur-Apances 64 A3
Fresnillo 148 D4
Fresno 146 C1
Fresno Reservoir 140 E1
Freudenstadt 64 D2
Freyung 54 J8
Frias 158 H4
Fribourg 64 C4
Friedburg 64 G2
Friedrichshafen 64 E3
Friesach 64 K4
Friesoythe 54 C3
Frisian Islands 56 H1
Fritzlar 54 E5
Frobisher Bay 136 T4
Frodsham 38 F2
Frolovo 72 H5
Frome 38 F4
Frontera 148 F5
Frontignan 60 J10
Frosinone 66 H7
Frøya 50 D5
Fruges 56 E4
Frýdek Místek 52 H8
Fudai 88 L4
Fuding 86 G5
Fuengirola 62 F8
Fuentesauco 62 E3
Fuerte Olimpo 158 K3
Fuerteventura 112 C3
Fugu 86 E3
Fuhai 82 R8
Fujieda 88 K6
Fujin 84 N7
Fuji-san 88 K6
Fukuchiyama 88 H6
Fukue 88 E7
Fukue-jima 88 E7
Fukui 88 J5
Fukuoka 88 F7
Fukushima 88 L5
Fukuyama 88 G6
Fulda 54 E6
Fulda 54 E6
Fuling 86 D5
Fulton 144 D2
Funabashi 88 L6
Funafuti 124 H6
Funchal 112 B2
Fundão 62 C4
Funing 90 D2
Funtua 114 F2
Furano 88 M2
Fürg 101 F2
Furmanovka 82 N9
Furmanovo 72 J5
Furneaux Group 126 J8
Furqlus 100 E2
Fürstenberg 54 J3
Fürstenfeldbruck 64 G2
Fürstenwalde 54 K4
Fürth 54 F7
Furukawa 88 L4
Fushun 88 B3
Fusong 88 D2
Füssen 64 F3
Futog 68 G4
Fuxhou 86 F5
Fu Xian 86 D3
Fuxin 86 G2
Fuyang 86 F4
Fuyu 86 G1
Fuyun 82 R8
Fuzhou 90 F1
Fyn 54 F1
Fynshav 54 F2

G

Gaalkacyo 116 H2
Gabès 112 H2
Gabon 114 G5
Gaborone 118 D4
Gābrik 101 H4
Gabrovo 68 N7
Gacé 56 C6
Gacko 68 F6
Gäddede 50 H4
Gadsden 144 D3
Găeşti 68 N5
Gaeta 66 H7
Gafsa 112 G2
Gaggenau 64 D2
Gagnoa 114 C3
Gagra 98 J2
Gaildorf 64 E2
Gaillac 60 G10
Gainesville, *Fla., United States* 144 E4
Gainesville, *Ga., United States* 144 E3
Gainesville, *Mo., United States* 144 C2
Gainesville, *Tex., United States* 144 B3
Gainsborough 38 H2
Gairloch 36 C4
Gai Xian 88 B3
Gala 94 E3
Galana 116 F4
Galanta 64 N2
Galapagos Islands =
Islas Galápagos 156 (1)B1
Galashiels 36 F6
Galatas 70 F7
Galaţi 68 R4
Galdhøpiggen 50 D6
Galena 146 (1)F3
Galesburg 142 B2
Galich 72 H3
Gallabat 110 G5
Gallan Head 36 A3
Galle 94 D7
Gallipoli 66 N8
Gallipolis 144 E2
Gällivare 50 L3
Galloway 36 D6
Gallup 146 E1
Galtat Zemmour 112 C3
Galveston Bay 138 G6
Galway 35 B3
Galway Bay 35 B3
Gamalakhe 118 E6
Gambēla 116 E2
Gambell 84 Z4
Gambier Islands 124 N8
Gamboma 116 B4
Gamboula 116 B3
Gan 84 L7
Ganado 146 E1
Gäncä 98 M3
Gandajika 116 C5
Gander 136 W7
Ganderkesee 54 D3
Gandesa 62 L3
Gāndhīdhām 94 B4
Gandhinagar 94 B4
Gandia 62 K6
Gandu 156 K6
Ganganagar 94 B3
Gangara 114 F2
Gangdise Shan 94 D2
Ganges 60 J10
Ganges 94 E3
Gangi 66 J11
Gangtok 94 E3
Gannett Peak 140 E2
Ganta 114 C3
Ganye 114 G3
Ganzhou 86 E5
Gao 112 E5
Gaoual 112 C6
Gap 64 B6
Gapan 90 G3
Garanhuns 156 K5
Garba 114 J3
Garbsen 54 E4
Gardelegen 54 G4
Garden City 140 F3
Gardēz 96 J3
Gardone Val Trompia 64 F5
Gargždai 52 L2
Gariau 93 D3
Garies 118 B6
Garissa 116 F4
Garland 144 B3
Garlasco 64 D5
Garliava 52 N3
Garmisch-Partenkirchen 64 G3
Garnett 144 B2
Garonne 60 E9
Garoowe 116 H2
Garoua 114 G3
Garoua Boulaï 114 G3
Garren Point 35 F1
Garry Lake 136 L3
Garsen 116 G4
Garut 92 D4
Garwa 94 D4
Garwolin 52 L6
Gary 138 J3
Garyarsa 94 D2
Garzê 86 B4
Gasan Kuli 96 F2
Gasht 96 H4
Gashua 114 G2
Gastonia 144 E2
Gastre 158 H7
Gatchina 72 F3
Gatehouse of Fleet 36 D7
Gateshead 36 G7
Gatesville 144 B3
Gatineau 142 E1
Gatley 38 F2
Gatrūyeh 101 F2
Gauja 50 N8
Gaula 50 F5
Gaurella 94 D4
Gauteng 118 D5
Gava 62 N3
Gāvbandī 101 E3
Gavdos 70 G10
Gävle 50 J6
Gawler 126 G6
Gawler Ranges 126 G6
Gaxun Nur 86 C2
Gaya, *India* 94 E4
Gaya, *Niger* 114 E2
Gaylord 142 D1
Gayndah 126 K5
Gayny 72 K2
Gaywood 38 J3
Gaza 100 B5
Gaz-Achak 82 L9
Gazandzhyk 82 K10
Gaza Strip 100 B5
Gaziantep 98 G5
Gazipaşa 70 Q8
Gazli 82 L9
Gaz Şāleh 101 G2
Gbaaka 114 C3
Gbarnga 114 C3
Gdańsk 52 H3
Gdov 50 P7
Gdyel 62 K9
Gdynia 52 H3
Gebel el Tīh 100 A7
Gebel Halâl 100 A6
Gebel Katherina 110 F2
Gebel Yi'allaq 100 A6
Gebze 70 M4
Gedaref 110 G5
Gediz 70 M6
Gediz 70 K6
Gedser 54 G2
Geel 56 H3
Geelong 126 H7
Geesthacht 54 F3
Gē'gvai 94 D2
Geidam 114 G2
Geilenkirchen 56 J4
Geilo 50 E6
Geinhausen 54 E6
Geislingen 64 E2
Geita 116 E4
Gejiu 90 C2
Gela 66 J11
Geladī 116 H2
Geldern 56 J3
Geleen 56 H4
Gelendzhik 98 H1
Gelibolu 70 J4
Gelibolu Yarimadasi 70 J4
Gelsenkirchen 56 K3
Gembloux 56 G4
Gembu 114 G3
Gemena 116 B3
Gemlik 70 M4
Gemlik Körfezi 70 L4
Gemona del Friuli 64 J4
Genalē Wenz 116 G2
General Acha 158 J6
General Alvear 158 H6
General Pico 158 J6
General Pinedo 158 J4
General Roca 158 H6
General Santos 90 H5
Geneva 142 E2
Genève 64 B4
Gengma 90 B2
Genil 62 F7
Genk 56 H4
Genoa = Genova 64 D6
Genova 64 D6
Gent 56 F3
Genteng 92 D4
Genthin 54 H4
Geographe Bay 126 B6
George 118 C6
George 136 T5
George Town, *Australia* 126 J8
George Town, *Malaysia* 92 C1
George Town, *United States* 144 F5
Georgetown, *Australia* 126 H3
Georgetown, *Gambia* 114 B2
Georgetown, *Guyana* 156 F2
Georgetown, *Ky., United States* 144 E2
Georgetown, *S.C., United States* 144 F3
Georgetown, *Tex., United States* 144 B3
George West 144 B4
Georgia 144 E3
Georgia 98 K2
Georgian Bay 142 D1
Gera 54 H6
Geraldine 128 C7
Geraldton, *Australia* 126 B5
Geraldton, *Canada* 138 J2
Gérardmer 64 B2
Gerāsh 101 F3
Gerede 98 E3
Gerefsried 64 G3
Gereshk 96 H3
Gérgal 62 H7
Gerik 90 C5
Gerlach 140 C2
Germantown 142 C3
Germany 54 E6
Germencik 70 K7
Germering 64 G2
Germersheim 56 L5
Gernika 62 H1
Gerolzhofen 54 F7
Gërzë 94 D2
Geser 93 D3
Getafe 62 G4
Gettysburg 140 F2
Getxo 62 H1
Geugnon 60 K7
Gevaş 98 K4
Gevgelija 70 E3
Gewanē 110 H5
Geyik Dağ 70 Q8
Geyser 140 D1
Geyve 70 N4
Ghabāghib 100 D3
Ghadāmis 112 G2
Ghadīr Minqār 100 E3
Ghana 114 D3
Ghanzi 118 C4
Gharandal 100 C6
Ghardaïa 112 F2
Gharo 96 J5
Gharyān 112 H2
Ghāt 110 B2
Ghazaouet 112 E1
Ghaziabad 94 C3
Ghazipur 94 D3
Ghazn 96 J3
Gheorgheni 68 N3
Gherla 68 L2
Ghizar 94 B1
Ghotāru 94 B3
Ghōwrī 101 F2
Ghunthur 100 E2
Giannitsa 70 E4
Giannutri 66 F6
Giarre 66 K11
Gibraleón 62 D7
Gibraltar 62 E8
Gibson Desert 126 D4
Gideån 50 K5
Gien 60 H6
Gießen 54 D6
Gifhorn 54 F4
Gifu 88 J6
Gigha 36 C6
Giglio 66 E6
Giglio Castello 66 E6
Gijón 62 E1
Gila 146 E2
Gila Bend 146 D2
Gilan Garb 98 L6
Gilău 68 L3
Gilazi 98 N3
Gilbert Islands 124 H5
Gilbués 156 H5
Gilching 64 G2
Gilf Kebir Plateau 110 E3
Gilgandra 126 J6
Gilgit 94 B1
Gilimanuk 92 E4
Gillam 136 N5
Gillette 140 E2
Gillingham 38 J4
Gills Rock 142 C1

Gilroy 140 B3
Gîmbī 116 F2
Gimli 136 M6
Gimol'skoe Ozero 50 R5
Gīnīr 116 G2
Gioia del Colle 66 L8
Gioia Tauro 66 K10
Gioura 70 F5
Girdle Ness 36 G4
Giresun 98 H3
Girga 110 F2
Girona 62 N3
Gironde 60 E8
Girvan 36 D6
Gisborne 128 G4
Gisenyi 116 D4
Gitega 116 D4
Giurgiu 68 N6
Givet 56 G4
Givors 60 K8
Giyon 116 F2
Gizhiga 84 U4
Gizhiginskaya Guba 84 T4
Giżycko 52 L3
Gjiri i Vlorës 70 B4
Gjirokastër 70 C4
Gjoa Haven 136 M3
Gjøvik 50 F6
Glacier Peak 140 B1
Gladstone 126 K4
Glamoč 68 D5
Glan 54 C7
Glan 93 C1
Glarner Alpen 64 D4
Glasgow, *United Kingdom* 36 D6
Glasgow, *Ky., United States* 142 C3
Glasgow, *Mont., United States* 140 E1
Glastonbury 38 F4
Glauchau 54 H6
Glazov 82 J6
Gleisdorf 64 L3
Glen Affric 36 D4
Glendale, *Ariz., United States* 146 D2
Glendale, *Calif., United States* 146 C2
Glendambo 126 G6
Glendive 140 F1
Glenfinnan 36 C5
Glengormley 35 F2
Glen Mor 36 D4
Glenmorgan 126 J5
Glennallen 146 (1)H3
Glenn Innes 126 K5
Glenrothes 36 E5
Glens Falls 142 F2
Glenveagh National Park 35 D1
Glenwood, *Ark., United States* 142 B4
Glenwood, *Minn., United States* 142 A1
Glenwood, *N. Mex., United States* 146 E2
Glenwood Springs 140 E3
Glidden 142 B1
Glina 64 M5
Gliwice 52 H7
Glodeni 68 Q2
Głogów 52 F6
Glomfjord 50 H3
Glomma 50 F5
Glorieuses 108 H7
Glossop 38 G2
Gloucester, *United Kingdom* 38 F4
Gloucester, *United States* 142 F2
Głowno 52 J6
Głuchołazy 52 G7
Glückstadt 54 E3
Gmünd, *Austria* 64 J4
Gmünd, *Austria* 64 L2
Gmunden 64 J3
Gniezno 52 G5
Gnjilane 70 D2
Gnoien 54 H3
Goalpara 94 F3
Goba 116 F2
Gobabis 118 B4
Gobernador Gregores 158 G8
Gobi Desert 86 C2
Gobo 88 H7
Gobustan 96 E1
Goch 56 J3
Gochas 118 B4
Godalming 38 H4
Godbout 142 G1
Godē 116 G2
Goderich 142 D2
Godhra 94 B4
Gödöllő 68 G2
Gods Lake 136 N6
Godthåb = Nuuk 136 W4
Goeree 56 F3
Goes 56 F3
Gogama 142 D1
Goiânia 156 H7
Goiás 156 G6
Goiás 156 G7
Gökçeada 70 H4
Gökova Körfezi 70 K8
Göksun 98 G5
Golaghat 94 F3
Golan Heights 100 C3
Golbāf 101 G2
Gölbasi 98 G5
Gol'chikha 82 Q3
Gölcük 70 K5
Gołdap 52 M3
Gold Coast 126 K5
Golden Bay 128 D5
Goldendale 140 B1
Golden Gate 146 B1
Golden Vale 35 C4
Goldfield 140 C3
Goldsboro 142 E3
Goldsworthy 126 C4
Göle 98 K3
Goleniów 52 D4
Golestānak 101 F1
Golfe d'Ajaccio 66 C7
Golfe de Gabès 112 H2
Golfe de Hammamet 112 H1
Golfe de Porto 66 C6
Golfe de Sagone 66 C6
Golfe de Saint-Malo 60 C5
Golfe de Tunis 66 E11
Golfe de Valinco 66 C7
Golfe du Lion 60 J10
Golfo de Almería 62 H8
Golfo de Batabanó 148 H4
Golfo de Cádiz 62 C7
Golfo de California 148 B3
Golfo de Chiriquí 148 H7
Golfo de Corcovado 158 F7
Golfo de Cupica 156 B2
Golfo de Fonseca 148 G6
Golfo de Guayaquil 156 A4
Golfo de Honduras 148 G5
Golfo del Darién 156 B2
Golfo dell' Asinara 66 C7
Golfo de los Mosquitos 156 A2
Golfo de Mazarrón 62 J7
Golfo de Morrosquillo 156 B1
Golfo de Panamá 148 J7
Golfo de Penas 158 F8
Golfo de San Jorge 158 H8
Golfo de Santa Clara 146 D2
Golfo de Tehuantepec 148 E5
Golfo de València 62 L5
Golfo de Venezuela 156 C1
Golfo di Augusta 66 K11
Golfo di Catania 66 K11
Golfo di Gaeta 66 H7
Golfo di Gela 66 J11
Golfo di Genova 66 C4
Golfo di Manfredonia 66 L7
Golfo di Olbia 66 D8
Golfo di Oristano 66 C9
Golfo di Orosei 66 D8
Golfo di Palmas 66 C10
Golfo di Policastro 66 K9
Golfo di Salerno 66 J8
Golfo di Santa Eufemia 66 K10
Golfo di Squillace 66 L10
Golfo di Taranto 66 L8
Golfo di Trieste 64 J5
Golfo di Venezia 64 H5
Golfo San Matías 158 J6
Gölhisar 70 M8
Golin Baixing 88 A1
Gölköy 98 G3
Gölmarmara 70 K6
Golyshmanovo 82 M6
Goma 116 D4
Gombe 114 G2
Gombi 114 G2
Gomera 112 B3
Gómez Palacio 146 F3
Gonam 84 M5
Gonbad-e Kavus 96 G2
Gonda 94 D3
Gonder 110 G5
Gondia 94 D4
Gondomar 62 B3
Gönen 70 K4
Gonfreville-Orcher 56 C5
Gongga Shan 86 C5
Gonghe 86 C3
Gongliu 82 Q9
Gongpoquan 86 B2
Gongshan 90 B1
Gonzáles 138 G7
Gonzales 144 B4
González 146 G4
Goodland 140 F3
Goodwick 38 D3
Goole 38 H2
Goolgowi 126 J6
Goomalling 126 C6
Goondiwindi 126 K5
Goose Lake 140 B2
Göppingen 64 E2
Góra 52 F6
Gora Bazardyuzi 98 M3
Gora Kamen 82 S4
Gorakhpur 94 D3
Gora Ledyanaya 84 W4
Gora Pobeda 84 R4
Gora Yenashimskiy Polkan 82 S6
Goražde 68 F6
Gorbitsa 84 K6
Goré 114 H3
Gorē 116 F2
Gore 128 B8
Gorey 35 E4
Gorgān 96 F2
Gorgona 64 E7
Gori 98 L2
Gorinchem 56 H3
Goris 98 M4
Gorizia 64 J5
Gorki 72 N1
Gorlice 52 L8
Görlitz 52 D6
Gorna Oryakhovitsa 68 N6
Gornji Milanovac 68 H5
Gorno-Altaysk 82 R7
Gorno Oryakhovitsa 70 H1
Gorodets 72 H3
Gorontalo 93 B2
Gort 35 C3
Gorumna 35 B3
Goryachiy Klyuch 98 H1
Gory Belukha 82 R8
Gory Ulutau 72 N5
Gorzów Wielkopolski 52 E5
Goslar 54 F5
Gospić 66 K4
Gosport 38 G5
Gossau 64 E3
Gossi 114 D1
Gostivar 70 C3
Gostyń 52 G6
Gostynin 52 J5
Göteborg 50 F8
Gotha 54 F6
Gothèye 114 E2
Gotland 50 K8
Gotō-rettō 88 E7
Gotse Delchev 70 F3
Gotska Sandön 50 K7
Göttingen 54 E5
Gouda 56 G2
Gough Island 108 B10
Goundam 112 E5
Gouraya 62 M8
Gourcy 114 D2
Gourdon 60 G9
Gournay-en-Bray 56 D5
Gourock 36 D6
Governador Valadares 156 J7
Governor's Harbour 144 F4
Govorovo 84 M3
Gowārān 96 J4
Gower 38 D4
Goya 158 K4
Gozha Co 94 D1
Gozo = Gwardex 66 J12
Graaff-Reinet 118 C6
Grabovica 68 K5
Gračac 64 L6
Gračanica 68 F5
Gradačac 68 F5
Gräfenhainichen 54 H5
Grafton, *Australia* 126 K5
Grafton, *United States* 140 G1
Graham Island 146 (1)L5
Grajaú 156 H5
Grajewo 52 M4
Gram 54 E1
Gramat 60 G9
Grampian Mountains 36 E5
Granada, *Nicaragua* 148 G6
Granada, *Spain* 62 G7
Granard 35 D3
Granby 142 F1
Gran Canaria 112 B3
Grand Bahama 144 F4
Grand Ballon 60 N6
Grand Bank 136 V7
Grand Canal 35 D3
Grand Canyon 140 D3
Grande, *Bolivia* 156 E7
Grande, *Brazil* 156 J6
Grande Cache 136 H6
Grande Prairie 136 H5
Grand Erg de Bilma 112 H5
Grand Erg Occidental 112 E3
Grand Erg Oriental 112 F3
Grand Falls, *N.B., Canada* 142 G1
Grand Falls, *Nfld., Canada* 136 V7
Grand Forks, *Canada* 138 C2
Grand Forks, *United States* 140 G1
Grand Haven 142 C2
Grand Island 140 G2
Grand Junction 140 E3
Grand Marais, *Mich., United States* 142 C1
Grand Marais, *Minn., United States* 142 B1
Grand-Mère 142 F1
Grândola 62 B6
Grand Portage 142 C1
Grand Rapids, *Canada* 136 M6
Grand Rapids, *Mich., United States* 142 C2
Grand Rapids, *Minn., United States* 142 B1
Grand Teton 140 D2
Grange 35 C2
Grangemouth 36 E5
Grangeville 140 C1
Granite Falls 142 A2
Granollers 62 N3
Gran Paradiso 64 C5
Grantham 38 H3
Grantown-on-Spey 36 E4
Grants 146 E1
Grants Pass 140 B2
Granville 60 D5
Granville Lake 136 M5
Gräsö 50 K6
Grasse 64 B7
Grassrange 140 E1
Grass Valley 140 B3
Graulhet 60 G10
Graus 62 L2
Gravelines 56 E3
Gravenhurst 142 E2
Gravesend 38 J4
Gravina in Puglia 66 L8
Gray 60 L6
Grayling 142 D2
Grays 38 J4
Grays Lake 140 D2
Grayville 142 C3
Graz 64 L3
Great Abaco 144 F4
Great Artesian Basin 126 H4
Great Australian Bight 126 E6
Great Bahama Bank 148 J4
Great Barrier Island 128 E3
Great Barrier Reef 126 J2
Great Basin 140 C3
Great Bear Lake 146 (1)M2
Great Bend 146 G1
Great Dividing Range 126 J4
Greater Antilles 148 J5
Greater Sunda Islands 124 B6
Great Exhibition Bay 128 D2
Great Exuma 138 L7
Great Falls 140 D1
Great Inagua 148 K4
Great Karoo 118 C6
Great Malvern 38 F3
Great Nicobar 94 F7
Great Ormes Head 36 E2
Great Ouse 38 J3
Great Plains 140 F2
Great Rift Valley 116 E5
Great Salt Lake 140 D2
Great Salt Lake Desert 140 D2
Great Sand Sea 110 D2
Great Sandy Desert 126 D4
Great Slave Lake 134 N3
Great Torrington 38 D5
Great Victoria Desert 126 E5
Great Wall 86 C3
Great Yarmouth 38 K3
Greece 70 D5
Greeley 140 F2
Green 140 D3
Green Bay 142 C2
Greenfield 144 D2
Greenland 134 G2
Greenland Sea 134 B2
Greenlaw 36 F6
Greenock 36 D6
Green River, *Wyo., United States* 140 E2
Green River, *Ut., United States* 140 D3
Greensboro 144 F2
Greensburg, *Ind., United States* 144 D2
Greensburg, *Pa., United States* 142 E2
Greenvale 126 J3
Green Valley 148 B2
Greenville, *Liberia* 114 C3
Greenville, *Al., United States* 144 D3
Greenville, *Fla., United States* 144 E3
Greenville, *Miss., United States* 144 C3
Greenville, *N.C., United States* 142 E3
Greenville, *S.C., United States* 144 E3
Greenwood, *Miss., United States* 144 C3
Greenwood, *S.C., United States* 144 E3
Gregory 140 G2
Gregory Lake 126 E4
Greifswald 54 J2
Greifswalder Bodden 54 J2
Greiz 54 H6
Grenada 138 J5
Grenada 156 E1
Grenchen 64 C3
Grenoble 60 L8
Gretna 144 C4
Gretna 36 E7
Greve in Chianti 64 G7
Greven 56 K2
Grevena 70 D4
Grevenbroich 56 J3
Grevesmühlen 54 G3
Greybull 140 E2
Greymouth 128 C6
Grey Range 126 H5
Griesheim 54 D7
Grieskirchen 64 J2
Grigoriopol 68 S2
Grimma 54 H5
Grimmen 54 J2
Grimsby 38 H2
Grimsey 50 (1)D1
Grimsstaðir 50 (1)E2
Grímsvötn 50 (1)E2
Grindsted 50 E9
Grobina 52 L1
Gröbming 64 J3
Grodekovo 86 J2
Grodzisk Wielkopolski 52 F5
Grójec 52 K6
Gronau 54 C4
Groningen 54 B3
Groote Eylandt 126 G2
Grootfontein 118 B3
Großenhain 54 J5
Großer Arber 54 J7
Grosser Beerberg 54 F6
Grosseto 66 F6
Groß-Gerau 54 D7
Großglockner 64 H3
Groß Mohrdorf 54 H2
Groswater Bay 136 V6
Grottaglie 66 M8
Groupe Actéon 124 N8
Grove Hill 144 D3
Groznyy 98 L2
Grubišno Polje 68 E4
Grudovo 70 K2
Grudziądz 52 H4
Gruinard Bay 36 C4
Grünau 118 B5
Grünberg 54 D6
Gryazi 72 G4
Gryazovets 72 H3
Gryfice 52 E4
Gryfino 54 K3
Grytøya 50 J2
Grytviken 158 P9
Gstaad 64 C4
Guadalajara, *Mexico* 148 D4
Guadalajara, *Spain* 62 G4
Guadalcanal 124 F7
Guadalope 62 K4
Guadalquivir 62 E7
Guadalupe 148 E3
Guadalupe 148 A3
Guadeloupe 154 E2
Guadiana 62 C7
Guadix 62 G7
Guaíra 158 L3
Guajará Mirim 156 D6
Guajarraã 156 D5
Guam 124 E4
Guanambi 156 J6
Guanare 156 D2
Guane 148 H4
Guangshui 86 E4
Guangyuan 86 D4
Guangzhou 90 E2
Guanipa 156 E2
Guanling 86 D5
Guantánamo 148 J4
Guanyun 86 F4
Guaporé 156 E6
Guaqui 156 D7
Guarabira 156 K5
Guarda 62 C4
Guardo 62 F2
Guasave 138 E6
Guastalla 64 F6
Guatemala 148 F5
Guatemala 148 F6
Guaviare 156 D3
Guayaquil 156 B4
Guayaramerín 156 D6
Guaymas 146 D3
Guba, *Dem. Rep. of Congo* 116 D6

Guba, *Ethiopia* 110 G5
Guba Buorkhaya 84 N2
Gubakha 72 L3
Guban 116 G2
Gubbi 94 C6
Gubbio 64 H7
Guben 54 K5
Gubin 52 D6
Gudaut'a 98 J2
Gudbrandsdalen 50 E6
Gudermes 98 M2
Gudvangen 50 D6
Guebwiller 54 C9
Guéckédou 114 B3
Guelma 112 G1
Guelph 142 D2
Guérande 60 C6
Guéret 60 B7
Guernsey 140 F2
Guernsey 38 (1)F6
Guérou 112 C5
Guerrero Negro 146 D3
Gugē 116 F2
Gūh Kūh 96 G4
Guiana 148 L7
Guiana Highlands 156 F3
Guider 114 G3
Guiglo 114 C3
Guijuelo 62 E4
Guildford 38 H4
Guilianova 66 H6
Guilin 90 E1
Guillaumes 64 B6
Guillestre 64 B6
Guimarães 62 B3
Guinea 114 B2
Guinea-Bissau 114 A2
Güines 148 H4
Guingamp 60 B5
Güiria 156 E1
Guisborough 36 G7
Guise 56 F5
Guitiriz 62 C1
Guiyang 86 D5
Gujranwala 94 B2
Gujrat 94 B2
Gulang 86 C3
Gulbarga 94 C5
Gulbene 50 P8
Gulf of Aden 96 E7
Gulf of Alaska 146 (1)H4
Gulf of Aqaba 96 B4
Gulf of Boothia 136 N2
Gulf of Bothnia 50 K6
Gulf of Carpentaria 126 G2
Gulf of Finland 50 M7
Gulf of Gdansk 52 J3
Gulf of Guinea 114 D4
Gulf of Mannar 94 C7
Gulf of Martaban 90 B3
Gulf of Mexico 148 F3
Gulf of Oman 101 G4
Gulf of Riga 50 M8
Gulf of St. Lawrence 136 U7
Gulf of Santa Catalina 146 C2
Gulf of Thailand 90 C4
Gulf of Tongking 90 D3
Gulfport 144 D3
Gulistan 82 M9
Gülşehir 70 S6
Gulu 116 E3
Gülübovo 70 H2
Gumdag 96 F2
Gumel 114 F2
Gumla 94 D4
Gummersbach 56 K3
Gummi 114 F2
Gümüşhane 98 H3
Guna 94 C4
Guna Terara 110 G5
Gungu 116 B5
Gunib 98 M2
Gunnbjørns Fjeld 160 (1)U2
Gunnedah 126 K6
Gunnison, *Colo., United States* 140 E3
Gunnison, *Ut., United States* 140 D3
Gunong Kinabalu 92 F1
Guntakal 94 C5
Guntur 94 D5
Gunung Kerinci 92 C3
Gunung Korbu 92 C2
Gunung Kwoka 93 D3
Gunung Leuser 92 B2
Gunung Mekongga 93 B3
Gunung Mulu 92 E2
Gunung Pangrango 92 D4
Gunungsitoli 92 B2
Gunung Togwomeri 93 D3
Günzburg 64 F2
Gunzenhausen 54 F7
Guoyang 86 F4
Gura Humorului 68 N2
Gurk 64 K4
Gurskoye 84 P6
Gürün 98 G4
Gurupi 156 H4
Gusau 114 F2
Gusev 52 M3
Gushgy 96 H2
Gusinoozersk 84 H6
Guspini 66 C9
Güssing 64 M3
Güstrow 52 B4
Gütersloh 54 D5
Guthrie, *Okla., United States* 140 G3
Guthrie, *Tex., United States* 146 F2
Gutsuo 94 E3
Guttenberg 142 B2
Guwahati 94 F3
Guyana 156 F2
Guyang 86 E2
Guymon 146 F1
Guyuan 86 D3
Guzar 96 J2
Gvardejsk 52 L3
Gwadar 96 H4
Gwalior 94 C3
Gwanda 118 D4
Gwardex 66 J12
Gwda 52 F4
Gweebarra Bay 35 C2
Gweru 118 D3
Gyangzê 94 E3
Gyaring Hu 86 B4
Gyaros 70 G7
Gyda 82 P3
Gydanskiy Poluostrov 82 P3
Gyirong 94 E3
Gyldenløves Fjord 136 Y4
Gympie 126 K5
Gyomaendrőd 68 H3
Gyöngyös 68 G2
Győr 68 E2
Gypsumville 136 M6
Gytheio 70 E8
Gyula 68 J3
Gyumri 98 K3
Gyzylarbat 96 G2

H

Haapajärvi 50 N5
Haapsalu 50 M7
Haar 64 G2
Haarlem 56 G2
Haast 128 B6
Habahe 82 R8
Habarūt 96 F6
Habaswein 116 F3
Habbān 96 E7
Habbānīyah 98 K7
Habirag 86 F2
Habomai-Shoto 84 R8
Haboro 88 L1
Hachijō-jima 88 K7
Hachinohe 88 L3
Hachiōji 88 K6
Hadadong 82 Q9
Haddington 36 F6
Haddunmahti Atoll 94 B8
Hadejia 114 G2
Hadejia 114 F2
Hadera 100 B4
Haderslev 54 E1
Ḩaḑramawt 96 E6
Hadilik 82 R10
Hadjout 62 N8
Hadleigh 38 J3
Hadrian's Wall 36 F6
Haeju 88 C4
Haenam 88 D6
Ḩafar al Bāţin 101 A2
Hafik 98 G4
Hafnarfjörður 50 (1)C2
Haft Gel 101 C1
Hagen 56 K3
Hagenow 54 G3
Hägere Hiywet 116 F2
Hagerstown 142 E3
Ha Giang 86 C6
Haguenau 56 K6
Haicheng 88 B3
Haifa = Hefa 100 B4
Haikou 90 E3
Hā'il 96 D4
Hailar 84 K7
Hailey 140 D2
Hailong 88 C2
Hailsham 38 J5
Hailuoto 50 N4
Hainan 90 D3
Haines Junction 146 (1)K3
Haining 86 G4
Hai Phong 90 D2
Haiti 148 K5
Haiya 110 G4
Hajdúböszörmény 68 J2
Hajdúhadház 52 L10
Hajdúnánás 52 L10
Hajdúszoboszló 52 L10
Hajipur 94 E3
Ḩājjīābād 101 F2
Hajmah 96 G6
Hajnówka 52 N5
Haka 94 F4
Hakkâri 98 K5
Hakodate 88 L3
Ḩalab 98 G5
Ḩalabān 110 H3
Ḩalabja 98 L6
Halaib 110 G3
Halba 100 D2
Halberstadt 54 G5
Halden 50 F7
Haldensleben 54 G4
Halesowen 38 F3
Halifax 136 U8
Halifax 38 G2
Halifax Bay 126 J3
Halkirk 36 E3
Hall 64 G3
Hall Beach 136 Q3
Halle 56 G4
Hallein 64 J3
Halligen 54 D2
Hallock 140 G1
Hall Peninsula 136 T4
Halls Creek 126 E3
Halmahera 93 C2
Halmahera Sea 93 C3
Halmstad 52 B1
Halstead 38 J4
Haltern 56 K3
Haltwhistle 36 F7
Hamada 88 G6
Hamadān 96 E3
Hamaguir 112 E2
Ḩamāh 98 G6
Hamamatsu 88 J6
Hamar 50 F6
Hamarøy 50 H2
Hamatonbetsu 88 M1
Hambantota 94 D7
Hamburg, *Germany* 54 E3
Hamburg, *Ark., United States* 144 C3
Hamburg, *N.Y., United States* 142 E2
Hämeenlinna 50 N6
Hameln 54 E4
Hamersley Range 126 C4
Hamhŭng 88 D3
Hami 82 S9
Hamīd 110 F3
Hamilton, *Australia* 126 H7
Hamilton, *Bermuda* 148 M2
Hamilton, *Canada* 142 E2
Hamilton, *New Zealand* 128 E3
Hamilton, *United Kingdom* 36 D6
Hamilton, *Al., United States* 144 D3
Hamilton, *Mont., United States* 140 D1
Hamilton, *Oh., United States* 142 D3
Hamina 50 P6
Hamirpur 94 D3
Hamm 54 C5
Hammada du Drâa 112 D3
Hammam Bou Hadjar 62 K9
Hammamet 66 E12
Hammam Lif 112 H1
Hammelburg 54 E6
Hammerfest 50 M1
Hammer Springs 128 D6
Hampden 128 C7
Hampshire Downs 38 G4
Hāmūn-e Jaz Mūrīān 101 H3
Ḩanalc 110 G2
Hanamaki 88 L4
Hanau 54 D6
Hâncești 68 R3
Hancheng 86 E3
Hancock 142 C1
Handan 86 E3
Handeni 116 F5
Handerslev 50 E9
Handlová 52 H9
Hanford 146 C1
Hangayn Nuruu 82 T8
Hangu 86 F3
Hangzhou 86 F4
Hanīdh 101 C3
Hanko 50 M7
Hanksville 140 D3
Hanna 136 K6
Hannibal 144 C2
Hannover 54 E4
Hanö 52 D2
Hanöbukten 52 D2
Ha Nôi 90 D2
Hanoi = Ha Nôi 90 D2
Hanover 142 F2
Han Shui 86 D4
Hanson Bay 128 (1)B1
Hanumangarh 94 B3
Hanzhong 86 D4
Hao 124 M7
Häora 94 E4
Haouza 112 C3
Haparanda 50 N4
Hāpoli 94 F3
Hapur 94 C3
Ḩaraḑ, *Saudi Arabia* 96 E5
Ḩaraḑ, *Yemen* 110 H4
Haramachi 88 L5
Harare 118 E3
Harbin 86 H1
Harbour Breton 136 V7
Harburg 54 F3
Hardangerfjorden 50 C7
Hardangervidda 50 D6
Hardenberg 56 J2
Harderwijk 56 H2
Hardin 140 E1
Hardy 144 C2
Haren 56 K2
Härer 116 G2
Hargeysa 116 G2
Har Hu 86 B3
Haridwar 94 C3
Harihari 128 C6
Harima-nada 88 H6
Hari Rud 96 H3
Harlan 142 A2
Hârlău 68 P2
Harlech 38 D3
Harlem 140 E1
Harlingen, *Netherlands* 56 H1
Harlingen, *United States* 144 B4
Harlow 38 J4
Harlowtown 140 E1
Harney Basin 138 B3
Harney Lake 140 C2
Härnösand 50 J5
Har Nur 84 K7
Har Nuur 82 S8
Haro 62 H2
Haroldswick 36 (1)H1
Harpenden 38 H4
Harricanaw 136 R6
Harrisburg, *Ill., United States* 142 C3
Harrisburg, *Pa., United States* 144 F1
Harrison 142 B3
Harrison Bay 146 (1)G1
Harrisville 142 D2
Harrogate 38 G2
Harrow 38 H4
Har Saggi 100 B6
Harsin 98 M6
Hârşova 68 Q5
Harstad 50 J2
Hartberg 64 L3
Hartford 142 F2
Hartland Point 38 D4
Hartlepool 36 G7
Har Us Nuur 82 S8
Harvey 140 G1
Harwich 38 K4
Harz 54 F5
Häsā 100 C6
Haselünne 54 C4
Hashtpar 98 N5
Häsik 96 G6
Haskell 144 B3
Haslemere 38 H4
Hassan 94 C6
Hasselfelde 54 F5
Hasselt 56 H4
Haßfurt 54 F6
Hassi Bel Guebbour 112 G3
Hassi Messaoud 112 G2
Hässleholm 50 G8
Hastings, *New Zealand* 128 F4
Hastings, *United Kingdom* 38 J5
Hastings, *Minn., United States* 142 B2
Hastings, *Nebr., United States* 140 G2
Haţeg 68 K4
Hatfield 38 H4
Hatgal 84 G6
Ha Tinh 90 D3
Hatteras 144 F2
Hattiesburg 144 D3
Hatvan 68 G2
Haud 110 H6
Haud Ogadēn 116 G2/H2
Haugesund 50 C7
Hauraki Gulf 128 E3
Haut Atlas 112 D2
Hauts Plateaux 112 E2
Havana 144 C1
Havana = La Habana 148 H4
Havant 38 H5
Havel 52 C5
Havelock, *New Zealand* 128 D5
Havelock, *United States* 144 F3
Havelock North 128 F4
Havenby 54 D1
Haverfordwest 38 D4
Haverhill 38 J3
Havlíčkův Brod 52 E8
Havre 140 E1
Havre-St-Pierre 136 U6
Havrylivtsi 68 P1
Havza 98 F3
Hawaii 146 (2)E2
Hawaii 146 (2)E4
Hawaiian Islands 124 J3
Hawera 128 E4
Hawes 36 F7
Hawi 146 (2)F3
Hawick 36 F6
Hawke Bay 128 F4
Hawker 126 G6
Hawr al'Awdah 101 B1
Hawr al Ḩammar 101 B1
Hawthorne 140 C3
Hay 126 H6
Hay 136 H5
Hayange 56 J5
Haydarābad 98 L5
Hayden 146 D2
Hayrabolu 70 K3
Hay River 136 H4
Hays 144 B2
Haywards Heath 38 H5
Hazard 142 D3
Hazārībāg 94 E4
Hazebrouck 56 E4
Hazel Grove 38 F2
Hazelton, *Canada* 136 F5
Hazelton, *United States* 142 E2
Head of Bight 126 F6
Hearne 144 B3
Hearst 142 D1
Hebbronville 146 G3
Hebgen Lake 140 D2
Hebi 86 E3
Hebron, *Canada* 136 U5
Hebron, *Israel* 100 C5
Hebron, *Nebr., United States* 140 G2
Hebron, *N.D., United States* 140 F1
Hecate Strait 136 E6
Hechi 90 D2
Hechingen 64 D2
Hede 50 G5
Heerenveen 56 H2
Heerlen 56 J4
Ḩefa 100 B4
Hefei 86 F4
Hegang 86 J1
Hegura-jima 88 J5
Hegyfalu 64 M3
Heide 54 E2
Heidelberg 54 D7
Heidenheim 64 F2
Heilbad Heiligenstadt 54 F5
Heilbronn 54 E7
Heiligenhafen 54 F2
Heimaey 50 (1)C3
Heinola 50 N6
Hejing 82 R9
Hekla 50 (1)D3
Helagsfjället 50 G5
Helena, *Ark., United States* 144 C3
Helena, *Mont., United States* 140 D1
Helen Reef 93 D2
Helensburgh 36 D5
Helensville 128 E3
Helgea 52 D1
Helgoland 54 C2
Helgoländer Bucht 54 D2
Hellin 62 J6
Helmand 96 H3
Helmond 56 H3
Helmsdale 36 E3
Helmsley 36 G7
Helmstedt 54 G4
Helodrano Antongila 118 H3
Helong 88 E2
Helsingborg 50 G8
Helsinge 52 B1
Helsingør 50 G8
Helsinki 50 N6
Helston 38 C5
Helwan 110 F2
Hemel Hempstead 38 H4
Hemsworth 38 G2

Henashi-zaki 88 K3
Hendek 70 N4
Henderson, *Ky., United States* 142 C3
Henderson, *Nev., United States* 140 D3
Henderson, *N.C. United States* 144 F2
Henderson Island 124 P8
Hendersonville 142 C3
Hendijarn 101 C1
Hengelo 56 J2
Hengyang 86 E5
Henichesk 72 F5
Hénin-Beaumont 56 E4
Henley-on-Thames 38 H4
Hennebont 60 B6
Hennigsdorf 54 J4
Henryetta 142 A3
Henzada 90 B3
Heppenheim 54 D7
Heppner 140 C1
Hepu 90 D2
Héradsflói 50 (1)F2
Herald Cays 126 J3
Herāt 96 H3
Herbert 128 C7
Herborn 54 D6
Herceg-Novi 68 F7
Hereford, *United Kingdom* 38 F3
Hereford, *United States* 148 D2
Herekino 128 D2
Herentals 56 G3
Herford 54 D4
Herisau 64 E3
Herlen Gol 86 E1
Herm 38 (1)F6
Hermagor 64 J4
Herma Ness 36 (1)H1
Hermel 100 D2
Hermiston 140 C1
Hermosillo 138 D6
Hernád 52 L9
Herne 54 C5
Herne Bay 38 K4
Herning 50 E8
Hérouville-St-Clair 56 B5
Herrenberg 64 D2
Hersbruck 54 G7
Herstat 56 H4
Hertford 38 H4
Hertlay 56 E6
Hervey Bay 126 K5
Herzberg 54 F5
Herzliyya 100 B4
Hesdin 56 E4
Heshan 90 D2
Hesselø 52 A1
Hessisch-Lichtenau 54 E5
Hetton-le-Hole 36 G7
Hettstedt Lutherstadt 54 G5
Heves 52 K10
Hexham 36 F7
He Xian 90 E2
Hexigten Qi 86 F2
Heysham 36 F7
Heze 86 F3
Hezuozhen 86 C3
Hialeah 144 E4
Hiawatha 144 B2
Hibbing 142 B1
Hickory 142 D3
Hidaka-sammyaku 88 M2
Hidalgo del Parral 148 C3
Hiddensee 54 H2
Hierro 112 B3
Higashi-suidō 88 E7
High Point 142 E3
High Wycombe 38 H4
Hiiumaa 50 M7
Hikurangi 128 E2
Hikurangi 128 G3
Hikutaia 128 E3
Hildburghausen 54 F6
Hildesheim 54 E4
Hillsboro, *Oh., United States* 144 E2
Hillsboro, *Oreg., United States* 140 B1
Hillsboro, *Tex., United States* 146 G2
Hillsville 142 D3
Hillswick 36 (1)G1
Hilo 146 (2)F4
Hilton Head Island 144 E3
Hilva 98 H5
Hilversum 56 H2
Himalayas 80 L6
Himarë 70 B4
Himatnagar 94 B4
Himeji 88 H6
Himi 88 J5
Himora 110 G5
Ḩimş 100 D2
Hinckley 38 G3
Hindu Kush 94 A1
Hindupur 94 C6
Hinesville 144 E3
Hingoli 94 C5
Hinnøya 50 H2
Hiroo 88 M2
Hirosaki 88 L3
Hiroshima 88 G6
Hirschaid 54 F7
Hirson 56 G5
Hirtshals 50 E8
Hisar 94 C3
Hischberg 54 G6
Hisdal 50 C6
Hispaniola 154 D2
Hisyah 100 D2
Hīt 98 K7
Hitachi 88 L5
Hitchin 38 H4
Hitoyoshi 88 F7
Hitra 50 D5
Hiuchi-nada 88 G6
Hiva Oa 124 M6
Hjälmaren 50 H7
Hjalmar Lake 136 K4
Hjelmsøya 50 M1
Hlinsko 52 E8
Hlohovec 64 N2
Hlyboka 68 N1
Hlybokaye 72 E3
Ho 114 E3
Hobart, *Australia* 126 J8
Hobart, *United States* 146 G1
Hobbs 146 F2
Hobro 50 E8
Hobyo 116 H3
Hô Chi Minh 90 D4
Höchstadt 54 F7
Hockenheim 54 D7
Hoddesdon 38 H4
Hódmezővásárhely 68 H3
Hodonín 52 G9
Hoek van Holland 56 G3
Hoeryŏng 88 E2
Hoeyang 88 D4
Hof 54 G6
Hofgeismar 54 E5
Höfn 50 (1)F2
Hofsjökull 50 (1)D2
Hofsos 50 (1)D2
Hōfu 88 F6
Hohe 64 H3
Hohe Dachstein 52 C10
Hohe Tauern 66 G1
Hohhot 86 E2
Hoh Xil Shan 94 E1
Hôi An 90 D3
Hoima 116 E3
Hokitika 128 C6
Hokkaidō 88 N2
Holbæk 52 A2
Holbeach 38 J3
Holbrook 146 D2
Holderness 38 H2
Holdrege 140 G2
Holguín 148 J4
Holič 64 N2
Hollabrunn 64 M2
Holland 142 C2
Hollis 146 G2
Hollywood 144 E4
Holman 136 H2
Hólmavík 50 (1)C2
Holmes Reefs 126 J3
Holstebro 50 E8
Holsteinische Schweiz 54 F2
Holsteinsborg = Sisimiut 136 W3
Holsworthy 38 D5
Holton 144 B2
Holyhead 38 D2
Holy Island, *Eng., United Kingdom* 36 G6
Holy Island, *Wales, United Kingdom* 38 D2
Holyoke 140 F2
Holywood 35 F2
Holzkirchen 64 G3
Holzminden 54 E5
Homa Bay 116 E4
Homberg 54 E5
Hombori 112 E5
Home Bay 136 T3
Homestead 144 E4
Homewood 144 D3
Homs = Ḩimş 100 D2
Homyel' 72 F4
Hondo, *N. Mex., United States* 146 E2
Hondo, *Tex., United States* 146 G3
Honduras 148 G6
Hønefoss 50 F6
Honey Lake 140 B2
Honfleur 56 C5
Hon Gai 90 D2
Hong Kong 90 E2
Hongliuyuan 86 B2
Hongor 86 E1
Honiara 124 F6
Honiton 38 E5
Honjō 88 K4
Honokaa 146 (2)F3
Honolulu 146 (2)D2
Honshū 88 L5
Hooge 54 D2
Hoogeveen 56 J2
Hoogezand-Sappemeer 56 J1
Hook Head 35 E4
Hooper Bay 146 (1)D3
Hoorn 56 H2
Hoorn Islands 124 H7
Hopa 98 J3
Hope, *Canada* 140 B1
Hope, *Ak., United States* 136 B4
Hope, *Ark., United States* 144 C3
Hopedale 136 U5
Hopetoun 126 H7
Hopin 94 G4
Hopkinsville 142 C3
Hoquiam 140 B1
Horadiz 98 M4
Horasan 98 K3
Horgo 84 F7
Horizon Depth 124 D8
Horley 38 H4
Hormak 96 H4
Hormoz 101 F3
Horn 64 L2
Hornavan 50 J3
Horncastle 38 H2
Hornsea 38 H2
Horodenka 68 N1
Horodok 52 N8
Horqin Youyi Qianqi 84 L7
Horsens 50 E9
Horsham, *Australia* 126 H7
Horsham, *United Kingdom* 38 H4
Horten 50 F7
Hortiguela 62 G2
Horton 146 (1)N2
Ḩoseynābād 101 G2
Hoshab 96 H4
Hoshangabad 94 C4
Hospet 94 C5
Hosséré Vokre 114 G3
Hotan 82 Q10
Hotan 82 Q10
Hot Springs, *Ark., United States* 142 B4
Hot Springs, *N.C., United States* 142 D3
Hottah Lake 136 H3
Houdan 56 D6
Houdelaincourt 64 A2
Houghton 142 C1
Houghton-le-Spring 36 G7
Houlton 142 G1
Houma, *China* 86 E3
Houma, *United States* 138 H6
Houmt Souk 112 H2
Houston 138 G6
Hovd 82 S8
Hövsgöl Nuur 84 F6
Hövüün 86 C2
Howard Junction 128 D5
Howden 38 H2
Howland 124 J5
Ḩowz-e Panj 101 G1
Hoxie 144 C2
Höxter 54 E5
Hoxud 82 R9
Hoy 36 E3
Høyanger 50 D6
Hoyerswerda 54 K5
Hradeç Králové 52 E7
Hranice 52 G8
Hrazdan 98 L3
Hrodna 52 N4
Hron 52 H9
Hrubieszów 52 N7
Hsin-chu 90 G2
Hsueh-Shan 90 G2
Hsweni 90 B2
Huacho 156 B6
Huade 86 E2
Huadian 88 D2
Huaibei 86 F4
Huaibin 86 F4
Huaihua 86 D5
Huainan 86 F4
Huaiyin 86 F4
Huaki 93 C4
Huallaga 156 B5
Huambo 118 B2
Huancayelica 156 B6
Huancayo 156 B6
Huang 86 F3
Huangchuan 86 F4
Huangshan 86 F5
Huangshi 86 F4
Huang Xian 86 G3
Huangyan, *China* 86 G5
Huangyan, *China* 86 C3
Huanren 88 C3
Huanuco 156 B5
Huaráz 156 B5
Huarmey 156 B6
Huasco 158 G4
Huashixia 86 B3
Huatabampo 138 E6
Hubli 94 C5
Huch'ang 88 D3
Hucknall 38 G2
Huddersfield 38 G2
Huddinge 50 K7
Hudiksvall 50 J6
Hudson 142 F2
Hudson 142 F2
Hudson Bay 136 L6
Hudson Bay 136 P5
Hudson Strait 136 S4
Huê 90 D3
Huelva 62 D7
Huercal Overa 62 J7
Huesca 62 K2
Huéscar 62 H7
Huftaroy 50 C6
Hughenden 126 H4
Hugh Town 38 B6
Hugo 144 B3
Hugo Lake 144 B3
Huia 128 E3
Huich'ŏn 88 D3
Huila Plateau 118 A3
Huinan 88 C2
Huinca Renancó 158 J5
Huizhou 90 E2
Hulin 84 N7
Hull 142 E1
Hulst 56 G3
Hulun Nur 84 K7
Huma 84 M6
Huma 84 M6
Humaitá 156 E5
Humbe 118 A3
Humble 54 F2
Humboldt 136 L6
Humboldt 140 C2
Hümedän 96 G4
Humenné 52 L9
Humphrey 140 D2
Humpolec 52 E8
Hün 110 C2
Húnaflói 50 (1)C2
Hunchun 88 F2
Hunedoara 68 K4
Hünfeld 54 E6
Hungary 68 F3
Hungen 54 D6
Hungerford, *Australia* 126 H5
Hungerford, *United Kingdom* 38 G4
Hŭngnam 88 D4
Hunjiang 88 D3
Hunsrück 54 B7
Hunstanton 38 J3
Hunte 54 D4
Hunter Island 124 H8
Huntingburg 144 D2
Huntingdon, *United Kingdom* 38 H3
Huntingdon, *United States* 144 E2
Huntington 144 D1
Huntington Beach 146 C2
Huntly, *New Zealand* 128 E3
Huntly, *United Kingdom* 36 F4
Huntsville, *Canada* 142 E1
Huntsville, *Al., United States* 144 D3
Huntsville, *Tex., United States* 148 E2
Hunyuan 86 E3
Ḩūr 101 G1
Hurdiyo 116 J1
Hurghada 110 F2
Huron 140 G2
Hürth 56 J4
Húsavík 50 (1)E1
Huşi 68 R3
Huslia 146 (1)F2
Husn 100 C4
Husum 54 E2
Hutag 84 G7
Hutanopan 92 B2
Hutchinson 146 G1
Ḩūth 110 H4
Huttwil 64 C3
Huvadu Atoll 94 B8
Huy 56 H4
Huzou 86 G4
Hvannadalshnúkur 50 (1)E2
Hvar 68 D6
Hvar 68 D6
Hvolsvöllur 50 (1)C3
Hwange 118 D3
Hyak 140 B1
Hyannis 140 F2
Hyargas Nuur 82 S8
Hyden 126 C6
Hyderabad, *India* 94 C5
Hyderabad, *Pakistan* 96 J4
Hyères 60 M10
Hyesan 88 E3
Hyndam Peak 140 D2
Hythe 38 K4
Hyūga 88 F7
Hyvinkää 50 N6

I

Iaco 156 D6
Ialomiţa 68 P5
Ianca 68 Q4
Iaşi 68 Q2
Ibadan 114 E3
Ibagué 156 B3
Ibar 68 H6
Ibb 110 H5
Ibbenbüren 54 C4
Iberia 156 C5
Ibiza = Eivissa 62 M5
Ibiza = Eivissa 62 M6
Ibotirama 156 J6
Ibrā' 96 G5
'Ibrī 101 G5
Ica 156 B6
Içana 156 D3
İçel 98 F5
Iceland 48 C1
Ichalkaranji 94 B5
Ichinoseki 88 L4
Idabel 144 C3
Ida Grove 142 A2
Idah 114 F3
Idaho 140 D2
Idaho Falls 140 D2
Idar-Oberstein 54 C7
Idfu 110 F3
Idhān Awbārī 112 H3
Idhan Murzūq 112 H4
Idiofa 116 C4
Idlib 98 G6
Idstein 54 D6
Ieper 56 E4
Ierapetra 70 H9
Ifakara 116 F5
Ifanadiana 118 H4
Ife 114 E3
Ifjord 50 P1
Igarka 82 R4
Iggesund 50 J6
Igizyar 96 L2
Iglesias 66 C9
Igli 112 E2
Igloolik 136 Q3
Ignace 142 B1
İğneada 70 K3
Igoumenitsa 70 C5
Igra 72 K3
Igrim 72 M2
Igualada 62 M3
Iguatu 156 K5
Ilharaña 118 H2
Ihosy 118 H4
Ihtiman 70 F2
Iida 88 J6
Iim 64 G2
Iisalmi 50 P5
Iiulissat 136 W3
Ijebu Ode 114 E3
IJmuiden 56 G2
IJssel 56 J2
IJsselmeer 56 H2
Ikaria 70 J7
Ikeda 88 M2
Ikela 116 C4
Ikhtiman 68 L7
Iki 88 E7
Ikire 114 E3
Ikom 114 F3
Ikopa 118 H3
Ikorodu 114 E3
Ilagan 90 G3
Īlām 96 E3
Iława 52 J4
Ilbenge 84 L4
Ilebo 116 C4
Île d'Anticosti 136 U7
Île de Jerba 112 H2
Île de la Gonâve 148 K5
Île de Noirmoutier 60 C7
Île de Ré 60 D7
Île d'Oléron 60 D8

Île d'Yeu 60 C7
Île Europa 118 G4
Ilek 72 K4
Ilek 72 K4
Île Plane 66 E11
Îles Cani 66 D11
Îles Chesterfield 124 F7
Îles Crozet 108 J10
Îles de la Madeleine 136 U7
Îles Désappointement 124 M7
Îles d'Hyères 60 M11
Îles Duc de Gloucester 124 M7
Îles Glorieuses 118 H2
Ilesha 114 E3
Îles Kerkenah 112 H2
Îles Maria 124 L8
Îles Palliser 124 M7
Île Tidra 112 B5
Île Zembra 66 E11
Ilfracombe 38 D4
Ilgın 98 D4
Ilha da Trindade 154 H6
Ilha de Marajó 156 H4
Ilha de São Luís 156 J4
Ilha do Bazaruto 118 F4
Ilha Fernando de Noronha 156 L4
Ilha Grande 156 E4
Ilha Grande de Gurupa 156 G4
Ilhas Martin Vaz 158 Q3
Ilhéus 156 K6
Iliamna Volcano 146 (1)G4
Iligan 90 G5
Il'kal 94 C5
Ilkeston 38 G3
Ilkley 38 G2
Iller 64 F3
Illertissen 64 F2
Illichivs'k 68 T3
Illinois 138 H3
Illinois 142 C2
Illizi 112 G3
Ilmenau 54 F6
Ilo 156 C7
Iloilo 90 G4
Ilorin 114 E3
Ilovlya 72 H5
Il'pyrskiy 84 U4
Ilwaco 140 B1
Ilych 72 L2
Imabari 88 G6
Imatra 50 Q6
Imeni-Babushkina 82 G6
Imeni Polinyosipenko 84 P6
Imese 116 B3
Imī 116 G2
İmişli 98 N4
Immeln 52 D1
Immenstadt 64 F3
Immingham 38 H2
Imola 64 G6
Imotski 68 E6
Imperatriz 156 H5
Imperia 64 D7
Imperial 140 F2
Impfondo 116 B3
Imphal 94 F4
Imrali Adası 70 L4
Imroz 70 H4
Ina 88 J6
Inambari 156 C6
In Aménas 112 G3
Inangahua 128 C5
Inanwatan 93 D3
Iñapari 156 D6
Inarijärvi 50 P2
Inca 62 N5
Ince Burun 98 F2
Inch'ŏn 88 D5
Incirliova 70 K7
Indalsälven 50 H5
Independence, *Kans., United States* 144 B2
Independence, *Mo., United States* 142 B3
India 94 C4
Indiana 138 J3
Indiana 142 E2
Indianapolis 144 D2
Indian Ocean 94 D8
Indianola 142 B2
Indian Springs 140 C3
Indiga 72 J1
Indio 146 C2
Indonesia 92 D3
Indore 94 C4
Indramayu 92 D4
Indre 60 G6
Indre Sula 50 C6
Indus 96 K3
İnebolu 98 E3
İnecik 70 K4
İnegöl 98 C3
In Ekker 112 G4
Ineu 68 J3
Ingelheim 56 L5
Ingeniero Jacobacci 158 H7
Ingham 126 J3
Ingoda 84 J6
Ingolstadt 64 G2
Ingrāj Bāzār 94 E3
I-n-Guezzam 112 G5
Ingushetiya 98 L2
Inhambane 118 F4
Inhaminga 118 E3
Inirida 156 D3
Inishark 35 A3
Inishbofin 35 A3
Inisheer 35 B3
Inishmaan 35 B3
Inishmore 35 B3
Inishmurray 35 C2
Inishowen 35 D1
Inishtrahull 35 D1
Inishturk 35 A3
Inkisi-Kisantu 114 H6
Inn 64 H2
Inner Hebrides 36 B5
Innerleithen 36 E6
Inner Mongolia = Nei Monggol 86 E2
Inner Sound 36 C4
Inneston 126 G7
Innisfail 126 J3
Innsbruck 64 G3
Inongo 116 B4
Inowrocław 52 H5
In Salah 112 F3
Insein 90 B3
Inta 82 K4
Interlaken 64 C4
International Falls 142 B1
Intsy 72 H1
Inubō-zaki 88 L6
Inukjuak 136 R5
Inuvik 146 (1)L2
Inveraray 36 C5
Inverbervie 36 F5
Invercargill 128 B8
Invergordon 36 D4
Inverness 36 D4
Inverurie 36 F4
Inverway 126 E3
Investigator Group 126 F6
Investigator Strait 126 G7
Inya 82 R7
Inya 84 R4
Ioannina 70 C5
Iokanga 82 F4
Iola 144 B2
Iona 36 B5
Ionești 68 M5
Ionian Sea 70 B6
Ionioi Nisoi 70 B5
Ios 70 H8
Ios 70 H8
Iowa 138 H3
Iowa City 142 B2
Iowa Falls 142 B2
Ipameri 156 H7
Ipatinga 158 N2
Ipatovo 72 H5
Ipiales 156 B3
Ipiaú 156 K6
Ipoh 92 C2
Iporá 156 G7
Ippy 116 C2
Ipsala 70 J4
Ipswich 38 K3
Iqaluit 136 T4
Iquique 158 G3
Iquitos 156 C4
Iracoubo 156 G2
Irakleia 70 F3
Irakleia 70 H8
Irakleio 70 H9
Iraklion = Irakleio 48 G4
Iran 96 F3
Irānshahr 96 H4
Irapuato 148 D4
Iraq 96 D3
Irbid 100 C4
Irbit 72 M3
Irecê 156 J6
Irgiz 72 M5
Irgiz 72 M5
Irhil M'Goun 112 D2
Irian Jaya 93 E3
Iringa 116 F5
Iriri 156 G4
Irish Sea 58 G8
Irkutsk 84 G6
Iron Mountain 142 C1
Ironton 144 E2
Ironwood 142 B1
Irrawaddy 94 F5
Irshava 68 L1
Irta 72 J2
Irtysh 72 P3
Irtyshsk 82 P7
Irumu 116 D3
Irún 62 J1
Irvine 36 D6
Irvinestown 35 D2
Irving 146 G2
Isabela 93 B1
Isabella 142 B1
Isabella Lake 146 C1
Ísafjarðardjúp 50 (1)A1
Ísafjörður 50 (1)B1
Isahaya 88 F7
Isar 64 G3
Ischia 66 H8
Ischia 66 H8
Ise 88 J6
Isel 64 H4
Isère 64 B5
Iserlohn 56 K3
Isernia 66 J7
Isetskoye 72 N3
Iseyin 114 E3
Isfana 96 J2
Ishikari-wan 88 L2
Ishim 72 N3
Ishim 72 N4
Ishinomaki 88 L4
Ishkoshim 96 K2
Isigny-sur-Mer 56 A5
Isiolo 116 F3
Isiro 116 D3
Iskăr 68 M6
İskenderun 98 G5
Iskitim 82 Q7
Isla Alejandro Selkirk 158 E5
Isla Campana 158 F8
Isla Clarence 158 G9
Isla Clarión 148 B5
Isla Coiba 148 H7
Isla Contreras 158 F9
Isla de Alborán 62 G9
Isla de Bioco 114 F4
Isla de Chiloé 158 G7
Isla de Coco 148 G7
Isla de Cozumel 148 G4
Isla de la Juventud 148 H4
Isla de los Estados 158 J9
Isla de Malpelo 156 A3
Isla de Margarita 156 E1
Isla de Providencia 148 H6
Isla de San Andrés 148 H6
Isla de São Francisco 158 M4
Isla de São Sebastião 158 M3
Isla Desolación 158 F9
Isla Española 156 (1)B2
Isla Fernandina 156 (1)A2
Isla Gorgona 156 B3
Isla Grande 158 N3
Isla Grande de Tierra del Fuego 158 H9
Isla Guafo 158 F7
Isla Hoste 158 G10
Isla Isabela 156 (1)A2
Isla La Tortuga 156 D1
Isla Londonderry 158 G9
Islamabad 94 B2
Isla Madre de Dios 158 F8/9
Isla Marchena 156 (1)A1
Islamgarh 94 B3
Islamorada 144 E5
Isla Navarino 158 H10
Island Lake 136 M6
Island Magee 35 F2
Islands of the Four Mountains 146 (1)C5
Isla Pinta 156 (1)A1
Isla Puná 156 A4
Isla Riesco 158 G9
Isla Robinson Crusoe 158 E5
Isla San Benedicto 148 B5
Isla San Cristóbal 156 (1)B2
Isla San Salvador 156 (1)A2
Isla Santa Cruz 156 (1)A2
Isla Santa Inés 158 F9
Isla Santa Maria 156 (1)A2
Islas Baleares 62 N5
Islas Canarias 108 A3
Islas Canarias 112 B3
Islas Columbretes 62 L5
Islas de la Bahía 148 G5
Islas de los Desventurados 158 E4
Islas Galápagos 156 (1)B1
Islas Juan Fernández 158 E5
Islas Los Roques 156 D1
Islas Marías 148 C4
Islas Socorro 148 B5
Islas Revillagigedo 148 B5
Islas Wollaston 158 H10
Islas Wellington 158 F8
Islay 36 B6
Isle 60 F8
Isle of Man 36 D7
Isle of Noss 36 (1)H1
Isle of Sheppey 38 J4
Isle of Wight 38 G5
Isle Royale 142 C1
Isles of Scilly 38 B6
Ismâ'ilîya 110 F1
İsmayıllı 98 N3
Isna 110 F2
Isoka 118 E2
Isola delle Correnti 66 J12
Isola di Capo Rizzuto 66 M10
Isola di Pantelleria 66 G12
Isole Égadi 66 F11
Isole Lipari 66 J10
Isole Ponziane 66 H8
Isole Tremiti 66 K6
Iso-Vietonen 50 N3
Isparta 70 N7
Ispica 66 J12
Israel 100 B5
Israelite Bay 126 D6
Issia 114 C3
Issimu 93 B2
Issoire 60 J8
Issoudun 60 H7
İstanbul 98 C3
İstanbul Boğazı 98 C3
Istiaia 70 F6
Istmo de Tehauntepec 148 F5
Istra 64 J5
Istres 60 K10
Itaberaba 156 J6
Itabira 156 J7
Itabuna 156 K6
Itacoatiara 156 F4
Itaituba 156 F4
Itajaí 158 M4
Italy 66 E4
Itambacuri 156 J7
Itanagar 94 F3
Itapebi 156 K7
Itapetinga 156 J7
Itapicuru 156 K6
Itapicuru Mirim 156 J4
Itapipoca 156 K4
Itarsi 94 C4
Ithaca 142 E2
Ithaki 70 C6
Ithaki 70 C6
Itiquira 156 F/G7
Ituí 156 C5
Ituiutaba 156 H7
Itumbiara 156 H7
Ituni 156 F2
Ituri 116 D3
Iturup 156 D5
Itzehoe 54 E3
Iuaretê 156 D3
Iutica 156 D3
Ivalo 50 P2
Ivanava 50 N10
Ivangrad 68 G7
Ivanhoe, *Australia* 126 H6
Ivanhoe, *United States* 142 A2
Ivano-Frankivs'k 72 D5
Ivanovo 72 H3
Ivatsevichy 50 N10
Ivdel' 72 M2
Ivittuut 136 X4
Ivohibe 118 H4
Ivory Coast 114 C3
Ivosjön 52 D1
Ivrea 64 C5
Ivujivik 136 R4
Ivybridge 38 E5
Iwaki 88 L5
Iwamizawa 88 L2
Iwo 114 E3
Iyo-nadā 88 G7
Izberbash 98 M2
Izegern 56 F4
Izhevsk 72 K3
Izhma 72 K1
Izhma 72 K2
Izk 96 G5
Izkī 101 G5
Izmayil 68 R4
İzmir 98 B4
İzmir Körfezi 70 J6
İzmit 98 C3
İznik 98 C3
İznik Gölü 98 C3
Izola 64 J5
Izra' 100 D4
Izuhara 88 E6
Izumo 88 G6
Izu-shotō 88 K6

J

Jabal ad Durūz 100 D4
Jabal Akhḍar 101 G5
Jabal al Nuṣayrīyah 100 D1
Jabal an Nabī Shu'ayb 110 H4
Jabal Ash Sham 101 G5
Jabal aẓ Ẓannah 101 E4
Jabalpur 94 C4
Jabal Shammar 110 G2
Jabal Thamar 110 J5
Jabiru 126 F2
Jablah 100 C1
Jablonec 52 E7
Jablunkov 52 H8
Jaboatão 156 K5
Jaca 62 K2
Jacareacanga 156 G5
Jackman 142 F1
Jacksboro 144 B3
Jackson, *Calif., United States* 140 B3
Jackson, *Minn., United States* 142 B2
Jackson, *Miss., United States* 144 C3
Jackson, *Oh., United States* 144 E2
Jackson, *Tenn., United States* 144 D2
Jackson Head 128 B6
Jackson Lake 140 D2
Jacksonville, *Fla., United States* 144 E3
Jacksonville, *Ill., United States* 142 B3
Jacksonville, *N.C., United States* 144 F3
Jacksonville, *Tex., United States* 144 B3
Jacmel 148 K5
Jacobabad 94 A3
Jacobina 156 J6
Jacunda 156 H4
Jacupiranga 158 M3
Jade 54 D3
Jadebusen 54 D3
Jādū 112 H2
Jaen 156 B5
Jaén 62 G7
Jaffna 94 D7
Jagdalpur 94 D5
Jagersfontein 118 D5
Jaggang 94 C2
Jagst 54 E7
Jahrom 101 E2
Jaipur 94 C3
Jaisalmer 94 B3
Jajce 68 E5
Jakarta 92 D4
Jäkkvik 50 J3
Jakobshavn = Ilulissat 136 W3
Jakobstad 50 M5
Jalālābād 94 B2
Jalandhar 94 C2
Jalapa Enriquez 148 E5
Jalgaon 94 C4
Jalībah 101 B1
Jalingo 114 G3
Jalna 94 C5
Jalón 62 J3
Jalpaiguri 94 E3
Jālū 110 D2
Jalūlā 98 L6
Jamaica 148 H5
Jamalpur 94 E3
Jambi 92 C3
James 140 G2
James Bay 136 Q6
Jamestown, *N.Y., United States* 142 E2
Jamestown, *N.D., United States* 140 G1
Jammerbugten 50 E8
Jammu 94 B2
Jammu and Kashmir 94 C2
Jamnagar 94 B4
Jämsä 50 N6
Jamshedpur 94 E4
Janakpur 94 E3
Janaúba 156 J7
Jandaq 96 F3
Jandongi 116 C3
Jane Peak 128 B7
Janesville 142 C2
Jan Mayen 134 C2
Jannatabad 82 L10
Janos 146 E2
Jánossomorja 64 N3
Janów Lubelski 52 M7
Jantarnyj 52 J3
Januária 156 J7
Jaora 94 C4
Japan 88 L5
Japan Trench 124 E2
Japurá 156 D4
Jarābulus 98 H5
Jaramillo 158 H8
Jarash 100 C4
Jardim 158 K3
Jarosław 52 M7

Järpen 50 G5
Jarud Qi 86 G2
Järvenpää 50 N6
Jarvis 124 K6
Jasel'da 50 N10
Jäsk 101 G4
Jason Islands 158 J9
Jasper, *Al., United States* 144 D3
Jasper, *Fla., United States* 144 E3
Jasper, *Tex., United States* 144 C3
Jastrebarsko 64 L5
Jászberény 68 G2
Jataí 156 G7
Jatapu 156 F4
Jaunpur 94 D3
Java = Jawa 92 E4
Javarthushuu 84 J7
Java Sea 92 E4
Javoriv 52 N8
Jawa 92 E4
Jawhar 116 H3
Jayapura 93 F3
Jayrūd 100 D3
Jaza'ïr Farasān 110 H4
Jazīrat Būbīyān 101 C2
Jazīrat-ye Khārk 101 D2
Jbail 100 C2
Jbel Ayachi 112 E2
Jbel Bou Naceur 112 E2
Jbel Toubkal 112 D2
Jean 140 C3
Jebba 114 E3
Jebel Bāqir 100 C7
Jebel el Atā'ita 100 C6
Jebel el Batrā 100 C7
Jebel-esh Sharqi 100 C3
Jebel Gimbala 110 D5
Jebel Ithrīyat 100 D6
Jebel Liban 100 C3
Jebel Mubrak 100 C6
Jebel Ram 100 C7
Jebel Uweinat 110 E3
Jedburgh 36 F6
Jedda = Jiddah 96 C5
Jedeida 66 D12
Jędrzejów 52 K7
Jefferson 142 B2
Jefferson City, *Mo., United States* 142 B3
Jefferson City, *Tenn., United States* 144 E2
Jeffersonville 142 C3
Jega 114 E2
Jēkabpils 50 N8
Jelgava 50 M8
Jemaja 92 D2
Jena 54 G6
Jendouba 112 G1
Jenin 100 C4
Jenkins 142 D3
Jequié 156 J6
Jequitinhonha 156 J7
Jerada 112 E2
Jeremoabo 156 K6
Jerez 146 F4
Jerez de la Frontera 62 D8
Jerez de los Caballeros 62 D6
Jericho, *Australia* 126 J4
Jericho, *Israel* 100 C5
Jerramungup 126 C6
Jersey 38 (1)F6
Jersey City 144 G1
Jerusalem = Yerushalayim 100 C5
Jesenice 68 B3
Jesenik 52 G7
Jesi 64 J7
Jessore 94 E4
Jesup 144 E3
Jeumont 56 G4
Jever 54 C3
Jeypore 94 D5
Jezioro 52 D4
Jezioro Gardno 50 J9
Jezioro Jeziorsko 52 H6
Jezioro Łebsko 52 F3
Jezioro Śniardwy 52 L4
Jezioro Wigry 52 N2
Jezzine 100 C3
Jhang Maghiana 94 B2
Jhansi 94 C3
Jharsuguda 94 D4
Jhelum 94 B2
Jialing Jiang 86 D4
Jiamusi 86 J1
Ji'an 86 E5
Jiangle 86 F5
Jiangling 86 E4
Jiangmen 86 E6
Jiangyou 86 C4
Jianyang 86 F5
Jiaonan 86 F3
Jiaozou 86 E3
Jiaxing 86 G4
Jiayuguan 86 B3
Jibou 68 L2
Jičín 52 E7
Jiddah 96 C5
Jiesjavrre 50 N2
Jiexiu 86 E3
Jihlava 52 E8
Jijia 68 Q2
Jijiga 116 G2
Jilib 116 G3
Jilin 88 D2
Jima 116 F2
Jimbolia 68 H4
Jiménez 146 F3
Jimsar 82 R9
Jinan 86 F3
Jinapo Hu 88 E2
Jinchang 86 C3
Jincheng 86 E3
Jindřichův Hradec 52 E8
Jingdezhen 86 F5
Jinggu 86 C6
Jinghe 82 Q9
Jinghong 86 C6
Jingmen 86 E4
Jingning 86 D3
Jingxi 86 D6
Jingyuan 86 C3
Jinhua 86 F5
Jining, *China* 86 F3
Jining, *China* 86 E2
Jinja 116 E3
Jinka 116 F2
Jinsha 86 C5
Jinshi 86 E5
Jinta 86 B2
Jinxi 86 G2
Jinzhou 86 G2
Jirgatol 96 K2
Jirin Gol 86 F2
Jirkov 54 J6
Jīroft 101 G2
Jirriiban 116 H2
Jishou 86 D5
Jisr ash Shughūr 98 G6
Jiu 68 L4
Jiujiang 86 F5
Jiwani 96 H4
Jixi 88 F1
Jīzān 110 H4
Jizera 52 D7
J. J. Castelli 156 D4
Joal-Fadiout 112 B6
João Pessoa 156 L5
Jódar 62 G7
Jodhpur 94 B3
Joensuu 72 E2
Jõetsu 88 K5
Jõgeva 50 P7
Johannesburg, *South Africa* 118 D5
Johannesburg, *United States* 146 C1
John Day 140 C2
John o' Groats 36 E3
John Redmond Reservoir 144 B2
Johnson 144 A2
Johnson City 142 D3
Johnson's Crossing 146 (1)L3
Johnston Island 124 J4
Johnstown 142 E2
Johor Bahru 92 C2
Joigny 60 J5
Joinville, *Brazil* 158 M4
Joinville, *France* 60 L5
Jokkmokk 50 K3
Jökulsa á Fjöllum 50 (1)E1
Jolfa 98 L4
Joliet 138 J3
Joliette 142 F1
Jolo 93 B1
Jolo 93 B1
Jonava 52 P2
Jonesboro 142 B3
Jones Sound 136 P1
Jonesville 144 C3
Jonglei Canal 116 E2
Jongunjärvi 50 P4
Joniškis 52 N1
Jönköping 50 H8
Jonquière 142 F1
Joplin 144 C2
Jordan 100 D5
Jordan 140 E1
Jordan Valley 140 C2
Jorhat 94 F3
Jörn 50 L4
Jos 114 F3
José de San Martin 158 G7
Joseph Bonaparte Gulf 126 E2
Joûnié 100 C2
Joure 56 H2
Juan de Nova 118 G3
Juàzeiro 156 J5
Juàzeiro do Norte 156 K5
Juba 116 E3
Jubba 116 G3
Júcar 62 J5
Juchitán 148 F5
Judenburg 64 K3
Juhre 84 L8
Juist 54 B3
Juiz de Fora 158 N3
Julesburg 140 F2
Juli 156 C7
Juliaca 156 C7
Juliana Top 156 F3
Julianstown 35 E3
Jülich 56 J4
Jullouville 56 A6
Jumilla 62 J6
Jumla 94 D3
Junagadh 94 B4
Junction 144 B3
Junction City 144 B2
Jundah 126 H4
Juneau 146 (1)L4
Jungfrau 64 C4
Junggar Pendi 82 R8
Junsele 50 J5
Jun Xian 86 E4
Jura 36 C5
Jūra 52 M2
Jura 64 B4
Jurbarkas 52 M2
Jurf ed Darāwīsh 100 C6
Jurhe 86 G2
Jurilovca 68 R5
Jūrmala 50 M8
Jūrmala 72 D3
Juruá 156 D4
Juruena 156 F6
Juruena 156 F5
Justo Daract 158 H5
Jutaí 156 D5
Jüterbog 54 J5
Juwain 96 H3
Ju Xian 86 F3
Jüymand 96 G3
Jüyom 101 F2
Juzur al Halaniyat 96 G6
Jylland 50 E8
Jyvädskylä 72 E2
Jyväskylä 50 N5

K

K2 94 C1
Kaakhka 96 G2
Kaamanen 50 P2
Kaaresuvanto 50 M2
Kaarta 112 C6
Kabaena 93 B4
Kabakly 96 H2
Kabala 114 B3
Kabale 116 E4
Kabalo 116 D5
Kabardino-Balkariya 98 K2
Kåbdalis 50 L3
Kabompo 118 C2
Kabongo 116 D5
Kabugao 90 G3
Kābul 96 J3
Kabwe 118 D2
Kachikattsy 84 M4
Kachug 84 H6
Kadama 94 B6
Kadañ 52 C7
Kadınhanı 70 Q6
Kadirli 98 G5
Kadoka 140 F2
Kadoma 118 D3
Kadugli 110 E5
Kaduna 114 F2
Kadzherom 72 L2
Kaédi 112 C5
Kaeo 128 D2
Kaesŏng 88 D5
Kāf 100 E5
Kafanchan 114 F3
Kaffrine 114 A2
Kafiau 93 C3
Kåfjord 50 N1
Kafr Buhum 100 D1
Kafr el Sheikh 110 F1
Kafue 118 D3
Kaga 88 J5
Kaga Bandoro 116 B2
Kagoshima 88 F8
Kahemba 116 B5
Kahnūj 101 G3
Kahraman Maraş 98 G5
Kahta 98 H5
Kahurangi Point 128 C5
Kaiama 114 E3
Kai Besar 93 D4
Kaifeng 86 E4
Kaihu 128 D2
Kaihua 86 F5
Kai Kecil 93 D4
Kaikohe 128 D2
Kaikoura 128 D6
Kaili 86 D5
Kailua 146 (2)D2
Kailua Kona 146 (2)E4
Kaimana 93 D3
Käina 50 M7
Kainji Reservoir 114 E2
Kaipara Harbour 128 D3
Kairouan 112 H1
Kaiserslautern 54 C7
Kaišiadorys 52 P3
Kaitaia 128 D2
Kaiwatu 93 C4
Kaiyuan 90 C2
Kajaani 50 P4
Kakamega 116 E3
Kakata 114 B3
Kakhovs'ke Vodoskhovyshche 72 F5
Kākī 101 D2
Käkinädä 94 D5
Kaktovik 146 (1)J1
Kalabagh 94 B2
Kalabahi 93 B4
Kalabakan 92 F2
Kalach 72 H4
Kalachinsk 72 P3
Kalach-na-Donu 72 H5
Kaladar 142 E2
Ka Lae 146 (2)F5
Kalahari Desert 118 C4
Kalajoki 50 M4
Kalakan 84 K5
Kalam 94 B1
Kalamata 70 E7
Kalamazoo 142 C2
Kalampaka 70 D5
Kalana 114 C2
Kalaotoa 93 B4
Kalapana 146 (2)G4
Kalaupapa 146 (2)E2
Kalavryta 70 E6
Kalbarri 126 B5
Kale 70 L7
Kalecik 98 E3
Kaledupa 93 B4
Kalemie 116 D5
Kalemyo 94 F4
Kalevala 50 R4
Kalewa 94 F4
Kalgoorlie 126 D6
Kalianda 92 D4
Kalibo 90 G4
Kalima 116 D4
Kalimantan 92 E2
Kaliningrad 52 K3
Kaliningradskij Zaliv 52 J3
Kalispell 140 D1
Kalisz 52 H6
Kalixälven 50 M3
Kalkan 70 M8
Kalkaring 126 F3
Kalkaska 142 C2
Kallavesi 50 P5
Kallsjön 50 G5
Kalmar 50 J8
Kalmykiya 98 M1
Kalmykovo 72 K5
Kalocsa 68 F3
Kalol 94 B4
Kalpakio 70 C5
Kalpeni 94 B6
Kaltag 146 (1)F3
Kaltenkirchen 54 E3
Kaluga 72 G4
Kalyan 94 B5
Kalymnos 70 J8
Kalymnos 70 J7
Kama 116 D4
Kama 48 K1
Kamaishi 88 L4
Kaman 98 E4
Kamande 116 D4
Kamango 82 U6
Kamares 70 G8
Kambarka 72 K3
Kambo Ho 88 E3
Kamchatka 84 U6
Kamchatskiy Zaliv 84 U5
Kamenica 70 E2
Kamenka, *Russia* 72 H1
Kamenka, *Russia* 72 H4
Kamen'-na-Obi 82 Q7
Kamen'-Rybolov 88 F1
Kamensk-Shakhtinskiy 72 H5
Kamensk-Ural'skiy 72 M3
Kamenz 52 D6
Kamet 94 C2
Kamiiso 88 L3
Kamina 116 C5
Kamitsushima 88 E6
Kamituga 116 D4
Kamiyaku 88 F8
Kamloops 136 G6
Kamoenai 88 L2
Kampala 116 E3
Kampen 56 H2
Kampong Cham 90 D4
Kâmpóng Chhnăng 90 C4
Kâmpot 90 C4
Kamsuuma 116 G3
Kam"yanets'-Podil's'kyy 72 E5
Kamyanyets 50 M10
Kämyärän 98 M6
Kamyshin 72 J4
Kamyzyak 72 J5
Kan 110 F6
Kanab 146 D1
Kananga 116 C5
Kanazawa 88 J5
Kanbalu 94 G4
Kanchipuram 94 C6
Kandahār 96 J3
Kandalaksha 50 S3
Kandalakshskiy Zaliv 72 F1
Kandi 114 E2
Kandira 70 N3
Kandy 94 D7
Kane 142 E2
Kaneohe 146 (2)D2
Kang 118 C4
Kangaatsiaq 136 W3
Kangal 98 G4
Kangān, *Iran* 101 E3
Kangān, *Iran* 101 G4
Kangar 92 C1
Kangaroo Island 126 G7
Kangchenjunga 94 E3
Kangding 86 C4
Kangeq 136 Y4
Kangerluarsoruseq 136 W4
Kangersuatsiaq 136 W2
Kangetet 116 F3
Kanggye 88 D3
Kangiqsualujjuaq 136 T5
Kangiqsujuaq 136 S4
Kangirsuk 136 S4
Kangmar 94 E3
Kangnŭng 88 E5
Kango 114 G4
Kangping 86 G2
Kaniama 116 C5
Kanin Nos 82 G4
Kanji Reservoir 108 D4
Kanjiža 68 H3
Kankaanpää 50 M6
Kankakee 142 C2
Kankan 114 C2
Kankossa 112 C5
Kannapolis 144 E2
Kano 114 F2
Kanoya 88 F8
Kanpur 94 D3
Kansas 144 A2
Kansas 144 B2
Kansas City, *Kans., United States* 144 C2
Kansas City, *Mo., United States* 144 C2
Kansk 82 T6
Kanta 116 F2
Kantchari 114 E2
Kantemirovka 72 G5
Kanye 118 C4
Kao-Hsiung 86 G6
Kaolack 112 B6
Kaoma 118 C2
Kapanga 116 C5
Kap Arkona 52 C3
Kapchagay 82 P9
Kap Cort Adelaer = Kangeq 136 Y4
Kap Farvel = Uummannarsuaq 136 Y5
Kapfenberg 64 L3
Kapıdağı Yarimadası 70 K4
Kapiri Mposhi 118 D2
Kapit 92 E2
Kapiti Island 128 E5
Kaplice 64 K2
Kapoeta 116 E3
Kaposvár 68 E3
Kappel 54 C6
Kappeln 54 E2
Kappl 64 F3
Kapsan 88 E3
Kapuskasing 138 K2
Kapuvár 68 E2

Kara 82 M4
Kara, *Russia* 82 M4
Kara, *Togo* 114 E3
Kara Ada 70 K8
Kara-Balta 82 N9
Karabekaul 96 H2
Kara-Bogaz-Gol 96 F1
Karabutak 72 M5
Karacabey 70 L4
Karacaköy 70 L3
Karacal Tepe 70 Q8
Karachayevo-Cherkesiya 98 J2
Karachayevsk 98 J2
Karachi 96 J5
Karaganda 82 N8
Karaginskiy Zaliv 84 V5
Karaj 96 F2
Karak 100 C5
Kara-Kala 96 G2
Karakalpakiya 82 K9
Karakoçan 98 J4
Karakol 82 P9
Kara-Köl 82 N9
Karakoram 80 L6
Karaksar 84 K6
Karam 84 H5
Karaman 98 E5
Karamay 82 R8
Karamea 128 D5
Karamea Bight 128 C5
Karamürsel 70 M4
Karand 98 M6
Karaoy 82 N8
Karapınar 70 R7
Kara-Say 82 P9
Karasburg 118 B5
Kara Sea = Karskoye More 82 L3
Karasu 98 D3
Karasuk 82 P7
Karasuk 82 P7
Karatal 82 P8
Karataş 98 F5
Karatobe 72 K5
Karaton 72 K5
Karatsu 88 E7
Karazhal 72 P5
Karbalā' 96 D3
Karcag 68 H2
Karditsa 70 D5
Kärdla 50 M7
Kareliya 50 R4
Karepino 72 L2
Karesuando 50 M2
Kargalinskaya 98 M2
Kargasok 82 Q6
Kargat 82 P6
Kargil 94 C2
Kargopol' 72 G2
Kariba 118 D3
Kariba Dam 118 D3
Karibib 118 B4
Karimata 92 D3
Karimnagar 94 C5
Karkaralinsk 82 P8
Karkinits'ka Zatoka 72 F5
Karlik Shan 86 A2
Karlovac 68 C4
Karlovasi 70 J7
Karlovo 70 G2
Karlovy Vary 54 H6
Karlshamn 52 D1
Karlskoga 50 H7
Karlskrona 50 H8
Karlsruhe 54 D8
Karlstad, *Norway* 50 G7
Karlstad, *United States* 142 A1
Karlstadt 54 E7
Karmala 94 C5
Karmi'el 100 C4
Karmøy 50 C7
Karnafuli Reservoir 94 F4
Karnal 94 C3
Karnische Alpen 64 H4
Karnobat 70 J2
Karodi 96 J4
Karonga 116 E5
Karpathos 70 K9
Karpathos 70 K9
Karpenisi 70 D6
Karpogory 72 H2
Karrabük 98 E3
Karratha 126 C4
Kars 98 K3
Karsakpay 72 N5
Kärsava 50 P8
Karshi 96 J2
Karskoye More 82 L3
Karslyaka 70 K6
Karstula 50 N5
Kartal 70 M4
Kartaly 72 M4
Kartayel' 72 K2
Kartuzy 52 H3
Karufa 93 D3
Karumba 126 H3
Karur 94 C6
Karvina 52 H8
Karwar 94 B6
Karystos 70 G6
Kasai 116 B4
Kasaji 118 C2
Kasama 118 E2
Kasansay 82 N9
Kasba Lake 136 L4
Kasempa 118 D2
Kasenga 118 D2
Kāshān 96 F3
Kashi 96 L2
Kashima 86 L3
Kashiwazaki 88 K5
Kāshmar 96 G2
Kāshmor 96 J4
Kasimov 72 H4
Kasli 72 M3
Kasongo 116 D4
Kasos 70 K9
Kaspi 98 L3
Kaspiysk 98 M2
Kassala 110 G4
Kassandreia 70 F4
Kassel 54 E5
Kasserine 112 G1
Kastamonu 98 E3
Kastelli 70 F9
Kastoria 70 D4
Kasulu 116 E4
Kasumkent 98 N3
Kasur 94 B2
Kata 84 G5
Katchall 94 F7
Katerini 70 E4
Katete 118 E2
Katha 94 G4
Katherine 126 F2
Kathiawar 96 K5
Kathmandu 94 E3
Kati 114 C2
Katihar 94 E3
Katiola 114 C3
Kato Nevrokopi 70 F3
Katonga 116 E3
Katoomba 126 K6
Katowice 52 J7
Katrineholm 50 J7
Katsina 114 F2
Katsina-Ala 114 F3
Katsuta 88 L5
Katsuura 88 L6
Kattakurgan 96 J2
Kattavia 70 K9
Kattegat 50 F8
Katun' 82 R7
Katwijkaan Zee 56 G2
Kauai 146 (2)B1
Kaufbeuren 64 F3
Kauhajoki 50 M5
Kaunas 52 N3
Kauno 52 P3
Kaunus 48 G2
Kaura Namoda 114 F2
Kavadarci 70 D3
Kavajë 70 B3
Kavala 70 G4
Kavali 94 C5
Kavār 101 E2
Kavaratti 94 B6
Kavarna 68 R6
Kawabe 88 L4
Kawagoe 88 K6
Kawakawa 128 E2
Kawambwa 116 D5
Kawasaki 88 K6
Kawau Island 128 E3
Kaweka 128 F4
Kawhia 128 E4
Kawkareik 90 B3
Kawthaung 90 B4
Kaya 114 D2
Kayak 82 U3
Kaycee 140 E2
Kayenta 146 D1
Kayes 114 B2
Kaymaz 70 P5
Kaynar 82 P8
Kayseri 98 F4
Kayyerkan 82 R4
Kazachinskoye 84 E5
Kazach'ye 84 P2
Kazakdar'ya 82 K9
Kazakhstan 82 L8
Kazan 136 M4
Kazan' 72 J3
Kazanlük 70 H2
Kazan-rettō 124 E3
Kazbek 98 L2
Kāzerūn 101 D2
Kazincbarcika 68 H1
Kazungula 118 D3
Kazuno 88 L3
Kazymskiy Mys 82 M5
Kea 70 G7
Kea 70 G7
Kearney 138 G3
Keban Barajı 98 H4
Kébémèr 112 B5
Kebkabiya 110 D5
Kebnekajse 50 K3
K'ebrī Dehar 116 G2
K'ech'a Terara 116 F2
Keçiborlu 70 N7
Kecskemet 68 G3
Kėdainiai 52 N2
Kedgwick 142 G1
Kediri 92 E4
Kédougou 114 B2
Kędzierzyn-Koźle 52 H7
Keele 146 (1)M3
Keene 142 F2
Keetmanshoop 118 B5
Keewatin 142 B1
Kefallonia 70 C6
Kefamenanu 93 B4
Keflavík 50 (1)B2
Kegen' 82 P9
Keg River 136 H5
Keheili 110 F4
Kehl 64 C2
Keighley 38 G2
Keila 50 N7
Keitele 50 N5
Keith 36 F4
Kekerengu 128 D5
Kékes 68 H2
Kelai Thiladhunmathee Atoll 94 B7
Kelheim 64 G2
Kelibia 66 F12
Kelkit 98 G3
Kells 35 E3
Kelmë 52 M2
Kélo 114 H3
Kelowna 136 H7
Kelso 140 B1
Kelso 36 F6
Keluang 92 C2
Kem' 72 F2
Kemaliye 98 H4
Kemalpaşa 70 K6
Kemasik 92 C2
Kemer, *Turkey* 70 M8
Kemer, *Turkey* 70 N8
Kemerovo 82 R6
Kemi 50 N4
Kemijärvi 50 P3
Kemijärvi 50 P3
Kemijoki 50 P3
Kemmerer 140 D3
Kemmuna 66 J12
Kemnath 54 G7
Kemp's Bay 144 F5
Kempten 64 F3
Kendal 36 F7
Kendall 144 E4
Kendari 93 B3
Kendawangan 92 E3
Kendégué 114 H2
Kendujhargarh 94 E4
Kenedy 144 B4
Kenema 114 B3
Keneurgench 96 G1
Kenge 116 B4
Kengtung 90 B2
Kenhardt 118 C5
Kenilworth 38 G3
Kénitra 112 D2
Kenmare 35 B5
Kenmare River 35 A5
Kennett 144 D2
Kennewick 140 C1
Keno Hill 146 (1)K3
Kenora 138 H2
Kenosha 142 C2
Kentau 82 M9
Kentucky 138 J4
Kentwood 144 C3
Kenya 108 G5
Keokuk 142 B2
Kępno 52 H6
Kepulauan Anambas 92 D2
Kepulauan Aru 93 E4
Kepulauan Ayu 93 D2
Kepulauan Balabalangan 92 F3
Kepulauan Banggai 93 B3
Kepulauan Barat Daya 93 C4
Kepulauan Batu 92 B3
Kepulauan Bonerate 93 A4
Kepulauan Kai 93 D4
Kepulauan Kangean 92 F4
Kepulauan Karimunjawa 92 D4
Kepulauan Karkaralong 93 B2
Kepulauan Laut Kecil 92 F3
Kepulauan Leti 93 C4
Kepulauan Lingga 92 C2
Kepulauan Lucipara 93 C4
Kepulauan Mentawai 92 B3
Kepulauan Nanusa 93 C2
Kepulauan Natuna 92 D2
Kepulauan Riau 92 C2
Kepulauan Sabalana 92 F4
Kepulauan Sangir 93 C2
Kepulauan Solor 93 B4
Kepulauan Sula 93 B3
Kepulauan Talaud 93 C2
Kepulauan Tanimbar 93 D4
Kepulauan Tengah 92 F4
Kepulauan Togian 93 B3
Kepulauan Tukangbesi 93 B4
Kepulauan Watubela 93 D3
Kerch 98 G1
Kerchevskiy 72 L3
Kerempe Burnu 70 R2
Keren 110 G4
Kericho 116 F4
Keri Keri 128 D2
Kerio 116 F3
Kerki 96 J2
Kerkrade 56 J4
Kerkyra 70 B5
Kerkyra 70 B5
Kerma 110 F4
Kermadec Islands 124 H8
Kermadec Trench 124 J9
Kermān 101 G1
Kermānshāh 96 E3
Kermānshāhān 101 F1
Keros 70 H8
Kerpen 56 J4
Kerrville 144 B3
Kerulen 84 J7
Keryneia 98 E6
Keşan 70 J4
Kesennuma 88 L4
Keşiş Dağları 96 C2
Keswick 36 E7
Keszthely 68 E3
Keta 114 E3
Ketapang 92 D3
Ketchikan 146 (1)L4
Kētou 114 E3
Kętrzyn 52 L3
Kettering 38 H3
Kettle Falls 138 C2
Kewanee 142 C2
Keweenaw Peninsula 142 C1
Key Largo 144 E4
Keynsham 38 F3
Keystone Lake 144 B2
Key West 144 E5
Kezhma 84 G5
Kežmarok 52 K8
Khabarovsk 84 P7
Khadyzhensk 98 H1
Khakasiya 82 R7
Khairwāra 94 B4
Khalafabād 101 C1
Khalīg el Suweis 110 F2
Khalīj Surt 110 C1
Khalūf 96 G5
Khambhat 94 B4
Khamis Mushay 96 D6
Khamis Mushayt 110 H4
Khamkkeut 90 C3
Khampa 84 L4
Khamrà 84 J4
Khān al Baghdādī 98 K7
Khān az Zabīb 100 D5
Khandagayty 82 S7
Khandwa 94 C4
Khanewal 94 B2
Khannya 82 X4
Khanpur 94 B3
Khān Shaykhūn 100 D1
Khantau 82 N9
Khantayka 84 D3
Khanty-Mansiysk 72 N2
Khān Yūnis 100 B5
Khapalu 94 C1
Kharabali 72 J5
Kharagpur 94 E4
Kharampur 84 B4
Kharan 96 J4
Khargon 94 C4
Kharkiv 72 G5
Kharlu 50 R6
Kharmanli 70 H3
Kharnmam 94 D5
Kharovsk 72 H3
Khartoum = El Khartum 110 F4
Khasavyurt 98 M2
Khāsh 96 H4
Khashgort 72 N1
Khashm el Girba 110 G4
Khashuri 98 K3
Khaskovo 70 H3
Khatanga 84 G2
Khātūnābād 101 F1
Khatyrka 84 X4
Khavda 96 J5
Khawr Fakkān 101 G4
Khaydarken 96 K2
Khayelitsha 118 B6
Khemis Miliana 112 F1
Khemisset 112 D2
Khenchela 112 G1
Kherāmeh 101 E2
Kherson 72 F5
Kheta 82 T3
Kheta 82 T3
Kheygiyakha 72 P2
Khilok 84 J6
Khirbat Isrīyah 100 E1
Khīyāv 98 M4
Khmel'nyts'kyy 72 E5
Khodā Afarīn 98 M4
Kholmsk 84 Q7
Khonj 101 E3
Khon Kaen 90 C3
Khonuu 84 Q3
Khoper 72 H4
Khor 84 P7
Khor 84 P7
Khoreyver 72 L1
Khorinsk 84 H6
Khorramābād 96 E3
Khorramshahr 101 C1
Khorugh 96 K2
Khoseda Khard 72 L1
Khouribga 112 D2
Khrebet Cherskogo 84 P3
Khrebet Dzhagdy 84 N6
Khrebet Dzhugdzhur 84 N5
Khrebet Khamar Daban 84 G6
Khrebet Kolymskiy 80 U3
Khrebet Kopet Dag 96 G2
Khrebet Suntar Khayata 84 P4
Khrebet Tarbagatay 82 Q8
Khroma 84 Q2
Khudoseya 84 C3
Khudzhakh 84 R4
Khujand 96 J1
Khulna 94 E4
Khurayş 101 B4
Khushab 94 B2
Khust 68 L1
Khuwei 110 E5
Khuzdar 96 J4
Khvormūj 101 D2
Khvoy 98 L4
Khyber Pass 96 K3
Kibaya 116 F4
Kibombo 116 D4
Kibondo 116 E4
Kibre Mengist 116 F2
Kičevo 70 C3
Kichmengskiy Gorodok 72 J3
Kicking Horse Pass 136 H6
Kidal 112 F5
Kidderminster 38 F3
Kidira 114 B2
Kidsgrove 38 F2
Kiel 54 F2
Kielce 52 K7
Kielder Water 36 F6
Kieler Bucht 54 F2
Kiev = Kyyiv 72 F4
Kiffa 112 C5
Kigali 116 E4
Kigoma 116 D4
Kihnu 50 M7
Kıkıköy 70 L3
Kikinda 68 H4
Kikonai 88 L3
Kikori 93 F4
Kikwit 116 B5
Kilbeggan 35 D3
Kilchu 88 E3
Kilcormac 35 D3
Kildare 35 E3
Kilifi 116 F4
Kilindoni 116 F5
Kilingi-Nõmme 50 N7
Kilis 98 G5
Kiliya 68 S4
Kilkee 35 B4
Kilkeel 35 E2

Kilkenny 35 D4
Kilkis 70 E4
Killala Bay 35 B2
Killarney, *Canada* 142 D1
Killarney, *Republic of Ireland* 35 B4
Killarney National Park 35 B5
Killorglin 35 B4
Killybegs 35 C2
Kilmarnock 36 D6
Kil'mez 72 K3
Kilosa 116 F5
Kilrush 35 B4
Kilsyth 36 D6
Kilttan 94 B6
Kilwa 116 D5
Kilwa Masoko 116 F5
Kimberley 118 C5
Kimberley Plateau 126 E3
Kimch'aek 88 E3
Kimolos 70 G8
Kimongo 114 G5
Kimry 72 G3
Kinango 116 F4
Kinbrace 36 E3
Kincardine 142 D2
Kinda 116 C5
Kinder 144 C3
Kinder Scout 38 G2
Kindia 114 B2
Kindu 116 D4
Kineshma 72 H3
Kingaroy 126 K5
King City 140 B3
King George Islands 136 R5
Kinghorn 36 E5
Kingisepp 50 Q7
King Island, *Australia* 126 H7
King Island, *Canada* 84 AA3
Kingman 146 D1
Kingri 96 J3
Kingsbridge 38 E5
Kingscote 126 G7
Kingsland 144 E3
King's Lynn 38 J3
King Sound 126 D3
Kings Peak 140 D2
Kingsport 144 E2
Kingston, *Canada* 142 E2
Kingston, *Jamaica* 148 J5
Kingston, *United States* 142 F2
Kingston upon Hull 38 H2
Kingston upon Thames 38 H4
Kingstown 156 E1
Kingsville 144 B4
Kings Worthy 38 G4
Kington 38 E3
Kingussie 36 D4
Kingville 148 E3
King William Island 136 M3
King William's Town 118 D6
Kinik 70 K5
Kinka-san 88 L4
Kinlochewe 36 C4
Kinna 50 G8
Kinnaird Head 36 G4
Kinnegad 35 D3
Kinross 36 E5
Kinsale 35 C5
Kinsale Harbour 35 C5
Kinshasa 116 B4
Kinsley 144 B2
Kinston 142 E3
Kintampo 114 D3
Kintore 36 F4
Kintyre 36 C6
Kinyeti 116 E3
Kinzig 54 E6
Kipini 116 G4
Kipnuk 146 (1)E3
Kirchheim 64 E2
Kirchheimbolanden 56 L5
Kircudbright 36 D7
Kirenga 84 H5
Kirensk 84 H5
Kiribati 124 J6
Kırıkhan 98 G5
Kırıkkale 98 E4
Kirillov 72 G3
Kirinyaga 116 F4
Kirishi 72 F3
Kiritimati 124 L5
Kirkağaç 70 K5
Kirk Bulāg Dāgh 96 E2
Kirkby 38 F2
Kirkby in Ashfield 38 G2
Kirkby Lonsdale 36 F7
Kirkcaldy 36 E5
Kirkconnel 36 D6
Kirkjubæjarklaustur 50 (1)E3
Kirkland Lake 142 D1
Kırklareli 70 K3
Kirkūk 98 L6
Kirkwall 36 F3
Kirov, *Kyrgyzstan* 82 N9
Kirov, *Russia* 72 J3
Kirov, *Russia* 72 F4
Kirovohrad 72 F5
Kiroyo-Chepetsk 72 K3
Kirriemuir 36 E5
Kirs 72 K3
Kirsanov 72 H4
Kırşehir 98 F4
Kiruna 50 L3
Kiryū 88 K5
Kisangani 116 D3
Kisbér 68 E2
Kiselevsk 82 R7
Kishanganj 94 E3
Kishangarh, *India* 94 B3
Kishangarh, *India* 94 B3
Kishi 114 E3
Kishiwada 88 H6
Kishtwar 94 C2
Kisii 116 E4
Kiska Island 146 (3)B1
Kiskőrös 68 G3
Kiskunfélegyháza 68 G3
Kiskunhalas 68 G3
Kiskunmajsa 68 G3
Kislovodsk 98 K2
Kismaayo 116 G4
Kissidougou 114 B3
Kisumu 116 E4
Kisvárda 68 K1
Kita 114 C2
Kitakami 88 L4
Kita-Kyūshū 86 H4
Kita-Kyūshū 88 F7
Kitami 88 M2
Kitchener 142 D2
Kitgum 116 E3
Kitimat 136 F6
Kittilä 50 N3
Kitunda 116 E5
Kitwe 118 D2
Kitzingen 54 F7
Kiuruvesi 50 P5
Kivijärvi 50 N5
Kivik 52 D2
Kiya 84 D5
Kıyıköy 98 C3
Kizel 72 L3
Kizilalan 70 R8
Kızılcahamam 98 E3
Kızılırmak 98 F3
Kızılkaya 70 N7
Kizil'skoye 72 L4
Kızıltepe 98 J5
Kizlyar 98 M2
Kizlyarskiy Zaliv 98 M1
Kizyl-Atrek 82 J10
Kladanj 68 F5
Kladno 52 D7
Klagenfurt 64 K4
Klaipėda 50 L9
Klamath 140 B2
Klamath 140 B2
Klamath Falls 140 B2
Klarälven 50 G6
Klatovy 54 J7
Klaus 64 K3
Klerksdorp 118 D5
Kleve 54 B5
Klin 72 G3
Klingenthal 54 H6
Klínovec 54 H6
Klintsy 72 F4
Ključ 64 M6
Kłobuck 52 H7
Kłodzko 52 F7
Kløfta 50 F6
Klosterneuburg 64 M2
Klosters 64 E4
Kluane 136 D4
Kluane Lake 146 (1)J3
Kluczbork 52 H7
Klyuchevskaya Sopka 84 U5
Klyuchi 84 U5
Knapdale 36 C6
Knaresborough 36 G7
Knezha 68 M6
Knighton 38 G3
Knin 68 D5
Knittelfeld 68 B2
Knjaževac 68 K6
Knokke-Heist 56 F3
Knoxville 142 D3
Knutsford 38 F2
Knysna 118 C6
Koba 92 D3
Kōbe 88 H6
Kobe 93 C2
København 50 G9
Kobenni 112 D5
Koblenz 54 C6
Kobo 94 G3
Kobroör 93 E4
Kobryn 52 P5
Kobuk 146 (1)F2
Kobuk 146 (1)F2
Kočani 70 E3
Koçarli 70 K7
Kočevje 68 B4
Köch'ang 88 E6
Ko Chang 90 C4
Kochechum 84 F3
Kōchi 88 G7
Kochi 94 C7
Kochkor 82 P9
Kochki 82 Q7
Kochubey 98 M1
Kodiak 146 (1)G4
Kodiak Island 146 (1)G4
Kodino 72 G2
Kodinsk 84 F5
Kodomari-misaki 88 L3
Kodyma 68 S1
Köflach 68 C2
Kōfu 88 K6
Køge 52 B2
Køge Bugt 52 B2
Kohat 94 B2
Kohima 94 F3
Koh-i-Qaisir 96 H3
Koh-i-Sangan 96 J3
Kohtla-Järve 50 P7
Koidu 114 B3
Koi Sanjaq 98 L6
Koitere 50 R5
Kokenau 93 E3
Kokkola 50 M5
Kokomo 144 D1
Kokpekty 82 Q8
Kokshetau 72 N4
Kokstad 118 D6
Kolaka 93 B3
Kolar 94 C6
Kolari 50 M3
Kolašin 68 G7
Kolda 114 B2
Kolding 50 E9
Kole 116 C4
Kolhapur 94 B5
Kolin 52 E7
Kollam 94 C7
Köln 54 B6
Kolno 52 L4
Koło 52 H5
Kołobrzeg 52 E3
Kologriv 72 H3
Kolomna 72 G3
Kolomyya 68 N1
Kolonedale 93 B3
Kolosovka 72 P3
Kolpashevo 82 Q6
Kolpos Agiou Orous 70 F4
Kolpos Kassandras 70 F4
Kolpos Murampelou 70 H9
Kolskijzaliv 50 S2
Kolskiy Poluostrov 72 G1
Kolumadulu Atoll 94 B8
Koluton 72 N4
Kolva 72 L2
Kolwezi 118 D2
Kolyma 84 R4
Kolymskaya Nizmennost' 84 S3
Kolymskaye 84 T3
Komandorskiye Ostrova 84 V5
Komárno 68 F2
Komárom 68 F2
Komatsu 88 J5
Kombe 116 D4
Komi 72 K2
Komló 68 F3
Kom Ombo 110 F3
Komotini 70 H3
Komsa 82 R5
Komsomol'skiy 72 J5
Komsomol'sk-na-Amure 84 P6
Konārka 94 E5
Konda 72 N3
Kondagaon 94 D5
Kondinskoye 72 N3
Kondoa 116 F4
Kondopoga 72 F2
Kondrat'yeva 82 V5
Kondūz 96 J2
Kong Frederick VI Kyst 136 Y4
Kongi 82 R9
Kongola 118 C3
Kongolo 116 D5
Kongsberg 50 E7
Kongur Shan 82 N10
Königsberg = Kaliningrad 52 K3
Königswinter 54 C6
Königs-Wusterhausen 54 J4
Konin 52 H5
Konispol 70 C5
Konitsa 70 C4
Köniz 64 C4
Konjic 68 E6
Konosha 72 H2
Konotop 72 F4
Konstanz 64 E3
Konstinbrod 68 L7
Kontagora 114 F2
Kon Tum 90 D4
Konya 98 E5
Konz 54 B7
Kookynie 126 D5
Kootenai 140 C1
Kootenay Lake 138 C2
Kópasker 50 (1)E1
Kópavogur 50 (1)C2
Koper 64 J5
Kopeysk 72 M3
Köping 50 J7
Koplik 68 G7
Koprivnica 68 D3
Korba, *India* 94 D4
Korba, *Tunisia* 66 E12
Korbach 54 D5
Korçë 70 C4
Korčula 68 D7
Kord Sheykh 101 E2
Korea Bay 88 B4
Korea Strait 88 E6
Korf 84 V4
Korhogo 114 C3
Korinthiakos Kolpos 70 E6
Korinthos 70 E7
Kōriyama 88 L5
Korkino 72 M4
Korkuteli 98 D5
Korla 82 R9
Korliki 84 C4
Körmend 68 D2
Kornat 68 C6
Koroba 93 F4
Köroğlu Dağları 70 Q4
Köroğlu Tepesi 70 P4
Korogwe 116 F5
Koronowo 52 G4
Koror 124 D5
Korosten' 72 E4
Koro Toro 110 C4
Korsakov 84 Q7
Korsør 54 G1
Korti 110 F4
Kortrijk 56 F4
Korumburra 126 J7
Koryakskiy Khrebet 84 V4
Koryazhma 82 H5
Kos 70 K8
Kos 70 K8
Kosa 72 L3
Ko Samui 90 C5
Kościan 52 F5
Kościerzyna 52 H3
Kosciusko 144 D3
Kosh Agach 82 R8
Koshoba 96 F1
Košice 52 L9
Koslan 72 J2
Kosŏng 88 E4
Kosovo 70 C2
Kosovska Mitrovica 70 C2
Kosrae 124 G5
Kostajnica 64 M5
Kostenets 70 F2
Kosti 110 F5
Kostino 84 D3
Kostomuksha 50 R4
Kostroma 72 H3
Kostrzyn 52 D5
Kos'yu 72 L1
Koszalin 52 F3
Kőszeg 68 D2
Kota 94 C3
Kotaagung 92 C4
Kotabaru 92 F3
Kota Belud 92 F1
Kota Bharu 92 C1
Kotabumi 92 C3
Kota Kinabalu 92 F1
Kotamubagu 93 B2
Kotapinang 92 B2
Kotel'nich 72 J3
Kotel'nikovo 72 H5
Köthen 54 G5
Kotido 116 E3
Kotka 50 P6
Kotlas 72 J2
Kotlik 146 (1)E3
Kotor Varoš 68 E5
Kotov'sk 72 E5
Kottagudem 94 D5
Kotte 94 D7
Kotto 116 C2
Kotuy 84 G3
Kotzebue 146 (1)E2
Kotzebue Sound 146 (1)D2
Kouango 114 H3
Koudougou 114 D2
Koufey 114 G2
Koulamoutou 114 G5
Koum 114 G3
Koumra 114 H3
Koundâra 114 B2
Koupéla 112 C6
Kourou 156 G2
Koutiala 114 C2
Kouvola 72 E2
Kovdor 50 R3
Kovel' 72 D4
Kovin 68 H5
Kovrov 72 H3
Kowanyama 126 H3
Köyceğiz 70 L8
Koygorodok 72 K2
Koykuk 146 (1)E3
Koynas 72 J2
Koyukuk 146 (1)F2
Kozan 98 F5
Kozani 70 D4
Kozheynikovo 82 W3
Kozhikode 94 C6
Kozienice 52 L6
Kozloduy 68 L6
Kozlu 70 P3
Kōzu-shima 88 K6
Kpalimé 114 E3
Kraai 118 D6
Krabi 90 B5
Kradeljevo 66 M5
Kragujevac 68 H5
Kraków 52 J7
Kraljeviča 64 K5
Kraljevo 68 H6
Kralovice 52 C8
Kramators'k 72 G5
Kramfors 50 J5
Kranj 68 B3
Krapina 66 K2
Krapinske Toplice 64 L4
Krasino 82 J3
Krāslava 50 P9
Kraśnik 52 M7
Krasnoarmeysk 72 N4
Krasnoborsk 72 J2
Krasnodar 72 G5
Krasnohrad 72 G5
Krasnokamensk 84 K6
Krasnosel'kup 84 C3
Krasnotur'insk 72 M3
Krasnoufimsk 72 L3
Krasnovishersk 72 L2
Krasnoyarsk 84 E5
Krasnoyarskoye Vodokhranilishche 82 S6
Krasnoznamensk 52 M3
Krasnystaw 52 N7
Krasnyy Chikoy 84 H6
Krasnyy Kut 72 J4
Krasnyy Yar 72 J5
Kratovo 70 E2
Kraynovka 98 M2
Krefeld 56 J3
Kremenchuk 72 F5
Kremmling 140 E2
Krems 64 L2
Kremsmünster 64 K2
Krestovka 72 K1
Krestyakh 84 K4
Kretinga 52 L2
Kribi 114 F4
Krichim 70 G2
Krieglach 64 L3
Krishna 94 C5
Krishnagiri 94 C6
Kristiansand 50 E7
Kristianstad 50 H8
Kristiansund 50 D5
Kristinehamn 50 H7
Kristinestad 50 L5
Kriti 70 H10
Kriva Palanka 70 E2
Križevci 68 D3
Krk 64 K5
Krk 64 K5
Kroměříž 52 G8
Kronach 54 G6
Krŏng Kaôh Kŏng 90 C4
Kronotskiy Zaliv 84 U6
Kroonstadt 118 D5

Kroper 66 H3
Kropotkin 72 H5
Krosno 52 L8
Krško 64 L5
Krugë 70 B3
Krui 92 C4
Krumbach 64 F2
Krung Thep 90 C4
Kruså 54 E2
Kruševac 68 J6
Krychaw 72 F4
Krym' 98 E1
Krymsk 98 H1
Krynica 52 L8
Krytiko Pelagos 70 G9
Kryve Ozero 68 T2
Kryvyy Rih 72 F5
Krzna 52 N5
Ksar el Boukhari 62 N9
Ksen'yevka 84 K6
Ksour Essaf 112 H1
Kuala Kerai 92 C1
Kuala Lipis 92 C2
Kuala Lumpur 92 C2
Kuala Terengganu 92 C1
Kuandian 88 C3
Kuantan 92 C2
Kuşadasi 70 K7
Kučevo 68 J5
Kuching 92 E2
Kucovë 70 B4
Kudat 92 F1
Kudus 92 E4
Kudymkar 72 K3
Kufstein 64 H3
Kugmallit Bay 136 E2
Kühbonän 101 G1
Kühdasht 98 M7
Küh-e Alījuq 101 D1
Küh-e Bābā 96 J3
Küh-e Būl 101 E1
Küh-e Dīnār 101 D1
Küh-e Fūrgun 101 G3
Küh-e Hazārān 101 G2
Küh-e Hormoz 101 F3
Küh-e Kalat 96 G3
Küh-e Kührän 101 H3
Küh-e Läleh Zär 101 G2
Küh-e Masāhūn 101 F1
Küh-e Safidār 101 E2
Kuh-e Sahand 98 M5
Kühestak 101 G3
Küh-e Taftān 96 H4
Kühhā-ye Bashäkerd 101 G3
Kühhā-ye Zāgros 101 D1
Kuhmo 50 Q4
Kühpäyeh 101 G1
Kuito 118 B2
Kuji 88 L3
Kukës 68 H7
Kukhtuy 84 Q4
Kukinaga 88 F8
Kula 68 K6
Kulagino 72 K5
Kulandy 82 K8
Kuldīga 50 L8
Kulgera 126 F5
Kulmbach 54 G6
Külob 96 J2
Kul'sary 72 K5
Kultsjön 50 H4
Kulu 98 E4
Kulunda 82 P7
Kulynigol 84 C4
Kuma 72 N3
Kumamoto 88 F7
Kumanovo 68 J7
Kumara, *New Zealand* 128 C6
Kumara, *Russia* 84 M6
Kumasi 114 D3
Kumba 114 F4
Kumbağ 70 K4
Kumbakonam 94 C6
Kumeny 72 K3
Kumertau 72 L4
Kumla 50 H7
Kumluca 70 N8
Kummerower See 54 H3
Kumo 114 G3
Kumta 94 B6
Kumukh 98 M2
Kunene 118 A3
Kungälv 50 F8
Kungrad 82 K9
Kungu 116 B3
Kungur 72 L3
Kunhing 90 B2
Kunlun Shan 94 D1
Kunming 86 C6
Kunsan 88 D6
Kunszetmarton 52 K11
Künzelsau 54 E7
Kuolayarvi 50 Q3
Kuopio 72 E2
Kupang 126 B2
Kupino 82 P7
Kupreanof Point 146 (1)F4
Kup"yans'k 72 G5
Kuqa 82 Q9
Kür 98 M3
Kura 96 E2
Kuragino 84 E6
Kurashiki 88 G6
Kurasia 94 D4
Kurchum 82 Q8
Kürdämir 98 N3
Kurduvadi 94 C5
Kürdzhali 70 H3
Kure 88 G6
Kure Island 124 J3
Kuressaare 50 M7
Kureyka 84 D3
Kureyka 84 E3
Kurgal'dzhinskiy 82 N7
Kurgan 72 N3
Kurikka 50 M5
Kuril Islands = Kuril'skiye Ostrova 84 S7
Kuril'sk 84 R7
Kuril'skiye Ostrova 84 S7
Kuril Trench 80 V5
Kuripapango 128 F4
Kurmuk 110 F5
Kurnool 94 C5
Kuroiso 88 K5
Kurow 128 C7
Kuršėnai 52 M1
Kursk 72 G4
Kuršumlija 68 J6
Kurşunlu 98 E3
Kuruman 118 C5
Kurume 88 F7
Kurumkan 84 J6
Kurunegala 94 D7
Kushikino 88 F8
Kushimoto 88 H7
Kushir 84 H6
Kushiro 88 N2
Kushmurun 72 M4
Kushum 72 K4
Kuskokwim Bay 146 (1)E4
Kuskokwim Mountains 146 (1)F3
Kussharo-ko 88 N2
Kustanay 72 M4
Kütahya 98 C4
K'ut'aisi 98 K2
Kutan 98 M1
Kutchan 88 L2
Kutina 68 D4
Kutno 52 J5
Kutu 114 H5
Kutum 110 D5
Kuujjua 136 J2
Kuujjuaq 136 T5
Kuujjuarapik 136 R5
Kuusamo 72 E1
Kuvango 118 B2
Kuwait 101 B2
Kuwait = Al Kuwayt 101 C2
Kuya 72 H1
Kuybyshev 82 P6
Kuygan 82 N8
Kuytun 82 R9
Kuyumba 84 F4
Kuznetsk 72 J4
Kuzomen' 72 G1
Kvaløya, *Norway* 50 M1
Kvaløya, *Norway* 50 J2
Kvalynsk 82 H7
Kwale 116 F4
Kwangju 88 D6
Kwango 116 B5
Kwazulu Natal 118 E5
Kwekwe 118 D3
Kwidzyn 50 K10
Kwilu 114 H5
Kyakhta 84 H6
Kyancutta 126 G6
Kyaukpyu 90 A3
Kyaukse 94 G4
Kyeburn 128 C7
Kyeintali 94 F5
Kyjov 64 N2
Kyklades 70 G7
Kyle of Lochalsh 36 C4
Kyll 56 J4
Kyllini 70 D7
Kymi 70 G6
Kyŏngju 88 E6
Kyōto 88 H6
Kyparissia 70 D7
Kyperissiakos Kolpos 70 C7
Kyra Panagia 70 G5
Kyren 84 G6
Kyrgyzstan 82 N9
Kyritz 54 H4
Kyrta 72 L2
Kyshtovka 82 P6
Kystatyam 84 L3
Kytalyktakh 84 N3
Kythira 70 E8
Kythira 70 F8
Kythnos 70 G7
Kyushe 82 K8
Kyūshū 88 F7
Kyūshū-sanchi 88 F7
Kyustendil 70 E2
Kyusyur 84 M2
Kyyiv 72 F4
Kyzyl 82 S7
Kzyl-Dzhar 72 N5
Kzyl-Orda 72 N6
Kzyltu 82 N7

L

Laascaanood 116 H2
Laatzen 54 E4
Laba 114 F2
La Banda 158 J4
La Bañeza 62 E2
La Baule 60 C6
La Bazoge 60 F5
Labbezenga 112 F5
Labé 114 B2
Labe 52 E7
Labin 64 K5
Labinsk 98 J1
Laboulaye 158 J5
Labrador 136 U6
Labrador City 136 T6
Labrador Sea 136 V4
Lábrea 156 E5
Labrieville 142 G1
Labuha 93 C3
Labuhan 92 D4
Labuhanbajo 93 A4
Labutta 90 A3
Labytnangi 82 M4
Laç 68 G8
Lac à l'Eau Claire 136 R5
Lacanau 60 D8
La Carlota 62 F7
La Carolina 62 G6
Lac Bienville 136 S5
Lac Brochet 136 L5
Laccadive Islands 94 B6
Lac d'Annecy 64 B5
Lac de Bizerte 66 D11
Lac Débo 112 E5
Lac de Kossou 114 C3
Lac de Lagdo 114 G3
Lac de Manantali 114 C2
Lac de Mbakaou 114 G3
Lac de Neuchâtel 64 B4
Lac de Retenue de la Lufira 116 D6
Lac de St-Croix 64 B7
Lac des Bois 136 G3
Lac de Sélingue 114 C2
Lac Do 112 E5
Lac du Bourget 64 A5
Lacedonia 66 K7
Lacepede Bay 126 G7
Lac Evans 136 R6
Lac Faguibine 112 E5
Lac Fitri 110 C5
La Charité-sur-Loire 60 J6
La Chaux-de-Fonds 64 B3
La Chorrera 156 C4
Lac Ichkeul 66 D11
La Ciotat 60 L10
Lac La Biche 136 J6
Lac La Martre 136 H4
Lac Léman = Lake Geneva 64 B4
Lac Mai-Ndombe 116 B4
Lac-Mégantic 142 F1
Lac Minto 136 R5
Lac Nzilo 116 D6
Lac Onangué 114 F5
Laconi 66 D9
Laconia 142 F2
Lac Payne 136 S5
La Crosse 142 B2
La Cruz 138 E7
Lac St-Jean 142 F1
Lac St. Joseph 136 N6
Lac Seul 136 N6
Lac Tumba 116 B4
Lacul Brateş 68 Q4
Lacul Razim 68 R5
Lacul Sinoie 68 R5
Lac Upemba 116 D5
La Dorada 156 C2
Ladozhskoye Ozero 72 F2
Ladysmith, *South Africa* 118 D5
Ladysmith, *United States* 142 B1
Ladyzhenka 72 N4
La Esmeralda, *Bolivia* 158 J3
La Esmeralda, *Venezuela* 156 D3
Læsø 50 F8
Lafayette, *Ind., United States* 142 C2
Lafayette, *La., United States* 144 C3
La Ferté-St-Aubin 60 G6
Lafia 114 F3
Lafiagi 114 F3
La Flèche 60 E6
Lafnitz 64 M3
Laft 101 F3
Lagan 50 G8
Lagan' 72 J5
Lage 56 L3
Lågen 50 E6
Lage's 140 D2
Laggan 36 D4
Laghouat 112 F2
Lagkadas 70 F4
Lagoa dos Patos 158 L5
Lagoa Mirim 158 L5
Lago Argentino 158 G9
Lago de Cahora Bassa 118 E3
Lago del Coghinas 66 C8
Lago del Flumendosa 66 D9
Lago de Maracaibo 156 C2
Lago de Nicaragua 148 G6
Lago de Poopó 156 D7
Lago di Bolsena 66 F6
Lago di Caine 64 D5
Lago di Como 64 E4
Lago di Garda 64 F5
Lago di Lecco 64 E5
Lago di Lugano 64 E5
Lago d'Iseo 64 E5
Lago di Varano 66 K7
Lago Maggiore 64 D5
Lago Omodeo 66 C8
Lago Rogaguado 156 D6
Lagos, *Nigeria* 114 E3
Lagos, *Portugal* 62 B7
Lago Titicaca 156 D7
Lago Trasimeno 66 G5
La Goulette 66 E12
La Grand-Combe 60 K9
La Grande 140 C1
Lagrange 126 D3
La Grange 144 E3
La Gran Sabana 156 E2
Laguna 158 M4
Laguna de Caratasca 148 H5
Laguna Madre 144 B4
Laguna Mar Chiquita 154 E7
Lagunillas 156 E7
La Habana 148 H4
Lahad Datu 90 F5
Lahat 92 C3
La Haye-du-Puits 56 A5
Lāhījān 96 F2
Lahn 56 L4
Lahnstein 56 K4
Laholmsbukten 52 B1
Lahore 94 B2
Lahr 64 C2
Lahti 50 N6
Laï 116 B2
Laiagam 93 F4
Lai Chau 90 C2
L'Aigle 56 C6
Laihia 50 M5
Laingsburg 118 C6
Lairg 36 D3
Laiwu 86 F3
Laiyuan 86 E3
Lajanurpekhi 98 K2
Lajes 158 L4
Lajosmizse 52 J10
La Junta 140 F3
Lake Abbe 116 G1
Lake Abitibi 142 E1
Lake Albert, *Dem. Rep. of Congo/ Uganda* 116 D3
Lake Albert, *United States* 140 B2
Lake Almanor 140 B2
Lake Amadeus 126 F4
Lake Andes 140 G2
Lake Argyle 126 E3
Lake Argyle Tourist Village 126 E3
Lake Athabasca 136 K5
Lake Austin 126 C5
Lake Balkhash = Ozero Balkhash 80 L5
Lake Bangweulu 118 E2
Lake Barlee 126 C5
Lake Benmore 128 C7
Lake Blanche 126 H5
Lake Buchanan 146 G2
Lake Callabonna 126 H5
Lake Carey 126 D5
Lake Carnegie 126 D5
Lake Chad 110 B5
Lake Charles 144 C3
Lake Chelan 140 B1
Lake Chilwa 118 F3
Lake City 144 E3
Lake Claire 136 J5
Lake Coleridge 128 C6
Lake Constance 64 E3
Lake Crowley 140 C3
Lake C. W. McConaughy 140 F2
Lake Diefenbaker 136 K6
Lake Disappointment 126 D4
Lake District National Park 36 E7
Lake Dojran 70 E3
Lake Dora 126 D4
Lake Dundas 126 B6
Lake Edward 116 D4
Lake Elwall 140 D1
Lake Erie 142 D2
Lake Eyasi 116 E4
Lake Eyre 124 D8
Lake Eyre Basin 126 G5
Lake Eyre North 126 G5
Lake Eyre South 126 G5
Lake Francis Case 140 G2
Lake Frome 126 H6
Lake Gairdner 126 G6
Lake Geneva 64 B4
Lake Gordon 126 H8
Lake Grace 126 C6
Lake Harbour 136 T4
Lake Hauroko 128 A7
Lake Havasu 146 C2
Lake Havasu City 146 D2
Lake Hopkins 126 E4
Lake Hudson 144 B2
Lake Huron 142 D1
Lake Jackson 144 B4
Lake Kariba 118 D3
Lake Kemp 144 B2
Lake Kerkinitis 68 L8
Lake Kivu 116 D4
Lake Kyoga 116 E3
Lake Ladoga = Ladozhskoye Ozero 72 F2
Lakeland 144 E4
Lake Lefroy 126 D6
Lake Louis 136 H6
Lake Macdonald 126 E4
Lake Mackay 126 E4
Lake Macleod 126 B4
Lake Manapouri 128 A7
Lake Manitoba 136 M6
Lake Manyara 116 F4
Lake Maurice 126 F5
Lake McDonald 140 D1
Lake McMillan 146 F2
Lake Mead 140 D3
Lake Melville 136 U6
Lake Michigan 142 C2
Lake Moore 126 C5
Lake Murray 93 F4
Lake Mweru 116 D5
Lake Mweru Wantipa 116 E5
Lake Nash 126 G4
Lake Nasser 110 F3
Lake Natron 116 F4
Lake Neale 126 E4
Lake Nipigon 136 P6/7
Lake Nipissing 142 E1
Lake Nyasa 118 E2
Lake Oahe 140 F2
Lake of the Woods 142 B1
Lake Ohau 128 B7
Lake Ohrid 70 C4
Lake Okeechobee 144 E4
Lake Onega = Onezhskoye Ozero 48 H1
Lake Ontario 142 E2
Lake O' The Cherokees 142 B3
Lake O' The Pines 144 C3
Lake Paringa 128 B6
Lake Peipus 50 P7
Lake Placid 144 E4
Lakeport 140 B3
Lake Poteriteri 128 A8
Lake Powell 140 D3
Lake Prespa 70 D4
Lake Providence 144 C3
Lake Pskov 50 P7
Lake Pukaki 128 C7
Lake Rotorua 128 F4
Lake Rukwa 116 E5
Lake St. Lucia 118 E5
Lake Sakakawea 140 F1
Lake Scutari 68 G7
Lake Simcoe 142 E2
Lake Superior 142 C1
Lake Tahoe 140 B3
Lake Tanganyika 116 D5

Lake Taupo	128	E4
Lake Te Anau	128	A7
Lake Tekapo	128	C6
Lake Tekapo	128	C6
Lake Texoma	144	B3
Lake Torrens	126	G6
Lake Travis	146	G2
Lake Tschida	140	F1
Lake Turkana	116	F3
Lake Victoria	116	E4
Lakeview	140	B2
Lake Volta	114	D3
Lake Waikare	128	E3
Lake Waikaremoana	128	F4
Lake Wakatipu	128	B7
Lake Wanaka	128	B7
Lake White	126	E4
Lake Wills	126	E4
Lake Winnipeg	136	M6
Lake Winnipegosis	136	L6
Lakewood	140	E3
Lake Woods	126	F3
Lake Xau	118	C4
Lake Yamma Yamma	126	H5
Lakhdaria	62	P8
Lakhimpur	94	D3
Lakhnadon	94	C4
Lakhpat	94	A4
Lakin	144	A2
Lakki	94	B2
Lakonikos Kolpos	70	E8
Lakota	140	G1
Lakselv	50	N1
Lalín	62	B2
La Línea	62	E8
Lalitpur	94	C4
Lal-Lo	90	G3
La Loche	136	K5
La Louvière	56	G4
La Maddalena	66	D7
Lamar, *Colo., United States*	146	F1
Lamar, *Mo., United States*	144	C2
Lamard	101	E3
La Marsa	66	E12
Lamballe	60	C5
Lambaréné	114	G5
Lambay	35	E3
Lambert's Bay	118	B6
Lam Chi	90	C3
Lamesa	146	F2
Lamia	70	E6
Lammermuir Hills	36	F6
Lamone	64	G6
Lampang	90	B3
Lampasas	146	G2
Lampedusa	112	H1
Lampeter	38	D3
Lamu	116	G4
Lanai	146	(2)D3
Lanai City	146	(2)E3
Lanark	36	E6
Lancang	90	B2
Lancaster, *United Kingdom*	36	F7
Lancaster, *Mo., United States*	142	B2
Lancaster, *N.H., United States*	142	F2
Lancaster, *Oh., United States*	142	D3
Lancaster, *Pa., United States*	142	E2
Lancaster, *S.C., United States*	144	E3
Lancaster Sound	136	Q2
Lanciano	66	J6
Landau, *Germany*	56	L5
Landau, *Germany*	64	H2
Landeck	64	F3
Lander	140	E2
Landerneau	60	A5
Landor	126	C5
Landsberg	64	F2
Land's End	38	C5
Landshut	64	H2
Landskrona	52	B2
Landstuhl	56	K5
Land Wursten	54	D3
La'nga Co	94	D2
Langarūd	98	N5
Langdon	140	G1
Langebæk	54	H1
Langeland	54	F2
Langen, *Germany*	54	D3
Langen, *Germany*	56	L5
Langenau	64	F2
Langenhagen	54	E4
Langeoog	54	C3
Langeoog	54	C3
Langfang	86	F3
Langholm	36	E6
Langjökull	50	(1)C2
Langkawi	90	B5
Langkon	90	F5
Langogne	60	J9
Langon	60	E9
Langøya	50	H2
Langreo	62	E1
Langres	64	A3
Langsa	90	B6
Langtry	146	F3
Langvatnet	50	G3
Länkäran	98	N4
Lannion	60	B5
L'Anse	142	C1
Lansing	142	D2
Lanxi	86	H1
Lanya	116	E2
Lanzarote	112	C3
Lanzhou	86	C3
Laoag	90	G3
Lao Cai	90	C2
Laohekou	86	E4
Laon	56	F5
La Oroya	156	B6
Laos	90	C3
Laotougou	88	E2
Lapa	158	M4
La Palma	112	B3
La Palma	148	J7
La Paragua	156	E2
La Paz, *Argentina*	158	K5
La Paz, *Bolivia*	156	D7
La Paz, *Mexico*	148	B4
La Pedrera	156	D4
La Perla	146	F3
La Pérouse Strait	86	L1
La Pesca	144	B5
La Pine	140	B2
Lapithos	100	A1
La Plant	140	F1
La Plata	158	K5
Lappajärvi	50	M5
Lappeenranta	50	Q6
Lappland	50	M2
Laptev Sea = More Laptevykh	84	L1
Lapua	50	M5
Łapy	52	M5
La Quiaca	158	H3
L'Aquila	66	H6
Lār	101	F3
Larache	112	D1
Laramie	140	E2
Laramie Range	140	E2
Larantuka	93	B4
Larat	93	D4
Larba	62	P8
Laredo, *Spain*	62	G1
Laredo, *United States*	146	G3
Largo	144	E4
Largs	36	D6
L'Ariana	66	E12
Lariang	93	A3
La Rioja	158	H4
Larisa	70	E5
Larkana	96	J4
Larkhall	36	E6
Larnaka	100	A2
Larne	35	F2
La Rochelle	60	D7
La Roche-sur-Yon	60	D7
La Roda	62	H5
La Romana	148	L5
La Ronge	136	K5
Larrimah	126	F3
Lar'yak	82	Q5
La Sarre	142	E1
Las Cabezas de San Juan	62	E7
Las Cruces	146	E2
La Serena	158	G4
La Seu d'Urgell	62	M2
La Seyne-sur-Mer	60	L10
Lashio	90	B2
Lashkar Gāh	96	H3
Las Horquetas	158	G8
Łask	52	J6
Las Lomitas	158	J3
La Solana	62	G6
Las Palmas	112	B3
Las Petas	156	F7
La Spezia	64	E6
Las Plumas	158	H7
Las Taques	156	C1
Last Chance	140	F3
Lastoursville	114	G5
Lastovo	68	D7
Las Varas	138	E7
Las Varillas	158	J5
Las Vegas, *Nev., United States*	140	C3
Las Vegas, *N. Mex., United States*	146	E1
La Teste	60	D9
Latina	66	G7
Latisana	64	J5
La Toma	158	H5
La Tuque	142	F1
Latur	94	C5
Latvia	50	M8
Lauchhammer	54	J5
Lauder	36	F6
Lauenburg	54	F3
Lauf	54	G7
Lau Group	124	J7
Launceston, *Australia*	126	J8
Launceston, *United Kingdom*	38	D5
La Union	62	K7
Laupheim	64	E2
Laura	126	H3
Laurel	144	D3
Laurencekirk	36	F5
Lauria	66	K8
Laurinburg	144	F3
Lausanne	64	B4
Laut, *Indonesia*	92	F3
Laut, *Malaysia*	92	D2
Lauter	56	K5
Lauterbach	54	E6
Lava	52	L3
Laval, *Canada*	142	F1
Laval, *France*	60	E5
La Vall d'Uixo	62	K5
Lavant	64	K4
Lāvar Kabkān	101	D2
La Vega	148	K5
Laviana	62	E1
La Vila Joiosa	62	K6
Lavras	158	N3
Lavrentiya	84	Z3
Lavrio	70	G7
Lawdar	110	J5
Lawra	114	D2
Lawrence, *New Zealand*	128	B7
Lawrence, *Kans., United States*	142	A3
Lawrence, *Mass., United States*	142	F2
Lawrenceville	144	D2
Lawton	144	B3
Laya	72	L1
Laylā	110	J3
Laysan Island	124	J3
Layton	140	D2
Lazarev	84	Q6
Lázaro Cárdenas	148	D5
Lazdijai	52	N3
Lāzeh	101	E3
Lazo	84	P3
Leadville	140	E3
Leamington	142	D2
Leatherhead	38	H4
Leavenworth, *Kans., United States*	142	A3
Leavenworth, *Wash., United States*	140	B1
Lebach	56	J5
Lebanon	100	C3
Lebanon, *Mo., United States*	142	B3
Lebanon, *N.H., United States*	142	F2
Lebanon, *Pa., United States*	142	E2
Lebanon, *Tenn., United States*	142	C3
Lebel-sur-Quévillon	142	E1
Lębork	52	G3
Lebrija	62	D8
Lebu	158	G6
Lecce	66	N8
Lecco	64	E5
Lech	64	F3
Leck	54	D2
Le Creusot	60	K7
Le Crotoy	56	D4
Łeczna	52	M6
Łęczyca	52	J5
Ledbury	38	F3
Ledmozero	50	R4
Lee	35	C5
Leech Lake	142	B1
Leeds	36	G8
Leek, *Netherlands*	56	J1
Leek, *United Kingdom*	38	F2
Leer	56	K1
Leesburg	144	E4
Leeston	128	D6
Leesville	144	C3
Leeuwarden	56	H1
Leeward Islands	148	M5
Lefkada	70	C6
Lefkada	70	C6
Lefkimmi	70	C5
Lefkonikon	100	A1
Lefkosia	70	R9
Legaspi	90	G4
Legionowo	52	K5
Legnago	64	G5
Legnica	52	F6
Leh	94	C2
Le Havre	56	C5
Lehre	54	F4
Lehrte	54	F4
Leiah	94	B2
Leibnitz	64	L4
Leicester	38	G3
Leiden	56	G2
Leie	56	F4
Leigh	38	F2
Leigh Creek	126	G6
Leighton Buzzard	38	H4
Leine	54	E4
Leinster	126	D5
Leinster	35	E3
Leipzig	54	H5
Leiria	62	B5
Leiyang	86	E5
Lek	56	G3
Lelystad	56	H2
Le Mans	60	F6
Le Mars	142	A2
Lemberg	54	D8
Lemesos	70	Q10
Lemgo	56	L2
Lemieux Islands	136	U4
Lemmer	56	H2
Lemmon	140	F1
Le Muret	60	E9
Lena	62	E1
Lena	84	L4
Lendava	64	M4
Lendinare	64	G5
Lengerich	56	K2
Lengshuijiang	86	E5
Lengshuitan	86	E5
Lenininsk-Kuznetskiy	82	R7
Leninskoye	72	J3
Lenmalu	93	D3
Lenne	56	K3
Lennestadt	56	L3
Lens	56	E4
Lensk	84	K4
Lenti	64	M4
Lentini	66	J11
Léo	114	D2
Leoben	64	L3
Leominster	38	F3
León, *Mexico*	148	D4
León, *Nicaragua*	148	G6
León, *Spain*	62	E2
Leonardville	118	B4
Leonberg	64	E2
Leonforte	66	J11
Leonidi	70	E7
Leonora	126	D5
Leova	68	R3
Le Palais	60	B6
Lepe	62	C7
Le Perthus	60	H11
Lepoura	70	G6
Lepsy	82	P8
Le Puy	60	J8
Léré	114	G3
Lerici	64	E6
Lerik	98	N4
Lerma	62	G2
Leros	70	J7
Lerwick	36	(1)G1
Lešak	68	H6
Les Andelys	56	D5
Lesatima	116	F4
Lesbos = Lesvos	70	H5
Les Escaldes	60	G11
Les Escoumins	136	T7
Leshan	86	C5
Les Herbiers	60	D7
Leshukonskoye	72	J2
Leskovac	68	J7
Lesosibirsk	82	S6
Lesotho	118	D5
Lesozavodsk	88	G1
Lesparre-Médoc	60	E8
Les Sables-d'Olonne	60	D7
Les Sept Îles	60	B5
Lesser Antilles	148	L6
Lesser Slave Lake	136	J5
Lesvos	70	H5
Leszno	52	F6
Letaba	118	E4
Letchworth	38	H4
Letenye	64	M4
Lethbridge	140	D1
Lethem	156	F3
Leticia	156	D4
Letpadan	90	B3
Le Tréport	56	D4
Letterkenny	35	D2
Leutkirch	64	F3
Leuven	56	G4
Leuze	56	F4
Levadeia	70	E6
Levanzo	66	G10
Levashi	98	M2
Levaya Khetta	72	P2
Leven	36	F5
Leverano	66	N8
Leverburgh	36	A4
Leverkusen	56	J3
Levice	52	H9
Levico Terme	64	G4
Levin	128	E5
Lévis	142	F1
Levitha	70	J7
Levoča	52	K9
Levski	68	N6
Lewe	90	B3
Lewes	38	J5
Lewis	36	B3
Lewis and Clark Lake	140	G2
Lewis Range	136	J7
Lewiston, *Id., United States*	140	C1
Lewiston, *Me., United States*	142	F2
Lewistown, *Mont., United States*	140	E1
Lewistown, *Pa., United States*	142	E2
Lexington, *Ky., United States*	142	D3
Lexington, *Nebr., United States*	140	G2
Lexington, *Va., United States*	142	E3
Lexington Park	144	F2
Leyburn	36	G7
Leyland	38	F2
Leyte	90	G4
Lezhë	68	G8
Lhari	94	F2
Lhasa	94	F3
Lhazê	94	E3
Lhokseumawe	90	B5
Lian Xian	90	E2
Lianyuan	90	E1
Lianyungang	86	F4
Liaocheng	86	F3
Liao He	88	B3
Liaoyang	88	B3
Liaoyuan	88	C2
Liard	136	F5
Liard River	136	F5
Libby	140	C1
Libenge	116	B3
Liberal	144	A2
Liberec	52	E7
Liberia	114	B3
Liberia	148	G6
Liberty	144	C1
Libjo	90	H4
Libourne	60	E9
Libreville	114	F4
Libya	110	C2
Libyan Desert	110	D2
Libyan Plateau	110	E1
Licata	66	H11
Lich	54	D6
Lichfield	38	G3
Lichinga	118	F2
Lichtenfels	54	G6
Lida	50	N10
Lidköping	50	G7
Lidodi Jesolo	64	H5
Lido di Ostia	66	G7
Lidzbark Warmiński	52	K3
Liebenwalde	54	J4
Liechtenstein	64	E3
Liège	56	H4
Lieksa	50	R5
Lienz	64	H4
Liepāja	52	L1
Lier	56	G3
Liezen	64	K3
Lifford	35	D2
Lignières	60	H7
Ligueil	60	F6
Ligurian Sea	64	D7
Lihue	146	B2
Lijiang	90	C1
Likasi	116	D6
Lilienfeld	64	L2
Lille	56	F4
Lillebonne	56	C5
Lillehammer	50	F6
Lillerto	64	G3
Lilongwe	118	E2
Liloy	90	G5
Lima, *Peru*	156	B6
Lima, *Mont., United States*	140	D2
Lima, *Oh., United States*	142	D2
Limanowa	52	K8
Limassol = Lemesos	70	Q10
Limavady	35	E1
Limbaži	50	N8
Limburg	56	L4
Limeira	158	M3
Limerick	35	C4
Limingen	50	G4
Limni Kastorias	70	C4
Limni Kerkinitis	70	E3
Limni Koronia	70	F4
Limni Trichonida	70	D6
Limni Vegoritis	70	D4
Limni Volvi	70	F4
Limnos	70	H5
Limoges	60	G8
Limon	140	F3

Limón	148	H7
Limoux	60	H10
Limpopo	118	D4
Linares, *Chile*	158	G6
Linares, *Mexico*	146	G4
Linares, *Spain*	62	G6
Linaria	70	G6
Lincang	90	C2
Linchuan	86	F5
Lincoln, *United Kingdom*	38	H2
Lincoln, *Ill., United States*	142	C2
Lincoln, *Me., United States*	142	G1
Lincoln, *Nebr., United States*	140	G2
Lincoln, *N.H., United States*	142	F2
Lincolnshire Wolds	38	H2
Lindenow Fjord	136	Y4
Lindesnes	50	D8
Lindi	116	F6
Lindi	116	D3
Lindos	70	L8
Line Islands	124	L5
Linfen	86	E3
Lingayen	90	G3
Lingen	56	K2
Lingga	92	C3
Lingshui	90	D3
Linguère	114	A1
Lingyuan	86	F2
Linhal	86	G5
Linhares	156	J7
Linhe	86	D2
Linjiang	88	D3
Linköping	50	H7
Linkou	88	F1
Linosa	66	G13
Lins	158	M3
Linton	140	F1
Linxi	86	F2
Linxia	86	C3
Lin Xian	86	E3
Linyi	86	F3
Linz	64	K2
Liobomil'	52	P6
Lipari	66	J10
Lipari	66	J10
Lipcani	68	P1
Lipetsk	72	G4
Lipin Bor	72	G2
Lipno	52	J5
Lipova	68	J3
Lippe	56	L3
Lippstadt	56	L3
Lipsoi	70	J7
Liptovský-Mikuláš	52	J8
Lipu	90	E2
Liqeni i Fierzës	68	H7
Liqeni Komanit	68	G7
Lira	116	E3
Liri	66	H7
Lisala	116	C3
Lisboa	62	A6
Lisbon = Lisboa	62	A6
Lisburn	35	E2
Liscannor Bay	35	B4
Lishi	86	E3
Lishui	86	F5
Lisieux	56	C5
Liskeard	38	D5
Liski	72	G4
L'Isle-sur-la-Sorgue	60	L10
Lismore	36	C5
Lisnaskea	35	D2
Lisse	56	G2
Lištica	66	M5
Listowel	35	B4
Listvyanka	84	H6
Litang	86	C5
Litani	156	G3
Litava	52	F8
Litchfield, *Ill., United States*	142	C3
Litchfield, *Minn., United States*	142	B1
Lithgow	126	K6
Lithuania	50	L9
Litke	84	Q6
Litomerice	54	K6
Litomyšl	52	F8
Litovel	52	G8
Litovko	84	P7
Little Abaco	144	F4
Little Andaman	94	F6
Little Barrier Island	128	E3
Littleborough	38	F2
Little Current	142	D1
Little Desert	126	H7
Little Falls	142	B1
Littlefield	146	F2
Littlehampton	38	H5
Little Inagua	148	K4
Little Karoo	118	C6
Little Minch	36	B4
Little Nicobar	94	F7
Little Rock	144	C3
Littleton	140	E3
Litvinov	54	J6
Liupanshui	86	C5
Liuzhou	86	D6
Live Oak	144	E3
Liverpool, *Canada*	136	U8
Liverpool, *United Kingdom*	38	F2
Liverpool Bay, *Canada*	136	F2
Liverpool Bay, *United Kingdom*	38	E2
Livingston, *United Kingdom*	36	E6
Livingston, *United States*	140	D1
Livingstone	118	D3
Livingstonia	118	E2
Livno	68	E6
Livny	72	G4
Livonia	142	D2
Livorno	64	F7
Liwale	116	F5
Lizard	38	C6
Lizard Point	38	C6
Ljubljana	64	K4
Ljugarn	50	K8
Ljungan	50	J5
Ljungby	50	G8
Ljusdal	50	J6
Ljusnan	72	C2
Llandeilo	38	E4
Llandovery	38	E4
Llandrindod Wells	38	E3
Llandudno	38	E2
Llanelli	38	D4
Llanes	62	F1
Llangollen	38	E3
Llanidloes	38	E3
Llanos	156	C2
Llanrwst	38	E2
Llanwrtyd Wells	38	E3
Lleida	62	L3
Llerena	62	E6
Lleyn	38	D3
Lli	82	P9
Lloret de Mar	62	N3
Llucmajor	62	N5
Loano	64	D6
Lobamba	118	E5
Lobatse	118	D5
Löbau	54	K5
Łobez	52	E4
Lobito	118	A2
Locarno	64	D4
Loch Awe	36	C5
Lochboisdale	36	A4
Loch Broom	36	C4
Lochearnhead	36	D5
Lochem	56	J2
Loch Eriboll	36	D3
Loch Ericht	36	D5
Loch Fyne	36	C5
Lochgilphead	36	C5
Loch Indaal	36	B6
Lochinver	36	C3
Loch Leven	36	E5
Loch Linnhe	36	C5
Loch Lochy	36	D5
Loch Lomond	36	D5
Lochmaddy	36	A4
Loch Maree	36	C4
Loch Morar	36	C5
Lochnagar	36	E5
Loch Ness	36	D4
Lochranza	36	C6
Loch Ryan	36	C6
Loch Shiel	36	C5
Loch Shin	36	D3
Loch Snizort	36	B4
Loch Tay	36	D5
Lockerbie	36	E6
Lockhart	144	B4
Lock Haven	142	E2
Lockport	142	E2
Locri	66	L10
Lodève	60	J10
Lodeynoye	72	F2
Lodge Grass	140	E1
Lodi, *Italy*	64	E5
Lodi, *United States*	140	B3
Lodja	116	C4
Lodwar	116	F3
Łódź	52	J6
Loei	90	C3
Lofoten	50	G3
Logan, *Ia., United States*	142	A2
Logan, *N. Mex., United States*	146	F1
Logan, *Ut., United States*	140	D2
Logansport	142	C2
Logatec	64	K5
Logroño	62	H2
Lohiniva	50	N3
Lohr	54	E7
Loikaw	90	B3
Loir	60	F6
Loire	60	D6
Loja, *Ecuador*	156	B4
Loja, *Spain*	62	F7
Lokan tekojärvi	50	P3
Lokeren	56	F3
Lokichar	116	F3
Lokichokio	116	E3
Lokoja	114	F3
Lokosovo	72	P2
Loks Land	136	U4
Lolland	54	G2
Lollondo	116	F4
Lolo	140	D1
Lom	68	L6
Lomami	116	C4
Lomas	156	C7
Lomas de Zamora	158	K5
Lombadina	126	D3
Lomblen	93	B4
Lombok	92	F4
Lombok	92	F4
Lomé	114	E3
Lomela	116	C4
Lomela	116	C4
Lommel	56	H3
Lomonosovka	72	N4
Lompoc	146	B2
Łomża	52	M4
London, *Canada*	142	D2
London, *United Kingdom*	38	H4
London, *United States*	144	E2
Londonderry	35	D2
Londrina	158	L3
Longarone	64	H4
Long Bay	148	J2
Long Beach	146	C2
Long Branch	142	F2
Long Eaton	38	G3
Longford	35	D3
Long Island, *Canada*	136	Q5
Long Island, *United States*	142	F2
Longlac	136	P7
Long Lake	140	F1
Longmont	140	E2
Long Prairie	142	B1
Long Range Mountains	136	V6
Longreach	126	H4
Longtown	36	F6
Longueuil	142	F1
Longview, *Tex., United States*	144	C3
Longview, *Wash., United States*	140	B1
Longwy	56	H5
Long Xuyên	90	D4
Longyan	90	F1
Löningen	56	K2
Lönsdalen	50	H3
Lons-le-Saunier	64	A4
Looe	38	D5
Lookout Pass	140	C1
Loop Head	35	B4
Lopez	90	G4
Lop Nur	82	S9
Lopphavet	50	L1
Loptyuga	72	J2
Lora del Rio	62	E7
Lorain	142	D2
Loralai	94	A2
Lorca	62	J7
Lordegān	101	D1
Lord Howe Island	126	L6
Lordsburg	146	E2
Loreto	148	B3
Lorient	60	B6
Lorn	36	C5
Lörrach	64	C3
Lorraine	126	G3
Los Alamos	146	E1
Los Angeles, *Chile*	158	G6
Los Angeles, *United States*	146	C2
Los Banos	140	B3
Los Blancos	158	J3
Losheim	56	J5
Losice	52	M5
Lošinj	64	K6
Los Mochis	148	C3
Lospalos	93	C4
Lossiemouth	36	E4
Los Telares	158	J4
Los Teques	156	D1
Lost Trail Pass	140	D1
Los'va	72	M2
Los Vientos	158	H3
Lotta	50	Q2
Lotte	56	K2
Louang Namtha	90	C2
Louangphrabang	90	C3
Loubomo	114	G5
Loudéac	60	C5
Louga	114	A1
Lough Allen	35	C2
Loughborough	38	G3
Lough Carra	35	B3
Lough Conn	35	B2
Lough Corrib	35	B3
Lough Derg	35	C4
Lough Derravaragh	35	D3
Lough Ennell	35	D3
Lough Foyle	35	D1
Lough Leane	35	B4
Lough Mask	35	B3
Lough Neagh	35	E2
Lough Owel	35	D3
Loughrea	35	C3
Lough Ree	35	D3
Lough Sheelin	35	D3
Louhans	60	L7
Louisa	142	D3
Louisiade Archipelago	126	K2
Louisiana	144	C3
Louis Trichardt	118	D4
Louisville, *Ga., United States*	144	E3
Louisville, *Ky., United States*	144	D2
Louisville, *Miss., United States*	144	D3
Loukhi	50	S3
Loulé	62	C7
Louny	54	J6
Loup	140	G2
Lourdes	60	E10
Louros	70	C5
Louth, *Australia*	126	J6
Louth, *United Kingdom*	38	H2
Loutra Aidipsou	70	F6
Louviers	56	D5
Lovech	68	M6
Lovell	140	E2
Lovelock	140	C2
Lovosice	54	K6
Lovran	64	K5
Lôvua	118	C2
Lowa	116	D4
Lowell	142	F2
Lower Hutt	128	E5
Lower Lake	140	B2
Lower Lough Erne	35	D2
Lower Post	136	F5
Lowestoft	38	K3
Łowicz	52	J5
Lowville	142	F2
Loxstedt	54	D3
Loyalty Islands	124	G8
Loyno	72	K3
Loznica	68	G5
L-Travemünde	54	F3
Luama	116	D4
Luampa	118	C3
Lu'an	86	F4
Luanda	116	A5
Luangwa	118	E3
Luangwa	118	E2
Lua Nova	156	F5
Luanping	86	F2
Luanshya	118	D2
Luarca	62	D1
Luau	118	C2
Lubaczów	52	N7
Lubań	52	E6
Lubango	118	A2
Lubāns	50	P8
Lubao	116	D5
Lubartów	52	M6
Lübbecke	56	L2
Lübben	54	J5
Lübbenau	54	J5
Lubbock	146	F2
Lübeck	54	F3
Lubefu	116	C4
Lubero	116	D4
Lubilash	116	C5
Lubin	52	F6
Lublin	52	M6
Lubliniec	52	H7
Lubny	72	F4
Luboń	52	F5
Lubsko	52	D6
Lubudi	116	D5
Lubuklinggau	92	C3
Lubumbashi	116	D6
Lubutu	116	D4
Lucala	116	B5
Lucan	35	E3
Lucas	156	F6
Lucca	64	F7
Luce Bay	36	D7
Lucedale	144	D3
Lucena, *Philippines*	90	G4
Lucena, *Spain*	62	F7
Lučenec	52	J9
Lucera	66	K7
Lucero	146	E2
Lucira	118	A2
Luckau	54	J5
Luckenwalde	54	J4
Lucknow	94	D3
Luçon	60	D7
Lucusse	118	C2
Ludden	140	G1
Lüdenscheid	56	K3
Lüderitz	118	B5
Ludhiana	94	C2
Ludington	142	C2
Ludlow, *United States*	146	C2
Ludlow, *United Kingdom*	38	F3
Ludogori	68	P6
Luduș	68	M3
Ludvika	50	H6
Ludwigsburg	64	E2
Ludwigsfelde	54	J4
Ludwigshafen	56	L5
Ludwigslust	54	G3
Ludza	50	P8
Luebo	116	C5
Luena	118	B2
Lufeng	90	F2
Lufira	116	D6
Lufkin	144	C3
Luga	50	Q7
Luga	72	E3
Lugano	64	D4
Lugela	118	F3
Lugenda	118	F2
Luggate	128	B7
Lugnaquilla	35	E4
Lugo	64	G6
Lugoj	68	J4
Lugovoy	82	N9
Lugu	94	D2
Luhans'k	72	G5
Luhuo	86	C4
Lui	90	E2
Luilaka	116	B4
Luing	36	C5
Luino	64	D4
Luis Moya	146	F4
Luiza	116	C5
Lukavac	68	F5
Lukovit	68	M6
Łuków	52	M6
Lukulu	118	C2
Lukumburu	116	F5
Lukuni	116	B5
Luleå	50	M4
Lüleburgaz	70	K3
Lulua	116	D5
Lumbala Kaquengue	118	C2
Lumberton	144	F3
Lumbrales	62	D4
Lumimba	118	E2
Lumsden	128	B7
Lund	52	C2
Lundazi	118	E2
Lundy	38	D4
Lune	36	F7
Lüneburg	54	F3
Lüneburger Heide	54	F4
Lunel	60	K10
Lünen	56	K3
Lunéville	64	B2
Lungau	64	J3
Luntai	82	Q9
Luohe	86	E4
Luoyang	86	E4
Luozi	116	A4
Lupeni	68	L4
Lūrā Shīrīn	98	L5
Lure	64	B3
Luremo	116	B5
Lurgan	35	E2
Lurio	118	F2
Lusaka	118	D3
Lusambo	116	C5
Lushnjë	70	B4
Lushui	86	B5
Lüshun	86	G3
Lusk	140	F2
Lutembo	118	C2
Lutherstadt Wittenberg	54	H5
Luton	38	H4
Luts'k	72	E4
Lutterworth	38	G3
Lutto	50	P2
Lützow-Holmbukta	160	(2)J3
Luuq	116	G3
Luverne	142	A2
Luvua	116	D5
Luwuk	93	B3
Luxembourg	56	H5
Luxembourg	56	J5
Luxeuil-les-Bains	64	B3
Luxor	110	F2
Luza	72	J2
Luza	72	J2

Luzern 64 D3
Luzhou 86 D5
Luzilândia 156 J4
Luznice 64 K1
Luzon 90 G3
Luzon Strait 90 G2
Luzy 60 J7
Luzzi 66 L9
L'viv 52 N8
Lyady 50 Q7
Lyapin 72 M2
Lybster 36 E3
Lycksele 72 C2
Lydenburg 118 E5
Lydney 38 F4
Lyme Bay 38 F5
Lyme Regis 38 F5
Lymington 38 G5
Lynchburg 142 E3
Lynn 142 F2
Lynn Lake 136 L5
Lynton 38 E4
Lynx Lake 136 K4
Lyon 60 K8
Lys 56 E4
Lys'va 72 L3
Lysychans'k 72 G5
Lytham St. Anne's 38 E2
Lyttelton 128 D6

M

Maalosmadulu Atoll 94 B7
Ma'ān 100 C6
Maardu 50 N7
Ma'arrat an Nu'mān 98 G6
Maas 56 J3
Maasin 90 G4
Maastricht 56 H4
Mabalane 118 E4
Mabanza-Ngungu 114 G6
Mabaruma 156 F2
Mabein 90 B2
Mablethorpe 38 J2
Macapá 156 G3
Macas 156 B4
Macassar Strait 124 B6
Macau, *Brazil* 156 K5
Macau, *China* 90 E2
Macaúba 156 G6
Macclesfield 38 F2
Macdonnell Ranges 126 F4
Macduff 36 F4
Macedonia 70 C3
Maceió 156 K5
Macerata 64 J7
Macgillycuddy's Reeks 35 B5
Machakos 116 F4
Machala 156 B4
Macheng 86 F4
Machilipatnam 94 D5
Machiques 156 C1
Machynlleth 38 E3
Macia 118 E4
Măcin 68 R4
Mack 146 E1
Mackay 126 J4
Mackay Lake 136 J4
Mackenzie 136 G4
Mackenzie Bay 136 D3
Mackenzie Mountains 136 E3
Mackinaw City 142 D1
Macmillan 136 E4
Macmillan Pass 136 F4
Macomb 142 B2
Macomer 66 C8
Macon, *Ga., United States* 144 E3
Macon, *Mo., United States* 144 C2
Mâcon 60 K7
Macroom 35 C5
Macuje 156 C3
Mādabā 100 C5
Madagascar 118 H3
Madan 68 M8
Madanapalle 94 C6
Madaoua 114 F2
Madeira 112 B2
Madeira 156 E5
Maden 98 H4
Madera 146 E3
Madikeri 94 C6
Madison 142 C2
Madison, *Ind., United States* 142 C3
Madison, *Minn., United States* 142 A1
Madison, *S.D., United States* 140 G2
Madisonville 142 C3
Madiun 92 E4
Mado Gashi 116 F3
Madoi 86 B4
Madona 50 P8
Madras = Chennai, *India* 94 D6
Madras, *United States* 140 B2
Madre de Dios 156 C6
Madrid, *Philippines* 90 H5
Madrid, *Spain* 62 G4
Madridejos 62 G5
Madura 92 E4
Madurai 94 C6
Maebashi 88 K5
Mae Hong Son 90 B3
Mae Nam Mun 90 C3
Mae Sariang 90 B3
Maevatanana 118 H3
Mafeteng 118 D5
Maffighofen 64 J2
Mafia Island 116 G5
Mafinga 116 F5
Mafra 158 M4
Mafraq 100 D4
Magadan 84 S5
Magadi 116 F4
Magdagachi 84 M6
Magdalena 156 C2
Magdalena, *Bolivia* 156 E6
Magdalena, *Mexico* 146 D2
Magdalena, *United States* 146 E2
Magdeburg 54 G4
Magdelaine Cays 126 K3
Magelang 92 E4
Magenta 64 D5
Magerøya 50 N1
Maghera 35 E2
Magherafelt 35 E2
Maglaj 68 F5
Maglie 66 N8
Magnitogorsk 72 L4
Magnolia 144 C3
Mago 84 P6
Magog 142 F1
Magta Lahjar 112 C5
Magu 116 E4
Magwe 90 A2
Mahābād 98 L5
Mahaboboka 118 G4
Mahagi 116 E3
Mahajamba 118 H3
Mahajanga 118 H3
Mahalapye 118 D4
Mahān 101 G1
Mahanadi 94 D4
Mahanoro 118 H3
Mahasamund 94 D4
Mahavavy 118 H3
Mahbubnagar 94 D5
Mahḍah 101 G4
Mahé Island 118 (2)C1
Mahenge 116 F5
Mahesāna 94 B4
Mahia Peninsula 128 F4
Mahilyow 72 F4
Mahnomen 142 A1
Mahón 62 Q5
Mahuva 96 K5
Maicao 156 C1
Maidenhead 38 H4
Maidstone 38 J4
Maiduguri 114 G2
Mai Gudo 116 F2
Maímédy 54 B6
Main 54 E7
Mainburg 64 G2
Main-Donau-Kanal 54 G7
Maine 142 G1
Maïné Soroa 114 G2
Maingkwan 90 B1
Mainland, *Orkney Is., United Kingdom* 36 E2
Mainland, *Shetland Is., United Kingdom* 36 (1)G1
Maintirano 118 G3
Mainz 54 D6
Maio 114 (1)B1
Majene 93 A3
Majicana 158 H4
Majuro 124 H5
Makale 93 A3
Makamba 116 D4
Makanza 116 B3
Makarora 128 B7
Makarov 84 Q7
Makarska 68 E6
Makar'yev 72 H3
Makat 72 K5
Makeni 114 B3
Makgadikgadi 118 C4
Makhachkala 98 M2
Makhorovka 82 M7
Makindu 116 F4
Makinsk 72 P4
Makiyivka 72 G5
Makkah 110 G3
Makó 68 H3
Makokou 114 G4
Makongolosi 116 E5
Makorako 128 F4
Makoua 114 H4
Maków Mazowiecka 52 L5
Makran 96 G4
Makronisi 70 G7
Mākū 98 L4
Makumbako 116 E5
Makurazaki 88 F8
Makurdi 114 F3
Makūyeh 101 E2
Makuyuni 116 F4
Malabar Coast 94 B6
Malabo 114 F4
Malack 52 F9
Malacky 64 M2
Malad City 140 D2
Maladzyechna 72 E4
Málaga 62 F8
Malahide 35 E3
Malaimbandy 118 H4
Malaita 124 G6
Malakal 116 E2
Malakanagiri 94 D5
Malakula 124 G7
Malamala 93 B3
Malang 92 E4
Malanje 116 B5
Malanville 114 E2
Malaryta 52 P6
Malatya 98 H4
Malaut 94 B2
Malāvi 98 M7
Malawi 118 E2
Malaya Baranikha 84 V3
Malaya Vishera 72 F3
Malaybalay 90 H5
Malāyer 96 E3
Malay Peninsula 90 C6
Malay Reef 126 J3
Malaysia 92 C2
Malbork 52 J3
Malchin, *Germany* 54 H3
Malchin, *Mongolia* 82 S8
Malden Island 124 L6
Maldives 94 B8
Maldon 38 J4
Maldonado 158 L5
Malé 64 F4
Male 94 B8
Male Atoll 94 B8
Malegaon 94 B4
Malé Karpaty 64 N2
Maleme 70 F9
Malesherbes 60 H5
Maleta 84 H6
Malheur 140 C2
Malheur Lake 140 C2
Mali 112 E5
Malindi 116 G4
Malin Head 35 D1
Malkara 70 J4
Malko Tŭrnovo 68 Q8
Mallaig 36 C4
Mallawi 110 F2
Mallorca 62 P5
Mallow 35 C4
Malmédy 56 J4
Malmesbury 118 B6
Malmesbury 38 F4
Malmö 52 C2
Malmyzh 72 K3
Maloca 156 F3
Malone 142 F2
Måløy 50 C6
Malozemel'skaya Tundra 72 K1
Målselv 50 K2
Malta 140 E1
Malta 66 J13
Malta Channel 66 J12
Maltahöhe 118 B4
Maltby 38 G2
Malton 36 H7
Malvern 142 B4
Malý Dunaj 64 N2
Malyy Uzen' 72 J4
Mama 84 J5
Mamadysh 72 K3
Mambasa 116 D3
Mamburao 90 G4
Mamelodi 118 D5
Mammoth Hot Springs 140 D2
Mamonovo 52 J3
Mamoré 156 D6
Mamou 114 B2
Mamoudzou 118 H2
Mamuju 93 A3
Ma'mūl 96 G6
Mamuno 118 C4
Man 114 C3
Mana 146 (2)A1
Manacapuru 156 E4
Manacor 62 P5
Manado 93 B2
Managua 148 G6
Manakara 118 H4
Manali 94 C2
Mananara 118 H4
Mananara Avaratra 118 H3
Mananjary 118 H4
Manankoro 114 C2
Manantenina 118 H4
Manassas 142 E3
Manaus 156 E4
Manavgat 70 P8
Manbij 98 G5
Manchester, *United Kingdom* 38 F2
Manchester, *Ia., United States* 142 B2
Manchester, *Ky., United States* 142 D3
Manchester, *Tenn., United States* 142 C3
Manchester, *Vt., United States* 142 F2
Mand 96 H4
Mandabe 118 G4
Mandal 50 D7
Mandalay 90 B2
Mandalgovĭ 86 D1
Mandan 140 F1
Mandera 116 G3
Mandi 94 C2
Mandi Burewala 94 B2
Mandimba 118 F2
Manding 112 D6
Mandla 94 D4
Mandø 54 D1
Mandritsara 118 H3
Mandsaur 94 C4
Mandurah 126 C6
Manduria 66 M8
Mandvi 94 A4
Mandya 94 C6
Manfredonia 66 K7
Manga 114 G2
Manga 156 J6
Mangaia 124 K8
Mangalia 68 R6
Mangalore 94 B6
Mangareva 124 N8
Mangatupopo 128 E4
Mangaweka 128 F4
Manggar 92 D3
Mangit 96 H1
Mangnai 82 S10
Mango 114 E2
Mangoky 118 G4
Mangole 93 C3
Mangonui 128 D2
Mangrove Cay 144 F5
Manhad 94 B5
Manhattan 144 B2
Manhuaçu 156 J8
Mania 118 H3
Maniamba 118 F2
Manicoré 156 E5
Manicouagan 136 T6
Manīfah 101 C3
Manihiki 124 K7
Maniitsoq 136 W3
Manila 90 G4
Manisa 70 K6
Manistee 142 C2
Manistique 142 C1
Manitoba 136 M6
Manitou 140 G1
Manitoulin Island 142 D1
Manitouwadge 142 C1
Manitowoc 142 C2
Maniwaki 142 E1
Manizales 156 B2
Manja 118 G4
Manjimup 126 C6
Mankato 142 B2
Manley Hot Springs 136 A4
Manlleu 62 N3
Manna 92 C3
Mannar 94 D7
Mannheim 56 L5
Manning, *Canada* 136 H5
Manning, *United States* 144 E3
Manokwari 93 D3
Manono 116 D5
Manorhamilton 35 C2
Mano River 114 B3
Manosque 60 L10
Manouane 142 F1
Manouane Lake 136 S6
Manp'o 88 D3
Manra 124 J6
Manresa 62 M3
Mansa 118 D2
Mansel Island 136 Q4
Mansfield, *United Kingdom* 38 G2
Mansfield, *La., United States* 144 C3
Mansfield, *Oh., United States* 142 D2
Manta 156 A4
Manteo 144 F2
Mantes-la-Jolie 56 D5
Mantova 64 F5
Manturovo 72 H3
Manú 156 C6
Manuelzinho 156 G5
Manūjān 101 G3
Manukan 90 G5
Manukau 128 E3
Manukau Harbour 128 E3
Manyberries 140 D1
Manyinga 118 C2
Manyoni 116 E5
Manzanares 62 G5
Manzanillo 148 J4
Manzhouli 84 K7
Manzil 100 D5
Manzini 118 E5
Mao 110 C5
Maoming 90 E2
Mapam Yumco 94 D2
Mapi 93 E4
Mapinhane 118 F4
Maple Creek 138 E2
Mapuera 156 E4
Maputo 118 E5
Maqueda 62 F4
Maquela do Zombo 116 B5
Maquinchao 158 H7
Maquoketa 142 B2
Māra 94 D4
Maraã 156 D4
Marabá 156 H5
Maracaibo 156 C1
Maracay 156 D1
Marādah 110 C2
Maradi 114 F2
Marāgheh 98 M5
Maralal 116 F3
Marand 98 L4
Maranhão 156 H5
Marañón 156 B4
Marans 60 E7
Marari 156 D5
Mărășești 68 Q4
Marathon, *Canada* 142 C1
Marathon, *United States* 146 F2
Marbella 62 F8
Marble Bar 126 C4
Marburg 56 L4
Marcal 64 N3
Marcali 64 N4
March 38 J3
Marche 56 H4
Marchena 62 E7
Mardan 94 B2
Mar del Plata 158 K6
Mardin 98 J5
Maré 124 G8
Mareeba 126 J3
Marettimo 66 F11
Marfa 146 F2
Margate 38 K4
Margherita di Savoia 66 L7
Marghita 68 K2
Margilan 96 K1
Marguerite Bay 160 (2)KK3
María Elena 158 H3
Marianas Trench 124 E4
Marianna 144 D3
Mariánské Lázně 54 H7
Mariazell 64 L3
Mar'ib 110 J4
Maribo 54 G2
Maribor 64 L4
Maridi 116 D2
Marie Byrd Land 160 (2)FF2
Marie Galante 148 M5
Mariehamn 50 K6
Marienberg 54 J6
Mariental 118 B4
Mariestad 50 G7
Marietta 144 E2
Marietta, *Oh., United States* 142 D3
Marietta, *Okla., United States* 144 B3
Mariinsk 82 R6
Marijampolė 52 N3
Marília 158 M3
Marín 62 B2
Marinette 142 C1
Maringá 158 L3
Marino 66 G7
Marion, *Ill., United States* 142 C3
Marion, *Ind., United States* 142 C2
Marion, *Oh., United States* 142 D2
Maripa 156 D2
Mariscal Estigarribia 158 J3

Name	Page	Grid
Maritime Alps	64	C6
Mariupol'	72	G5
Marīvān	98	M6
Mariy El	72	J3
Marjayoûn	100	C3
Marka	116	G3
Markam	86	B5
Markaryd	52	C1
Marked Tree	144	C2
Marken	56	H2
Markermeer	56	H2
Market Drayton	38	F3
Market Harborough	38	H3
Market Rasen	38	H2
Market Weighton	38	H2
Markham	142	E2
Marki	52	L5
Markit	82	P10
Markkleeberg	54	H5
Markovo	84	W4
Marktoberdorf	64	F3
Marktredwitz	54	H7
Marla	126	F5
Marlborough	38	G4
Marlborough Downs	38	G4
Marle	56	F5
Marmande	60	F9
Marmara Adası	70	K4
Marmara Denizi	70	L4
Marmaris	70	L8
Marmolada	64	G4
Marne	56	F5
Marne-la-Vallée	56	E6
Maro	114	H3
Maroansetra	118	H3
Marolambo	118	H4
Maroni	156	G3
Maros	93	A3
Marotiri	124	M8
Maroua	114	G2
Marquesas Islands	124	M6
Marquette	142	C1
Marradi	64	G6
Marrakech	112	D2
Marra Plateau	110	D5
Marree	126	G5
Marrupa	118	F2
Marsa Alam	110	F2
Marsabit	116	F3
Marsala	66	G11
Marsberg	56	L3
Marsden	126	J6
Marseille	60	L10
Marseille-en-Beauvaisis	56	D5
Marshall, *Ill., United States*	144	D2
Marshall, *Tex., United States*	144	C3
Marshall Islands	124	G4
Marshalltown	142	B2
Marsh Harbour	144	F4
Marsh Island	144	C4
Martapura, *Indonesia*	92	E3
Martapura, *Indonesia*	92	C3
Martigny	64	C4
Martigues	60	L10
Martin, *Slovakia*	52	H8
Martin, *United States*	140	F2
Martina Franca	66	M8
Martinborough	128	E5
Martinique	148	M6
Martinsburg	142	E3
Martinsville, *Ind., United States*	142	C3
Martinsville, *Va., United States*	142	E3
Marton	128	E5
Martos	62	G7
Maruchak	96	H2
Mårvatn	50	E6
Mary	96	H2
Maryborough	126	K5
Maryland	142	E3
Maryport	36	E7
Marysville, *Canada*	142	G1
Marysville, *Calif., United States*	146	B1
Marysville, *Kans., United States*	144	B2
Maryville	142	B2
Masai Steppe	116	F4
Masaka	116	E4
Masalembu Besar	92	E4
Masallı	98	N4
Masamba	93	B3
Masan	88	E6
Masasi	116	F6
Masbate	90	G4
Masbate	90	G4
Mascara	112	F1
Maseru	118	D5
Mashhad	96	G2
Masi-Manimba	116	B4
Masindi	116	E3
Maşīrah	96	G5
Masjed Soleymān	96	E3
Maskanah	98	H5
Mason	144	B3
Mason Bay	128	A8
Mason City	142	B2
Masqaţ	101	H5
Massa	64	F6
Massachusetts	142	F2
Massachusetts Bay	142	G2
Massafra	66	M8
Massa Marittimo	66	E5
Massawa	110	G4
Massena	142	F2
Masset	136	E6
Massif Central	60	H8
Massif de Guéra	110	C5
Massif de l'Aïr	112	G5
Massif des Écrins	64	B5
Massif du Chaillu	114	G5
Massif du Tsaratanana	118	H2
Massif Ennedi	110	D4
Massillon	142	D2
Massinga	118	F4
Masteksay	72	K5
Masterton	128	E5
Mastung	96	J4
Masty	50	N10
Masuda	88	F6
Masuguru	118	F2
Masvingo	118	E4
Maşyāf	100	D1
Matadi	116	A5
Matagami	142	E1
Matagorda Island	144	B4
Matakana Island	128	F3
Matakawau	128	E3
Matale	94	D7
Matam	114	B1
Matamoros, *Mexico*	146	G3
Matamoros, *Mexico*	146	F3
Matane	142	G1
Matanzas	138	K7
Matara	94	D7
Mataram	92	F4
Mataranka	126	F3
Mataró	62	N3
Mataura	128	B8
Matawai	128	F4
Matehuala	146	F4
Matera	66	L8
Mátészalka	68	K2
Mateur	66	D11
Matheson	142	D1
Mathraki	70	B5
Mathura	94	C3
Mati	90	H5
Matlock	38	G2
Matmata	112	G2
Mato Grosso	156	F6
Mato Grosso	156	F6
Mato Grosso do Sul	156	F7
Matosinhos	62	B3
Maţraḩ	101	H5
Matrei	64	H4
Matrûh	110	E1
Matsiatra	118	H4
Matsu	86	G5
Matsue	88	G6
Matsumae	88	L3
Matsumoto	88	J5
Matsusaka	88	J6
Matsuyama	88	G7
Mattawa	142	E1
Matterhorn	64	C5
Matthews Ridge	156	E2
Mattighofen	54	J8
Mattoon	142	C3
Maturín	156	E2
Maubeuge	56	F4
Mauchline	36	D6
Mauganj	94	D4
Maui	146	(2)F3
Maullín	158	G7
Maumturk Mountains	35	B3
Maun	118	C3
Maun	64	K6
Mauna Kea	146	(2)F4
Mauna Loa	146	(2)F4
Mauritania	112	C5
Mauritius	118	(1)B2
Mauron	60	C5
Mauthen	64	H4
Mavinga	118	C3
Mawlaik	90	A2
Max	140	F1
Maya	84	P5
Maya	92	D3
Mayādīn	98	J6
Mayaguana	148	K4
Mayagüez	148	L5
Mayamba	116	B4
Maybole	36	D6
Maych'ew	110	G5
Maydh	116	H1
Mayenne	60	E5
Mayenne	60	E5
Mayer	146	D2
Maykamys	82	P8
Maykop	98	J1
Mayly-Say	96	K1
Maymecha	84	G3
Mayn	84	W4
Mayo	136	D4
Mayor Island	128	F3
Mayotte	118	H2
Mayrhofen	64	G3
Mayskiy	84	M6
Mayumba	114	G5
Mayya	84	N4
Mazagão	156	G4
Mazagran	60	K4
Mazama	140	B1
Mazamet	60	H10
Mazār	100	C5
Mazar	82	P10
Mazara del Vallo	66	G11
Mazār-e Sharīf	96	J2
Mazatlán	148	C4
Mažeikiai	52	M1
Mazocahui	146	D3
Mazomora	116	F5
Mazra	100	C5
Mazyr	72	E4
Mazzarino	66	J11
Mbabane	118	E5
Mbäiki	114	H4
Mbala	116	E5
Mbale	116	E3
Mbalmayo	114	G4
Mbamba Bay	118	E2
Mbandaka	116	B3
Mbanga	114	F4
M'banza Congo	116	A5
Mbarara	116	E4
Mbeya	116	E5
Mbomou	116	C3
Mbour	114	A2
Mbout	112	C5
Mbuji-Mayi	116	C5
Mbuyuni	116	F5
McAlester	144	B3
McBride	136	G6
McCamey	146	F2
McCammon	140	D2
McClintock	136	N5
McClintock Channel	136	L2
McComb	144	C3
McCook	140	F2
McDermitt	140	C2
McGehee	144	C3
McGrath	146	(1)F3
Mchinga	116	F5
McKinlay	126	H4
McKinney	144	B3
McLaughlin	140	F1
McLennan	136	H5
McMinnville	142	C3
McPherson	144	B2
McRae	144	E3
Meadow Lake	136	K6
Meadville	142	D2
Meander River	136	H5
Meaux	56	E6
Mecca = Makkah	110	G3
Mechelen	56	G3
Mechernich	56	J4
Mecidiye	70	J4
Mecklenburger Bucht	54	G2
Mecula	118	F2
Meda	62	C4
Medak	94	C5
Medan	92	B2
Médéa	62	N8
Medellín	156	B2
Medenine	112	H2
Mederdra	112	B5
Medford	140	B2
Medgidia	68	R5
Mediaş	68	M3
Medicine Bow	140	E2
Medicine Hat	136	J7
Medicine Lodge	144	B2
Medina = Al Madīnah	110	G3
Medinaceli	62	H3
Medina de Campo	62	F3
Medina Sidonia	62	E8
Mediterranean Sea	48	E4
Mednogorsk	72	L4
Medveditsa	72	H4
Medvezh'yegorsk	72	F2
Meekatharra	126	C5
Meeker	140	E2
Meerane	54	H6
Meerut	94	C3
Mēga	116	F3
Mega	93	D3
Megalopoli	70	E7
Meganisi	70	C6
Megara	70	F6
Megisti	70	M8
Mehrān	98	M7
Mehriz	96	F3
Meiktila	90	B2
Meiningen	54	F6
Meiringen	64	D4
Meißen	54	J5
Meizhou	90	F2
Mejez El Bab	66	D12
Mékambo	114	G4
Mek'elē	110	G5
Meknès	112	D2
Mekong	90	D4
Melaka	92	C2
Melanesia	124	F5
Melbourne, *Australia*	126	H7
Melbourne, *United States*	144	E4
Melchor de Mencos	148	G5
Meldorf	54	D2
Meldrum Bay	142	D1
Meleuz	72	L4
Mélfi	110	C5
Melfi	66	K8
Melfort	136	L6
Melide	62	B2
Melilla	62	H9
Melita	140	F1
Melitopol'	72	G5
Melk	64	L2
Melkosopochnik	82	N8
Melksham	38	F4
Mělník	54	K6
Melo	158	L5
Melton Mowbray	38	H3
Melun	60	H5
Melut	110	F5
Melvern Lake	144	B2
Melville	136	L6
Melville Island, *Australia*	126	F2
Melville Island, *Canada*	134	N2
Melville Peninsula	136	P3
Memba	118	G2
Memberamo	93	E3
Memboro	93	A4
Memmert	56	J1
Memmingen	64	F3
Mempawah	92	D2
Memphis, *Mo., United States*	142	B2
Memphis, *Tenn., United States*	142	C3
Mena	144	C3
Menai Bridge	38	D2
Menai Straight	38	D2
Ménaka	112	F5
Mendawai	92	E3
Mende	60	J9
Menden	56	K3
Mendī	116	F2
Mendip Hills	38	F4
Mendoza	158	H5
Menemen	70	K6
Menen	56	F4
Menfi	66	G11
Menggala	92	D3
Meniet	112	F4
Menindee	126	H6
Menkere	84	L3
Menominee	142	C1
Menomonee Falls	142	C2
Menongue	118	B2
Menorca	62	Q4
Mentok	92	D3
Menunu	93	B2
Menyuan	86	C3
Menzel Bourguiba	66	D11
Menzel Bouzelfa	66	E12
Menzel Temime	66	E12
Menzies	126	D5
Meppel	56	J2
Meppen	56	K2
Merano	64	G4
Merauke	93	F4
Mercato Saraceno	64	H7
Merced	140	B3
Mercedes, *Argentina*	158	H5
Mercedes, *Argentina*	158	K4
Mercedes, *United States*	144	B4
Mercedes, *Uruguay*	158	K5
Mercury Islands	128	E3
Mere	56	F4
Mergenevo	72	K5
Mergui	90	B4
Mergui Archipelago	90	B4
Merichas	70	G7
Mérida, *Mexico*	148	G4
Mérida, *Spain*	62	D6
Mérida, *Venezuela*	148	K7
Meridian	144	D3
Mérignac	60	E9
Merinha Grande	62	B5
Meriruma	156	G3
Merke	82	N9
Merkys	50	N9
Merowe	110	F4
Merredin	126	C6
Merrick	36	D6
Merrill	142	C1
Merriman	140	F2
Merritt	136	G6
Mersch	56	J5
Merseburg	54	H5
Mers el Kébir	62	K9
Mersey	38	F2
Mersin = Icel	70	S8
Mersing	92	C2
Mērsrags	50	M8
Merthyr Tydfil	38	E4
Meru	116	F3
Méru	56	E5
Merzifon	98	F3
Merzig	56	J5
Mesa	146	D2
Mesa de Yambi	156	C3
Mesagne	66	M8
Meschede	56	L3
Mesöaria Plain	100	A1
Mesolongi	70	D6
Mesopotamia	98	K6
Messaad	112	F2
Messina, *Italy*	66	K10
Messina, *South Africa*	118	D4
Messini	70	E7
Messiniakos Kolpos	70	D8
Mestre	64	H5
Meta	156	C2
Metairie	144	C4
Metaline Falls	140	C1
Metán	158	J4
Metangula	118	E2
Metema	110	G5
Meteor Depth	154	J9
Metković	68	E6
Metlika	64	L5
Metro	92	D4
Metsovo	70	D5
Mettet	56	G4
Mettlach	56	J5
Metz	56	J5
Metzingen	64	E2
Meulaboh	90	B6
Meuse	56	G4
Mexia	144	B3
Mexicali	146	C2
Mexican Hat	146	E1
Mexico	142	B3
Mexico	148	D4
Meymaneh	96	H2
Meynypil'gyno	84	X4
Mezdra	68	L6
Mezen'	72	H1
Mezenskaya Guba	72	H1
Mezhdurechensk	82	R7
Mezőberény	68	J3
Mezőkövesd	68	H2
Mezőtúr	68	H2
Mfuwe	118	E2
Miajadas	62	E5
Miami, *Fla., United States*	144	E4
Miami, *Okla., United States*	144	C2
Miandowāb	98	M5
Miandrivazo	118	H3
Mīāneh	98	M5
Miangyang	86	E4
Mianning	86	C5
Mianwali	94	B2
Mianyang	86	C4
Miaodao Qundao	86	G3
Miao'ergou	82	Q8
Miass	72	M4
Miastko	52	G4
Michalovce	52	L9
Michigan	142	C1
Michipicoten Island	142	C1
Michurin	68	Q7
Michurinsk	72	H4
Mickleover	38	G3
Micronesia	124	F4
Mid-Atlantic Ridge	154	G1
Middelburg, *Netherlands*	56	F3
Middelburg, *South Africa*	118	D6
Middelfart	54	E1
Middelkerke	56	E3
Middle America Trench	134	L8
Middle Andaman	90	A4
Middlebury	142	F2
Middle Lake	140	C2
Middlesboro	142	D3

Middlesbrough 36 G7
Middleton 38 F2
Middletown, *N.Y., United States* 142 F2
Middletown, *Oh., United States* 142 D3
Middlewich 38 F2
Midhurst 38 H5
Mīdī 110 H4
Midland, *Canada* 142 E2
Midland, *Mich., United States* 142 D2
Midland, *Tex., United States* 146 F2
Midway Islands 124 J3
Midwest City 144 B2
Mid Yell 36 (1)G1
Midzor 68 K6
Miechów 52 K7
Międzyrzec Podlaski 52 M5
Miedzyrzecz 52 E5
Mielan 60 F10
Mielec 52 L7
Miembwe 116 F5
Mien 52 D1
Miercurea-Ciuc 68 N3
Mieres 62 E1
Miesbach 64 G3
Mī'ēso 116 G2
Miging 94 F3
Miguel Auza 146 F4
Mikhaylovka 72 H4
Mikhaylovskiy 82 P7
Mikino 84 U4
Mikkeli 50 P6
Mikulov 64 M2
Mikun' 72 K2
Mikuni-sammyaku 88 K5
Mikura-jima 88 K7
Mila 112 G1
Milaca 142 B1
Miladhunmadulu Atoll 94 B7
Milan = Milano, *Italy* 64 E5
Milan, *United States* 144 D2
Milano 64 E5
Milas 70 K7
Milazzo 66 K10
Mildenhall 38 J3
Miles 126 K5
Miles City 140 E1
Milford, *Del., United States* 142 E3
Milford, *Ut., United States* 140 D3
Milford Haven 38 C4
Milford Sound 128 A7
Milford Sound 128 A7
Miliana 62 N8
Milicz 52 G6
Milk 136 J7
Mil'kovo 84 T6
Millau 60 J9
Millbank 140 G1
Milledgeville 144 E3
Miller 140 G2
Millerovo 72 H5
Millington 142 C3
Millinocket 142 G1
Millom 36 E7
Miloro 116 E5
Milos 70 G8
Milton, *New Zealand* 128 B8
Milton, *United States* 144 D3
Milton Keynes 38 H3
Miluo 86 E5
Milwaukee 142 C2
Mily 82 L8
Mimizan-Plage 60 D9
Mīnāb 101 G3
Mina Jebel Ali 101 F4
Minas, *Indonesia* 92 C3
Minas, *Uruguay* 158 K5
Mīnā' Sa'ūd 101 C2
Minas Gerais 156 H7
Minas Novas 156 J7
Minatitián 148 F5
Minbu 90 A2
Minchinmávida 158 G7
Mincivan 98 M4
Mindanao 90 G5
Mindelheim 64 F2
Mindelo 114 (1)B1
Minden 56 L2
Mindoro 90 G4
Mindoro Strait 90 G4
Minehead 38 E4
Mineola 144 B3
Mineral'nyye Vody 98 K1
Minerva Reefs 124 J8
Minfeng 82 Q10
Minga 116 D6
Mingäçevir 98 M3
Mingäçevir Su Anbarı 98 M3
Mingulay 36 A5
Minhe 86 C3
Minicoy 94 B7
Minilya Roadhouse 126 B4
Minna 114 F3
Minneapolis 142 B2
Minnesota 142 A1
Minnesota 142 A2
Miño 62 C2
Minot 140 F1
Minsk 72 E4
Mintlaw 36 F4
Minturn 140 E3
Minusinsk 82 S7
Min Xian 86 C4
Min'yar 72 L3
Miquelon 142 E1
Miraflores 156 C3
Miramas 60 K10
Mirambeau 60 E8
Miranda 156 F8
Miranda de Ebro 62 H2
Miranda do Douro 62 D3
Mirandela 62 C3
Mirbāt 96 F6
Mīrjāveh 96 H4
Mirnyy 84 J4
Mirow 54 H3
Mirpur Khas 94 A3
Mirtoō Pelagos 70 F7
Mirzapur 94 D3
Miskolc 68 H1
Misoōl 93 D3
Mişrātah 110 C1
Missinaibi 136 Q6
Missinipe 136 L5
Mission 140 F2
Mississippi 144 C3
Mississippi 144 D2
Mississippi River Delta 144 D4
Missoula 140 D1
Missouri 140 F1
Missouri 142 B3
Missouri City 144 B4
Mistassibi 136 S7
Mistelbach 64 M2
Mitchell 140 G2
Mitchelstown 35 C4
Mithankot 96 K4
Mithaylov 72 G4
Mithymna 70 J5
Mito 88 L5
Mitsamiouli 118 G2
Mitsinjo 118 H3
Mits'iwa 96 C6
Mittellandkanal 56 K2
Mittersill 64 H3
Mittweida 54 H6
Mitú 156 C3
Mitzic 114 G4
Miyake-jima 88 K6
Miyako 88 L4
Miyakonojō 88 F8
Miyazaki 88 F8
Miyoshi 88 G6
Mīzan Teferī 116 F2
Mizdah 112 H2
Mizen Head 35 B5
Mizhhir"ya 68 L1
Mizil 68 P4
Mizpe Ramon 100 B6
Mjölby 50 H7
Mjøsa 50 F6
Mkuze 118 E5
Mladá Boleslav 52 D7
Mladenovac 68 H5
Mława 52 K4
Mljet 68 E7
Mmabatho 118 D5
Moa 126 H2
Moanda 114 G5
Moapa 140 D3
Moate 35 D3
Moba 116 D5
Mobaye 116 C3
Mobayi-Mbongo 116 C3
Moberly 142 B3
Mobile 144 D3
Moçambique 118 G3
Môc Châu 90 C2
Mochudi 118 D4
Mocímboa da Praia 118 G2
Mocuba 118 F3
Modane 64 B5
Modena 64 F6
Modesto 140 B3
Modica 66 J12
Mödling 64 M2
Modowi 93 D3
Modriča 68 F5
Moenkopi 146 D1
Moers 56 J3
Moffat 36 E6
Moffat Peak 128 B7
Mogadishu = Muqdisho 116 H3
Mogaung 90 B1
Mogilno 52 G5
Mogocha 84 K6
Mogochin 82 Q6
Mogok 90 B2
Mohács 68 F4
Mohammadia 62 L9
Mohe 84 L6
Mohembo 118 C3
Mohoro 116 F5
Mohyliv-Podil's'kyy 68 Q1
Moi 50 D7
Moincêr 94 D2
Moineşti 68 P3
Mo i Rana 50 H3
Moissac 60 G9
Mojave 146 C1
Mojave Desert 146 C2
Mokau 128 E4
Mokohinau Island 128 E2
Mokolo 114 G2
Mokoreta 128 B8
Mokp'o 88 D6
Mol 56 H3
Mola di Bari 66 M7
Molat 64 K6
Mold 38 E2
Molde 50 D5
Moldova 68 R2
Moldova 68 P2
Moldova Nouă 68 J5
Molepolole 118 C4
Molfetta 66 L7
Molina de Aragón 62 J4
Molina de Segura 62 J6
Moline 142 B2
Möll 64 J4
Mollendo 156 C7
Molokai 146 (2)D2
Molopo 118 C5
Molsheim 64 C2
Molucca Sea 93 C2
Moma 118 F3
Mombasa 116 G4
Momchilgrad 68 N8
Møn 54 H2
Monach Islands 36 A4
Monaco 64 C7
Monaco 64 C7
Monadhliath Mountains 36 D4
Monaghan 35 E2
Monahans 146 F2
Mona Passage 148 L5
Monasterevin 35 D3
Monbetsu, *Japan* 88 M1
Monbetsu, *Japan* 88 M2
Moncalieri 64 C5
Monchegorsk 50 S3
Mönchengladbach 56 J3
Monchique 62 B7
Monclova 146 F3
Moncton 136 U7
Mondovi 64 C6
Mondragone 66 H7
Mondy 84 G6
Monemvasia 70 F8
Monfalcone 64 J5
Monforte 62 C5
Monforte de Lemos 62 C2
Monfredónia 66 K7
Monga 116 C3
Mongkung 90 B2
Mongo 110 C5
Mongolia 86 B2
Mongonu 114 G2
Mongora 94 B2
Mongu 118 C3
Mong Yai 90 B2
Mong Yu 90 B2
Monkoto 116 C4
Monmouth 142 B2
Monmouth 38 F4
Mono 114 E3
Mono Lake 140 C3
Monopoli 66 M8
Monor 52 J10
Monowai 128 A7
Monreal del Campo 62 J4
Monreale 66 H10
Monroe, *La., United States* 144 C3
Monroe, *Mich., United States* 142 D2
Monroe, *N.C., United States* 144 E3
Monroe, *Wash., United States* 140 B1
Monroe City 144 C2
Monrovia 114 B3
Mons 56 F4
Monschau 56 J4
Monselice 64 G5
Montabaur 56 K4
Montague Island 154 J9
Montalbán 62 K4
Montalto Uffugo 66 L9
Montana 140 E1
Montana 68 L6
Montargis 60 H6
Montauban 60 G10
Montauk 142 F2
Mont aux Sources 118 D5
Montbard 60 K6
Montbéliard 64 B3
Montblanc 62 M3
Mont Blanc 64 B5
Montbrison 60 K8
Mont Cameroun 114 F4
Montceau-les-Mines 60 K7
Mont-de-Marsan 60 E10
Montdidier 56 E5
Monte Alegre 156 G4
Monte Azul 156 J7
Montebello 142 F1
Monte Bello Islands 126 B4
Montebelluna 64 H5
Monte Calvo 66 K7
Monte Cinto 66 C6
Montecristo 66 E6
Monte Etna 66 J11
Montefiascone 66 G6
Montego Bay 148 J5
Montélimar 60 K9
Monte Limbara 66 D8
Monte Lindo 158 K4
Montemorelos 144 B4
Monte Namuli 118 F3
Montenegro = Crna Gora 68 F7
Monte Perdino 62 L2
Monte Pollino 66 L9
Montepuez 118 F2
Montepulciano 66 F5
Monte Quemado 158 J4
Montereau-faut-Yonne 60 H5
Monterey 142 E3
Monterey Bay 140 B3
Montería 156 B2
Montero 156 E7
Monte Rosa 64 C5
Monterotondo 66 G6
Monterrey 146 F3
Monte Sant'Angelo 66 K7
Montes Claros 156 J7
Montesilvano 66 J6
Montevarchi 64 G7
Montevideo, *United States* 142 A1
Montevideo, *Uruguay* 158 K5
Monte Viso 64 C6
Monte Vista 146 E1
Montgomery 144 D3
Monthey 64 B4
Monticello 140 E3
Montijo 62 D6
Montilla 62 F7
Mont Joli 142 G1
Mont-Laurier 142 E1
Montluçon 60 H7
Montmagny 142 F1
Montmedy 56 H5
Mont Mézenc 60 K9
Montone 64 G6
Montoro 62 F6
Mont Pelat 60 M9
Montpelier, *Id., United States* 140 D2
Montpelier, *Vt., United States* 142 F2
Montpellier 60 J10
Montréal 142 F1
Montreul 56 D4
Montreux 64 B4
Montrose, *United Kingdom* 36 F5
Montrose, *United States* 140 E3
Monts Bagzane 112 G5
Mont Serkout 112 G4
Montserrat 148 M5
Monts Nimba 114 C3
Monts Otish 136 S6
Mont Tahat 112 G4
Monywa 90 A2
Monza 64 E5
Monzón 62 L3
Moonie 126 K5
Moorcroft 140 F2
Moorhead 142 A1
Moosburg 64 G1
Moose Jaw 136 K6
Moose Lake 136 M6
Moosomin 136 L6
Moosonee 136 Q6
Mopeia 118 F3
Mopti 112 E6
Moqor 96 J3
Mór 68 F2
Mora 50 H6
Móra 62 B6
Moradabad 94 C3
Morafenobe 118 G3
Morag 52 J4
Moramanga 118 H3
Moran 140 D2
Morane 124 N8
Moratuwa 94 D7
Morava 52 G8
Moravské Budějovice 64 L1
Morawhanna 156 F2
Moray Firth 36 E4
Morbach 56 K5
Morbegno 64 E4
Morbi 94 B4
Morcenx 60 E9
Mordaga 84 L6
Mordoviya 72 H4
Moreau 140 F1
Morecambe 36 F7
Morecambe Bay 38 E1
Moree 126 J5
Morehead, *Papua New Guinea* 93 F4
Morehead, *United States* 142 D3
More Laptevykh 84 L1
Morelia 148 D5
Morella 62 K4
Moresby Island 146 (1)L5
Moreton Island 126 K5
Morez 60 M7
Morfou 70 Q9
Morgan 126 G6
Morgan City 144 C4
Morgantown 142 D3
Morges 64 B4
Mori 88 L2
Morioka 88 L4
Morkoka 84 J4
Morlaix 60 B5
Morningside 36 E6
Mornington Island 126 G3
Morocco 108 C2
Morogoro 116 F5
Moro Gulf 90 G5
Morombe 118 G4
Mörön 84 G7
Morondava 118 G4
Morón de la Frontera 62 E7
Moroni 118 G2
Moron Us He 94 F2
Morotai 93 C2
Moroto 116 E3
Morpeth 36 G6
Morris 140 G1
Morristown 144 E2
Mors 50 E8
Morshansk 72 H4
Mortain 56 B6
Morteros 158 J5
Morvern 36 C5
Morwell 126 J7
Mosbach 54 E7
Mosby 140 D1
Moscow = Moskva 72 G3
Mosel 56 K4
Moselle 56 G6
Moses Lake 140 C1
Mosgiel 128 C7
Moshi 116 F4
Mosjøen 50 G4
Moskenesøy 50 F3
Moskva 72 G3
Mosonmagyaróvár 64 N3
Mosquero 146 F1
Moss 50 F7
Mossburn 128 B7
Mosselbaai 118 C6
Mossoró 156 K5
Most 54 J6
Mostaganem 62 L9
Mostar 68 E6
Mostoles 62 G4
Møsvatn 50 E7
Mot'a 110 G5
Motala 50 H7
Motherwell 36 E6
Motihari 94 D3
Motilla del Palancar 62 J5
Motiti Island 128 F3
Motril 62 G8
Motru 68 K5
Motu One 124 L7
Motygino 82 S6
Mouchard 64 A4
Moudjéria 112 C5
Moudros 70 H5
Mouila 114 G5
Moulins 60 J7
Moulmein 90 B3
Moultrie 144 E3
Moundou 110 C6
Mount Adam 158 J9
Mount Adams 140 B1

Mountain Grove 142 B3
Mountain Home 142 B3
Mountain Nile = Bahr el Jebel 116 E2
Mount Alba 128 B7
Mount Aloysius 126 E5
Mount Anglem 128 A8
Mount Apo 90 H5
Mount Ararat 98 L4
Mount Arrowsmith 128 C6
Mount Aspiring 128 B7
Mount Assiniboine 136 H6
Mount Augustus 126 C4
Mount Baco 90 G3
Mount Baker 140 B1
Mount Bartle Frere 126 J3
Mount Bogong 126 J7
Mount Brewster 128 B7
Mount Bruce 126 C4
Mount Cameroun 108 D5
Mount Carmel 140 D3
Mount Columbia 136 H6
Mount Cook 128 C6
Mount Cook 128 C6
Mount Donald 128 A7
Mount Douglas 126 J4
Mount Egmont 128 E4
Mount Elbert 140 E3
Mount Elgon 116 E3
Mount Essendon 126 D4
Mount Evelyn 126 F2
Mount Everest 94 E3
Mount Fairweather 136 D5
Mount Gambier 126 H7
Mount Garnet 126 J3
Mount Hermōn 100 C3
Mount Hood 140 B1
Mount Hutt 128 C6
Mount Huxley 128 B7
Mount Isa 126 G4
Mount Jackson 160 (2)MM2
Mount Karisimbi 116 D4
Mount Kendall 128 D5
Mount Kenya = Kirinyaga 116 F4
Mount Kilimanjaro 116 F4
Mount Kirkpatrick 160 (2)AA1
Mount Kosciuszko 126 J7
Mount Liebig 126 F4
Mount Lloyd George 136 G5
Mount Logan 136 C4
Mount Magnet 126 C5
Mount Maunganui 128 F3
Mount McKinley 146 (1)G3
Mount Meharry 126 C4
Mountmellick 35 D3
Mount Menzies 160 (2)L2
Mount Minto 160 (2)Y2
Mount Mulanje 118 F3
Mount Murchison 128 C6
Mount Nyiru 116 F3
Mount Olympus 140 B1
Mount Ord 126 E3
Mount Ossa 126 J8
Mount Owen 128 D5
Mount Paget 158 P9
Mount Pleasant, *Ia., United States* 142 B2
Mount Pleasant, *Mich., United States* 142 D2
Mount Pleasant, *S.C., United States* 144 F3
Mount Pleasant, *Tex., United States* 144 B3
Mount Pleasant, *Ut., United States* 140 D3
Mount Pulog 90 G3
Mount Rainier 140 B1
Mountrath 35 D3
Mount Ratz 136 E5
Mount Richmond 128 D5
Mount Roberts 126 K5
Mount Robson 136 H6
Mount Roosevelt 136 F5
Mount Roraima 156 E2
Mount Ross 128 E5
Mount's Bay 38 C5
Mount Shasta 140 B2
Mount Somers 128 C6
Mount Stanley 116 D3
Mount Tahat 108 D3
Mount Travers 128 D6
Mount Tuun 88 D3
Mount Usborne 158 K9
Mount Vernon, *Al., United States* 144 D3
Mount Vernon, *Ill., United States* 142 C3
Mount Vernon, *Oh., United States* 142 D2
Mount Vernon, *Wash., United States* 140 B1
Mount Victoria, *Myanmar* 90 A2
Mount Victoria, *Papua New Guinea* 124 E6
Mount Waddington 136 F6
Mount Washington 136 S8
Mount Whitney 140 C3
Mount Wilson 140 E3
Mount Woodroffe 126 F5
Mount Ziel 126 F4
Moura 62 C6
Mourne Mountains 35 E2
Mousa 36 (1)G2
Moussoro 110 C5
Moutamba 114 G5
Mouth of the Shannon 35 B4
Mouths of the Amazon 154 G3
Mouths of the Danube 68 S4
Mouths of the Ganges 94 E4
Mouths of the Indus 96 J5
Mouths of the Irrawaddy 90 A3
Mouths of the Krishna 94 D5
Mouths of the Mekong 90 D5
Mouths of the Niger 114 F4
Moûtiers 64 B5
Moutong 93 B2
Mouzarak 114 H2
Moville 35 D1
Moyale 116 F3
Moyen Atlas 112 D2
Moyenvic 56 J6
Moyeroo 82 U4
Moyynty 82 N8
Mozambique 118 E3
Mozambique Channel 118 F4
Mozdok 98 L2
Mozhga 72 K3
Mozirje 64 K4
Mpanda 116 E5
Mpika 118 E2
Mporokoso 116 E5
Mpumalanga 118 D5
Mrągowo 52 L4
Mrkonjić-Grad 64 N6
M'Sila 112 F1
Mtsensk 72 G4
Mtwara 116 G6
Muang Khammouan 90 C3
Muang Không 90 D4
Muang Khôngxédôn 90 D3
Muang Khoua 90 C2
Muang Pakxan 90 C3
Muang Phin 90 D3
Muang Sing 90 C2
Muang Xai 90 C2
Muar 92 C2
Muarabungo 92 C3
Muaradua 92 C3
Muarasiberut 92 B3
Muaratewen 92 E3
Muarawahau 92 F2
Mubarek 82 M10
Mubende 116 E3
Mubrani 93 D3
Much Wenlock 38 F3
Muck 36 B5
Muckadilla 126 J5
Muckle Roe 36 (1)G1
Muconda 116 C6
Mucur 70 S5
Mudanjiang 88 E1
Mudanya 70 L4
Muddy Gap 140 E2
Mudurnu 70 P4
Mufulira 118 D2
Mughshin 96 F6
Muğla 70 L7
Mugodzhary 72 L5
Muhammad Qol 110 G3
Mühldorf 64 H2
Mühlhausen 54 F5
Muhos 50 N4
Muhu 50 M7
Muhulu 116 D4
Muir of Ord 36 D4
Mukacheve 52 M9
Mukdahan 90 C3
Mukomuko 92 C3
Mukry 96 J2
Mukuku 118 D2
Mulaku Atoll 94 B8
Mulde 54 H5
Muleshoe 146 F2
Mulgrave Island 126 H2
Mulhacén 62 G7
Mülheim 56 J3
Mulhouse 64 C3
Muling 88 G1
Mull 36 C5
Mullaittivu 94 D7
Mullewa 126 C5
Müllheim 64 C3
Mullingar 35 D3
Mull of Galloway 36 D7
Mull of Kintyre 36 C6
Mulobezi 118 D3
Multan 96 K3
Mumbai 94 B5
Mumbwa 118 D2
Muna 93 B4
Münchberg 54 G6
München 64 G2
Münden 54 E5
Mundo Novo 156 J6
Mundrabilla 126 E6
Muneðarnes 50 (1)C1
Munera 62 H5
Mungbere 116 D3
Munger 94 E3
Munich = München 64 G2
Munster 35 C4
Munster, *France* 64 C2
Münster, *Germany* 54 F4
Münster, *Germany* 56 K3
Munte 93 A2
Muojärvi 50 Q4
Muonio 50 M3
Muqdisho 116 H3
Mur 64 L4
Muradiye 98 K4
Murang'a 116 F4
Murashi 72 J3
Murat 98 K4
Muratlı 70 K3
Murchison 128 D5
Murcia 62 J7
Murdo 140 F2
Mureș 68 J3
Muret 60 G10
Murfreesboro, *N.C., United States* 144 F2
Murfreesboro, *Tenn., United States* 144 D2
Murghob 96 K2
Muriaé 156 J8
Müritz 54 H3
Muriwai 128 F4
Murmansk 50 S2
Murnau 64 G3
Murom 72 H3
Muroran 88 L2
Muros 62 A2
Muroto 88 H7
Murphy 144 E2
Murray 126 H6
Murray 142 C3
Murray Bridge 126 G7
Murray River Basin 126 H6
Murska Sobota 64 M4
Murter 64 L7
Murtosa 62 B4
Murud 94 B5
Murupara 128 F4
Mururoa 124 M8
Murwara 94 D4
Murzūq 112 H3
Mürzzuschlag 64 L3
Muş 98 J4
Mūša 52 N1
Musala 70 F2
Musandam Peninsula 101 G3
Musay'īd 101 D4
Muscat = Masqaţ 101 H5
Musgrave Ranges 126 E5
Mushin 114 E3
Muskegon 142 C2
Muskogee 144 B2
Musmar 110 G4
Musoma 116 E4
Musselburgh 36 E6
Mussende 116 B6
Mustafakemalpaşa 70 L4
Mut, *Egypt* 110 E2
Mut, *Turkey* 70 R8
Mutare 118 E3
Mutarnee 126 J3
Mutnyy Materik 72 L1
Mutoray 82 U5
Mutsamudu 118 G2
Mutsu 88 L3
Mutsu-wan 88 L3
Muttaburra 126 H4
Mutur 94 D7
Muyezerskiy 50 R5
Muyinga 116 E4
Muynak 82 K9
Muzaffarnagar 94 C3
Muzaffarpur 94 E3
Muzillac 60 C6
Múzquiz 146 F3
Muztagata 82 N10
Mwali 118 G2
Mwanza 116 E4
Mweka 116 C4
Mwenda 116 D6
Mwene-Ditu 116 C5
Mwenezi 118 E4
Mwenezi 118 E4
Mwinilunga 118 C2
Myanmar 90 B2
Myaungmya 90 A3
Myingyan 90 B2
Myitkyina 90 B1
Myjava 64 N2
Myjava 64 N2
Mykolayiv 52 N8
Mykonos 70 H7
Mymensingh 94 F4
Mynbulak 82 L9
Myndagayy 84 N4
Myōjin 86 K4
Myonggan 88 E3
Myrdalsjökull 50 (1)D3
Myrina 70 H5
Myrtle Beach 144 F3
Mys Alevina 84 S5
Mys Aniva 86 L1
Mys Buorkhaya 84 N2
Mys Dezhneva 84 Z3
Mys Elizavety 84 Q6
Mys Enkan 84 P5
Mys Govena 84 V5
Mys Kanin Nos 72 H1
Mys Kekurskij 50 S2
Mys Kril'on 86 L1
Myślenice 52 J8
Myślibórz 52 D5
Mys Lopatka, *Russia* 84 T6
Mys Lopatka, *Russia* 84 S2
Mys Navarin 84 X4
Mys Olyutorskiy 84 W5
Mysore 94 C6
Mys Peschanyy 82 J9
Mys Povorotnyy 88 G2
Mys Prubiynyy 72 F5
Mys Shelagskiy 84 V2
Mys Sivuchiy 84 U5
Mys Terpeniya 84 Q7
Mys Tolstoy 84 T5
Mys Yuzhnyy 84 T5
Mys Zhelaniya 82 M2
Myszksw 52 J7
My Tho 90 D4
Mytilini 70 J5
Mývatn 50 (1)E2
Mže 54 H7
Mzimba 118 E2
Mzuzu 118 E2

N

Naalehu 146 (2)F4
Naas 35 E3
Nabas 90 G4
Naberezhnyye Chelny 72 K3
Nabeul 66 E12
Nabīd 101 G2
Nabire 93 E3
Nablus 100 C4
Nacala 118 G2
Nacaroa 118 F2
Náchod 52 F7
Nacogdoches 144 C3
Nadiad 94 B4
Nador 112 E2
Nadvirna 68 M1
Nadym 72 P1
Nadym 72 P2
Næstved 54 G1
Nafpaktos 70 D6
Nafplio 70 E7
Naga 90 G4
Nagano 88 K5
Nagaoka 88 K5
Nagaon 94 F3
Nagarzê 94 F3
Nagasaki 88 E7
Nagaur 94 B3
Nagercoil 94 C7
Nago 86 H5
Nagold 54 D8
Nagorsk 72 K3
Nagoya 88 J6
Nagpur 94 C4
Nagqu 94 F2
Nagyatád 64 N4
Nagykállš 68 J2
Nagykanizsa 64 N4
Nagykáta 52 J10
Nagykőrös 68 G2
Naha 86 H5
Nahanni 136 G4
Nahanni Butte 136 G4
Nahr en Nile = Nile 110 F2
Nailsworth 38 F4
Naiman Qi 86 G2
Nain 136 U5
Nairn 36 E4
Nairobi 116 F4
Naivasha 116 F4
Naizishan 88 D2
Najafābād 96 F3
Nájera 62 H2
Najibabad 94 C3
Najin 88 F2
Najrān 110 H4
Naju 88 D6
Nakamura 88 G7
Nakatsu 88 F7
Nakhl 100 A7
Nakhodka, *Russia* 82 P4
Nakhodka, *Russia* 88 G2
Nakhon Ratchasima 90 C3
Nakhon Sawan 90 B3
Nakhon Si Thammarat 90 B5
Nakina 136 P6
Nakło nad Notecią 52 G4
Naknek 146 (1)F4
Nakonde 116 E5
Nakskov 54 G2
Nakten 50 H5
Nakuru 116 F4
Nal'chik 98 K2
Nallıhan 70 P4
Nālūt 112 H2
Namagan 82 N9
Namakzar-e Shadad 101 G1
Namanga 116 F4
Namapa 118 F2
Namasagali 116 E3
Nam Can 90 C5
Nam Co 94 F2
Namdalen 50 G4
Nam Dinh 90 D2
Namib Desert 118 A4
Namibe 118 A3
Namibia 118 B4
Namidobe 118 F3
Namlea 93 C3
Namo 93 A3
Nampa 140 C2
Nampala 114 C1
Nam Ping 90 B3
Namp'o 88 C4
Nampula 118 F3
Namsos 50 F4
Namtsy 84 M4
Namur 56 G4
Namwala 118 D3
Namwŏn 88 D6
Nan 90 C3
Nanaimo 140 B1
Nanao 88 J5
Nanchang 86 F5
Nanchong 86 D4
Nancy 64 B2
Nanda Devi 94 C2
Nanded 94 C5
Nandurbar 94 B4
Nandyal 94 C5
Nanfeng 86 F5
Nangalala 126 G2
Nangapinoh 92 E3
Nangatayap 92 E3
Nangis 60 J5
Nangong 86 F3
Nang Xian 94 F3
Nanjing 86 F4
Nankoku 88 G7
Nannine 126 C5
Nanning 90 D2
Nanortalik 136 X4
Nanpan 90 D2
Nanping 86 F5
Nansei-shotō 86 H5
Nantes 60 D6
Nanton 138 D1
Nantong 86 G4
Nantwich 38 F2
Nanumea 124 H6
Nanuque 156 J7
Nanutarra Roadhouse 126 C4
Nanyang 86 E4
Napa 140 B3
Napalkovo 82 N3
Napamute 146 (1)F3
Napas 84 C4
Napasoq 136 W3
Napier 128 F4
Naples 144 E4
Naples = Napoli 66 J8
Napo 156 C4
Napoli 66 J8
Naqb Ashtar 100 C6
Nara, *Japan* 88 H6
Nara, *Mali* 112 D5
Narathiwat 90 C5
Narberth 38 D4
Narbonne 60 H10
Nardò 66 N8
Nares Strait 134 J2
Narew 52 N5
Narew 52 L5
Narib 118 B4
Narmada 94 C4
Narnaul 94 C3

Narni 66 G6
Narok 116 F4
Närpes 50 L5
Narrabi 126 J6
Narrandera 126 J6
Narsimhapur 94 C4
Nart 86 F2
Narva 50 Q7
Narva 50 P7
Narva Bay 50 P7
Narvik 50 J2
Nar'yan Mar 72 K1
Naryn 84 F6
Năsăud 68 M2
Nashua 142 F2
Nashville 144 D2
Našice 68 F4
Nasik 94 B4
Nasir 116 E2
Nassarawa 114 F3
Nassau 144 F4
Nässjö 50 H8
Nastapoka Islands 136 R5
Nasugbu 90 G4
Naswá 101 G5
Nata 118 D4
Natal 156 K5
Natara 84 L3
Natashquan 136 U6
Natchez 144 C3
Natchitoches 144 C3
National Park 128 E4
Natitingou 114 E2
Natori 88 L4
Natuna Besar 92 D2
Naucelle 60 H9
Nauchas 118 B4
Nauders 64 F4
Naujoji Akmenė 52 M1
Naumburg 54 G5
Na'ūr 100 C5
Nauru 124 G6
Nauta 156 C4
Nautonwa 94 D3
Navahermosa 62 F5
Navahrudak 50 N10
Navajo Reservoir 140 E3
Navalero 62 H3
Navalmoral de la Mata 62 E5
Navalvillar de Pela 62 E5
Navan 35 E3
Navapolatsk 72 E3
Navlya 72 F4
Navoi 82 M9
Navojoa 138 E6
Navrongo 114 D2
Navsari 94 B4
Nawá 100 D4
Nawabshah 96 J4
Nāwah 96 J3
Naxçıvan 98 L4
Naxos 70 H7
Naxos 70 H7
Nayakhan 84 T4
Nāy Band, *Iran* 101 E3
Nāy Band, *Iran* 96 G3
Nayoro 88 M1
Nazaré 62 A5
Nazareth 100 C4
Nazarovo 82 S6
Nazca 156 C6
Nazca Ridge 158 E3
Naze 86 H5
Nazilli 70 L7
Nazino 82 P6
Nazran' 98 L2
Nazrēt 116 F2
Nazwá 96 G5
Nazyvayevsk 72 P3
Ncojane 118 C4
Ndélé 116 C2
Ndjamena 110 B5
Ndjolé 114 G5
Ndola 118 D2
Nea Ionia 70 E5
Neale Junction 126 E5
Neapoli 70 F8
Nea Roda 70 F4
Neath 38 E4
Nea Zichni 70 F3
Nebbi 116 E3
Nebitdag 96 F2
Nebo 126 J4
Nebraska 140 G2
Neckar 54 D7
Neckar 54 D8
Neckarsulm 54 E7
Necker Island 124 K3
Necochea 158 K6
Nédély 110 C4
Nedre Soppero 50 L3
Needles 146 D2
Nefedovo 72 P3
Nefta 112 G2
Neftçala 98 N4
Neftekamsk 72 K3
Neftekumsk 98 L1
Nefteyugansk 72 P2
Nefyn 38 D3
Nefza 66 D12
Negage 116 B5
Negār 101 G2
Negēlē 116 F2
Negele 116 F2
Negev 100 B6
Negomane 118 F2
Negombo 94 C7
Negotin 68 K5
Negotino 70 E3
Négrine 112 G2
Negro, *Argentina* 158 J7
Negro, *Brazil* 156 E4
Negros 90 G5
Negru Vodă 68 R6
Nehbandān 96 G3
Nehe 84 M7
Nehoiu 68 P4
Neijiang 86 C5
Nei Monggol 86 E2
Neiva 156 B3
Neixiang 86 E4
Nejanilini Lake 136 M5
Nek'emtē 116 F2
Nelidovo 72 F3
Neligh 140 G2
Nellore 94 C6
Nel'ma 84 P7
Nelson 136 N5
Nelson, *Canada* 140 C1
Nelson, *New Zealand* 128 D5
Nelson, *United Kingdom* 38 F2
Nelspruit 118 E5
Nēma 112 D5
Nëman 50 N10
Neman 52 M2
Nemours 60 H5
Nemperola 93 B5
Nemunas 52 P3
Nemuro 88 N2
Nen 84 L7
Nenagh 35 C4
Nenana 146 (1)H3
Nene 38 H3
Nenjiang 84 M7
Neosho 142 B3
Nepa 84 H5
Nepal 94 D3
Nepalganj 94 D3
Nepean 142 E1
Nephin Beg Mountains 35 B2
Nepomuk 54 J7
Ner 52 H5
Nera 66 G6
Neratovice 54 K6
Neris 52 P2
Nerja 62 G8
Neryungri 84 L5
Nesebūr 68 Q7
Ness City 144 B2
Neston 38 E2
Netanya 100 B4
Netherlands 56 H2
Netherlands Antilles 148 L6
Nettilling Lake 136 S3
Neubrandenburg 54 J3
Neuburg 54 G8
Neuchâtel 64 B3
Neuenhagen 54 J4
Neufchâteau, *Belgium* 56 H5
Neufchâteau, *France* 60 L5
Neufchâtel-en-Bray 56 D5
Neuhof 54 E6
Neukirchen 54 D2
Neumarkt 54 G7
Neumünster 54 F2
Neunkirchen, *Austria* 64 M3
Neunkirchen, *Germany* 54 C7
Neuquén 158 H6
Neuruppin 54 H4
Neusiedler 52 F10
Neusiedler See 64 M3
Neuss 56 J3
Neustadt, *Germany* 54 F2
Neustadt, *Germany* 54 F7
Neustadt, *Germany* 54 G6
Neustadt, *Germany* 54 G8
Neustadt, *Germany* 54 H7
Neustadt, *Germany* 56 L5
Neustrelitz 54 J3
Neu-Ulm 54 F8
Neuwerk 54 D3
Neuwied 56 K4
Nevada 140 C3
Nevada 142 B3
Nevado Auzangate 156 C6
Nevado de Colima 148 D5
Nevado de Cumbal 156 B3
Nevado de Huascaran 156 B5
Nevado de Illampu 156 D7
Nevado Sajama 156 D7
Nevados de Cachi 158 H4
Never 84 L6
Nevers 60 J7
Nevesinje 68 F6
Nevėžis 50 M9
Nevinnomyssk 98 J1
Nevşehir 70 S6
Newala 116 F6
New Albany, *Ind., United States* 142 C3
New Albany, *Miss., United States* 144 D3
New Amsterdam 156 F2
Newark, *N.J., United States* 142 F2
Newark, *Oh., United States* 142 D3
Newark-on-Trent 38 H2
New Bedford 142 F2
Newberg 140 B1
New Bern 144 F2
Newberry 144 E3
New Braunfels 144 B4
New Britain 124 F6
New Brunswick 136 T7
Newburgh 142 F2
Newbury 38 G4
New Bussa 114 E3
Newcastle 35 F2
Newcastle, *Australia* 126 K6
Newcastle, *United States* 140 F2
Newcastle Emlyn 38 D3
Newcastle-under-Lyme 38 F2
Newcastle-upon-Tyne 36 G7
Newcastle Waters 126 F3
Newcastle West 35 B4
New Cumnock 36 D6
New Delhi 94 C3
New England 140 F1
Newe Zohars 100 C5
New Forest 38 G5
Newfoundland 136 V7
Newfoundland 136 V5
New Georgia Island 124 F6
New Glasgow 136 U7
New Guinea 80 S10
New Hampshire 142 F2
New Hampton 142 B2
New Hanover 124 F6
New Haven 142 F2
Newhaven 38 J5
New Iberia 144 C3
New Ireland 124 F6
New Jersey 142 F2
New Liskeard 142 E1
New London 142 F2
Newman 126 C4
Newmarket 38 J3
New Meadows 140 C2
New Mexico 146 E2
New Milton 38 G5
Newnan 144 E3
New Orleans 144 D4
New Plymouth 128 E4
Newport, *Republic of Ireland* 35 B3
Newport, *Eng., United Kingdom* 38 G5
Newport, *Wales, United Kingdom* 38 F4
Newport, *Ark., United States* 144 C2
Newport, *Oreg., United States* 140 B2
Newport, *R.I., United States* 142 F2
Newport, *Vt., United States* 142 F2
Newport, *Wash., United States* 140 C1
Newport Pagnell 38 H3
New Providence 144 F5
Newquay 38 C5
New Romney 38 J5
New Ross 35 E4
Newry 35 E2
New Siberia Islands = Novosibirskiye Ostrova 84 P1
New Smyrna Beach 144 E4
New South Wales 126 H6
Newton, *Ia., United States* 142 B2
Newton, *Kans., United States* 144 B2
Newton Abbot 38 E5
Newton Aycliffe 36 G7
Newtonmore 36 D4
Newton Stewart 36 D7
Newtown 38 E3
Newtownabbey 35 F2
Newtownards 35 F2
Newtownbutler 35 D2
Newtownstewart 35 D2
New Ulm 142 B2
New York 142 E2
New York 142 F2
New Zealand 128 B5
Neya 72 H3
Neyrīz 101 F2
Neyshābūr 96 G2
Ngabang 92 D2
Ngalu 93 B5
Ngamring 94 E3
Ngaoundéré 114 G3
Ngara 116 E4
Ngawihi 128 E5
Ngo 114 H5
Ngoura 110 C5
Ngozi 116 D4
Nguigmi 114 G2
Nguru 114 G2
Nhachengue 118 F4
Nha Trang 90 D4
Nhulunbuy 126 G2
Niafounké 112 E5
Niagara Falls 142 E2
Niakaramandougou 114 C3
Niamey 114 E2
Niangara 116 D3
Nia-Nia 116 D3
Nias 92 B2
Nicaragua 148 G6
Nicastro 66 L10
Nice 64 C7
Nicholls Town 144 F4
Nicobar Islands 90 A5
Nicosia = Lefkosia 70 R9
Nida 52 K7
Nidd 38 G1
Nidym 84 F4
Nidzica 52 K4
Niebüll 54 D2
Niedere Tauern 64 J3
Niefang 114 G4
Niemegk 54 H4
Nienburg 54 E4
Niesky 54 K5
Nieuw Amsterdam 156 F2
Nieuw Nickerie 156 F2
Nieuwpoort 56 E3
Niğde 70 S7
Niger 112 G5
Niger 114 E2
Nigeria 114 F2
Nigoring Hu 86 B3
Niigata 88 K5
Niihau 146 (2)A2
Nii-jima 88 K6
Nijar 62 H8
Nijmegen 56 H3
Nikel' 50 R2
Nikolayevsk-na-Amure 84 Q6
Nikol'sk 72 J3
Nikol'skoye 84 V5
Nikopol' 72 F5
Nik Pey 98 N5
Nikšić 68 F7
Nilande Atoll 94 B8
Nile 110 F3
Niles 142 C2
Nimach 94 B4
Nîmes 60 K10
Nimule 116 E3
Nin 64 L6
Nine Degree Channel 94 B7
9 de Julio 158 J6
Ning'an 88 E1
Ningbo 86 G5
Ningde 86 F5
Ninghai 86 G5
Ninh Binh 90 D2
Ninh Hoa 90 D4
Ninohoe 88 L3
Niobrara 140 G2
Niobrara 140 F2
Nioro 112 D5
Nioro du Sahel 114 C1
Niort 60 E7
Nipigon 142 C1
Niquelândia 156 H6
Nirmal 94 C5
Niš 68 J6
Nisa 62 C5
Niscemi 66 J11
Nishinoomote 88 F8
Nisporeni 68 R2
Nisyros 70 K8
Niţă 101 C3
Niterói 158 N3
Nitra 52 H9
Nitra 52 H9
Nitsa 72 M3
Niue 124 K7
Nivelles 56 G4
Nizamabad 94 C5
Nizhnekamsk 72 K3
Nizhnekamskoye Vodokhranilishche 72 K3
Nizhneudinsk 84 F5
Nizhnevartovsk 72 Q2
Nizhneyansk 84 P2
Nizhniy Lomov 72 H4
Nizhniy Novgorod 72 H3
Nizhniy Tagil 72 M3
Nizhnyaya Tunguska 84 H4
Nizhyn 72 F4
Nizip 98 G5
Nizza Monferrato 64 D6
Njazidja 118 G2
Njombe 116 E5
Njombe 116 E5
Nkambe 114 G3
Nkhotakota 118 E2
Nkongsamba 114 F4
Nkurenkuru 118 B3
Noatak 146 (1)F2
Nobeoka 88 F7
Noboribetsu 88 L2
Noci 66 M8
Nogales, *Mexico* 146 D2
Nogales, *United States* 146 D2
Nogat 52 J3
Nogent-le-Rotrou 60 F5
Noginsk 72 G3
Noginskiy 82 S5
Nogliki 84 Q6
Noheji 88 L3
Noia 62 B2
Noire 90 C2
Noirmoutier-en-l'Île 60 C6
Nojima-zaki 88 K6
Nok Kundi 96 H4
Nokou 112 H6
Nola, *Central African Republic* 116 B3
Nola, *Italy* 66 J8
Nolinsk 72 J3
Noma-misaki 88 F8
Nome 146 (1)D3
Nomoi Islands 124 F5
Nomo-saki 88 E7
Nong'an 88 C1
Nong Khai 90 C3
Noord-Beveland 56 F3
Noord-Oost-Polder 56 H2
Noordwijk aan Zee 56 G2
Norak 96 J2
Noranda 142 E1
Nordaustlandet 160 (1)L1
Nordborg 54 E1
Norden 54 C3
Nordenham 54 D3
Norderney 54 C3
Norderney 54 C3
Norderstedt 54 F3
Nordfjordeid 50 D6
Nordfriesische Inseln 54 D2
Nordhausen 54 F5
Nordhorn 56 K2
Nordkapp 50 N1
Nordkinn 50 P1
Nordkinnhalvøya 50 P1
Nordkvaløya 50 J1
Nordli 50 G4
Nördlingen 54 F8
Nord-Ostsee-Kanal 54 E2
Nordstrand 54 D2
Nordvik 82 W3
Nore 35 D4
Norfolk, *Nebr., United States* 140 G2
Norfolk, *Va., United States* 142 E3
Norfolk Island 124 G8
Noril'sk 82 R4
Norman 144 B2
Normandia 156 F3
Normanton 126 H3
Norman Wells 136 F3
Nørre Åby 54 E1
Nørre Alslev 54 G2
Norristown 142 E2
Norrköping 50 J7
Norrtälje 50 K7
Norseman 126 D6
Norsk 84 N6
Northallerton 36 G7
Northam 126 C6
North America 124 P2
Northampton, *Australia* 126 B5
Northampton, *United Kingdom* 38 H3
North Andaman 90 A4
North Battleford 136 K6
North Bay 142 E1
North Berwick 36 F5
North Cape 128 D2
North Carolina 144 F2
North Channel 36 C7
North Charleston 144 F3
North Dakota 140 F1
North Dorset Downs 38 F5
North Downs 38 J4

Northeast Providence Channel 144 F4
Northeim 54 F5
Northern Cape 118 C5
Northern Ireland 35 E2
Northern Mariana Islands 124 E4
Northern Province 118 D4
Northern Territory 126 F4
North Foreland 38 K4
North Harris 36 B4
North Horr 116 F3
North Iberia 148 F2
North Island 128 D3
North Korea 88 C4
North Little Rock 144 C3
North Platte 138 F3
North Platte 140 F2
North Roe 36 (1)G1
North Ronaldsay 36 F2
North Sea 58 N4
North Shields 36 G6
North Stradbroke Island 126 K5
North Taranaki Bight 128 D4
North Uist 36 A4
Northumberland National Park 36 F6
Northumberland Strait 136 U7
North Vancouver 140 B1
North Walsham 38 K3
North West 118 C5
North West Basin 126 C4
North West Cape 126 B4
North West Christmas Island Ridge 124 K4
North West Highlands 36 C4
Northwest Territories 136 G4
Northwich 38 F2
North York Moors National Park 36 H7
Norton 144 B2
Norton Sound 146 (1)E3
Nortorf 54 E2
Norway 50 F5
Norwegian Sea 50 B4
Norwich, *United Kingdom* 38 K3
Norwich, *United States* 142 F2
Nos 72 H1
Nos Emine 68 Q7
Nosevaya 72 K1
Noshiro 88 K3
Nos Kaliakra 68 R6
Noşratābād 96 G4
Nossen 54 J5
Nos Shabla 68 R6
Nosy Barren 118 G3
Nosy Bé 118 H2
Nosy Boraha 118 J3
Nosy Mitsio 118 H2
Nosy Radama 118 H2
Nosy-Varika 118 H4
Notec 52 G4
Notia Pindos 70 D5
Notios Evvoïkos Kolpos 70 F6
Notre Dame Bay 136 V7
Notsé 114 E3
Nottingham 38 G3
Nottingham Island 136 R4
Nouâdhibou 112 B4
Nouakchott 112 B5
Nouâmghar 112 B5
Nouméa 124 G8
Nouvelle Calédonie 124 G8
Nova Gorica 64 J5
Nova Gradiška 68 E4
Nova Iguaçu 158 N3
Nova Mambone 118 F4
Nova Pazova 68 H5
Novara 64 D5
Nova Scotia 136 T8
Nova Xavantina 156 G6
Novaya Igirma 84 G5
Novaya Karymkary 72 N2
Novaya Kasanka 72 J5
Novaya Lyalya 72 M3
Novaya Zemlya 82 J3
Nova Zagora 68 P7
Novelda 62 K6
Nové Město 52 F8
Nové Mesto 52 G9
Nové Zámky 52 H10
Novgorod 72 F3
Novi Bečej 68 H4
Novigrad 66 H3
Novi Iskŭr 68 L7
Novi Ligure 64 D6
Novi Marof 64 M4
Novi Pazar, *Bulgaria* 68 Q6
Novi Pazar, *Yugoslavia* 68 H6
Novi Sad 68 G4
Novi Vinodolski 64 K5
Novoaleksandrovsk 72 H5
Novoalekseyevka 72 L4
Novoanninsky 72 H4
Novocheboksarsk 72 J3
Novocherkassk 72 H5
Novodvinsk 72 H2
Novo Hamburgo 158 L4
Novohrad-Volyns'kyy 72 E4
Novokazalinsk 72 M5
Novokutznetsk 82 R7
Novokuybyshevsk 72 J4
Novoletov'ye 82 U3
Novo Mesto 64 L5
Novomikhaylovskiy 98 H1
Novomoskovsk 72 G4
Novonazimovo 84 E5
Novorossiysk 98 G1
Novorybnoye 84 H2
Novoselivka 68 S2
Novosergiyevka 72 K4
Novosibirsk 82 Q6
Novosibirskiye Ostrova 84 P1
Novosil' 72 G4
Novotroitsk 72 L4
Novouzensk 72 J4
Novozybkov 72 F4
Novvy 82 V3
Nový Bor 54 K6
Nóvý Jičín 52 H8
Novyy Port 82 N4
Novyy Uoyan 84 J5
Novyy Urengoy 82 P4
Novyy Urgal 84 N6
Novyy Uzen' 82 J9
Nowa Dęba 52 L7
Nowa Ruda 52 F7
Nowata 144 B2
Nowogard 52 E4
Nowo Warpno 54 K3
Nowra 126 K6
Now Shahr 96 F2
Nowy Dwór Mazowiecki 52 K5
Nowy Sącz 52 K8
Nowy Targ 52 K8
Nowy Tomyśl 52 F5
Noyabr'sk 82 P5
Noyon 56 E5
Nsombo 118 D2
Ntem 114 G4
Ntwetwe Pan 118 C4
Nu 94 G2
Nuasjärvi 50 Q4
Nubian Desert 110 F3
Nudo Coropuna 156 C7
Nueltin Lake 136 M4
Nueva Lubecka 158 G7
Nueva Rosita 146 F3
Nueva San Salvador 148 G6
Nuevo Casas Grandes 146 E2
Nuevo Laredo 146 G3
Nugget Point 128 B8
Nuhaka 128 F4
Nuku'alofa 124 J8
Nuku Hiva 124 M6
Nukumanu Islands 124 F6
Nukunonu 124 J6
Nukus 82 K9
Nullagine 126 D4
Nullarbor Plain 126 E6
Numan 114 G3
Numata 88 K5
Numazu 88 K6
Numbulwar 126 G2
Numfor 93 E3
Numto 72 P2
Nunarsuit 136 X4
Nunavut 136 M3
Nuneaton 38 G3
Nungnain Sum 86 F1
Nunivak Island 146 (1)D3
Nunligram 84 Y3
Nuoro 66 D8
Nuquí 156 B2
Nura 72 P4
Nurābād 101 D1
Nurata 96 J1
Nurmes 50 Q5
Nürnberg 54 G7
Nürtingen 64 E2
Nurzec 52 M5
Nusaybin 98 J5
Nushki 96 J4
Nutak 136 U5
Nuuk 136 W4
Nuussuaq 136 W2
Nyagan' 72 N2
Nyahururu 116 F3
Nyala 110 D5
Nyalam 94 E3
Nyamlell 116 D2
Nyamtumbo 116 F6
Nyandoma 72 H2
Nyantakara 116 E4
Nyborg 54 F1
Nybro 50 H8
Nyda 82 N4
Nyima 94 E2
Nyingchi 94 F3
Nyírbátor 68 K2
Nyíregyháza 52 L10
Nykarleby 50 M5
Nykøbing 54 G2
Nyköping 50 J7
Nylstroom 118 D4
Nymburk 52 E7
Nynäshamn 50 J7
Nyngan 126 J6
Nyon 64 B4
Nysa 52 G7
Nysa 52 D6
Nysted 54 G2
Nyukhcha 72 J2
Nyunzu 116 D5
Nyurba 84 K4
Nyuya 84 K4
Nzega 116 E4
Nzérékoré 114 C3
N'zeto 116 A5
Nzwami 118 G2

O

Oadby 38 G3
Oahe 146 (2)D2
Oahu 124 L3
Oakdale 144 C3
Oakham 38 H3
Oak Lake 140 F1
Oakland 140 B3
Oak Lawn 142 C2
Oakley 144 A2
Oak Ridge 142 D3
Oamaru 128 C7
Oaxaca 148 E5
Ob' 72 N2
Obama 88 H6
Oban 36 C5
O Barco 62 D2
Oberdrauburg 64 H4
Oberhausen 56 J3
Oberkirch 54 D8
Oberlin 144 A2
Oberndorf 64 H3
Oberstdorf 64 F3
Oberursel 54 D6
Obervellach 52 C11
Oberwart 64 M3
Obi 93 C3
Obidos 156 F4
Obigarm 96 K2
Obihiro 88 M2
Obluch'ye 84 N7
Obninsk 72 G3
Obo, *Central African Republic* 116 D2
Obo, *China* 86 C3
Oborniki 52 F5
Obouya 114 H5
Oboyan' 72 G4
Obskaya Guba 82 N4
Obuasi 114 D3
Ob'yachevo 72 J2
Ocala 144 E4
Ocaña, *Colombia* 156 C2
Ocaña, *Spain* 62 G5
Ocean City 142 E3
Ocean Falls 136 F6
Oceanside 146 C2
Och'amch'ire 98 J2
Ochil Hills 36 E5
Ochsenfurt 54 E7
Oconto 142 C2
Oda 114 D3
Ōda 88 G6
Ōdate 88 L3
Odda 50 D6
Odemira 62 B7
Ödemiş 70 L6
Odense 54 F1
Oder = Odra 52 F6
Oderzo 64 H5
Odesa 72 F5
Odessa = Odesa, *Ukraine* 72 F5
Odessa, *United States* 146 F2
Odienné 114 C3
Odorheiu Secuiesc 68 N3
Odra 52 F6
Odžaci 68 G4
Oeh 86 C2
Oeiras 156 J5
Oelrichs 140 F2
Oelsnitz 54 H6
Oeno 124 N8
Oestev 158 H7
Ofaqim 100 B5
Offenbach 54 D6
Offenburg 64 C2
Ōgaki 88 J6
Ogasawara-shotō 80 T7
Ogbomosho 114 E3
Ogden 140 D2
Ogdensburg 136 R8
Ogilvie Mountains 136 C4
Oglio 64 E5
Ogosta 68 L6
Ogre 50 N8
Ogre 50 N8
O Grove 62 B2
Ogulin 64 L5
Ohai 128 A7
Ohanet 112 G3
Ohio 142 D2
Ohio 142 C3
Ohre 54 J6
Ohrid 70 C3
Ohura 128 E4
Oia 70 H8
Oiapoque 156 G3
Oil City 142 E2
Oise 56 E5
Ōita 88 F7
Ojinaga 146 F3
Ojiya 88 K5
Ojos del Salado 158 H4
Oka 84 G6
Okaba 93 E4
Okahandja 118 B4
Okanagan Lake 138 C2
Okano 114 G4
Okanogan 140 C1
Okara 94 B2
Okarem 96 F2
Okato 128 D4
Okavango Delta 118 C3
Okaya 88 K5
Okayama 88 G6
Okehampton 38 D5
Okene 114 F3
Oker 54 F4
Okha, *India* 96 J5
Okha, *Russia* 84 Q6
Okhansk 72 L3
Okhotsk 84 Q5
Okhtyrka 72 F4
Okinawa 86 H5
Okinawa 86 H5
Oki-shotō 88 G5
Okitipupa 114 E3
Oklahoma 144 B2
Oklahoma City 144 B2
Okoppe 88 M1
Okoyo 114 H5
Okranger 50 E5
Oksino 72 K1
Oktinden 50 H4
Oktyabr'sk 72 L5
Oktyabr'skiy 72 K4
Okurchan 84 S5
Okushiri-tō 88 K2
Ólafsvík 50 (1)B2
Olancha 140 C3
Öland 50 J8
Olanga 50 Q3
Olathe 144 C2
Olava 54 J7
Olavarría 158 J6
Oława 52 G7
Olbia 66 D8
Olching 64 G2
Old Crow 146 (1)K2
Oldenburg, *Germany* 54 D3
Oldenburg, *Germany* 54 F2
Oldenzaal 56 J2
Oldham 38 F2
Old Head of Kinsale 35 C5
Oldmeldrum 36 F4
Olean 142 E2
Olecko 52 M3
Olekma 84 L5
Olekminsk 84 L4
Oleksandriya 72 F5
Olenegorsk 50 S2
Olenek 84 J3
Olenëk 84 L2
Olenëkskiy Zaliv 84 L2
Oleśnica 52 G6
Olesno 52 H7
Olhão 62 C7
Olib 64 K6
Olinda 156 L5
Oliva 62 K6
Olivet, *France* 60 G6
Olivet, *United States* 140 G2
Olivia 142 B2
Ollerton 38 F2
Olmos 156 B5
Olney 144 B3
Olochi 84 K6
Olonets 72 F2
Olongapo 90 G4
Oloron-Ste-Marie 60 E10
Olot 62 N2
Olovyannaya 84 K6
Olpe 56 K3
Olsztyn 52 K4
Olt 68 M4
Olten 64 C3
Oltenița 68 P5
Oltu 98 K3
Oluan-pi 90 G2
Olvera 62 E8
Olympia 140 B1
Olympos 70 E4
Olympus 70 Q10
Olyutorskiy 84 W4
Olyutorskiy Zaliv 84 V4
Om' 82 N6
Oma 94 D2
Omae-saki 88 K6
Omagh 35 D2
Omaha 140 G2
Omak 140 C1
Omakau 128 B7
Oman 96 G5
Omapere 128 D2
Omarama 128 B7
Omaruru 118 B4
Omba, *China* 94 E2
Omba, *Russia* 82 E4
Omboué 114 F5
Ombrone 66 F6
Omdurman = Umm Durman 110 F4
Omegna 64 D5
Omeo 126 J7
Om Hajer 110 G5
Omīdeyeh 101 C1
Omis 64 M7
Ommen 56 J2
Omolon 84 T3
Omoloy 84 N3
Omo Wenz 116 F2
Omsk 82 N6
Omsukchan 84 S4
Ōmū 88 M1
Omulew 52 L4
Ōmura 88 F7
Ōmuta 88 F7
Onang 93 A3
Onda 62 K5
Ondangwa 118 B3
Ondjiva 118 B3
Ondo 114 E3
Öndörhaan 86 E1
One and a Half Degree Channel 94 B8
Onega 72 G2
O'Neill 140 G2
Oneonta 142 F2
Onești 68 P3
Onezhskoye Ozero 72 F2
Ongjin 88 C5
Ongole 94 D5
Onguday 82 R7
Oni 98 K2
Onilahy 118 G4
Onitsha 114 F3
Ono 88 J6
Onon 84 J7
Onon 84 J7
Onslow Bay 148 J2
Onsong 88 E2
Ontario 136 N6
Ontinyent 62 K6
Ontonagon 142 C1
Onyx 146 C1
Oodnadatta 126 G5
Oologah Lake 144 B2
Oostburg 56 F3
Oostelijk-Flevoland 56 H2
Oostende 56 E3
Oosterhout 56 G3
Oosterschelde 56 F3
Oost-Vlieland 56 H1
Ootsa Lake 136 F6
Opala 116 C4
Oparino 72 J3
Opava 52 G8
Opelika 144 D3
Opelousas 144 C3
Opheim 140 E1
Opochka 72 E3
Opoczno 52 K6
Opole 52 G7
Opornyy 82 J8
Opotiki 128 F4
Opp 144 D3
Opunake 128 D4
Opuwo 118 A3
Oradea 68 J2

Orahovac 68 H7
Orai 94 C3
Orán 158 J3
Oran 62 K9
Orange 118 C5
Orange, *Australia* 126 J6
Orange, *France* 60 K9
Orange, *United States* 144 C3
Orangeburg 144 E3
Orangemund 118 B5
Orangeville 142 D2
Orango 114 A2
Oranienburg 54 J4
Oranmore 35 C3
Orapa 118 D4
Orăștie 68 L4
Oravița 68 J4
Orbec 60 F4
Orbetello 66 F6
Orco 64 C5
Ordes 62 B1
Ordes Santa Comba 62 B1
Ordu 98 G3
Ordway 140 F3
Öreälven 50 K4
Örebro 50 H7
Oregon 140 B2
Oregon 142 A3
Orekhovo-Zuyevo 72 G3
Orel 72 G4
Orem 140 D2
Ören 70 K7
Orenburg 72 L4
Orestiada 70 J3
Orewa 128 E3
Orford Ness 38 K3
Orhei 68 R2
Orihuela 62 K6
Orillia 142 E2
Orinoco 156 D2
Orinoco Delta = Delta del Orinoco 156 E2
Orissaare 50 M7
Oristano 66 C9
Orivesi 50 Q5
Orkla 50 F5
Orkney Islands 36 F3
Orlando 144 E4
Orléans 60 G6
Orlik 84 F6
Orly 56 E6
Ormara 96 H4
Ormoc 90 G4
Ormos Almyrou 70 G9
Ormos Mesara 70 G9
Ormskirk 38 F2
Ornans 60 M6
Ornö 50 K7
Örnsköldsvik 50 K5
Orocué 156 C3
Orofino 140 C1
Oromocto 142 G1
Orona 124 J6
Oronoque 156 F3
Oronsay 36 B5
Oroqen Zizhiqi 84 L6
Orosei 66 D8
Orosháza 68 H3
Oroszlany 52 H10
Orotukan 84 S4
Oroville 140 B3
Orpington 38 J4
Orroroo 126 G6
Orsa 50 H6
Orsay 60 H5
Orsha 72 F4
Orsk 72 L4
Orșova 68 K5
Ørsta 50 D5
Ortaklar 70 K7
Orthez 60 E10
Ortigueira 62 C1
Ortisei 64 G4
Ortles 64 F4
Ortona 66 J6
Ortonville 142 A1
Orümīyeh 98 L5
Oruro 156 D7
Orvieto 66 G6
Orville 60 L6
Ōsaka 88 H6
Osām 68 M6
Osceola 142 B2
Oschatz 54 J5
Oschersleben 54 G4
O Seixo 62 B3
Osh 82 N9
Oshamambe 88 L2
Oshawa 142 E2
Oshkosh, *Nebr., United States* 140 F2
Oshkosh, *Wis., United States* 142 C2
Oshogbo 114 E3
Osijek 68 F4
Osimo 64 J7
Oskaloosa 142 B2
Oskarshamn 50 J8
Oslo 50 F7
Oslofjorden 50 F7
Osmancık 98 F3
Osmaniye 98 G5
Osnabrück 56 L2
Osor 64 K6
Osorno 158 G7
Osprey Reef 126 J2
Oss 56 H3
Ossa de Montiel 62 H6
Osseo 142 B2
Ossora 84 U5
Ostashkov 72 F3
Oste 54 E3
Osterburg 54 G4
Østerdalen 50 F6
Osterholz-Scharmbeck 54 D3
Osterode 54 F5
Östersund 50 H5
Ostfriesische Inseln 54 C3
Ostiglia 64 G5
Ostrava 52 H8
Ostróda 52 K4
Ostrołęka 52 L4
Ostrov, *Czech Republic* 54 H6
Ostrov, *Russia* 72 E3
Ostrova Arkticheskogo Instituta 82 P2
Ostrova Medvezh'i 84 T2
Ostrov Atlasova 84 S6
Ostrova Vrangelya 134 V4
Ostrov Ayon 84 V2
Ostrov Belyy 82 N3
Ostrov Beringa 84 V6
Ostrov Bol'shevik 82 V2
Ostrov Bol'shoy Begichev 84 J2
Ostrov Bol'shoy Lyakhovskiy 84 Q2
Ostrov Bol'shoy Shantar 84 P6
Ostrov Chechen' 98 M2
Ostrov Iturup 88 P1
Ostrov Karaginskiy 84 U5
Ostrov Kil'din 50 T2
Ostrov Kolguyev 82 H4
Ostrov Komsomolets 82 T1
Ostrov Kotel'nyy 84 P1
Ostrov Kunashir 88 P1
Ostrov Mednyy 84 V6
Ostrov Mezhdusharskiy 82 H3
Ostrov Novaya Sibir' 84 S2
Ostrov Ogurchinskiy 96 F2
Ostrov Oktyabr'skoy 82 S2
Ostrov Onekotan 84 S7
Ostrov Paramushir 84 T6
Ostrov Rasshua 84 S7
Ostrov Shiashkotan 84 S7
Ostrov Shumshu 84 T6
Ostrov Simushir 84 S7
Ostrov Urup 84 S7
Ostrov Ushakova 82 Q1
Ostrov Vaygach 82 K3
Ostrov Vise 82 P2
Ostrov Vosrozhdeniya 82 K9
Ostrov Vrangelya 84 W2
Ostrowiec Świętokrzyski 52 L7
Ostrów Mazowiecka 52 L5
Ostrów Wielkopolski 52 G6
Ostuni 66 M8
Osum 70 C4
Ōsumi-shotō 88 F8
Osuna 62 E7
Oswego 142 E2
Oswestry 38 E3
Oświęcim 52 J7
Otago Peninsula 128 C7
Otaki 128 E5
Otaru 88 L2
Oțelu Roșu 68 K4
Othonoi 70 B5
Oti 114 E3
Otira 128 C6
Otjiwarongo 118 B4
Otley 38 G2
Otočac 64 L6
Otog Qi 86 D3
Otoineppu 88 M1
Otorohanga 128 E4
Otranto 66 N8
Otrøy 50 D5
Otrozhnyy 84 W3
Ōtsu 88 H6
Otta 50 E6
Ottawa 142 E1
Ottawa, *Canada* 142 E1
Ottawa, *Ill., United States* 142 C2
Ottawa, *Kans., United States* 144 B2
Ottawa Islands 136 Q5
Otterburn 36 F6
Otterøy 50 F4
Ottobrunn 64 G2
Ottumwa 142 B2
Otukpo 114 F3
Ouachita Mountains 144 C3
Ouadâne 112 C4
Ouadda 116 C2
Ouagadougou 114 D2
Oualàta 112 D5
Ouallam 114 E2
Ouanda-Djallé 116 C2
Ouargla 112 G2
Ouarzazate 112 D2
Oudenaarde 56 F4
Oudenbosch 56 G3
Oudtshoorn 118 C6
Oued Laou 62 E9
Oued Medjerda 66 D12
Oued Meliane 66 D12
Oued Tiélat 62 K9
Oued Zem 112 D2
Ouélésségougou 114 C2
Ouésso 114 H4
Ouezzane 112 D2
Oughterard 35 B3
Oujda 112 E2
Oujeft 112 C4
Oulainen 50 N4
Ould Yenjé 112 C5
Oulu 50 N4
Oulujärvi 50 P4
Oulujoki 50 P4
Oulx 64 B5
Oum-Chalouba 110 D4
Oum-Hadjer 110 C5
Ounarjoki 50 N3
Our 56 J4
Ouray 140 E3
Ourense 62 C2
Ouricuri 156 J5
Ourthe 56 H4
Ouse 38 G2
Oustreham 56 B5
Outer Hebrides 36 A3
Outjo 118 B4
Outokumpu 50 Q5
Out Skerries 36 (1)H1
Ouyen 126 H7
Ovacık 70 R8
Ovada 64 D6
Ovalle 158 G5
Ovareli 98 L3
Overflakkee 56 G3
Overlander Roadhouse 126 B5
Overland Park 144 C2
Overton 140 D3
Övertorneå 50 M3
Ovidiopol' 68 T3
Oviedo 62 E1
Owaka 128 B8
Owando 114 H5
Owase 88 J6
Owatonna 142 B2
Owen River 128 D5
Owensboro 142 C3
Owens Lake 140 C3
Owen Sound 142 D2
Owerri 114 F3
Owo 114 F3
Owosso 142 D2
Owyhee 140 C2
Owyhee 140 C2
Oxford, *New Zealand* 128 D6
Oxford, *United Kingdom* 38 G4
Oxnard 146 C2
Oxted 38 J4
Oyama 88 K5
Oyapock 156 G3
Oyem 114 G4
Oyen 138 D1
Oyonnax 64 A4
Ózd 52 K9
Ozernovskiy 84 T6
Ozero Alakol' 82 Q8
Ozero Aralsor 72 J5
Ozero Aydarkul' 82 M9
Ozero Balkhash 82 N8
Ozero Baykal 84 H6
Ozero Beloye 72 G2
Ozero Chany 82 P7
Ozero Chernoye 72 N3
Ozero Il'men' 72 F3
Ozero-Imandra 50 R2
Ozero Inder 82 J8
Ozero Janis'jarvi 50 R5
Ozero Kamennoje 50 R4
Ozero Kanozero 50 T3
Ozero Khanka 88 G1
Ozero Kolvitskoye 50 S3
Ozero Kovdozero 50 S3
Ozero Kulundinskoye 82 P7
Ozero Kushmurun 72 N4
Ozero Lama 84 D2
Ozero Leksozero 50 R5
Ozero Lovozero 50 T2
Ozero Morzhovets 72 H1
Ozero Njuk 50 R4
Ozero Ozhogino 84 R3
Ozero Pirenga 50 R3
Ozero Pyaozero 50 R3
Ozero Saltaim 72 P3
Ozero Sarpa 72 J5
Ozero Segozeroskoye 72 F2
Ozero Seletyteniz 82 N7
Ozero Sredneye Kuyto 50 R4
Ozero Taymyr 82 U3
Ozero Teletskoye 82 R7
Ozero Tengiz 72 N4
Ozero Topozero 50 R4
Ozero Umbozero 50 T3
Ozero Vygozero 72 G2
Ozero Yalpug 68 R4
Ozero Zaysan 82 Q8
Ozero Zhaltyr 72 K5
Ozero Zhamanakkol' 72 M5
Ozersk 52 M3
Ozhogina 84 R3
Ozhogino 84 R3
Ozieri 66 C8
Ozinki 72 J4
Ozona 146 F2
Ozurget'i 98 J3

P

Paamiut 136 X4
Paar 54 G8
Paarl 118 B6
Pabbay 36 A4
Pabianice 52 J6
Pabna 94 E4
Pacasmayo 156 B5
Pachino 66 K12
Pachuca 148 E4
Pacific Ocean 124 M3
Pacitan 92 E4
Packwood 140 B1
Padalere 93 B3
Padang 92 C3
Padangpanjang 92 C3
Padangsidempuan 92 B2
Padborg 54 E2
Paderborn 54 D5
Padova 64 G5
Padre Island 144 B4
Padrón 62 B2
Padstow 38 D5
Paducah, *Ky., United States* 142 C3
Paducah, *Tex., United States* 146 F2
Padum 94 C2
Paekdu San 88 D3
Paeroa 128 E3
Pafos 70 Q10
Pag 64 L6
Pag 64 K6
Paga Conta 156 G4
Pagadian 90 G5
Pagai Selatan 92 B3
Pagai Utara 92 B3
Pagalu = Annobón 114 F5
Pagan 124 E4
Pagatan 92 F3
Page, *Ariz., United States* 146 D1
Page, *Okla., United States* 144 C3
Pagosa Springs 140 E3
Pagri 94 E3
Pahiatua 128 E5
Paia 146 (2)E3
Paide 50 N7
Paignton 38 E5
Päijänne 50 N6
Painan 92 C3
Painesville 142 D2
Paisley 36 D6
Paita 156 A5
Pakaraima Mountains 156 E2
Pakch'ŏn 88 C4
Pakhachi 84 V4
Paki 114 F2
Pakistan 96 J4
Pakokku 90 A2
Pakotai 128 D2
Pakrac 64 N5
Paks 68 F3
Pakxé 90 D3
Pala 110 B6
Palafrugell 62 P3
Palagonia 66 J11
Palagruža 66 L6
Palaiochora 70 F9
Palamós 62 P3
Palana 84 U5
Palanan 90 G3
Palanga 52 L2
Palangkaraya 92 E3
Palanpur 94 B4
Palantak 96 H4
Palapye 118 D4
Palatka, *Russia* 84 S4
Palatka, *United States* 144 E4
Palau 124 D5
Palau 124 D5
Palau 66 D7
Palaw 90 B4
Palawan 90 F5
Palazzolo Arceide 66 J11
Palembang 92 C3
Palencia 62 F2
Paleokastritsa 70 B5
Palermo 66 H10
Palestine 144 B3
Palestrina 66 G7
Paletwa 90 A2
Palghat 94 C6
Pali 94 B3
Palikir 124 F5
Palimbang 90 G5
Pälkohda 94 D5
Palk Strait 94 C7
Palma 62 N5
Palma del Rio 62 E7
Palma di Montechiaro 66 H11
Palmanova 64 J5
Palmares 156 K5
Palmarola 66 G8
Palmas 156 H6
Palmas 158 L4
Palm Bay 144 E4
Palmdale 146 C2
Palmerston 128 C7
Palmerston Island 124 K7
Palmerston North 128 E5
Palm Harbor 144 E4
Palmi 66 K10
Palmira 156 B3
Palmyra Island 124 K5
Palojärvi 50 M2
Palopo 93 B3
Palu, *Indonesia* 93 A3
Palu, *Turkey* 98 J4
Palyavaam 84 W3
Pama 114 E2
Pamekasan 92 E4
Pamhagen 64 M3
Pamiers 60 G10
Pamlico Sound 144 F2
Pampa 146 F1
Pampas 158 J6
Pamplona, *Colombia* 148 K7
Pamplona, *Spain* 62 J2
Pana 142 C3
Panagyurishte 68 M7
Panaji 94 B5
Panama 148 H7
Panamá 156 B2
Panama Canal = Canal de Panamá 148 J7
Panama City 144 D3
Panarea 66 K10
Panarik 92 D2
Panaro 64 G6
Panay 90 G4
Pančevo 68 H5
Panciu 68 Q4
Pandan 90 G4
Pandharpur 94 C5
Panevėžys 52 P2
Pangani 116 F5
Pangin 94 F3
Pangkajene 93 A3
Pangkalanbuun 92 E3
Pangkalpinang 92 D3
Pangnirtung 136 T3
Panguitch 140 D3
Pangutaran Group 90 G5
Panhandle 146 F1
Panipat 94 C3
Panjāb 96 J3
Panjgur 96 H4
Pankshin 114 F3
Pantanal 156 F7
Pantar 93 B4
Pantelleria 112 H1
Pantemakassar 93 B4
Paola 66 L9
Paoua 116 B2
Papa 146 (2)F4
Pápa 68 E2
Papakura 128 E3
Papantla 148 E4
Paparoa 128 E3
Papa Stour 36 (1)G1
Papatowi 128 B8

Papa Westray	36	F2
Papenburg	54	C3
Papey	50	(1)F2
Papua New Guinea	124	E6
Papun	90	B3
Pará	156	G5
Para	156	H4
Parabel'	82	Q6
Paracatu	156	H7
Paracel Islands	90	E3
Paraćin	68	J6
Pará de Minas	156	J7
Paragould	144	C2
Paragua, *Bolivia*	156	E6
Paragua, *Venezuela*	156	E2
Paraguay	154	F6
Paraguay	158	J3
Paraíba	156	K5
Parakou	114	E3
Paralia	70	E8
Paralimni	100	A1
Paramaribo	156	F2
Paranã	156	H6
Paranã	156	H6
Paraná	158	J5
Paraná	158	K4
Paraná	158	L3
Paranaguá	158	M4
Paranaíba	156	G7
Paranaíba	156	G7
Paranavaí	158	L3
Paranestio	70	G3
Paraparaumu	128	E5
Paray-le Monial	60	K7
Parbhani	94	C5
Parchim	54	G3
Pardo	156	J7
Pardubice	52	E7
Pareh	98	L4
Parepare	93	A3
Parga	70	C5
Parigi	93	B3
Parika	156	F2
Parintins	156	F4
Paris, *France*	60	H5
Paris, *Tenn., United States*	144	D2
Paris, *Tex., United States*	144	B3
Parkersburg	142	D3
Park Rapids	142	A1
Parla	62	G4
Parma	64	F6
Parma, *Italy*	64	F6
Parma, *United States*	142	D2
Parnaíba	156	J4
Parnassus	128	D6
Pärnu	50	N7
Pärnu	50	N7
Paros	70	H7
Paros	70	H7
Parry Bay	136	Q3
Parry Islands	136	L1
Parry Sound	142	D2
Parsons	144	B2
Parthenay	60	E7
Partinico	66	H10
Partizansk	88	G2
Paru	156	G4
Parvatipuram	94	D5
Paryang	94	D2
Pasadena, *Calif., United States*	146	C2
Pasadena, *Tex., United States*	144	B4
Paşalimani Adası	70	K4
Pasawng	90	B3
Paşcani	68	P2
Pasco	140	C1
Pascual	90	G4
Pasewalk	54	K3
Pasig	90	G4
Pasinler	98	J3
Pasłęk	52	J3
Pasłek	52	J3
Pasleka	50	L9
Pašman	64	L7
Pasni	96	H4
Paso de Hachado	158	G6
Paso de Indios	158	H7
Paso de la Cumbre	158	H5
Paso de San Francisco	158	H4
Paso Río Mayo	158	G8
Paso Robles	146	B1
Passage de la Déroute	38	(1)F6
Passau	54	J8
Passo Fundo	158	L4
Passos	156	H8
Pastavy	50	P9
Pasto	156	B3
Pastos Bons	156	J5
Pasvalys	52	P1
Pásztó	68	G2
Patagonia	158	G8
Patan, *India*	94	B4
Patan, *Nepal*	94	E3
Patchway	38	F4
Patea	128	E4
Pate Island	116	G4
Paterna	62	K5
Paternò	66	J11
Paterson	142	F2
Pathankot	94	C2
Pathein	90	A3
Pathfinder Reservoir	140	E2
Patia	156	B3
Patiala	94	C2
Patmos	70	J7
Patna	94	E3
Patnos	98	K4
Patos de Minas	156	H7
Patra	70	D6
Patraikis Kolpos	70	D6
Patreksfjörður	50	(1)B2
Pattani	90	C5
Pattaya	90	C4
Patti	66	J10
Paturau River	128	D5
Pau	62	K1
Pauini	156	D5
Pauini	156	D5
Paulatuk	146	(1)N2
Paulo Afonso	156	K5
Paul's Valley	144	B3
Päveh	98	M6
Pavia	64	E5
Pāvilosta	50	L8
Pavlikeni	68	N6
Pavlodar	82	P7
Pavlohrad	72	G5
Pavlovsk	72	H4
Pavlovskaya	72	G5
Pavullo nel Frignano	64	F6
Paxoi	70	C5
Paxson	146	(1)H3
Payerne	64	B4
Payette	140	C2
Payne's Find	126	C5
Paysandu	158	K5
Payson	146	D2
Payturma	82	S3
Pazar	98	J3
Pazardzhik	68	M7
Pazin	64	J5
Peace	136	H5
Peacehaven	38	H5
Peace River	136	H5
Peach Springs	146	D1
Peak District National Park	38	G2
Pearsall	144	B4
Pebane	118	F3
Pebas	156	C5
Peć	68	H7
Pecan Island	144	C4
Pechora	72	L1
Pechora	72	K1
Pechorskoye More	82	J4
Pechory	50	P8
Pecos	146	F2
Pecos	146	F2
Pécs	68	F3
Pedja	50	P7
Pedra Azul	156	J7
Pedra Lume	114	(1)B1
Pedreiras	156	J4
Pedro Afonso	156	H5
Pedro Juan Caballero	158	K3
Pedro Luro	158	J6
Peebles	36	E6
Peel	36	D7
Peel Sound	136	M2
Peene	54	J3
Peenemünde	54	J2
Pegasus Bay	128	D6
Pegnitz	54	G7
Pegu	90	B3
Pegunungan Barisan	92	B2
Pegunungan Iban	92	F2
Pegunungan Maoke	93	E3
Pegunungan Meratus	92	F3
Pegunungan Schwaner	92	E3
Pegunungan Van Rees	93	E3
Pehuajó	158	J6
Peine	54	F4
Peißenberg	64	G3
Peixe	156	H6
Pekalongan	92	D4
Pekanbaru	92	C2
Peking = Beijing	86	F3
Pelaihari	92	E3
Peleduy	84	J5
Peleng	93	B3
Pelhřimov	52	E8
Pelješac	66	M6
Pello	50	N3
Pellworm	54	D2
Pelly Bay	136	P3
Peloponnisos	70	D7
Pelotas	158	L5
Pelym	72	M2
Pemangkat	92	D2
Pematangsiantar	92	B2
Pemba	118	G2
Pemba Island	116	F5
Pembina	140	G1
Pembine	142	C1
Pembroke, *Canada*	142	E1
Pembroke, *United Kingdom*	38	D4
Pembroke, *United States*	144	E3
Pembroke Dock	38	D4
Pembrokeshire Coast National Park	38	C4
Peñafiel	62	F3
Peñaranda de Bracamonte	62	E4
Peñarroya-Pueblonuevo	62	E6
Penarth	38	E4
Pendik	70	M4
Pendleton	140	C1
Pendolo	92	G3
Pend Oreille Lake	140	C1
Pen Hills	142	E2
Peniche	62	A5
Penicuik	36	E6
Península de Azuero	148	H7
Península de Guajira	148	K6
Península Valdés	158	J7
Péninsule de Gaspé	136	T7
Péninsule d'Ungava	136	R4
Penmarch	60	A6
Penne	66	H6
Pennines	36	F7
Pennsylvania	142	E2
Penrith	36	F7
Pensacola	148	G2
Penticton	140	C1
Pentland Firth	36	E3
Pentland Hills	36	E6
Pen y Fan	38	E4
Penza	72	J4
Penzance	38	C5
Penzhina	84	V4
Penzhinskaya Guba	84	U4
Penzhinskiy Khrebet	84	V4
Peoria, *Ariz., United States*	146	D2
Peoria, *Ill., United States*	142	C2
Percival Lakes	126	D4
Peregrebnoye	72	N2
Pereira	156	B3
Pergamino	158	J5
Périers	60	D4
Périgueux	60	F8
Peristera	70	G5
Perito Moreno	158	G8
Perleberg	54	G3
Perm'	72	L3
Përmet	70	C4
Pernambuco	156	K5
Pernik	68	L7
Péronne	56	E5
Perpignan	60	H11
Perrine	144	E4
Perry, *Fla., United States*	144	E3
Perry, *Ga., United States*	144	E3
Persepolis	101	E2
Persian Gulf	101	C2
Perth, *Australia*	126	C6
Perth, *United Kingdom*	36	E5
Pertuis Breton	60	D7
Peru	142	C2
Peru	156	C6
Peru-Chile Trench	154	D5
Perugia	66	G5
Pervomays'k	72	F5
Pervoural'sk	72	L3
Pesaro	64	H7
Pescara	66	J6
Pescia	64	F7
Peshawar	94	B2
Peshkopi	70	C3
Peshtera	70	G2
Peski Karakumy	96	G2
Peski Kzyylkum	82	L9
Peski Priaral'skiye Karakumy	82	L8
Pesnica	64	L4
Pessac	60	E9
Petah Tiqwa	100	B4
Petalioi	70	G7
Petaluma	140	B3
Pétange	56	H5
Petare	148	L6
Petauke	118	E2
Peterborough, *Canada*	142	E2
Peterborough, *United Kingdom*	38	H3
Peterhead	36	G4
Peter I Øy	160	(2)JJ3
Peterlee	36	G7
Petersburg	142	E3
Petersfield	38	H4
Petershagen	54	D4
Petit Mécatina	136	U6
Peto	148	G4
Petre Bay	128	(1)B1
Petrich	70	F3
Petrila	68	L4
Petrinja	64	M5
Petrolina	156	J5
Petropavlovka	84	H6
Petropavlovsk	72	N4
Petropavlovsk-Kamchatskiy	84	T6
Petrópolis	158	N3
Petroşani	68	L4
Petrovac	68	J5
Petrovsk-Zabaykal'skiy	84	H6
Petrozavodsk	72	F2
Petrun	72	M1
Petukhovo	72	N3
Pevek	84	W3
Pezinok	52	G9
Pfaffenhofen	54	G8
Pfarrkirchen	54	H8
Pflach	64	F3
Pforzheim	54	D8
Pfunds	64	F4
Pfungstadt	54	D7
Phalaborwa	118	E4
Phalodi	94	B3
Phan Rang	90	D4
Phan Thiêt	90	D4
Phatthalung	90	C5
Phet Buri	90	B4
Phichit	90	C3
Philadelphia, *Miss., United States*	144	D3
Philadelphia, *Pa., United States*	144	F2
Philippeville	56	G4
Philippines	90	G5
Philippine Trench	80	R8
Philips	136	K7
Phillipsburg	140	G3
Phitsanulok	90	C3
Phnum Penh	90	C4
Phoenix	118	(1)B2
Phoenix	146	D2
Phoenix Islands	124	J6
Phôngsali	90	C2
Phuket	90	B5
Phumĭ Sâmraông	90	C4
Piacenza	64	E5
Piadena	64	F5
Pianoro	64	G6
Pianosa	66	E6
Piatra-Neamţ	68	P3
Piauí	156	J5
Piazza Armerina	66	J11
Pibor Post	116	E2
Picacho del Centinela	146	F3
Picayune	144	D3
Pichilemu	158	G5
Pickering	36	H7
Pico	112	(1)B2
Pico Almanzor	62	E4
Pico Cristóbal Colón	148	K6
Pico da Bandeira	158	N3
Pico da Neblina	156	D3
Pico de Itambé	158	N2
Pico de Teide	112	B3
Pico Duarte	148	K5
Picos	156	J5
Picton, *New Zealand*	128	D5
Picton, *United States*	142	E2
Pic Tousside	110	C3
Piedras Negras	146	F3
Pieksämäki	50	P5
Pielinen	50	Q5
Pierre	140	F2
Pierrelatte	60	K9
Piers do Rio	156	H7
Piešťany	52	G9
Pietermaritzburg	118	E5
Pietersburg	118	D4
Pietrasanta	64	F6
Piet Retief	118	E5
Pieve di Cadore	64	H4
Pihlájavesi	50	P6
Pik Aborigen	84	R4
Piketberg	118	B6
Pik Kommunizma	96	K2
Pik Pobedy	82	P9
Piła	52	F4
Pilaya	158	H3
Pilcomayo	156	E8
Pilibhit	94	C3
Pilica	52	J7
Pimba	126	G6
Pimenta Bueno	156	E6
Pinamalayan	90	G4
Pinamar	158	K6
Pinang	90	B5
Pınarbaşı	98	G4
Pinar del Río	148	H4
Pinarhisar	70	K3
Pińczów	52	K7
Pindaré Mirim	156	H4
Pine Bluff	142	B4
Pine Bluffs	140	F2
Pine City	142	B1
Pine Creek	126	F2
Pine Creek Reservoir	142	A4
Pinega	72	H2
Pineios	70	E5
Pine Island Bay	160	(2)GG3
Pineland	144	C3
Pinerolo	64	C6
Pineville, *Ky., United States*	142	D3
Pineville, *La., United States*	144	C3
Pingdingshan	86	E4
Pingguo	90	D2
Pingle	90	E2
Pingliang	86	D3
Pingshi	86	E5
P'ing-tung	90	G2
Pingxiang, *China*	90	D2
Pingxiang, *China*	90	E1
Pinhel	62	C4
Pini	92	B2
Pinka	64	M3
Pink Mountain	136	G5
Pinneberg	54	E3
Pinsk	72	E4
Pioche	140	D3
Piombino	66	E6
Pioneer	146	D2
Pioneer Mountains	140	D1
Pionerskiī	52	K3
Pionerskiy	72	M2
Piopio	128	E4
Piotrków Trybunalski	52	J6
Piove di Sacco	64	H5
Piperi	70	G5
Pipestone	142	A2
Pipiriki	128	E4
Piqua	142	D2
Piracicaba	158	M3
Pireas	70	F7
Pirin	70	F3
Piripiri	156	J4
Pirmasens	54	C7
Pirna	54	J6
Pirot	68	K6
Piru	93	C3
Pisa	52	L4
Pisa	64	F7
Pisco	156	B6
Písek	52	D8
Pishīn	96	H4
Pishin	96	J3
Piska	52	L4
Pisticci	66	L8
Pistoia	64	F7
Pisz	52	L4
Pitcairn Islands	124	P8
Piteå	50	L4
Piteälven	72	C1
Piteşti	68	M5
Pithara	126	C6
Pithiviers	60	H5
Pitkyaranta	72	F2
Pitlochry	36	E5
Pitlyar	72	N1
Pitt Island	128	(1)B2
Pittsburg	144	C2
Pittsburgh	142	D2
Pitt Strait	128	(1)B2
Piura	156	A5
Pivka	64	K5
Placer	90	G4
Placerville	146	B1
Plaiamonas	70	E5
Plains	146	F2
Plainview	146	F2
Plampang	92	F4
Planalto Central	156	H6
Planalto da Borborema	156	K5
Planalto do Mato Grosso	156	G6
Plankinton	140	G2
Plano	144	B3
Plasencia	62	D5
Plast	72	M4
Plateau du Djado	112	H4
Plateau du Limousin	60	F8
Plateau du Tademaït	112	F3
Plateau of Tibet = Xizang Gaoyuan	94	D2
Plateaux Batéké	114	G5
Platinum	146	(1)E4
Plato	148	K7
Plato Ustyurt	82	J9
Platte	144	B1
Platteville	142	B2
Plattling	54	H8
Plattsburgh	142	F2

Plattsmouth 144 B1
Plau 54 H3
Plauen 54 H6
Plavnik 64 K6
Plavsk 72 G4
Playa de Castilla 62 D7
Playas 156 A4
Plây Cu 90 D4
Pleasanton 146 G3
Pleiße 54 H5
Plentywood 140 F1
Plesetsk 72 H2
Pleven 68 M6
Pljevlja 68 G6
Płock 52 J5
Pločno 68 E6
Ploërmel 60 C6
Ploiești 68 P5
Plomari 70 J6
Plön 54 F2
Płońsk 52 K5
Plovdiv 68 M7
Plumtree 118 D4
Plungė 52 L2
Plymouth, *United Kingdom* 38 D5
Plymouth, *United States* 142 C2
Plyussa 50 Q7
Plyussa 72 E3
Plzeň 52 C8
Po 64 E5
Pocahontas 148 F1
Pocatello 140 D2
Pochet 84 F5
Pochinok 72 F4
Pocking 64 J2
Pocomoke City 142 E3
Podgorica 68 G7
Podkamennaya Tunguska 84 F4
Podol'sk 72 G3
Podravska Slatina 68 E4
Poel 54 G2
Pofadder 118 B5
Poggibonsi 64 G7
Pogradec 70 C4
P'ohang 88 E5
Pohnpei 124 F5
Pohokura 128 F4
Pohořelice 64 M2
Point Arena 138 B4
Point Barrow 146 (1)F1
Point Conception 146 B2
Point Culver 126 D6
Point d'Entrecasteaux 126 B6
Pointe-Noire 114 G5
Point Hope 146 (1)D2
Point Hope 146 (1)D2
Point of Ardnamurchan 36 B5
Point of Ayre 36 D7
Point Pedro 94 D7
Point Sur 140 B3
Poitiers 60 F7
Pokaran 94 B3
Pokhara 94 D3
Poko 116 D3
Pokrovsk 84 M4
Pola de Siero 62 E1
Poland 52 G6
Polar Bluff 148 F1
Polatlı 70 Q5
Polatsk 72 E3
Police 54 K3
Polichnitos 70 J5
Policoro 66 L8
Poligny 60 L7
Poligus 82 S5
Polillo Islands 90 G4
Poliocastro 66 L9
Polis 70 Q9
Polistena 66 L10
Pollachi 94 C6
Pollença 62 P5
Polohy 72 G5
Polomoloc 90 H5
Polonnaruwa 94 D7
Poltava 72 F5
Poltavka 88 F1
Põltsamaa 50 N7
Poluostrov Shmidta 84 Q6
Poluostrov Taymyr 82 R3
Poluostrov Yamal 82 M3
Poluy 82 M4
Põlva 50 P7
Polyaigos 70 G8
Polyarnye Zori 50 S3
Polyarnyy 84 X3
Polykastro 70 E4
Polynesia 124 J6
Pombal 62 B5
Pomeranian Bay 52 D3
Pomeroy 140 C1
Pomorie 68 Q7
Pompano Beach 144 E4
Pompei 66 J8
Ponca City 144 B2
Ponce 148 L5
Pondicherry 94 C6
Pond Inlet 136 R2
Ponferrada 62 D2
Poniatowa 52 M6
Ponoy 72 H1
Pons 60 E8
Ponta Delgada 112 (1)B2
Ponta do Podrão 114 G6
Ponta do Sol 114 (1)B1
Ponta Grossa 158 L4
Ponta Khehuene 118 E5
Pont-à-Mousson 60 M5
Ponta Porã 158 K3
Pontarlier 60 M7
Pontassieve 64 G7
Ponta Zavora 118 F4
Pont-d'Alin 60 L7
Ponteareas 62 B2
Ponte da Barca 62 B3
Pontedera 64 F7
Ponte de Sor 62 C5
Pontefract 38 G2
Ponteland 36 G6
Pontevedra 62 B2
Pontiac 142 C2
Pontianak 92 D3
Pontivy 60 C5
Pontoise 56 E5
Pontorson 60 D5
Pontremoli 64 E6
Pontypool 38 E4
Pontypridd 38 E4
Ponza 66 G8
Poogau 64 J3
Poole 38 G5
Poole Bay 38 G5
Pooncarie 126 H6
Poopó 156 D7
Poopó Challapata 158 H2
Poor Knights Islands 128 E2
Popayán 148 J8
Poperinge 56 E4
Popigay 82 W3
Poplar Bluff 142 B3
Poplarville 144 D3
Popocatépetl 148 E5
Popoh 92 E4
Popokabaka 114 H6
Popovača 64 M5
Popovo 68 P6
Poprad 52 K8
Poprad 52 K8
Porangatu 156 H6
Porbandar 96 J5
Porcupine 146 (1)K2
Pordenone 64 H5
Poreč 64 J5
Poret 66 H3
Pori 50 L6
Porirua 128 E5
Porlamar 148 M6
Poronaysk 84 Q7
Poros 70 F7
Porosozero 72 F2
Porozina 64 K5
Porpoise Bay 160 (2)T3
Porriño 62 B2
Porsangen 50 N1
Porsgrunn 50 E7
Portadown 35 E2
Portaferry 35 F2
Portage 142 C2
Portage la Prairie 140 G1
Port Alberni 140 B1
Port Albert 126 J7
Portalegre 62 C5
Portales 146 F2
Port Arthur, *Australia* 126 J8
Port Arthur, *United States* 144 C4
Port Askaig 36 B6
Port Augusta 126 G6
Port-au-Prince 148 K5
Port Austin 142 D2
Port Blair 90 A4
Port Burwell 136 U4
Port Charlotte 144 E4
Port Douglas 126 J3
Portel, *Brazil* 156 G4
Portel, *Portugal* 62 C6
Port Elizabeth 118 D6
Port Ellen 36 B6
Port Erin 36 D7
Porterville 146 C1
Port Fitzroy 128 E3
Port-Gentil 114 F5
Port Harcourt 114 F4
Port Hardy 136 F6
Port Hawkesbury 136 U7
Porthcawl 38 E4
Port Hedland 126 C4
Porthmadog 38 D3
Port Hope Simpson 136 V6
Port Huron 142 D2
Portimão 62 B7
Port Jefferson 142 F2
Portland, *Australia* 126 H7
Portland, *New Zealand* 128 E2
Portland, *Ind., United States* 142 D2
Portland, *Me., United States* 142 F2
Portland, *Oreg., United States* 140 B1
Portland Island 128 F4
Port Laoise 35 D3
Port Lavaca 144 B4
Port Lincoln 126 G6
Port Loko 114 B3
Port Louis 118 (1)B2
Port Macquarie 126 K6
Port-Menier 136 U7
Port Moresby 126 J1
Port Nis 36 B3
Port Nolloth 118 B5
Porto, *Corsica* 66 C6
Porto, *Portugal* 62 B3
Porto Alegre, *R.G.S., Brazil* 158 L5
Porto Alegre, *Pará, Brazil* 156 G4
Porto Amboim 118 A2
Portocheli 70 F7
Porto do Son 62 A2
Pôrto Esperidião 156 F7
Portoferraio 66 E6
Pôrto Franco 156 H5
Port of Spain 156 E1
Pôrto Grande 156 G3
Portogruaro 64 H5
Porto Inglês 114 (1)B1
Portomaggiore 64 G6
Pôrto Murtinho 158 K3
Pôrto Nacional 156 H6
Porto-Novo 114 E3
Port Orford 140 B2
Porto San Giorgio 66 H5
Pôrto Santana 156 G3
Porto Santo 112 B2
Pôrto Seguro 156 K7
Porto Tolle 64 H6
Porto Torres 66 C8
Porto-Vecchio 66 D7
Pôrto Velho 156 E5
Portoviejo 156 A4
Port Pire 126 G6
Portree 36 B4
Port Renfrew 140 B1
Portrush 35 E1
Port Said = Bûr Sa'îd 110 F1
Port St. Johns 118 D6
Port Shepstone 118 E6
Portslade-by-Sea 38 H5
Portsmouth, *United Kingdom* 38 G5
Portsmouth, *N.H., United States* 142 F2
Portsmouth, *Oh., United States* 142 D3
Portsmouth, *Va., United States* 142 E3
Port Sudan = Bur Sudan 110 G4
Port Sulphur 144 D4
Port Talbot 38 E4
Portugal 62 B5
Portugalete 62 G1
Port-Vendres 60 J11
Port-Vila 124 G7
Port Warrender 126 E2
Posadas 158 K4
Poschiavo 64 F4
Poshekhon'ye 72 G3
Poso 93 B3
Posŏng 88 D6
Posse 156 H6
Pößneck 54 G6
Post 146 F2
Postmasburg 118 C5
Postojna 64 K5
Post Weygand 112 F4
Posušje 68 E6
Pota 92 G4
Potapovo 82 R4
Poteau 144 C2
Potenza 64 J7
Potenza 66 K8
Potgietersrus 118 D4
P'ot'i 98 J2
Potiskum 114 G2
Potlatch 140 C1
Potosi 156 D7
Potsdam, *Germany* 54 J4
Potsdam, *United States* 142 F2
Potters Bar 38 H4
Pottuvil 94 D7
Poughkeepsie 142 F2
Poulton-le-Fylde 38 F2
Pourerere 128 F5
Pouto 128 E3
Póvoa de Varzim 62 B3
Povorino 72 H4
Powder 140 E1
Powder River 140 E2
Powell River 136 G7
Poyang Hu 86 F5
Požarevac 68 J5
Poza Rica 148 E4
Požega 68 H6
Poznań 52 F5
Pozoblanco 62 F6
Pozzuoli 66 J8
Prabumulih 92 C3
Prachatice 52 D8
Prachuap Khiri Khan 90 B4
Prado 156 K7
Præstø 54 H1
Prague = Praha 52 D7
Praha 52 D7
Praia 114 (1)B2
Prainha 156 G4
Prairie du Chien 142 B2
Prapat 92 B2
Praslin Island 118 (2)B1
Pratas = Dongsha Qundao 90 F2
Prato 64 G7
Pratt 140 G3
Prattville 144 D3
Prawle Point 38 E5
Praya 92 F4
Preetz 54 F2
Preganziòl 64 H5
Preiļi 50 P8
Premnitz 54 H4
Premuda 64 K6
Prentice 142 B1
Prenzlau 52 C4
Preobrazhenka 84 H4
Preparis Island 90 A4
Preparis North Channel 90 A3
Preparis South Channel 90 A4
Přerov 52 G8
Presa de la Boquilla 146 E3
Presa de las Adjuntas 146 G4
Presa Obregón 146 E3
Prescott 140 D4
Preševo 68 J7
Presho 140 G2
Presidencia Roque Sáenz Peña 158 J4
Presidente Prudente 158 L3
Presidio 146 F3
Preslav 68 P6
Presnogorkovka 72 N4
Prešov 52 L9
Presque Isle 142 G1
Přeštice 54 J7
Preston, *United Kingdom* 38 F2
Preston, *Minn., United States* 142 B2
Preston, *Mo., United States* 142 B3
Prestwick 36 D6
Pretoria 118 D5
Preveza 70 C6
Priargunsk 84 K6
Pribilof Islands 146 (1)D4
Priboj 68 G6
Příbram 52 D8
Price 140 D3
Prichard 144 D3
Priego de Córdoba 62 F7
Priekule 50 L8
Prienai 52 N3
Prieska 118 C5
Priest Lake 140 C1
Prievidza 52 H9
Prijedor 68 D5
Prijepolje 68 G6
Prikaspiyskaya Nizmennost' 72 K5
Prilep 70 D3
Primolano 64 G5
Primorsk 50 Q6
Primorsko Akhtarsk 72 G5
Prince Albert 136 K6
Prince Albert Peninsula 136 H2
Prince Albert Sound 136 H2
Prince Charles Island 136 R3
Prince Edward Island 108 G10
Prince Edward Island 136 U7
Prince George 136 G6
Prince of Wales Island, *Australia* 126 H2
Prince of Wales Island, *Canada* 136 L2
Prince of Wales Island, *United States* 136 E5
Prince of Wales Strait 136 H2
Prince Patrick Island 134 Q2
Prince Regent Inlet 136 N2
Prince Rupert 136 E6
Princess Charlotte Bay 126 H2
Princeton, *Canada* 140 B1
Princeton, *Ill., United States* 142 C2
Princeton, *Ky., United States* 142 C3
Princeton, *Mo., United States* 142 B2
Prince William Sound 136 B4
Príncipe 114 F4
Prineville 140 B2
Priozersk 50 R6
Priština 68 J7
Pritzwalk 54 H3
Privas 60 K9
Privolzhskaya Vozvyshennost 72 H4
Prizren 68 H7
Probolinggo 92 E4
Proddatur 94 C6
Progreso 148 G4
Prokhladnyy 98 L2
Prokop'yevsk 82 R7
Prokuplje 68 J6
Proletarsk 72 H5
Proliv Longa 84 X2
Proliv Matochkin Shar 82 K3
Proliv Vil'kitskogo 82 U2
Prophet 136 G5
Propriano 66 C7
Prorer Wiek 54 J2
Proserpine 126 J4
Prosna 52 G6
Prosperidad 90 H5
Prostojov 52 G8
Proti 70 D7
Provadiya 68 Q6
Prøven = Kangersuatsiaq 136 W2
Providence 142 F2
Providence Island 118 (2)B2
Provideniya 84 Z4
Provincetown 142 F2
Provins 60 J5
Provo 140 D2
Provost 136 J6
Prudhoe Bay 146 (1)H1
Prudnik 52 G7
Prüm 56 J4
Pruszków 52 K5
Prut 68 R4
Pružany 52 P5
Prvić 64 K6
Pryluky 72 F4
Prypyats' 48 G2
Przasnysz 52 K4
Przemyśl 52 M8
Przeworsk 52 M7
Psara 70 H6
Psebay 98 J1
Pskov 72 E3
Ptolemaïda 70 D4
Ptuj 64 L4
Pucallpa 156 C5
Pucheng 86 F5
Puch'ŏn 88 D5
Púchov 52 H8
Pucioasa 68 N4
Puck 52 H3
Pudasjärvi 50 P4
Pudozh 72 G2
Puebla 148 E5
Puebla de Don Rodrigo 62 F5
Pueblo 140 F3
Puelches 158 H6
Puelén 158 H6
Puente-Genil 62 F7
Puerto Acosta 156 D7
Puerto Aisén 158 G8
Puerto Alegre 156 E6
Puerto Angel 148 E5
Puerto Ayacucho 148 L7
Puerto Barrios 148 G5
Puerto Berrío 156 C2
Puerto Cabezas 148 H6
Puerto Carreño 148 L7
Puerto del Rosario 112 C3
Puerto de Navacerrada 62 G4
Puerto Guarini 156 F8
Puerto Heath 156 D6
Puerto Inírida 156 D3
Puerto Leguízamo 156 C4
Puerto Libertad 146 D3
Puerto Limón 156 B3
Puertollano 62 F6
Puerto Madryn 158 J7
Puerto Maldonado 156 D6
Puerto Montt 158 G7
Puerto Natáles 158 G9
Puerto Nuevo 148 K7
Puerto Páez 156 D2
Puerto Peñasco 146 D2
Puerto Princesa 90 F5
Puerto Real 62 D8
Puerto Rico 148 L5
Puerto Rico 156 D6
Puerto Rico Trench 154 E1
Puerto Santa Cruz 158 H9
Puerto Suárez 156 F7
Pukapuka 124 N7

Pukatawagen 136 L5
Pukch'ŏng 88 E3
Pukë 68 G7
Pukeuri Junction 128 C7
Pula 64 J6
Pulaski 142 E2
Puławy 52 M6
Pullman 140 C1
Pułtusk 50 L10
Pultusk 52 L5
Pulu 82 Q10
Pülümür 98 H4
Puncak Jaya 93 E3
Puncak Mandala 93 F3
Pune 94 B5
P'ungsan 88 E3
Punia 116 D4
Puno 156 C7
Punta Albina 118 A3
Punta Alice 66 M9
Punta Angamos 158 G3
Punta Arena 140 B3
Punta Arenas 158 G9
Punta Ballena 158 G4
Punta da Estaca de Bares 62 C1
Punta Dungeness 158 H9
Punta Eugenia 148 A3
Punta Galera 158 G6
Punta Gallinas 148 K6
Punta Gorda 144 E4
Punta La Marmora 66 D8
Punta Lavapié 158 G6
Punta Lengua de Vaca 158 G5
Punta Mala 156 B2
Punta Mariato 148 H7
Punta Medanosa 158 H8
Punta Negra 156 A5
Punta Norte, *Argentina* 158 J7
Punta Norte, *Argentina* 158 K6
Punta Pariñas 156 A5
Punta Rasa 158 J7
Puntarenas 148 H6
Punta San Gabriel 146 D3
Punta San Telmo 148 D5
Punta Sarga 112 B4
Puponga 128 D5
Puqi 86 E5
Pur 82 P4
Puri 94 E5
Purmerend 56 G2
Purpe 84 B4
Purukcahu 92 E3
Purus 156 E5
Puruvesi 50 Q6
Pusan 88 E6
Pushkin 72 F3
Püspökladany 52 L10
Putao 90 B1
Putaruru 128 E3
Putian 86 F5
Putna 68 P4
Puttalami 94 C7
Putten 56 G3
Puttgarden 54 G2
Putumayo 156 C4
Putusibau 92 E2
Puuwai 146 (2)A2
Puvurnituq 136 R5
Puy de Dôme 60 H8
Puy de Sancy 60 H8
Puysegur Point 128 A8
Pweto 116 D5
Pwllheli 38 D3
Pyal'ma 72 G2
Pyasina 82 R3
Pyatigorsk 98 K1
Pyè 90 B3
Pyhäjärvi 50 M6
Pylos 70 D8
Pyŏktong 88 C3
P'yŏnggang 88 D4
P'yŏngyang 88 C4
Pyramid Island 128 (1)B2
Pyramid Lake 140 C2/3
Pyrenees 60 E11
Pyrgos 70 D7
Pyrzyce 52 D4
Pyshchug 72 J3
Pytalovo 50 P8

Q

Qā 'Azamān 100 E5
Qadīmah 96 C5
Qādub 96 F7
Qagan Nur 86 F2
Qal'aikhum 96 K2
Qalamat Nadqān 101 D5
Qalāt 96 J3
Qal'at Bīshah 96 D5
Qal'eh-ye Now 96 H3
Qamdo 86 B4
Qamīnīs 110 C1
Qandala 116 H1
Qaraaoun 98 F7
Qardho 116 H2
Qartaba 100 C2
Qasr el Azraq 100 D5
Qasr el Kharana 100 D5
Qasr Farafra 110 E2
Qaṭanā 100 D3
Qatar 101 D4
Qatrāna 100 D5
Qattâra Depression 110 E2
Qax 98 M3
Qāyen 96 G3
Qazangöldag 98 M4
Qazax 98 L3
Qazımämmäd 98 N3
Qazvīn 96 E2
Qena 110 F2
Qeqertarsuatsiaat 136 W4
Qeqertarsuatsiaq 136 V2
Qeqertarsuup Tunua 136 V3
Qeshm 101 G3
Qeshm 101 F3
Qeys 101 E3
Qezel Owzan 98 N5
Qezi'ot 100 B6
Qianshanlaoba 82 Q8
Qiaowan 86 B2
Qidukou 94 G2
Qiemo 82 R10
Qijiang 86 D5
Qijiaojing 82 S9
Qila Saifullah 96 J3
Qilian 86 C3
Qilian Shan 86 B3
Qingdao 86 G3
Qinghai Hu 86 B3
Qinghai Nanshan 86 B3
Qingjiang 86 F4
Qingshuihe 86 E3
Qingyang 86 D3
Qingyuan, *China* 86 E6
Qingyuan, *China* 86 G2
Qinhuangdao 86 F3
Qinzhou 90 D2
Qionghai 90 E3
Qiqian 84 L6
Qiqihar 84 L7
Qīr 101 E2
Qira 82 Q10
Qiryat Ata 100 C4
Qiryat Motzkin 100 C4
Qiryat Shemona 100 C3
Qishn 96 F6
Qolleh-ye Damāvand 96 F2
Qom 96 F3
Qomishëh 96 F3
Qornet es Saouda 100 D2
Qorveh 98 M6
Qoṭbābād 101 G3
Qotūr 98 L4
Quang Ngai 90 D3
Quangolodougou 114 C3
Quang Tri 90 D3
Quanzhou 90 F2
Quaqtaq 136 T4
Quarto Sant'Elena 66 D9
Quba 98 N3
Quchan 96 G2
Québec 142 F1
Quedlinburg 54 G5
Queen Charlotte 136 E6
Queen Charlotte Islands 136 E6
Queen Charlotte Sound 136 E6
Queen Charlotte Strait 136 F6
Queen Elizabeth Islands 134 M2
Queen Maud Gulf 136 L3
Queensland 126 G4
Queenstown, *Australia* 126 J8
Queenstown, *New Zealand* 128 B7
Queenstown, *South Africa* 118 D6
Queets 140 B1
Quelimane 118 F3
Quemado 146 E2
Querétaro 148 D4
Quesnel 136 G6
Quetta 96 J3
Quezaltenango 148 F6
Quezon 90 F5
Quezon City 90 G4
Qufu 86 F3
Quibala 118 A2
Quibdó 148 J7
Quiberon 60 B6
Quijotoa 146 D2
Quillagua 158 H3
Quilmes 158 K5
Quilpie 126 H5
Quimbele 116 B5
Quimilí 158 J4
Quimper 60 A5
Quimperlé 60 B6
Quincy 142 B3
Qui Nhon 90 D4
Quionga 116 G6
Quirindi 126 K6
Quito 156 B4
Qujing 90 C1
Qumar He 94 F1
Qumaryan 94 F1
Qurayyāt 96 G5
Qurghonteppa 96 J2
Qurlurtuuq 136 H3
Qus 110 F2
Qusar 98 N3
Quseir 110 F2
Quzhou 86 F5

R

Raab 64 L3
Raahe 50 N4
Raalte 56 J2
Raasay 36 B4
Raas Caseyr 96 F7
Rab 64 K6
Rab 64 K6
Rába 68 E2
Raba 93 A4
Răbăgani 68 K3
Rabak 110 F5
Rabat, *Malta* 66 J13
Rabat, *Morocco* 112 D2
Rabca 64 N3
Rābigh 96 C5
Rabka 52 K8
Rach Gia 90 D5
Racine 142 C2
Ráckeve 68 F2
Rădăuți 68 N2
Radbuza 54 H7
Radcliffe on Trent 38 G3
Radeberg 54 J5
Radebeul 54 J5
Radhanpur 94 B4
Radnevo 68 N7
Radom 52 L6
Radomir 68 K7
Radomsko 52 J6
Radoviš 70 E3
Radstadt 52 C10
Radstock 38 F4
Raduznny 82 P5
Radviliškis 52 N2
Radzyń Podlaski 52 M6
Rae-Edzo 136 H4
Raetihi 128 E4
Raevavae 124 M8
Rafaela 158 J4
Rafah 100 B5
Rafaï 116 C3
Rafḥā 96 D4
Rafsanjān 101 G1
Raglan 128 E3
Ragusa 66 J12
Raha 93 B3
Rahad el Berdi 110 D5
Rahimyar Khan 96 K4
Raichur 94 C5
Raiganj 94 E3
Raigarh 94 D4
Rainach 64 L4
Rainbow Lake 136 H5
Rainier 140 B1
Rainy Lake 142 B1
Rainy River 142 B1
Raipur 94 D4
Rai Valley 128 D5
Rajahmundry 94 D5
Raja-Jooseppi 50 Q2
Rajapalaiyam 94 C7
Rajgarh 94 C3
Rajkot 96 K5
Raj Nangaon 94 D4
Rajsamand 94 B3
Rajshahi 94 E4
Rakhiv 68 M1
Rakovica 64 L6
Rakovnik 52 C7
Rakovski 68 M7
Rakvere 50 P7
Raleigh 144 F2
Ralik Chain 124 G5
Ram 100 C7
Rama 148 H6
Ramallah 100 C5
Rambouillet 60 G5
Rameswaram 94 C7
Rāmhormoz 101 C1
Ramla 100 B5
Ramlat Rabyānah 110 C3
Râmnicu Sărat 68 Q4
Râmnicu Vâlcea 68 M4
Ramonville-St-Agne 60 G10
Rampur, *India* 94 C3
Rampur, *India* 94 C2
Ramree Island 90 A3
Ramsey 36 D7
Ramsgate 38 K4
Ramtha 100 D4
Ranau 92 F1
Rancagua 158 G5
Ranchi 94 E4
Randalstown 35 E2
Randazzo 66 J11
Randers 50 F8
Randijaure 50 K3
Randolph 140 G2
Rånes 56 B6
Rangamati 94 F4
Rangiora 128 D6
Rangoon = Yangon 90 B3
Rankin 146 F2
Rankin Inlet 136 N4
Rannoch Moor 36 D5
Ranong 90 B5
Ransiki 93 D3
Rānya 98 L5
Rapa 124 M8
Rapalla 66 D4
Rapallo 64 E6
Rapar 96 K5
Raperswil 64 D3
Rapid City 140 F2
Rapid River 142 C1
Rapla 50 N7
Rapur 96 J5
Raroia 124 N7
Rarotonga 124 K8
Râs Abu Shagara 110 G3
Ra's al Ḥadd 96 G5
Ra's al Ḥazrah 101 D4
Ra's al Hilāl 110 D1
Ra's al Khajī 101 C2
Ra's al Khaymah 101 F4
Ra's al Kūh 101 G4
Ra's al Muraysah 110 E1
Ra's al 'Udayd 101 D4
Ra's az Zawr 101 C3
Râs Banâs 110 G3
Ras Beddouza 112 C1
Ras Bir 110 H5
Ras Dashen Terara 110 G5
Ra's-e Barkan 101 C2
Raseiniai 50 M9
Râs el Nafas 100 B7
Ra's Fartak 96 F6
Râs Ghârib 110 F2
Rasht 98 N5
Rāsk 96 H4
Raška 68 H6
Ras Kasar 110 G4
Ra's Madrakah 96 G6
Râs Nouâdhibou 112 B4
Rason Lake 126 D5
Rass Ajdir 112 H2
Rass Jebel 66 E11
Rass Mostefa 66 F12
Rassokha 84 H2
Rast 68 L6
Ras Tannūrah 101 D3
Rastatt 56 L6
Rastede 54 D3
Ratak Chain 124 H4
Ratangarh 96 K4
Rat Buri 90 B4
Rath 94 C3
Rathcoole 35 E3
Rathdrum 35 E4
Rathenow 54 H4
Rathfriland 35 E2
Rathkeale 35 C4
Rathlin 35 E1
Rath Luirc 35 C4
Ratlam 94 C4
Ratnagiri 96 K6
Raton 140 F3
Ratta 84 C4
Ratten 64 D4
Ratzeburg 54 F3
Rauðamýri 50 (1)B2
Raudhatain 101 B1
Raukumara Range 128 F4
Rauma 50 L6
Raurimu 128 E4
Rausu 88 N1
Răut 68 R2
Ravalli 140 D1
Ravānsar 98 M6
Rāvar 101 G1
Ravenna 64 H6
Ravensburg 64 E3
Ravensthorpe 126 D6
Ravnina 96 H2
Rāwah 98 J6
Rawaki 124 J6
Rawalpindi 96 K3
Rawa Mazowiecka 52 K6
Rawāndiz 98 L5
Rawicz 52 F6
Rawlinna 126 E6
Rawlins 140 E2
Rawmarsh 38 G2
Rawson 158 J7
Rawu 94 G3
Raychikhinsk 84 M7
Rayleigh 38 J4
Raymond 140 B1
Raymondville 146 G3
Rayong 90 C4
Razdol'noye 88 F2
Razgrad 68 P6
Razlog 68 L8
Reading, *United Kingdom* 38 H4
Reading, *United States* 142 E2
Realicó 158 J6
Rebaa 112 G2
Rebbenesøya 50 J1
Rebun-tō 86 L1
Rechytsa 72 F4
Recife 156 L5
Recklinghausen 56 K3
Recknitz 54 H3
Reconquista 158 K4
Recreo 158 H4
Red, *Canada/United States* 140 G1
Red, *United States* 144 B3
Reda 52 H3
Red Bluff 146 B1
Redcar 36 G7
Red Cloud 144 B1
Red Deer 136 J6
Redding 140 B2
Redditch 38 G3
Redfield 140 G2
Redhill 38 H4
Red Lake 136 N6
Red Lakes 138 H2
Red Lodge 140 E1
Red Oak 142 A2
Redon 60 C6
Redondela 62 B2
Red River = Song Hông 90 C2
Redruth 38 C5
Red Sea 110 G3
Redwater 136 J6
Red Wing 142 B2
Redwood City 140 B3
Redwood Falls 142 A2
Reed City 142 C2
Reedsport 140 B2
Reefton 128 C6
Rega 52 E4
Regen 54 J8
Regen 54 H7
Regensburg 54 H7
Regenstauf 54 H7
Reggane 112 F3
Reggio di Calabria 66 K10
Reggio nell'Emilia 64 F6
Reghin 68 M3
Regina, *Brazil* 156 G3
Regina, *Canada* 138 F1
Rehau 54 H6
Rehoboth 118 B4
Rehovot 100 B5
Reichenbach 54 H6
Reigate 38 H4
Reims 56 G5
Reinach Bad 64 C3
Reindeer Lake 136 L5
Reinosa 62 F1
Reisi 66 J11
Reliance 136 K4
Relizane 112 F1
Remada 112 H2
Remagen 56 K4
Rembang 92 E4
Remeshk 101 H3
Remiremont 60 M6
Remscheid 56 K3
Rena 50 F6
Rendina 70 F4
Rendsburg 54 E2
Rengat 92 C3
Reni 68 R4
Renmark 126 H6
Rennes 60 D5
Reno 140 C3

Reno 64 G6
Rentería 62 J1
Renton 140 B1
Renukut 94 D4
Reo 93 B4
Replot 50 L5
Reprêsa de Balbina 156 F4
Represa de Samuel 156 E5
Represa de Sao Simao 156 G7
Represa Ilha Solteira 156 G7
Represa Tucuruí 156 H4
Republic 140 C1
Republic of Ireland 35 C3
Repulse Bay 126 J4
Repulse Bay 136 P3
Requena, *Peru* 156 C5
Requena, *Spain* 62 J5
Reşadiye 98 G3
Resen 68 J8
Réservoir Cabonga 142 E1
Réservoir Caniapiscau 136 T6
Réservoir de La Grande 2 136 R6
Réservoir de La Grande 3 136 R6
Réservoir de La Grande 4 136 S6
Réservoir Gouin 142 F1
Réservoir Manicouagan 136 T6
Réservoir Opinaca 136 R6
Réservoir Pipmuacan 142 G1
Reshteh-ye Kūhhā-ye Alborz 96 F2
Resistencia 158 K4
Reşiţa 68 J4
Resolute 136 N2
Resolution Island, *Canada* 136 U4
Resolution Island, *New Zealand* 128 A7
Resovo 70 K3
Rethel 56 G5
Rethymno 70 G9
Réunion 118 (1)B2
Reus 62 M3
Reutlingen 54 E8
Revda 72 L3
Revillagigedo Island 146 (1)L4
Revin 56 G5
Revivim 100 B5
Revúca 52 K9
Rewa 94 D4
Rexburg 140 D2
Reykjanes 50 (1)B3
Reykjavík 50 (1)C2
Reynosa 144 B4
Rezat 54 F7
Rezé 60 D6
Rēzekne 50 P8
Rezina 68 R2
Rezovo 68 R8
Rezzato 64 F5
Rhayader 38 E3
Rheda-Wiedenbrück 54 D5
Rhein = Rhine 64 C2
Rheinbach 56 K4
Rheine 56 K2
Rheinfelden 64 C3
Rhin = Rhine 64 C2
Rhine 64 C2
Rhinelander 142 C1
Rho 64 E5
Rhode Island 142 F2
Rhodes = Rodos 70 L8
Rhondda 38 E4
Rhône 60 K9
Rhyl 38 E2
Rhymney 38 E4
Rhynie 36 F4
Ribadeo 62 C1
Ribas do Rio Pardo 158 L3
Ribble 38 F2
Ribe 50 E9
Ribeauvillé 60 N5
Ribeirão Prêto 158 M3
Ribeira = Santa Eugenia 62 A2
Ribera 66 H11
Riberalta 156 D6
Ribnica 66 J3
Rîbniţa 68 S2
Ribnitz-Damgarten 54 H2
Říčany 54 K6
Riccione 64 H7
Richardson Mountains 146 (1)K2
Richfield 140 D3
Richland 140 C1
Richlands 142 D3
Richmond, *Australia* 126 H4
Richmond, *New Zealand* 128 D5
Richmond, *United Kingdom* 36 G7
Richmond, *Ky., United States* 142 D3
Richmond, *Va., United States* 142 E3
Richmond-upon-Thames 38 H4
Rickmansworth 38 H4
Ridgecrest 146 C1
Ridgway 142 E2
Ried 64 J2
Riesa 54 J5
Rieti 66 G6
Rifle 140 E3
Rīga 50 N8
Rīgān 101 H2
Riggins 140 C1
Rigolet 136 V6
Rijeka 64 K5
Riley 140 C2
Rimava 52 J9
Rimavská Sobota 52 K9
Rimini 64 H6
Rimouski 142 G1
Rineia 70 H7
Ringe 54 F1
Ringkøbing 50 E8
Ringkøbing Fjord 50 D9
Ringsted 54 G1
Ringvassøya 50 J1
Ringwood 38 G5
Rinteln 54 E4
Rio Branco 156 D5
Río Colorado 158 J6
Río Cuarto 158 J5
Rio de Janeiro 158 N3
Rio de Janeiro 158 N3
Río de la Plata 158 K6
Río Gallegos 158 H9
Rio Grande 146 E2
Río Grande, *Argentina* 158 H9
Río Grande, *Mexico* 146 F4
Rio Grande 158 L5
Rio Grande City 144 B4
Rio Grande do Norte 156 K5
Rio Grande do Sul 158 L4
Riohacha 148 K6
Río Largartos 148 G4
Riom 60 J8
Rio Mulatos 156 D7
Rionero in Vulture 66 K8
Rio Tigre 156 B4
Rio Verde, *Brazil* 156 G7
Rio Verde, *Chile* 158 G9
Rio Verde de Mato Grosso 156 G7
Ripley, *Oh., United States* 142 D3
Ripley, *Tenn., United States* 142 C3
Ripley, *W. Va., United States* 142 D3
Ripoll 62 N2
Ripon 36 G7
Rishiri-tō 84 Q7
Rishon le Ziyyon 100 B5
Risør 50 E7
Ritchie's Archipelago 90 A4
Ritzville 140 C1
Rivadavia 158 G4
Riva del Garda 64 F5
Rivarolo Canavese 64 C5
Rivas 148 G6
Rivera, *Argentina* 158 J6
Rivera, *Uruguay* 158 K5
River Cess 114 C3
Riversdale 118 C6
Riversdale Beach 128 E5
Riverton, *Canada* 136 M6
Riverton, *New Zealand* 128 A8
Rivesaltes 60 H11
Rivière-du-Loup 142 G1
Rivne 72 E4
Rivoli 64 C5
Riwoqê 94 G2
Riyadh = Ar Riyāḑ 101 B4
Rize 98 J3
Rizhao 86 F3
Roanne 60 K7
Roanoke 142 D3
Roanoke Rapids 144 F2
Roaringwater 35 B5
Robāţ 101 G1
Robe 126 G7
Robertsfors 50 L4
Robertval 142 F1
Roboré 156 F7
Robstown 144 B4
Roccastrada 66 F6
Rochdale 38 F2
Rochefort, *Belgium* 56 H4
Rochefort, *France* 60 E8
Rochelle 142 C2
Rocher River 136 J4
Rochester, *United Kingdom* 38 J4
Rochester, *Minn., United States* 142 B2
Rochester, *N.H., United States* 142 F2
Rochester, *N.Y., United States* 142 E2
Rockall 48 C2
Rockefeller Plateau 160 (2)EE2
Rockford 142 C2
Rockhampton 126 K4
Rock Hill 142 D4
Rock Island 142 B2
Rocklake 140 G1
Rockport 140 B1
Rock Rapids 142 A2
Rock Springs 140 E2
Rocksprings 146 F3
Rocky Mount 142 E3
Rocky Mountains 136 F5
Rødby Havn 54 G2
Roddickton 136 V6
Roden 56 J1
Rodez 60 H9
Rodi Garganico 66 K7
Roding 54 H7
Rodney 142 D2
Rodopi Planina 68 M7
Rodos 70 L8
Rodos 70 L8
Roebourne 126 C4
Roermond 56 J3
Roeselare 56 F4
Roes Welcome Sound 136 P4
Rogers City 142 D1
Rogerson 140 D2
Rogliano 66 D6
Rogozno 52 G5
Rogue 140 B2
Rohrbach 64 K2
Rohtak 94 C3
Roi Et 90 C3
Roja 50 M8
Rokiškis 50 N9
Rokycany 52 C8
Rolla 142 B3
Rolleston 128 D6
Rolvsøya 50 M1
Roma 93 C4
Roma, *Australia* 126 J5
Roma, *Italy* 66 G7
Roman 68 P3
Romania 68 L4
Romans-sur-Isère 60 L8
Rombas 56 J5
Rome = Roma 66 G7
Rome, *Ga., United States* 144 D3
Rome, *N.Y., United States* 142 E2
Romford 38 J4
Romney 142 E3
Romny 72 F4
Rømø 54 D1
Romorantin-Lanthenay 60 G6
Romsey 38 G5
Rona, *Scot., United Kingdom* 36 C4
Rona, *Scot., United Kingdom* 36 C2
Ronan 138 D2
Ronas Hill 36 (1)G1
Ronay 36 A4
Roncesvalles 62 J2
Ronda 62 E8
Rondônia 156 E6
Rondônia 156 E6
Rondonópolis 156 G7
Rondu 96 L2
Rongcheng 86 G3
Rønne 52 D2
Ronneby 50 H8
Ronne Entrance 160 (2)JJ3
Ronne Ice Shelf 160 (2)MM2
Ronse 56 F4
Roosendaal 56 G3
Roper Bar 126 F2
Roquetas de Mar 62 H8
Roraima 156 E3
Røros 50 F5
Rosário 156 J4
Rosario, *Argentina* 158 J5
Rosario, *Mexico* 138 D6
Rosario, *Mexico* 138 E7
Rosario, *Paraguay* 158 K3
Rosário Oeste 156 F6
Rosarito 138 C6
Rosarno 66 K10
Roscommon 35 C3
Roscrea 35 D4
Roseau 148 M5
Roseburg 140 B2
Roseires Reservoir 110 F5
Rose Island 124 K7
Rosenburg 146 G3
Rosenheim 64 H3
Roses 62 P2
Rosetown 136 K6
Rosica 68 N6
Rosignano Marittimo 64 F7
Roşiori de Vede 68 N5
Rosita 68 Q6
Roskilde 50 G9
Roslavl' 72 F4
Rossano 66 L9
Rossan Point 35 C2
Ross Ice Shelf 160 (2)Z1
Ross Lake 140 B1
Rosslare Harbour 35 E4
Roßlau 54 H5
Rosso 112 B5
Ross-on-Wye 38 F4
Rossosh' 72 G4
Ross River 136 E4
Ross Sea 160 (2)AA2
Røssvatnet 50 G4
Røst 50 G3
Rostāq 101 E3
Rosthern 136 K6
Rostock 54 H2
Rostov 72 G3
Rostov-na-Donu 72 G5
Rostrenen 60 B5
Rostrevor 35 E2
Roswell 146 F2
Rota 124 E4
Rote 93 B5
Rotenburg, *Germany* 54 E3
Rotenburg, *Germany* 54 E5
Roth 54 G7
Rothenburg 54 F7
Rotherham 38 G2
Rothesay 36 C6
Rothwell 38 H3
Roto 126 J6
Rotorua 128 F4
Rott 64 H2
Rottenmann 64 K3
Rotterdam 60 K2
Rottnen 52 E1
Rottumeroog 56 J1
Rottumerplaat 56 J1
Rottweil 64 D2
Rotuma 124 H7
Roubaix 56 F4
Rouen 56 D5
Rouiba 62 P8
Round Mountain 126 K6
Round Rock 144 B3
Roundup 140 E1
Rousay 36 E2
Rouyn 142 E1
Rovaniemi 50 N3
Rovato 64 E5
Rovereto 64 G5
Rovigo 64 G5
Rovinari 68 L5
Rovinj 64 J5
Rovuma 116 F6
Rowley Island 136 R3
Rowley Shoals 126 C3
Roxas 90 G4
Roxburgh 128 B7
Royal Canal 35 E3
Royal Leamington Spa 38 G3
Royal Tunbridge Wells 38 J4
Royan 60 D8
Roye 56 E5
Royston 38 H3
Rozdil'na 68 T3
Rožňava 52 K9
Rozzano 64 E5
Rrëshen 70 B3
Rtishchevo 72 H4
Ruacana 118 A3
Ruahine Range 128 E5
Ruapehu 128 E4
Ruapuke Island 128 B8
Ruarkela 94 D4
Ruatahuna 128 F4
Ruatoria 128 G3
Ruawai 128 D3
Rub' al Khālī 96 E6
Rubeshibe 88 M2
Rubi 116 C3
Rubtsovsk 82 Q7
Ruby 146 (1)F3
Rudan 101 G3
Ruda Śląska 52 H7
Rudbar 96 H3
Rüdersdorf 54 J4
Rudkøbing 54 F2
Rudnaya Pristan' 88 H2
Rudnyy 72 M4
Rudolstadt 54 G6
Rue 56 D4
Ruffec 60 F7
Rufiji 116 F5
Rugby, *United Kingdom* 38 G3
Rugby, *United States* 138 G2
Rugeley 38 G3
Rügen 52 C3
Ruhnu 50 M8
Ruhr 56 L3
Rui'an 86 G5
Rum 36 B4
Ruma 68 G4
Rumāh 101 B4
Rumaylah 101 B1
Rumbek 116 D2
Rum Cay 148 K4
Rumigny 56 G5
Rum Jungle 126 F2
Rumoi 88 L2
Runanaga 128 C6
Runcorn 38 F2
Rundu 118 B3
Rundvik 50 K5
Ruoqiang 82 R10
Ruo Shui 86 C2
Rupa 64 K5
Rupat 92 C2
Rupert 136 R6
Rupert 140 D2
Rurutu 124 L8
Ruse 68 N6
Rushden 38 H3
Rushon 94 G3
Rushville, *Ill., United States* 142 B2
Rushville, *Ind., United States* 142 C3
Rushville, *Nebr., United States* 140 F2
Russell 140 G3
Russellville, *Ark., United States* 144 C2
Russellville, *Ky., United States* 144 D2
Rüsselsheim 54 D7
Russia 50 L9
Russia 80 M3
Russoye Ust'ye 84 R2
Rust'avi 98 L3
Ruston 144 C3
Rutana 116 D4
Rute 62 F7
Ruteng 93 B4
Ruthin 38 E2
Rutland 142 F2
Rutland Water 38 H3
Rutog 94 C2
Ruvo di Puglia 66 L7
Ruvuma 116 F6
Ruzayevka 72 H4
Ružomberok 52 J8
Rwanda 116 D4
R-Warnemünde 54 H2
Ryazan' 72 G4
Ryazhsk 72 H4
Rybinsk 72 G3
Rybinskoye Vodokhranilishche 72 G3
Rybnik 52 H7
Rychnov 52 F7
Ryde 38 G5
Rye 38 J5
Rye Patch Reservoir 140 C2
Ryki 52 L6
Ryl'sk 72 F4
Ryn-Peski 72 J5
Ryōtsu 88 K4
Rypin 52 J4
Ryukyu Islands = Nansei-shotō 86 H5
Rzeszów 52 M7
Rzhev 72 F3

S

Sa'ādatābād, *Iran* 101 E1
Sa'ādatābād, *Iran* 101 F2
Saale 54 G6
Saalfeld 54 G6
Saalfelden 64 H3
Saanen 66 B2
Saar 56 J5
Saarbrücken 56 J5
Saarburg 56 J5
Saaremaa 50 L7
Saarlouis 56 J5
Saatli 98 N4
Saatly 96 E2
Saba 148 M5
Sab' Ābār 100 E3
Šabac 68 G5
Sabadell 62 N3
Sabah 92 F1
Sabang 90 B5
Sabhā 112 H3
Sabiñánigo 62 K2
Sabinas 146 F3
Sabinas Hidalgo 146 F3
Sabine 144 B3
Sabine Lake 144 C3
Sabinov 52 L8
Sabkhet el Bardawîl 100 A5
Sable Island 136 V8
Sablé-sur-Sarthe 60 E6
Sabôr 62 D3
Sabres 60 E9
Sabun 82 Q5
Sabzevār 96 G2
Săcele 68 N4
Sachanga 118 B2
Sachs Harbour 136 G2
Sacile 64 H5

Säckingen 64 C3
Sacramento 140 B3
Sacramento 140 B3
Şad'ah 96 D6
Sadiqabad 96 K4
Sadiya 94 G3
Sado 62 B6
Sadoga-shima 88 K4
Sadon 98 K2
Sado-shima 86 K3
Sa Dragonera 62 N5
Sadût 100 B5
Säffle 50 G7
Safford 146 E2
Saffron Walden 38 J3
Safi, *Jordan* 100 C5
Safi, *Morocco* 112 D2
Safonovo, *Russia* 72 F3
Safonovo, *Russia* 72 J1
Safranbolu 70 Q3
Saga, *China* 94 E3
Saga, *Japan* 88 F7
Sagami-nada 88 K6
Sagar 94 C4
Sagastyr 82 Z3
Sage 140 D2
Saginaw 142 D2
Sagiz 72 K5
Sagiz 72 K5
Sagres 62 B7
Saguache 140 E3
Sagua la Grande 148 H4
Sagunt 62 K5
Sahāb 100 D5
Sahagún 62 E2
Sahara 108 C3
Saharah el Gharbîya 110 E2
Saharanpur 94 C3
Saharsa 94 E3
Şahbuz 98 L4
Sahel 108 C4
Sahiwal 96 K3
Sahuaripa 146 E3
Šahy 68 F1
Saïda, *Algeria* 112 F2
Saïda, *Lebanon* 100 C3
Sa'īdābād 101 F2
Saidpur 94 E3
Saigo 88 G5
Saigon = Hô Chi Minh 90 D4
Saiha 94 F4
Saihan Toroi 86 C2
Saiki 88 F7
Saimaa 50 P6
Saimbeyli 98 G4
Sā'in 101 F1
Saindak 96 H4
St. Abb's Head 36 F6
St. Albans 38 H4
St-Amand-Montrond 60 H7
St. Andrä 64 K4
St. Andrews 36 F5
St. Anthony 136 V6
St. Arnaud 128 D5
St-Augustin 136 V6
St. Augustin 56 K4
St. Augustine 144 E4
St. Austell 38 D5
St. Austell Bay 38 D5
St-Avertin 60 F6
St-Avold 56 J5
St. Barthélémy 148 M5
St. Bee's Head 36 E7
St. Brides Bay 38 C4
St-Brieuc 60 C5
St. Catharines 138 L3
St. Catherine's Point 38 G5
St-Chamond 60 K8
St-Claude 60 L7
St. Cloud 142 B1
St. David's 38 C4
St. David's Head 38 C4
St-Denis, *France* 56 E6
St-Denis, *Réunion* 118 (1)B2
St-Dié 64 B2
St-Dizier 60 K5
Ste-Anne-de-Beaupré 142 F1
Ste-Maxime 60 M10
Ste-Menehould 56 G5
Saintes 60 E8
Stes-Maries-de-la-Mer 60 K10
St-Étienne 60 K8
St-Étienne-du-Rouvray 56 D5
St-Félicien 142 F1
St-Florent 66 D6
St-Florentin 60 J5
St-Flour 60 J8
St. Francis 140 F3
St. Gallen 64 E3
St-Gaudens 60 F10
St. George, *Australia* 126 J5
St. George, *United States* 140 D3
St. Georgen 64 D2
St. Georges 142 F1
St. George's 148 M6
St. George's Channel 38 C4
St-Germain-en-Laye 56 E6
St-Girons 60 G11
St. Govan's Head 38 D4
St. Helena 108 C7
St. Helena Bay 118 B6
St. Helens, *United Kingdom* 38 F2
St. Helens, *United States* 140 B1
St. Helier 38 (1)F6
St-Hubert 56 H4
St. Ignace 142 D1
St. Ives 38 C5
St-Jean-d'Angely 60 E8
St-Jean-de-Luz 60 D10
St-Jean-de-Maurienne 64 B5
St-Jean-sur-Richelieu 142 F1
St. John 136 T7
St. John's 136 W7
St. Johnsbury 142 F2
St. Joseph 142 B3
St-Jovité 142 F1
St-Junien 60 F8
St. Kilda 58 D4
St. Kitts-Nevis 148 M5
St. Laurent 156 G2
St-Laurent-en-Grandvaux 64 A4
St. Lawrence 142 G1
St. Lawrence Island 146 (1)C3
St-Léonard 142 G1
St-Lô 56 A5
St. Louis, *Senegal* 112 B5
St. Louis, *United States* 142 B3
St. Lucia 148 M6
St. Maarten 148 M5
St. Magnus Bay 36 (1)G1
St-Malo 60 D5
St. Marys 142 D2
St. Matthew Island 146 (1)C3
St-Mihiel 56 H6
St. Moritz 64 E4
St-Nazaire 60 C6
St. Neots 38 H3
St-Nicolas-de-Port 64 B2
St. Niklaas 56 G3
St-Omer 56 E4
St-Palais 60 D10
St-Pamphile 142 G1
St-Paul 64 B6
St. Paul, *Minn., United States* 142 B2
St. Paul, *Nebr., United States* 140 G2
St. Peter 142 B2
St. Peter Ording 54 D2
St. Peter Port 38 (1)F6
St. Petersburg 144 E4
St. Petersburg = Sankt-Peterburg 72 F3
St-Pierre 118 (1)B2
St-Pierre-et-Miquelon 136 V7
St. Pierre Island 118 (2)A2
St-Pol-de-Léon 60 A5
St-Pol-sur-Ternoise 56 E4
St. Pölten 64 L2
St-Quentin 56 F5
St-Raphaël 64 B7
St. Siméon 142 G1
St. Stephen 142 G1
St. Thomas 142 D2
St-Tropez 64 B7
St. Truiden 56 H4
St-Valéry-sur-Somme 56 D4
St. Veit 64 K4
St. Veit an der Glan 68 B3
St. Vincent and the Grenadines 148 M6
St-Vincent-les-Forts 64 B6
St-Vith 56 J4
Saipan 124 E4
Sajószentpéter 52 K9
Sākākah 96 D4
Sakaraha 118 G4
Sakarya 70 N4
Sakarya 70 N4
Sakata 88 K4
Sakchu 88 C3
Sakha 84 N3
Sakhalin 84 Q6
Sakhalinskiy Zaliv 84 Q6
Sakhon Nakhon 90 C3
Şäki 98 M3
Sakishima-shotō 86 H6
Sakskøbing 54 G2
Sal 114 (1)B1
Sal 72 H5
Sala 50 J7
Šal'a 52 G9
Salacgrīva 50 N8
Sala Consilina 66 K8
Saladillo 158 K6
Salado 158 J4
Şalālah 96 F6
Salamanca, *Mexico* 148 D4
Salamanca, *Spain* 62 E4
Salamanca, *United States* 142 E2
Salamina 70 F7
Salamīyah 100 E1
Salar de Uyuni 158 H3
Salawati 93 D3
Salayar 93 B4
Salbris 60 H6
Salcombe 38 E5
Saldus 50 M8
Sale 126 J7
Sale 38 F2
Salekhard 82 M4
Salem 140 B2
Salem, *India* 94 C6
Salem, *United States* 142 C3
Salerno 66 J8
Salford 38 F2
Salgótarján 52 J9
Salida 140 E3
Salihli 70 L6
Salihorsk 72 E4
Salima 118 E2
Salina 66 J10
Salina, *Kans., United States* 140 G3
Salina, *Ut., United States* 140 D3
Salinas, *Brazil* 156 J7
Salinas, *Ecuador* 156 A4
Salinas, *Mexico* 146 F4
Salinas, *United States* 146 B1
Salinas Grandes 158 J4
Salinópolis 156 H4
Salisbury, *United Kingdom* 38 G4
Salisbury, *Md., United States* 142 E3
Salisbury, *N.C., United States* 142 D3
Salisbury Island 136 R4
Salisbury Plain 38 F4
Şalkhad 100 D4
Salla 50 Q3
Salluit 136 R4
Salmās 98 L4
Salmon 140 D1
Salmon 140 C1/D1
Salmon Arm 136 H6
Salmon River Mountains 140 C1
Salo 50 M6
Salò 64 F5
Salon-de-Provence 60 L10
Salonta 68 J3
Sal'sk 72 H5
Salsomaggiore Terme 64 E6
Salt 100 C4
Salta 158 H3
Saltash 38 D5
Saltburn-by-the-Sea 36 H7
Saltee Islands 35 E4
Saltillo 146 F3
Salt Lake City 140 D2
Salto 158 K5
Salto del Guairá 158 K3
Salton Sea 146 C2
Saluda 144 E3
Salûm 110 E1
Saluzzo 64 C6
Salvador 156 K6
Salvadore 154 H5
Salween 90 B2
Salyan 98 N4
Salyersville 142 D3
Salym 72 P3
Salym 64 H2
Salzach 64 J3
Salzburg 54 F4
Salzgitter 54 G4
Salzwedel 156 E7
Samaipata 90 H4
Samar 72 K4
Samara 92 F3
Samarinda 96 J2
Samarkand 98 K6
Sāmarrā' 98 N3
Şamaxı 94 D4
Sambalpur 92 D2
Sambas 118 J2
Sambava 94 C3
Sambhal 52 N8
Sambir 93 A3
Sambo 92 F3
Samboja 56 F4
Sambre 88 E6
Samch'ŏnp'o 116 F4
Same 70 C6
Sami 98 M3
Sāmkir 124 J7
Samoa 64 L5
Samobor 72 H2
Samoded 68 L7
Samokov 52 G9
Šamorín 70 J7
Samos 70 J7
Samos 70 H4
Samothraki 70 H4
Samothraki 92 E3
Sampit 144 C3
Sam Rayburn Reservoir 94 D2
Samsang 50 F9
Samsø 98 G3
Samsun 98 K2
Samtredia 90 B4
Samut Songkhram 114 D2
San 52 L7
San 110 H4
Şan'ā 114 G4
Sanaga 158 F4
San Ambrosio 93 C3
Sanana 93 C3
Sanana 98 M6
Sanandaj 146 F2
San Angelo 62 M6
San Antonia Abad 158 G5
San Antonio, *Chile* 148 E3
San Antonio, *United States* 158 H3
San Antonio de los Cobres 158 H7
San Antonio-Oeste 96 F6
Sanäw 66 H6
San Benedetto del Tronto 146 C2
San Bernardino 158 H5
San Bernardo 156 D6
San Borja 158 G6
San Carlos, *Chile* 90 G3
San Carlos, *Philippines* 156 D3
San Carlos, *Venezuela* 158 G7
San Carlos de Bariloche 158 J6
San Carlos de Bolivár 156 C2
San Carlos del Zulia 146 D2
San Carlos Lake 66 H11
San Cataldo 88 C1
Sanchahe 82 P10
Sanchakou 94 B4
Sanchor 72 J3
Sanchursk 146 C2
San Clemente Island 124 G7
San Cristóbal 158 J5
San Cristóbal, *Argentina* 156 C2
San Cristóbal, *Venezuela* 148 F5
San Cristóbal de las Casas 148 J4
Sancti Spíritus 36 C6
Sanda 92 F1
Sandakan 50 D6
Sandane 70 F3
Sandanski 36 F2
Sanday 54 G2
Sandby 50 F7
Sandefjord 146 E1
Sanders 146 F2
Sanderson 126 D3
Sandfire Flat Roadhouse 146 C2
San Diego 70 N6
Sandıklı 50 C7
Sandnes 50 G4
Sandnessjøen 116 C5
Sandoa 52 L7
Sandomierz 64 H5
San Donà di Piave 94 F5
Sandoway 38 G5
Sandown 140 C1
Sandpoint 36 A5
Sandray 50 J6
Sandviken 140 D2
Sandy 126 K4
Sandy Cape 126 D2
Sandy Island 136 N6
Sandy Lake 136 N6
Sandy Lake 144 E3
Sandy Springs
San Felipe 138 D5
San Félix 158 E4
San Fernando, *Chile* 158 G5
San Fernando, *Mexico* 144 B5
San Fernando, *Philippines* 90 G3
San Fernando, *Spain* 62 D8
San Fernando de Apure 156 D2
San Fernando de Atabapo 156 D3
Sanford, *Fla., United States* 144 E4
Sanford, *N.C., United States* 144 F2
San Francis 144 A2
San Francisco, *Argentina* 158 J5
San Francisco, *United States* 140 B3
Sangamner 94 B5
Sangān 96 H3
Sangar 84 M4
Sangāreddi 94 C5
Sangasanga 92 F3
Sângeorz-Băi 68 M2
Sangerhausen 54 G5
Sanggau 92 E2
Sangha 114 H4
Sanghar 96 J4
San Gimignano 64 G7
San Giovanni in Fiore 66 L9
San Giovanni Valdarno 64 G7
Sangir 93 C2
Sangkhla Buri 90 B3
Sangkulirang 92 F2
Sangli 94 B5
Sangmélima 114 G4
Sangre de Cristo Range 146 E1
Sangsang 94 E3
Sangue 156 F6
Sangüesa 62 J2
Sanjō 88 K5
San Joaquin Valley 140 B3
San Jose 140 B3
San José 148 H7
San Jose de Buenavista 90 G4
San José de Chiquitos 156 E7
San José de Jáchal 158 H5
San José del Cabo 148 C4
San José de Ocuné 156 C3
San Juan 148 H4
San Juan, *Argentina* 158 H5
San Juan, *Costa Rica* 148 H6
San Juan, *Puerto Rico* 148 L5
San Juan, *United States* 146 E1
San Juan, *Venezuela* 156 D2
San Juan Bautista, *Paraguay* 158 K4
San Juan Bautista, *Spain* 62 M5
San Juan de los Cayos 156 D1
San Juan de los Morros 156 D2
San Juan Mountains 140 E3
San Julián 158 H8
Sankt-Peterburg 72 F3
Sankuru 116 C4
Sanlıurfa 98 H5
San Lorenzo 146 D3
Sanlúcar de Barrameda 62 D8
San Lucas 148 C4
San Luis 158 H5
San Luis Obispo 146 B1
San Luis Potosí 148 D4
San Luis Río Colorado 146 D2
San Marcos 144 B4
San Marino 64 H7
San Marino 64 H7
San Martín 156 E6
Sanmenxia 86 E4
San Miguel 148 G6
San Miguel 156 E7
San Miguel de Tucumán 158 H4
San Miguel Island 146 B2
San Miniato 64 F7
San Nicolás de los Arroyos 158 J5
San Nicolás de los Garzas 144 A4
San Nicolas Island 146 C2
Sânnicolau Mare 68 H3
Sanok 52 M8
San Pablo 90 G4
San-Pédro 114 C4
San Pedro, *Argentina* 158 J3
San Pedro, *Bolivia* 156 E7
San Pedro, *Paraguay* 158 K3
San Pedro, *Philippines* 90 G4
San Pedro de las Colonias 146 F3
San Pedro Sula 148 G5
San Pellegrino Terme 64 E5
San Pietro 66 C9
Sanqaçal 98 N3
Sanquhar 36 E6
San Rafael 158 H5
San Remo 64 C7
San Roque 62 E8
Sansalé 114 B2
San Salvador 144 G5
San Salvador 148 G6
San Salvador de Jujuy 158 H3
Sansar 94 C4
San Sebastián = Donostia 62 J1
San Sebastian de los Reyes 62 G4
Sansepolcro 64 H7
San Severo 66 K7
Sanski Most 64 M6
Santa Ana, *Bolivia* 156 D7
Santa Ana, *El Salvador* 148 G6
Santa Ana, *Mexico* 146 D2
Santa Ana, *United States* 146 C2
Santa Bárbara 138 E6
Santa Barbara 146 C2
Santa Barbara Island 146 C2
Santa Catalina 158 H4
Santa Catalina Island 146 C2
Santa Catarina 158 L4
Santa Clara, *Columbia* 156 D4
Santa Clara, *Cuba* 138 K7
Santa Clarita 146 C2
Santa Comba Dão 62 B4
Santa Cruz 158 G9
Santa Cruz, *Bolivia* 156 E7
Santa Cruz, *Philippines* 90 G3
Santa Cruz, *United States* 146 B1
Santa Cruz de Tenerife 112 B3
Santa Cruz Island 146 B2

Santa Cruz Islands 124 G7
Santa Elena 156 E3
Santa Eugenia 62 A2
Santa Fe 140 E3
Santa Fé 158 J5
Sant'Agata di Militello 66 J10
Santa Isabel 124 F6
Santa Isabel 158 H6
Santa la Grande 138 K7
Santa Margarita 138 D7
Santa Margherita Ligure 64 E6
Santa Maria 112 (1)B2
Santa Maria, *Brazil* 158 L4
Santa Maria, *United States* 146 B2
Santa Maria das Barreiras 156 H5
Santa Marinella 66 F6
Santa Marta, *Colombia* 148 K6
Santa Marta, *Spain* 62 D6
Santana do Livramento 158 K5
Santander 62 G1
Sant'Antioco 66 C9
Sant'Antioco 66 C9
Santanyí 62 P5
Santa Pola 62 K6
Santarém, *Brazil* 156 G4
Santarém, *Spain* 62 B5
Santa Rosa, *Argentina* 158 J6
Santa Rosa, *R.G.S., Brazil* 158 L4
Santa Rosa, *Acre, Brazil* 156 C5
Santa Rosa, *Calif., United States* 140 B3
Santa Rosa, *N. Mex., United States* 146 F2
Santa Rosa Island 146 B2
Santa Vitória do Palmar 158 L5
Sant Boi 62 N3
Sant Carlos de la Ràpita 62 L4
Sant Celoni 62 N3
Sant Feliu de Guixols 62 P3
Santiago 158 G5
Santiago, *Brazil* 158 L4
Santiago, *Dominican Republic* 148 K5
Santiago, *Philippines* 90 G3
Santiago, *Spain* 62 B2
Santiago de Cuba 148 J5
Santiago del Estero 158 J4
Santo André 158 M3
Santo Antão 114 (1)A1
Santo Antônio de Jesus 156 K6
Santo Antônio do Içá 156 D4
Santo Domingo 148 L5
Santo Domingo de los Colorados 156 B4
Santoña 62 G1
Santos 158 M3
San Vicente 90 G3
San Vincenzo 66 E5
Sanya 90 D3
Sao Bernardo do Campo 156 E4
São Borja 158 K4
São Carlos 158 M3
São Félix, *M.G., Brazil* 156 G6
São Félix, *Pará, Brazil* 156 G5
São Filipe 114 (1)B2
São Francisco 156 J6
São João de Madeira 62 B4
São Jorge 112 (1)B2
São José do Rio Prêto 158 L3
São Luís 156 J4
São Miguel 112 (1)B2
Saône 60 K7
São Nicolau 114 (1)B1
São Paulo 158 L3
São Paulo 158 M3
São Paulo de Olivença 156 D4
São Raimundo Nonato 156 J5
São Tiago 114 (1)B1
São Tomé 114 F4
São Tomé 114 F4
São Tomé and Príncipe 114 F4
São Vicente 114 (1)A1
São Vicente 158 M3
Sapanca 70 M4
Saparua 93 C3
Sapele 114 F3
Sapes 70 H4
Sapientza 70 D8
Sa Pobla 62 P5
Sapporo 88 L2
Sapri 66 K8
Sapudi 92 E4
Sapulpa 144 B2
Saqqez 98 M5
Sarāb 98 M5
Sara Buri 90 C4
Sarajevo 68 F6
Sarakhs 96 H2
Saraktash 72 L4
Saramati 94 G3
Saran 82 N8
Saranac Lake 142 F2
Sarandë 70 C5
Sarangani Islands 93 C1
Saranpul 72 M2
Saransk 72 J4
Sarapul 72 K3
Sarapul'skoye 84 P7
Sarasota 144 E4
Sarata 68 S3
Saratoga 140 E2
Saratoga Springs 142 F2
Saratov 72 J4
Saravan 96 H4
Sarawak 92 E2
Saray 70 K3
Sarayköy 70 L7
Sarayönü 70 Q6
Sarbāz 96 H4
Sarbīsheh 96 G3
Sárbogárd 68 F3
Sar Dasht 98 L5
Sardegna 66 E8
Sardinia = Sardegna 66 E8
Sardis Lake 144 B3
Sar-e Pol 96 J2
Sargodha 96 K3
Sarh 114 H3
Sārī 96 F2
Saria 70 K9
Sarıkamış 98 K3
Sarıkaya 98 F4
Sarikei 92 E2
Sarina 126 J4
Sariñena 62 K3
Sarīr Tibesti 110 C3
Sariwŏn 88 C4
Sarıyer 70 M3
Sark 38 (1)F6
Sarkad 68 J3
Sarkand 82 P8
Sarkikaraağaç 70 P6
Şarkişla 98 G4
Şarköy 70 K4
Sarmi 93 E3
Särna 50 G6
Sarnia 142 D2
Sarny 72 E4
Sarolangun 92 C3
Saronno 64 E5
Saros Körfezi 70 J4
Sárospatak 52 L9
Sarre 60 M5
Sarrebourg 60 N5
Sarreguemines 60 N4
Sarria 62 C2
Sartène 66 C7
Sartyn'ya 72 M2
Saruhanli 70 K6
Sárur 98 L4
Sárvár 64 M3
Sarvestān 101 E2
Sarviz 68 F2
Sarykamyshkoye Ozero 82 K9
Saryozek 82 P9
Saryshagan 82 N8
Sarysu 82 M8
Sary-Tash 96 K2
Sarzana 64 E6
Sasaram 94 D4
Sasebo 88 E7
Saskatchewan 136 K6
Saskatchewan 136 L6
Saskatoon 136 K6
Saskylakh 82 W3
Sassandra 114 C4
Sassari 66 C8
Sassnitz 54 J2
Sasso Marconi 64 G6
Sassuolo 64 F6
Satadougou 114 B2
Satara 94 B5
Satna 94 D4
Sátoraljaújhely 52 L9
Satti 94 C2
Sättna 50 J5
Satu Mare 68 K2
Satun 92 B1
Sauce 158 K5
Saudi Arabia 96 D4
Sauk Center 142 B1
Saulgau 64 E2
Saulieu 60 K6
Sault Ste. Marie, *Canada* 142 D1
Sault Ste. Marie, *United States* 142 D1
Saumlakki 93 D4
Saumur 60 E6
Saunders Island 154 J9
Saura 82 J9
Saurimo 116 C5
Sauðarkrókur 50 (1)D2
Sava 64 L5
Savaii 124 J7
Savalou 114 E3
Savannah 134 K6
Savannah, *Ga., United States* 144 E3
Savannah, *Tenn., United States* 144 D2
Savannakhet 90 C3
Savaştepe 70 K5
Savè 114 E3
Save 118 E4
Sāveh 96 F2
Saverne 54 C8
Savigliano 64 C6
Savona 64 D6
Savonlinna 50 Q6
Savu 93 B5
Sawahlunto 92 C3
Sawai Madhopur 94 C3
Sawqirah 96 G6
Sawu Sea 93 B4
Sayanogorsk 82 S7
Sayansk 84 G6
Sayhūt 96 F6
Sāylac 110 H5
Saynshand 86 E2
Sayram Hu 82 Q9
Say'ūn 96 E6
Say-Utes 82 J9
Sazan 70 B4
Sazin 96 K2
Sbaa 112 E3
Scafell Pike 36 E7
Scalea 66 K9
Scalpay, *Scot., United Kingdom* 36 C4
Scalpay, *Scot., United Kingdom* 36 B4
Scapa Flow 36 E3
Scarba 36 C5
Scarborough 36 H7
Scargill 128 D6
Scarp 36 A3
Schaalsee 54 F3
Schaffhausen 64 D3
Schagen 56 G2
Scharbeutz 54 F2
Schärding 64 J2
Scharhörn 54 D3
Scheeßel 54 E3
Schefferville 136 T6
Scheibbs 64 L3
Schelde 56 F3
Schenectady 142 F2
Scheveningen 56 G2
Schiedam 56 G3
Schiermonnikoog 56 H1
Schiermonnikoog 56 J1
Schio 64 G5
Schiza 70 D8
Schkeuditz 54 H5
Schlei 54 E2
Schleiden 56 J4
Schleswig 54 E2
Schlieben 54 J5
Schlüchtern 54 E6
Schneeberg 54 H6
Schneeberg 54 G6
Schönebeck 54 G4
Schongau 64 F3
Schöningen 54 F4
Schouwen 56 F3
Schramberg 64 D2
Schreiber 142 C1
Schrems 64 L2
Schull 35 B5
Schwabach 54 G7
Schwäbische Alb 64 E2
Schwäbisch-Gmünd 64 E2
Schwäbisch-Hall 54 E7
Schwalmstadt 54 E6
Schwandorf 54 H7
Schwarzenbek 54 F3
Schwarzenberg 54 H6
Schwarzwald 64 D3
Schwaz 64 G3
Schwechat 52 F9
Schwedt 52 D4
Schweich 56 J5
Schweinfurt 54 F6
Schwenningen 64 D2
Schwerin 54 G3
Schweriner See 54 G3
Schwetzingen 54 D7
Schwyz 64 D3
Sciacca 66 H11
Scicli 66 J12
Scobey 140 E1
Scotia Ridge 158 K9
Scotia Sea 160 (2)A4
Scotland 36 D5
Scott City 140 F3
Scott Inlet 136 T2
Scott Island 160 (2)Z3
Scott Reef 126 D2
Scottsbluff 140 F2
Scottsboro 142 C4
Scotty's Junction 146 C1
Scourie 36 C3
Scranton 142 E2
Scunthorpe 38 H2
Seaham 36 G7
Seal 136 M5
Seamill 36 D6
Sea of Azov 72 G5
Sea of Galilee 100 C4
Sea of Japan 88 G3
Sea of Marmara = Marmara Denizi 70 L4
Sea of Okhotsk 84 Q5
Sea of the Hebrides 36 A4
Searchlight 146 D1
Searcy 142 B3
Seaside 140 B1
Seaton 38 E5
Seattle 140 B1
Sebeş 68 L4
Sebkha Azzel Matti 112 F3
Sebkha de Timimoun 112 E3
Sebkha de Tindouf 112 D3
Sebkha Mekerrhane 112 F3
Sebkha Oum el Drouss Telli 112 C4
Sebkhet de Chemchâm 112 C4
Sebnitz 54 K6
Sebring 144 E4
Secchia 64 F6
Sechura 156 A5
Secretary Island 128 A7
Secunderabad 94 C5
Sécure 156 D7
Sedalia 142 B3
Sedan 56 G5
Sedano 62 G2
Seddon 128 D5
Seddonville 128 C5
Sede Boqer 100 B6
Sedeh 96 G3
Sederot 100 B5
Sedico 64 H4
Sedom 100 C5
Seeheim 118 B5
Seelow 54 K4
Sées 60 F5
Seesen 54 F5
Seevetal 54 E3
Sézé 64 B5
Seferihisar 70 J6
Segamat 92 C2
Segezha 72 F2
Seghnān 96 K2
Ségou 114 C2
Segovia 62 F4
Segré 60 E6
Séguédine 112 H4
Seguin 144 B4
Segura 62 H6
Sehithwa 118 C4
Sehnde 54 E4
Seil 36 C5
Seiland 50 M1
Seiling 144 B2
Seinäjoki 50 M5
Seine 60 F4
Sekayu 92 C3
Sekondi 114 D3
Selassi 93 D3
Selat Bangka 92 D3
Selat Berhala 92 C3
Selat Dampir 93 D3
Selat Karimata 92 D3
Selat Makassar 92 F3
Selat Mentawai 92 B3
Selat Sunda 92 D4
Selawik 146 (1)F2
Selb 54 H6
Selby 140 G1
Selby 38 G2
Selçuk 70 K7
Selebi-Phikwe 118 D4
Sélestat 64 C2
Selfoss 50 (1)C3
Sélibabi 112 C5
Seligman 146 D1
Seljord 50 E7
Selkirk 138 G1
Selkirk 36 F6
Selkirk Mountains 138 C1
Sells 146 D2
Selm 56 K3
Selmer 142 C3
Selpele 93 D3
Selsey Bill 38 H5
Selvas 156 C5
Selwyn Lake 136 L5
Selwyn Mountains 146 (1)L3
Semanit 70 B4
Semarang 92 E4
Sematan 92 D2
Sembé 114 G4
Seminoe Reservoir 140 E2
Seminole, *Okla., United States* 140 G3
Seminole, *Tex., United States* 146 F2
Semiozernoye 82 L7
Semipalatinsk 82 Q7
Semiyarka 82 P7
Semois 56 H5
Semporna 92 F2
Sena Madureira 156 D5
Senanga 118 C3
Senatobia 144 D3
Sendai 88 L4
Senec 64 N2
Seneca 144 E3
Senegal 114 A2
Sénégal 114 B1
Senftenberg 54 J5
Sengerema 116 E4
Senhor do Bonfim 156 J6
Senica 52 G9
Senigallia 64 J7
Senj 64 K6
Senja 50 J2
Senlis 56 E5
Sennar 96 B7
Senneterre 142 E1
Sens 60 J5
Senta 68 H4
Seoni 94 C4
Seoul = Sŏul 88 D5
Separation Point 128 D5
Sepinang 92 F2
Sept-Îles 136 T6
Seraing 56 H4
Serakhs 96 H2
Seram 93 D3
Seram Sea 93 C3
Serang 92 D4
Serbia = Srbija 68 H6
Serdobsk 72 H4
Serebryansk 82 Q8
Sered' 68 E1
Şereflikoçhisar 70 R6
Seregno 64 E5
Serein 60 J6
Seremban 92 C2
Serenje 118 E2
Sergelen 86 E1
Sergeyevka 72 N4
Sergipe 156 K6
Sergiyev Posad 72 G3
Seria 92 E2
Serifos 70 G7
Serifos 70 G7
Serik 70 P8
Seringapatam Reef 126 D2
Sermata 93 C4
Seronga 118 C3
Serov 72 M3
Serowe 118 D4
Serpa 62 C7
Serpneve 68 S3
Serpukhov 72 G4
Serra Acari 156 F3
Serra Curupira 156 E3
Serra da Chela 118 A3
Serra da Espinhaço 156 J7
Serra da Ibiapaba 156 J4
Serra da Mantiqueira 158 M3
Serra de Maracaju 158 K3
Serra do Cachimbo 156 F5
Serra do Caiapó 156 G7
Serra do Roncador 156 G6
Serra dos Carajás 156 G5
Serra dos Dois Irmãos 156 J5
Serra dos Parecis 156 E6
Serra do Tiracambu 156 H4
Serra Estrondo 156 H5
Serra Formosa 156 F6
Serra Geral de Goiás 156 H6
Serra Geral do Paranã 156 H7
Serra Lombarda 156 G3
Serra Pacaraima 156 E3
Serra Parima 156 E3
Serra Tumucumaque 156 F3
Serre da Estrela 62 C4
Serres, *France* 60 L9
Serres, *Greece* 70 F3
Serrinha 156 K6
Sertã 62 B5
Serui 93 E3
Servia 70 D4
Sêrxü 86 B4
Sese Islands 116 E4
Sesfontein 118 A3
Sesheke 118 C3
Sessa Aurunca 66 H7
Sestri Levante 64 E6
Sestroretsk 50 Q6
Sestrunj 64 K6
Sestu 66 D9
Sesvete 64 M5

Setana	88	K2
Sète	60	J10
Sete Lagoas	156	J7
Setesdal	50	D7
Sétif	112	G1
Settat	112	D2
Settle	36	F7
Setúbal	62	B6
Sŏul	124	C2
Seurre	60	L7
Sevana Lich	98	L3
Sevastopol'	98	E1
Seven Lakes	146	E1
Sevenoaks	38	J4
Sévérac-le-Château	60	J9
Severn, *Canada*	136	P5
Severn, *United Kingdom*	38	F4
Severnaya Dvina	72	H2
Severnaya Osetiya	98	L2
Severnaya Zemlya	82	U1
Severn Estuary	38	E4
Severnoye	72	K4
Severnyy	82	L4
Severobaykal'sk	84	H5
Severodvinsk	72	G2
Severo-Kuril'sk	84	T6
Severomorsk	50	S2
Severoural'sk	72	M2
Severo-Yeniseyskiy	82	S5
Sevier Lake	140	D3
Sevilla	62	E7
Sevlievo	68	N7
Seward Peninsula	146	(1)E2
Seyakha	82	N3
Seychelles	118	(2)B2
Seychelles Islands	108	J6
Seydişehir	70	P7
Seydisfjöður	50	(1)G2
Seyhan	98	F5
Seymchan	84	S4
Seymour, *Australia*	126	J7
Seymour, *Ind., United States*	144	D2
Seymour, *Tex., United States*	144	B3
Sézanne	60	J5
Sezze	66	H7
Sfakia	70	G9
Sfântu Gheorghe, *Romania*	68	N4
Sfântu Gheorghe, *Romania*	68	S5
Sfax	112	H2
's-Gravenhage	56	G2
Sgùrr Mòr	36	C4
Sha'am	101	G3
Shabla	68	R6
Shabunda	116	D4
Shabwah	96	E6
Shache	82	P10
Shādegān	101	C1
Shadehill Reservoir	140	F1
Shaftesbury	38	F4
Shagamu	114	E3
Shagonar	82	S7
Shag Rocks	158	N9
Shahbā'	100	D4
Shahdāb	101	G1
Shahdol	94	D4
Shah Fuladi	96	J3
Shahjahanpur	94	C3
Shahrak	96	H3
Shahr-e Bābāk	101	F1
Shahrtuz	96	J2
Shakhrisabz	96	J2
Shakhtërsk	84	Q7
Shakhty	72	H5
Shakhun'ya	72	J3
Shaki	114	E3
Shakotan-misaki	88	L2
Shama	116	E5
Shamattawa	136	N5
Shamis	101	E5
Shamrock	146	F1
Shand	96	H3
Shandan	86	C3
Shandong Bandao	86	G3
Shangani	118	D3
Shangdu	86	E2
Shanghai	86	G4
Shanghang	86	F6
Shangqui	86	F4
Shangrao	86	F5
Shangzhi	86	H1
Shangzhou	86	D4
Shannon	35	C3
Shantarskiye Ostrova	84	P5
Shantou	86	F6
Shanwei	90	F2
Shanyin	86	E3
Shaoguan	86	E6
Shaoxing	86	G5
Shaoyang	86	E5
Shapinsay	36	F2
Shapkina	72	K1
Shaqrā'	101	A4
Sharga	82	T8
Sharjah = Ash Shāriqah	101	F4
Shark Bay	124	B8
Shark Reef	126	J2
Sharmah	110	G2
Sharm el Sheikh	110	F2
Sharūrah	96	E6
Shashe	118	D4
Shashi	86	E4
Shasta Lake	140	B2
Shats'k	52	N6
Shatsk	72	H4
Shaubak	100	C6
Shawano	142	C2
Shaykh Miskīn	100	D4
Shcherbakove	84	U3
Shchigry	72	G4
Shchuch'ye	82	L6
Shchuchyn	50	N10
Sheberghān	96	J2
Sheboygan	142	C2
Sheerness	38	J4
Sheffield, *New Zealand*	128	D6
Sheffield, *United Kingdom*	38	F4
Sheffield, *Al., United States*	142	C4
Sheffield, *Tex., United States*	146	F2
Shegmas	72	J2
Shelburne	136	T8
Shelby	140	D1
Shelbyville	142	C3
Shelikof Strait	146	(1)F4
Shenandoah	142	A2
Shendam	114	F3
Shendi	110	F4
Shenkursk	72	H2
Shenyang	88	B3
Shenzhen	86	E6
Shepetivka	72	E4
Shepparton	126	J7
Shepton Mallet	38	F4
Sherborne	38	F5
Sherbro Island	114	B3
Sherbrooke	142	F1
Sheridan	140	E2
Sheringham	38	K3
Sherkaly	72	N2
Sherkin Island	35	B5
Sherlovaya Gora	84	K6
Sherman	144	B3
's-Hertogenbosch	56	H3
Sherwood Forest	38	G2
Shetland Islands	36	(1)H1
Shetpe	82	J9
Sheyenne	140	G1
Sheykh Sho'eyb	101	E3
Shiant Islands	36	B4
Shibata	88	K5
Shibetsu, *Japan*	88	M1
Shibetsu, *Japan*	88	N2
Shibotsu-jima	88	P2
Shiderty	82	N7
Shiel Bridge	36	C4
Shihezi	82	R9
Shijiazhuang	86	E3
Shikarpur	96	J4
Shikoku	88	G7
Shikoku-sanchi	88	G7
Shikotan-tō	88	P2
Shikotsu-ko	88	L2
Shiliguri	94	E3
Shilka	84	K6
Shilka	84	K6
Shillong	94	F3
Shilovo	72	H4
Shimabara	88	F7
Shimla	94	C2
Shimoda	88	K6
Shimoga	94	C6
Shimo-Koshiki-jima	88	E8
Shimoni	116	F4
Shimonoseki	88	F7
Shinâş	101	G4
Shīndan	96	H3
Shingū	88	H7
Shinjō	88	L4
Shinyanga	116	E4
Shiono-misaki	88	H7
Shiprock	140	E3
Shiquan	86	D4
Shirakawa	88	L5
Shīrāz	101	E2
Shire	118	E3
Shiretoko-misaki	88	N1
Shiriya-zaki	88	L3
Shīr Kūh	96	F3
Shiv	94	B3
Shivpuri	94	C3
Shiyan	86	E4
Shizuishan	86	D3
Shizuoka	88	K6
Shkodër	68	G7
Shomishko	82	K8
Shorap	96	J4
Shoreham-by-Sea	38	H5
Shoshone, *Calif., United States*	140	C3
Shoshone, *Id., United States*	140	D2
Shoshoni	140	E2
Shostka	72	F4
Show Low	146	E2
Shoyna	72	H1
Shreveport	144	C3
Shrewsbury	38	F3
Shuangliao	88	B2
Shuangyashan	84	N7
Shubarkuduk	82	K8
Shulan	88	D1
Shumagin Islands	146	(1)E5
Shumen	68	P6
Shumikha	72	M3
Shuqrah	96	E7
Shurchi	96	J2
Shūr Gaz	101	H2
Shurinda	84	J5
Shuryshkary	72	N1
Shuya	72	H3
Shuyang	86	F4
Shwebo	90	B2
Shymkent	82	M9
Sia	93	D4
Sialkot	96	K3
Siatista	70	D4
Šiauliai	52	N2
Sibay	72	L4
Šibenik	68	C6
Siberia = Sibir	80	N3
Siberut	92	B3
Sibi	96	J4
Sibigo	92	B2
Sibir	80	N3
Sibiu	68	M4
Sibolga	92	B2
Sibu	92	E2
Sibuco	90	G5
Sibut	116	B2
Sicilia	66	G11
Sicilian Channel	66	F11
Sicily = Sicilia	66	G11
Šid	68	G4
Siddipet	94	C5
Siderno	66	L10
Sidi Barrani	110	E1
Sidi Bel Abbès	112	E1
Sidi Kacem	112	D2
Sidirokastro	70	F3
Sidlaw Hills	36	E5
Sidmouth	38	E5
Sidney	140	F2
Sidoan	93	B2
Sidorovsk	82	Q4
Sieburg	56	K4
Siedlce	52	M5
Sieg	56	K4
Siegen	56	L4
Siemiatycze	52	M5
Siĕmréab	90	C4
Siena	64	G7
Sieradz	52	H6
Sierpc	52	J5
Sierra Blanca	146	E2
Sierra Colorada	158	H7
Sierra de Calalasteo	158	H4
Sierra de Córdoba	158	H5
Sierra de Gata	62	D4
Sierra de Gúdar	62	K4
Sierra del Nevado	158	H6
Sierra de Perija	148	K7
Sierra Grande	158	H7
Sierra Leone	114	B3
Sierra Madre	148	F5
Sierra Madre del Sur	148	E5
Sierra Madre Occidental	138	E6
Sierra Madre Oriental	146	F3
Sierra Morena	62	E6
Sierra Nevada, *Spain*	62	G7
Sierra Nevada, *United States*	146	B1
Sierra Vizcaino	138	D6
Sierre	64	C4
Sifnos	70	G8
Sig	62	K9
Sigean	60	H10
Sighetu Marmației	68	L2
Sighișoara	68	M3
Siglufjörður	50	(1)D1
Sigmaringen	64	E2
Signal Mountain	142	C3
Siguiri	114	C2
Sihanoukville	90	C4
Siilinjärvi	50	P5
Siirt	98	J5
Sikar	94	C3
Sikasso	114	C2
Sikea	70	F4
Sikeston	142	C3
Sikhote Alin	88	H1
Sikinos	70	G8
Siklós	68	F4
Siktyakh	84	L3
Sil	62	C2
Šilalė	52	M2
Silandro	64	F4
Silba	64	K6
Silchar	94	F4
Şile	70	M3
Silhouette Island	118	(2)B1
Siliana	66	D12
Silifke	98	E5
Siling Co	94	E2
Silistra	68	Q5
Silivri	70	L3
Siljan	50	H6
Sillamäe	50	P7
Silsbee	144	C3
Siluas	92	D2
Šilutė	52	L2
Silvan	98	J4
Silver Bay	142	B1
Silver City	146	E2
Silver Lake	140	B2
Silvermine Mountains	35	C4
Silver Plains	126	H2
Simanggang	92	E2
Simao	86	C6
Simav	98	C4
Simcoe	142	D2
Simeonovgrad	68	N7
Simeria	52	N12
Simeuluë	92	A2
Simferopol'	98	F1
Șimleu Silvaniei	68	K2
Simmerath	56	J4
Simojärvi	50	P3
Simpang	92	C3
Simpson Desert	126	G4
Sinabang	92	B2
Sinai	110	F2
Sinaia	68	N4
Şinak	98	K5
Sinalunga	66	F5
Sinanju	88	C4
Sinbaungwe	90	B3
Sincelejo	156	B2
Sinclair's Bay	36	E3
Sindangbarang	92	D4
Sindelfingen	54	E8
Sines	62	B7
Singa	110	F5
Singapore	92	C2
Singapore	92	C2
Singaraja	92	E4
Singen	64	D3
Sîngerei	68	R2
Singida	116	E4
Singkawang	92	D2
Singkep	92	C3
Singkilbaru	92	B2
Singleton	126	K6
Siniscola	66	D8
Sinj	68	D6
Sinjai	93	B4
Sinjār	98	J5
Sinkat	110	G4
Sinni	66	L8
Sinop	98	F2
Sinsheim	54	D7
Sintang	92	E2
Sinton	144	B4
Sinŭiju	88	C3
Sinyaya	84	L4
Sió	68	F3
Siófok	68	F3
Sion	64	C4
Sioux City	142	A2
Sioux Falls	142	A2
Sioux Lookout	138	H2
Siping	88	C2
Sipiwesk	136	M5
Sipura	92	B3
Sira	50	D7
Siracusa	66	K11
Sir Banī 'Yās	101	E4
Sir Edward Pellew Group	126	G3
Siret	68	P2
Siret	68	Q4
Sīrgān	96	H4
Şiria	52	L11
Siri Kit Dam	90	B3
Sirk	101	G3
Sirohi	94	B4
Sirsa	94	C3
Sirsi	94	B6
Sisak	68	D4
Sisian	98	L4
Sisimiut	136	W3
Sisŏphŏn	90	C4
Sisseton	140	G1
Sistema Central	62	E4
Sistema Iberico	62	H3
Sisteron	64	A6
Sitapur	94	D3
Sitasjaure	50	J3
Siteia	70	J9
Sitges	62	M3
Sithonia	70	F4
Sitka	136	D5
Sittard	56	H4
Sittingbourne	38	J4
Sittwe	94	F4
Sivand	101	E1
Sivas	98	G4
Siverek	98	H5
Sivrihisar	70	P5
Siwa	110	E1
Siyăzăn	98	N3
Sjælland	50	F9
Sjenica	68	H6
Sjenica Jezero	68	G6
Sjöbo	52	C2
Skädlderviken	52	B1
Skaerbaek	54	D1
Skagen	50	F8
Skagerrak	50	D8
Skala	70	E8
Skantzoura	70	G5
Skardu	96	L2
Skarżysko-Kamienna	52	K6
Skaulo	50	L3
Skawina	52	J8
Skaymat	112	B4
Skegness	38	J2
Skellefteå	50	L4
Skelmersdale	38	F2
Ski	50	F7
Skiathos	70	F5
Skibotn	50	L2
Skidal'	52	P4
Skiddaw	36	E7
Skien	50	E7
Skikda	112	G1
Skipton	38	F2
Skjern	50	E9
Škofja Loka	64	K4
Skopelos	70	F5
Skopje	68	J7
Skövde	50	G7
Skovorodino	84	L6
Skowhegan	142	G2
Skuodas	50	L8
Skye	36	B4
Skyros	70	G6
Skyros	70	G6
Slagelse	54	G1
Slagnäs	50	K4
Slane	35	E3
Slaney	35	E4
Slano	68	E7
Slantsy	50	Q7
Slaný	54	K6
Slatina	68	M5
Slave	134	N3
Slave Lake	136	J5
Slavonska Požega	68	E4
Slavonski Brod	68	F4
Slavyanka	88	F2
Slavyansk-na-Kubani	98	H1
Sławno	52	F3
Sleaford	38	H3
Sleeper Islands	136	Q5
Slidell	144	D3
Slieveardagh Hills	35	D4
Slieve Aughty Mountains	35	C3
Slieve Bloom Mountains	35	D3
Sligachan	36	B4
Sligo	35	C2
Sligo Bay	35	C2
Slite	50	K8
Sliven	68	P7
Slobozia, *Moldova*	68	S3
Slobozia, *Romania*	68	Q5
Slonim	50	N10
Slough	38	H4
Slovakia	52	H9
Slovenia	64	K4
Slovenj Gradec	64	L4
Slovenska Bistrica	64	L4
Slov"yans'k	72	G5
Słubice	52	D5
Slunj	64	L5
Słupca	52	G5
Słupsk	52	G3
Slussfors	50	J4
Slutsk	72	E4
Slyne Head	35	A3

Slyudyanka 84 G6
Smålandsfarvandet 54 G1
Smallwood Reservoir 136 U6
Smargon' 50 P9
Smederevo 68 H5
Smila 72 F5
Smirnykh 84 Q7
Smiths Falls 142 E2
Smokey Hills 144 B2
Smoky 136 H6
Smøla 50 D5
Smolensk 72 F4
Smolyan 70 G3
Smooth Rock Falls 142 D1
Smyrna 144 E3
Snæfell 50 (1)F2
Snake 140 C1
Snake River Plain 140 D2
Snåsavatnet 50 F4
Sneek 56 H1
Snezhnogorsk 82 R4
Snežnik 64 K5
Snina 52 M9
Snøhetta 50 E5
Snøtinden 50 G3
Snowdon 38 D2
Snowdonia National Park 38 E3
Snowdrift 136 J4
Snowville 140 D2
Snyder 146 F2
Soalala 118 H3
Soanierana-Ivongo 118 H3
Soa-Siu 93 C2
Soay 36 B4
Sobral 156 J4
Sochaczew 52 K5
Sochaux 64 B3
Sochi 98 H2
Socorro 146 E2
Socotra = Suquṭrā 96 F7
Socuéllamos 62 H5
Sodankylä 50 P3
Söderhamn 50 J6
Södertälje 50 J7
Sodo 116 F2
Soe 93 B4
Soest 56 L3
Sofia = Sofiya 68 L7
Sofiya 68 L7
Sofiysk, *Russia* 84 N6
Sofiysk, *Russia* 84 P6
Sofporog 50 R4
Sōfu-gan 86 L5
Sogamoso 156 C2
Sognefjorden 50 C6
Sogod 90 G4
Sog Xian 94 F2
Sohâg 110 F2
Soignies 56 G4
Soissons 56 F5
Sokch'o 88 E4
Söke 70 K7
Sokhumi 98 J2
Sokode 114 E3
Sokol 72 H3
Sokółka 50 M10
Sokolo 114 C2
Sokolov 54 H6
Sokołów Podlaski 52 M5
Sokoto 114 F2
Sokoto 114 F2
Sokyryany 68 Q1
Solander Island 128 A8
Solapur 94 C5
Sölden 64 F4
Solent 38 G5
Solenzara 66 D7
Solhan 98 J4
Solihull 38 G3
Solikamsk 72 L3
Sol'-Iletsk 72 L4
Soliman 66 E12
Solingen 56 K3
Sollefteå 50 J5
Soller 62 N5
Solna 50 J7
Solomon Islands 124 F6
Solothurn 64 C3
Solov'yevsk 84 K6
Šolta 68 D6
Soltau 54 E4
Sol'tsy 72 F3
Solway Firth 36 E7
Solwezi 118 D2
Soma 70 K5
Sōma 88 L5
Somalia 116 H2
Sombor 68 G4
Sombrerete 146 F4
Somerset, *Australia* 126 H2
Somerset, *Ky., United States* 142 C3
Somerset, *Pa., United States* 142 E2
Somerset Island 136 N2
Someș 68 K2
Somme 56 E4
Sommen 50 H8
Sömmerda 54 G5
Sømna 50 F4
Sondags 118 D6
Sønderborg Ærø 54 E2
Sondershausen 54 F5
Sondrio 64 E4
Songavatn 50 D7
Songea 116 F6
Song Hông 90 C2
Songhua 86 H1
Songhua Hu 88 D2
Songhua Jiang 88 D1
Songkan 86 D5
Songkhla 90 C5
Songnam 88 D5
Songnim 88 C4
Songo 118 E3
Songololo 114 G6
Songpan 86 C4
Sonid Yuoqi 86 E2
Sonid Zuoqi 86 E2
Son La 90 C2
Sonneberg 54 G6
Sono 156 H6
Sonora 146 B1
Sonora 146 D3
Sonoyta 146 D2
Sonsorol Islands 93 D1
Sonthofen 64 F3
Sopot 50 K9
Sopron 64 M3
Sora 66 H7
Soracaba 158 M3
Sorel 142 F1
Sorgun 98 F4
Soria 62 H3
Sorø 54 G1
Soroca 68 R1
Sorochinsk 72 K4
Sorong 93 D3
Soroti 116 E3
Sørøya 50 L1
Sorrento 66 J8
Sorsele 50 J4
Sorso 66 C8
Sorsogon 90 G4
Sort 62 M2
Sortavala 50 R6
Sørvagen 50 G3
Sōsan 88 D5
Sosnogorsk 82 J5
Sosnovka 82 G4
Sosnovo 50 R6
Sosnowiec 52 J7
Sos'va 72 M3
Sos'vinskaya 72 M2
Soto la Marina 146 G4
Soubré 114 C3
Soufli 70 J3
Souilly 56 H5
Souk Ahras 66 B12
Sōul 88 D5
Soulac-sur-Mer 60 D8
Soumussalmi 50 Q4
Sound of Arisaig 36 C5
Sound of Barra 36 A4
Sound of Bute 36 C6
Sound of Harris 36 A4
Sound of Jura 36 C6
Sound of Raasay 36 B4
Sound of Sleat 36 C4
Soûr 100 C3
Soure 62 B5
Sour el Ghozlane 62 P8
Souris 138 G2
Souris 138 F2
Sousa 156 K5
Sousse 112 H1
South Africa 118 C6
South America 134 J9
Southampton, *Canada* 142 D2
Southampton, *United Kingdom* 38 G5
Southampton Island 136 Q4
South Andaman 94 F6
South Atlantic Ocean 158 P6
South Australia 126 F5
South Baymouth 142 D1
South Bend 142 C2
Southborough 38 J4
South Boston 142 E3
South Carolina 144 E3
South Charleston 144 E2
South China Sea 90 E4
South Dakota 140 F2
South Dorset Downs 38 F5
South Downs 38 H5
South East Cape 126 J8
South East Point 126 J7
Southend-on-Sea 38 J4
Southern Alps 128 B6
Southern Cross 126 C6
Southern Indian Lake 136 M5
Southern Uplands 36 E6
South Foreland 38 K4
South Georgia 158 P9
South Harris 36 A4
South Haven 142 C2
South Hayling 38 H5
South Hill 142 E3
South Island 128 B6
South Korea 88 D5
South Lake Tahoe 140 B3
South Orkney Islands 160 (2)A3
South Pacific Ocean 158 P6
South Platte 140 F2
Southport 38 E2
South Queensferry 36 E6
South Ronaldsay 36 F3
South Sandwich Islands 160 (2)C4
South Sandwich Trench 154 H9
South Saskatchewan 138 D1
South Shetland Islands 160 (2)MM4
South Shields 36 G7
South Taranaki Bight 128 D4
South Uist 36 A4
South West Cape, *Auckland Island* 128 (2)A1
South West Cape, *Australia* 126 H8
Southwest Cape 128 A8
South West Pacific Basin 124 L9
Southwold 38 K3
Sovata 68 N3
Soverato 66 L10
Sovetsk, *Russia* 50 L9
Sovetsk, *Russia* 72 J3
Soweto 118 D5
Sōya-misaki 88 L1
Sozopol 68 Q7
Spa 56 H4
Spain 62 F5
Spalding 38 H3
Sparks 146 C1
Spartanburg 144 E3
Sparti 70 E7
Sparwood 140 D1
Spassk-Dal'niy 88 G1
Spean Bridge 36 D5
Spearfish 140 F2
Spencer 142 A2
Spencer Gulf 126 G6
Spennymoor 36 G7
Sperrin Mountains 35 E2
Spetses 70 F7
Spey 36 E4
Spey Bay 36 E4
Speyer 56 L5
Spiekeroog 54 C3
Spiez 64 C4
Spilimbergo 64 H4
Spišska Nová Ves 52 K9
Spitsbergen 160 (1)P2
Spittal 64 J4
Split 68 D6
Spokane 140 C1
Spoleto 66 G6
Spooner 142 B1
Sprague 140 C1
Spratly Islands 90 E4
Spray 140 C2
Spree 54 K4
Spremberg 54 K5
Sprimont 56 H4
Spring 144 B3
Springbok 118 B5
Springe 54 E4
Springer 146 F1
Springerville 146 E2
Springfield, *Colo., United States* 146 F1
Springfield, *Ill., United States* 142 C3
Springfield, *Mass., United States* 142 F2
Springfield, *Mo., United States* 142 B3
Springfield, *Oh., United States* 142 D3
Springfield, *Oreg., United States* 140 B2
Springfield, *Vt., United States* 142 F2
Spring Hill 144 E4
Springs 118 D5
Springs Junction 128 D6
Springsure 126 J4
Springville, *Al., United States* 144 D3
Springville, *N.Y., United States* 142 E2
Spulico 66 L9
Spurn Head 38 J2
Squamish 140 B1
Squinzano 66 N8
Srbija 68 H6
Srbobran 68 G4
Srebrenica 68 G5
Sredenekolymsk 84 S3
Sredinnyy Khrebet 84 T6
Srednesibirskoye Ploskogor'ye 84 F3
Srednogorie 70 G2
Srem 52 G5
Sretensk 84 K6
Sri Jayawardenapura-Kotte 94 D7
Srikakulam 94 D5
Sri Lanka 94 D7
Srinagar 94 B2
Stack Skerry 36 D3
Stade 50 E10
Stadlandet 50 C5
Stadskanaal 56 J2
Stadtallendorf 54 E6
Stadthagen 54 E4
Staffa 36 B5
Staffelstien 54 F6
Stafford 38 F3
Staines 38 H4
Stainz 64 L4
Stakhanov 72 G5
Stalowa Wola 52 M7
Stambolijski 70 G2
Stamford, *United Kingdom* 38 H3
Stamford, *United States* 142 F2
Standish 142 D2
Stanford 142 D3
Stanke Dimitrov 70 F2
Stanley 36 G7
Stanley, *Australia* 126 J8
Stanley, *Falkland Islands* 158 K9
Stanley, *United States* 140 F1
Stanovaya 84 T3
Stanovoye Nagor'ye 84 J5
Stanovoy Khrebet 84 L5
Staphorst 56 J2
Stapleton 140 F2
Starachowice 52 L6
Stara L'ubovňa 52 K8
Stara Pazova 68 H5
Stara Planina 70 F1
Staraya Russa 72 F3
Stara Zagora 68 N7
Starbuck Island 124 L6
Stargard Szczeciński 50 H10
Starkville 144 D3
Starnberg 64 G2
Starnberger See 64 G3
Starogard Gdański 52 H4
Staro Oryakhovo 68 Q7
Start Point 38 E5
Staryy Oskol 72 G4
Staszów 52 L7
Statesboro 144 E3
Statesville 144 E2
Staunton 144 F2
Stavanger 50 C7
Staveley 38 G2
Stavoron 56 H2
Stavropol' 98 J1
Stavropol'skaya Vovyshennost' 72 H5
Steamboat Springs 140 E2
Steens Mountains 140 C2
Steenwijk 56 J2
Stefansson Island 136 L2
Stege 54 H1
Ștei 68 K3
Stein 54 G7
Steinach am Brenner 64 G3
Steinfurt 56 K2
Steinhausen 118 B4
Steinjker 50 F4
Stenay 56 H5
Stendal 54 G4
Steno Antikythiro 70 F9
Stephenville 144 B3
Sterling 140 F2
Sterling City 146 F2
Sterling Heights 142 D2
Sterlitamak 72 L4
Sternberk 52 G8
Stettiner Haff 50 G10
Stevenage 38 H4
Stevens Point 142 C2
Stevenston 36 D6
Stevens Village 146 (1)H2
Stewart 136 F5
Stewart 146 (1)K3
Stewart Island 128 A8
Steyr 64 K2
Stillwater 144 B2
Stinnett 146 F1
Štip 70 E3
Stirling 36 E5
St. Ives Bay 38 C5
Stjørdal 50 F5
Stockach 64 E3
Stockerau 64 M2
Stockholm 50 K7
Stockport 38 F2
Stockton, *Calif., United States* 146 B1
Stockton, *Kans., United States* 146 G1
Stockton-on-Tees 36 G7
Stœng Trêng 90 D4
Stoke-on-Trent 38 F2
Stokksnes 50 (1)F2
Stolac 68 F6
Stolberg 56 J4
Stolin 72 E4
Stollberg 54 H6
Stomio 70 E5
Stone 38 F3
Stonehaven 36 F5
Stonehenge 38 G4
Stony Rapids 136 K5
Stör 54 E2
Stora Lulevatten 50 K3
Stord 50 C7
Store Bælt 54 F1
Støren 50 F5
Store Sotra 50 B6
Storjord 50 H3
Storlien 50 G5
Storm Bay 126 J8
Storm Lake 142 A2
Stornoway 36 B3
Storozhevsk 72 K2
Storozhynets' 68 N1
Storsjøen 50 F6
Storsjön, *Sweden* 50 G5
Storsjön, *Sweden* 50 J6
Storuman 50 J4
Storuman 50 J4
Stour 38 J3
Stourbridge 38 F3
Stourport-on-Severn 38 F3
Stowmarket 38 J3
Stow-on-the-Wold 38 G4
Strabane 35 D2
Stradella 64 E5
Strait of Belle Isle 136 V6
Strait of Bonifacio 66 D7
Strait of Dover 38 K5
Strait of Georgia 140 B1
Strait of Gibraltar 62 E9
Strait of Hormuz 101 G3
Strait of Juan de Fuca 140 B1
Strait of Malacca 92 C2
Straits of Florida 144 E5
Strakonice 54 J7
Stralsund 50 G9
Strand 118 B6
Stranda 50 D5
Strandavatn 50 D6
Strangford Lough 35 F2
Stranraer 36 C7
Strasbourg 64 C2
Strasburg 146 F1
Strășeni 68 R2
Stratford, *Canada* 142 D2
Stratford, *New Zealand* 128 E4
Stratford, *United States* 140 F3
Stratford-upon-Avon 38 G3
Strathcarron 36 C4
Strathmore 36 F5
Strathroy 142 D2
Strath Spey 36 E4
Strathy 36 E3
Strathy Point 36 D3
Stratoni 70 F4
Stratton 142 F1
Straubing 64 H2
Straumnes 50 (1)B1
Strausberg 54 J4
Streaky Bay 126 F6
Streator 142 C2
Street 38 F4
Strehaia 68 L5
Strelka, *Russia* 84 E5
Strelka, *Russia* 84 S4
Strezhevoy 72 Q2
Strimonas 70 F4
Strofades 70 C7
Strokestown 35 C3
Stroma 36 E3
Stromboli 66 K10
Stromness 36 E3
Strömsund 50 H5
Stronsay 36 F2
Stroud 38 F4
Struga 70 C3
Strugi-Krasnyye 50 Q7
Strumica 70 E3
Stryjama 68 M7
Stryy 52 N8
Stryy 52 N8
Strzegom 52 F7
Strzelce Opolskie 52 H7
Strzelin 52 G7
Strzelno 52 H5
Studholme Junction 128 C7

Sturgeon Bay 142 C2
Sturgeon Falls 142 E1
Sturgis, *Ky., United States* 142 C3
Sturgis, *S.D., United States* 140 F2
Sturkö 52 E1
Štúrova 52 H10
Sturt Stony Desert 126 G5
Stuttgart, *Germany* 64 E2
Stuttgart, *United States* 144 C3
Stykkishólmur 50 (1)B2
Suai 93 C4
Suakin 110 G4
Subcule 110 H5
Subi Besar 92 D2
Sublette 146 F1
Subotica 68 G3
Suceava 68 P2
Suck 35 C3
Suckow 54 G3
Sucre 156 D7
Sudak 98 F1
Sudan 110 E5
Sudan 114 D2
Suday 72 H3
Sudbury, *Canada* 142 D1
Sudbury, *United Kingdom* 38 J3
Sudd 116 E2
Sudová Vyshnya 52 N8
Suez = El Suweis 110 F2
Suez Canal 110 F1
Suffolk 144 F2
Sugun 96 L2
Suḥār 101 G4
Suhl 54 F6
Suide 86 E3
Suifenhe 88 F1
Suigam 94 B4
Suihua 84 M7
Suippes 56 G5
Suir 35 D4
Suixi 86 E6
Suizhong 86 G2
Suizhou 86 E4
Sukabumi 92 D4
Sukadana 92 D3
Sukhinichi 72 G4
Sukhona 72 H3
Sukkertoppen = Maniitsoq 136 W3
Sukkur 96 J4
Sula 72 K1
Sula 72 K1
Sula Sgei 36 C2
Sulawesi 93 A3
Sulby 36 D7
Sulejówek 52 L5
Sule Skerry 36 D2
Sulgachi 84 N4
Sulina 68 S4
Sulingen 56 L2
Sullana 156 A4
Sullivan 144 C2
Sulmona 66 H6
Sulphur Springs 144 B3
Sultan 110 D1
Sultanhanı 70 R6
Sultanpur 94 D3
Sulu Archipelago 90 G5
Sulu Sea 90 F5
Sulzbach 56 K5
Sulzbach-Rosenberg 54 G7
Sulzberger Bay 160 (2)CC2
Sumatera 92 C2
Sumatra = Sumatera 92 C2
Sumba 93 A5
Sumbawa 93 A4
Sumbawabesar 93 A4
Sumbawanga 116 E5
Sumbe 118 A2
Sumburgh 36 (1)G2
Sumburgh Head 36 (1)G2
Sumeih 116 D2
Šumen 98 B2
Sumenep 92 E4
Sumisu-jima 88 L8
Sumkino 72 N3
Summer Lake 140 B2
Summerville 144 E3
Summit 136 B4
Šumperk 52 G8
Sumqayıt 98 N3
Sumter 144 E3
Sumy 72 F4
Sunbury 142 E2
Sunch'ŏn 88 D6
Sun City 118 D5
Sundance 140 F2
Sundarbans 94 E4
Sunday Strait 126 D3
Sunderland 36 G7
Sundridge 142 E1
Sundsvall 50 J5
Sundsvallsbukten 50 J5
Sungaipenuh 92 C3
Sungei Petani 90 C5
Sungurlu 98 F3
Sunnyvale 140 B3
Sun Prairie 142 C2
Suntar 84 K4
Suntsar 96 H4
Sunwu 84 M7
Sunyani 114 D3
Suomussalmi 72 E2
Suō-nada 88 F7
Suonenjoki 50 P5
Suordakh 84 P3
Suoyarvi 72 F2
Superior 138 H2
Supetar 68 D6
Süphan Daği 98 K4
Sūqash Shuyūkh 101 B1
Suqian 86 F4
Suquṭrā 96 F7
Sūr 96 G5
Sura 72 J4
Surab 96 J4
Surabaya 92 E4
Sūrak 101 H4
Surakarta 92 E4
Šurany 68 F1
Surat 94 B4
Surat Thani 90 B5
Surdulica 68 K7
Sûre 56 H5
Surfers Paradise 126 K5
Surgut 82 N5
Surgutikha 82 R5
Surigao 90 H5
Surin 90 C4
Surinam 156 F3
Surkhet 94 D3
Sürmaq 101 E1
Surovikino 72 H5
Surskoye 72 J4
Surt 112 J2
Surtsey 50 (1)C3
Susa 64 C5
Şuşa 98 M4
Sušac 68 D7
Susak 64 K6
Susanville 140 B2
Suşehri 98 H3
Sušice 54 J7
Susitna 146 (1)G3
Susuman 84 R4
Susurluk 70 L5
Sutak 94 C2
Sutherland 118 C6
Sutlej 94 B3
Sutton 38 H4
Sutton Coldfield 38 G3
Sutton-in-Ashfield 38 G2
Suusamyr 82 N9
Suva 124 H7
Suvorov Island 124 K7
Suwałki 52 M3
Suwannaphum 90 C3
Suweilih 100 C4
Suweima 100 C5
Suwŏn 88 D5
Suzak 72 N6
Suzhou, *China* 86 G4
Suzhou, *China* 86 F4
Suzuka 88 J6
Suzu-misaki 88 J5
Svalbard 160 (1)Q2
Svalyaya 68 L1
Svappavaara 50 L3
Svartenhuk Halvø 136 V2
Svatove 72 G5
Sveg 50 H5
Svendborg 50 F9
Šventoji 50 N9
Sverdrup Islands 160 (1)DD2
Svetac 68 C6
Sveti Nikole 70 D3
Svetlaya 84 P7
Svetlogorsk 52 K3
Svetlograd 98 K1
Svetlyy, *Russia* 52 K3
Svetlyy, *Russia* 82 L7
Svidník 52 L8
Svilengrad 70 J3
Svishtov 68 N6
Svitava 52 F8
Svitovy 52 F8
Svobodnyy 84 M6
Svratka 52 F8
Svyetlahorsk 72 E4
Swadlincote 38 G3
Swaffham 38 J3
Swain Reefs 126 K4
Swains Island 124 J7
Swakopmund 118 A4
Swale 36 F7
Swan 154 C2
Swanage 38 G5
Swan Hill 126 H7
Swan Islands 148 H5
Swan River 136 L6
Swansea, *Australia* 126 J8
Swansea, *United Kingdom* 38 E4
Swansea Bay 38 E4
Swaziland 118 E5
Sweden 50 H6
Sweetwater 146 F2
Swider 52 L5
Świdnica 52 F7
Świdnik 52 M6
Świdwin 52 E4
Świebodzin 52 E5
Świecie 52 H4
Swift Current 138 E1
Swindon 38 G4
Swinford 35 C3
Świnoujście 50 H10
Switzerland 64 C4
Swords 35 E3
Syalakh 84 L3
Syamzha 72 H2
Syców 52 G6
Sydney, *Australia* 126 K6
Sydney, *Canada* 136 U7
Syke 56 L2
Syktyvkar 72 K2
Sylacauga 144 D3
Sylhet 94 F4
Sylt 50 E9
Sylvania 142 D2
Sym 82 R5
Sym 82 R5
Symi 70 K8
Synya 72 L1
Syracuse, *Kans., United States* 146 F1
Syracuse, *N.Y., United States* 142 E2
Syrdar'ya 82 L8
Syrdar'ya 96 J1
Syria 96 C3
Syrian Desert = Bādiyat ash Shām 100 D4
Syrna 70 J8
Syros 70 G7
Sytomino 72 P2
Syzran' 72 J4
Szamos 68 K1
Szamotuły 52 F5
Szarvas 52 K11
Szczecin 52 D4
Szczecinek 52 F4
Szczytno 52 K4
Szeged 68 H3
Szeghalom 68 J2
Székesfehérvár 68 F2
Szekszárd 68 F3
Szentendre 68 G2
Szentes 68 H3
Szerencs 52 L9
Szigetvár 68 E3
Szolnok 68 H2
Szombathely 68 D2
Szprotawa 52 E6
Sztum 52 J4
Szydlowiec 52 K6

T

Tab 68 F3
Tabarka 66 C12
Tabas 96 G3
Tabāsin 101 G1
Taber 140 D1
Table Cape 128 G4
Tabong 94 G3
Tábor 52 D8
Tabor 84 R2
Tabora 116 E5
Tabou 114 C4
Tabrīz 98 M4
Tabuaeran 124 K5
Tabūk 96 C4
Tacheng 82 Q8
Tachov 54 H7
Tacloban 90 H4
Tacna 156 C7
Tacoma 138 B2
Tacuarembó 158 K5
Tacurong 93 B1
Tadcaster 38 G2
Tadjoura 110 H5
Tadmur 98 H6
Tadoussac 142 G1
Taech'ŏn 88 D5
Taegu 88 E6
Taejŏn 86 H3
Tafahi 124 J7
Tafalla 62 J2
Tafila 100 C6
Tafi Viejo 158 H4
Tagab 110 F4
Taganrog 72 G5
Taganrogskiy Zaliv 72 G5
Tagbilaran 90 G5
Tagul 84 F6
Tagum 90 H5
Tagus 62 B5
Taharoa 128 E4
Taheke 128 D2
Tahiti 124 M7
Tahoe Lake 136 K2
Tahoka 146 F2
Tahoua 114 F2
Tahrūd 101 G2
Tahuna 90 H6
Tai'an 86 F3
T'ai-chung 86 G6
Taihape 128 E4
Taihe 86 E5
Taikeng 86 E4
Tailem Bend 126 G7
Tain 36 D4
T'ai-nan 86 G6
T'ai-Pei 86 G6
Taiping 92 C1
Taipingchuan 88 B1
T'ai-tung 90 G2
Taivalkoski 50 Q4
Taiwan 90 G2
Taiwan Strait 90 F2
Taiyuan 86 E3
Taizhou 86 F4
Ta'izz 96 D7
Tajikistan 96 J2
Tajima 88 K5
Tajo 48 D3
Tak 90 B3
Takaka 128 D5
Takamatsu 88 H6
Takaoka 88 J5
Takapuna 128 E3
Takasaki 88 K5
Takayama 88 J5
Takefu 88 J6
Takengon 92 B2
Takestān 96 E2
Ta Khmau 90 D4
Takht 84 P6
Takhta-Bazar 96 H2
Takhtabrod 82 M7
Takhtakupyr 82 L9
Takijuq Lake 136 J3
Takikawa 88 L2
Takoradi 114 D4
Taksimo 84 J5
Takua Pa 90 B5
Takum 114 G3
Talak 112 F5
Talara 156 A4
Talas 82 N9
Tal'at Mūsā 98 G6
Talavera de la Reina 62 F5
Talaya 84 S4
Talbotton 144 E3
Talca 158 G6
Talcahuano 158 G6
Taldykorgan 82 P9
Tālesh 96 E2
Taliabu 93 B3
Talibon 90 G4
Talitsa 72 M3
Tall 'Afar 98 K5
Tallahassee 144 E3
Tallaimannar 94 C7
Tall al Laḥm 101 B1
Tallinn 50 N7
Tall Kalakh 100 D2
Tallowbridge 35 C4
Tallulah 138 H5
Tall 'Uwaynāt 98 K5
Tălmaciu 68 M4
Tal'menka 82 Q7
Talon 84 R5
Tāloqān 82 N10
Taloyoak 136 N3
Talsi 50 M8
Taltal 158 G4
Tama 142 B2
Tamale 114 D3
Tamanrasset 112 G4
Tamanthi 94 G3
Tamar 38 D5
Tamási 68 F3
Tamazunchale 138 G7
Tambacounda 114 B2
Tambey 82 N3
Tambo 126 J4
Tambov 72 H4
Tambu 93 A3
Tambura 116 D2
Tampa 144 E4
Tamp-e Gīrān 101 H3
Tampere 50 M6
Tampico 148 E4
Tamsagbulag 86 F1
Tamsweg 64 J3
Tamworth, *Australia* 126 K6
Tamworth, *United Kingdom* 38 G3
Tana, *Kenya* 116 G4
Tana, *Norway* 50 P2
Tanabe 88 H7
Tana bru 50 P1
Tanacross 146 (1)J3
Tanafjorden 50 Q1
Tanaga Island 146 (3)C1
T'ana Hāyk' 110 G5
Tanahgrogot 92 F3
Tanahjampea 93 A4
Tanahmerah 93 F4
Tanami 126 E4
Tanami Desert 126 F3
Tanaro 64 C6
Tanch'ŏn 88 E3
Tanda 114 D3
Tandag 90 H5
Tăndărei 68 Q5
Tandil 158 K6
Tandragee 35 E2
Tanega-shima 88 F8
Tanew 52 M7
Tanezrouft 112 E4
Tanga, *Russia* 84 J6
Tanga, *Tanzania* 116 F5
Tanger 112 D1
Tangermünde 54 G4
Tanggu 86 F3
Tangmai 94 G2
Tangra Yumco 94 E2
Tangshan 86 F3
Tanimbar 124 D6
Tanjona Ankaboa 118 G4
Tanjona Bobaomby 118 H2
Tanjona Masoala 118 J3
Tanjona Vilanandro 118 G3
Tanjona Vohimena 118 H5
Tanjung 92 F3
Tanjungbalai 92 B2
Tanjung Cangkuang 92 C4
Tanjung Datu 92 D2
Tanjung d'Urville 93 E3
Tanjungkarang Telukbetung 92 D4
Tanjung Libobo 93 C3
Tanjung Lumut 92 D3
Tanjung Mengkalihat 92 F2
Tanjungpandan 92 D3
Tanjung Puting 92 E3
Tanjungredeb 92 F2
Tanjung Selatan 92 E3
Tanjungselor 92 F2
Tanjung Vals 93 E4
Tankovo 82 R5
Tankse 94 C2
Tanlovo 72 P1
Tanney 56 G5
Tanout 114 F2
Tanta 110 F1
Tan-Tan 112 C3
Tanzania 116 E5
Tao'an 86 G1
Taomasina 118 H3
Taongi 124 J4
Taormina 66 K11
Taos 146 E1
Taoudenni 112 E5
Taourirt 112 E2
T'ao-yuan 90 G2
Tapa 50 N7
Tapachula 148 F6
Tapajós 156 F4
Tapauá 156 E5
Tapolca 68 E3
Tappahannock 144 F2
Tapsuy 72 M2
Tapuaenuku 128 D6
Taquari 156 F7
Tara 72 Q3
Tara 82 N6
Tarābulus 112 H2
Taraclia 68 R4
Taracua 156 D3
Tarāghin 112 H3
Tarakan 90 F6
Taran 82 N3
Taranaki = Mount Egmont 128 E4
Tarancón 62 H5
Taransay 36 A4
Taranto 66 M8

Tarapoto	156	B5
Tarare	60	K8
Tarascon	60	K10
Tarauacá	156	C5
Tarauacá	156	C5
Tarawa	124	H5
Tarawera Lake	128	F4
Tarazona	62	J3
Tarbat Ness	36	E4
Tarbert, *Republic of Ireland*	35	B4
Tarbert, *Scot., United Kingdom*	36	B4
Tarbert, *Scot., United Kingdom*	36	C6
Tarbes	60	F10
Tarbet	36	D5
Tarcoola	126	F6
Taree	126	K6
Tareya	82	S3
Tarfaya	112	C3
Târgovişte	68	N5
Târgu Frumos	68	Q2
Târgu Jiu	68	L4
Târgu Lăpuş	68	L2
Târgu Mureş	68	M3
Târgu-Neamţ	68	P2
Târgu Ocna	68	P3
Târgu Secuiesc	68	P3
Tarhunah	112	H2
Tarif	101	E4
Tarifa	62	E8
Tarija	158	J3
Tarim	82	Q9
Tarīm	96	E6
Tarim Pendi	82	Q10
Tarīn Kowt	96	J3
Tariskay Shan	82	Q9
Taritatu	93	E3
Tarkio	144	B1
Tarko Sale	82	P5
Tarlac	90	G3
Tarn	60	H10
Tarna	52	K10
Tärnaby	50	H4
Târnăveni	68	M3
Tarnogskiy Gorodok	72	H2
Tărnovo	70	K2
Tarnów	52	K7
Tarnowskie Góry	52	H7
Taro	64	E6
Ţārom	101	F2
Taroom	126	J5
Taroudannt	112	D2
Tarquinia	66	F6
Tarragona	62	M3
Tarras	128	B7
Tàrrega	62	M3
Tarso Emissi	110	C3
Tarsus	98	F5
Tartagal	158	J3
Tartu	50	P7
Ţarţūs	100	C2
Tarutyne	68	S3
Tarvisio	64	J4
Tasbuget	82	M9
Tashigang	94	F3
Tashir	98	L3
Tashkent	82	M9
Tash-Kömür	82	N9
Tashtagol	82	R7
Tasiilaq	136	Z3
Tasikmalaya	92	D4
Taskesken	82	Q8
Taşköprü	98	F3
Tasman Bay	128	D5
Tasmania	124	E10
Tasmania	126	H8
Tasman Mountains	128	D5
Tasman Sea	128	B3
Tăşnad	68	K2
Taşova	98	G3
Tassili du Hoggar	112	F4
Tassili-n'-Ajjer	112	G3
Tasty	82	M9
Tasūj	98	L4
Tata, *Hungary*	68	F2
Tata, *Morocco*	112	D3
Tataba	93	B3
Tatabánya	68	F2
Tataouine	112	H2
Tatarbunary	68	S4
Tatariya	72	J3
Tatarsk	82	P6
Tatarskiy Proliv	84	P7
Tateyama	88	K6
Tathlina Lake	136	H4
Tatta	96	J5
Tatvan	98	K4
Tauá	156	J5
Tauberbischofsheim	54	E7
Tauern	64	J4
Taumarunui	128	E4
Taungdwingyi	90	B2
Taung-gyi	94	G4
Taungup	94	F5
Taunsa	94	B2
Taunton, *United Kingdom*	38	E4
Taunton, *United States*	142	F2
Taunus	56	L4
Taunusstein	56	L4
Taupo	128	F4
Tauragė	52	M2
Tauranga	128	F3
Tauroa Point	128	D2
Tavda	72	N3
Tavda	72	N3
Tavira	62	C7
Tavistock	38	D5
Tavoy	90	B4
Tavşanli	98	C4
Taw	38	E5
Tawas City	142	D2
Tawau	92	F2
Tawitawi	92	F1
Taxkorgan	82	P10
Tay	36	E5
Tayga	82	R6
Taylorville	144	D2
Taym	96	C4
Taymā'	110	G2
Taymura	84	F4
Taymylyr	84	L2
Tay Ninh	90	D4
Taynuilt	36	C5
Tayshet	84	F5
Tayuan	84	L6
Tayyebād	96	H3
Taza	112	E2
Tazeh Kand	98	M4
Tazenakht	112	D2
Tāzirbū	110	D2
Tazovskaya Guba	82	N4
Tazovskiy	82	P4
Tazovskiy Poluostrov	82	N4
Tazungdam	90	B1
T'bilisi	98	L3
Tchamba	114	G3
Tchibanga	114	G5
Tchin Tabaradene	112	G5
Tczew	52	H3
Te Anau	128	A7
Te Araroa	128	G3
Te Aroha	128	E3
Te Awamutu	128	E4
Teberda	98	J2
Tébessa	112	G1
Tebingtinggi	92	B2
Téboursouk	66	D12
Techa	72	M3
Techiman	114	D3
Tecuala	146	D4
Tecuci	68	Q4
Tedzhen	96	H2
Tees	38	F7
Tegal	92	D4
Tegernsee	64	G3
Tegina	114	F2
Teglio	64	F4
Tegucigalpa	148	G6
Tegul'det	82	R6
Te Hapua	128	D2
Te Haroto	128	F4
Tehek Lake	136	M3
Teheran = Tehrān	96	F2
Tehrān	96	F2
Teignmouth	38	E5
Tejo = Tagus	62	B5
Te Kaha	128	F3
Te Kao	128	D2
Tekirdağ	70	K4
Tekirdağ	98	B3
Teknaf	94	F4
Teku	93	B3
Te Kuiti	128	E4
T'elavi	98	L3
Tel Aviv-Yafo	100	B4
Telegraph Creek	146	(1)L4
Telén	158	H6
Teles Pires	156	F5
Telford	38	F3
Telfs	64	G3
Teller	146	(1)D2
Telsen	158	H7
Telšiai	52	M2
Teltow	54	J4
Teluk Berau	93	D3
Teluk Bone	93	B3
Teluk Cenderawasih	93	E3
Telukdalem	92	B2
Teluk Kumai	92	E3
Telukpakedai	92	D3
Teluk Sampit	92	E3
Teluk Sukadana	92	D3
Teluk Tomini	93	B2
Tema	114	D3
Tembenchi	82	T4
Temerin	68	G4
Temerloh	90	C6
Teminabuan	93	D3
Temochic	146	E3
Tempe	146	D2
Tempio Pausaria	66	D8
Temple	146	G2
Templemore	35	D4
Temryuk	98	G1
Temuco	158	G6
Tenali	94	D5
Tendaho	110	H5
Ten Degree Channel	94	F7
Tendo	88	L4
Tendrara	112	E2
Ténéré	112	G5
Ténéré du Tafassasset	112	G4
Tenerife	112	B3
Ténès	112	F1
Tenggarong	92	F3
Tenke	118	D2
Tenkodogo	114	D2
Tennant Creek	126	F3
Tennessee	134	K6
Tennessee	138	J4
Tenojoki	50	P2
Tenteno	93	B3
Tenterden	38	J4
Tenterfield	126	K5
Teo	62	B2
Teófilo Otoni	156	J7
Tepa	93	C4
Tepehuanes	138	E6
Tepic	138	F7
Teplice	52	C7
Ter	62	N2
Terceira	112	(1)B2
Terek	98	L2
Teresina	156	J5
Tergnier	56	F5
Terme	98	G3
Termez	96	J2
Termini Imerese	66	H11
Termirtau	82	N7
Termoli	68	C8
Ternate	93	C2
Terneuzen	56	F3
Terni	66	G6
Ternitz	64	M3
Ternopil'	72	E5
Ternuka	128	C7
Terracina	66	H7
Terrassa	62	N3
Terre Haute	144	D2
Terry	140	E1
Tersa	72	H4
Terschelling	56	H1
Teruel	62	J4
Tervel	98	B2
Tervola	50	N3
Teseney	110	G4
Teshekpuk Lake	146	(1)F1
Teshikaga	88	N2
Teshio	88	L1
Teslin	146	(1)L3
Teslin	146	(1)L3
Tessalit	112	F4
Têt	60	H11
Tete	118	E3
Teterow	54	H3
Teteven	70	G2
Tétouan	112	D1
Tetovo	68	H8
Teuco	158	J3
Teulada	66	C10
Tevere	66	G6
Teverya	100	C4
Teviothead	36	F6
Tevriz	72	P3
Te Waewae Bay	128	A8
Tewkesbury	38	F4
Texarkana	144	C3
Texas	138	F5
Texel	56	G1
Teya	82	S5
Teykovo	72	H3
Tfarity	112	C3
Thaba Putsoa	118	D5
Thabazimbi	118	D4
Thailand	90	C4
Thai Nguyên	90	D2
Thal	94	B2
Thale Luang	90	C5
Thamarīt	96	F6
Thame	38	H4
Thames	38	G4
Thamūd	96	E6
Thane	94	B5
Thanh Hoa	90	D3
Thanjavur	94	C6
Thann	64	C3
Tharad	94	B4
Thar Desert	94	B3
Thargomindah	126	H5
Tharwāniyyah	101	E5
Thasos	70	G4
Thasos	70	G4
Thaton	90	B3
Thaya	52	E9
The Bahamas	144	F4
The Bluff	144	F4
The Broads	38	K3
The Burren	35	B3
The Cheviot	36	F6
The Cheviot Hills	36	F6
The Dalles	140	B1
Thedford	140	F2
The Fens	38	J3
The Gambia	114	A2
The Granites	126	E4
The Hague = 's-Gravenhage	56	G2
Thelon	136	L4
The Minch	36	C3
The Naze	38	K4
Thenia	62	P8
Theniet el Had	62	N9
The North Sound	36	F2
Theodore Roosevelt	156	E5
Theodore Roosevelt Lake	146	D2
The Pas	136	L6
The Rhins	36	C7
Thermaikos Kolpos	70	E4
Thermopolis	140	E2
The Sandlings	38	K3
The Sisters	128	(1)B1
Thessalon	142	D1
Thessaloniki	70	E4
Thetford	38	J3
Thetford Mines	142	F1
The Twins	128	D5
The Wash	38	J3
The Weald	38	H4
The Whitsundays	126	J4
Thief River Falls	142	A1
Thiers	60	J8
Thiès	114	A2
Thika	116	F4
Thimphu	94	E3
Þingvallavatn	50	(1)C2
Thionville	56	J5
Thira	70	H8
Thira	70	H8
Thirasia	70	H8
Thirsk	36	G7
Thiruvananthapuram	94	C7
Thisted	50	E8
Þistilfjöður	50	(1)F1
Thiva	70	F6
Thiviers	60	F8
Þjórsá	50	(1)D2
Tholen	56	G3
Thomastown	35	D4
Thomasville	144	E3
Thompson	136	M5
Thompson	136	H6
Thompson Falls	140	C1
Thomson	144	E3
Thonon-les-Bains	64	B4
Þórisvatn	50	(1)D2
Þorlákshöfn	50	(1)C3
Thornbury	38	F4
Thorne	38	H2
Thornhill	36	E6
Þorshöfn	50	(1)F1
Thouars	60	E7
Thrakiko Pelagos	70	H4
Three Forks	140	D1
Three Kings Island	128	C2
Three Rivers	142	C2
Throckmorton	144	B3
Thuin	56	G4
Thun	64	C4
Thunder Bay	142	C1
Thuner See	64	C4
Thung Song	90	B5
Thüringer Wald	54	F6
Thurles	35	D4
Thurso	36	E3
Thurso	36	E3
Thusis	64	E4
Tīāb	101	G3
Tianjin	86	F3
Tianmen	86	E4
Tianqiaoling	88	E2
Tianshifu	88	C3
Tianshui	86	D4
Tianshuihai	96	L2
Tianyang	86	D6
Tiaret	112	F1
Tibati	114	G3
Tibboburra	126	H5
Tibesti	110	C3
Tibet = Xizang	94	E2
Tiburón	148	B3
Tîchît	112	D5
Tichla	112	C4
Ticino	64	D4
Ticul	148	G4
Tidjikdja	112	C5
Tieling	88	B2
Tielongtan	94	C1
Tielt	56	F3
Tienen	56	G4
Tien Shan	82	Q9
Tien Yen	90	D2
Tierra Amarilla	140	E3
Tiétar	62	E4
Tiflis = T'bilisi	108	H1
Tifton	144	E3
Tifu	93	C3
Tighina	68	S3
Tignère	114	G3
Tigre	156	B4
Tigris	98	K6
Tijuana	138	C5
Tikanlik	82	R9
Tikhoretsk	72	H5
Tikhvin	72	F3
Tikrīt	98	K6
Tiksi	84	M2
Tilburg	56	H3
Tilichiki	84	V4
Tillabéri	114	E2
Tillamook	140	B1
Tillicoultry	36	E5
Tilos	70	K8
Timanskiy Kryazh	72	K2
Timaru	128	C7
Timashevsk	72	G5
Timber Creek	126	F3
Timerloh	92	C2
Timimoun	112	F3
Timişoara	68	J4
Timmins	142	D1
Timon	156	J5
Timor	93	C4
Timor Sea	126	E2
Tinaca Point	124	C5
Tin Alkoum	112	H4
Tinchebray	56	B6
Tindivanam	94	C6
Tindouf	112	D3
Tineo	62	D1
Tinfouchy	112	D3
Tinglev	54	E2
Tingo Maria	156	B5
Tingri	94	E3
Tingsryd	52	E1
Tiniroto	128	F4
Tinnsjø	50	E7
Tinogasta	158	H4
Tinos	70	H7
Tinos	70	H7
Tinsukia	94	G3
Tîntâne	112	C5
T'i'o	110	H5
Tipperary	35	C4
Tirana = Tiranë	70	B3
Tiranë	70	B3
Tirari Desert	126	G5
Tiraspol	68	S3
Tire	70	K6
Tiree	36	B5
Tiroungoulou	116	C2
Tirschenreuth	54	H7
Tirso	66	C9
Tiruchchirāppalli	94	C6
Tirunelveli	94	C7
Tirupati	94	C6
Tiruppur	94	C6
Tiruvannamalai	94	C6
Tisa	68	H4
Ţisīyah	100	D4
Tišnov	52	F8
Tisza	52	M9
Tiszafoldvár	68	H3
Tiszafüred	68	H2
Tiszaújváros	52	L10
Tit-Ary	82	Z3
Titel	68	H4
Titlagarh	94	D4
Titova Korenica	64	L6
Titovo Velenje	66	K2
Titu	68	N5
Titusville	144	E4
Tivaouane	112	B6
Tiverton	38	E5
Tivoli	66	G7
Tiyās	100	E2
Tizi Ouzou	112	F1

Tiznit 112 D3
Tjeldøya 50 H2
Tjørkolm 50 D7
Tlemcen 112 E2
Tmassah 110 C2
Toad River 136 F5
Tobago 148 M6
Tobelo 93 C2
Tobermorey 126 G4
Tobermory, *United Kingdom* 36 B5
Tobermory, *United States* 142 D1
Tobi 93 D2
Toboali 92 D3
Tobol 72 M4
Tobol 72 M4
Tobol'sk 72 N3
Tobseda 72 K1
Tocantins 156 H5
Tocantins 156 H5
Toce 64 D4
Tocopilla 158 G3
Todeli 93 B3
Todi 66 G6
Tofino 140 A1
Togo 114 E3
Toimin 66 H2
Toi-misaki 88 F8
Tōjō 88 G6
Tok 146 (1)J3
Tokar 110 G4
Tokat, *Sudan* 96 C6
Tokat, *Turkey* 96 C1
Tokelau 124 J6
Tokmak 82 P9
Tokoroa 128 E4
Tokounou 114 C3
Toksun 82 R9
Tok-tō 86 J3
Toktogul 82 N9
Tokushima 88 H6
Tokuyama 88 F6
Tōkyō 88 K6
Tolaga Bay 128 G4
Tôlañaro 118 H4
Tolbo 82 S8
Toledo, *Brazil* 158 L3
Toledo, *Spain* 62 F5
Toledo, *United States* 142 D2
Toliara 118 G4
Tolitoli 93 B2
Tol'ka 82 Q5
Tol'ka 82 Q5
Tollense 54 J3
Tolmezzo 64 J4
Tolmin 64 J4
Tolna 68 F3
Tolosa 62 H1
Tol'yatti 72 J4
Tolybay 82 L7
Tom' 82 R6
Tomah 142 B2
Tomakomai 88 L2
Tomamae 88 L1
Tomar, *Brazil* 156 E4
Tomar, *Portugal* 62 B5
Tomari 84 Q7
Tomaszów Lubelski 52 N7
Tomaszów Mazowiecki 52 K6
Tomatin 36 D4
Tombouctou 112 E5
Tombua 118 A3
Tomé 158 G6
Tomelloso 62 H5
Tomini 93 B2
Tommot 84 M5
Tomo 156 D2
Tompo 84 P4
Tom Price 126 C4
Tomra 94 E2
Tomsk 82 Q6
Tomtor 84 Q4
Tomu 93 D3
Tonalá 148 F5
Tonbridge 38 J4
Tondano 93 B2
Tønder 54 D2
Tonga 116 E2
Tonga 124 J7
Tonga Islands 124 J8
Tongareva 124 K6
Tonga Trench 124 J8
Tongbai 86 E4
Tongchuan 86 D4
Tongduch'ŏn 88 D5
Tongeren 56 H4
Tonghae 88 E5
Tonghua 88 C3
Tongliao 86 G2
Tongling 86 F4
Tongshi 90 D3
Tongue 140 E1
Tongue 36 D3
Tongue Bay 36 D3
Tongyu 86 G2
Tónichi 138 E6
Tonj 116 D2
Tonk 94 C3
Tonkābon 96 F2
Tônlé Sab 90 C4
Tonnay-Charente 60 E8
Tönning 54 D2
Tonopah 140 C3
Tooele 140 D2
Toora-Khem 82 T7
Toowoomba 126 K5
Topeka 138 G4
Topki 82 R6
Toplița 68 N3
Topock 146 D2
Topol'čany 52 H9
Topolobampo 138 E6
Torbali 70 K6
Torbat-e Heydarīyeh 96 G2
Torbat-e Jām 96 H2
Torbay 38 E5
Tordesillas 62 F3
Töre 50 M4
Torells 62 N2
Torgau 54 H5
Torgelow 52 C4
Torhout 56 F3
Torino 64 C5
Tori-shima 88 L8
Torneälven 50 L3
Torneträsk 50 K2
Tornio 50 N4
Toro 62 E3
Toronto 142 E2
Tororo 116 E3
Toros Dağları 98 E5
Torquay 38 E5
Torrance 146 C2
Torreblanca 62 L4
Torre de Moncorvo 62 C3
Torrejón de Ardoz 62 G4
Torrelapaja 62 J3
Torrelavega 62 F1
Torremolinos 62 F8
Torrent 62 K5
Torreón 146 F3
Torre-Pacheco 62 K7
Torres Strait 126 H2
Torres Vedras 62 A5
Torrevieja 62 K6
Torrington 140 F2
Tortoli 66 D9
Tortona 64 D6
Tortosa 62 L4
Tortum 98 J3
Torūd 96 G2
Toruń 52 H4
Tory 35 C1
Tory Sound 35 C1
Torzhok 72 G3
Tosa-wan 88 G7
Tostedt 54 E3
Tosya 70 S3
Totaranui 128 D5
Tôtes 56 D5
Tot'ma 72 H3
Totnes 38 E5
Totora 156 D7
Tottenham 38 H4
Tottori 88 H6
Touba, *Ivory Coast* 114 C3
Touba, *Senegal* 114 A2
Tougan 114 D2
Touggourt 112 G2
Tougouri 114 D2
Touil 112 C5
Toul 60 L5
Toulépleu 114 C3
Toulon 60 L10
Toulouse 60 G10
Toummo 112 H4
Toungoo 90 B3
Tourcoing 56 F4
Tournai 56 F4
Tournon-sur-Rhône 60 K8
Tours 60 F6
Touws River 118 C6
Tovuz 98 L3
Towanda 142 E2
Towari 93 B3
Towcester 38 H3
Towner 140 F1
Townsend 140 D1
Townshend Island 126 K4
Townsville 126 J3
Toxkan 82 P9
Toyama 88 J5
Toyohashi 88 J6
Toyooka 88 H6
Toyota 88 J6
Tozeur 112 G2
Tqvarch'eli 98 J2
Trāblous 100 C2
Trabzon 98 H3
Tracy 142 A2
Trail 140 C1
Traiskirchen 64 M2
Trakai 50 N9
Tralee 35 B4
Tralee Bay 35 B4
Tramán Tepuí 156 E2
Tranås 50 H7
Trancoso 62 C4
Trang 90 B5
Trangan 93 D4
Transantarctic Mountains 160 (2)B1
Trapani 66 G11
Trappes 56 E6
Traun 64 K2
Traunreut 64 H3
Traunsee 64 J3
Traversay Islands 154 H9
Traverse City 142 C2
Travnik 68 E5
Trbovlje 64 L4
Trebbia 64 E6
Třebíč 52 E8
Trebinje 68 F7
Trebišov 68 J1
Trebnje 64 L5
Trebon 64 K1
Tredegar 38 E4
Tregaron 38 E3
Tregosse Islets 126 K3
Treherbert 38 E4
Trélazé 60 E6
Trelew 158 H7
Trelleborg 50 G9
Tremadog Bay 38 D3
Tremonton 140 D2
Tremp 62 L2
Trenčín 52 H9
Trent 38 H2
Trento 64 G4
Trenton, *Canada* 142 E2
Trenton, *United States* 142 F2
Trepassey 136 W7
Tres Arroyos 158 J6
Três Corações 156 H8
Tres Esquinas 156 B3
Treshnish Isles 36 B5
Tres Lagos 158 G8
Trespaderne 62 G2
Tretower 38 E4
Treuchtlingen 64 F2
Treviglio 64 E5
Treviso 64 H5
Triangle 118 E4
Tricase 66 N9
Trichur 94 C6
Trier 56 J5
Trieste 64 J5
Triglav 64 J4
Trikala 70 D5
Trikomon 100 A1
Trilj 64 M7
Trincomalee 94 D7
Tring 38 H4
Trinidad 156 E1
Trinidad, *Bolivia* 156 E6
Trinidad, *United States* 146 F1
Trinidad, *Uruguay* 158 K5
Trinidad and Tobago 156 E1
Trinity Islands 146 (1)G4
Trino 64 D5
Trion 144 D3
Tripoli, *Greece* 70 E7
Tripoli = Trâblous, *Lebanon* 100 C2
Tripoli = Tarābulus, *Libya* 112 H2
Trischen 54 D2
Tristan da Cunha 108 B9
Trivandrum = Thiruvananthapuram 94 C7
Trjavna 98 A2
Trnava 68 E1
Trogir 68 D6
Troina 66 J11
Troisdorf 54 C6
Trois Rivières 142 F1
Troitsk 72 M4
Troitsko-Pechorsk 72 L2
Trojan 70 G2
Trollhättan 50 G7
Trombetas 156 F4
Tromsø 50 K2
Trona 140 C3
Trondheim 50 F5
Trondheimsfjörden 50 E5
Troodos 98 E6
Trotuș 68 P3
Trout Lake, *N.W.T., Canada* 136 G4
Trout Lake, *Ont., Canada* 136 N6
Trowbridge 38 F4
Troy, *Al., United States* 144 D3
Troy, *N.Y., United States* 142 F2
Troyan 68 M7
Troyes 60 K5
Trstenik 68 J6
Trudovoye 88 G2
Trujillo, *Peru* 156 B5
Trujillo, *Spain* 62 E5
Truro, *Canada* 136 U7
Truro, *United Kingdom* 38 C5
Trusovo 82 J4
Truth or Consequences 146 E2
Trutnov 52 E7
Tryavana 70 H2
Trzcianka 52 F4
Trzebnica 52 G6
Tržič 64 K4
Tsetserleg 84 G7
Tshabong 118 C5
Tshane 118 C4
Tshikapa 116 C5
Tshuapa 116 C4
Tsiafajavona 118 H3
Tsimlyanskoy Vodokhranilishche 72 H5
Tsiroanomandidy 118 H3
Ts'khinvali 98 K2
Tsuchiura 88 L5
Tsugaru-kaikyō 88 L3
Tsumeb 118 B3
Tsumkwe 118 C3
Tsuruga 88 J6
Tsuruoka 88 K4
Tsushima 88 E6
Tsuyama 88 H6
Tua 62 C3
Tual 93 D4
Tuam 35 C3
Tuân Giao 90 C2
Tuapse 98 H1
Tubarão 158 M4
Tubas 100 C4
Tübingen 64 E2
Tubize 56 G4
Tubruq 110 D1
Tubuai 124 M8
Tubuai Islands 124 L8
Tucano 156 K6
Tuchola 52 G4
Tucson 146 D2
Tucumcari 146 F1
Tucupita 156 E2
Tucuruí 156 H4
Tudela 62 J2
Țufayḥ 101 C3
Tuffley 38 F4
Tuguegarao 90 G3
Tugur 84 P6
Tui 62 B2
Tuktoyaktuk 146 (1)L2
Tula, *Mexico* 146 G4
Tula, *Russia* 72 G4
Tulare 140 C3
Tulcea 68 R4
Tulkarm 100 B4
Tullamore 35 D3
Tulle 60 G8
Tulln 64 M2
Tullow 35 E4
Tuloma 50 S2
Tulsa 138 G4
Tulsequah 146 (1)L4
Tulun 84 G6
Tulung La 94 F3
Tulu Weiel 116 E2
Tumaco 156 B3
Tumān 96 H2
Tumen 88 E2
Tumereng 156 E2
Tumkur 94 C6
Tumut 126 J7
Tunca 70 J3
Tunceli 98 H4
Tunduru 118 F2
Tundzha 68 P8
Tungir 84 L5
Tungku 92 F1
Tungsten 146 (1)M3
Tungusk 82 S5
Tunis 112 H1
Tunisia 112 E2
Tunja 156 C2
Tupelo 144 D3
Tupik 84 L6
Tupiza 158 H3
Tupper Lake 142 F2
Tuquan 86 G1
Tura, *India* 94 F3
Tura, *Russia* 84 G4
Turan 82 S7
Turangi 128 E4
Turayf 110 G1
Turbat 96 H4
Turbo 156 B2
Turda 68 L3
Turek 52 H5
Turgay 82 L8
Turgay 82 L8
Turgayskaya Stolovaya Strana 82 L7
Tŭrgovishte 68 P6
Turgutlu 70 K6
Turhal 98 G3
Turin = Torino 64 C5
Turinsk 72 M3
Turiy Rog 88 F1
Turka 84 H6
Türkeli Adası 70 K4
Turkestan 82 M9
Turkey 98 D4
Turkmenbashi 96 F1
Turkmenistan 96 G2
Turks and Caicos Islands 148 K4
Turks Islands 148 K4
Turku 50 M6
Turma 84 N6
Turnhout 56 G3
Turnov 52 E7
Turnu Măgurele 68 M6
Turpan 82 R9
Turpan Pendi 82 S9
Turquino 154 D2
Turriff 36 F4
Turtas 72 N3
Turtkul' 96 H1
Turtle Island 126 K3
Turu 82 U5
Turugart Pass 82 P9
Turukhan 84 C3
Turukhansk 82 R4
Turukta 84 K4
Tuscaloosa 144 D3
Tuscola 144 D2
Tuticorin 94 C7
Tutonchany 84 E4
Tutrakan 68 P5
Tuttle Creek Reservoir 144 B2
Tuttlingen 64 D3
Tutuila 124 K7
Tuvalu 124 H6
Tuxpan, *Mexico* 138 G7
Tuxpan, *Mexico* 138 E7
Tuxtla Gutiérrez 148 F5
Tuyên Quang 90 D2
Tuy Hoa 90 D4
Tuymazy 72 K4
Tuz Gölü 98 E4
Tuz Khurmātū 98 L6
Tuzla 68 F5
Tver' 72 G3
Twatt 36 E2
Tweed 36 F6
Twentynine Palms 146 C2
Twilight Cove 126 E6
Twin Buttes Reservoir 146 F2
Twin Falls 140 D2
Twizel 128 C7
Two Harbors 142 B1
Tyachiv 68 L1
Tygda 84 M6
Tyler 138 G5
Tylkhoy 84 U4
Tym 82 Q6
Tynda 84 L5
Tyne 36 F6
Tynemouth 36 G6
Tynset 50 F5
Tyra 82 S7
Tyrifjorden 50 F6
Tyrnavos 70 E5
Tyrrhenian Sea 66 F8
Tyry 84 P4
Tysa 52 N9
Tyukyan 84 K4
Tyumen' 82 M6
Tyung 84 K3
Tyva 84 F6

U

Uarini 156 D4
Uaupés 156 D3
Ubá 156 J8
Ubaitaba 156 K6
Ubangi 116 B3
Ube 88 F7
Úbeda 62 G6
Uberaba 156 H7
Uberlândia 156 H7

Überlingen 64 E3
Ubon Ratchathani 90 C3
Ubrique 62 E8
Ucayali 156 B5
Uchami 82 T5
Ucharal 82 Q8
Uchiura-wan 88 L2
Uchkuduk 82 L9
Uckermark 54 J3
Uckfield 38 J5
Ucluelet 140 A1
Uda, *Russia* 84 F5
Uda, *Russia* 84 N6
Udachnyy 84 J3
Udagamandalam 94 C6
Udaipur 94 B4
Uddevalla 50 F7
Uddjaure 72 C1
Uddjaure Storavan 50 K4
Udine 64 J4
Udmurtiya 72 K3
Udon Thani 90 C3
Udupi 94 B6
Uecker 54 J3
Ueckermünde 54 J3
Ueda 88 K5
Uele 116 C3
Uelen 84 AA3
Uel'kal 84 Y3
Uelzen 54 F4
Ufa 72 L4
Ufa 72 L3
Uganda 116 E3
Ugep 114 F3
Ugine 64 B5
Uglegorsk 84 Q7
Uglich 72 G3
Ugljan 64 L6
Ugol'naya Zyryanka 84 R3
Ugol'nyye Kopi 84 X4
Ugulan 84 S4
Uh 68 K1
Uherské Hradiště 52 G8
Uherský Brod 52 G8
Uig 36 B4
Uiju 88 C3
Uil 72 K5
Uil 72 K5
Uinta Mountains 140 D2
Uitenhage 118 D6
Újfehértó 68 J2
Ujiji 116 D4
Ujjain 94 C4
Ujung Pandang 93 A4
Ukerewe Island 116 E4
Ukhta 82 J5
Ukiah 140 B3
Ukkusissat 136 W2
Ukmergė 52 P2
Ukraine 48 G3
Ulaanbaatar 84 H7
Ulaangom 82 S8
Ulan 86 B3
Ulan Bator = Ulaanbaatar 86 D1
Ulan-Ude 84 H6
Ulaş 98 G4
Ulchin 88 E5
Ulcinj 68 G8
Uldz 84 J7
Ulety 84 J6
Ulhasnagar 94 B5
Uliastay 82 T8
Ulindi 116 D4
Ullapool 36 C4
Ullŭng do 88 F5
Ulm 64 F2
Ulog 68 F6
Ulongue 118 E2
Ulsan 88 E6
Ulster 35 D2
Ulu 84 M4
Ulubat Gölü 70 L4
Ulugqat 96 K2
Ulukışla 98 F5
Ulungur Hu 82 R8
Ulunkhan 84 J5
Uluru 126 F5
Ulu-Yul 84 D5
Ulva 36 B5
Ulverston 36 E7
Ulya 84 Q5
Ul'yanovsk 72 J4
Ulytau 82 M8
Umag 66 H3
Uman' 72 F5
Umarkot 96 J4
Umba 72 F1
Umeå 50 L5
Umeälven 50 J4
Umfolozi 118 E5
Ummal Arānib 112 H3
Umm al Jamājim 101 A3
Umm Durman 110 F4
Umm Keddada 110 E5
Umm Lajj 110 G3
Umm Qaşr 101 B1
Umm Ruwaba 110 F5
Umnak Island 146 (1)E5
Umtata 118 D6
Umuarama 158 L3
Unalakleet 146 (1)E3
Unalaska Island 146 (1)E5
'Unayzah 100 C6
Underberg 118 D5
Ungava Bay 136 T5
Ungheni 68 Q2
Ungwana Bay 116 G4
União da Vitória 158 L4
Unije 64 K6
Unimak Island 146 (1)D5
Unim Bāb 101 D4
Unini 156 E4
Union 142 B3
Union City 148 G1
Union Springs 144 D3
United Arab Emirates 96 F5
United Kingdom 58 G6
United States 134 M5
Unna 56 K3
Unraven 146 E1
Unst 36 (1)H1
Unstrut 54 G5
Unzha 72 H3
Upernavik 136 W2
Upernavik Kujalleq 136 V2
Upington 118 C5
Upolu 124 J7
Upper Hutt 128 E5
Upper Klamath Lake 140 B2
Upper Lake 140 C2
Upper Lough Erne 35 D2
Upper Sandusky 142 D2
Uppsala 50 J7
Upsala 142 B1
'Uqlat al 'Udhaybah 101 B2
Urad Houqi 86 D2
Urakawa 88 M2
Ural 72 K5
Ural Mountains = Ural'skiy Khrebet 48 L1
Ural'sk 72 K4
Ural'skiy Khrebet 48 L1
Urambo 116 E5
Uranium City 136 K5
Uraricoera 156 E3
Uraricoera 156 E3
Uray 72 M2
Urbana, *Ill., United States* 142 C2
Urbana, *Oh., United States* 142 D2
Urbania 64 H7
Urbino 64 H7
Urdzhar 82 Q8
Ure 36 G7
Uren' 72 J3
Urengoy 82 P4
Urgench 96 H1
Urho 82 R8
Uritskiy 72 N4
Urla 70 J6
Urlaţi 68 P5
Urmston 38 F2
Uroševac 68 J7
Uro-teppa 96 J2
Urt 86 C2
Uruaçu 156 H6
Uruapan 148 D5
Urucurituba 156 F4
Uruguaiana 158 K4
Uruguay 158 K5
Uruguay 158 K5
Ürümqi 82 R9
Urus Martan 98 L2
Uruti 128 E4
Uryupino 84 L6
Uryupinsk 72 H4
Urzhum 72 K3
Urziceni 68 P5
Usa 82 L4
Usa 88 F7
Uşak 98 C4
Usedom 54 J3
Useless Loop 126 B5
Usfān 96 C5
Ushtobe 82 P8
Usingen 54 D6
Usk 38 E4
Usman' 72 G4
Usol'ye Sibirskoye 84 G6
Ussel 60 H8
Ussuri 88 G1
Ussuriysk 86 J2
Usta 72 J3
Ust'-Alekseyevo 72 J2
Ust'-Barguzin 84 H6
Ust' Chaun 84 W3
Ústí 52 F8
Ustica 66 H10
Ust'-Ilimsk 84 G5
Ústí nad Labem 52 D7
Ust'-Ishim 82 N6
Ustka 52 F3
Ust'-Kamchatsk 84 U5
Ust'-Kamenogorsk 82 Q8
Ust'-Kamo 82 T5
Ust'-Karenga 84 K6
Ust'-Khayryuzovo 84 T5
Ust'-Kulom 72 K2
Ust'-Kut 84 G5
Ust'-Kuyga 84 P3
Ust'-Labinsk 98 H1
Ust'-Maya 84 N4
Ust'-Mukduyka 82 R4
Ust'-Muya 84 K5
Ust' Nem 72 K2
Ust'-Nera 84 Q4
Ust'-Nyukzha 84 L5
Ust'-Olenek 84 K2
Ust'-Omchug 84 R4
Ust' Ozernoye 84 D5
Ust' Penzhino 84 V4
Ust'-Pit 84 E5
Ustrem 72 N2
Ust'-Sopochnoye 84 T5
Ust' Tapsuy 72 M2
Ust'-Tarka 82 P6
Ust'-Tatta 84 N4
Ust'-Tsil'ma 82 J4
Ust' Un'ya 72 L2
Ust'-Urkima 84 L5
Ust' Usa 72 L1
Ust'-Uyskoye 82 L7
Usu 82 Q9
Usuki 88 F7
Utah 138 D4
Utah Lake 140 D2
Utata 84 G6
Utena 50 N9
Uthal 96 J4
Utica 142 E2
Utiel 62 J5
Utrecht 56 H2
Utrera 62 E7
Utsjoki 50 P2
Utsunomiya 88 K5
Uttaradit 90 C3
Uttoxeter 38 G3
Utva 72 K4
Uummannaq Fjord 136 V2
Uummannarsuaq 136 Y5
Uusikaupunki 50 L6
Uvalde 148 E3
Uvargin 84 X3
Uvat 72 N3
Uvinza 116 E5
Uvira 116 D4
Uvs Nuur 82 S7
Uwajima 88 G7
Uxbridge 38 H4
Uy 72 M4
Uyar 82 S6
Uyuk 82 N9
Uyuni 158 H3
Uzbekistan 82 L9
Uzhhorod 68 K1
Užice 68 G6
Uzunköprü 68 P8

V

Vaal 118 D5
Vaasa 50 L5
Vác 68 G2
Vacaria 158 M4
Vachi 96 E1
Vadodara 94 B4
Vado Ligure 64 D6
Vadsø 50 Q1
Vaduz 64 E3
Værøy 50 G3
Vaganski Vhr 64 L6
Vagay 72 N3
Váh 52 H8
Vakh 72 Q2
Valbonnais 64 A6
Valcheta 158 H7
Valdagno 64 G5
Valday 72 F3
Val-de-Meuse 64 A2
Valdemoro 62 G4
Valdepeñas 62 G6
Valdez 136 B4
Valdivia 158 G6
Val-d'Or 142 E1
Valdosta 138 K5
Valdres 50 E6
Valea lui Mihai 68 K2
Valence 60 K9
Valencia, *Spain* 62 K5
Valencia, *Venezuela* 156 D1
Valencia de Alcántara 62 C5
Valenciennes 56 F4
Vălenii de Munte 68 P4
Valentia 35 A5
Valentine 140 F2
Valenza 64 D5
Vale of York 36 G7
Valera 156 C2
Valga 72 E3
Val Horn 138 F5
Valjevo 68 G5
Valka 50 N8
Val'karay 84 X3
Valkeakoski 50 N6
Valkenswaard 56 H3
Valladolid, *Mexico* 148 G4
Valladolid, *Spain* 62 F3
Valle 50 D7
Valledupar 156 C1
Vallée de Azaouagh 112 F5
Vallée du Tîlemsi 112 F5
Vallée-Jonction 142 F1
Vallejo 140 B3
Vallentuna 50 K7
Valletta 66 J13
Valley City 140 G1
Valley Falls 140 B2
Valley of the Kings 110 F2
Valli di Comacchio 64 H6
Vallorbe 64 B4
Valls 62 M3
Valmiera 50 N8
Valognes 56 A5
Val-Paradis 142 E1
Valparai 94 C6
Valparaíso, *Chile* 158 G5
Valparaíso, *Mexico* 146 F4
Valsad 94 B4
Val'tevo 72 H2
Valuyki 72 G4
Valverde del Camino 62 D7
Vammala 50 M6
Van 98 K4
Vanadzor 98 L3
Vanavara 84 G4
Van Buren 142 G1
Vancouver, *Canada* 140 B1
Vancouver, *United States* 140 B1
Vancouver Island 136 F7
Vandalia 144 D2
Vanderbijlpark 118 D5
Vanderhoof 136 G6
Van Diemen Gulf 126 F2
Vänern 50 G7
Vangaindrano 118 H4
Van Gölü 98 K4
Van Horn 146 F2
Vanimo 93 F3
Vanino 84 Q7
Vankarem 84 Y3
Vanna 50 K1
Vännäs 50 K5
Vannes 60 C6
Vanrhynsdorp 118 B6
Vantaa 50 N6
Vanua Levu 124 H7
Vanuatu 124 G7
Van Wert 142 D2
Vanzevat 72 N2
Vanzhil'kynak 84 C4
Varāmīn 96 F2
Varanasi 94 D3
Varangerfjorden 50 R2
Varaždin 68 D3
Varazze 64 D6
Varberg 50 G8
Varda 70 D6
Vardar 70 E3
Varde 50 E9
Vardenis 98 L3
Vardø 50 R1
Varel 54 D3
Varena 52 P3
Varese 64 D5
Vârful Moldoveanu 68 M4
Vårfurile 68 K3
Varginha 158 M3
Varkaus 50 P5
Varna 98 B2
Värnamo 50 H8
Varnsdorf 54 K6
Várpalota 68 F2
Varto 98 J4
Varzi 64 E6
Varzy 60 J6
Vásárosnamény 68 K1
Vasilikos 100 A2
Vaslui 68 Q3
Västerås 50 J7
Västervik 50 J8
Vasto 66 J6
Vasvár 64 M3
Vatan 60 G6
Vatersay 36 A5
Vathia 70 E8
Vatican City 66 F7
Vatnajökull 50 (1)E2
Vatomandry 118 H3
Vatra Dornei 68 N2
Vättern 50 H7
Vaughn 146 E2
Vawkavysk 52 P4
Växjö 50 H8
Vayuniya 94 D7
Vazhgort 72 J2
Vecht 56 J2
Vechta 56 L2
Vecsés 68 G2
Vedaranniyam 94 C6
Vedea 68 N6
Vedi 98 L4
Veendam 56 J1
Veenendaal 56 H2
Vega 146 F1
Vega 50 F4
Vegreville 136 J6
Vejen 54 E1
Vejer de la Frontera 62 E8
Vejle 50 E9
Vel' 82 G5
Vela Luka 68 D7
Velenje 64 L4
Veles 70 D3
Vélez-Málaga 62 F8
Velika Gorica 64 M5
Velika Plana 68 J5
Velikaya 84 W4
Velikiye Luki 72 F3
Velikiy Ustyug 72 J2
Veliko Tŭrnovo 68 N6
Vélingara 114 B2
Velingrad 68 L7
Velita Kladuša 64 L5
Velké Meziříčí 52 F8
Velký Krtíš 52 J9
Velletri 66 G7
Vellinge 52 C2
Vellore 94 C6
Velopoula 70 F8
Vel'sk 72 H2
Velten 54 J4
Velva 140 F1
Venaria 64 C5
Vence 64 C7
Venda Nova 62 C3
Vendôme 60 G6
Venev 72 G4
Venezia 64 H5
Venezuela 156 D2
Vengurla 94 B5
Veniaminof Volcano 146 (1)F4
Venice 144 D4
Venice = Venezia 64 H5
Venlo 56 J3
Venray 56 H3
Venta 72 D3
Venta de Baños 62 F3
Ventimiglia 64 C7
Ventnor 38 G5
Ventotene 66 H8
Ventspils 50 L8
Vera, *Argentina* 158 J4
Vera, *Spain* 62 J7
Veracruz 148 E5
Veraval 94 B4
Verbania 64 D5
Vercelli 64 D5
Verdalsøra 50 F5
Verde 156 G8
Verden 54 E4
Verdun 56 H5
Vereeniging 118 D5
Vereshchagino 84 D4
Verín 62 C3
Verkhneimbatsk 84 D4
Verkhne-Imbatskoye 82 R5
Verkhnetulomskoe Vodokhranilishche 50 R2
Verkhneural'sk 72 L4
Verkhniy Baskunchak 72 J5
Verkhnyaya Amga 84 M5
Verkhnyaya Toyma 72 J2
Verkhnyaya Tura 72 L3
Verkhovyna 68 M1
Verkhoyansk 84 N3
Verkhoyanskiy Khrebet 84 M3

Vermillion 140 G2
Vermont 138 M3
Vernal 140 E2
Verneuil 56 C6
Vernon, *France* 56 D5
Vernon, *United States* 144 B3
Vero Beach 144 E4
Veroia 70 E4
Verona 64 F5
Versailles 56 E6
Verviers 56 H4
Veselí 64 N2
Vesijarvi 50 N6
Vesoul 54 B9
Vesterålen 50 G2
Vestfjorden 50 G3
Vestmannaeyjar 50 (1)C3
Vestvagøy 50 G2
Vesuvio 66 J8
Veszprém 68 E2
Vet 118 D5
Vetluga 72 J3
Vetluga 72 J3
Veurne 56 E3
Vevey 64 B4
Vezirköprü 98 F3
Viana do Castelo 62 B3
Vianden 56 J5
Viangchan 90 C3
Viareggio 64 F7
Viborg 50 E8
Vibo Valentia 66 L10
Vibraye 60 F5
Vic 62 N3
Vicenza 64 G5
Vichuga 72 H3
Vichy 60 J7
Vicksburg 144 C3
Victor Harbor 126 G7
Victoria 126 H7
Victoria, *Argentina* 158 J5
Victoria, *Canada* 140 B1
Victoria, *Chile* 158 G6
Victoria, *Malta* 66 J12
Victoria, *Romania* 68 M4
Victoria, *Seychelles* 118 (2)C1
Victoria, *United States* 144 B4
Victoria de las Tunas 148 J4
Victoria Falls 118 D3
Victoria Island 136 J2
Victoria Land 160 (2)W2
Victoria River 126 F3
Victoria Strait 136 M3
Victoriaville 142 F1
Victoria West 118 C6
Vidalia 138 K5
Vidamlja 52 N5
Videle 68 N5
Vidin 68 K6
Viedma 158 J7
Vienenburg 54 F5
Vienna 142 C3
Vienna = Wien 64 M2
Vienne 60 K8
Vienne 60 F7
Vientiane = Viangchan 90 C3
Vierzon 60 H6
Vieste 66 L7
Vietnam 90 D3
Viêt Tri 90 D2
Vigan 90 G3
Vigevano 64 D5
Vigia 156 H4
Vigo 62 B2
Vigo di Cadore 64 H4
Viho Valentia 66 L10
Vijaywada 94 D5
Vik 50 (1)D3
Vikna 50 E4
Vila de Conde 62 B3
Vilafranca del Penedäs 62 M3
Vila Franca de Xira 62 A6
Vila Nova de Gaia 62 B3
Vilanova y la Geltru 62 M3
Vila Real 62 C3
Vila-real 62 K5
Vilar Formoso 62 D4
Vila Velha 156 G3
Vilhelmina 50 J4
Vilhena 156 E6
Vilija 50 N9
Viljandi 50 N7
Vilkaviškis 52 N3
Villa Ahumada 148 C2
Villablino 62 D2
Villacarrillo 62 G6
Villach 64 J4
Villacidro 66 C9
Villa Constitución 138 D7
Villa de Cos 148 D4
Villafranca de los Barros 62 D6
Villafranca di Verona 64 F5
Villagarcia 62 B2
Villagrán 146 G4
Villahermosa 148 F5
Villa Huidobro 158 J5
Villalba 62 C1
Villaldama 146 F3
Villalpando 62 E3
Villamartín 62 E8
Villa Montes 158 J3
Villanueva 146 F4
Villanueva de Cordoba 62 F6
Villa Ocampo 146 E3
Villaputzu 66 D9
Villarrobledo 62 H5
Villa San Giovanni 66 K10
Villavelayo 62 H2
Villavicencio 156 C3
Villaviciosa 62 E1
Villazon 158 H3
Villedieu-les-Poêles 56 A6
Villefranche-de-Rouergue 60 H9
Villefranche-sur-Saône 60 K8
Villena 62 K6
Villeneuve-sur-Lot 60 F9
Villers-Bocage 56 B5
Villers-Cotterêts 56 F5
Villerupt 56 H5
Villeurbanne 60 K8
Villingen 64 D2
Vilnius 50 N9
Vilsbiburg 64 H2
Vilshofen 64 J2
Vilvoorde 56 G4
Vilyuy 84 L4
Vilyuysk 84 L4
Vilyuyskoye Vodokhranilishche 84 J4
Vimoutiers 56 C6
Vimperk 64 J1
Viña del Mar 158 G5
Vinaròs 62 L4
Vincennes 144 D2
Vineland 142 F3
Vinh 90 D3
Vinkovci 68 F4
Vinnytsya 72 E5
Vinson Massif 160 (2)JJ2
Vinstri 50 E6
Vinzili 72 N3
Viöl 54 E2
Vioolsdrift 118 B5
Vipava 64 J5
Vipiteno 64 G4
Vir 64 L6
Virac 90 G4
Viranşehir 98 H5
Virawah 94 B4
Virden 140 F1
Vire 56 B6
Virginia 138 L4
Virginia 142 B1
Virginia 35 D3
Virginia Beach 142 E3
Virgin Islands, *United Kingdom* 154 E2
Virgin Islands, *United States* 154 E2
Virihaure 50 J3
Virôchey 90 D4
Virovitica 68 E4
Virton 56 H5
Virtsu 50 M7
Virudunagar 94 C7
Vis 68 D6
Visalia 140 C3
Visby 50 K8
Viscount Melville Sound 136 J2
Viseu, *Brazil* 156 H4
Viseu, *Portugal* 62 C4
Vişeu de Sus 68 M2
Vishakhapatnam 94 D5
Vishera 82 K5
Vishnevka 82 N7
Visoko 68 F6
Visp 64 C4
Vissegrad 68 G6
Visselhövede 54 E4
Vistula = Wisła 48 F2
Viterbo 66 G6
Vitez 68 E5
Viti Levu 124 H7
Vitim 84 J5
Vitolište 70 D3
Vitória 158 N3
Vitória da Conquista 156 J6
Vitoria-Gasteiz 62 H2
Vitré 60 D5
Vitry-le-François 56 G6
Vitsyebsk 72 F3
Vitteaux 60 K6
Vittel 64 A2
Vittoria 66 J12
Vittorio Veneto 64 H5
Viveiro 62 C1
Vivi 82 T4
Vivonne 60 F7
Vize 70 K3
Vizhas 72 J1
Vizianagaram 94 D5
Vizinga 82 H5
Vizzini 66 J11
Vjosë 70 C4
Vladikavkaz 98 L2
Vladimir 72 H3
Vladivostok 88 F2
Vlasotince 68 K7
Vlasovo 84 N2
Vlieland 56 G1
Vlissingen 56 F3
Vlorë 70 B4
Vltava 52 D8
Vöcklabruck 64 J2
Vodice 64 L7
Vodnjan 64 J6
Vogelsberg 54 E6
Voghera 64 D6
Vohipeno 118 H4
Vöhringen 64 F2
Voi 116 F4
Voinjama 114 C3
Voiron 60 L8
Voitsberg 64 L3
Vojens 54 E1
Vojmsjön 50 J4
Vojvodina 68 G4
Volary 54 J8
Volcán Antofalla 158 H4
Volcán Barú 148 H7
Volcán Cayambe 156 B3
Volcán Citlaltépetl 134 L7
Volcán Corcovado 158 G7
Volcán Cotopaxi 156 B4
Volcán Domuyo 158 G6
Volcán Lanin 158 G6
Volcán Llullaillaco 158 H3
Volcán San Pedro 158 H3
Volcán Tajumulco 148 F5
Volga 72 J5
Volgodonsk 72 H5
Volgograd 72 H5
Völkermarkt 64 K4
Volkhov 72 F3
Völklingen 56 J5
Volksrust 118 D5
Volochanka 82 S3
Volodarskoye 72 N4
Vologda 72 H3
Volonga 72 J1
Volos 70 E5
Volosovo 50 Q7
Volta Redonda 156 J8
Volterra 64 F7
Voltri 64 D6
Volzhskiy 72 H5
Voorne 56 F3
Voranava 50 N9
Vorderrhein 64 E4
Vordingborg 54 G1
Voreios Evvoïkos Kolpos 70 E6
Voreria Pindos 70 C4
Vorkuta 72 M1
Vormsi 50 M7
Vorona 72 H4
Voronezh 72 G4
Vorstershoop 118 C5
Võru 50 P8
Vosges 64 C2
Voss 50 D6
Vostochno-Sibirskoye More 84 U2
Vostochnyy Sayan 82 T7
Vostok Island 124 L6
Votkinsk 82 J6
Vozhgora 72 J2
Vranje 68 J7
Vranov 52 L9
Vranov nad Toplau 68 J1
Vratsa 68 L6
Vrbas 68 G4
Vrbas 68 E5
Vrbovsko 64 L5
Vrendenburg 118 B6
Vriddhachalam 94 C6
Vršac 68 J4
Vryburg 118 C5
Vryheid 118 E5
Vsetín 52 G8
Vstrechnyy 84 V3
Vućitrh 68 J7
Vukovar 68 G4
Vuktyl' 72 L2
Vulcăneşti 68 R4
Vulcano 66 J10
Vung Tau 90 D4
Vuollerim 50 L3
Vuotso 50 P2
Vyatka 72 K3
Vyazemskiy 84 N7
Vyaz'ma 72 F3
Vyborg 50 Q6
Vychegda 72 K2
Vyksa 72 H3
Vylkove 68 S4
Vynohradiv 52 N9
Vyshniy Volochek 72 F3
Vyškov 52 G8
Vytegra 72 G2

W

Wa 114 D3
Waal 56 H3
Waalwijk 56 H3
Wabē Shebelē Wenz 116 G2
Wabush 136 T6
Waco 144 B3
Wad Banda 110 E5
Waddān 110 C2
Waddeneilanden 56 G1
Waddenzee 56 H1
Waddington 38 H2
Wadebridge 38 D5
Wadena 142 A1
Wādī al Fārigh 110 C1
Wādī al Hamīm 110 D1
Wadi Halfa 110 F3
Wādi Mūsā 100 C6
Wad Medani 110 F5
Wadsworth 146 C1
Wafangdian 86 G3
Wafangdian 88 A4
Wager Bay 136 P3
Wagga Wagga 126 J7
Wahai 93 C3
Wahiawa 146 (2)C2
Wahpeton 140 G1
Waiau 128 D6
Waiblingen 64 E2
Waidhofen 64 K3
Waidhofen an der Ybbs 68 B2
Waigeo 93 D3
Waiheke Island 128 E3
Waihi 128 E3
Waikabubak 93 A4
Waikaia 128 B7
Waikaremoana 128 F4
Waikato 128 E4
Waikawa 128 B8
Wailuku 146 (2)E3
Waimana 128 F4
Waimate 128 C7
Waingapu 126 B1
Wainwright 146 (1)F1
Waiouru 128 E4
Waipara 128 D6
Waipawa 128 F4
Waipiro 128 G4
Waipu 128 E2
Waipukurau 128 F5
Wairoa 128 F4
Waitakaruru 128 E3
Waitaki 128 C7
Waitangi 128 (1)B1
Waitara 128 E4
Waitotara 128 E4
Waiuku 128 E3
Wajima 88 J5
Wajir 116 G3
Wakasa-wan 88 H6
Wakayama 88 H6
Wakeeney 146 G1
Wakefield 38 G2
Wake Island 124 G4
Wakkanai 88 L1
Waku-Kungo 118 B2
Wałbrzych 52 F7
Walcheren 56 F3
Wałcz 52 F4
Waldmünchen 54 H7
Waldshut-Tiengen 64 D3
Walen See 64 E3
Wales 38 E3
Wales Island 136 P3
Walgett 126 J6
Walker Lake 146 C1
Walkerville 126 J7
Wall 140 F2
Wallaceburg 142 D2
Wallasey 38 E2
Walla Walla 140 C1
Wallis et Futuna 124 J7
Walney Island 36 E7
Walpole 126 C6
Walsall 38 G3
Walsenburg 140 F3
Walsrode 54 E4
Waltershausen 54 F6
Walvis Bay 118 A4
Wamba 116 D3
Wana 96 J3
Wanaaring 126 H5
Wanaka 128 B7
Wandel Sea 134 A1
Wandingzhen 90 B2
Wando 88 D6
Wanganui 128 E4
Wanganui 128 E4
Wangen 64 E3
Wangerooge 54 D3
Wangiwangi 93 B4
Wan Hsa-la 90 B2
Wantage 38 G4
Wanxian 86 D4
Wanyuan 86 D4
Warangal 94 C5
Warburg 54 D5
Ward 128 E5
Wardha 94 C4
Waregem 56 F4
Wareham 38 F5
Waremme 56 H4
Waren 54 H3
Warendorf 56 K3
Warka 52 L6
Warla 52 H6
Warmandi 93 D3
Warminster 38 F4
Warm Springs 140 C3
Warren, *Mich., United States* 142 D2
Warren, *Oh., United States* 142 D2
Warren, *Pa., United States* 142 E2
Warrenpoint 35 E2
Warrensburg 142 B3
Warrenton 118 C5
Warri 114 F3
Warrington, *United Kingdom* 38 F2
Warrington, *United States* 144 D3
Warrnambool 126 H7
Warroad 142 A1
Warsaw = Warszawa 52 K5
Warstein 54 D5
Warszawa 52 K5
Warta 52 F5
Warwick 38 G3
Wasatch Range 146 D1
Wasco 146 C1
Washap 96 H4
Washburn Lake 136 K2
Washington 140 B1
Washington, *United Kingdom* 36 G7
Washington, *N.C., United States* 142 E3
Washington, *Pa., United States* 142 D2
Washington, *Ut., United States* 140 D3
Washington D.C. 134 J6
Wassenaar 56 G2
Wasserburg 64 H2
Watampone 93 B3
Watansoppeng 93 A3
Waterbury 142 F2
Waterford 35 D4
Waterloo, *Belgium* 56 G4
Waterloo, *United States* 142 B2
Watersmeet 142 C1
Watertown, *N.Y., United States* 142 E2
Watertown, *S.D., United States* 140 G1
Watertown, *Wis., United States* 142 C2
Waterville 142 G2
Watford 38 H4
Watford City 140 F1
Wath upon Dearne 38 G2
Watmuri 93 D4
Watrous 136 K6
Watsa 116 D3
Watseka 144 D1
Watson Lake 146 (1)M3
Wau 116 D2
Waubay Lake 140 G1
Waukegan 142 C2
Waukesha 142 C2
Waurika 144 B3
Wausau 138 J3
Waveney 38 K3
Waverley 128 E4
Waverly 142 C3
Wavre 56 G4
Wawa 142 D1
Wāw al Kabīr 110 C2
Waxxari 82 R10
Waycross 144 E3
Waynesboro, *Ga., United States* 144 E3
Waynesboro, *Miss., United States* 144 D3
Waynesville 142 D3
Weaverville 140 B2
Weber 128 F5
Webi Shaabeelle 116 G3

Webster 140 G1
Weddell Island 158 J9
Weddell Sea 160 (2)A2
Wedel 54 E3
Weed 140 B2
Weert 56 H3
Węgorzewo 52 L3
Wei 86 D4
Weichang 86 F2
Weida 54 H6
Weiden 54 H7
Weifang 86 F3
Weihai 86 G3
Weilburg 54 D6
Weilheim 64 G3
Weimar 54 G6
Weinan 86 D4
Weinheim 54 D7
Weining 86 C5
Weipa 126 H2
Weiser 140 C2
Weißenburg 54 F7
Weißenfels 54 G5
Weißwasser 54 K5
Weixi 90 B1
Wejherowo 52 H3
Welkom 118 D5
Welland 38 H3
Wellawaya 94 D7
Wellesley Islands 126 G3
Wellingborough 38 H3
Wellington 38 E5
Wellington, *New Zealand* 128 E5
Wellington, *Colo., United States* 140 F2
Wellington, *Kans., United States* 144 B2
Wells, *United Kingdom* 38 F4
Wells, *United States* 140 C2
Wellsboro 142 E2
Wellsford 128 E3
Wellton 146 D2
Wels 64 K2
Welshpool 38 E3
Welwyn Garden City 38 H4
Wenatchee 140 B1
Wenchang 90 E3
Wenga 116 B3
Wenman 156 (1)A1
Wentworth 126 H6
Wen Xian 86 C4
Wenzhou 86 G5
Werdër 116 H2
Werder 54 H4
Werl 56 K3
Werneck 54 F7
Wernigerode 54 F5
Werra 54 F6
Wertheim 54 E7
Wesel 56 J3
Wesel Dorsten 54 B5
Weser 54 E4
Wessel Islands 126 G2
West Antarctica 160 (2)GG2
West Bank 100 C4
West Branch 142 D2
West Bromwich 38 G3
West Burra 36 (1)G1
Westbury 38 F4
West Cape 124 G10
West End 144 F4
Westerland 54 D2
Western Australia 126 D5
Western Cape 118 B6
Western Ghats 94 B5
Western Reef 128 (1)B1
Western Sahara 112 C4
Wester Ross 36 C4
Westerschelde 56 F3
Westerstede 56 K1
Westervoort 56 J3
Westerwald 56 K4
West Falkland 158 J9
West Frankfort 144 D2
West Glacier 140 D1
West Heath 38 G3
West Kirby 38 E2
West Lunga 118 C2
West Memphis 144 C2
Weston 142 D3
Weston-super-Mare 38 F4
West Palm Beach 144 E4
West Plains 142 B3
Westport, *New Zealand* 128 C5
Westport, *Republic of Ireland* 35 B3
Westray 36 F2
West Siberian Plain = Zapadno-Sibirskaya Ravnina 80 L3
West-Terschelling 56 H1
West Virginia 142 D3
West Wendover 140 D2
West Yellowstone 140 D2
Wetar 93 C4
Wetaskiwin 136 J6
Wete 116 F5
Wetherby 38 G2
Wetumpka 144 D3
Wetzlar 54 D6
Wewak 93 F3
Wexford 35 E4
Wexford Harbour 35 E4
Weyburn 138 F2
Weymouth 38 F5
Weymouth Bay 38 F5
Whakatane 128 F3
Whale Cove 136 N4
Whalsay 36 (1)H1
Whangamata 128 E3
Whangamomona 128 E4
Whangarei 128 E2
Wharfe 38 G1
Wheeler Peak 146 E1
Wheeler Ridge 146 C2
Wheeling 144 E1
Whitby 36 H7
Whitchurch 38 F4
White, *Nev., United States* 140 C3
White, *S.D., United States* 136 L8
White Bay 136 V6
White Cliffs 126 H6
Whitecourt 136 H6
Whitefish Point 142 C1
Whitehaven 36 E7
Whitehead 35 F2
Whitehorse 146 (1)L3
White Island 128 F3
Whitemark 126 J8
White Mountain Peak 140 C3
White Mountains 136 S8
Whitemouth 140 G1
White Nile = Bahr el Abiad 110 F5
White River, *Canada* 142 C1
White River, *United States* 140 F2
White Sea = Beloye More 72 G1
White Sulphur Springs 140 D1
Whiteville 144 F3
White Volta 114 D3
Whithorn 36 D7
Whitley Bay 36 G6
Whitney 142 E1
Whitsand Bay 38 D5
Whyalla 126 G6
Wiay 36 A4
Wichita 144 B2
Wichita Falls 144 B3
Wick 36 E3
Wickenburg 146 D2
Wickford 38 J4
Wicklow 35 E4
Wicklow Mountains 35 E3
Wicklow Mountains National Park 35 E3
Widawka 52 J6
Widnes 38 F2
Wieluń 52 H6
Wien 64 M2
Wiener Neustadt 64 M3
Wieringermeer Polder 56 G2
Wiesbaden 54 D6
Wiesloch 54 D7
Wiesmoor 54 C3
Wigan 38 F2
Wiggins 140 F2
Wigton 36 E7
Wigtown 36 D7
Wigtown Bay 36 D7
Wil 64 E3
Wilbur 140 C1
Wilcannia 126 H6
Wildeshausen 54 D4
Wilhelmshaven 54 D3
Wilkes-Barre 142 E2
Wilkes Land 160 (2)U2
Willapa Bay 140 B1
Willemstad 156 D1
Williams, *Australia* 126 C6
Williams, *Ariz., United States* 140 D3
Williams, *Calif., United States* 140 B3
Williamsburg 142 E3
Williams Lake 136 G6
Williamson 144 E2
Williamsport 142 E2
Willis Group 126 K3
Williston, *South Africa* 118 C6
Williston, *Fla., United States* 144 E4
Williston, *N.D., United States* 140 F1
Williston Lake 136 G5
Willmar 142 A1
Willow 146 (1)H3
Willowmore 118 C6
Willow River 142 B1
Willow Springs 142 B3
Wilmington, *Del., United States* 142 E3
Wilmington, *N.C., United States* 144 F3
Wilmslow 38 F2
Wilson 142 E3
Wilson Reservoir 144 B2
Wilson's Promontory 126 J7
Wilton 38 G4
Wiluna 126 D5
Wimborne Minster 38 G5
Winamac 142 C2
Winchester, *United Kingdom* 38 G4
Winchester, *Ky., United States* 142 D3
Winchester, *Va., United States* 142 E3
Windermere 36 F7
Windhoek 118 B4
Windischgarsten 64 K3
Windom 142 A2
Windorah 126 H5
Windsor, *Canada* 142 D2
Windsor, *United Kingdom* 38 H4
Windsor, *United States* 144 F2
Windward Islands 148 N6
Windward Passage 154 D2
Winfield, *Al., United States* 144 D3
Winfield, *Kans., United States* 146 G1
Wingate Mountains 126 E2
Winisk 136 P5
Winisk 136 P6
Winisk Lake 136 P6
Winnemucca 140 C2
Winner 140 G2
Winnfield 138 H5
Winnipeg 136 M7
Winona, *Minn., United States* 142 B2
Winona, *Miss., United States* 144 D3
Winschoten 56 K1
Winsen 54 F3
Winsford 38 F2
Winslow 146 D1
Winston-Salem 142 D3
Winterberg 54 D5
Winter Harbour 136 J2
Winterswijk 56 J3
Winterthur 64 D3
Winton, *Australia* 126 H4
Winton, *New Zealand* 128 B8
Wisbech 38 J3
Wisconsin 138 H2
Wisconsin 142 B2
Wisconsin Dells 142 C2
Wisconsin Rapids 142 C2
Wisil Dabarow 116 H2
Wisła 52 H8
Wisła 52 H4
Wisłoka 52 L8
Wismar 54 G3
Wissembourg 54 C7
Witham 38 J4
Withernsea 38 J2
Witney 38 G4
Witten 56 K3
Wittenberge 54 G3
Wittenoom 126 C4
Wittingen 54 F4
Wittlich 56 J5
Wittmund 54 C3
Wittstock 54 H3
Witzenhausen 54 E5
W. J. van Blommesteinmeer 156 G2
Wkra 52 K5
Władysławowo 52 H3
Włocławek 52 J5
Włodawa 52 N6
Wodzisław Śląski 52 H7
Wohlen 64 D3
Wokam 93 D4
Woking 38 H4
Wokingham 38 H4
Wolf Creek 140 D1
Wolfen 54 H5
Wolfenbüttel 54 F4
Wolf Point 140 E1
Wolfratshausen 64 G3
Wolfsberg 64 K4
Wolfsburg 54 F4
Wolgast 54 J2
Wollaston Lake 136 K5
Wollaston Peninsula 136 H3
Wollongong 126 K6
Wołomin 52 L5
Wolsztyn 52 F5
Wolvega 56 J2
Wolverhampton 38 F3
Wombourne 38 F3
Wŏnju 88 D5
Wŏnsan 88 D4
Woodbridge 38 K3
Woodburn 140 B1
Woodford 38 J4
Woodland 140 B3
Woodstock, *Canada* 142 G1
Woodstock, *United Kingdom* 38 G4
Woodstock, *United States* 142 C2
Woodville, *New Zealand* 128 E5
Woodville, *Miss., United States* 144 C3
Woodville, *Tex., United States* 144 C3
Woodward 140 G3
Woody Head 128 E3
Wooler 36 F6
Woonsocket, *R.I., United States* 142 F2
Woonsocket, *S.D., United States* 140 G2
Worcester, *South Africa* 118 B6
Worcester, *United Kingdom* 38 F3
Worcester, *United States* 138 M3
Wörgl 64 H3
Workington 36 E7
Worksop 38 G2
Worland 140 E2
Worms 54 D7
Wörth 54 D7
Worthing 38 H5
Worthington 138 G3
Wosu 93 B3
Wotu 93 B3
Wowoni 93 B3
Wrangell 136 E5
Wrangell Mountains 136 C4
Wray 138 F3
Wrexham 38 F2
Wrigley 136 G4
Wrocław 52 G6
Września 52 G5
Wu 86 D5
Wubin 126 C6
Wubu 86 E3
Wuchang 86 H2
Wuchuan 86 E2
Wuday'ah 96 E6
Wudu 86 C4
Wuhai 86 D3
Wuhan 86 E4
Wuhu 86 F4
Wüjang 94 C2
Wukari 114 F3
Wuli 94 F2
Wunsiedel 54 G6
Wunstorf 54 E4
Wuppertal 54 C5
Würzburg 54 E7
Wurzen 54 H5
Wushi 82 P9
Wusuli 86 J1
Wutach 64 D3
Wuwei 86 C3
Wuxi 86 G4
Wuxu 90 D2
Wuyuan 86 D2
Wuzhong 86 D3
Wuzhou 90 E2
Wye 38 E3
Wymondham 38 K3
Wyndham 126 E3
Wynniatt Bay 136 J2
Wyoming 138 E3
Wyszków 52 L5
Wytheville 144 E2

X

Xaafuun 116 J1
Xàbia 62 L6
Xaçmaz 98 N3
Xaidulla 82 P10
Xainza 94 E2
Xai-Xai 118 E4
Xam Nua 90 C2
Xankändi 98 M4
Xanten 56 J3
Xanthi 70 G3
Xapuri 156 D6
Xar Moron 84 K8
Xàtiva 62 K6
Xiahe 86 C3
Xiamen 90 F2
Xi'an 86 D4
Xiangcheng 86 E4
Xiangfan 86 E4
Xianghoang 90 C3
Xianghuang Qi 86 E2
Xiangtan 86 E5
Xianning 86 E5
Xianyang 86 D4
Xiaogan 86 E4
Xiao Hinggan Ling 84 M7
Xiaonanchuan 94 F1
Xichang 90 C1
Xigazê 94 E3
Xi Jiang 86 E6
Xilinhot 86 F2
Xincai 86 E4
Xingcheng 86 G2
Xinghe 86 E2
Xinghua 86 F4
Xingtai 86 F3
Xingu 156 G5
Xingyi 90 C1
Xinhe 82 Q9
Xining 86 C3
Xinjie 86 D3
Xinjin 86 G3
Xinmin 88 B2
Xintai 86 F3
Xinxiang 86 E3
Xinyang 86 E4
Xinyu 86 F5
Xinyuan 82 Q9
Xinzhou 86 E3
Xinzo de Limia 62 C2
Xique Xique 156 J6
Xi Ujimqin Qi 86 F2
Xiushu 86 E5
Xiwu 94 G2
Xixia 86 E4
Xi Xiang 86 D4
Xizang 94 E2
Xizang Gaoyuan 94 D2
Xuanhua 86 E2
Xuchang 86 E4
Xuddur 116 G3
Xuwen 90 E2
Xuzhou 86 F4

Y

Ya'an 86 D3
Yabassi 114 F4
Yabēlo 116 F3
Yablonovyy Khrebet 84 J6
Yabrūd 100 D3
Yabuli 88 E1
Yacuma 156 D6
Yadgir 94 D5
Yagel'naya 82 P4
Yagodnyy 72 N3
Yahk 136 H7
Yakima 140 B1
Yako 114 D2
Yakoma 116 C3
Yaksha 72 L2
Yakumo 88 L2
Yaku-shima 88 F8
Yakutat 146 (1)K4
Yakutsk 84 M4
Yala 90 C5
Yalova 70 M4
Yalta 98 F1
Yalu 88 D3
Yalutorovsk 72 N3
Yamagata 88 L4
Yamaguchi 88 F6
Yamarovka 84 J6
Yambio 116 D3
Yambol 68 P7
Yamburg 82 P4
Yamdena 93 D4
Yammit 100 B5
Yamoussoukro 114 C3
Yampa 140 E2
Yampil' 68 R1
Yamsk 84 S5
Yan'an 86 D3
Yanbu'al Baḩr 96 C5
Yancheng 86 G4
Yandun 86 A2
Yangambi 116 C3
Yangbajain 94 F2
Yangdok 88 D4
Yangi Kand 98 N5
Yangjiang 90 E2
Yangon 90 B3
Yangquan 86 E3
Yangshuo 90 E2
Yangtze = Chang Jiang 86 D4
Yangzhou 86 F4
Yanhuqu 94 D2
Yani-Kurgan 82 M9
Yanji 88 E2
Yankton 140 G2
Yano-Indigirskaya Nizmennost' 84 N2
Yanqi 82 R9
Yanqing 86 F2
Yanshan 90 C2
Yanskiy Zaliv 84 N2
Yantai 86 G3
Yaoundé 114 G4
Yap 124 D5
Yapen 93 E3
Yaqui 138 E6
Yaraka 126 H4
Yaransk 72 J3
Yardımcı Burnu 70 E8
Yare 38 K3
Yaren 124 G6

Yarensk 72 J2
Yari 156 C3
Yarkant 96 L2
Yarkovo 72 N3
Yarlung Zangbo 94 F3
Yarm 36 G7
Yarmouth, *Canada* 136 T8
Yarmouth, *United Kingdom* 38 G5
Yaroslavl' 72 G3
Yar Sale 72 P1
Yartsevo 72 F3
Yashkul' 72 J5
Yasnyy 72 L4
Yāsūj 101 D1
Yatağan 70 L7
Yathkyed Lake 136 M4
Yatsushiro 88 F7
Yatta 100 C5
Yavari 156 C5
Yawatongguzlangar 82 Q10
Yaya 82 R6
Yayladağı 98 F6
Yazd 96 F3
Yazdān 96 H3
Yazd-e Khvāst 101 E1
Yazoo City 144 C3
Ydra 70 F7
Ye 90 B3
Yea 126 J7
Yecheng 96 L2
Yecla 62 J6
Yefremov 72 G4
Yegendybulak 82 P8
Yei 116 E3
Yekaterinburg 72 M3
Yelets 72 G4
Yelizovo 84 T6
Yell 36 (1)G1
Yellowknife 136 J4
Yellow River = Huang He 86 C3
Yellow Sea 86 G3
Yellowstone 140 E1
Yellowstone Lake 140 D2
Yell Sound 36 (1)G1
Yeloten 96 H2
Yelva 82 J5
Yelwa 114 E2
Yemen 96 D7
Yemetsk 72 H2
Yenakiyeve 72 G5
Yengisar 96 L2
Yenihisar 70 K7
Yenisey 82 S6
Yeniseysk 82 S6
Yeniseyskiy Kryazh 82 S5
Yeo Lake 126 D5
Yeovil 38 F5
Yeppoon 126 K4
Yeraliyev 82 J9
Yerbogachen 84 H4
Yerevan 98 L3
Yerington 140 C3
Yerkov 70 S5
Yerkoy 98 F4
Yermak 82 P7
Yermitsa 72 K1
Yernva 82 J5
Yershov 72 J4
Yerupaja 156 B6
Yerushalayim 100 C5
Yesil' 72 N4
Yeşilhisar 98 F4
Yeşilköy 70 L4
Yessey 82 U4
Yevlax 98 M3
Yevpatoriya 72 F5
Yeyik 82 Q10
Yeysk 72 G5
Yibin 86 C5
Yichang 86 E4
Yichun, *China* 86 H1
Yichun, *China* 86 E5
Yilan 86 H1
Yıldız Dağları 70 K2
Yıldızeli 98 G4
Yinchuan 86 D3
Yingcheng 86 E4
Yingkou 86 G2
Yingtan 86 F5
Yining 82 Q9
Yirga Alem 116 F2
Yitomio 50 M3
Yitulihe 84 L6
Yiyang 86 E5
Yli-Kitka 50 Q3
Ylivieska 50 N4
Ylöjärvi 50 M6
Yoakum 144 B4
Yoboki 110 H5
Yogyakarta 92 E4
Yohuma 116 C3
Yokadouma 114 G4
Yoko 114 G3
Yokohama, *Japan* 88 K6
Yokohama, *Japan* 88 L3
Yokosuka 88 K6
Yokote 88 L4
Yola 114 G3
Yonago 88 G6
Yonezawa 88 L5
Yong'an 90 F1
Yongdeng 86 C3
Yŏnghŭng 88 D4
Yongren 90 C1
Yongxiu 86 F5
Yonkers 142 F2
York, *United Kingdom* 38 G2
York, *Nebr., United States* 140 G2
York, *Pa., United States* 142 E3
Yorkshire Dales National Park 36 F7
Yorkshire Wolds 36 H7
Yorkton 136 L6
Yoshkar Ola 72 J3
Yŏsu 88 D6
Yotvata 100 C7
You 90 D2
Youghal 35 D5
Youghal Bay 35 D5
Youngstown 142 D2
Youvarou 114 D1
Yozgat 98 F4
Yreka 140 B2
Ystad 52 C2
Ystradgynlais 38 E4
Ysyk-Köl 82 P9
Ytre Sula 50 B6
Ytyk-Kyuyel' 84 N4
Yu 90 D2
Yuan 90 C2
Yuanjiang 90 C2
Yuanmou 90 C1
Yuanping 86 E3
Yucatán 148 F5
Yucatan Channel 148 G4
Yuci 86 E3
Yudoma 84 Q4
Yuendumu 126 F4
Yueyang 86 E5
Yugorenok 84 P5
Yugoslavia 68 H6
Yugo-Tala 84 S3
Yukagirskoye Ploskogor'ye 84 S3
Yukon 146 (1)E3
Yukon Territory 146 (1)K2
Yukorskiy Poluostrov 82 L4
Yüksekova 98 L5
Yukta 84 H4
Yuli 82 R9
Yulin, *China* 86 D3
Yulin, *China* 90 E2
Yuma 146 C2
Yumen 86 B3
Yumin 82 Q8
Yunak 98 D4
Yuncheng 86 E3
Yun Xian 90 C2
Yuogi Feng 82 R8
Yurga 82 Q6
Yurimaguas 156 B5
Yurla 72 K3
Yuroma 72 J1
Yur'yevets 72 H3
Yu Shan 90 G2
Yushkozero 50 S4
Yushu, *China* 86 B4
Yushu, *China* 86 H2
Yusufeli 98 J3
Yutian 82 Q10
Yuxi 86 C6
Yuyao 86 G4
Yuzawa 88 L4
Yuzhno Kuril'sk 88 N1
Yuzhno-Sakhalinsk 84 Q7
Yuzhno-Sukhokumsk 98 L1
Yuzhnoural'sk 72 M4
Yverdon-les-Bains 64 B4
Yvetot 56 C5

Z

Zaanstad 56 G2
Ząbkowice Śląskie 52 F7
Zabok 64 L4
Zābol 96 H3
Zabrze 52 H7
Zacatecas 146 F4
Zadar 64 L6
Zadonsk 72 G4
Zafora 70 J8
Zafra 62 D6
Zāgheh-ye-Bālā 98 M6
Zagora 112 D2
Zagreb 64 L5
Zagyva 52 K10
Zāhedān 96 H4
Zahirabad 94 C5
Zahlé 100 C3
Zahrān 96 D6
Zaječar 68 K6
Zakamensk 84 G6
Zākhō 98 K5
Zakopane 52 J8
Zakynthos 70 C7
Zakynthos 70 C7
Zala 64 M4
Zalaegerszeg 64 M4
Zalakomár 68 E3
Zalari 84 G6
Zalaszentgrót 64 N4
Zalău 68 L2
Ẓalim 96 D5
Zalingei 110 D5
Zaliv Aniva 84 Q7
Zaliv Kara-Bogaz Gol 96 F1
Zaliv Kresta 84 Y3
Zaliv Paskevicha 72 L5
Zaliv Shelikhova 84 T5
Zaliv Terpeniya 84 Q7
Zamakh 96 E6
Zambezi 118 C2
Zambezi 118 E3
Zambia 118 D2
Zamboanga 90 G5
Zambrów 52 M5
Zamora 62 E3
Zamość 52 N7
Zanda 94 C2
Zandvoort 56 G2
Zanesville 144 E2
Zangguy 96 L2
Zanjān 98 N5
Zannone 66 H8
Zanzibar 116 F5
Zanzibar Island 116 F5
Zaouatallaz 112 G4
Zaozernyy 82 S6
Zapadnaya Dvina 72 E3
Zapadno-Sibirskaya Ravnina 82 L5
Zapadnyy Sayan 82 S7
Zapata 146 G3
Zapolyarnyy 50 R2
Zaporizhzhya 72 G5
Zaprešić 64 L5
Zaqatala 98 M3
Zara 98 G4
Zarafshan 82 L9
Zaragoza 62 K3
Zarand 101 G1
Zaranj 96 H3
Zarasai 50 P9
Zaraza 156 D2
Zarechensk 50 R3
Zaria 114 F2
Zărnești 68 N4
Zarqā' 100 D4
Zarqān 101 E2
Żary 52 E6
Zarzadilla de Totana 62 J7
Žatec 52 C7
Zavetnoye 72 H5
Zavidoviči 68 F5
Zavitinsk 84 M6
Zayarsk 82 U6
Zaysan 82 Q8
Zayü 90 B1
Zazafotsy 118 H4
Zbraslav 52 D8
Zēbāk 96 K2
Zēbār 98 L5
Zeebrugge 56 F3
Ẕefat 100 C4
Zehdenick 54 J4
Zeilona Góra 52 E6
Zeist 56 H2
Zeitz 54 H5
Zelenoborskiy 50 S3
Zelenograd 72 G3
Zelenogradsk 52 K3
Zelenokumsk 98 K1
Zelina 68 D4
Zella-Mehlis 54 F6
Zell am See 64 H3
Zémio 116 D2
Zemlya Alexsandry 82 G1
Zemlya Frantsa-Iosifa 82 J2
Zemlya Vil'cheka 82 L1
Zempoalteptl 148 E5
Zenica 68 E5
Zerbst 54 H5
Zermatt 64 C4
Zeta Lake 136 K2
Zeulenroda 54 G6
Zeven 54 E3
Zevenaar 56 J3
Zeya 84 M6
Zeya 84 M6
Zeydābād 101 F2
Zeyskoye Vodokhranilishche 84 M5
Zgharta 100 C2
Zgierz 52 J6
Zgorzelec 52 E6
Zhailma 72 M4
Zhaksy 72 N4
Zhaksykon 72 N5
Zhaltyr 72 N4
Zhambyl 82 N9
Zhanatas 82 M9
Zhangbei 86 E2
Zhangguangcai Ling 86 H2
Zhangjiakou 86 E2
Zhangling 84 L6
Zhangwu 86 G2
Zhangye 86 B3
Zhangzhou 90 F2
Zhanjiang 90 E2
Zhaodong 84 M7
Zhaoqing 90 E2
Zhaosu 82 Q9
Zhaotong 86 C5
Zhaoyuan 86 H1
Zharkamys 82 K8
Zharkent 82 P9
Zharma 82 Q8
Zharyk 82 N8
Zhaxigang 94 C2
Zheleznogorsk 72 G4
Zhengzhou 86 E4
Zhenjiang 86 F4
Zherdevka 72 H4
Zhetybay 82 J9
Zhezkazgan 82 M8
Zhigalovo 84 H5
Zhigansk 84 L3
Zhilinda 84 J2
Zhob 96 J3
Zholymbet 82 N7
Zhongba 94 D3
Zhongdian 86 B5
Zhongning 86 D3
Zhongshan 90 E2
Zhongze 86 G5
Zhoukou 86 E4
Zhuanghe 86 G3
Zhucheng 86 F3
Zhumadian 86 E4
Zhuo Xian 86 F3
Zhytomyr 72 E4
Žiar 52 H9
Zibo 86 F3
Zichang 86 D3
Zieriksee 56 F3
Ziesar 54 H4
Zighan 110 D2
Zigon 90 B3
Zigong 86 C5
Ziguinchor 112 B6
Zikhron Ya'aqov 100 B4
Žilina 52 H8
Zillah 110 C2
Zima 84 G6
Zimbabwe 118 D3
Zimmi 114 B3
Zimnicea 68 N6
Zinder 114 F2
Zinjibār 110 J5
Zinnowitz 54 J2
Zirc 52 G10
Žirje 66 K5
Zistersdorf 64 M2
Zitava 52 H9
Zittau 54 K6
Ziway Hāyk' 116 F2
Zixing 90 E1
Zlaté Moravce 52 H9
Zlatoust 72 L3
Zlín 52 G8
Zlīṭan 112 H2
Złocieniec 52 F4
Złoczew 52 H6
Złotów 52 G4
Zmeinogorsk 82 Q7
Znamenskoye 82 N6
Żnin 52 G5
Znojmo 64 M2
Zoigê 86 C4
Zolotinka 84 M5
Zomba 118 F3
Zongo 116 B3
Zonguldak 70 P3
Zouar 110 C3
Zouérat 112 C4
Zovka 52 N7
Zrenjanin 68 H4
Zschopau 54 J6
Zug 64 D3
Zugdidi 98 J2
Zuger See 64 D3
Zugspitze 54 F9
Zuid-Beveland 56 F3
Zuni 146 E1
Zunyi 86 D5
Županja 68 F4
Zürich 64 D3
Zuru 114 F2
Žut 66 K5
Zutphen 56 J2
Zuwārah 110 B1
Zuyevka 82 J6
Zvishavane 118 E4
Zvolen 52 J9
Zvornik 68 G5
Zwedru 114 C3
Zweibrücken 56 K5
Zwettl 64 L2
Zwickau 54 H6
Zwiesel 54 J7
Zwoleń 52 L6
Zwolle 56 J2
Zyryanka 84 S3
Zyryanovsk 82 Q8
Żywiec 52 J8